Introduction to Financial Accounting
Second Edition

PEARSON CUSTOM PUBLISHING

Introduction to Financial Accounting

Second Edition

Compiled from:

Frank Wood's
Business Accounting 1
Twelfth Edition
by Frank Wood and Alan Sangster

Frank Wood's
Business Accounting 2
Eleventh Edition
by Frank Wood and Alan Sangster

ALWAYS LEARNING   PEARSON

Harlow, England • London • New York • Boston • San Francisco • Toronto • Sydney • Auckland • Singapore • Hong Kong
Tokyo • Seoul • Taipei • New Delhi • Cape Town • Sao Paulo • Mexico City • Madrid • Amsterdam • Munich • Paris • Milan

Pearson Education Limited
Edinburgh Gate
Harlow
Essex CM20 2JE

And associated companies throughout the world

Visit us on the World Wide Web at:
www.pearsoned.co.uk

This Custom Book Edition © Pearson Education Limited 2012

Compiled from:

Frank Wood's
Business Accounting 1
Twelfth Edition
by Frank Wood and Alan Sangster
ISBN 978 0 273 75918 8
Copyright © Frank Wood 1967
Copyright © Longman Group UK Limited 1972, 1979, 1984, 1989, 1993
Copyright © Pearson Professional Limited 1996
Copyright © Financial Times Professional Limited 1999
Copyright © Pearson Education Limited 2002, 2007, 2008, 2012

Frank Wood's
Business Accounting 2
Eleventh Edition
by Frank Wood and Alan Sangster
ISBN 978 0 273 71213 8
Copyright © Frank Wood 1967
Copyright © Longman Group UK Limited 1972, 1979, 1984, 1989, 1993
Copyright © Pearson Professional Limited 1996
Copyright © Financial Times Professional Limited 1999
Copyright © Pearson Education Limited 2002, 2005, 2007, 2008

ISBN 978 1 78086 321 4

Printed in Great Britain by Clays Ltd, St Ives plc

Contents

Books of Original Entry

Adjustments for Financial Statements 1

Adjustments for Financial Statements 2

Adjustments for Financial Statements 3

Introduction to the Financial Statements of Limited Companies

The Financial Statements of Limited Companies

Interpretation of Financial Statements 1

Interpretation of Financial Statements 2

Corporate Governance

Statements of Cash Flows 1

Statements of Cash Flows 2

Bank Reconciliations and Control Accounts

Correction of Errors and Suspense Accounts

Single Entry and Incomplete Records

Answers

Introduction to Financial Accounting

The accounting equation and the statement of financial position

Learning objectives

After you have studied this chapter, you should be able to:

- explain what accounting is about
- briefly describe the history of accounting
- explain the relationship between bookkeeping and accounting
- list the main users of accounting information and what accounting information they are interested in
- present and explain the accounting equation
- explain the relationship between the accounting equation and the layout of the statement of financial position [balance sheet]
- explain the meaning of the terms assets, capital, liabilities, accounts receivable (debtors), and accounts payable (creditors)
- describe how accounting transactions affect the items in the accounting equation
- draw up statements of financial position after different accounting transactions have occurred

Introduction

In this chapter, you will learn: what accounting is; what led to its development into what it is today; who uses accounting information; and the relationship between the various components that, together, comprise what is known as the 'accounting equation'.

1.1 What is accounting?

What do you think of when you read or hear the word, 'accounting'? What do you believe it means or represents?

If you have already attended some accounting classes or if you have spoken to someone who knows something about accounting, you will probably have a fairly good idea of what accounting is and what it is used for. If not, you may find it useful to have this knowledge before you start studying the subject. During the course of the next few pages, let's see if you can gain that knowledge and learn what accounting is.

Accounting can be defined as:

The process of identifying, measuring, and communicating economic information to permit informed judgements and decisions by users of that information.

A bit of a mouthful really but, what it means is that accounting involves deciding what amounts of money are, were, or will be involved in transactions (often buying and selling transactions) and then organising the information obtained and presenting it in a way that is useful for decision-making.

Despite what some people think, accounting is not a branch of mathematics, although the man credited with writing the first book to be printed on the subject, Luca Pacioli (c. 1445–1517), was a mathematician and teacher. He wrote on the topic *'in order that the subjects of the most gracious Duke of Urbino* [his sponsor or benefactor] *may have complete instructions in the conduct of business'*, and to *'give the trader without delay information as to his assets and liabilities'*. ('Assets' are things that you own; 'liabilities' are things that you owe.)

What Pacioli wrote is contained in 27 pages of a school textbook and reference manual for merchants on business and mathematics (*Summa de arithmetica, geometria, proportioni et proportionalita* – Everything about Arithmetic, Geometry and Proportion) which was first published in Italy in 1494. His treatise has been translated into many languages, including English, and is acknowledged as the chief reason why we maintain accounts in the way we do today.

Accounting may not require a knowledge of mathematics but you do need to be able to add, subtract, multiply and divide – things you need to be able to do in your daily life anyway. Otherwise, you would not know how much money you had with you, how much you would have if you spent some of it, or whether the change you received was correct. So, let's remove one big misconception some people have concerning accounting: you do not need to be good at arithmetic to be good at accounting, though you will find it easier to 'do' accounting if you are.

1.2   The history of accounting

Accounting began because people needed to:

- record business transactions; and
- know how much they owned and how much they owed.

It is known to have existed in one form or another for at least 10,000 years. (Records exist which indicate its use at that time in Mesopotamia.) There is also considerable evidence of accounting being practised in ancient times in Egypt, China, India, Greece and Rome. In England, the 'Pipe Roll', the oldest surviving accounting record in the English language, contains an annual description of rents, fines and taxes due to the King of England, from 1130 to 1830.

In India, a system of accounting, called *Bahi-khata*, was developed many centuries ago but it did not spread beyond that region, probably because a description of it was never written down until the twentieth century. It spread by word of mouth and, even today, is a standardised method of keeping accounting records in parts of that region.

In the rest of the world, accounting appears to have developed slowly for thousands of years. The first known example of business records maintained using what we call 'double entry bookkeeping' – the method described by Pacioli and the method used universally today – was in a branch of an Italian firm in southern France in 1299. But, it was another 150 years before it became relatively commonly used by northern Italian partnerships and joint ventures. The rest of the world took considerably longer to adopt the method. That this system of double entry bookkeeping came to be universally adopted is due to Pacioli, and what he wrote about it in 1494.

It has been suggested that no standard system for maintaining accounting records had been developed before this because the circumstances of the day did not make it practicable for anyone to do so – there was little point, for example, in anyone devising a formal system of accounting if the people who would be required to 'do' accounting did not know how to read or write. Were such a system developed, there was no point in writing about it if people could not read what was written.

One accounting scholar (A. C. Littleton) has suggested that seven key ingredients were required before a formal system could be developed and that all seven existed when Pacioli wrote his treatise:

- *Private property.* The power to change ownership exists and there is a need to record the transaction.
- *Capital.* Wealth is productively employed such that transactions are sufficiently important to make their recording worthwhile and cost-effective.
- *Commerce.* The exchange of goods on a widespread level. The volume of transactions needs to be sufficiently high to motivate someone to devise a formal, organised system that could be applied universally to record transactions.
- *Credit.* The present use of future goods. Cash transactions, where money is exchanged for goods, do not require that any details be recorded of who the customer or supplier was. The existence of a system of buying and selling on credit (i.e. paying later for goods and services purchased today) led to the need for a formal organised system that could be applied universally to record credit transactions.
- *Writing.* A mechanism for making a permanent record in a common language. Writing had clearly been around for a long time prior to Pacioli but it was, nevertheless, an essential element required before accounting could be formalised.
- *Money.* There needs to be a common denominator for exchange. So long as barter was used rather than payment with currency, there was no need for a bookkeeping system based upon transactions undertaken using a uniform set of monetary values.
- *Arithmetic.* As with writing, this has clearly been in existence far longer than accounting. Nevertheless, it is clearly the case that without an ability to perform simple arithmetic, there was no possibility that a formal organised system of accounting could be devised.

Of these, the most important catalyst for the emergence of double entry bookkeeping was almost certainly the use of credit in business. In the middle ages, a businessman who did not know how much was owed to him and how much he owed, could lose his business, his home, and everything he owned.

During the Crusades (1096–1292), trade routes to the east were opened and merchants, many from the Italian ports like Venice, began to expand their activities along the new routes. Venice dominated trade and along with another Italian city, Florence, was the major banking centre in the western world up to at least the mid-fifteenth century.

This expansion of trade led merchants to start operating in joint ventures (where they shared costs and profits) with businessmen located elsewhere. The merchants employed agents to conduct business on their behalf. The need to record details of these arrangements was obvious.

When accounting information was recorded in the Middle Ages it sometimes simply took the form of a note of the details of each transaction and each receipt and payment. These notes were used by the owner mainly in order to keep track of moneys due.

In Florence, a custom had emerged in the twelfth century of maintaining a record of important personal events in a book called a *Ricordanze*. It was a very popular practice and Florentine merchants started to record transactions, receipts and payments in their *Ricordanze*.

The larger the business, the greater the number of entries that were made. The entries were made when they occurred and it could be some time before the next transaction with the same person occurred. Even with these records in the *Ricordanze*, it became difficult to tell what total amounts were owed and due.

To address this problem, merchants started transferring details from the *Ricordanze* into another book and entries in that book were organised into what we now call, 'accounts', one for each person or item.

This was the beginning of the system of double entry bookkeeping described by Pacioli. In his system, a book called a *Memorandum* replaced the *Ricordanze*. The details recorded in it were abbreviated, organised and transferred into another book called a *Journal*. Details from that book were then further summarised and entered into accounts maintained in a third book called a *Ledger*.

The accountant of the Middle Ages was someone who knew how to enter data relating to financial transactions into the accounting books. He was what we call a 'bookkeeper'. Quite often, it would be the owner of the business who performed all the accounting tasks. Otherwise, an employee would be given the job of maintaining the accounting records.

As businesses grew in size, it became less common for the owner to personally maintain the accounting records and more usual for someone to be employed as a bookkeeper. Then, as companies began to dominate the business environment, managers became separated from owners – the owners of companies (shareholders) often have no involvement in the day-to-day running of the business. This led to a need for some monitoring of the managers. Auditing of the financial records became the norm and this, effectively, established the accounting profession.

The first association of accountants, the *Collegio dei Rexonati*, was formed in Venice in 1581 and had a role in training auditors, but the widespread emergence of an accounting profession was slow. It was not until the nineteenth century that the majority of Italian states required accountants to be members of a recognised association, but organisation was regional not national.

In 1854, the first national body of accountants was formed: the Institute of Chartered Accountants of Scotland. Thereafter, other national bodies began to emerge gradually throughout the world, with the English Institute of Chartered Accountants being formed in 1880 and the first US national accounting body being formed in 1887.

If you wish to discover more about the history of accounting, you will find that it is readily available on the Internet. Perform a search on either of the terms 'history of accounting' or 'accounting history' and you should find more information than you could ever realistically read on the subject.

1.3 Accountants

From its roots among the scribes of Mesopotamia, accounting is one of the oldest professions in the world. Today, there are around 200 professional accountancy bodies, each with its own entry requirements. While there are notable exceptions, nowadays these generally consist of a series of examinations plus relevant work experience, the same requirement as applied to anyone seeking admission to the Venetian *Collegio dei Rexonati* in 1581.

Today, accountants go beyond the role of the bookkeepers of the Middle Ages. As they did then, accountants record and manipulate financial data in order to provide financial information. In addition, today's accountants are also expected to interpret the information they produce, all in order to assist in decision-making.

Unlike Italy of the nineteenth century, in most of the world, it is not necessary to be member of a professional accountancy body in order to work as an accountant, although few without such membership are likely today to rise above the level of a bookkeeper.

Being a member of a professional accountancy body indicates a minimum level of knowledge and expertise that would be expected and upon which employers and others using information provided by such accountants may rely. Because membership of such a body presents an image of professional expertise and understanding, it is important that accountants act in a manner that is consistent with what is expected of them. Any failure to do so places the image of the profession at risk.

1.4 Professional ethics

It is for this reason that it is now recognised that accountants have a responsibility to be 'ethical'. This is a relatively new development. For many years, ethics were an informal element of the training of accountants. However, an apparently never-ending stream of high-profile financial scandals since the 1960s has threatened the reputation of the accounting profession. As a result, the informal approach to ethics has been formalised in an attempt to stop such events occurring.

It is for this reason that some accountancy bodies now include a separate ethics course in their training. Others have embedded ethics into some of their courses and examinations. But, what does it mean to be 'ethical'?

Being ethical involves showing integrity, fairness, respect and openness in behaviour and attitude in all situations. Members of all professions have a responsibility to society because they have the specialist knowledge and expertise to deal with certain situations in a more informed way than those who are not so qualified. For accountants, their professional ethics are not just concerned with how an accountant should be in the workplace, they relate to how accountants should behave in all aspects of their public life.

Ethics apply not only to what an accountant does, and to his or her interaction with those who are not accountants. Ethics also apply to how accountants conduct themselves with each other and with those aspiring to be accountants. Managers and trainers of accountants have an ethical responsibility to present themselves as respectful, honest, and trustworthy; and to ensure that their accounting trainees embrace those same values.

The International Federation of Accountants is the world umbrella body for professional accountancy bodies. It has currently (in 2011) 165 member bodies in 125 countries. Its 2010 *Code of Ethics for Professional Accountants* forms the basis for many of the ethical codes applied by its member bodies. The IFAC Code is available at **http://web.ifac.org/publications/ international-ethics-standards-board-for-accountants/code-of-ethics**

In the IFAC Code, it is stated that a professional accountant must comply with the following fundamental principles:

(a) *Integrity* – to be straightforward and honest in all professional and business relationships.
(b) *Objectivity* – to not allow bias, conflict of interest or undue influence of others to override professional or business judgements.
(c) *Professional competence and due care* – to maintain professional knowledge and skill at the level required to ensure that a client or employer receives competent professional services based on current developments in practice, legislation and techniques and act diligently and in accordance with applicable technical and professional standards.
(d) *Confidentiality* – to respect the confidentiality of information acquired as a result of professional and business relationships and, therefore, not to disclose any such information to third parties without proper and specific authority, unless there is a legal or professional right or duty to disclose, nor to use the information for the personal advantage of the professional accountant or third parties.
(e) *Professional behaviour* – to comply with relevant laws and regulations and avoid any action that discredits the profession.

To supplement their ethical codes, accountancy bodies worldwide operate their own disciplinary code which establishes what steps may be taken should a member act unethically. These disciplinary codes are designed to protect non-accountants and to maintain the reputation of the profession and the demand for its services. Accountants found guilty of unethical behaviour risk the possibility of fines or even expulsion from their professional body.

Activity 1.1 Do you think that such a system of self-regulation is appropriate?

1.5   The objectives of accounting

Accounting has many objectives, including letting people and organisations know:

- if they are making a profit or a loss;
- what their business is worth;
- what a transaction was worth to them;
- how much cash they have;
- how wealthy they are;
- how much they are owed;
- how much they owe to someone else;
- enough information so that they can keep a financial check on the things they do.

However, the primary objective of accounting is to provide information for decision-making. The information is usually financial, but can also be given in volumes, for example, the number of cars sold in a month by a car dealership or the number of cows in a farmer's herd.

So, for example, if a business recorded what it sold, to whom, the date it was sold, the price at which it was sold, and the date it received payment from the customer, along with similar data concerning the purchases it made, certain information could be produced summarising what had taken place. The profitability of the business and the financial status of the business could also be identified, at any particular point in time. It is the primary objective of accounting to take such information and convert it into a form that is useful for decision-making.

People and businesses

Accounting is something that affects people in their personal lives just as much as it affects very large businesses. We all use accounting ideas when we plan what we are going to do with our money. We have to plan how much of it we will spend and how much we will save. We may write down a plan, known as a **budget**, or we may simply keep it in our minds.

Recording accounting data

However, when people talk about accounting, they are normally referring to accounting as used by businesses and other organisations. The owners cannot remember all the details so they have to keep records of it.

Organisations not only record cash received and paid out. They will also record goods bought and sold, items bought to use rather than to sell, and so on. This part of accounting is usually called the *recording of data*.

Classifying and summarising

When the data is being recorded it has to be organised so as to be most useful to the business. This is known as *classifying* and *summarising* data.

Following such classifications and summaries it will be possible to work out how much profit or loss has been made by the business during a particular period. It will also be possible to show what resources are owned by the business, and what is owed by it, on the closing date of the period.

Communicating information

From the data, people skilled in accounting should be able to tell whether or not the business is performing well financially. They should be able to ascertain the strengths and weaknesses of the business.

Finally, they should be able to tell or *communicate* their results to the owners of the business, or to others allowed to receive this information.

Accounting is, therefore, concerned with:

- recording data;
- classifying and summarising data;
- communicating what has been learnt from the data.

1.6 What is bookkeeping?

Until about one hundred years ago all accounting data was *kept* by being recorded manually in *books*, and so the part of accounting that is concerned with recording data is often known as **bookkeeping**.

Nowadays, although handwritten books may be used (particularly by smaller organisations), most accounting data is recorded electronically and stored electronically using computers.

Bookkeeping is the process of recording data relating to accounting transactions in the accounting books.

1.7 Accounting is concerned with . . .

Accounting is concerned with the uses which accountants might make of the bookkeeping information given to them. This book will cover many such uses.

1.8 Users of accounting information

Possible users of accounting information include:

- *Managers*. These are the day-to-day decision-makers. They need to know how well things are progressing financially and about the financial status of the business.
- *Owner(s) of the business*. They want to be able to see whether or not the business is profitable. In addition they want to know what the financial resources of the business are.
- *A prospective buyer*. When the owner wants to sell a business the buyer will want to see such information.
- *The bank*. If the owner wants to borrow money for use in the business, then the bank will need such information.
- *Tax inspectors*. They need it to be able to calculate the taxes payable.
- *A prospective partner*. If the owner wants to share ownership with someone else, then the would-be partner will want such information.
- *Investors*, either existing ones or potential ones. They want to know whether or not to invest their money in the business.
- *Creditors*. They want to know if there is any risk of not being paid what they are due.

There are many other users of accounting information – suppliers and employees, for example. One obvious fact is that without properly recorded accounting data a business would have many difficulties providing the information these various users (often referred to as '**stakeholders**') require.

 Activity 1.2 Which two of these stakeholder groups do you think are considered to be the most important? Why?

However, the information produced by accounting needs to be a compromise – so many different groups of stakeholders make it impossible to produce accounting information at a reasonable cost in a form that suits them all. As a result, accounting focuses on producing information for owners. The other stakeholder groups often find the accounting information provided fails to tell them what they really want to know. However, if organisations made the effort to satisfy the information needs of all stakeholders, accounting would be a very costly exercise indeed!

1.9   The accounting equation

By adding up what the accounting records say belongs to a business and deducting what they say the business owes, you can identify what a business is worth according to those accounting records. The whole of financial accounting is based upon this very simple idea. It is known as the *accounting equation*.

It can be explained by saying that if a business is to be set up and start trading, it will need resources. Let's assume first that it is the owner of the business who has supplied all of the resources. This can be shown as:

> **Resources supplied by the owner = Resources in the business**

In accounting, special terms are used to describe many things. The amount of the resources supplied by the owner is called **capital**. The actual resources that are then in the business are called **assets**. This means that when the owner has supplied all of the resources, the accounting equation can be shown as:

> Capital = Assets

Usually, however, people other than the owner have supplied some of the assets. **Liabilities** is the name given to the amounts owing to these people for these assets. The accounting equation has now changed to:

> Capital = Assets – Liabilities

This is the most common way in which the accounting equation is presented. It can be seen that the two sides of the equation will have the same totals. This is because we are dealing with the same thing from two different points of view – the value of the owners' investment in the business and the value of what is owned by the owners.

 Activity 1.3   What piece of useful information that is available from these three items is not directly shown by this equation? (*Hint*: you were introduced to it at the start of this section.)

Unfortunately, with this form of the accounting equation, we can no longer see at a glance what value is represented by the resources in the business. You can see this more clearly if you switch assets and capital around to produce the alternate form of the accounting equation:

> Assets = Capital + Liabilities

This can then be replaced with words describing the resources of the business:

> **Resources: what they are = Resources: who supplied them**
> **(Assets)   (Capital + Liabilities)**

It is a fact that no matter how you present the accounting equation, the totals of both sides will *always* equal each other, and that this will *always* be true no matter how many transactions there may be. The actual assets, capital and liabilities may change, but the total of the assets will always equal the total of capital + liabilities. Or, reverting to the more common form of the accounting equation, the capital will always equal the assets of the business minus the liabilities.

Assets consist of property of all kinds, such as buildings, machinery, inventories (stocks) of goods and motor vehicles. Other assets include debts owed by customers and the amount of money in the organisation's bank account.

Liabilities include amounts owed by the business for goods and services supplied to the business and for expenses incurred by the business that have not yet been paid for. They also include funds borrowed by the business.

Capital is often called the owner's **equity** or net worth. It comprises the funds invested in the business by the owner plus any profits retained for use in the business less any share of profits paid out of the business to the owner.

 Activity 1.4 What else would affect capital? (*Hint*: this item causes the value of capital to fall.)

1.10 The statement of financial position and the effects of business transactions

The accounting equation is expressed in a financial report called the **statement of financial position**.

 Activity 1.5 Without looking back, write down the commonly used form of the accounting equation.

The statement of financial position shows the financial position of an organisation at a point in time. In other words, it presents a snapshot of the organisation at the date for which it was prepared. The statement of financial position is not the first accounting record to be made, nor the first that you will learn how to do, but it is a convenient place to start to consider accounting.

Let's now look at how a series of transactions affects the statement of financial position.

1 The introduction of capital

On 1 May 2011, B. Blake started in business and deposited £60,000 into a bank account opened specially for the business. The statement of financial position would show:

B. Blake
Statement of Financial Position as at 1 May 2011

	£
Assets: Cash at bank	60,000
Capital	60,000

Note how the top part of the statement of financial position contains the assets and the bottom part contains the capital. This is always the way the information is presented in a statement of financial position.

2 The purchase of an asset by cheque

On 3 May 2011, Blake buys a small shop for £32,000, paying by cheque. The effect of this transaction on the statement of financial position is that the cash at the bank is decreased and the new asset, shop, is added:

B. Blake
Statement of financial position as at 3 May 2011

Assets	£
Shop	32,000
Cash at bank	28,000
	60,000
Capital	60,000

Note how the two parts of the statement of financial position 'balance'. That is, their totals are the same. This is always the case with statements of financial position, and is why they used to be called, 'balance sheets'.

3 The purchase of an asset and the incurring of a liability

On 6 May 2011, Blake buys some goods for £7,000 from D. Smith, and agrees to pay for them some time within the next two weeks. The effect of this is that a new asset, **inventory**, is acquired, and a liability for the goods is created. A person to whom money is owed for goods is known in accounting language as a **creditor**, and is described in the statement of financial position as an **account payable**. The statement of financial position becomes:

B. Blake
Statement of financial position as at 6 May 2011

Assets	£
Shop	32,000
Inventory	7,000
Cash at bank	28,000
	67,000
Less: Account payable	(7,000)
	60,000
Capital	60,000

Note how the liability (the account payable) is shown as a deduction from the assets. This is exactly the same calculation as is presented in the most common form of the accounting equation.

 Activity 1.6   Why do you think the £7,000 value for account payable is shown in brackets?

Now, let's return to our example.

4 Sale of an asset on credit

On 10 May 2011, goods which cost £600 were sold to J. Brown for the same amount, the money to be paid later. The effect is a reduction in the amount of goods held, i.e. inventory, and the creation of a new asset. A person who owes the business money is known in accounting language as a **debtor**, and is described in the statement of financial position as an **account receivable**. The statement of financial position is now:

B. Blake
Statement of financial position as at 10 May 2011

Assets	£
Shop	32,000
Inventory	6,400
Account receivable	600
Cash at bank	28,000
	67,000
Less: Account payable	(7,000)
	60,000
Capital	60,000

5 Sale of an asset for immediate payment

On 13 May 2011, goods which cost £400 were sold to D. Daley for the same amount. Daley paid for them immediately by cheque. Here one asset, inventory, is reduced, while another asset, cash at bank, is increased. The statement of financial position becomes:

B. Blake
Statement of financial position as at 13 May 2011

Assets	£
Shop	32,000
Inventory	6,000
Account receivable	600
Cash at bank	28,400
	67,000
Less: Account payable	(7,000)
	60,000
Capital	60,000

6 The payment of a liability

On 15 May 2011, Blake pays a cheque for £3,000 to D. Smith in part payment of the amount owing. The asset of cash at bank is therefore reduced, and the liability to the creditor is also reduced. The statement of financial position is now:

B. Blake
Statement of financial position as at 15 May 2011

Assets	£
Shop	32,000
Inventory	6,000
Account receivable	600
Cash at bank	25,400
	64,000
Less: Account payable	(4,000)
	60,000
Capital	60,000

Note how the total of each part of the statement of financial position has not changed. The business is still worth £60,000 to the owner.

7 Collection of an asset

J. Brown, who owed Blake £600, makes a part payment of £200 by cheque on 31 May 2011. The effect is to reduce one asset, account receivable, and to increase another asset, cash at bank. The statement of financial position becomes:

B. Blake
Statement of financial position as at 31 May 2011

Assets	£
Shop	32,000
Inventory	6,000
Account receivable	400
Cash at bank	25,600
	64,000
Less: Account payable	(4,000)
	60,000
Capital	60,000

1.11   Equality of the accounting equation

It can be seen that every transaction has affected two items. Sometimes it has changed two assets by reducing one and increasing the other. In other cases, the effect has been different. However, in each case other than the very first (when the business was started by the owner injecting some cash into it), no change was made to the total of either section of the statement of financial position and the equality between their two totals has been maintained. The accounting equation has held true throughout the example, and it always will. The effect of each of these seven accounting transactions upon the two sections of the statement of financial position is shown below:

Number of transaction as above	Assets	Capital and Liabilities	Effect on statement of financial position totals
1	+	+	Each side added to equally
2	+ −		A *plus* and a *minus* both on the assets side *cancelling each other out*
3	+	+	Each side has equal additions
4	+ −		A *plus* and a *minus* both on the assets side *cancelling each other out*
5	+ −		A *plus* and a *minus* both on the assets side *cancelling each other out*
6	−	−	Each side has equal deductions
7	+ −		A *plus* and a *minus* both on the assets side *cancelling each other out*

These are not the only types of accounting transactions that can take place. Two other examples arise when

(8) the owner withdraws resources from the business for his or her own use; and where
(9) the owner pays a business expense personally.

A summary of the effect upon assets, liabilities and capital of each type of transaction you've been introduced to so far is shown below:

Example of transaction	Effect	
(1) Owner pays capital into the bank	↑ Increase asset (Bank)	↑ Increase capital
(2) Buy inventory by cheque	↓ Decrease asset (Bank)	↑ Increase asset (Inventory)
(3) Buy inventory on credit	↑ Increase asset (Inventory)	↑ Increase liability (Accounts payable)
(4) Sale of inventory on credit	↓ Decrease asset (Inventory)	↑ Increase asset (Accounts receivable)
(5) Sale of inventory for cash (cheque)	↓ Decrease asset (Inventory)	↑ Increase asset (Bank)
(6) Pay creditor	↓ Decrease asset (Bank)	↓ Decrease liability (Accounts payable)
(7) Debtor pays money owing by cheque	↑ Increase asset (Bank)	↓ Decrease asset (Accounts receivable)
(8) Owner takes money out of the business bank account for own use	↓ Decrease asset (Bank)	↓ Decrease capital
(9) Owner pays creditor from private money outside the firm	↓ Decrease liability (Accounts payable)	↑ Increase capital

Transactions (8) and (9) cause the totals of each part of the statement of financial position to change (as did the very first, when capital was introduced to the business by the owner). When the capital changes, the totals of the two parts of the statement of financial position both change.

1.12 More detailed presentation of the statement of financial position

Let's now look at the statement of financial position of B. Blake as at 31 May 2011, presented according to how you will learn to present the information later in the book:

B. Blake
Statement of financial position as at 31 May 2011

	£	£
Non-current assets		
Shop		32,000
Current assets		
Inventory	6,000	
Account receivable	400	
Cash at bank	25,600	
		32,000
Total assets		64,000
Less Current liabilities		
Account payable		(4,000)
Net assets		60,000
Capital		60,000

You will have noticed in this statement of financial position the terms 'non-current assets', 'current assets' and 'current liabilities'. Chapter 8 contains a full explanation of these terms. At this point we will simply say:

- **Non-current assets** (fixed assets) are assets which have a long life bought with the intention to use them in the business and not with the intention to simply resell them, e.g. buildings, machinery, fixtures, motor vehicles.
- **Current assets** are assets consisting of cash, goods for resale or items having a short life (i.e. no more than a year remaining on the date of the statement of financial position). For example, the value of inventory in hand goes up and down as it is bought and sold. Similarly, the amount of money owing to us by debtors will change quickly, as we sell more to them on credit and they pay their debts. The amount of money in the bank will also change as we receive and pay out money.
- **Current liabilities** are those liabilities which have to be paid within no more than a year from the date on the statement of financial position, e.g. accounts payable for goods purchased.

Don't forget that there is a Glossary of accounting terms at the back of the book.

Learning outcomes

You should now have learnt:

1 Accounting is concerned with the recording, classifying and summarising of data, and then communicating what has been learnt from it.

2 Accounting has existed for at least 10,000 years but a formal, generally accepted method of recording accounting data has only been in existence for the last 500 years.

3 It may not only be the owner of a business who will need the accounting information. It may need to be shown to others, e.g. the bank or the Inspector of Taxes.

4 Accounting information can help the owner(s) of a business to plan for the future.

5 The accounting equation is: Capital = Assets − Liabilities.

6 The two sides of the accounting equation are represented by the two parts of the statement of financial position.

7 The total of one part of the statement of financial position should always be equal to the total of the other part.

8 Every transaction affects two items in the accounting equation. Sometimes that may involve the same item being affected twice, once positively (going up) and once negatively (going down).

9 Every transaction affects two items in the statement of financial position.

Note: Generally, the values used in exhibits and exercises have been kept down to relatively small amounts. This has been done deliberately to make the work of the student that much easier. Constantly handling large figures does not add anything to the study of the principles of accounting. It simply wastes a lot of the student's time, and he/she will probably make far more errors if larger figures are used.

Doing this may lead to the authors being accused of not being 'realistic' with the figures given, but we believe that it is far more important to make learning easier for the student.

Answers to activities

1.1   As with all professions, enforcement of a code of ethics in a manner which encourages outsiders to believe that accountancy bodies are serious on this issue is not simply a case of having a disciplinary code. Outsiders can be very sceptical about self-regulation, especially if accountants found guilty of unethical conduct are let off with a warning or a minor fine. This is a difficult situation to address: non-accountants lack the technical knowledge and expertise to interpret accounting practice and so are incapable of truly understanding many of the situations that may arise. Finding something more appropriate is difficult, if not impossible.

1.2   Owners and creditors are considered to be the most important stakeholders because they have most to lose if the business fails.

1.3   Who supplied the resources of the business.

1.4   Capital will be reduced if a business makes a loss. The loss means that assets have been reduced and capital is reduced by the same amount so as to maintain the balance in the accounting equation.

1.5   Capital = Assets – Liabilities

1.6   It is a negative number. In accounting, we *always* use brackets to indicate negative numbers.

Review questions

If you haven't already started answering them, you now have a set of graded review questions to try. 'Graded' means that they get more difficult as you go through them. Ideally, they should be done in the sequence they appear. *However, don't forget that the questions with an 'A' after the question number do not have any answers provided in this book.* Your teacher or lecturer will be able to provide you with the answers to those questions but be sure to attempt them first before asking for the answers! The answers to the other questions can be found at the back of the book.

We realise that you would like to have *all* the answers in the book. However, teachers and lecturers would not then be able to test your knowledge with questions from this book, as you would already possess the answers. It is impossible to please everyone, and the compromise reached is that of putting a large number of review questions in the book.

This means that appropriate reinforcement of what you have learnt can take place, even if you are studying on your own and have to miss out all the 'A' questions because you have no access to the answers.

Multiple choice questions. In addition to these Review Questions, there are questions relating to the material in this chapter in a bank of multiple choice questions at the end of Chapter 6. You should wait and attempt them when you reach them, not before.

1.1   Complete the gaps in the following table:

	Assets	Liabilities	Capital
	£	£	£
(a)	20,000	3,400	?
(b)	23,000	8,800	?
(c)	19,200	?	3,200
(d)	8,100	?	6,500
(e)	?	7,900	17,300
(f)	?	18,500	51,900

1.2A   Complete the gaps in the following table:

	Assets	Liabilities	Capital
	£	£	£
(a)	55,000	16,900	?
(b)	?	17,200	34,400
(c)	36,100	?	28,500
(d)	119,500	15,400	?
(e)	88,000	?	62,000
(f)	?	49,000	110,000

1.3   Which of the items in the following list are liabilities and which of them are assets?

(a)   Loan from A. Sangster
(b)   We owe a supplier
(c)   Equipment
(d)   Bank overdraft
(e)   Inventory of goods held for sale
(f)   Loan to F. Wood

1.4A   Classify the following items into liabilities and assets:

(a)   Motor vehicles
(b)   Premises
(c)   Accounts payable for inventory
(d)   Inventory
(e)   Accounts receivable
(f)   Owing to bank
(g)   Cash in hand
(h)   Loan from D. Jones
(i)   Machinery

1.5   State which of the following are wrongly classified:

Assets	Liabilities
Loan to C. Smith	Delivery van
Mortgage on office building	Accounts payable
Accounts receivable	Office supplies
Warehouse	Computers
Our business website	Cash in hand

1.6A   Which of the following are shown under the wrong headings?

Assets	Liabilities
Cash at bank	Loan from J. Graham
Fixtures	Machinery
Accounts payable	Motor vehicles
Building	
Inventory	
Accounts receivable	
Capital	

1.7   Luca Pacioli is setting up a new business. Before actually selling anything, he bought a van for £13,000, a transportable market stall for £1,050; a computer for £450; and an inventory of goods for £8,000. He did not pay in full for his inventory of goods and still owes £3,000 for them. He borrowed £10,000 from Basil Yamey. After the events just described, and before trading starts, he has £1,400 cash in hand and £4,700 in the bank. Calculate the amount of his capital.

1.8A   F. Flint is starting a business. Before actually starting to sell anything, he bought fixtures for £1,200, a van for £6,000 and an inventory of goods for £2,800. Although he has paid in full for the fixtures and the van, he still owes £1,600 for some of the inventory. B. Rub lent him £2,500. After the above, Flint has £200 in the business bank account and £175 cash in hand. You are required to calculate his capital.

1.9 Draw up N. Marriott's statement of financial position from the following information as at 31 December 2011:

	£
Capital	20,700
Accounts receivable	800
Car	8,300
Accounts payable	3,600
Equipment	7,900
Inventory	5,700
Cash at bank	1,600

1.10A Draw up M. Kelly's statement of financial position as at 30 June 2012 from the following items:

	£
Capital	10,200
Equipment	3,400
Accounts payable	4,100
Inventory	3,600
Accounts receivable	4,500
Cash at bank	2,800

1.11 Complete the columns to show the effects of the following transactions:

	Effect upon		
	Assets	Liabilities	Capital
(a) We pay a creditor £310 by cheque.			
(b) Bought fixtures £175 paying in cash.			
(c) Bought goods on credit £630.			
(d) The proprietor introduces another £1,200 cash into the business.			
(e) J. Walker lends the business £2,500 in cash.			
(f) A debtor pays us £50 in cash.			
(g) We return goods costing £90 to a supplier whose bill we had not paid.			
(h) Bought an office computer paying £610 by cheque.			

1.12A Complete the columns to show the effects of the following transactions:

	Effect upon		
	Assets	Liabilities	Capital
(a) Bought a van on credit £8,700.			
(b) Repaid by cash a loan owed to F. Duff £10,000.			
(c) Bought goods for £1,400 paying by cheque.			
(d) The owner puts a further £4,000 cash into the business.			
(e) A debtor returns to us goods worth £150. We agree to make an allowance for them.			
(f) Bought goods on credit £760.			
(g) The owner takes out £200 cash for his personal use.			
(h) We pay a creditor £1,150 by cheque.			

1.13   A. Park has the following items in her statement of financial position on 30 April 2012: Capital £31,700; Accounts payable £7,400; Fixtures £9,600; Car £12,300; Inventory £8,600; Accounts receivable £4,100; Cash at bank £1,600; Cash in hand £2,900.

During the first week of May 2012

(a)   She bought extra inventory for £1,100 on credit.
(b)   One of the debtors paid her £450 by cheque.
(c)   She bought a computer by cheque £610.

You are asked to draw up a statement of financial position as at 7 May 2012 after the above transactions have been completed.

1.14A   J. Hill has the following assets and liabilities on 30 November 2012: Accounts payable £2,800; Equipment £6,200; Car £7,300; Inventory £8,100; Accounts receivable £4,050; Cash at bank £9,100; Cash in hand £195.

You are not given the capital amount at that date.

During the first week of December 2012

(a)   Hill bought extra equipment on credit for £110.
(b)   Hill bought extra inventory by cheque £380.
(c)   Hill paid creditors by cheque £1,150.
(d)   Debtors paid Hill £640 by cheque and £90 by cash.
(e)   Hill put an extra £1,500 into the business, £1,300 by cheque and £200 in cash.

You are to draw up a statement of financial position as at 7 December 2012 after the above transactions have been completed.

Need more practice? Instant feedback?
Visit **www.myaccountinglab.com**

Featuring unlimited practice questions, a personalised study plan that identifies the areas where you need to focus for better marks, and interactive material designed to help all kinds of learners, MyAccountingLab is a vital tool for maximising your understanding, confidence, and success. Log in at **www.myaccountinglab.com** to see why 92 per cent of students surveyed last year recommend MyAccountingLab.

The Double Entry System

The double entry system for assets, liabilities and capital

2.1 Nature of a transaction

In Chapter 1, you saw how various events had changed two items in the statement of financial position. Events which result in such changes are known as 'transactions'. This means that if the proprietor asks the price of some goods, but does not buy them, then there is no transaction. If the proprietor later asks the price of some other goods, and then buys them, then there would be a transaction, and two statement of financial position items would then have to be altered.

2.2 The double entry system

We have seen that every transaction affects two items. We need to show these effects when we first record each transaction. That is, when we enter the data relating to the transaction in the accounting books we need to ensure that the items that were affected by the transaction, and only those items, are shown as having changed. This is the bookkeeping stage of accounting and the process we use is called **double entry**. You will often hear it referred to as **double entry bookkeeping**. Either term is correct.

Activity 2.1   Why do you think it is called 'double entry'?

If we want to show the double effect of every transaction when we are doing our bookkeeping, we have to show the effect of each transaction on each of the two items it affects. For each transaction this means that a bookkeeping entry will have to be made to show an increase or decrease of one item, and another entry to show the increase or decrease of the other item. From this description, you will probably see that the term 'double entry bookkeeping' is a good one, as each entry is made twice (double entry).

At this point, you may be wondering why you can't just draw up a new statement of financial position after each transaction, and so provide all the information required.

 Activity 2.2   Why can't we just adjust the statement of financial position and forget about making entries in any of the accounting books?

Instead of constantly drawing up statements of financial position after each transaction, what we have instead is the 'double entry' system. The basis of this system is that the transactions which occur are entered in a set of **accounts** within the accounting books. An account is a place where all the information referring to a particular asset or liability, or to capital, is recorded.

Thus, there will be an account where all the information concerning office equipment will be entered. Similarly, there will be an account for buildings, where all the information concerned with buildings will be shown. This will be extended so that every asset, every liability and capital will each have its own account for transactions involving that item.

2.3   The accounts for double entry

Each account should be shown on a separate page in the accounting books. The double entry system divides each page into two halves. The left-hand side of each page is called the **debit** side, while the right-hand side is called the **credit** side. The title of each account is written across the top of the account at the centre.

This is the layout of a page of an accounts book:

Title of account written here

Left-hand side of the page	Right-hand side of the page
This is the 'debit' side.	This is the 'credit' side.

Do you see how the shape resembles a 'T'? Not surprisingly, these are commonly referred to as **T-accounts**:

Account title here – the top stroke of the T

This line separates the two sides and is the downstroke of the T

Many students find it very difficult to make correct entries in the accounts because they forget that *debit* and *credit* have special accounting meanings. Don't fall into that trap. You must not confuse any other meanings you know for these two terms with the accounting ones.

You describe the entries in the accounts by saying something like 'debit account "x" with £z and credit account "y" with £z', inserting the names of the accounts and the actual amount in place of x, y and z. So, for example, if you paid £10 by cheque for a kettle, you could say 'debit the kettle account with £10 and credit the bank account with £10'.

To actually make this entry, you enter £10 on the left-hand (i.e. debit) side of the kettle account and on the right-hand (i.e. credit) side of the bank account.

Kettle account				Bank account	
£					£
10					10

You learnt in Chapter 1 that transactions increase or decrease assets, liabilities or capital. In terms of the assets, liabilities and capital:

- to **increase** an **asset** we make a DEBIT entry
- to **decrease** an **asset** we make a CREDIT entry
- to **increase** a **liability/capital** account we make a CREDIT entry
- to **decrease** a **liability/capital** account we make a DEBIT entry.

Placing these in a table organised by type of item, the double entry rules for bookkeeping are:

Accounts	To record	Entry in the account
Assets	an increase a decrease	Debit Credit
Liabilities	an increase a decrease	Credit Debit
Capital	an increase a decrease	Credit Debit

Let's look once again at the accounting equation:

	Capital =	Assets −	Liabilities
To increase each item	Credit	Debit	Credit
To decrease each item	Debit	Credit	Debit

The double entry rules for liabilities and capital are the same, but they are the opposite of those for assets. Looking at the accounts the rules will appear as:

Capital account		Any asset account		Any liability account	
Decreases	*Increases*	*Increases*	*Decreases*	*Decreases*	*Increases*
−	+	+	−	−	+

In a real business, at least one full page would be taken for each account in the accounting books. However, as we have not enough space in this textbook to put each account on a separate page, we will list the accounts under each other.

2.4   Worked examples

The entry of a few transactions can now be attempted.

1 The owner starts the business with £10,000 in cash on 1 August 2012.

The effects of this transaction are entered as follows:

Effect	Action
1 Increases the *asset* of cash 2 Increases the capital	Debit the cash account Credit the capital account

Cash

2012	£		
Aug 1	10,000		

Capital

		2012	£
		Aug 1	10,000

The date of the transaction has already been entered. (**Never forget to enter the date of each transaction.**) Now there remains the description (often referred to as the 'narrative') which is to be entered alongside the amount. This is completed by a cross-reference to the title of the other account in which the double entry is completed. The double entry to the item in the cash account is completed by an entry in the capital account. Therefore the word 'Capital' will appear as the narrative in the cash account:

Cash

2012		£	
Aug 1 Capital		10,000	

Similarly, the double entry to the item in the capital account is completed by an entry in the cash account, so the word 'Cash' will appear in the capital account:

Capital

		2012	£
		Aug 1 Cash	10,000

2 A van is bought for £4,500 cash on 2 August 2012.

Effect	Action
1 Increases the *asset* of van 2 Decreases the *asset* of cash	Debit the van account Credit the cash account

Van

2012		£	
Aug 2 Cash		4,500	

Cash

			2012			£
			Aug	2	Van	4,500

3 Fixtures (e.g. shelves) are bought on credit from Shop Fitters for £1,250 on 3 August 2008.

Effect	Action
1 Increases the *asset* of fixtures	Debit the fixtures account
2 Increases the *liability* to Shop Fitters	Credit the Shop Fitters account

Fixtures

2012			£	
Aug	3	Shop Fitters	1,250	

Shop Fitters

			2012			£
			Aug	3	Fixtures	1,250

Note how the liability of accounts payable is split in the accounting books so that a separate account is maintained for each account payable.

4 Paid the amount owing to Shop Fitters in cash on 17 August 2012.

Effect	Action
1 Decreases the *liability* to Shop Fitters	Debit the Shop Fitters account
2 Decreases the *asset* of cash	Credit the cash account

Shop Fitters

2012			£	
Aug	17	Cash	1,250	

Cash

			2012			£
			Aug	17	Shop Fitters	1,250

5 Transactions to date.

Combining all four of these transactions, the accounts now contain:

Cash

2012			£	2012			£
Aug	1	Capital	10,000	Aug	2	Van	4,500
					17	Shop Fitters	1,250

Capital

			2012			£
			Aug	1	Cash	10,000

Van

2012		£	
Aug 2	Cash	4,500	

Shop Fitters

2012		£	2012		£
Aug 17	Cash	1,250	Aug 3	Fixtures	1,250

Fixtures

2012		£	
Aug 3	Shop Fitters	1,250	

Note how you enter each transaction in an account in date order and how, once you open an account (e.g. Shop Fitters), you continue to make entries in it rather than opening a new account for every entry.

Before you read further, work through Review Questions 2.1 and 2.2A.

2.5 A further worked example

Have you noticed how each column of figures is headed by a '£' sign? This is important. You always need to indicate what the figures represent. In this case, it is pounds; in other cases you will meet during this book, the figures may be thousands of pounds (represented by '£000') or they could be in a different currency altogether. **Always include appropriate column headings.**

Now you have actually made some entries in accounts, go carefully through the following example. Make certain you can understand every entry and, if you have any problems, reread the first four sections of this chapter until you are confident that you know and understand what you are doing.

First, here is a table showing a series of transactions, their effects and the double entry action to take:

Transactions	Effect	Action
2012 May 1 Started a household machines business putting £25,000 into a business bank account.	↑ Increases *asset* of bank. ↑ Increases *capital* of owner.	Debit bank account. Credit capital account.
3 Bought equipment on credit from House Supplies £12,000.	↑ Increases *asset* of equipment. ↑ Increases *liability* to House Supplies.	Debit equipment account. Credit House Supplies account.
4 Withdrew £150 cash from the bank and placed it in the cash box.	↑ Increases *asset* of cash. ↓ Decreases *asset* of bank.	Debit cash account. Credit bank account.

Transactions	Effect	Action
2012 **May 7** Bought a van paying by cheque, £6,800.	↑ Increases *asset* of van. ↓ Decreases *asset* of bank.	Debit van account. Credit bank account.
10 Sold some equipment that was not needed at cost of £1,100 on credit to J. Rose.	↑ Increases *asset* of money owing from J. Rose. ↓ Decreases *asset* of equipment.	Debit J. Rose account. Credit equipment account.
21 Returned some of the equipment costing £2,300 to House Supplies.	↓ Decreases *liability* to House Supplier. ↓ Decreases *asset* of equipment.	Debit House Supplies. Credit equipment account.
28 J. Rose pays the amount owing, £1,100, by cheque.	↑ Increases *asset* of bank. ↓ Decreases *asset* of money owing by J. Rose.	Debit bank account. Credit J. Rose account.
30 Bought another van paying by cheque £4,300.	↑ Increases *asset* of vans. ↓ Decreases *asset* of bank.	Debit van account. Credit bank account.
31 Paid £9,700 to House Supplies by cheque.	↓ Decreases *liability* to House Supplies. ↓ Decreases *asset* of bank.	Debit House Supplies. Credit bank account.

You may find it worthwhile trying to enter all these transactions in T-accounts before reading any further. You will need to know that, similarly to accounts payable, the asset of accounts receivable is split in the accounting books so that a separate account is maintained for each debtor. You will need accounts for Bank, Cash, Capital, Equipment, Vans, House Supplies and J. Rose.

In T-account form this is shown:

Bank

2012			£	2012			£
May	1	Capital	25,000	May	4	Cash	150
					7	Van	6,800
	28	J. Rose	1,100		30	Van	4,300
					31	House Supplies	9,700

Cash

2012			£		
May	4	Bank	150		

Capital

2012				2012			£
				May	1	Bank	25,000

Equipment

2012			£	2012				£
May	3	House Supplies	12,000	May	10	J. Rose		1,100
					21	House Supplies		2,300

Vans

2012			£	
May	7	Bank	6,800	
	30	Bank	4,300	

House Supplies

2012			£	2012			£
May	21	Equipment	2,300	May	3	Equipment	12,000
	31	Bank	9,700				

J. Rose

2012			£	2012			£
May	10	Equipment	1,100	May	28	Bank	1,100

If you tried to do this before looking at the answer, be sure you understand any mistakes you made before going on.

2.6 Abbreviation of 'limited'

In this book, when we come across transactions with limited companies the letters 'Ltd' are used as the abbreviation for 'Limited Company'. So, if you see that the name of a business is 'W. Jones Ltd', it is a limited company. In our accounting books, transactions with W. Jones Ltd will be entered in the same way as for any other customer or supplier. It will be seen later that some limited companies use plc (which stands for 'public limited company') instead of Ltd.

2.7 Value Added Tax (VAT)

You may have noticed that VAT has not been mentioned in the examples covered so far. This is deliberate, so you are not confused as you learn the basic principles of accounting. In Chapter 19, you will be introduced to VAT and shown how to make the entries relating to it.

2.8 The mystery of making double entries

Double entry bookkeeping appears very simple: for every debit entry there is an equal credit entry. However, students often find that they cannot decide which account to debit and which account to credit. If you have this problem, you are not alone – virtually everyone struggles with this from time to time. However, if you learn the technique we describe in this section – the *Rule of Benefit* – you will find that you can always correctly identify which accounts are to be debited and which are to be credited.

A number of methods have been suggested in various books to help you make entries to the correct account and some students find them sufficient. I was taught to debit increases in assets and expenses and to credit increases in income and liabilities, a useful rule, but one that is sadly incomplete. Another rule often suggested is debit the receiver and credit the giver; again, a useful but sadly incomplete principle to adopt.

To overcome these deficiencies, students are sometimes given lists of transactions and told to learn the double entries for each example, so that they may then recall the appropriate example and make the correct entries for new transactions of the same form as the example. In some countries today, this case-based approach is a common element of accounting teaching and learning. Yet, even this is flawed – who can remember everything they memorise?

A simpler and far more effective approach is to be found in the first ever book to contain a detailed description of double entry bookkeeping, the bookkeeping treatise written by Fra' Luca Pacioli in 1494. In his book, he describes double entry from three perspectives: capital of the owner; cash; and credit. All transactions involve at least one of these. Taking each in turn:

Capital from the owner

If the owner of a business uses his or her own resources to provide the business with something, the capital account is credited and an account for the item provided is debited.

If the owner withdraws resources from the business, the capital account is debited and the account for the item withdrawn is credited.

You always know how to record the entry in the capital account so the other account must be treated in the opposite way – that is, if the capital account is credited, the other account is debited; if the capital account is debited, the other account is credited.

This rule always works for any transaction involving the owner's capital account.

Cash

If cash increases, you debit the cash account and credit the account of the item which gave rise to the cash. For example, if you sell goods for £30 in cash, you debit the cash account with £30 and credit the sales account with £30.

If cash decreases, you credit the cash account and debit the account of the item for which cash was expended. For example, if you pay someone wages of £100, you credit the cash account with £100 and debit the wages account with £100.

This rule always works for any cash transaction.

Credit

If a transaction *increases* the amount you are *owed*, you debit the account of the person who owes you money and you credit the account of the item that you gave that person in exchange for the promise to pay you later. For example, if you sell something on credit for £40 to Simon Stevin, you debit Simon Stevin's account with £40 and you credit the sales account with £40. You do the opposite if a transaction *decreases* the amount you are *owed*.

If a transaction *increases* the amount you owe, you credit the account of the person to whom you owe money and you debit the account of the item that you received from that person in exchange for the promise you made to pay later. For example, if you buy goods for resale on credit for £80 from Domenico Manzoni, you credit Domenico Manzoni's account with £80 and you debit the purchases account with £80. You do the opposite if a transaction *decreases* the amount you *owe*.

This rule always works for any credit transaction.

The Rule of Benefit

There is an even simpler way of looking at all this: consider every transaction from the perspective of the benefit inherent in the transaction.

Every asset is a benefit. Every expense represents payment for a benefit received by the business – expenditure is made so as to obtain a benefit. Thus, if a business pays a telephone bill, it is paying for the benefit it received (use of a phone), and so on. So,

1 if a business receives cash, the asset of cash has increased, which is a benefit to the business: *debit* the cash account;
2 if a business pays cash for something, the asset of cash has decreased, which is a reduction in benefit to the business: *credit* the cash account;
3 if a business receives a promise to pay from someone, that is a benefit to the business: *debit* that person's account;
4 if a business promises to pay someone for something, that promise represents a reduction in benefit to the business: *credit* that person's account;
5 if a business buys a van, the van is a new asset of the business and assets bring benefit to the business: *debit* the van account;
6 if a business sells an asset, such as a van, that is a reduction in benefit to the business – it no longer has the van: *credit* the van account;
7 if a business pays wages, the work they are for represents a benefit to the business: *debit* the wages account;
8 if a business pays for electricity, the electricity it received is a benefit to the business: *debit* the electricity account.

In each case, the other account involved will be treated in the opposite way. For example, wages paid in (7) are debited to the wages account. If they were paid in cash, the other account involved is the cash account. It should be credited.

This *Rule of Benefit* always works for every transaction:

> **Identify the accounts affected by a transaction. Debit the account for which there has been an increase in benefit; credit the account for which there has been a reduction in benefit.**

When you combine the *Rule of Benefit* with the rules mentioned above for capital, cash, and credit, you will always make the correct debit and credit entries in the accounts.

Learning outcomes

You should now have learnt:

1 That double entry follows the rules of the accounting equation.
2 That double entry maintains the principle that every debit has a corresponding credit entry.
3 That double entries are made in accounts in the accounting books.
4 Why each transaction is entered into accounts rather than directly into the statement of financial position.
5 How transactions cause increases and decreases in asset, liability and capital accounts.
6 How to record transactions in T-accounts.

Answers to activities

2.1 Each transaction is entered twice. In an accounting transaction, something always 'gives' and something 'receives' and both aspects of the transaction must be recorded. In other words, there is a double entry in the accounting books – each transaction is entered twice.

2.2   A statement of financial position is a financial report that summarises the financial position of an organisation at a point in time. It does not present enough information about the organisation to make it appropriate to enter each transaction directly on to the statement of financial position. It does not, for instance, tell us who the debtors are or how much each one of them owes the organisation, nor who the creditors are or the details of the amounts owing to each of them. We need to maintain a record of each individual transaction so that (a) we know what occurred and (b) we can check to see that it was correctly recorded.

Review questions

2.1   Complete the following table:

		Account to be debited	Account to be credited
(a)	Bought computer on credit from C. Ure Ltd.		
(b)	The proprietor paid a creditor, P. Took, from his private funds.		
(c)	A debtor, J. Pike, paid us by cheque.		
(d)	Repaid part of loan from J. Syme in cash.		
(e)	Returned the computer to C. Ure Ltd.		
(f)	A debtor, F. Wilson, pays us by cheque.		
(g)	Bought car on credit from Wiley Motors.		

2.2A   Complete the following table:

		Account to be debited	Account to be credited
(a)	Bought lorry for cash.		
(b)	Paid creditor, T. Lake, by cheque.		
(c)	Repaid P. Logan's loan by cash.		
(d)	Sold lorry for cash.		
(e)	Bought office machinery on credit from Ultra Ltd.		
(f)	A debtor, A. Hill, pays us by cash.		
(g)	A debtor, J. Cross, pays us by cheque.		
(h)	Proprietor puts a further amount into the business by cheque.		
(i)	A loan of £200 in cash is received from L. Lowe.		
(j)	Paid a creditor, D. Lord, by cash.		

2.3   Write up the asset and liability and capital accounts to record the following transactions in the records of J. Beach.

2013
July   1   Started business with £62,000 in the bank.
      2   Bought office furniture by cheque £3,700.
      3   Bought computers £1,710 on credit from VPC Ltd.
      5   Bought a van paying by cheque £9,800.
      8   Sold some of the office furniture – not suitable for the business – for £450 on credit to D. Bush & Sons.
    15   Paid the amount owing to VPC Ltd £1,710 by cheque.
    23   Received the amount due from D. Bush & Sons £450 by cheque.
    31   Bought machinery by cheque £310.

2.4   You are required to open the asset and liability and capital accounts and record the following transactions for June 2013 in the records of P. Bernard.

2013
June   1   Started business with £17,500 in cash.
        2   Paid £9,400 of the opening cash into a bank account for the business.
        5   Bought office furniture on credit from Dream Ltd for £2,100.
        8   Bought a van paying by cheque £5,250.
        12 Bought equipment from Pearce & Sons on credit £2,300.
        18 Returned faulty office furniture costing £260 to Dream Ltd.
        25 Sold some of the equipment for £200 cash.
        26 Paid amount owing to Dream Ltd £1,840 by cheque.
        28 Took £130 out of the bank and added to cash.
        30 F. Brown lent us £4,000 – giving us the money by cheque.

2.5A   Write up the asset, capital and liability accounts in the books of D. Gough to record the following transactions:

2012
June   1   Started business with £16,000 in the bank.
        2   Bought van paying by cheque £6,400.
        5   Bought office fixtures £900 on credit from Old Ltd.
        8   Bought van on credit from Carton Cars Ltd £7,100.
        12 Took £180 out of the bank and put it into the cash till.
        15 Bought office fixtures paying by cash £120.
        19 Paid Carton Cars Ltd a cheque for £7,100.
        21 A loan of £500 cash is received from B. Berry.
        25 Paid £400 of the cash in hand into the bank account.
        30 Bought more office fixtures paying by cheque £480.

2.6A   Write up the accounts to record the following transactions:

2010
March   1   Started business with £750 cash and £9,000 in the bank.
        2   Received a loan of £2,000 from B. Blane by cheque.
        3   Bought a computer for cash £600.
        5   Bought display equipment on credit from Clearcount Ltd £420.
        8   Took £200 out of the bank and put it in the cash till.
        15 Repaid part of Blane's loan by cheque £500.
        17 Paid amount owing to Clearcount Ltd £420 by cheque.
        24 Repaid part of Blane's loan by cash £250.
        31 Bought a printer on credit from F. Jones for £200.

Inventory

3.1 Inventory movements

In the examples in Section 1.10 of Chapter 1, inventory was sold at the same price at which it was bought. This is, of course, extremely unusual. In fact, any new business doing this wouldn't last terribly long. Businesses need to make profits to survive, as many 'dot.com' Internet companies discovered in 2000 when their bubble burst and all the losses they had been making took effect.

Normally, goods and services are sold above cost price, the difference being **profit**. As you know, when goods and services are sold for less than their cost, the difference is a **loss**.

Activity 3.1

Let's think about the double entry implications if all sales were at cost price. Fill in the blanks in the following:

As we did in Chapter 1, it would be possible to have an inventory account with goods purchased being _____ to the inventory account (as purchases represent __ _____ in the asset, inventory) and goods sold being _____ to it (as sales represent __ _____ in the asset, inventory).

The difference between the two sides of the inventory account would then represent the cost of the goods unsold at that date. (We'll ignore things like wastage, obsolescence and losses of inventory for now.)

Because most sales are not priced at cost, the sales figures include elements of profit or loss. Because of this, in most cases, the difference between the two sides of the inventory account would not represent the cost of the inventory.

At face value, maintaining an inventory account on this basis would serve no useful purpose. However, as pointed out by the distinguished scholar and accounting historian, G.N. Stoner, this 'early perpetual inventory records' system served a very useful purpose: it reveals the basic profit to date on each item of inventory once all the units of the item have been sold – a very useful piece of information for the managers of a business, which can be extended to be even more useful if the number of units of inventory involved in each transaction is also noted in the account.

Activity 3.2

How does adding the units to the entry in the account result in more useful information?

However, when preparing the financial statements of a business, we seek to identify the over-all profit, not just the profit on one item. Consequently, rather than using the 'early perpetual inventory records' system, many businesses use what is known as the 'periodic inventory valuation' system. Under this approach, we subdivide the way inventory is reported into several accounts, each one showing a movement of inventory. Firstly, we must distinguish between transactions that cause inventory to increase and those that cause it to decrease. Let's deal with each of these in turn.

1 **Increase in inventory.** This can be due to one of two causes:
   (a) The purchase of additional goods.
   (b) The return in to the business of goods previously sold. The reasons for this are numerous. The goods may have been the wrong type; they may, for example, have been surplus to requirements or faulty.

To distinguish the two aspects of the increase of inventory, two accounts are opened:
   (i) **a Purchases Account** – in which purchases of goods are entered; and
   (ii) **a Returns Inwards Account** – in which goods being returned into the business are entered. (Another name for this account is the **Sales Returns Account**.)

So, for *increases* in inventory, we need to choose which of these two accounts to use to record the *debit* side of the transaction.

2 **Decrease in inventory.** Ignoring things like wastage and theft, this can be due to one of two causes:
   (a) The sale of goods.
   (b) Goods previously bought by the business now being returned to the supplier.

Once again, in order to distinguish the two aspects of the decrease of inventory, two accounts are opened:

(*i*) **a Sales Account** – in which sales of goods are entered; and

(*ii*) **a Returns Outwards Account** – in which goods being returned out to a supplier are entered. (This is also known as the **Purchases Returns Account**.)

So, for *decreases* in inventory, we need to choose which of these two accounts to use to record the *credit* side of the transaction.

As inventory is an asset, and these four accounts are all connected with this asset, the double entry rules are those used for assets.

Activity 3.3   What are the double entry rules for assets?

Accounts	To record	Entry in the account
Assets	an increase a decrease	_____ _____

We shall now look at some entries in the following sections.

3.2 Purchase of inventory on credit

On 1 August 2012, goods costing £165 are bought on credit from D. Henry. First, the twofold effect of the transaction must be considered so that the bookkeeping entries can be worked out.

1 The asset of inventory is increased. An increase in an asset needs a debit entry in an account. Here the account is one designed for this type of inventory movement. It is clearly a 'purchase' movement so that the account to use must be the purchases account.

2 There is an increase in a liability. This is the liability of the business to D. Henry because the goods bought have not yet been paid for. An increase in a liability needs a credit entry. In this case, it would be a credit entry to D. Henry's account.

These two entries appear in the accounts as:

Purchases		
2012	£	
Aug 1 D. Henry	165	

D. Henry		
	2012	£
	Aug 1 Purchases	165

Note that these entries look identical to those you would make if you were using an inventory account rather than a purchases account. (The word 'inventory' would replace 'purchases' if an inventory account were being used.)

3.3 Purchases of inventory for cash

On 2 August 2012, goods costing £310 are bought, cash being paid for them immediately at the time of purchase.

1 As before, it is the asset of inventory that is increased, so a debit entry will be needed. The movement of inventory is that of a 'purchase', so the purchases account needs to be debited.
2 The asset of cash is decreased. To reduce an asset a credit entry is called for, and the asset is cash, so we need to credit the cash account.

Purchases

2012		£	
Aug 2 Cash		310	

Cash

			2012		£
			Aug 2 Purchases		310

3.4 Sales of inventory on credit

On 3 August 2012, goods were sold on credit for £375 to J. Lee.

1 An asset account is increased. The increase in the asset of trade receivables requires a debit and the debtor is J. Lee, so that the account concerned is that of J. Lee.
2 The asset of inventory is decreased. For this a credit entry to reduce an asset is needed. The movement of inventory is clearly the result of a 'sale' and so it is the sales account that needs to be credited.

J. Lee

2012		£	
Aug 3 Sales		375	

Sales

			2012		£
			Aug 3 J. Lee		375

3.5 Sales of inventory for cash

On 4 August 2012, goods are sold for £55, cash being received immediately at the time of sale.

1 The asset of cash is increased, so the cash account must be debited.
2 The asset of inventory is reduced. The reduction of an asset requires a credit and the movement of inventory is represented by 'sales'. Thus the entry needed is a credit in the sales account.

Cash

2012		£	
Aug 4 Sales		55	

Sales

			2012		£
			Aug 4 Cash		55

So far, so good. Apart from replacing the inventory account with the purchases account for inventory increases and the sales account for inventory decreases, you've done nothing different in your entries to the accounts compared with what you learnt in Chapters 1 and 2.

Go back to Chapters 1 and 2, and refresh your understanding of account entries.

Now let's look at the other inventory-related transactions that cause inventory to increase and decrease – returns inwards (sales that are being returned) and returns outwards (purchases that are being returned to the supplier).

3.6 Returns inwards

On 5 August 2012, goods which had been previously sold to F. Lowe for £29 are now returned *to the business*. This could be for various reasons such as:

- we sent goods of the wrong size, the wrong colour or the wrong model;
- the goods may have been damaged in transit;
- the goods are of poor quality.

1 The asset of inventory is increased by the goods returned. Thus, a debit representing an increase of an asset is needed. This time, the movement of inventory is that of 'returns inwards'. The entry required is a debit in the *Returns Inwards Account*.
2 There is a decrease in an asset. The debt of F. Lowe to the business is now reduced. A credit is needed in F. Lowe's account to record this.

Returns inwards			
2012	£		
Aug 5 F. Lowe	29		

	F. Lowe		
		2012	£
		Aug 5 Returns inwards	29

(Remember, another name for the Returns Inwards account is the 'Sales Returns account'.)

3.7 Returns outwards

On 6 August 2012, goods previously bought for £96 are returned *by the business* to K. Howe.

1 The liability of the business to K. Howe is decreased by the value of the goods returned. The decrease in a liability needs a debit, this time in K. Howe's account.
2 The asset of inventory is decreased by the goods sent out. Thus, a credit representing a reduction in an asset is needed. The movement of inventory is that of 'returns outwards' so the entry will be a credit in the *Returns Outwards Account*.

K. Howe			
2012	£		
Aug 6 Returns outwards	96		

	Returns outwards		
		2012	£
		Aug 6 K. Howe	96

(Remember, another name for the Returns Outwards account is the 'Purchases Returns account'.)

You're probably thinking this is all very straightforward. Well, let's see how much you have learnt by looking at two review questions.

Before you read further, work through Review Questions 3.1 and 3.2.

3.8 A worked example

2013
May   1   Bought goods on credit £220 from D. Small.
       2   Bought goods on credit £410 from A. Lyon & Son.
       5   Sold goods on credit to D. Hughes for £60.
       6   Sold goods on credit to M. Spencer for £45.
      10   Returned goods £15 to D. Small.
      11   Goods sold for cash £210.
      12   Goods bought for cash £150.
      19   M. Spencer returned £16 goods to us.
      21   Goods sold for cash £175.
      22   Paid cash to D. Small £205.
      30   D. Hughes paid the amount owing by him £60 in cash.
      31   Bought goods on credit £214 from A. Lyon & Son.

You may find it worthwhile trying to enter all these transactions in T-accounts before reading any further. You will need the following accounts: Purchases, Sales, Returns Outwards, Returns Inwards, D. Small, A. Lyon & Son, D. Hughes, M. Spencer and Cash.

Purchases

2013			£	
May	1	D. Small	220	
	2	A. Lyon & Son	410	
	12	Cash	150	
	31	A. Lyon & Son	214	

Sales

				2013			£
				May	5	D. Hughes	60
					6	M. Spencer	45
					11	Cash	210
					21	Cash	175

Returns outwards

				2013			£
				May	10	D. Small	15

Returns inwards

2013			£	
May	19	M. Spencer	16	

D. Small

2013			£	2013			£
May	10	Returns outwards	15	May	1	Purchases	220
	22	Cash	205				

A. Lyon & Son

			2013			£
			May	2	Purchases	410
				31	Purchases	214

D. Hughes

2013			£	2013			£
May	5	Sales	60	May	30	Cash	60

M. Spencer

2013			£	2013			£
May	6	Sales	45	May	19	Returns inwards	16

Cash

2013			£	2013			£
May	11	Sales	210	May	12	Purchases	150
	21	Sales	175		22	D. Small	205
	30	D. Hughes	60				

If you tried to do this before looking at the answer, be sure you understand any mistakes you made before going on.

3.9   Special meaning of 'sales' and 'purchases'

You need to remember that 'sales' and 'purchases' have a special meaning in accounting when compared to ordinary language usage.

Purchases in accounting means the *purchase of those goods which the business buys with the sole intention of selling*. Obviously, sometimes the goods are altered, added to, or used in the manufacture of something else, but it is the element of resale that is important. To a business that deals in computers, for instance, computers constitute purchases.

If something else is bought *which the business does not intend to sell*, such as a van, such an item cannot be called 'purchases', even though in ordinary language you would say that a van has been purchased. The van was bought to be used and *not* for resale.

Similarly, **sales** means the *sale of those goods in which the business normally deals and which were bought with the sole intention of resale*. The word 'sales' must never be given to the disposal of other items, such as vans or buildings that were purchased to be used and *not* to be sold.

If we did not keep to these meanings, we would find it very difficult to identify which of the items in the purchases and sales accounts were inventory and which were assets that had been bought to be used.

Let's now look at another of the small complications accountants need to deal with – the differences between the treatment of cash transactions and credit transactions.

3.10   Comparison of cash transactions and credit transactions for purchases and sales

As you saw in the last example, when goods are purchased for cash, the entries are:

● Debit the purchases account.
● Credit the cash account.

On the other hand, the complete set of entries for the purchase of goods on credit can be broken down into two stages: first, the purchase of the goods, and second, the payment for them.

The first part is:

● **Debit the purchases account.**
● **Credit the supplier's account.**

The second part is:

● **Debit the supplier's account.**
● **Credit the cash account.**

Activity 3.4　What is the difference between the treatment of cash purchases and credit purchases?

A study of cash sales and credit sales reveals a similar difference in treatment:

Cash sales	Credit sales
Complete entry: 　Debit cash account 　Credit sales account	First part: 　Debit customer's account 　Credit sales account Second part: 　Debit cash account 　Credit customer's account

Learning outcomes

You should now have learnt:

1 That it is *not* appropriate to use an inventory account to record increases and decreases in inventory because inventory is normally sold at a price greater than its cost.

2 That inventory increases either because some inventory has been purchased or because inventory that was sold has been returned by the buyer.

3 That inventory decreases either because some inventory has been sold or because inventory previously purchased has been returned to the supplier.

4 That a purchase account is used to record purchases of inventory (as debit entries in the account) and that a returns inwards account is used to record inventory returned by customers (as debit entries in the account).

5 That a sales account is used to record sales of inventory (as credit entries in the account) and that a returns outwards account is used to record inventory returned to suppliers (as credit entries in the account).

6 How to record increases and decreases of inventory in the appropriate accounts.

7 That in accounting, the term 'purchases' refers to purchases of inventory. Acquisitions of any other assets, such as vans, equipment and buildings, are *never* described as purchases.

8 That in accounting, the term 'sales' refers to sales of inventory. Disposals of any other assets, such as vans, equipment and buildings, are *never* described as sales.

9 That purchases for cash are *never* entered in the supplier's account.

10 That purchases on credit are *always* entered in the supplier's (creditor's) account.

11 That sales for cash are *never* entered in the customer's account.

12 That sales on credit are *always* entered in the customer's (debtor's) account.

Answers to activities

3.1 As we did in Chapter 1, it would be possible to have an inventory account with goods purchased being DEBITED to the inventory account (as purchases represent AN INCREASE in the asset, inventory) and goods sold being CREDITED to it (as sales represent A DECREASE in the asset, inventory).

3.2 If the inventory account shows a debit of £100 and two credit entries totalling £120, the basic profit so far on the goods is £20. If there are no units left, the figure of £20 represents the basic profit earned from that good – a 20 per cent profit.

Assume that the debit entry includes a note that 5 units were purchased, and the credit entries include notes indicating that 1 unit was sold for £40 and then 2 units were sold for £80. Overall basic profit would still be £20 but there are still 2 units in inventory.

Managers know a profit has already been made on the item. They may decide to sell off the remaining units at a lower price, or to increase the selling price, or to do nothing to the selling price. The point is that they have the information in the inventory account with which to make such a decision.

An extra column could be added to each side of the account in order to do this, and this was often done during the 300 or so years when this method of recording inventory was widely used. It is no longer used in financial accounting.

3.3

Accounts	To record	Entry in the account
Assets	an increase	Debit
	a decrease	Credit

3.4 With cash purchases, no entry is made in the supplier's account. This is because cash passes immediately and therefore there is no need to keep a check of how much money is owing to that supplier. On the other hand, with credit purchases, the records should show to whom money is owed until payment is made and so an entry is always made in the supplier's (creditor's) account.

Review questions

3.1   Complete the following table:

	Account to be debited	Account to be credited
(1) Goods sold for cash.		
(2) Vans bought on credit from H. Thomas.		
(3) Machinery sold for cash.		
(4) Goods sold on credit to B. Perkins.		
(5) Goods purchased by us returned to supplier, H. Hardy.		
(6) Goods bought on credit from J. Reid.		
(7) Goods sold, a cheque being received immediately.		
(8) Goods we returned to H. Forbes.		
(9) Goods sold returned to us by customer, J. Nelson.		
(10) Goods bought on credit from D. Simpson.		

3.2A   Complete the following table:

	Account to be debited	Account to be credited
(a) Goods bought on credit from T. Morgan.		
(b) Goods returned to us by J. Thomas.		
(c) Machinery returned to L. Jones Ltd.		
(d) Goods bought for cash.		
(e) Van bought on credit from D. Davies Ltd.		
(f) Goods returned by us to I. Prince.		
(g) D. Picton paid us his account by cheque.		
(h) Goods bought by cheque.		
(i) We paid creditor, B. Henry, by cheque.		
(j) Goods sold on credit to J. Mullings.		

3.3   You are to write up the following in the books:

2012

July	1	Started in business with £1,600 cash.
	3	Bought goods for cash £220.
	7	Bought goods on credit £600 from F. Herd.
	10	Sold goods for cash £86.
	14	Returned goods to F. Herd £730.
	18	Bought goods on credit £120 from D. Exodus.
	21	Returned goods to D. Exodus £52.
	24	Sold goods to B. Squire £146 on credit.
	25	Paid F. Herd's account by cash £480.
	31	B. Squire paid us his account in cash £146.

3.4A   Enter the following transactions in the appropriate accounts:

2012
Aug   1   Started in business with £7,400 cash.
2   Paid £7,000 of the opening cash into the bank.
4   Bought goods on credit £410 from J. Watson.
5   Bought a van by cheque £4,920.
7   Bought goods for cash £362.
10   Sold goods on credit £218 to L. Less.
12   Returned goods to J. Watson £42.
19   Sold goods for cash £54.
22   Bought fixtures on credit from Firelighters Ltd £820.
24   F. Holmes lent us £1,500 paying us the money by cheque.
29   We paid J. Watson his account by cheque £368.
31   We paid Firelighters Ltd by cheque £820.

3.5   Enter the following transactions in the accounts of L. Linda:

2013
July   1   Started in business with £20,000 in the bank.
2   D. Rupert lent us £5,000 in cash.
3   Bought goods on credit from B. Brown £1,530 and I. Jess £4,162.
4   Sold goods for cash £1,910.
6   Took £200 of the cash and paid it into the bank.
8   Sold goods on credit to H. Rise £1,530.
10   Sold goods on credit to P. Taylor £341.
11   Bought goods on credit from B. Brown £560.
12   H. Rise returned goods to us £65.
14   Sold goods on credit to G. Pate £535 and R. Sim £262.
15   We returned goods to B. Brown £94.
17   Bought van on credit from Aberdeen Cars Ltd £9,100.
18   Bought office furniture on credit from J. Winter Ltd £1,800.
19   We returned goods to I. Jess £130.
20   Bought goods for cash £770.
24   Goods sold for cash £110.
25   Paid money owing to B. Brown by cheque £1,924.
26   Goods returned to us by G. Pate £34.
27   Returned some of office furniture costing £180 to J. Winter Ltd.
28   L. Linda put a further £2,500 into the business in the form of cash.
29   Paid Aberdeen Cars Ltd £9,100 by cheque.
31   Bought office furniture for cash £365.

3.6A Enter the following transactions in the accounts:

2012

May
1 Started in business with £18,000 in the bank.
2 Bought goods on credit from B. Hind £1,455.
3 Bought goods on credit from G. Smart £472.
5 Sold goods for cash £210.
6 We returned goods to B. Hind £82.
8 Bought goods on credit from G. Smart £370.
10 Sold goods on credit to P. Syme £483.
12 Sold goods for cash £305.
18 Took £250 of the cash and paid it into the bank.
21 Bought a printer by cheque £620.
22 Sold goods on credit to H. Buchan £394.
23 P. Syme returned goods to us £160.
25 H. Buchan returned goods to us £18.
28 We returned goods to G. Smart £47.
29 We paid Hind by cheque £1,373.
31 Bought machinery on credit from A. Cobb £419.

The effect of profit or loss on capital and the double entry system for expenses and revenues

Learning objectives

After you have studied this chapter, you should be able to:

- calculate profit by comparing revenue with expenses
- explain how the accounting equation is used to show the effects of changes in assets and liabilities upon capital after goods or services have been traded
- explain why separate accounts are used for each type of expense and revenue
- explain why an expense is entered as a debit in the appropriate expense account
- explain why an item of revenue is entered as a credit in the appropriate revenue account
- enter a series of expense and revenue transactions into the appropriate T-accounts
- explain how the use of business cash and business goods for the owner's own purposes are dealt with in the accounting records

Introduction

In this chapter, you will learn how to calculate profits and losses and how to enter expense and revenue transactions into the ledger. You will also learn about drawings (i.e. amounts withdrawn from the business by the owner), and how to record them.

4.1 The nature of profit or loss

To an accountant, **profit** means the amount by which **revenue** is greater than **expenses** for a set of transactions. The term revenue means the sales value of goods and services that have been supplied to customers. The term expenses means the cost value of all the assets that have been used up to obtain those revenues.

If, therefore, we supplied goods and services valued for sale at £100,000 to customers, and the expenses incurred by us in order to supply those goods and services amounted to £70,000 the result would be a profit of £30,000:

		£
Revenue:	goods and services supplied to our customers for the sum of	100,000
Less Expenses:	value of all the assets used up to enable us to supply these goods and services	(70,000)
Profit is therefore:		30,000

On the other hand, it is possible for our expenses to exceed our revenues for a set of transactions. In this case the result is a **loss**. For example, a loss would be incurred given the following:

		£
Revenue:	what we have charged to our customers in respect of all the goods and services supplied to them	60,000
Less Expenses:	value of all the assets used up to supply these goods and services to our customers	(80,000)
Loss is therefore:		(20,000)

> **Activity 4.1** In each of these two examples, a different explanation was given for the terms 'revenue' and 'expenses'. What is the difference between the two explanations given for 'revenue'? What is the difference between the two explanations given for 'expenses'?

4.2   The effect of profit and loss on capital

Businesses exist to make a profit and so increase their capital. Let's look at the relationship between profit and capital in an example.

On 1 January the assets and liabilities of a business are:

Assets: Fixtures £10,000; Inventory £7,000; Cash at the bank £3,000.
Liabilities: Accounts payable £2,000.

The capital is found from the accounting equation:

$$\text{Capital} = \text{Assets} - \text{Liabilities}$$

In this case, capital is £10,000 + £7,000 + £3,000 − £2,000 = £18,000.

During January, the whole of the £7,000 inventory is sold for £11,000 cash. On 31 January the assets and liabilities have become:

Assets: Fixtures £10,000; Inventory nil; Cash at the bank £14,000.
Liabilities: Accounts payable £2,000.

The capital is now £22,000:

$$\text{Assets (£10,000 + £14,000)} - \text{Liabilities £2,000}$$

So capital has increased by £4,000 from £18,000 to £22,000. It has increased by £4,000 because the £7,000 inventory was sold at a profit of £4,000 for £11,000. Profit, therefore, increases capital:

$$\text{Old capital} + \text{Profit} = \text{New capital}$$

£18,000 + £4,000 = £22,000

A loss, on the other hand, would reduce the capital:

$$\boxed{\text{Old capital} - \text{Loss} = \text{New capital}}$$

4.3 Profit or loss and sales

Profit will be made when goods or services are sold for more than they cost, while the opposite will result in a loss.

(You will learn later that there are different types of profit, some of which you may have heard of, such as 'gross profit' and 'net profit'. For now, we're not going to complicate things by going into that level of detail so, whatever you may already know about these different types of profit, try to focus for the time being on the simple definition of profit presented here.)

4.4 Profit or loss and expenses

Once profits or losses have been calculated, you can update the capital account. How often this will be done will depend on the business. Some only attempt to calculate their profits and losses once a year. Others do it at much more frequent intervals. Generally speaking, the larger the business, the more frequently profits are calculated.

In order to calculate profits and losses, revenue and expenses must be entered into appropriate accounts. All the expenses could be charged to one Expenses Account, but you would be able to understand the calculations of profit better if full details of each type of expense were shown in those profit calculations. The same applies to each type of revenue.

For this reason, a separate account is opened for each type of expense and for each type of revenue. For example, accounts in use may include:

Commissions account	Subscriptions account	Rent account
Bank interest account	Motor expenses account	Postages account
Royalties receivable account	Telephone account	Stationery account
Rent receivable account	General expenses account	Wages account
Overdraft interest account	Audit fees account	Insurance account

It is purely a matter of choice in a business as to the title of each expense or revenue account. For example, an account for postage stamps could be called 'Postage stamps account', 'Postages account', 'Communication expenses account', and so on. Also, different businesses amalgamate expenses, some having a 'Rent and telephone account', others a 'Rent, telephone and insurance account', etc. Infrequent or small items of expense are usually put into a 'Sundry expenses account' or a 'General expenses account'.

Most organisations use names for their accounts that make it obvious which accounts are for revenue and which accounts are for expenses. However, some don't. When in doubt as to whether an account is for revenue or expenses, you have two obvious indicators to consult. The first is on which side the entries are mainly appearing in the account. If it is the debit side, the account is almost certainly an expense account. The other indicator is the nature of the business. For example, a commission account in the accounting books of a firm of stockbrokers is almost certainly a revenue account.

Activity 4.2 Identify which of the accounts listed in the table above are expense accounts and which ones are revenue accounts.

4.5 Debit or credit

You need to know whether expense accounts should be debited or credited with the amounts involved. You know that assets involve expenditure by the business and are shown as debit entries. Expenses also involve expenditure by the business and should, therefore, also be debit entries. Why? Because assets and expenses must ultimately be paid for. This payment involves a credit to the bank account (or to the cash account) so the original entry in the asset account or in the expense account must be a debit.

Even where an expense is incurred on credit, the creditor must eventually be paid. The first entry will be to credit the supplier's (i.e. creditor's) account and debit the expense account. When payment is made to the supplier, the bank account is credited and the supplier's account is debited.

For example, if you pay rent of £500 in cash, the asset cash is decreased by £500. The accounting equation tells you that this means that the capital is reduced by each expense – if assets decrease, so does capital; if liabilities increase, capital decreases (otherwise the accounting equation won't balance). Expense accounts contain debit entries for expenses. The second part of the entry will either be a credit against an asset account, such as cash, or it will be a credit against a liability account, such as creditors.

> **Activity 4.3**
>
> Some students find this explanation involving the capital account very difficult to understand, so try this example to ensure you have followed it. Write down the accounting equation and see if you can work out what happens to it if (a) a business spends £30 in cash hiring a van for a day and (b) if a business hires a van for a day at a cost of £30 and is given 1 month to pay the bill. Assume in each case that the business has assets of £200, liabilities of £80 and capital of £120 before the transaction. What happens to capital in each case?

Revenue is the opposite of expenses and, therefore, is treated in the opposite way – revenue entries appear on the credit side of the revenue accounts. You've already seen this when you've entered sales figures as credits into the sales account. Thus, revenue is collected together in appropriately named accounts, where it is shown as a credit until it is transferred to the profit calculations at the end of the period.

Consider too the use of funds to pay for expenses which are used up in the short term, or assets which are used up in the long term, both for the purpose of getting revenue. Both of these forms of transactions are entered on the debit side of the appropriate accounts (expense accounts or asset accounts respectively), while the revenue which they generate is shown on the credit side of the appropriate revenue accounts.

So, to summarise, profit belongs to the owners. Revenues increase profits, so they increase capital, and that makes them credits. Expenses decrease profits, so they reduce capital, and that makes them debits. The treatment of expenses is the same as the treatment of assets. Increases in expenses result in debit entries to the appropriate expense accounts, while decreases (such as refunds for overpayment of an electricity bill) result in credit entries to those same accounts. Revenue is treated the same as liabilities. Increases in revenue are credited to the appropriate revenue accounts, while decreases are debited to the same accounts.

In other words:

Debit	Credit
Expenses	Revenues
Losses	Profits
Assets	Liabilities
	Capital

4.6 Double entries for expenses and revenues

Let's look at some examples that demonstrate the double entry required:

1 Rent of £200 is paid in cash.
   Here the twofold effect is:

   (a) The total of the expenses of rent is increased. As expense entries are shown as debits, and the expense is rent, the action required is to debit the rent account with £200.
   (b) The asset of cash is decreased. This means the cash account must be credited with £200 to show the decrease of the asset.

   Summary: Debit the *rent account* with £200.
   Credit the *cash account* with £200.

2 Motor expenses of £355 are paid by cheque.
   The twofold effect is:

   (a) The total of the motor expenses paid is increased. The amount in expense accounts is increased through debit entries, so the action required is to debit the motor expenses account with £355.
   (b) The asset of funds in the bank is decreased. This means the bank account must be credited with £355 to show the decrease of the asset.

   Summary: Debit the *motor expenses account* with £355.
   Credit the *bank account* with £355.

3 £60 cash is received for commission earned by the business.

   (a) The asset of cash is increased. This needs a debit entry of £60 in the cash account to increase the asset.
   (b) The revenue account, commissions received, is increased. Revenue is shown by a credit entry, so, to increase the revenue account, the commissions received account is credited with £60.

   Summary: Debit the *cash account* with £60.
   Credit the *commissions received account* with £60.

Now look at some more transactions and their effect upon the accounts in the following table:

	Increase	Action	Decrease	Action
June 1 Paid for postage stamps by cash £50	Expense of postage	Debit postage account	Asset of cash	Credit cash account
2 Paid for electricity by cheque £229	Expense of electricity	Debit electricity account	Asset of bank	Credit bank account
3 Received rent in cash £138	Asset of cash	Debit cash account	—	—
	Revenue of rent	Credit rent received account		
4 Paid insurance by cheque £142	Expense of insurance	Debit insurance account	Asset of bank	Credit bank account

Entering these four examples into the appropriate accounts results in:

Cash

	£			£
June 3 Rent received	138	June 1 Postage		50

Bank

			£
	June 2 Electricity		229
	4 Insurance		142

Electricity

	£	
June 2 Bank	229	

Insurance

	£	
June 4 Bank	142	

Postage

	£	
June 1 Cash	50	

Rent received

		£
	June 3 Cash	138

4.7   Drawings

Sometimes the owners will want to take cash out of the business for their private use. This is known as **drawings**. Any money taken out as drawings will reduce capital. Drawings are *never* expenses of a business. An increase in drawings is a debit entry in the drawings account, with the credit being against an asset account, such as cash or bank.

In theory, the debit entry should be made in the capital account (as drawings decrease capital). However, to prevent the capital account becoming full of lots of small transactions, drawings are not entered in the capital account. Instead, a *drawings account* is opened, and the debits are entered there.

The following example illustrates the entries for drawings:

On 25 August, the owner takes £50 cash out of the business for his own use.

Effect	Action
1 Capital is decreased by £50 2 Cash is decreased by £50	Debit the drawings account £50 Credit the cash account £50

Drawings

	£	
Aug 25 Cash	50	

Cash

		£
	Aug 25 Drawings	50

Sometimes goods are taken for private use. This form of withdrawal by the owner is also known as drawings. In Section 3.2, you learnt that when goods are purchased, the purchases account is debited. As a result, when goods are withdrawn it is the purchases account which should be credited.

The following example illustrates the entries for this form of drawings.

On 28 August, the owner takes £400 of goods out of the business for his own use.

Effect	Action
1 Capital is decreased by £400 2 Inventory is decreased by £400	Debit the drawings account £400 Credit the purchases account £400

Drawings

	£	
Aug 28 Purchases	400	

Purchases

		£
	Aug 28 Drawings	400

Learning outcomes

You should now have learnt:

1 How to calculate profit by comparing revenue with expenses.

2 That the accounting equation is central to any explanation of the effect of trading upon capital.

3 Why every different type of expense is shown in a separate expense account.

4 Why every different type of revenue is shown in a separate revenue account.

5 Why an expense is shown as a debit entry in the appropriate expense account.

6 Why revenue is shown as a credit entry in the appropriate revenue account.

7 How to enter a series of expense and revenue transactions into the appropriate T-accounts.

8 What is meant by the term 'drawings'.

9 That drawings are *always* a reduction in capital and *never* an expense of a business.

10 How to record drawings of cash in the accounting books.

11 How to record drawings of goods in the accounting books.

Answers to activities

4.1   There is no difference between either the two meanings given for revenue or the two meanings given for expenses. In each case, you are being given a slightly different wording so as to help you understand what the two terms mean.

4.2   *Expense accounts*
Rent account
Postages account
Commissions account
Stationery account
Wages account
Insurance account
Bank interest account
Motor expenses account
Telephone account
General expenses account
Overdraft interest account
Audit fees account

Revenue accounts
Subscriptions account
Rent receivable account
Royalties receivable account

Note that the answer has assumed that *unless* words like 'received' or 'receivable' follow the name of an account, the account is an expense. For example, the Commission Account and the Bank Interest Account could easily be for revenue rather than expenses. However, accounting practice is that as most accounts are for expenses, where there may be some confusion as to whether an account is for revenue or expenses, the name of the revenue account should make it clear that it is for revenue, not expenses. You can see an example in this question if you compare the names of the two rent accounts. Accounts like Subscriptions tend to appear mainly in the accounting books of clubs and societies and so there is no need in that case to indicate in the name that it is a revenue account. You can tell whether subscriptions are revenue or expenditure items from the type of organisation whose accounting books you are looking at. The same would apply, but even more so, to Audit Fees which are only ever revenue accounts in the accounting books of a firm of accountants. In all other cases, they are expense accounts.

4.3   The accounting equation is Capital = Assets − Liabilities. In this example, it starts as £120 = £200 − £80. Each transaction is entered twice. In both cases, the debit entry is £30 to a van hire expense account. The credit in (a) is to the cash account. In (b) it is to the car hire company's account (the creditor's account). In order for the accounting equation to balance, in (a) an asset (i.e. cash) has been reduced by £30 so capital must be reduced by the same amount, £30. In the case of (b) liabilities (i.e. the van hire company's account) have increased by £30 and so capital must also be reduced by that amount, £30. In the case of (a) the accounting equation becomes £90 = £170 − £80. In (b) it becomes £90 = £200 − £110. The effect on capital in both cases is that it decreases by the amount of the expense.

Review questions

4.1   Enter the following transactions, completing the double entry in the books for the month of May 2013:

2013
May   1   Started in business with £18,000 in the bank and £2,000 in cash.
   2   Purchased goods £580 on credit from D. Monty.
   3   Bought fixtures and fittings £2,300 paying by cheque.
   5   Sold goods for cash £280.
   6   Bought goods on credit £650 from C. George.
   10   Paid rent by cash £400.
   12   Bought stationery £90, paying in cash.
   18   Goods returned to D. Monty £82.
   21   Received rent of £240 by cheque for sublet of corner space.
   23   Sold goods on credit to G. Field for £1,600.

24 Bought a van paying by cheque £8,200.
30 Paid the month's wages by cash £610.
31 The proprietor took cash for his own personal use £510.

4.2 Write up the following transactions in the books of P. Hewitt:

2013
March 1 Started in business with cash £16,000.
2 Bought goods on credit from W. Young £420.
3 Paid rent by cash £870.
4 Paid £12,500 of the cash of the business into a bank account.
5 Sold goods on credit to D. Unbar £192.
7 Bought stationery £85 paying by cheque.
11 Cash sales £312.
14 Goods returned by us to W. Young £54.
17 Sold goods on credit to J. Harper £212.
20 Paid for repairs to the building by cash £78.
22 D. Unbar returned goods to us £31.
27 Paid W. Young by cheque £366.
28 Cash purchases £470.
29 Bought a van paying by cheque £3,850.
30 Paid motor expenses in cash £216.
31 Bought a computer £730 on credit from B. Coal.

4.3A Prepare the double entries (*not* the T-accounts) for the following transactions using the format:

Date		Dr	Cr
	Account name	£x	
	Account name		£x

July 1 Started in business with £5,000 in the bank and £1,000 cash.
2 Bought stationery by cheque £75.
3 Bought goods on credit from T. Smart £2,100.
4 Sold goods for cash £340.
5 Paid insurance by cash £290.
7 Bought a computer on credit from J. Hott £700.
8 Paid expenses by cheque £32.
10 Sold goods on credit to C. Biggins £630.
11 Returned goods to T. Smart £550.
14 Paid wages by cash £210.
17 Paid rent by cheque £225.
20 Received cheque £400 from C. Biggins.
21 Paid J. Hott by cheque £700.
23 Bought stationery on credit from News Ltd £125.
25 Sold goods on credit to F. Tank £645.
31 Paid News Ltd by cheque £125.

4.4A Write up the following transactions in the T-accounts of F. Fernandes:

Feb 1 Started in business with £11,000 in the bank and £1,600 cash.
2 Bought goods on credit: J. Biggs £830; D. Martin £610; P. Lot £590.
3 Bought goods for cash £370.
4 Paid rent in cash £75.
5 Bought stationery paying by cheque £62.
6 Sold goods on credit: D. Twigg £370; B. Hogan £290; K. Fletcher £410.
7 Paid wages in cash £160.
10 We returned goods to D. Martin £195.

11 Paid rent in cash £75.
13 B. Hogan returns goods to us £35.
15 Sold goods on credit to: T. Lee £205; F. Sharp £280; G. Rae £426.
16 Paid business rates by cheque £970.
18 Paid insurance in cash £280.
19 Paid rent by cheque £75.
20 Bought van on credit from B. Black £6,100.
21 Paid motor expenses in cash £24.
23 Paid wages in cash £170.
24 Received part of amount owing from K. Fletcher by cheque £250.
28 Received refund of business rates £45 by cheque.
28 Paid by cheque: J. Biggs £830; D. Martin £415; B. Black £6,100.

4.5 From the following statements which give the cumulative effects of individual transactions, you are required to state as fully as possible what transaction has taken place in each case. That is, write descriptions similar to those given in questions 4.1–4.4. There is no need to copy out the table. The first column of data gives the opening position. Each of the other columns represents a transaction. It is these transactions (A–I) that you are to describe.

Transaction:		A	B	C	D	E	F	G	H	I
Assets	£000	£000	£000	£000	£000	£000	£000	£000	£000	£000
Land and buildings	450	450	450	450	575	575	275	275	275	275
Motor vehicles	95	100	100	100	100	100	100	100	100	100
Office equipment	48	48	48	48	48	48	48	48	48	48
Inventory	110	110	110	110	110	110	110	110	110	93
Accounts receivable	188	188	188	188	188	108	108	108	108	120
Bank	27	22	22	172	47	127	427	77	77	77
Cash	15	15	11	11	11	11	11	11	3	3
	933	933	929	1,079	1,079	1,079	1,079	729	721	716
Liabilities										
Capital	621	621	621	621	621	621	621	621	621	616
Loan from Lee	200	200	200	350	350	350	350	–	–	–
Accounts payable	112	112	108	108	108	108	108	108	100	100
	933	933	929	1,079	1,079	1,079	1,079	729	721	716

Note: the heading £000 means that all the figures shown underneath it are in thousands of pounds, e.g. Office Equipment book value is £48,000. It saves constantly writing out 000 after each figure, and is done to save time and make comparison easier.

4.6A The following table shows the cumulative effects of a succession of separate transactions on the assets and liabilities of a business. The first column of data gives the opening position.

Transaction:		A	B	C	D	E	F	G	H	I
Assets	£000	£000	£000	£000	£000	£000	£000	£000	£000	£000
Land and buildings	500	500	535	535	535	535	535	535	535	535
Equipment	230	230	230	230	230	230	230	200	200	200
Inventory	113	140	140	120	120	120	120	120	119	119
Trade accounts receivable	143	143	143	173	160	158	158	158	158	158
Prepaid expenses*	27	27	27	27	27	27	27	27	27	27
Cash at bank	37	37	37	37	50	50	42	63	63	63
Cash on hand	9	9	9	9	9	9	9	9	9	3
	1,059	1,086	1,121	1,131	1,131	1,129	1,121	1,112	1,111	1,105
Liabilities										
Capital	730	730	730	740	740	738	733	724	723	717
Loan	120	120	155	155	155	155	155	155	155	155
Trade accounts payable	168	195	195	195	195	195	195	195	195	195
Accrued expenses*	41	41	41	41	41	41	38	38	38	38
	1,059	1,086	1,121	1,131	1,131	1,129	1,121	1,112	1,111	1,105

Required:

Identify clearly and as fully as you can what transaction has taken place in each case. Give two possible explanations for transaction I. Do not copy out the table but use the reference letter for each transaction.

(*Association of Accounting Technicians*)

Authors' note: You have not yet been told about 'prepaid expenses' and 'accrued expenses'. Prepaid expenses are expenses that have been paid in advance, the benefits of which will only be felt by the business in a later accounting period. Because the benefit of having incurred the expense will not be received until a future time period, the expense is not included in the calculation of profit for the period in which it was paid. As it was not treated as an expense of the period when profit was calculated, the debit in the account is treated as an asset when the statement of financial position is prepared, hence the appearance of the term 'prepaid expenses' among the assets in the question. Accrued expenses, on the other hand, are expenses that have not yet been paid for benefits which have been received. In F, £8,000 was paid out of the bank account (50–42) of which £3,000 was used to pay off some of the accrued expenses (41–38).

The Trial Balance

Balancing-off accounts

Learning objectives

After you have studied this chapter, you should be able to:

- close-off accounts when appropriate
- balance-off accounts at the end of a period and bring down the opening balance to the next period
- distinguish between a debit balance and a credit balance
- describe and prepare accounts in three-column format

Introduction

In this chapter, you'll learn how to discover what the amount outstanding on an account is at a particular point in time. You'll also learn how to close accounts that are no longer needed and how to record appropriate entries in accounts at the end and beginning of periods. Finally, you'll learn that T-accounts are not the only way to record accounting transactions.

5.1 Accounts for debtors

Where debtors have paid their accounts

So far you have learnt how to record transactions in the accounting books by means of debit and credit entries. At the end of each accounting period the figures in each account are examined in order to summarise the situation they present. This will often, but not always, be once a year if you are calculating profit. If you want to see what is happening with respect to particular accounts, it will be more frequently done. For example, if you want to find out how much your customers owe you for goods you have sold to them, you would probably do this at the end of each month.

Activity 5.1 Why do you think we would want to look at the accounts receivable in the accounting books as often as once a month?

Let's look at the account of one of our customers, K. Tandy, for transactions in August 2012:

K. Tandy

2012			£	2012			£
Aug	1	Sales	144	Aug	22	Bank	144
	19	Sales	300		28	Bank	300

If you add up the figures on each side, you will find that they both sum to £444. In other words, during the month we sold a total of £444 worth of goods to Tandy, and have been paid a total of £444 by her. This means that at the end of August she owes us nothing. As she owes us nothing, we do not need her account to prepare the statement of financial position (there is no point in showing a figure for accounts receivable of zero in the statement of financial position). We can, therefore, **close off** her account on 31 August 2012. This is done by inserting the totals on each side:

K. Tandy

2012			£	2012			£
Aug	1	Sales	144	Aug	22	Bank	144
	19	Sales	300		28	Bank	300
			444				444

Notice that totals in accounting are always shown with a single line above them, and a double line underneath. As shown in the following completed account for C. Lee, totals on accounts at the end of a period are always shown on a level with one another, even when there are less entries on one side than on the other.

Now, let's look at the account for C. Lee.

C. Lee

2012			£	2012			£
Aug	11	Sales	177	Aug	30	Bank	480
	19	Sales	203				
	22	Sales	100				
			480				480

In this account, C. Lee also owed us nothing at the end of August 2012, as he had paid us for all the sales we made to him.

Note: In handwritten accounts, you will often see this layout enhanced by two intersecting lines, one horizontal and one diagonal on the side which has less entries. If this were done, C. Lee's account would look like this:

C. Lee

2012			£	2012			£
Aug	11	Sales	177	Aug	30	Bank	480
	19	Sales	203				
	22	Sales	100				
			480				480

We won't use this layout in this book, but your teacher or lecturer may want you to use it whenever you are preparing T-accounts.

Activity 5.2   Why do you think we would want to draw these two extra lines onto the hand-written account?

If an account contains only one entry on each side and they are equal, you don't need to include totals. For example:

K. Wood

2012		£	2012		£
Aug 6	Sales	<u>214</u>	Aug 12	Bank	<u>214</u>

Now let's look at what happens when the two sides do not equal each other.

Where debtors still owe for goods

It is unlikely that everyone will have paid the amounts they owe us by the end of the month. In these cases, the totals of each side would not equal one another. Let's look at the account of D. Knight for August 2012:

D. Knight

2012		£	2012		£
Aug 1	Sales	158	Aug 28	Bank	158
15	Sales	206			
30	Sales	118			

If you add the figures you will see that the debit side adds up to £482 and the credit side adds up to £158. You should be able to see what the difference of £324 (i.e. £482 – £158) represents. It consists of the last two sales of £206 and £118. They have not been paid for and so are still owing to us on 31 August 2012.

In double entry, we only enter figures as totals if the totals on both sides of the account agree. We do, however, want to **balance-off** the account for August showing that Knight owes us £324. (While there would be nothing wrong in using the term 'close off', 'balance-off' is the more appropriate term to use when there is a difference between the two sides of an account.)

If Knight owes us £324 at close of business on 31 August 2012, then the same amount will be owed to us when the business opens on 1 September 2012.

Balancing the accounts is done in five stages:

1 Add up both sides to find out their totals. Note: do not write anything in the account at this stage.
2 Deduct the smaller total from the larger total to find the balance.
3 Now enter the balance on the side with the smallest total. This now means the totals will be equal.
4 Enter totals level with each other.
5 Now enter the balance on the line below the totals on the *opposite* side to the balance shown above the totals.

Against the balance above the totals, complete the date column by entering the last day of that period – for August, this will always be '31' even if the business was shut on that date because it fell on a weekend or was a holiday. Below the totals, show the first day of the next period against the balance – this will always be the day immediately after the last day of the previous period, in this case, September 1. The balance above the totals is described as the **balance *carried down*** (often abbreviated to 'balance c/d'). The balance below the total is described as the **balance *brought down*** (often abbreviated to 'balance b/d').

Knight's account when 'balanced-off' will appear as follows:

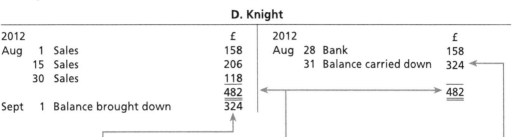

D. Knight

2012			£	2012			£
Aug	1	Sales	158	Aug	28	Bank	158
	15	Sales	206		31	Balance carried down	324
	30	Sales	118				
			482				482
Sept	1	Balance brought down	324				

Stage 5: finally, enter balance to start off entries for following month.

Stage 4: now enter totals level with each other.

Stage 3: enter balance here so that totals will be equal.

Note for students

- From now on, we will use the abbreviations 'c/d' and 'b/d'.
- The date given to balance c/d is the last day of the period which is finishing, and balance b/d is given the opening date of the next period.
- As the total of the debit side originally exceeded the total of the credit side, the balance is said to be a 'debit balance'. This being a personal account (for a person), the person concerned is said to be a debtor – the accounting term for anyone who owes money to the business.

Just as when the two sides each have only one entry and the two sides are equal, if an account contains only one entry it is unnecessary to enter the total after entering the balance carried down (because the balance becomes the only entry on the other side and it is equal to the other entry). A double line ruled under the entry will mean that the entry is its own total. For example:

B. Walters

2012			£	2012			£
Aug	18	Sales	51	Aug	31	Balance c/d	51
Sept	1	Balance b/d	51				

Note: T-accounts should *always* be closed off at the end of each period, even when they contain only one entry.

5.2 Accounts for creditors

Exactly the same principles will apply when the balances are carried down to the credit side. This balance is known as a 'credit balance'. We can look at the accounts of two of our suppliers which are to be balanced-off:

E. Williams

2012			£	2012			£
Aug	21	Bank	100	Aug	2	Purchases	248
					18	Purchases	116

K. Patterson

2012			£	2012			£
Aug	14	Returns outwards	20	Aug	8	Purchases	620
	28	Bank	600		15	Purchases	200

We now add up the totals and find the balance, i.e. Stages 1 and 2. When balanced-off, these will appear as:

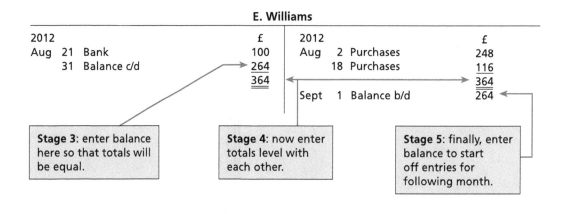

E. Williams

2012			£	2012			£
Aug	21	Bank	100	Aug	2	Purchases	248
	31	Balance c/d	264		18	Purchases	116
			364				364
				Sept	1	Balance b/d	264

Stage 3: enter balance here so that totals will be equal.

Stage 4: now enter totals level with each other.

Stage 5: finally, enter balance to start off entries for following month.

K. Patterson

2012			£	2012			£
Aug	14	Returns outwards	20	Aug	8	Purchases	620
	28	Bank	600		15	Purchases	200
	31	Balance c/d	200				
			820				820
				Sept	1	Balance b/d	200

The accounts of E. Williams and K. Patterson have credit balances. They are 'creditors' – the accounting term for someone to whom money is owed.

Before you read further attempt Review Questions 5.1 and 5.2.

5.3 Three-column accounts

Through the main part of this book, the type of account used is the T-account, where the left-hand side of the account is the debit side, and the right-hand side is the credit side. However, when computers are used the style of the ledger account is sometimes different. It appears as three columns of figures, one column for debit entries, another column for credit entries, and the last column for the balance. If you have an account at a bank, your bank statements will normally be shown using this three-column format.

The accounts used in this chapter will now be redrafted to show the ledger accounts drawn up in this way.

K. Tandy

			Debit	Credit	Balance (and whether debit or credit)	
2012			£	£	£	
Aug	1	Sales	144		144	Dr
	19	Sales	300		444	Dr
	22	Bank		144	300	Dr
	28	Bank		300	0	

C. Lee

2012			Debit £	Credit £	Balance £	
Aug	11	Sales	177		177	Dr
	19	Sales	203		380	Dr
	22	Sales	100		480	Dr
	30	Bank		480	0	

K. Wood

2012			Debit £	Credit £	Balance £	
Aug	6	Sales	214		214	Dr
	12	Bank		214	0	

D. Knight

2012			Debit £	Credit £	Balance £	
Aug	1	Sales	158		158	Dr
	15	Sales	206		364	Dr
	28	Bank		158	206	Dr
	31	Sales	118		324	Dr

B. Walters

2012			Debit £	Credit £	Balance £	
Aug	18	Sales	51		51	Dr

E. Williams

2012			Debit £	Credit £	Balance £	
Aug	2	Purchases		248	248	Cr
	18	Purchases		116	364	Cr
	21	Bank	100		264	Cr

K. Patterson

2012			Debit £	Credit £	Balance £	
Aug	8	Purchases		620	620	Cr
	14	Returns	20		600	Cr
	15	Purchases		200	800	Cr
	28	Bank	600		200	Cr

Note how the balance is calculated after every entry. This can be done quite simply when using a computer because the software can automatically calculate the new balance as soon as an entry is made.

When manual methods are being used it is often too much work to have to calculate a new balance after each entry. Also, the greater the number of calculations, the greater the possibility of errors. For these reasons, it is usual for students to use T-accounts *except* when required to use three-column accounts in an exam! However, it is important to note that there is no difference in principle – the final balances are the same using either method.

Learning outcomes

You should now have learnt:

1 How to close off accounts upon which there is no balance oustanding.

2 How to balance-off accounts at the end of a period.

3 How to bring down the opening balance on an account at the start of a new period.

4 That when an opening balance on an account is a debit, that account is said to have a debit balance. It also has a debit balance during a period whenever the total of the debit side exceeds the total of the credit side.

5 That when an opening balance on an account is a credit, that account is said to have a credit balance. It also has a credit balance during a period whenever the total of the credit side exceeds the total of the debit side.

6 That 'debtors' are people or organisations whose account in your accounting books has a greater value on the debit side. They owe you money. They are included in the amount shown for accounts receivable in the statement of financial position.

7 That 'creditors' are people or organisations whose account in your accounting books has a greater value on the credit side. You owe them money. They are included in the amount shown for accounts payable in the statement of financial position.

8 That T-accounts and three-column accounts disclose the same balance, given identical information about transactions.

9 That three-column accounts update and show the balance on the account after every transaction.

10 How to prepare three-column accounts.

Answers to activities

5.1 In order to survive, businesses must, in the long term, make profits. However, even profitable businesses go 'bust' if they do not have enough funds to pay their bills when they are due. Debtors represent a resource that is not yet in the form of funds (e.g. cash) that can be used to pay bills. By regularly monitoring the position on the account of each debtor, a business can tell which debtors are being slow to pay and, very importantly, do something about it.

5.2 The purpose is to prevent any more entries being made in the account. The entries would *always* be made in ink, so as to prevent their being erased and replaced with different entries. In a computerised accounting system, there is no need for measures such as these, because the controls and checks built into the computerised system prevent such things from happening.

Review questions

5.1   Enter the following items in the appropriate debtors' accounts (i.e. your customers' accounts) only; do *not* write up other accounts. Then balance-off each of these personal accounts at the end of the month. (Keep your answer; it will be used as a basis for Review Question 5.3.)

2012
May   1   Sales on credit to B. Flyn £810; F. Lane £1,100; T. Fey £413.
       4   Sales on credit to F. Start £480; B. Flyn £134.
      10   Returns inwards from B. Flyn £124; T. Fey £62.
      18   F. Lane paid us by cheque £1,100.
      20   T. Fey paid us £351 by cheque.
      24   B. Flyn paid us £440 by cash.
      31   Sales on credit to F. Start £240.

5.2   Enter the following in the appropriate creditors' accounts (i.e. your suppliers' accounts) only. Do *not* write up the other accounts. Then balance-off each of these personal accounts at the end of the month. (Keep your answer; it will be used as the basis for Review Question 5.4.)

2012
June   1   Purchases on credit from J. Saville £240; P. Todd £390; J. Fry £1,620.
       3   Purchases on credit from P. Todd £470; P. Rake £290.
      10   We returned goods to J. Fry £140; J. Saville £65.
      15   Purchases on credit from J. Saville £210.
      19   We paid P. Rake by cash £290.
      28   We paid J. Saville by cash £300.
      30   We returned goods to P. Todd £39.

5.3   Redraft each of the accounts given in your answer to 5.1 in three-column style.

5.4   Redraft each of the accounts given in your answer to 5.2 in three-column style.

5.5   Enter the following in the personal accounts (i.e. the creditor and debtor accounts) only. Do *not* write up the other accounts. Balance-off each personal account at the end of the month. After completing this, state which of the balances represent debtors and which represent creditors.

2012
Sept   1   Sales on credit to J. Bee £1,040; T. Day £1,260; J. Soul £480.
       2   Purchases on credit D. Blue £780; F. Rise £1,020; P. Lee £560.
       8   Sales on credit to T. Day £340; L. Hope £480.
      10   Purchases on credit from F. Rise £92; R. James £870.
      12   Returns inwards from J. Soul £25; T. Day £190.
      17   We returned goods to F. Rise £12; R. James £84.
      20   We paid D. Blue by cheque £780.
      24   J. Bee paid us by cheque £900.
      26   We paid R. James by cheque £766.
      28   J. Bee paid us by cash £80.
      30   L. Hope pays us by cheque £480.

5.6A   Enter the following transactions in personal accounts only. Bring down the balances at the end of the month. After completing this, state which of the balances represent debtors and which represent creditors.

2013

May	1	Credit sales G. Wood £310; K. Hughes £42; F. Dunn £1,100; M. Lyons £309.
	2	Credit purchases from T. Sim £190; J. Leech £63; P. Tidy £210; F. Rock £190.
	8	Credit sales to K. Hughes £161; F. Dunn £224.
	9	Credit purchases from J. Leech £215; F. Rock £164.
	10	Goods returned to us by F. Dunn £31; M. Lyons £82.
	12	Cash paid to us by M. Lyons £227.
	15	We returned goods to T. Sim £15; F. Rock £21.
	19	We received cheques from F. Dunn £750; G. Wood £310.
	21	We sold goods on credit to G. Wood £90; K. Hughes £430.
	28	We paid by cheque the following: T. Sim £175; F. Rock £100; P. Tidy £180.
	31	We returned goods to F. Rock £18.

5.7A   Redraft each of the accounts given in your answer to 5.6A in three-column style.

MyAccountingLab

Need more practice? Instant feedback?
Visit **www.myaccountinglab.com**

Featuring unlimited practice questions, a personalised study plan that identifies the areas where you need to focus for better marks, and interactive material designed to help all kinds of learners, MyAccountingLab is a vital tool for maximising your understanding, confidence, and success. Log in at **www.myaccountinglab.com** to see why 92 per cent of students surveyed last year recommend MyAccountingLab.

The trial balance

Introduction
....

In this chapter, you'll learn how to prepare a trial balance from the accounts in the accounting books. You'll discover that the alternate version of the accounting equation can be a useful guide to understanding why a trial balance must balance if all the double entries in the accounts are correct. You'll also learn that the trial balance is no guarantee that the double entries have all been recorded correctly. Finally, at the end of the chapter, you'll have the opportunity to do twenty multiple choice questions covering the material in Chapters 1–6.

6.1 Total debit entries = Total credit entries

You've learnt that under double entry bookkeeping

● for each debit entry there is a credit entry
● for each credit entry there is a debit entry

Let's see if you can remember the basics of double entry.

Activity 6.1

What is the double entry for each of the following transactions:

(a) Purchase of a new van for £9,000 which was paid in full by cheque

Dr   £

       Cr   £

(b) Goods which cost £40 taken out by the owner for her own use

Dr   £

       Cr   £

The total of all the items recorded in all the accounts on the debit side should equal the total of all the items recorded on the credit side of the accounts.

Activity 6.2   Do you remember the alternate form of the accounting equation you were shown in Chapter 1? What does it tell you has happened when it does not balance?

We need to check that for each debit entry there is also an equal credit entry. In order to check that there is a matching credit entry for every debit entry, we prepare something called a **trial balance**.

A type of trial balance could be drawn up by listing all the accounts and then entering the total of all the debit entries in each account in one column and the total of all the credit entries in each account into another column. Finally, you would add up the two columns of figures and ensure they are equal. Using the worked example in Section 3.8, this trial balance would be:

Trial balance as at 31 May 2013		
	Dr £	Cr £
Purchases	994	
Sales		490
Returns outwards		15
Returns inwards	16	
D. Small	220	220
A. Lyon & Son		624
D. Hughes	60	60
M. Spencer	45	16
Cash	445	355
	1,780	1,780

6.2   Total debit balances = Total credit balances

The method described in Section 6.1 is *not* the accepted method of drawing up a trial balance, but it is the easiest to understand at first. The form of trial balance used by accountants is a list of account balances arranged according to whether they are debit balances or credit balances.

Let's balance-off the accounts you saw in Section 3.8. The new entries are in blue so that you can see the entries required to arrive at the closing balances that are used in the trial balance.

You may find it worthwhile trying to balance these accounts yourself before reading any further.

Purchases

2013			£	2013			£
May	1	D. Small	220	May	31	Balance c/d	994
	2	A. Lyon & Son	410				
	12	Cash	150				
	31	A. Lyon & Son	214				
			994				994
June	1	Balance b/d	994				

Sales

2013			£	2013			£
May	31	Balance c/d	490	May	5	D. Hughes	60
					6	M. Spencer	45
					11	Cash	210
					21	Cash	175
			490				490
				June	11	Balance b/d	490

Returns outwards

2013			£	2013			£
May	31	Balance c/d	15	May	10	D. Small	15
				June	1	Balance b/d	15

Returns inwards

2013			£	2013			£
May	19	M. Spencer	16	May	31	Balance c/d	16
June	1	Balance b/d	16				

D. Small

2013			£	2013			£
May	10	Returns outwards	15	May	1	Purchases	220
	22	Cash	205				
			220				220

A. Lyon & Son

2013			£	2013			£
May	31	Balance c/d	624	May	2	Purchases	410
					31	Purchases	214
			624				624
				June	1	Balance b/d	624

D. Hughes

2013			£	2013			£
May	5	Sales	60	May	30	Cash	60

M. Spencer

2013			£	2013			£
May	6	Sales	45	May	19	Returns inwards	16
					31	Balance c/d	29
			45				45
June	1	Balance b/d	29				

Cash

2013			£	2013			£
May	11	Sales	210	May	12	Purchases	150
	21	Sales	175		22	D. Small	205
	30	D. Hughes	60		31	Balance c/d	90
			445				445
June	1	Balance b/d	90				

If you tried to do this before looking at the answer, be sure you understand any mistakes you made before going on.

If the trial balance was drawn up using the closing account balances, it would appear as follows:

Trial balance as at 31 May 2013		
	Dr £	Cr £
Purchases	994	
Sales		490
Returns outwards		15
Returns inwards	16	
A. Lyon & Son		624
M. Spencer	29	
Cash	90	
	1,129	1,129

The trial balance always has the date of the *last* day of the accounting period to which it relates. It is a snapshot of the balances on the ledger accounts at that date.

Just like the trial balance you saw in Section 6.1, the two sides of this one also 'balance'. However, the totals are lower. This is because the £220 in D. Small's account, £60 in D. Hughes' account, £16 in M. Spencer's account and £355 in the cash account have been cancelled out from each side of these accounts by taking only the *balances* instead of the *totals*. As equal amounts have been cancelled from each side, £651 in all, the new totals should still equal one another, as in fact they do at £1,129. (You can verify this if you subtract the new total of £1,129 from the previous one of £1,780. The difference is £651 which is the amount cancelled out from both sides.)

This form of trial balance is the easiest to extract when there are more than a few transactions during the period and it is the one accountants use.

Note that a trial balance can be drawn up at any time. However, it is normal practice to prepare one at the end of an accounting period before preparing an 'income statement' and a 'statement of financial position'. The income statement shows what profit has been earned in a period. (You will be looking at income statements in the next chapter.) The statement of financial position shows what the assets and liabilities of a business are at the end of a period.

Go back to Chapter 1 to refresh your understanding of the statement of financial position.

Activity 6.3 What advantages are there in preparing a trial balance when you are about to prepare an income statement and statement of financial position?

As you've just learnt from Activity 6.3, trial balances are not just done to find errors.

6.3 Trial balances and errors

Many students new to accounting assume that when the trial balance 'balances', the entries in the accounts must be correct. **This assumption is incorrect.** While it means that certain types of error have not been made (such as forgetting to enter the credit side of a transaction), there are several types of error that will not affect the balancing of a trial balance – omitting a transaction altogether, for example.

Examples of the errors which would be revealed, provided there are no compensating errors which cancel them out, are addition errors, using one figure for the debit entry and another figure for the credit entry, and entering only one side of a transaction.

We shall consider addition errors in greater detail in Chapter 33.

 Activity 6.4   If a trial balance fails to agree, what steps would you take in order to find the cause of the difference?

6.4 Multiple choice self-test questions

A growing practice of examining boards is to set multiple choice questions in accounting. In fact, this has become so popular with examiners that all the largest professional accounting bodies now use them, particularly in their first-level examinations.

Multiple choice questions give an examiner the opportunity to cover large parts of the syllabus briefly, but in detail. Students who omit to study areas of the syllabus will be caught out by an examiner's use of multiple choice questions. It is no longer possible to say that it is highly probable a certain topic will not be tested – the examiner can easily cover it with a multiple choice question.

We have deliberately included sets of 20 multiple choice questions at given places in this textbook, rather than a few at the end of each chapter. Such questions are relatively easy to answer a few minutes after reading the chapter. Asking the questions later is a far better test of your powers of recall and understanding. It also gives you practice at answering questions covering a range of topics in one block, as in an examination.

Each multiple choice question has a 'stem' (a part which poses the problem), a 'key' (which is the one correct answer), and a number of 'distractors', i.e. incorrect answers. The key plus the distractors are known as the 'options'.

If you do not know the answer, you should guess. You may be right by chance, or you may remember something subconsciously. In any event, unless the examiner warns otherwise, you will be expected to guess if you don't know the answer.

Read through the Learning Outcomes for this chapter and then attempt Multiple Choice Set 1.

Answers to all the multiple choice questions are given in Appendix 2 at the end of this book.

6.5 Closing inventory

Inventory at the end of a period is not usually to be found in an account in the ledger. It has to be found from inventory records and physical stocktaking. As it is not generally to be found in the ledger, it does not generally appear among the balances in a trial balance. However, opening inventory is often recorded in a ledger account, in which case the inventory balance at the start of a period would be included in the trial balance prepared at the end of that period.

Mnemonic

The following acronym may help you remember which accounts to debit and credit when they *increase* in value:

PEARLS
P – Purchases
E – Expenses   } Debit
A – Assets

R – Revenue
L – Liabilities   } Credit
S – Sales

Learning outcomes

You should now have learnt:

1 How to prepare a trial balance.

2 That trial balances are one form of checking the accuracy of entries in the accounts.

3 That errors can be made in the entries to the accounts that will not be shown up by the trial balance.

4 That the trial balance is used as the basis for preparing income statements and statements of financial position.

Answers to activities

6.1   (a)   *Dr*   Van account   £9,000
              Cr   Bank account   £9,000
        (b)   *Dr*   Drawings account   £40
              Cr   Purchases account   £40

6.2   The alternate form of the accounting equation is Assets = Capital + Liabilities. All the accounts with debit balances are assets and all the accounts with credit balances are either capital or liabilities. This means that so long as you enter a debit for every credit, the alternate accounting equation must always balance. If the alternate accounting equation does not balance, you've made an error somewhere, either in your double entries, or in your arithmetic within the individual accounts. Virtually all occurrences where the accounting equation does not balance that arise in practice are the result of double entry errors.

6.3   Firstly, you can verify whether the total of the debit balances equals the total of the credit balances. They need to be equal, or your income statement and statement of financial position will be incorrect and your statement of financial position will not balance. (That is, the accounting equation will not balance.) Secondly, you need to know what the balance is on every account so that you can enter the appropriate figures into the income statement and statement of financial position. If you don't prepare a trial balance, you will find it much more difficult to prepare these two accounting statements.

6.4   You need to check each entry to verify whether or not it is correct but firstly, it is best to start by checking that the totals in the trial balance have been correctly summed. Then, check that no account has been omitted from the trial balance. Then, check each account in turn.

Multiple choice questions: Set 1

Now attempt Set 1 of multiple choice questions. (Answers to all the multiple choice questions are given in Appendix 2 at the end of this book.)

Each of these multiple choice questions has four suggested answers, (A), (B), (C) and (D). You should read each question and then decide which choice is best, either (A) or (B) or (C) or (D). *Write down your answers on a separate piece of paper.* You will then be able to redo the set of questions later without having to try to ignore your answers.

MC1   Which of the following statements is **incorrect**?

(A)   Assets – Capital = Liabilities
(B)   Liabilities + Capital = Assets
(C)   Liabilities + Assets = Capital
(D)   Assets – Liabilities = Capital

MC2 Which of the following is **not** an asset?

(A) Buildings
(B) Cash balance
(C) Accounts receivable
(D) Loan from K. Harris

MC3 Which of the following is a liability?

(A) Machinery
(B) Accounts payable for goods
(C) Motor vehicles
(D) Cash at bank

MC4 Which of the following is **incorrect**?

	Assets £	Liabilities £	Capital £
(A)	7,850	1,250	6,600
(B)	8,200	2,800	5,400
(C)	9,550	1,150	8,200
(D)	6,540	1,120	5,420

MC5 Which of the following statements is correct?

		Effect upon	
		Assets	Liabilities
(A)	We paid a creditor by cheque	−Bank	−Accounts payable
(B)	A debtor paid us £90 in cash	+Cash	+Accounts receivable
(C)	J. Hall lends us £500 by cheque	+Bank	−Loan from Hall
(D)	Bought goods on credit	+Inventory	+Capital

MC6 Which of the following are correct?

	Accounts	To record	Entry in the account
(i)	Assets	an increase	Debit
		a decrease	Credit
(ii)	Capital	an increase	Debit
		a decrease	Credit
(iii)	Liabilities	an increase	Credit
		a decrease	Debit

(A) (i) and (ii)
(B) (ii) and (iii)
(C) (i) and (iii)
(D) (i), (ii) and (iii)

MC7 Which of the following are correct?

		Account to be debited	Account to be credited
(i)	Bought office furniture for cash	Office furniture	Cash
(ii)	A debtor, P. Sangster, pays us by cheque	Bank	P. Sangster
(iii)	Introduced capital by cheque	Capital	Bank
(iv)	Paid a creditor, B. Lee, by cash	B. Lee	Cash

(A) (i), (ii) and (iii) only
(B) (ii), (iii) and (iv) only
(C) (i), (ii) and (iv) only
(D) (i) and (iv) only

→

→ **MC8**   Which of the following are **incorrect**?

		Account to be debited	*Account to be credited*
(i)	Sold van for cash	Cash	Van
(ii)	Returned some of Office Equipment to Suppliers Ltd	Office Equipment	Suppliers Ltd
(iii)	Repaid part of loan from C. Charles by cheque	Loan from C. Charles	Bank
(iv)	Bought machinery on credit from Betterways Ltd	Betterways Ltd	Machinery

(A)   (ii) and (iv) only
(B)   (iii) and (iv) only
(C)   (ii) and (iii) only
(D)   (i) and (iii) only

MC9   Which of the following best describes the meaning of 'Purchases'?

(A)   Items bought
(B)   Goods bought on credit
(C)   Goods bought for resale
(D)   Goods paid for

MC10   Which of the following should not be called 'Sales'?

(A)   Office fixtures sold
(B)   Goods sold on credit
(C)   Goods sold for cash
(D)   Sale of item previously included in 'Purchases'

MC11   Of the following, which are correct?

		Account to be debited	*Account to be credited*
(i)	Goods sold on credit to R. Williams	R. Williams	Sales
(ii)	S. Johnson returns goods to us	Returns inwards	S. Johnson
(iii)	Goods bought for cash	Cash	Purchases
(iv)	We returned goods to A. Henry	A. Henry	Returns inwards

(A)   (i) and (iii) only
(B)   (i) and (ii) only
(C)   (ii) and (iv) only
(D)   (iii) and (iv) only

MC12   Which of the following are **incorrect**?

		Account to be debited	*Account to be credited*
(i)	Goods sold for cash	Cash	Sales
(ii)	Goods bought on credit from T. Carter	Purchases	T. Carter
(iii)	Goods returned by us to C. Barry	C. Barry	Returns outwards
(iv)	Van bought for cash	Purchases	Cash

(A)   (i) and (iii) only
(B)   (iii) only
(C)   (ii) and (iv) only
(D)   (iv) only

MC13   Given the following, what is the amount of Capital? Assets: Premises £20,000; Inventory £8,500; Cash £100. Liabilities: Accounts payable £3,000; Loan from A. Adams £4,000

(A)   £21,100
(B)   £21,600
(C)   £32,400
(D)   £21,400

MC14   Which of the following is correct?

(A)   Profit does not alter capital
(B)   Profit reduces capital
(C)   Capital can only come from profit
(D)   Profit increases capital

MC15   Which of the following are correct?

		Account to be debited	*Account to be credited*
(*i*)	Received commission by cheque	Bank	Commission received
(*ii*)	Paid rates by cash	Rates	Cash
(*iii*)	Paid motor expenses by cheque	Motor expenses	Bank
(*iv*)	Received refund of insurance by cheque	Insurance	Bank

(A)   (*i*) and (*ii*) only
(B)   (*i*), (*ii*) and (*iii*) only
(C)   (*ii*), (*iii*) and (*iv*) only
(D)   (*i*), (*ii*) and (*iv*) only

MC16   Of the following, which are **incorrect**?

		Account to be debited	*Account to be credited*
(*i*)	Sold van for cash	Cash	Sales
(*ii*)	Bought stationery by cheque	Stationery	Bank
(*iii*)	Took cash out of business for private use	Cash	Drawings
(*iv*)	Paid general expenses by cheque	General expenses	Bank

(A)   (*ii*) and (*iv*) only
(B)   (*i*) and (*ii*) only
(C)   (*i*) and (*iii*) only
(D)   (*ii*) and (*iii*) only

MC17   What is the balance on the following account on 31 May 2013?

C. De Freitas

2013			£	2013			£
May	1	Sales	205	May	17	Cash	300
	14	Sales	360		28	Returns	50
	30	Sales	180				

(A)   A credit balance of £395
(B)   A debit balance of £380
(C)   A debit balance of £395
(D)   There is a nil balance on the account

MC18   What would have been the balance on the account of C. De Freitas in MC17 on 19 May 2013?

(A)   A debit balance of £265
(B)   A credit balance of £95
(C)   A credit balance of £445
(D)   A credit balance of £265

→

→ **MC19**   Which of the following best describes a trial balance?

(A) It shows the financial position of a business
(B) It is a special account
(C) It shows all the entries in the books
(D) It is a list of balances on the books

MC20   Is it true that the trial balance totals should agree?

(A) No, there are sometimes good reasons why they differ
(B) Yes, except where the trial balance is extracted at the year end
(C) Yes, always
(D) No, because it is not a statement of financial position

Review questions

6.1 You are to enter up the necessary accounts for the month of May from the following information relating to a small printing firm. Then balance-off the accounts and extract a trial balance as at 31 May 2013.

2013
May   1   Started in business with capital in cash of £1,800 and £4,200 in the bank.
        2   Bought goods on credit from: J. Ward £610; P. Green £515; M. Taylor £174; S. Gemmill £345; P. Tone £542.
        4   Sold goods on credit to: J. Sharpe £340; G. Boycott £720; F. Titmus £1,152.
        6   Paid rent by cash £410.
        9   J. Sharpe paid us his account by cheque £340.
       10   F. Titmus paid us £1,000 by cheque.
       12   We paid the following by cheque: M. Taylor £174; J. Ward £610.
       15   Paid carriage in cash £38.
       18   Bought goods on credit from P. Green £291; S. Gemmill £940.
       21   Sold goods on credit to G. Boycott £810.
       31   Paid rent by cheque £490.

6.2 Enter the following transactions of an antiques shop in the accounts and extract a trial balance as at 31 March 2013.

2013
March   1   Started in business with £8,000 in the bank.
        2   Bought goods on credit from: L. Frank £550; G. Byers £540; P. Lee £610.
        5   Cash sales £510.
        6   Paid wages in cash £110.
        7   Sold goods on credit to: J. Snow £295; K. Park £360; B. Tyler £640.
        9   Bought goods for cash £120.
       10   Bought goods on credit from: G. Byers £410; P. Lee £1,240.
       12   Paid wages in cash £110.
       13   Sold goods on credit to: K. Park £610; B. Tyler £205.
       15   Bought shop fixtures on credit from Stop Ltd £740.
       17   Paid G. Byers by cheque £700.
       18   We returned goods to P. Lee £83.
       21   Paid Stop Ltd a cheque for £740.

24   B. Tyler paid us his account by cheque £845.
27   We returned goods to L. Frank £18.
30   G. Prince lent us £1,000 by cash.
31   Bought a van paying by cheque £6,250.

6.3A   Record the following details relating to a carpet retailer for the month of November 2013 and extract a trial balance as at 30 November 2013.

2013
Nov

1   Started in business with £15,000 in the bank.
3   Bought goods on credit from: J. Small £290; F. Brown £1,200; T. Rae £610; R. Charles £530.
5   Cash sales £610.
6   Paid rent by cheque £175.
7   Paid business rates by cheque £130.
11   Sold goods on credit to: T. Potts £85; J. Field £48; T. Gray £1,640.
17   Paid wages by cash £290.
18   We returned goods to: J. Small £18; R. Charles £27.
19   Bought goods on credit from: R. Charles £110; T. Rae £320; F. Jack £165.
20   Goods were returned to us by: J. Field £6; T. Potts £14.
21   Bought van on credit from Turnkey Motors £4,950.
23   We paid the following by cheque: J. Small £272; F. Brown £1,200; T. Rae £500.
25   Bought another van, paying by cheque immediately £6,200.
26   Received a loan of £750 cash from B. Bennet.
28   Received cheques from: T. Potts £71; J. Field £42.
30   Proprietor brings a further £900 into the business, by a payment into the business bank account.

6.4A   Record the following transactions for the month of January of a small finishing retailer, balance-off all the accounts, and then extract a trial balance as at 31 January 2012.

2012
Jan

1   Started in business with £10,500 cash.
2   Put £9,000 of the cash into a bank account.
3   Bought goods for cash £550.
4   Bought goods on credit from: T. Dry £800; F. Hood £930; M. Smith £160; G. Low £510.
5   Bought stationery on credit from Buttons Ltd £89.
6   Sold goods on credit to: R. Tong £170; L. Fish £240; M. Singh £326; A. Tom £204.
8   Paid rent by cheque £220.
10   Bought fixtures on credit from Chiefs Ltd £610.
11   Paid salaries in cash £790.
14   Returned goods to: F. Hood £30; M. Smith £42.
15   Bought van by cheque £6,500.
16   Received loan from B. Barclay by cheque £2,000.
18   Goods returned to us by: R. Tong £5; M. Singh £20.
21   Cash sales £145.
24   Sold goods on credit to: L. Fish £130; A. Tom £410; R. Pleat £158.
26   We paid the following by cheque: F. Hood £900; M. Smith £118.
29   Received cheques from: R. Pleat £158; L. Fish £370.
30   Received a further loan from B. Barclay by cash £500.
30   Received £614 cash from A. Tom.

6.5   Note, this question should not be attempted until cash discounts and trade discounts have been covered (see Chapters 13 and 14). It should also be noted that this is an example of the exception to the rule that closing inventory does not generally appear in a trial balance.

On 1 October 2012, the owner of the USS Enterprise, Mr Kirk, decides that he will boldly go and keep his records on a double entry system. His assets and liabilities at that date were:

	£
Fixtures and equipment	20,000
Inventory including weapons	15,000
Balance at Universe Bank	17,500
Cash	375
Accounts payable – Spock	3,175
– Scott	200
– McCoy	500

Kirk's transactions during October were as follows:

1 Sold faulty phasers, original cost £500, to Klingon Corp, for cash £5,000
2 Bought Photon Torpedoes (weapons), on credit from Central Council £2,500
3 Sold goods to Aardvarks, original cost £250, on credit, £1,500
4 Bought Cloaking Device (Fixture and Fittings) from Klingon Corp £3,500
5 Paid the balance owed to Spock at 1 October less a 5 per cent cash discount
6 Paid Central Council full amount due by cheque
7 Received full amount due from Aardvarks by cheque
8 Paid Klingon Corp by cheque after deducting 20 per cent trade discount
9 Paid, by bankers order, £10,000 for repairs to Enterprise following disagreement over amount owing to Klingon Corp and faulty phasers.

Required:
Open Enterprise's ledger accounts at 1 October, record all transactions for the month, balance the ledger accounts, and prepare a trial balance as at 31 October.

Financial Statements 1

Income statements: an introduction

Learning objectives

After you have studied this chapter, you should be able to:

- explain why income statements are not part of the double entry system
- explain why profit is calculated
- calculate cost of goods sold, gross profit, and net profit
- explain the difference between gross profit and net profit
- explain the relationship between the trading account and the profit and loss account
- explain how the trading account and the profit and loss account fit together to create the income statement
- explain how to deal with closing inventory when preparing the trading account section of an income statement
- close down the appropriate accounts and transfer the balances to the trading account
- close down the appropriate accounts and transfer the balances to the profit and loss account
- prepare an income statement from information given in a trial balance
- make appropriate double entries to incorporate net profit and drawings in the capital account

Introduction

In this chapter, you will learn how to close down revenue and expenditure accounts in order to calculate profit and prepare an income statement. You will learn how to adjust purchases with inventory and arrive at the cost of goods sold, and will discover the difference between gross profit and net profit. You will learn how to prepare an income statement, and, finally, you will learn how to transfer net profit and drawings to the capital account at the end of a period.

7.1   Purpose of income statements

The main reason why people set up businesses is to make profits. Of course, if the business is not successful, it may well incur losses instead. The calculation of such profits and losses is probably the most important objective of the accounting function. The owners will want to know how the actual profits compare with the profits they had hoped to make. Knowing what profits are being made helps businesses to do many things, including:

- planning ahead
- obtaining loans from banks, from other businesses, or from private individuals
- telling prospective business partners how successful the business is
- telling someone who may be interested in buying the business how successful the business is
- calculating the tax due on the profits so that the correct amount of tax can be paid to the tax authorities.

Chapter 4 dealt with the grouping of revenue and expenses prior to bringing them together to compute profit. In the case of a trader (someone who is mainly concerned with buying and selling goods), the profits are calculated by drawing up an **income statement**.

When it is shown in detail rather than in summary form (as is the case for the published income statements of companies), it contains something called the **trading account**. The trading account is prepared in order to arrive at a figure for **gross profit**.

Below the trading account is shown a summary of another account – the **profit and loss account**. The profit and loss account is prepared so as to arrive at the figure for **net profit**.

It is these two accounts that together comprise the income statement. Both the trading account and the profit and loss account *are* part of the double entry system. At the end of a financial period, they are closed off. They are then summarised and the information they contain is then copied into an income statement. **Income statements are not part of the double entry system.**

7.2   Gross profit

One of the most important uses of income statements is that of comparing the results obtained with the results expected. In a trading organisation, a lot of attention is paid to how much profit is made, before deducting expenses, for every £1 of sales revenue. As mentioned in Section 7.1, so that this can easily be seen in the profit calculation, the statement in which profit is calculated is split into two sections – one in which the gross profit is found (this is the trading account section of the statement), and the next section in which the **net profit** is calculated (this is the 'profit and loss account' section of the statement).

Gross profit is the excess of sales revenue over the cost of goods sold. Where the cost of goods sold is greater than the sales revenue, the result is a **gross loss**. By taking the figure of sales revenue less the cost of goods sold to generate that sales revenue, it can be seen that the accounting custom is to calculate a trader's profits only on goods that have been sold.

Activity 7.1   What does this tell you about the costs and revenues that are included in the calculation of gross profit? (*Hint*: what do you not include in the calculation?)

To summarise:

Gross profit (calculated in the **trading account**)	is the excess of sales revenue over the cost of goods sold in the period.

Activity 7.2

Calculate the gross profit or gross loss of each of the following businesses:

	Cost of goods purchased £	Sales £	Gross profit/(Gross loss) £
A	9,820	10,676	_____
B	7,530	14,307	_____
C	10,500	19,370	_____
D	9,580	9,350	_____
E	8,760	17,200	_____

7.3 Net profit

Net profit, found in the profit and loss account section of the income statement, consists of the gross profit plus any revenue other than that from sales, such as rents received or commissions earned, less the total costs used up during the period other than those already included in the 'cost of goods sold'. Where the costs used up exceed the gross profit plus other revenue, the result is said to be a **net loss**. Thus:

Net profit (calculated in the profit and loss account)	is what is left of the gross profit after all other expenses have been deducted.

Activity 7.3

Using the answer to Activity 7.2, complete the following table:

	Other revenues £	Expenses £	Net profit/(Net loss) £
A	–	2,622	_____
B	4,280	2,800	_____
C	500	2,500	_____
D	–	1,780	_____
E	3,260	2,440	_____

7.4 Information needed

Before drawing up an income statement you should prepare the trial balance. This contains nearly all the information needed. (Later on in this book you will see that certain adjustments have to be made, but we will ignore these at this stage.)

We can now look at the trial balance of B. Swift, drawn up as on 31 December 2012 after the completion of his first year in business.

Exhibit 7.1

B. Swift Trial balance as at 31 December 2012	Dr	Cr
	£	£
Sales		38,500
Purchases	29,000	
Rent	2,400	
Lighting expenses	1,500	
General expenses	600	
Fixtures and fittings	5,000	
Accounts receivable	6,800	
Accounts payable		9,100
Bank	15,100	
Cash	200	
Drawings	7,000	
Capital		20,000
	67,600	67,600

Note: To make this easier to follow, we shall assume that purchases consist of goods that are resold without needing any further work. You'll learn later that these are known as 'finished goods' but, for now, we'll simply refer to them as 'goods'.

We have already seen that gross profit is calculated as follows:

> Sales – Cost of goods sold = Gross profit

It would be easier if all purchases in a period were always sold by the end of the same period. In that case, cost of goods sold would always equal purchases. However, this is not normally the case and so we have to calculate the cost of goods sold as follows:

What we bought in the period:	Purchases
Less Goods bought but not sold in the period:	(Closing inventory)
	= Cost of goods sold

In Swift's case, there are goods unsold at the end of the period. However, there is no record in the accounting books of the value of this unsold inventory. The only way that Swift can find this figure is by checking his inventory at the close of business on 31 December 2008. To do this he would have to make a list of all the unsold goods and then find out their value. The value he would normally place on them would be the cost price of the goods, i.e. what he paid for them. Let's assume that this is £3,000.

The cost of goods sold figure will be:

	£
Purchases	29,000
Less Closing inventory	(3,000)
Cost of goods sold	26,000

Based on the sales revenue of £38,500 the gross profit can be calculated:

$$\text{Sales} - \text{Cost of goods sold} = \text{Gross profit}$$
$$£38,500 - £26,000 \qquad = £12,500$$

We now have the information we need to complete the trading account section of the income statement. Next, we need to close off the sales and purchases accounts at the end of the period so that they start the next period with no balance. To do so, we need to create a trading account (this is *not* the same as the trading part of the income statement, though it does produce the same gross profit figure) and then make the following entries:

(A) The balance of the sales account is transferred to the trading account by:

    1 Debiting the sales account (thus closing it).
    2 Crediting the trading account.

(B) The balance of the purchases account is transferred to the trading account by:

    1 Debiting the trading account.
    2 Crediting the purchases account (thus closing it).

(C) There is, as yet, no entry for the closing inventory in the double entry accounts. This is achieved as follows:

    1 Debit a closing inventory account with the value of the closing inventory.
    2 Credit the trading account (thus completing the double entry).

The trading account will look like this:

Trading

2012			£	2012				£
Dec 31	Purchases	**(B)**	29,000	Dec 31	Sales	**(A)**	38,500
				31	Closing inventory	**(C)**	3,000

We now close off the trading account in the normal way. In this case, revenues exceed costs so we describe the balance as 'gross profit'.

Trading

2012			£	2012			£
Dec 31	Purchases	**(B)**	29,000	Dec 31	Sales	**(A)**	38,500
31	Gross profit		12,500	31	Closing inventory	**(C)**	3,000
			41,500				41,500

Note that the balance shown on the trading account is described as 'gross profit' rather than being described as a balance. Also, note that the balance (i.e. the gross profit) is not brought down to the next period. The other accounts used in these double entries appear as shown below. (Note that there is no detail of the entries prior to the end of the period as all the information we have been given is the closing balances. These closing balances are simply described here as 'balance'.)

Sales

2012		£	2012		£
Dec 31	Trading	38,500	Dec 31	Balance	38,500

Purchases

2012		£	2012		£
Dec 31	Balance	29,000	Dec 31	Trading	29,000

Closing inventory

2012		£	2012		£
Dec 31	Trading	3,000	Dec 31	Balance	3,000

The entry of the closing inventory on the credit side of the trading account is, in effect, a deduction from the purchases on the debit side. As you will see when we look later at the trading account part of the income statement, the closing inventory is shown as a deduction from the purchases and the figure then disclosed is described as 'cost of goods sold'.

It must be remembered that we are concerned here with the very first year of trading when, for obvious reasons, there is no opening inventory. In Chapter 9, we will examine how to account for inventory in the later years of a business.

We can now draw up a profit and loss account (which is an 'account' opened so that the end-of-period double entries can be completed). Double entries are then prepared, firstly transferring the gross profit from the trading account to the credit of the profit and loss account. To do this, you would change the entry in the trading account to read 'Gross profit transferred to profit and loss':

Trading

2012		£	2012		£
Dec 31	Purchases	29,000	Dec 31	Sales	38,500
31	Gross profit transferred to		31	Closing inventory	3,000
	Profit and loss	12,500			
		41,500			41,500

Then, any revenue account balances, other than sales (which have already been dealt with in the trading account), are transferred to the credit of the profit and loss account. Typical examples are commissions received and rent received. In the case of B. Swift, there are no such revenue accounts.

The costs used up in the year, in other words, the expenses of the year, are then transferred to the debit of the profit and loss account. (It may also be thought, quite rightly, that, as the fixtures and fittings have been used during the year with subsequent deterioration of the assets, something should be charged for this use. This charge is known as 'depreciation'. The methods for calculating this are left until Chapter 26.)

The profit and loss account will now appear as follows:

Profit and loss

2012		£	2012		£
Dec 31	Rent	2,400	Dec 31	Gross profit transferred	
31	Lighting expenses	1,500		from Trading	12,500
31	General expenses	600			
31	Net profit	8,000			
		12,500			12,500

The expense accounts closed off will now appear as:

Rent

2012		£	2012		£
Dec 31	Balance	2,400	Dec 31	Profit and loss	2,400

Lighting expenses

2012		£	2012			£
Dec 31	Balance	1,500	Dec 31	Profit and loss		1,500

General expenses

2012		£	2012			£
Dec 31	Balance	600	Dec 31	Profit and loss		600

You now have all the information you need in order to prepare the income statement for the year ending 31 December 2012. It looks like this:

Exhibit 7.2

B. Swift
Income statement for the year ending 31 December 2012

	£	£
Sales		38,500
Less Cost of goods sold:		
Purchases	29,000	
Less Closing inventory	(3,000)	
		(26,000)
Gross profit		12,500
Less Expenses		
Rent	2,400	
Lighting expenses	1,500	
General expenses	600	
		(4,500)
Net profit		8,000

Note: 'Revenue' is often used instead of 'Sales' in this statement.

7.5 Effect on the capital account

Although the net profit has been calculated at £8,000 and is shown as a balancing figure on the debit side of the profit and loss account, no credit entry has yet been made to complete the double entry. In other accounts, the credit entry would normally be the 'balance b/d' at the start of the next period. However, as net profit increases the capital of the owner, the credit entry must be made in the capital account by transferring the net profit from the profit and loss account. (You would change the entry in the profit and loss account from 'net profit' to read 'net profit transferred to capital'.)

The trading account and the profit and loss account, and, indeed, all the revenue and expense accounts, can thus be seen to be devices whereby the capital account is saved from being concerned with unnecessary detail. Every sale made at a profit increases the capital of the proprietor, as does each item of revenue, such as rent received. On the other hand, each sale made at a loss, or each item of expense, decreases the capital of the proprietor.

Instead of altering the capital after each transaction, the respective bits of profit and loss, and of revenue and expense, are collected together using suitably described accounts. Then all the balances are brought together in one financial statement, the 'income statement', and the increase in the capital, i.e. the net profit, is determined. Alternatively, in the case of a net loss, the decrease in the capital is ascertained.

The fact that a separate drawings account has been in use can now also be seen to have been in keeping with the policy of avoiding unnecessary detail in the capital account. There will, therefore, only be one figure for drawings entered in the debit side of the capital account – the total of the drawings for the whole of the period.

The capital account, showing these transfers, and the drawings account now closed are as follows:

Capital

2012			£	2012				£
Dec	31	Drawings	7,000	Jan	1	Cash		20,000
	31	Balance c/d	21,000	Dec	31	Net profit		8,000
			28,000					28,000
				2006				
				Jan	1	Balance b/d		21,000

Drawings

2012			£	2012			£
Dec	31	Balance	7,000	Dec	31	Capital	7,000

Activity 7.4

Bertram Quigley opened a pet shop on 1 January 2012. He invested £10,000 in the business. The following information was obtained from his accounting records at the end of the year: Purchases of goods for resale £7,381; Sales £13,311; Expenses £1,172; Drawings £800; Inventory £410. What is the balance on Bertram Quigley's capital account at 31 December 2012?

7.6 The balances still in our books

It should be noticed that not all the items in the trial balance have been used in the income statement. The remaining balances are assets or liabilities or capital, they are not expenses or revenue. These will be used later when a statement of financial position is drawn up. (You'll remember learning in Chapter 1 that assets, liabilities and capital are shown in statements of financial position.)

Go back to Chapter 1 to refresh your understanding of assets, liabilities and capital.

Exhibit 7.3 shows the trial balance after the entries to the trading account and the profit and loss account have been made and the income statement prepared. All the accounts that were closed off in that process have been removed, and drawings and net profit have been transferred to the capital account. Notice also that the inventory account, which was not originally in the trial balance, is in the redrafted trial balance, as the item was not created as a balance in the books until the trading account was prepared. We will be using this trial balance when we start to look at statements of financial position in the next chapter.

Note: As the income statement was prepared using all this information, the trial balance shown in Exhibit 7.3 can also be described as having been prepared following preparation of the income statement.

Exhibit 7.3

B. Swift		
Trial balance as at 31 December 2012		
(after the trading account and the profit and loss account have been completed and the income statement prepared and the capital account adjusted for net profit and drawings)		
	Dr	Cr
	£	£
Fixtures and fittings	5,000	
Accounts receivable	6,800	
Accounts payable		9,100
Inventory	3,000	
Bank	15,100	
Cash	200	
Capital		21,000
	30,100	30,100

Note for students: Now that you have learnt how to prepare a T-account for the trading account and a T-account for the profit and loss account, we will only rarely ask you to prepare them again. You should remember how they are used to calculate gross profit and net profit and the typical entries they may contain. From now on, we will concentrate on producing the financial statement that combines these two accounts: the income statement.

Note also that under UK GAAP (i.e. UK accounting rules) the income statement was called the 'profit and loss account'. This confusing use of the same title for a financial statement and for an account in the ledger caused many problems. However, even though we now use the term 'income statement' for the financial statement you may sometimes see such a statement with the old title, or you may even be asked to prepare a financial statement using that title. If so, remember that it is the same as the one we call an income statement.

Learning outcomes
....

You should now have learnt:

1 Why income statements are not part of the double entry system.

2 Why profit is calculated.

3 How to calculate cost of goods sold, gross profit and net profit.

4 The double entries required in order to close off the relevant expense and revenue accounts at the end of a period and post the entries to the trading account and to the profit and loss account.

5 How to deal with inventory at the end of a period.

6 How to prepare an income statement from a trial balance.

7 How to transfer the net profit and drawings to the capital account at the end of a period.

8 That balances on accounts not closed off in order to prepare the income statement are carried down to the following period, that these balances represent assets, liabilities and capital, and that they are entered in the statement of financial position.

Answers to activities

7.1   You only include the costs that were incurred in creating those goods that were sold. These costs include the cost of buying those goods and any costs incurred in converting goods purchased into the goods that were sold – for example, the costs of converting raw materials into finished goods. The only costs you include are those that relate to the goods sold. The costs relating to goods that have not yet been sold are not included. You do not include other costs of the business, such as postage, motor expenses, office expenses, salaries of managers, and advertising costs. Nor do you include any costs relating to the purchase or use of any assets, such as motor vehicles, computers, machinery, fixtures and fittings, and buildings.

7.2

	Cost of goods purchased	Sales	Gross profit/(Gross loss)
	£	£	£
A	9,820	10,676	856
B	7,530	14,307	6,777
C	10,500	19,370	8,870
D	9,580	9,350	(230)
E	8,760	17,200	8,440

7.3

	Other revenues	Expenses	Net profit/(Net loss)
	£	£	£
A	–	2,622	(1,766)
B	4,280	2,800	8,257
C	500	2,500	6,870
D	–	1,780	(2,010)
E	3,260	2,440	9,260

7.4   £14,368. That is, £10,000 + £13,311 – (£7,381 – £410) – £1,172 – £800.

Review questions

7.1   From the following trial balance of B. Cork, extracted after one year's trading, prepare an income statement for the year ending 31 December 2012. A statement of financial position is not required.

Trial balance as at 31 December 2012

	Dr	Cr
	£	£
Sales		200,500
Purchases	120,800	
Salaries	58,600	
Motor expenses	2,400	
Rent	1,900	
Insurance	300	
General expenses	170	
Premises	95,600	
Motor vehicles	17,200	
Accounts receivable	26,800	
Accounts payable		17,600
Cash at bank	16,400	
Cash in hand	600	
Drawings	8,400	
Capital		131,070
	349,170	349,170

Inventory at 31 December 2012 was £15,600.

(Keep your answer; it will be used later in Review Question 8.1.)

7.2 From the following trial balance of G. Foot after his first year's trading, you are required to draw up an income statement for the year ending 30 June 2012. A statement of financial position is not required.

Trial balance as at 30 June 2012

	Dr	Cr
	£	£
Sales		266,000
Purchases	154,000	
Rent	3,800	
Lighting and heating expenses	700	
Salaries and wages	52,000	
Insurance	3,000	
Buildings	84,800	
Fixtures	2,000	
Accounts receivable	31,200	
Sundry expenses	300	
Accounts payable		16,000
Cash at bank	15,000	
Drawings	28,600	
Vans	16,000	
Motor running expenses	4,600	
Capital		114,000
	396,000	396,000

Inventory at 30 June 2012 was £18,000.

(Keep your answer; it will be used later in Review Question 8.2.)

7.3A From the following trial balance of B. Morse drawn-up on conclusion of his first year in business, draw up an income statement for the year ending 31 December 2013. A statement of financial position is not required.

Trial balance as at 31 December 2013

	Dr	Cr
	£	£
General expenses	305	
Business rates	2,400	
Motor expenses	910	
Salaries	39,560	
Insurance	1,240	
Purchases	121,040	
Sales		235,812
Car	4,300	
Accounts payable		11,200
Accounts receivable	21,080	
Premises	53,000	
Cash at bank	2,715	
Cash in hand	325	
Capital		23,263
Drawings	23,400	
	270,275	270,275

Inventory at 31 December 2013 was £14,486.

(Keep your answer; it will be used later in Review Question 8.3A.)

7.4A Extract an income statement for the year ending 30 June 2012 for G. Graham. The trial balance as at 30 June 2012 after his first year of trading was as follows:

	Dr	Cr
	£	£
Equipment rental	940	
Insurance	1,804	
Lighting and heating expenses	1,990	
Motor expenses	2,350	
Salaries and wages	48,580	
Sales		382,420
Purchases	245,950	
Sundry expenses	624	
Lorry	19,400	
Accounts payable		23,408
Accounts receivable	44,516	
Fixtures	4,600	
Shop	174,000	
Cash at bank	11,346	
Drawings	44,000	
Capital		194,272
	600,100	600,100

Inventory at 30 June 2012 was £29,304.

(Keep your answer; it will be used later in Review Question 8.4A.)

7.5 Bill Sankey is a sole proprietor who keeps records of his cash and bank transactions. His transactions for the month of March were as follows:

March 1 Cash in hand £400, Cash at bank £6,000.
      4 Sankey received a cheque for £1,200 from W. Abbot which was paid directly into the bank. This represented sales.
      6 Paid wages in cash £60.
      8 Sold goods for cash £300.
    10 Received cheque from G. Smart for £600, in full settlement of a debt of £640; this was paid directly into the bank.
    11 Paid sundry expenses in cash £48.
    14 Purchased goods by cheque for £1,400.
    18 Paid J. Sanders a cheque of £190 in full settlement of a debt of £210.
    23 Withdrew £25 from the bank to pay the office cleaning company.
    24 Paid wages in cash £60.
    26 Sold goods for cash £380.
    28 Paid salaries by cheque £240.
    31 Retained cash amounting to £600 and paid the remainder into the bank.

Required:
(a) Enter the above transactions within T-accounts and bring down the balances.
(b) Assuming no opening accounts receivable, accounts payable, or inventory, prepare an income statement for the month ended 31 March.

MyAccountingLab

Need more practice? Instant feedback?
Visit **www.myaccountinglab.com**

Featuring unlimited practice questions, a personalised study plan that identifies the areas where you need to focus for better marks, and interactive material designed to help all kinds of learners, MyAccountingLab is a vital tool for maximising your understanding, confidence, and success. Log in at **www.myaccountinglab.com** to see why 92 per cent of students surveyed last year recommend MyAccountingLab.

Statements of financial position

Learning objectives

After you have studied this chapter, you should be able to:

- explain why statements of financial position are not part of the double entry system
- explain why it is important that account balances are shown under appropriate headings in the statement of financial position
- explain the meanings of the terms non-current asset, current asset, current liability, and non-current liability
- describe the sequence in which each of the five main categories of items appear in the statement of financial position
- describe the sequence in which each non-current asset is entered in the statement of financial position
- describe the sequence in which each current asset is entered in the statement of financial position
- draw up a statement of financial position from information given in a trial balance

Introduction

In this chapter, you'll learn how to present asset, liability and capital balances in a statement of financial position and of the importance of adopting a consistent and meaningful layout.

8.1   Contents of the Statement of financial position

In Chapter 1, you learnt that statements of financial position contain details of assets, liabilities and capital. The items and amounts to be entered in the statement of financial position are found in the accounting books. As shown in the previous chapter, they comprise those **accounts with balances** that were *not* included in the income statement. All these accounts that continue to have balances must be assets, capital or liabilities.

Because it is these balances that are entered in the statement of financial position, it used to be called the 'balance sheet'. You should be aware of this: you may meet this term in an examination question or in a textbook – many people still use the old term.

Activity 8.1   Why have the accounts entered into the income statement been removed from the trial balance? (*Hint*: it is *not* because they were entered in that statement.)

8.2 Drawing up a Statement of financial position

Let's look again at the post-income-statement trial balance of B. Swift (from Exhibit 7.3):

Exhibit 8.1

B. Swift
Trial balance as at 31 December 2012
(after the trading account and the profit and loss account have been completed and
the income statement prepared and the capital account adjusted for net profit and drawings)

	Dr	Cr
	£	£
Fixtures and fittings	5,000	
Accounts receivable	6,800	
Accounts payable		9,100
Inventory	3,000	
Bank	15,100	
Cash	200	
Capital		21,000
	30,100	30,100

You'll probably remember seeing examples of statements of financial position in Chapter 1. If not, this would be a good time to spend a few minutes reading that chapter again.

Based on what you learnt in Chapter 1, let's now draw up the statement of financial position for B. Swift as at 31 December 2012.

Exhibit 8.2

B. Swift
Statement of financial position as at 31 December 2012

	£
Assets	
Fixtures and fittings	5,000
Inventory	3,000
Accounts receivable	6,800
Bank	15,100
Cash	200
Total assets	30,100
Liabilities	
Accounts payable	(9,100)
Net assets	21,000
Capital	21,000

8.3 No double entry in Statements of financial position

After the way we used the double entry system in the previous chapter to prepare the information we needed in order to draw up the income statement, it should not surprise you to learn that statements of financial position are also not part of the double entry system.

Activity 8.2 Why do you think it is that the statement of financial position is not part of the double entry system?

When we draw up accounts such as a cash account, a rent account, a sales account, a trading account, or a profit and loss account, we are preparing them as part of the double entry system. We make entries on the debit side and the credit side of these accounts.

As with income statements, when we draw up a statement of financial position, we do not enter anything in the various accounts. We do not actually transfer the fixtures and fittings balance or the accounts payable balance, or any of the other balances, to the statement of financial position.

All we do is to *list* the asset, capital and liabilities balances so as to form a statement of financial position. This means that none of these accounts have been closed off. *Nothing is entered in the ledger accounts.*

When the next accounting period starts, these accounts are still open and they all contain balances. As a result of future transactions, entries are then made in these accounts that add to or deduct from these opening balances using double entry.

If you see the word 'account', you will know that what you are looking at is part of the double entry system and will include debit and credit entries. If the word 'account' is not used, it is not part of double entry. For instance, the following items are not 'accounts', and are therefore *not* part of the double entry:

Trial balance: this is a list of the debit and credit balances in the accounts.
Income statement: this is a list of revenues and expenditures arranged so as to produce figures for gross profit and net profit for a specific period of time.
Statement of financial position: this is a list of balances arranged according to whether they are assets, capital or liabilities and so depict the financial situation on a specific date.

8.4 Layout of the Statement of financial position

Have you ever gone into a shop and found that the goods you were interested in were all mixed up and not laid out in a helpful or consistent way? You can see an example of this in most large shops specialising in selling CDs. They mix up some of their inventory, particularly anything on 'special offer', so that you need to search through everything in order to find what you want. In the process of doing so, the shop hopes that you will come across other things that you will buy that you would otherwise never have thought of. Some of Richard Branson's first Virgin music shops in the early 1970s used this technique and it seems to have developed from there as an effective way to sell music.

Unfortunately, this mix-up presentation technique would be of no benefit to the users of a statement of financial position. They would never find anything they didn't set out to find, but they would still have to go through the hassle of sorting through all the information in order to produce a meaningful statement of financial position for themselves. Because the statement of financial position is intended to be helpful and informative, we take great care in ensuring that it portrays the information it contains in a consistent and meaningful way.

As a result, not only can a user who is only interested in looking at the statement of financial position of one organisation find it easy to find information within it, other users who look at lots of different statements of financial position, such as bank managers, accountants and investors, find it straightforward making comparisons between different statements of financial position.

While the statement of financial position layout used in Exhibit 8.2 could be considered useful, it can be improved. Let's look at how we can do this. Firstly, we'll look at how assets could be presented in a more helpful and more meaningful way.

Assets

We are going to show the assets under two headings, non-current assets and current assets.

Non-current assets

Non-current assets are assets that:

1 were not bought primarily to be sold; but
2 are to be used in the business; and
3 are expected to be of use to the business for a long time.

Examples: buildings, machinery, motor vehicles, fixtures and fittings.

Non-current assets are listed first in the statement of financial position starting with those the business will keep the longest, down to those which will not be kept so long. For instance:

Non-current assets
1 Land and buildings
2 Fixtures and fittings
3 Machinery
4 Motor vehicles

Current assets

Current assets are assets that are likely to change in the short term and certainly within twelve months of the date of the statement of financial position. They include items held for resale at a profit, accounts receivable, cash in the bank, and cash in hand.

These are listed in increasing order of liquidity – that is, starting with the asset furthest away from being turned into cash, and finishing with cash itself. For instance:

Current assets
1 Inventory
2 Accounts receivable
3 Cash at bank
4 Cash in hand

Some students feel that accounts receivable should appear before inventory because, at first sight, inventory would appear to be more easily realisable (i.e. convertible into cash) than accounts receivable. In fact, accounts receivable can normally be more quickly turned into cash – you can often **factor** them by selling the rights to the amounts owed by debtors to a finance company for an agreed amount.

As all retailers would confirm, it is not so easy to quickly turn inventory into cash. Another advantage of using this sequence is that it follows the order in which full realisation of the assets in a business takes place: before there is a sale, there must be an inventory of goods which, when sold on credit, turns into accounts receivable and, when payment is made by the debtors, turns into cash.

Liabilities

There are two categories of liabilities, current liabilities and non-current liabilities.

Current liabilities

Current liabilities are items that have to be paid within a year of the date of the statement of financial position.

Examples: bank overdrafts, accounts payable resulting from the purchase on credit of goods for resale.

Non-current liabilities

Non-current liabilities are items that have to be paid more than a year after the date of the statement of financial position.

Examples: bank loans, loans from other businesses.

8.5 A properly drawn up statement of financial position

Exhibit 8.3 shows Exhibit 8.2 drawn up in a more appropriate way. You should also read the notes following the exhibit.

Exhibit 8.3

B. Swift
Statement of financial position as at 31 December 2012

	£	£
Non-current assets		
Fixtures and fittings		5,000
Current assets		
Inventory	3,000	
Accounts receivable	6,800	
Bank	15,100	
Cash	200	
		25,100
Total assets		30,100
Current liabilities		
Accounts payable		(9,100)
Net assets		21,000
Capital		
Cash introduced		20,000
Add Net profit for the year		8,000
		28,000
Less Drawings		(7,000)
		21,000

Notes:
(*a*) There are four categories of entries shown in this statement of financial position. In practice, the fifth, non-current liabilities, often appears. It is positioned after the current liabilities; and its total is added to the total of current liabilities to get the figure for total liabilities. Exhibit 8.4 shows where this would be if B. Swift had any non-current liabilities.

(b) The figure for each item within each category should be shown and a total for the category produced. An example of this is the £25,100 total of current assets. The figures for each asset are listed, and the total is shown below them.

(c) The total for non-current assets is added to the total for current assets and the total is labelled 'total assets'.

(d) The total for current liabilities is added to the total for non-current liabilities and the total is labelled 'total liabilities'.

(e) The total liabilities amount is subtracted from the total assets to get an amount labelled 'net assets'. This amount will be the same as the total capital (which, in company financial statements, is called 'total equity').

(f) You do not write the word 'account' after each item.

(g) The owners will be most interested in their capital and the reasons why it has changed during the period. To show only the final balance of £21,000 means that the owners will not know how it was calculated. So we show the full details of the capital account.

(h) Look at the date on the statement of financial position. Now compare it with the dates put on the top of the income statement in the previous chapter. The statement of financial position is a position statement – it is shown as being at one point in time, e.g. 'as at 31 December 2012'. The income statement is different. It is for a period of time, in this case for a whole year, and so it uses the phrase 'for the year ending'.

Note: the difference between current assets and total liabilities is known as 'net current assets' or 'working capital' and is the amount of resources the business has in a form that is readily convertible into cash. This figure is not shown in the statement of financial position but is easy to produce from a completed statement of financial position.

Exhibit 8.4

B. Swift
Statement of financial position as at 31 December 2012
(showing the position of non-current liabilities)

	£	£
Non-current assets		
Fixtures and fittings		5,000
Current assets		
Inventory	3,000	
Account receivable	6,800	
Bank	15,100	
Cash	200	
		25,100
Total assets		30,100
Current liabilities		
Accounts payable	9,100	
Non-current liabilities	–	
Total liabilities		(9,100)
Net assets		21,000
Capital		
Cash introduced		20,000
Add Net profit for the year		8,000
		28,000
Less Drawings		(7,000)
Total capital		21,000

Learning outcomes

You should now have learnt:

1 That all balances remaining on a trial balance after the income statement for a period has been drawn up are displayed in a statement of financial position dated 'as at' the last day of the period.

2 That the statement of financial position is *not* part of double entry.

3 That the statement of financial position starts with non-current assets at the top, then current assets, then current liabilities, then non-current liabilities, then capital.

4 The meanings of the terms non-current asset, current asset, current liability, and non-current liability.

5 That you list non-current assets in descending order starting with those that will remain in use in the business for the longest time.

6 That you list current assets from top to bottom in increasing order of liquidity.

7 That current assets less current liabilities are known as 'net current assets' or 'working capital'.

8 Why the figure for net current assets is very important.

Answers to activities

8.1 All these accounts should have been closed off when the trading account and the profit and loss account were completed and the income statement prepared. Only accounts with balances appear in a trial balance.

8.2 A statement of financial position is a financial statement that summarises the position at the end of a period. It contains all the balances on the accounts held in the accounting books at that time. As it is prepared after the income statement, all the accounts have already been balanced-off. All we do with the statement of financial position is copy the balances carried forward from the accounts and place them in an appropriate position in the statement.

Review questions

8.1   Return to Review Question 7.1 and prepare a statement of financial position as at 31 December 2013.

8.2   Return to Review Question 7.2 and prepare a statement of financial position as at 30 June 2012.

8.3A   Return to Review Question 7.3A and prepare a statement of financial position as at 31 December 2013.

8.4A   Return to Review Question 7.4A and prepare a statement of financial position as at 30 June 2012.

8.5   A. Bell started in business on 1 July 2012, with £60,000 capital in cash. During the first year he kept very few records of his transactions.
   The assets and liabilities of the business at 30 June 2013 were:

	£
Freehold premises	80,000
Mortgage on the premises	40,000
Inventory	28,000
Accounts receivable	1,600
Cash and bank balances	3,800
Accounts payable	6,200

During the year, Bell withdrew £12,000 cash for his personal use but he also paid £4,000 received from the sale of his private car into the business bank account.

Required:
From the above information, prepare a statement of financial position showing the financial position of the business at 30 June 2013 and indicating the net profit for the year.

8.6A   The following information relates to A. Trader's business:

Assets and liabilities at	1 January 2012	31 December 2012
	£	£
Fixtures	18,000	16,200
Account receivable	4,800	5,800
Inventory	24,000	28,000
Accounts payable	8,000	11,000
Cash	760	240
Balance at bank	15,600	4,600
Loan from B. Burton	6,000	2,000
Motor vehicle	–	16,000

During the year, Trader had sold private investments for £4,000 which he paid into the business bank account, and he had drawn out £200 weekly for private use.

Required:
Prepare a statement of financial position as at 31 December 2012 and give the net profit as at that date.

Financial Statements 2

Income statements and statements of financial position: further considerations

Learning objectives

After you have studied this chapter, you should be able to:

- explain the terms returns inwards, returns outwards, carriage inwards and carriage outwards
- record returns inwards and returns outwards in the income statement
- explain the difference between the treatment of carriage inwards and carriage outwards in the income statement
- explain why carriage inwards is treated as part of the cost of purchasing goods
- explain why carriage outwards is *not* treated as part of the cost of purchasing goods
- prepare an inventory account showing the entries for opening and closing inventory
- prepare an income statement and a statement of financial position containing the appropriate adjustments for returns, carriage and other items that affect the calculation of the cost of goods sold
- explain why the costs of putting goods into a saleable condition should be charged to the trading account

Introduction

This chapter contains material that *many* students get wrong in examinations. Take care as you work through it to understand and learn the points as they are presented to you.

In this chapter, you'll learn how to treat goods returned from customers and goods returned to suppliers in the trading account. You'll also learn how to deal with the costs of transporting goods into and out of a business. You will learn how to record inventory in an inventory account and then carry it forward in the account to the next period. You'll also learn how to enter opening inventory in the trading account. You'll learn that there are other costs that must be added to the cost of goods in the trading account. Finally, you'll learn how to prepare an income statement and a statement of financial position when any of these items are included in the list of balances at the end of a period.

9.1 Returns inwards and returns outwards

In Chapter 3, the idea of different accounts for different movements of inventory was introduced. There are four accounts involved. The sales account and the **returns inwards account** deal with goods sold and goods returned by customers. The purchases account and the **returns outwards account** deal with goods purchased and goods returned to the supplier respectively. In our first look at the preparation of a trading account in Chapter 7, returns inwards and returns outwards were omitted. This was done deliberately, so that your first sight of income statements would be as straightforward as possible.

Activity 9.1 Why do you think organisations bother with the two returns accounts? Why don't they just debit sales returned to the sales account and credit purchases returned to the purchases account?

Just as you may have done yourself, a large number of businesses return goods to their suppliers (**returns outwards**) and will have goods returned to them by their customers (**returns inwards**). When the gross profit is calculated, these returns will have to be included in the calculations.

Let us look again at the trial balance shown in Exhibit 7.1:

Exhibit 7.1 (extract)

B. Swift Trial balance as at 31 December 2012	Dr	Cr
	£	£
Sales		38,500
Purchases	29,000	

Now, suppose that in Exhibit 7.1 the trial balance of B. Swift, rather than simply containing a sales account balance of £38,500 and a purchases account balance of £29,000 the balances included those for returns inwards and outwards:

Exhibit 9.1

B. Swift Trial balance as at 31 December 2012 (extract)	Dr	Cr
	£	£
Sales		40,000
Purchases	31,200	
Returns inwards	1,500	
Returns outwards		2,200

Comparing these two exhibits reveals that they amount to the same thing as far as gross profit is concerned. Sales were £38,500 in the original example because returns inwards had already been deducted in arriving at the amount shown in Exhibit 7.1. In the amended version, returns inwards should be shown separately in the trial balance and then deducted on the face of the income statement to get the correct figure for goods sold to customers and *kept* by them, i.e. £40,000 – £1,500 = £38,500. Purchases were originally shown as being £29,000. In the new version, returns outwards should be deducted to get the correct figure of purchases *kept* by Swift. Both the returns accounts are included in the calculation of gross profit, which now becomes:

> (Sales *less* Returns inwards) – (Cost of goods sold *less* Returns outwards) = Gross profit

The gross profit is therefore unaffected and is the same as in Chapter 7: £12,500.

The trading account section of the income statement will appear as in Exhibit 9.2:

Exhibit 9.2

B. Swift
Trading account section of the income statement for the year ending 31 December 2012

	£	£
Sales		40,000
Less Returns inwards		(1,500)
		38,500
Less Cost of goods sold:		
Purchases	31,200	
Less Returns outwards	(2,200)	
	29,000	
Less Closing Inventory	(3,000)	
		(26,000)
Gross profit		12,500

9.2 Carriage

If you have ever purchased anything by telephone, by letter or over the Internet, you have probably been charged for 'postage and packing'. When goods are delivered by suppliers or sent to customers, the cost of transporting the goods is often an additional charge to the buyer. In accounting, this charge is called 'carriage'. When it is charged for delivery of goods purchased, it is called **carriage inwards**. Carriage charged on goods sent out by a business to its customers is called **carriage outwards**.

When goods are purchased, the cost of carriage inwards may either be included as a hidden part of the purchase price, or be charged separately. For example, suppose your business was buying exactly the same goods from two suppliers. One supplier might sell them for £100 and not charge anything for carriage. Another supplier might sell the goods for £95, but you would have to pay £5 to a courier for carriage inwards, i.e. a total cost of £100. In both cases, the same goods cost you the same total amount. It would not be appropriate to leave out the cost of carriage inwards from the 'cheaper' supplier in the calculation of gross profit, as the real cost to you having the goods available for resale is £100.

As a result, in order to ensure that the true cost of buying goods for resale is *always* included in the calculation of gross profit, carriage inwards is *always* added to the cost of purchases in the trading account.

Carriage outwards is not part of the selling price of goods. Customers could come and collect the goods themselves, in which case there would be no carriage outwards expense for the seller to pay or to recharge customers. **Carriage outwards is *always* entered in the profit and loss account section of the income statement. It is *never* included in the calculation of gross profit.**

Suppose that in the illustration shown in this chapter, the goods had been bought for the same total figure of £31,200 but, in fact, £29,200 was the figure for purchases and £2,000 for carriage inwards. The trial balance extract would appear as in Exhibit 9.3.

Exhibit 9.3

B. Swift
Trial balance as at 31 December 2012 (extract)

	Dr	Cr
	£	£
Sales		40,000
Purchases	29,200	
Returns inwards	1,500	
Returns outwards		2,200
Carriage inwards	2,000	

The trading account section of the income statement would then be as shown in Exhibit 9.4:

Exhibit 9.4

B. Swift
Trading account section of the income statement for the year ending 31 December 2012

	£	£
Sales		40,000
Less Returns inwards		(1,500)
		38,500
Less Cost of goods sold:		
Purchases	29,200	
Less Returns outwards	(2,200)	
	27,000	
Carriage inwards	2,000	
	29,000	
Less Closing inventory	(3,000)	
		(26,000)
Gross profit		12,500

It can be seen that the three versions of B. Swift's trial balance have all been concerned with the same overall amount of goods bought and sold by the business, at the same overall prices. Therefore, in each case, the same gross profit of £12,500 has been found.

Before you proceed further, attempt Review Questions 9.1 and 9.2A.

9.3   The second year of a business

At the end of his second year of trading, on 31 December 2013, B. Swift draws up another trial balance.

Exhibit 9.5

		Dr	Cr
B. Swift **Trial balance as at 31 December 2013**			
		£	£
Sales			67,000
Purchases		42,600	
Lighting and heating expenses		1,900	
Rent		2,400	
Wages: shop assistant		5,200	
General expenses		700	
Carriage outwards		1,100	
Buildings		20,000	
Fixtures and fittings		7,500	
Accounts receivable		12,000	
Accounts payable			9,000
Bank		1,200	
Cash		400	
Drawings		9,000	
Capital			31,000
Inventory (at 31 December 2012)		3,000	
		107,000	107,000

Adjustments needed for inventory

So far, we have been looking at new businesses only. When a business starts, it has no inventory brought forward. B. Swift started in business in 2012. Therefore, when we were preparing Swift's income statement for 2012, there was only closing inventory to worry about.

When we prepare the income statement for the second year we can see the difference. If you look back to the income statement in Exhibit 9.4, you can see that there was closing inventory of £3,000. This is, therefore, the opening inventory figure for 2013 that we will need to incorporate in the trading account. It is also the figure for inventory that you can see in the trial balance at 31 December 2013.

The closing inventory for one period is *always* brought forward as the opening inventory for the next period.

Swift checked his inventory at 31 December 2013 and valued it at that date at £5,500.

We can summarise the opening and closing inventory account positions for Swift over the two years as follows:

Trading account for the period ➡	Year ending 31 December 2012	Year ending 31 December 2013
Opening inventory 1.1.2012	None	
Closing inventory 31.12.2012	£3,000	
Opening inventory 1.1.2013		£3,000
Closing inventory 31.12.2013		£5,500

Inventory account

Before going any further, let's look at the inventory account for both years:

Inventory

2012		£	2012		£
Dec 31 Trading		3,000	Dec 31 Balance c/d		3,000
2013			2013		
Jan 1 Balance b/d		3,000	Dec 31 Trading		3,000
Dec 31 Trading		5,500	31 Balance c/d		5,500
		8,500			8,500

You can see that in 2013 there is both a debit and a credit double entry made at the end of the period to the trading account. First, the inventory account is credited with the opening inventory amount of £3,000 and the trading account is debited with the same amount. Then, the inventory account is debited with the closing inventory amount of £5,500 and the trading account is credited with the same amount.

Thus, while the first year of trading only includes one inventory figure in the trading account, for the second year of trading both opening and closing inventory figures will be in the calculations.

Let's now calculate the cost of goods sold for 2013:

	£
Inventory of goods at start of year	3,000
Add Purchases	42,600
Total goods available for sale	45,600
Less What remains at the end of the year (i.e. closing inventory)	(5,500)
Therefore the cost of goods that have been sold is	40,100

We can look at a diagram to illustrate this:

Exhibit 9.6

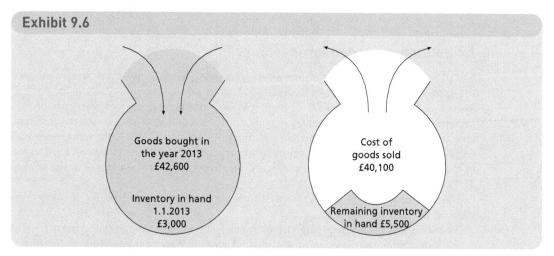

You can see that the left-hand container in the exhibit contains all the inventory available to be sold during the year. In the right-hand container, the closing inventory at the end of the year is now lying at the bottom and the empty space above it must, therefore, represent the inventory that has been sold.

The calculation of gross profit can now be done. You know from the trial balance that sales were £67,000 and from the calculation above that the cost of goods sold was £40,100. Gross profit is, therefore, £26,900.

Now the income statement and the statement of financial position can be drawn up, as shown in Exhibits 9.7 and 9.8:

Exhibit 9.7

B. Swift
Income statement for the year ending 31 December 2013

	£	£
Sales		67,000
Less Cost of goods sold:		
Opening inventory	3,000	
Add Purchases	42,600	
	45,600	
Less Closing inventory	(5,500)	
		(40,100)
Gross profit		26,900
Less Expenses:		
Wages	5,200	
Lighting and heating expenses	1,900	
Rent	2,400	
General expenses	700	
Carriage outwards	1,100	
		(11,300)
Net profit		15,600

Exhibit 9.8

B. Swift
Statement of financial position as at 31 December 2013

	£	£
Non-current assets		
Buildings		20,000
Fixtures and fittings		7,500
		27,500
Current assets		
Inventory	5,500	
Accounts receivable	12,000	
Bank	1,200	
Cash	400	
		19,100
Total assets		46,600
Current liabilities		
Accounts payable		(9,000)
Net assets		37,600
Capital		
Balance at 1 January 2013		31,000
Add Net profit for the year		15,600
		46,600
Less Drawings		(9,000)
Total capital		37,600

Financial statements

Financial statements is the term given to all the summary statements that accountants produce at the end of accounting periods. They are often called **'final accounts'**, but this term is quite misleading (as none of the financial statements are 'accounts' in the accounting sense). Nevertheless, some do still refer to them as the 'final accounts' or simply as **the accounts** of a business. You will, therefore, need to be aware of these terms, just in case you read something that uses these terms, or your teacher or lecturer, or an examiner, uses them at some time.

Other expenses in the trading account

You already know that carriage inwards is added to the cost of purchases in the trading account. You also need to add to the cost of goods in the trading account any costs incurred in converting purchases into goods for resale. In the case of a trader, it is very unusual for any additional costs to be incurred getting the goods ready for sale.

 Activity 9.2 What costs do you think a trader may incur that would need to be added to the cost of the goods in the trading account?

For goods imported from abroad it is usual to find that the costs of import duty and insurance are treated as part of the cost of the goods, along with any costs incurred in repackaging the goods. Any such additional costs incurred in getting goods ready for sale are debited to the trading account.

Note: Students often find it difficult to remember how to treat returns and carriage when preparing the income statement. You need to be sure to learn and remember that all returns, inwards and outwards, and carriage inwards appear in the calculation of gross profit. Carriage outwards appears as an expense in the profit and loss account section of the income statement.

9.4   A warning

Students lose a lot of marks on the topics covered in this chapter because they assume that the topics are easy and unlikely to be things that they will forget. Unfortunately, they are fairly easy to understand, and that is why they are easily forgotten and confused. You would be wise to make sure that you have understood and learnt everything presented to you in this chapter before you go any further in the book.

9.5   Review questions: the best approach

Before you attempt the review questions at the end of this chapter, you should read the section on review questions in the Notes for Students (pp. xv–xxiv).

Learning outcomes

You should now have learnt:

1 That returns *inwards* should be deducted from sales in the *trading* account.

2 That returns *outwards* should be deducted from purchases in the *trading* account.

3 That carriage *inwards* is shown as an expense item in the *trading* account.

4 That carriage *outwards* is shown as an expense in the *profit and loss* account.

5 How to prepare the inventory account and carry forward the balance from one period to the next.

6 That in the second and later years of a business, both opening and closing inventory are brought into the trading account.

7 That it is normal practice to show cost of goods sold as a separate figure in the trading account.

8 How to prepare an income statement that includes the adjustments for carriage inwards and both opening and closing inventory in the trading section and carriage outwards as an expense in the profit and loss section.

9 That expense items concerned with getting goods into a saleable condition are charged in the trading account.

10 That where there is import duty or insurance charged on goods purchased, these costs are treated as part of the cost of goods sold.

Answers to activities

9.1 Organisations want to know how much they sold as a separate item from how much of those goods sold were returned. The same goes for purchases and the goods sent back to the supplier. It is useful to know what proportion of goods sold are returned and whether there is any pattern in which customers are returning them. On the purchases side, knowing how many times goods have been returned and the proportion of purchases from individual suppliers that are being returned helps with monitoring the quality of the goods being purchased. While this information could be gathered if returns accounts were not used, it would be a more complicated task obtaining it. Most of all, however, the sales account is a revenue account. Entering returns inwards amounts in the sales account is contrary to the nature of the sales account. The same holds for returns outwards and the purchases account, which is an expense account.

9.2 In the case of a trader, it is very unusual for any additional costs to be incurred getting the goods ready for sale. However, a trader who sells clocks packed in boxes might buy the clocks from one supplier, and the boxes from another. Both of these items would be charged in the trading account as purchases. In addition, if someone was paid to pack the clocks into the boxes, then the wages paid for that to be done would also be charged in the trading account as part of the cost of those goods. Be careful not to confuse this with the wages of shop assistants who sell the clocks. Those wages *must* be charged in the profit and loss account because they are selling costs rather than extra costs incurred getting the goods ready for sale. The wages of the person packing the clocks would be the only wages in this case that were incurred while 'putting the goods into a saleable condition'.

Review questions

9.1 From the following information, draw up the trading account section of the income statement of J. Bell for the year ending 31 December 2012, which was his first year in business:

	£
Carriage inwards	1,000
Returns outwards	900
Returns inwards	1,300
Sales	165,000
Purchases	120,000
Inventory of goods: 31 December 2012	11,600

9.2A The following information is available for the year ending 31 March 2013. Draw up the trading account section of the income statement of P. Frank for that year.

	£
Inventory: 31 March 2013	52,400
Returns inwards	16,220
Returns outwards	19,480
Purchases	394,170
Carriage inwards	2,490
Sales	469,320

9.3 From the following trial balance of G. Still, draw up an income statement for the year ending 30 September 2013, and a statement of financial position as at that date.

	Dr	Cr
	£	£
Inventory: 1 October 2012	41,600	
Carriage outwards	2,100	
Carriage inwards	3,700	
Returns inwards	1,540	
Returns outwards		3,410
Purchases	188,430	
Sales		380,400
Salaries and wages	61,400	
Warehouse rent	3,700	
Insurance	1,356	
Motor expenses	1,910	
Office expenses	412	
Lighting and heating expenses	894	
General expenses	245	
Premises	92,000	
Motor vehicles	13,400	
Fixtures and fittings	1,900	
Accounts receivable	42,560	
Accounts payable		31,600
Cash at bank	5,106	
Drawings	22,000	
Capital		68,843
	484,253	484,253

Inventory at 30 September 2013 was £44,780.

9.4   The following trial balance was extracted from the books of F. Sorley on 30 April 2013. From it, and the note about inventory, prepare his income statement for the year ending 30 April 2013, and a statement of financial position as at that date.

	Dr	Cr
	£	£
Sales		210,420
Purchases	108,680	
Inventory: 1 May 2012	9,410	
Carriage outwards	1,115	
Carriage inwards	840	
Returns inwards	4,900	
Returns outwards		3,720
Salaries and wages	41,800	
Motor expenses	912	
Rent	6,800	
Sundry expenses	318	
Motor vehicles	14,400	
Fixtures and fittings	912	
Accounts receivable	23,200	
Accounts payable		14,100
Cash at bank	4,100	
Cash in hand	240	
Drawings	29,440	
Capital		18,827
	247,067	247,067

Inventory at 30 April 2013 was £11,290.

9.5A   The following is the trial balance of T. Owen as at 31 March 2012. Draw up a set of financial statements for the year ended 31 March 2012.

	Dr	Cr
	£	£
Inventory: 1 April 2011	52,800	
Sales		276,400
Purchases	141,300	
Carriage inwards	1,350	
Carriage outwards	5,840	
Returns outwards		2,408
Wages and salaries	63,400	
Business rates	3,800	
Communication expenses	714	
Commissions paid	1,930	
Insurance	1,830	
Sundry expenses	208	
Buildings	125,000	
Accounts receivable	45,900	
Accounts payable		24,870
Fixtures	1,106	
Cash at bank	31,420	
Cash in hand	276	
Drawings	37,320	
Capital		210,516
	514,194	514,194

Inventory at 31 March 2012 was £58,440.

9.6A   F. Brown drew up the following trial balance as at 30 September 2011. You are to draft the income statement for the year ending 30 September 2011 and a statement of financial position as at that date.

	Dr	Cr
	£	£
Capital		49,675
Drawings	28,600	
Cash at bank	4,420	
Cash in hand	112	
Accounts receivable	38,100	
Accounts payable		26,300
Inventory: 30 September 2010	72,410	
Van	5,650	
Office equipment	7,470	
Sales		391,400
Purchases	254,810	
Returns inwards	2,110	
Carriage inwards	760	
Returns outwards		1,240
Carriage outwards	2,850	
Motor expenses	1,490	
Rent	8,200	
Telephone charges	680	
Wages and salaries	39,600	
Insurance	745	
Office expenses	392	
Sundry expenses	216	
	468,615	468,615

Inventory at 30 September 2011 was £89,404.

9.7   Enter the following transactions in the ledger of A. Baker and prepare a trial balance at 31 May, together with a calculation of the profit for the month and a statement of financial position at 31 May.

May	1	Started in business with £1,500 in the bank and £500 cash.
	2	Purchased goods to the value of £1,750 from C. Dunn, agreeing credit terms of 60 days.
	3	Bought fixtures and fittings for the bakery for £150, paying by cheque.
	6	Bought goods on credit from E. Farnham for £115.
	10	Paid rent of £300 paying cash.
	12	Bought stationery – cash book and invoices – for £75 – paying by cash.
	14	Sold goods on credit, value £125, to G. Harlem.
	20	Bought an old van for deliveries for £2,000 on credit from I. Jumpstart.
	30	Paid wages of £450 net for the month by cheque.
	31	Summarised cash sales for the month and found them to be £2,500. Took a cheque for £500 as own wages for the month. Banked £2,000 out of the cash sales over the month.
	31	Closing inventory was £500.

9.8A   Ms Porter's business position at 1 July was as follows:

	£
Inventory	5,000
Equipment	3,700
Creditor (OK Ltd)	500
Debtor (AB Ltd)	300
Bank balance	1,200

During July, she:

	£
Sold goods for cash – paid to bank	3,200
Sold goods to AB Limited	600
Bought goods from OK Ltd on credit	3,900
Paid OK Ltd by cheque	3,000
Paid general expenses by cheque	500
AB Ltd paid by cheque	300

Inventory at 31 July was £6,200

Required:
(a) Open ledger accounts (including capital) at 1 July
(b) Record all transactions
(c) Prepare a trial balance
(d) Prepare an income statement for the period
(e) Prepare a statement of financial position as at 31 July

9.9 From the following trial balance of Kingfire, extracted after one year of operations, prepare an income statement for the year ending 30 June 2012, together with a statement of financial position as at that date.

	£	£
Sales		35,800
Purchases	14,525	
Salaries	2,325	
Motor expenses	9,300	
Rent and business rates	1,250	
Insurances – building	750	
– vehicles	1,200	
Motor vehicles	10,000	
Fixtures	17,500	
Cash in hand	500	
Cash at bank		1,250
Drawings	12,000	
Long-term loan		15,000
Capital		19,275
Accounts receivable	11,725	
Accounts payable		9,750
	81,075	81,075

Inventory on 30 June 2012 was £3,000.

Accounting concepts and assumptions

Learning objectives

After you have studied this chapter, you should be able to:

- describe the assumptions which are made when recording accounting data
- explain why one set of financial statements has to serve many purposes
- explain the implications of objectivity and subjectivity in the context of accounting
- explain what accounting standards are and why they exist
- explain the underlying concepts of accounting
- explain how the concepts and assumptions of materiality, going concern, comparability through consistency, prudence, accruals, separate determination, substance over form and other concepts and assumptions affect the recording and adjustment of accounting data and the reporting of accounting information

Introduction

What you have been reading about so far has been concerned with the recording of transactions in the books and the subsequent preparation of trial balances, income statements, and statements of financial position. Such recording has been based on certain assumptions. Quite deliberately, these assumptions were not discussed in detail at the time. This is because it is much easier to look at them with a greater understanding *after* basic double entry has been covered. These assumptions are known as the *concepts of accounting*.

The income statements and statements of financial position shown in the previous chapters were drawn up for the owner of the business. As shown later in the book, businesses are often owned by more than just one person and these accounting statements are for the use of all the owners.

If the financial statements were solely for the use of the owner(s), there would be no need to adopt a common framework for the preparation and presentation of the information contained within them. However, as you learnt at the start of this book, there are a lot of other people who may be interested in seeing these financial statements, and they need to be able to understand them. It is for this reason that there has to be a commonly established practice concerning how the information in the financial statements is prepared and presented.

In this chapter, you will learn about some of the agreed practices that underpin the preparation of accounting information, and about some of the regulations that have been developed to ensure that they are adhered to.

10.1 Objective of financial statements

Financial statements should provide information about the financial position, performance and changes in the financial position of an entity that is useful to a wide range of users in making economic decisions. In order to achieve this objective, financial statements are prepared on the basis of a number of established concepts and assumptions and must adhere to the rules and procedures set down in regulations called, '*accounting standards*'.

10.2 One set of financial statements for all purposes

If it had always been the custom to draft different financial statements for different purposes, so that one version was given to a banker, another to someone wishing to buy the business, etc., then accounting would be very different from what it is today. However, this has not occurred. Identical copies of the financial statements are given to all the different external stakeholders, irrespective of why they wish to look at them.

This means that the banker, the prospective buyer of the business, shareholders, etc. all see the same income statement and statement of financial position. This is not an ideal situation as the interests of each party are different and each party seeks different kinds of information from those wanted by the others. For instance, bank managers would really like to know how much the assets would sell for if the business ceased trading. They could then see what the possibility would be of the bank obtaining repayment of its loan or the overdraft. Other people would also like to see the information in the way that is most useful to them.

 Activity 10.1 This doesn't sound very ideal for anyone, does it? What benefits do you think there may be that outweigh these disadvantages of one set of financial statements for all?

Because everyone receives the same income statement and statement of financial position, in order to be of any use, all the various stakeholders have to believe that the assumptions upon which these financial statements are based are valid and appropriate. If they don't, they won't trust the financial statements.

Assume that you are in a class of students and that you have the problem of valuing your assets, which consist of four textbooks. The first value you decide is based upon how much you could sell them for. Your own guess is £60, but the other members of your class suggest they should be valued at anything from £30 to £80.

Suppose that you now decide to put a value on their use to you. You may well think that the use of these textbooks will enable you to pass your examinations and that you'll then be able to get a good job. Another person may have the opposite idea concerning the use of the textbooks. The use value placed on the textbooks by others in the class will be quite different. Your value may be higher than those of some of your colleagues and lower than others.

Finally, you decide to value them by reference to cost. You take out the receipts you were given when you purchased the textbooks, which show that you paid a total of £120 for them. If the rest of the class does not think that you have altered the receipts, then they will all agree with you that the value of the books, expressed at original cost, is £120. At last, you have found a way of valuing the textbooks where everyone agrees on the same figure. As this is the only valuation that you can all agree upon, each of you decides to use the idea of valuing the asset of textbooks at their cost price so that you can have a meaningful discussion about what you are worth (in terms of your assets, i.e. your textbooks) compared with everyone else in the class. It probably won't come as a surprise to you to learn that this is precisely the basis upon which the assets of a business are valued. Accountants call it the **historical cost concept**.

10.3   Objectivity and subjectivity

The use of a method which arrives at a value that everyone can agree to *because it is based upon a factual occurrence* is said to be **objective**. Valuing your textbooks at their cost is, therefore, objective – you are adhering to and accepting the facts. You are not placing your own interpretation on the facts. As a result, everyone else knows where the value came from and can see that there is very good evidence to support its adoption.

If, instead of being objective, you were **subjective**, you would use your own judgement to arrive at a cost. This often results in the value you arrive at being biased towards your own views and preferences – as in the example above when the usefulness of the textbooks to you for examinations was the basis of their valuation. Subjective valuations seem right to the person who makes them, but many other people would probably disagree with the value arrived at, because it won't appear to them to be objectively based.

The desire to provide the same set of financial statements for many different parties, and so provide a basis for measurement that is generally acceptable, means that objectivity is sought in financial accounting. If you are able to understand this desire for objectivity, then many of the apparent contradictions in accounting can be understood, because objectivity is at the heart of the financial accounting methods we all use.

Financial accounting, therefore, seeks objectivity and it seeks consistency in how information is prepared and presented. To achieve this, there must be a set of rules which lay down the way in which the transactions of the business are recorded. These rules have long been known as 'accounting concepts'. A group of these have become known as 'fundamental accounting concepts' or 'accounting principles' and have been enforced through their incorporation in accounting standards issued on behalf of the accountancy bodies by accounting standards boards, and by their inclusion in the relevant legislation governing companies.

10.4   Accounting Standards and Financial Reporting Standards in the UK

At one time, there used to be quite wide differences in the ways that accountants calculated profits. In the late 1960s a number of cases led to a widespread outcry against this lack of uniformity in accounting practice.

In response, the UK accounting bodies formed the Accounting Standards Committee (ASC). It issued a series of accounting standards, called *Statements of Standard Accounting Practice* (SSAPs). The ASC was replaced in 1990 by the Accounting Standards Board (ASB), which also issued accounting standards, this time called *Financial Reporting Standards* (FRSs). Both these forms of accounting standards were compulsory, enforced by company law.

From time to time, the ASB also issued *Urgent Issue Task Force Abstracts* (UITFs). These were generally intended to be in force only while a standard was being prepared or an existing standard amended to cover the topic dealt with in the UITF. Of course, some issues do not merit a full standard and so a few UITFs were never replaced by a new standard. UITFs carried the same weight as accounting standards and their application was compulsory for financial statements prepared under *UK GAAP* – the term for the set of regulations and legislation applicable to and created for UK financial statements.

SSAPs and FRSs were generally developed with the larger company in mind. In an effort to make adherence to standards more manageable for smaller companies, in 1997 the ASB issued a third category of standard – the *Financial Reporting Standard for Smaller Entities* (FRSSE). It was, in effect, a collection of some of the rules from virtually all the other accounting standards. Small entities could choose whether to apply it or continue to apply all the other accounting standards.

The authority, scope and application of each document issued by the ASB was announced when the document was issued. Thus, even though each accounting standard and UITF must be applied by anyone preparing financial statements under UK GAAP, in some cases certain classes of organisations were exempted from applying some or all of the rules contained within them. You can find out more about the work of the ASB and the standards and UITFs currently in issue at its website (**www.frc.org.uk/asb/technical/standards/accounting.cfm**).

 Activity 10.2 What benefits do you think there are if all entities adopt the same set of accounting standards?

In 2005, most companies whose shares were quoted on the London Stock Exchange were required to switch to International Accounting Standards, and other entities could do so if they wished. By 2010, many had switched voluntarily to International GAAP. Among those that had not switched to International GAAP, many had changed from UK GAAP terminology in their financial statements (such as 'stock' and 'Profit and Loss Account') to International GAAP terminology (such as 'inventory' and 'income statement').

The usefulness of UK accounting standards was clearly in the wane. Consequently, in 2010 the ASB published an exposure draft on the future of financial reporting in the UK and Republic of Ireland. It proposed a three-tier reporting framework, aimed at balancing the needs of preparers and users of financial statements; and sought to simplify UK standards into a concise, coherent and updated form. The new framework would be effective from 1 July 2013.

Two draft FRSs were proposed:

- *Application of Financial Reporting Requirements*, which describes the three-tier system; and
- *The Financial Reporting Standard for Medium-sized Entities* based on the International Accounting Standard Board (IASB)'s IFRS for Small and Medium-Sized Enterprises (SMEs), and applicable to entities which are not small and not publicly accountable.

The proposed three-tier system comprises:

1 Quoted groups will continue to report under international financial reporting standards (IFRS), as adopted by the EU. In addition, other companies which are *'publicly accountable'* would also report under IFRS. A company is considered to be 'publicly accountable' if its debt is traded on public markets, or if it holds deposits or manages other people's money.
2 Other entities other than the smallest companies would report under a new standard based on the IFRS for SMEs: the *FRSME*, as it would be called, would comply with UK and EU law and be designed so as to facilitate tax reporting.
3 The smallest companies, which will continue to use the simplified version of UK standards, known as the FRSSE.

All existing ASB standards would be replaced under the new system, except the existing FRSSE and the proposed FRSME.

 Activity 10.3 What do you think the benefits of a change to this new three-tier framework will be?

10.5   International Accounting Standards

The Accounting Standards Board deals with the United Kingdom and Ireland. Besides this and other national accounting boards, there is an international organisation concerned with accounting standards. The International Accounting Standards Committee (IASC) was established in 1973 and changed its name to the International Accounting Standards Board (IASB) in 2000.

The need for an IASB was due to:

(a) The considerable growth in international investment. This means that it is desirable to have similar accounting methods the world over so that investment decisions are more compatible.
(b) The growth in the number of multinational organisations. These organisations have to produce financial statements covering a large number of countries. Standardisation between countries makes the accounting work that much easier, and reduces costs.
(c) As quite a few countries now have their own standard-setting bodies, it is desirable that their efforts be harmonised.
(d) The need for accounting standards in countries that cannot afford a standard-setting body of their own.

The work of the IASB is overseen by 22 trustees, six from Europe, six from North America, six from Asia/Oceania, one from Africa, one from South America, and two from the rest of the world. The IASB has 15 members and will have 16 from 2012. Its members are appointed by the Trustees and must reflect an appropriate balance of auditors, financial statement preparers, users of financial statements and academics.

The IASC issued International Accounting Standards (IASs) and the IASB issues International Financial Reporting Standards (IFRSs). When the IASC was founded, it had no formal authority and IASs were entirely voluntary and initially intended for use in countries that either did not have their own accounting standards or would have had considerable logistical difficulty in establishing and maintaining the infrastructure necessary to sustain a national accounting standards board.

While the ASB has been at pains to ensure that most of the provisions of the relevant IASs are incorporated in existing SSAPs or FRSs and each FRS indicates the level of compliance with the relevant IAS, there do remain some differences between the two sets of standards. However, as mentioned in Section 10.4, the ASB is moving to eliminate any significant impact of this situation by the adoption of international standards by all but the smallest entities.

This textbook describes and discusses the contents of International Accounting Standards, and the terminology used throughout the book is that typically used under those standards.

10.6   Accounting standards and the legal framework

Accounting standards are given legal status under the Companies Acts and comply with European Union Directives. This ensures that there is no conflict between the law and accounting standards. Anyone preparing financial statements which are intended to show a 'true and fair view' (i.e. truly reflect what has occurred and the financial position of the organisation) must observe the rules laid down in the accounting standards.

10.7   Underlying accounting concepts

A number of accounting concepts have been applied ever since financial statements were first produced for external reporting purposes. These have become second nature to accountants and are not generally reinforced, other than through custom and practice.

The historical cost concept

The need for this has already been described in the textbook valuation example. It means that assets are normally shown at cost price, and that this is the basis for valuation of the assets.

The money measurement concept

Accounting information has traditionally been concerned only with those facts covered by (*a*) and (*b*) which follow:

(*a*) it can be measured in monetary units; and
(*b*) most people will agree to the monetary value of the transaction.

This limitation is referred to as the **money measurement concept**, and it means that accounting can never tell you everything about a business. For example, accounting does not show the following:

(*c*) whether the business has good or bad managers;
(*d*) whether there are serious problems with the workforce;
(*e*) whether a rival product is about to take away many of the best customers;
(*f*) whether the government is about to pass a law which will cost the business a lot of extra expense in future.

The reason that (*c*) to (*f*) or similar items are not recorded is that it would be impossible to work out a monetary value for them which most people would agree to.

Some people think that accounting and financial statements tell you everything you want to know about a business. The above shows that this is not the case.

The business entity concept

The **business entity concept** implies that the affairs of a business are to be treated as being quite separate from the non-business activities of its owner(s).

The items recorded in the books of the business are, therefore, restricted to the transactions of the business. No matter what activities the proprietor(s) get up to outside the business, they are completely disregarded in the books kept by the business.

The only time that the personal resources of the proprietor(s) affect the accounting records of a business is when they introduce new capital into the business, or take drawings out of it.

The dual aspect concept

This states that there are two aspects of accounting, one represented by the assets of the business and the other by the claims against them. The concept states that these two aspects are always equal to each other. In other words, this is the alternate form of the accounting equation:

$$\text{Assets} = \text{Capital} + \text{Liabilities}$$

As you know, double entry is the name given to the method of recording transactions under the **dual aspect concept**.

The time interval concept

One of the underlying principles of accounting, the **time interval concept**, is that financial statements are prepared at regular intervals of one year. Companies which publish further financial statements between their annual ones describe the others as 'interim statements'. For internal management purposes, financial statements may be prepared far more frequently, possibly on a monthly basis or even more often.

10.8   Underlying assumptions

The IASB Framework lists two assumptions that must be applied if financial statements are to meet their objectives: the **accrual basis** (also called the **accruals concept**) and the **going concern concept**.

Accrual basis

The effects of transactions and other events are recognised when they occur and they are recorded in the books and reported in the financial statements of the period to which they relate.

Net profit is the difference between revenues and the expenses incurred in generating those revenues, i.e.

$$\boxed{\text{Revenues} - \text{Expenses} = \text{Net Profit}}$$

Determining the expenses used up to obtain the revenues is referred to as *matching* expenses against revenues. The key to the application of the concept is that all income and charges relating to the financial period to which the financial statements relate should be taken into account without regard to the date of receipt or payment.

This concept is particularly misunderstood by people who have not studied accounting. To many of them, actual payment of an item in a period is taken as being matched against the revenue of the period when the net profit is calculated. The fact that expenses consist of the assets used up in a particular period in obtaining the revenues of that period, and that cash paid in a period and expenses of a period are usually different, as you will see later, comes as a surprise to a great number of them.

This assumption requires that adjustments are made to some figures in the trial balance before the financial statements can be prepared. The process of doing so is covered in Chapter 28.

Going concern

It is assumed that the business will continue to operate for at least twelve months after the end of the reporting period.

Suppose, however, that a business is drawing up its financial statements at 31 December 2012. Normally, using the historical cost concept, the assets would be shown at a total value of £100,000. It is known, however, that the business will be forced to close down in February 2013, only two months later, and the assets are expected to be sold for only £15,000.

In this case it would not make sense to keep to the going concern concept, and so we can reject the historical cost concept for asset valuation purposes. In the statement of financial position at 31 December 2012, the assets will be shown at the figure of £15,000. Rejection of the going concern concept is the exception rather than the rule.

Examples where the going concern assumption should be rejected are:

● if the business is going to close down in the near future;
● where shortage of cash makes it almost certain that the business will have to cease trading;
● where a large part of the business will almost certainly have to be closed down because of a shortage of cash.

10.9   Qualitative characteristics of financial statements

A useful diagram (Exhibit 10.1) illustrating the qualitative characteristics of accounting information was included by the ASB in an early draft of its equivalent of the IASB principles (upon which it was based).

Exhibit 10.1 The qualitative characteristics of accounting information

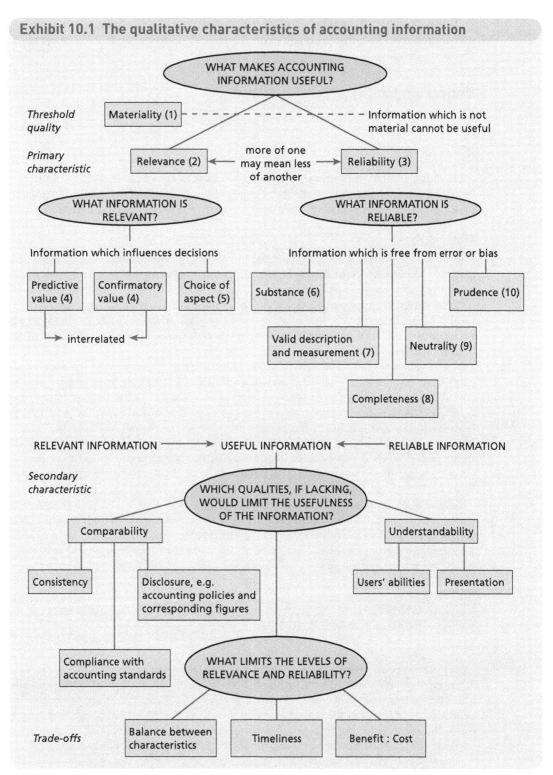

These are the attributes that make the information provided in financial statements useful to users. There are four principal qualitative characteristics: understandability, relevance, reliability and comparability.

Understandability

Information in financial statements should be readily understandable by users.

Relevance

Information in financial statements must be relevant to the decision-making needs of users. To be relevant, information must influence the economic decisions of users by helping them evaluate past, present or future events or confirming, or correcting, their past evaluation.

Materiality

Information is **material** if its omission or misstatement could influence the economic decisions of users. Materiality depends on the size of the item or error judged in the particular circumstances of its omission or misstatement.

Everything that appears in a financial accounting statement should be 'material'. That is, it should be of interest to the stakeholders, those people who make use of financial accounting statements. It need not be material to every stakeholder, but it must be material to a stakeholder before it merits inclusion.

Accounting does not serve a useful purpose if the effort of recording a transaction in a certain way is not worthwhile. Thus, if a box of paper-clips was bought it would be used up over a period of time, and this cost is used up every time someone uses a paper-clip. It is possible to record this as an expense every time a paper-clip is used but, obviously, the price of a paper-clip is so small that it is not worth recording it in this fashion, nor is the entire box of paper-clips. The paper-clips are not a material item and, therefore, the box would be charged as an expense in the period when it was bought, irrespective of the fact that it could last for more than one accounting period. In other words, do not waste your time in the elaborate recording of trivial items.

Similarly, the purchase of a cheap metal ashtray would also be charged as an expense in the period when it was bought because it is not a material item, even though it may in fact last for twenty years. A lorry would, however, be deemed to be a material item in most businesses, and so, as will be seen in Chapter 26, an attempt is made to charge each period with the cost consumed in each period of its use.

 Activity 10.4   Which fundamental accounting concept is what is being described in the previous paragraph an example of?

Businesses fix all sorts of arbitrary rules to determine what is material and what is not. There is no law that lays down what these should be – the decision as to what is material and what is not is dependent upon judgement. A business may well decide that all items under £100 should be treated as expenses in the period in which they were bought, even though they may well be in use in the business for the following 10 years. Another business, especially a large one, may fix the limit at £1,000. Different limits may be set for different types of item.

It can be seen that the size and the type of business will affect the decisions as to which items are material. With individuals, an amount of £1,000 may well be more than you, as a student, possess. For a multi-millionaire, what is a material item and what is not will almost certainly not be comparable. Just as individuals vary, then, so do businesses. Some businesses have a great deal of machinery and may well treat all items of machinery costing less than £1,000 as not being material, whereas another business which makes about the same amount of profit, but has very little machinery, may well treat a £600 machine as being a material item as they have fixed their materiality limit at £250.

Reliability

To be useful, information must also be reliable. To be reliable, information must be free from material error and bias and able to be depended upon by users to represent faithfully what it claims to represent.

Faithful representation

A statement of financial position should represent faithfully the transactions and other events that result in assets, liabilities and equity of the entity at the reporting date.

Substance over form

Transactions and other events must be accounted for and presented in accordance with their substance and economic reality and not merely their legal form. This is referred to as **substance over form**.

The legal form of a transaction can differ from its real substance. Where this happens, accounting should show the transaction in accordance with its real substance which is, basically, how the transaction affects the economic situation of the business. This means that accounting in this instance will not reflect the exact legal position concerning that transaction.

You have not yet come across the best and easiest illustration of this concept. Later in your studies you may have to learn about accounting for fixed assets being bought on hire purchase. We will take a car as an example.

- From a legal point of view, the car does not belong to the business until all the hire purchase instalments have been paid, and an option has been taken up whereby the business takes over legal possession of the car.
- From an economic point of view, you have used the car for business purposes, just as any other car owned by the business which was paid for immediately has been used. In this case, the business will show the car being bought on hire purchase in its ledger accounts and statement of financial position as though it were legally owned by the business, but also showing separately the amount still owed for it.

In this way, therefore, the substance of the transaction has taken precedence over the legal form of the transaction.

Neutrality

Information in financial statements must be free of bias.

Prudence

This is the inclusion of a degree of caution in the exercise of the judgement needed in making the estimates required under conditions of uncertainty (e.g. decisions relating to bad debts and allowances for doubtful debts), such that assets and income are not overstated and liabilities and expenses are not understated.

Very often accountants have to use their judgement to decide which figure to take for an item. Suppose a debt has been owing for quite a long time, and no one knows whether it will ever be paid. Should the accountant be optimistic and think that it will be paid, or be more pessimistic?

It is the accountant's duty to see that people get the proper facts about a business. The accountant should make certain that assets are not valued too highly. Similarly, liabilities should not be shown at values that are too low. Otherwise, people might inadvisedly lend money to a business, which they would not do if they had been provided with the proper facts.

The accountant should always exercise caution when dealing with uncertainty while, at the same time, ensuring that the financial statements are neutral – that gains and losses are neither overstated nor understated – and this is known as **prudence**.

It is true that, in applying the prudence concept, an accountant will normally make sure that all losses are recorded in the books, but that profits and gains will not be anticipated by recording them before they should be recorded. Although it emphasises neutrality, many people feel that the prudence concept means that accountants will normally take the figure relating to unrealised profits and gains which will understate rather than overstate the profit for a period. That is, they believe that accountants tend to choose figures that will cause the capital of the business to be shown at a lower amount rather than at a higher amount.

Do you agree with this view that the prudence concept results in accountants producing financial statements that understate profits and gains and therefore present a value for capital that is lower than it should be? Justify your answer.

The recognition of profits at an appropriate time has long been recognised as being in need of guidelines and these have long been enshrined in what is known as the **realisation concept**. This is not so much a separate concept as a part of the broader concept of prudence.

The realisation concept holds to the view that profit and gains can only be taken into account when realisation has occurred and that realisation occurs only when the ultimate cash realised is capable of being assessed (i.e. determined) with reasonable certainty. Several criteria have to be observed before realisation can occur:

- goods or services are provided for the buyer;
- the buyer accepts liability to pay for the goods or services;
- the monetary value of the goods or services has been established;
- the buyer will be in a situation to be able to pay for the goods or services.

Notice that it is not the time

- when the order is received; or
- when the customer pays for the goods.

However, it is only when you can be reasonably certain as to how much will be received that you can recognise profits or gains.

Of course, recognising profits and gains now that will only be 100 per cent known in future periods is unlikely to ever mean that the correct amount has been recognised. Misjudgements can arise when, for example, profit is recognised in one period, and later it is discovered that this was incorrect because the goods involved have been returned in a later period because of some deficiency. Also, where services are involved rather than goods, the services might turn out to be subject to an allowance being given in a later period owing to poor performance.

What do you think the accountant should do about these possibilities when applying the realisation concept?

The accountant needs to take every possibility into account yet, at the same time, the prudence concept requires that the financial statements are 'neutral', that is, that neither gains nor losses should be overstated or understated.

As you will see if you take your studies to a more advanced stage, there are times other than on completion of a sale when profit may be recognised. These could include profits on long-term contracts spanning several years, such as the building of a hotel or a very large bridge. In this case, profit might be calculated for each year of the contract, even though the work is not finished at that date.

Completeness

To be reliable, information in financial statements must be complete within the bounds of materiality and cost.

Comparability

Comparability requires **consistency**. The measurement and display of the financial effect of similar transactions and other events must be done in a consistent way throughout an entity and over time for that entity, and in a consistent way for different entities. Users must be informed of the accounting policies used in the preparation of the financial statements. They must be informed of any changes in those policies and of the effects of such changes. Financial statements must include corresponding information for the preceding periods.

10.10 Constraints on relevant and reliable information

Timeliness

Information must be reported in a timely manner.

Balance between benefit and cost

The benefits of information should exceed the costs of obtaining it.

Balance between qualitative characteristics

The aim should be to achieve a balance among the characteristics that best meets the objective of financial statements – see Section 10.1.

10.11 Other assumptions

Separate determination

In determining the aggregate amount of each asset or liability, the amount of each individual asset or liability should be determined separately from all other assets and liabilities. This is called **separate determination**. For example, if you have three machines, the amount at which machinery is shown in the statement of financial position should be the sum of the values calculated individually for each of the three machines. Only when individual values have been derived should a total be calculated.

Stability of currency

Accounting follows the historical cost concept, so assets are normally shown at their original cost. This has the effect of distorting the financial statements if inflation has caused the value of money to change over time – assets purchased 20 years ago for £50,000 would cost considerably more today, yet they would appear at that cost, not at the equivalent cost today. Users of financial statements need to be aware of this. There are techniques for eliminating these distortions, and they are covered in *Business Accounting 2*.

10.12 Accounting concepts and assumptions in action

This is too early a stage in your studies for you to be able to appreciate more fully how these concepts and assumptions work in practice. It is far better left towards the end of this book and, therefore, we consider this topic further in Chapter 47.

Learning outcomes

You should now have learnt:

1 Why one set of financial statements has to serve many purposes.

2 Why the need for general agreement has given rise to the concepts and conventions that govern accounting.

3 The implications of objectivity and subjectivity in the context of accounting.

4 What accounting standards are and why they exist.

5 The assumptions which are made when recording accounting data.

6 The underlying concepts of accounting.

7 How the concepts and assumptions of materiality, going concern, comparability through consistency, prudence, accruals, separate determination, substance over form, and other concepts and assumptions affect the recording and adjustment of accounting data and the reporting of accounting information.

8 That an assumption is made that monetary measures remain stable, i.e. that accounts are not normally adjusted for inflation or deflation.

Answers to activities

10.1 Although this is hardly ideal, at least everyone receives the same basic financial information concerning an organisation and, because all financial statements are prepared in the same way, comparison between them is reasonably straightforward. Also, some of the users of these financial statements have other sources of information, financial and otherwise, about a business – the banker, for example, will also have access to the financial statements produced for use by the managers of the business. These 'management accounts' are considerably more detailed than the financial statements and most bankers insist upon access to them when large sums of money are involved. (The financial statements produced for internal use are dealt with in Chapter 45.) The banker will also have information about other businesses in the same industry and about the state of the market in which the business operates, and will thus be able to compare the performance of the business against that of its competitors.

10.2 The use of accounting standards does *not* mean that two identical businesses will show exactly the same revenue, expenditure and profits year by year in their financial statements. However, it does considerably reduce the possibilities of very large variations in financial reporting, facilitates comparison between entities, and encourages consistency in the preparation of financial statements.

10.3 If all but the smallest companies report under international GAAP, this will reduce training costs of accountants and reduce the potential for auditing errors. At present, small and medium entities have a choice of which version of GAAP to apply when preparing their financial statements. Having all financial statements prepared according to which tier the entity that produced them lies in, should facilitate interpretation and comparison.

10.4 The accruals assumption (which is also sometimes referred to as the 'accruals concept').

10.5 Although accountants do include all the losses that have been identified in the financial statements, they also include all the gains that can be identified with reasonable certainty. In effect, by doing so, an accountant is being neutral and so, in practice, the amount of capital shown in the statement of financial position should be a true reflection of the position as known when the financial statements were produced.

10.6 When applying the realisation concept, the accountant will endeavour to estimate as accurately as possible the returns or allowances that are reasonably likely to arise and will build that information into the calculation of the profit and gains to be recognised in the period for which financial statements are being prepared.

Review questions

10.1 What is meant by the 'money measurement concept'?

10.2 Explain the concept of prudence in relation to the recognition of profits and losses.

10.3 Explain the term 'materiality' as it is used in accounting.

10.4 'The historical cost convention looks backwards but the going concern convention looks forwards.'

Required:
(*a*) Explain clearly what is meant by:
   (*i*) the historical cost convention;
   (*ii*) the going concern convention.
(*b*) Does traditional financial accounting, using the historical cost convention, make the going concern convention unnecessary? Explain your answer fully.
(*c*) Which do you think a shareholder is likely to find more useful – a report on the past or an estimate of the future? Why?

(*Association of Chartered Certified Accountants*)

Books of Original Entry

Books of original entry and ledgers

Introduction
....

In this chapter, you will learn about the books in which details of accounting transactions are recorded. You will learn that Day Books and Journals are used to record all transactions made on credit and that the Cash Book is used to record all cash and bank transactions. Then, you will learn that these entries are transferred from the books of original entry to a set of books called Ledgers and that each Ledger is for a particular type of item and that, by having a set of Ledgers, entries in accounts of items of a similar nature are recorded in the same place.

11.1 The growth of the business

When a business is very small, all the double entry accounts can be kept in one book, which we would call a 'ledger'. As the business grows it would be impossible just to use one book, as the large number of pages needed for a lot of transactions would mean that the book would be too big to handle. Also, suppose we have several bookkeepers. They could not all do their work properly if there were only one ledger.

The answer to this problem is for us to use more books. When we do this, we put similar types of transactions together and have a book for each type. In each book, we will not mix together transactions which are different from one another.

11.2 Books of original entry

When a transaction takes place, we need to record as much as possible of the details of the transaction. For example, if we sold four computers on credit to a Mr De Souza for £1,000 per computer, we would want to record that we sold four computers for £1,000 each to Mr De Souza on credit. We would also want to record the address and contact information of Mr De Souza and the date of the transaction. Some businesses would also record information like the identity of the person who sold them to Mr De Souza and the time of the sale.

Books of original entry are the books in which we first record transactions, such as the sale of the four computers. We have a separate book for each kind of transaction.

Thus, the nature of the transaction affects which book it is entered into. Sales will be entered in one book, purchases in another book, cash in another book, and so on. We enter transactions in these books, recording

- the date on which each transaction took place – the transactions should be shown in date order; and
- details relating to the sale (as listed in the computer example above), which are entered in a 'details' column.

Also,

- a folio column entry is made cross-referencing back to the original 'source document', e.g. the invoice; and
- the monetary amounts are entered in columns included in the books of original entry for that purpose.

11.3 Types of books of original entry

Books of original entry are known as either 'journals' or '**day books**'. However, in the case of the last book of original entry shown below, it is always a 'journal' and the second last is always known as the 'cash book'. The term 'day book' is, perhaps, more commonly used, as it more clearly indicates the nature of these books of original entry – entries are made to them every day. The commonly used books of original entry are:

- **Sales day book** (or *Sales journal*) – for credit sales.
- **Purchases day book** (or *Purchases journal*) – for credit purchases.
- **Returns inwards day book** (or *Returns inwards journal*) – for returns inwards.
- **Returns outwards day book** (or *Returns outwards journal*) – for returns outwards.
- **Cash book** – for receipts and payments of cash and cheques.
- General journal (or **Journal** if the term 'day book' is used for the other books of original entry) – for other items.

Most students find it less confusing if 'day book' is used rather than 'journal', as it makes it very clear what is meant when someone refers to 'the journal'. During the remainder of this book, we will use the term 'day book'. However, never forget that the term 'journal' can always be substituted for the term 'day book'. Be sure to remember this. Examiners may use either term.

11.4 Using more than one ledger

Entries are made in the books of original entry. The entries are then summarised and the summary information is entered, using double entry, to accounts kept in the various ledgers of the business. One reason why a set of ledgers is used rather than just one big ledger is that this makes it easier to divide the work of recording all the entries between different bookkeepers.

Activity 11.1 Why else do you think we have more than one ledger?

11.5 Types of ledgers

The different types of ledgers most businesses use are:

- **Sales ledger**. This is for customers' personal accounts – the accounts receivable.
- **Purchases ledger**. This is for suppliers' personal accounts – the accounts payable.
- **General ledger**. This contains the remaining double entry accounts, such as those relating to expenses, non-current assets, and capital.

11.6 A diagram of the books commonly used

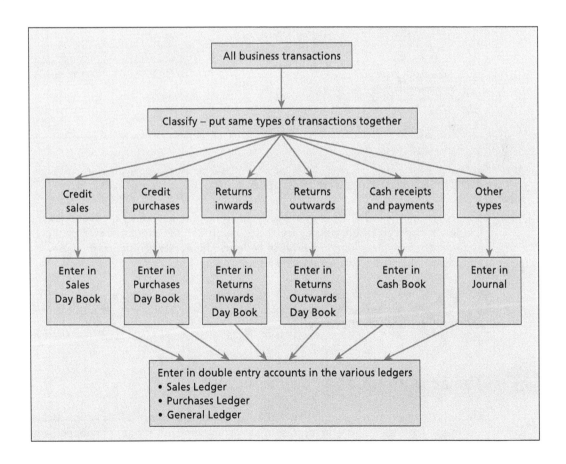

11.7 Description of books used

In the next few chapters we will look at the books used in more detail.

11.8   Types of accounts

Some people describe all accounts as personal accounts or as impersonal accounts.

- **Personal accounts** – these are for debtors and creditors (i.e. customers and suppliers).
- **Impersonal accounts** – divided between 'real' accounts and 'nominal' accounts:
  - **Real accounts** – accounts in which possessions are recorded. Examples are buildings, machinery, fixtures and inventory.
  - **Nominal accounts** – accounts in which expenses, income and capital are recorded.

A diagram may enable you to follow this better:

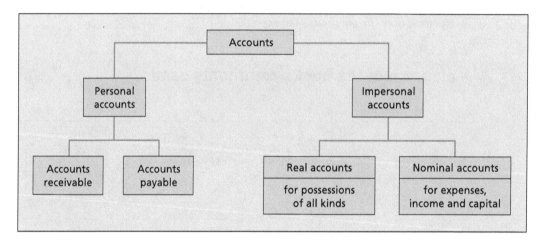

11.9   Nominal and private ledgers

The ledger in which the impersonal accounts are kept is known as the **Nominal** (or 'General') **Ledger**. In order to ensure privacy for the proprietor(s), the capital, drawings and other similar accounts are sometimes kept in a **Private Ledger**. This prevents office staff from seeing details of items which the proprietors want to keep secret.

Activity 11.2   Why bother with *books of original entry*? Why don't we just enter transactions straight into the ledgers?

11.10   The accountant as a communicator

The impression is often given that all that an accountant does is produce figures arranged in various ways. This has led to a perception that accountants are boring, pragmatic people with no sense of humour. While it is true that such work does take up quite a lot of an accountant's time, it does not account for all of a typical accountant's work. **Accountants also need to be good communicators,** not just in the way they present accounting information on paper, but also in how they verbally communicate the significance of the information they prepare.

An accountant can obviously arrange the financial figures so as to present the information in as meaningful a way as possible for the people who are going to use that information. That is, after all, what accountants are trained to do. If the financial figures are to be given to several people, all of whom are very knowledgeable about accounting, an accountant will simply apply all the conventions and regulations of accounting in order to present the information in the 'normal' accounting way, knowing full well that the recipients of the information will understand it.

On the other hand, accounting figures may well be needed by people who have absolutely no knowledge at all of accounting. In such a case, a typical accounting statement would be of little or no use to them. They would not understand it. In this case, an accountant might set out the figures in a completely different way to try to make it easy for them to grasp. For instance, instead of preparing a 'normal' income statement, the accountant might show the information as follows:

	£	£
In the year ended 31 December 2012 you sold goods for		100,000
Now, how much had those goods cost you to buy?		
At the start of the year you had inventory costing	12,000	
+ You bought some more goods in the year costing	56,000	
So altogether you had goods available to sell that cost	68,000	
− At the end of the year, you had inventory of goods unsold that cost	(6,000)	
So, the goods you had sold in the year had cost you	62,000	
Let us deduct this from what you had sold the goods for		(62,000)
This means that you had made a profit on buying and selling goods, before any other expenses had been paid, amounting to		38,000
(We call this type of profit the **gross** profit)		
But, during the year, you suffered other expenses such as wages, rent and electricity. The amount of these expenses, not including anything you took for yourself, amounted to		(18,000)
So, in this year your sales value exceeded all the costs involved in running the business (so that the sales could be made) by		20,000
(We call this type of profit the **net** profit)		

An accountant is failing to perform his or her role appropriately and effectively if the figures are not arranged so as to make them meaningful to the recipient. The accountant's job is not just to produce figures for the accountant's own consumption, it is to communicate the results to other people, many of whom know nothing about accounting.

Activity 11.3   Reconcile this observation with the standardisation of the presentation of financial accounting information as contained in accounting standards and the Companies Acts.

Nowadays, communication skills are a very important part of the accountant's role. Very often, the accountant will have to talk to people in order to explain the figures, or send a letter or write a report about them. The accountant will also have to talk or write to people to find out exactly what sort of accounting information is needed by them, or to explain to them what sort of information could be provided.

If accounting examinations contained only computational questions, they would not test the ability of candidates to communicate in any way other than writing down accounting figures and, as a result, the examinations would fail to examine these other important aspects of the job.

In recent years much more attention has been paid by examining boards to these other aspects of an accountant's work.

Learning outcomes

You should now have learnt:

1 That transactions are classified and details about them are entered in the appropriate book of original entry.

2 That the books of original entry are used as a basis for posting the transactions in summary form to the double entry accounts in the various ledgers.

3 That there is a set of books of original entry, each of which serves a specific purpose.

4 That there is a set of ledgers, each of which serves a specific purpose.

5 That accountants need to be good communicators.

Answers to activities

11.1 The most important reason is to aid analysis by keeping similar items together.

11.2 Books of original entry contain all the important information relating to a transaction. Ledgers just contain a summary. In fact, some of the entries in the ledgers are often just one-line entries covering an entire month of transactions.

11.3 There really is no conflict so far as financial information prepared for internal use is concerned. Financial statements produced for consumption by users outside the business do have to conform to the conventions relating to content and layout. However, those prepared for internal use do not. There is no reason why they could not be prepared along the lines of the unconventionally laid-out income statement shown on p. 133. External stakeholders will never receive their financial statements in this highly user-friendly form. It is simply too much work to customise the financial statement for every class of stakeholder.

MyAccountingLab Need more practice? Instant feedback?
Visit **www.myaccountinglab.com**

Featuring unlimited practice questions, a personalised study plan that identifies the areas where you need to focus for better marks, and interactive material designed to help all kinds of learners, MyAccountingLab is a vital tool for maximising your understanding, confidence, and success. Log in at **www.myaccountinglab.com** to see why 92 per cent of students surveyed last year recommend MyAccountingLab.

Cash books

Learning objectives

After you have studied this chapter, you should be able to:

- explain the format of two-column and three-column cash books
- enter up and balance-off cash books
- use folio columns for cross-referencing purposes
- make the entries for discounts allowed and discounts received both in the cash book and, at the end of a period, in the discount accounts in the general ledger
- make similar entries in separate columns in the cash book for other recurring items

Introduction

In this chapter, you'll learn how businesses record cash and cheque transactions in the cash book. You'll learn that a memorandum column, called the 'folio column', is included in the cash book; and you'll learn the reasons why this is done. You will learn how to make the necessary entries in the cash book and how to include entries for discounts received from creditors and allowed to debtors, both in the cash book and in the general ledger.

13.1 Drawing up a cash book

The cash book consists of the cash account and the bank account put together in one book. We used to show these two accounts on different pages of the ledger. Now it is easier to put the two sets of account columns together. This means that we can record all money received and paid out on a particular date on the same page.

In the cash book, the debit column for cash is put next to the debit column for bank. The credit column for cash is put next to the credit column for bank.

Exhibit 13.1 shows how a cash account and a bank account would appear if they had been kept separately. In Exhibit 13.2, they are shown as if the transactions had, instead, been kept in a cash book.

The bank column contains details of the payments made by cheque and direct transfer from the bank account and of the money received and paid into the bank account. The bank will have a copy of the account in its own books.

Periodically, or on request from the business, the bank sends a copy of the account in its books to the business. This document is known as the **bank statement**. When the business receives the bank statement, it checks it against the bank columns in its cash book to ensure that there are no errors.

Exhibit 13.1

Cash

2012			£	2012			£
Aug	2	T. Moore	33	Aug	8	Printing	20
	5	K. Charles	25		12	C. Potts	19
	15	F. Hughes	37		28	Office stationery	25
	30	H. Howe	18		31	Balance c/d	49
			113				113
Sept	1	Balance b/d	49				

Bank

2012			£	2012			£
Aug	1	Capital	10,000	Aug	7	Rent	205
	3	W. P. Ltd	244		12	F. Small Ltd	95
	16	K. Noone	408		26	K. French	268
	30	H. Sanders	20		31	Balance c/d	10,104
			10,672				10,672
Sept	1	Balance b/d	10,104				

Exhibit 13.2

Cash book

			Cash	Bank				Cash	Bank
2012			£	£	2012			£	£
Aug	1	Capital		10,000	Aug	7	Rent		205
	2	T. Moore	33			8	Printing	20	
	3	W. P. Ltd		244		12	C. Potts	19	
	5	K. Charles	25			12	F. Small Ltd		95
	15	F. Hughes	37			26	K. French		268
	16	K. Noone		408		28	Office stationery	25	
	30	H. Sanders		20		31	Balances c/d	49	10,104
	30	H. Howe	18						
			113	10,672				113	10,672
Sept	1	Balances b/d	49	10,104					

13.2 Cash paid into the bank

In Exhibit 13.2, the payments into the bank were cheques received by the business. They have been banked immediately upon receipt. We must now consider cash being paid into the bank.

1 Let's look at the position when customers pay their account in cash and, later, a part of this cash is paid into the bank. The receipt of the cash is debited to the cash column on the date received, the credit entry being in the customer's personal account. The cash banked has the following effect needing action:

Effect	Action
1 Asset of cash is decreased	Credit the asset account, i.e. the cash account which is represented by the cash column in the cash book.
2 Asset of bank is increased	Debit the asset account, i.e. the bank account which is represented by the bank column in the cash book.

A cash receipt of £100 from M. Davies on 1 August 2012 which was followed by the banking on 3 August of £80 of this amount would appear in the cash book as follows:

		Cash	Bank			Cash	Bank
		£	£			£	£
2012		100		2012		80	
Aug 1	M. Davies			Aug 3	Bank		
3	Cash		80				

Cash book

The details column shows entries against each item stating the name of the account in which the completion of double entry has taken place. Against the cash payment of £80 appears the word 'bank', meaning that the debit of £80 is to be found in the bank column, and the opposite applies.

2 Where the whole of the cash received is banked immediately the receipt can be treated in exactly the same manner as a cheque received, i.e. it can be entered directly into the bank column.

3 If the business requires cash, it may withdraw cash from the bank. Assuming this is done by use of a cheque, the business would write out a cheque to pay itself a certain amount in cash. The bank will give cash in exchange for the cheque over the counter. It could also be done using a cash card. The effect on the accounts is the same.

The twofold effect and the action required is:

Effect	Action
1 Asset of bank is decreased	Credit the asset account, i.e. the bank column in the cash book.
2 Asset of cash is increased	Debit the asset account, i.e. the cash column in the cash book.

A withdrawal of £75 cash on 1 June 2012 from the bank would appear in the cash book as:

Cash book

		Cash	Bank			Cash	Bank
		£	£			£	£
2012		75		2012			75
June 1	Bank			June 1	Cash		

Both the debit and credit entries for this item are in the same book. When this happens it is known as a **contra** item.

13.3   The use of folio columns

As you have already seen, the details column in an account contains the name of the account in which the other part of the double entry has been entered. Anyone looking through the books should, therefore, be able to find the other half of the double entry in the ledgers.

However, when many books are being used, just to mention the name of the other account may not be enough information to find the other account quickly. More information is needed, and this is given by using **folio columns**.

In each account and in each book being used, a folio column is added, always shown on the left of the money columns. In this column, the name of the other book and the number of the page in the other book where the other part of the double entry was made is stated against each and every entry.

So as to ensure that the double entry is completed, the folio column should only be filled in when the double entry has been completed.

An entry for receipt of cash from C. Kelly whose account was on page 45 of the sales ledger, and the cash recorded on page 37 of the cash book, would have the following folio column entries:

- in the cash book, the folio column entry would be SL 45
- in the sales ledger, the folio column entry would be CB 37

Note how each of the titles of the books is abbreviated so that it can fit into the space available in the folio column. Each of any contra items (transfers between bank and cash) being shown on the same page of the cash book would use the letter '¢' (for 'contra') in the folio column. There is no need to also include a page number in this case.

The act of using one book as a means of entering transactions into the accounts, so as to perform or complete the double entry, is known as **posting**. For example, you 'post' items from the sales day book to the appropriate accounts in the sales ledger and to the sales account and you 'post' items from the cash book to the appropriate accounts in the sales ledger.

 Activity 13.1 Why do you think only one account is posted to from the cash book rather than two, which is what happens with postings from the other day books (i.e. the other books of original entry)?

13.4   Advantages of folio columns

As described in Section 13.3, folio entries speed up the process of finding the other side of the double entry in the ledgers.

Activity 13.2 What other advantage can you think of for using a folio column?

13.5   Example of a cash book with folio columns

The following transactions are written up in the form of a cash book. The folio columns are filled in as though all the double entries had been completed to other accounts.

2012				£
Sept	1	Proprietor puts capital into a bank account for the business.		10,940
	2	Received cheque from M. Boon.		315
	4	Cash sales.		802
	6	Paid rent by cash.		135
	7	Banked £50 of the cash held by the business.		50
	15	Cash sales paid direct into the bank.		490
	23	Paid cheque to S. Wills.		277
	29	Withdrew cash from bank for business use.		120
	30	Paid wages in cash.		518

Cash book										(page 1)	
			Folio	Cash	Bank				Folio	Cash	Bank
2012				£	£	2012				£	£
Sept	1	Capital	GL1		10,940	Sept	6	Rent	GL65	135	
	2	M. Boon	SL98		315		7	Bank	¢	50	
	4	Sales	GL87	802			23	S. Wills	PL23		277
	7	Cash	¢		50		29	Cash	¢		120
	15	Sales	GL87		490		30	Wages	GL39	518	
	29	Bank	¢	120			30	Balances	c/d	219	11,398
				922	11,795					922	11,795
Oct	1	Balances	b/d	219	11,398						

The abbreviations used in the folio column are:

GL = general ledger   SL = sales ledger   ¢ = contra   PL = purchases ledger

13.6 Cash discounts

Businesses prefer it if their customers pay their accounts quickly. A business may accept a smaller sum in full settlement if payment is made within a certain period of time. The amount of the reduction of the sum to be paid is known as a 'cash discount'. The term 'cash discount' thus refers to the allowance given for quick payment. It is still called cash discount, even if the account is paid by cheque or by direct transfer into the bank account.

The rate of cash discount is usually stated as a percentage. Full details of the percentage allowed, and the period within which payment is to be made, are quoted on all sales documents by the seller. A typical period during which discount may be allowed is one month from the date of the original transaction.

Note: Cash discounts *always* appear in the profit and loss section of the income statement. They are not part of the cost of goods sold. Nor are they a deduction from selling price. Students often get this wrong in examinations – be careful!

13.7 Discounts allowed and discounts received

A business may have two types of cash discounts in its books. These are:

1 **Discounts allowed**: cash discounts allowed by a business to its customers when they pay their accounts quickly.

2 Discounts received: cash discounts received by a business from its suppliers when it pays what it owes them quickly.

We can now see the effect of discounts by looking at two examples.

Example 1

W. Clarke owed us £100. He pays us in cash on 2 September 2012, which is within the time limit applicable for a 5 per cent cash discount. He pays £100 – £5 = £95 in full settlement of his account.

Effect	Action
1 Of cash: Cash is increased by £95. Asset of accounts receivable is decreased by £95.	Debit cash account, i.e. enter £95 in debit column of cash book. Credit W. Clarke £95.
2 Of discounts: Asset of accounts receivable is decreased by £5. (After the cash was paid there remained a balance of £5. As the account has been paid, this asset must now be cancelled.) Expense of discounts allowed increased by £5.	Credit W. Clarke £5. Debit discounts allowed account £5.

Example 2

The business owed S. Small £400. It pays him by cheque on 3 September 2012, which is within the time limit laid down by him for a 2½ per cent cash discount. The business will pay £400 – £10 = £390 in full settlement of the account.

Effect	Action
1 Of cheque: Asset of bank is reduced by £390. Liability of accounts payable is reduced by £390.	Credit bank, i.e. entry in the credit bank column for £390. Debit S. Small's account £390.
2 Of discounts: Liability of accounts payable is reduced by £10. (After the cheque was paid, a balance of £10 remained. As the account has been paid the liability must now be cancelled.) Revenue of discounts received increased by £10.	Debit S. Small's account £10. Credit discounts received account £10.

The entries made in the business's books would be:

	Folio	Cash	Bank		Folio	Cash	Bank
		£	£			£	£
2012 Sept 2 W. Clarke	SL12	95		2012 Sept 3 S. Small	PL75		390

Cash book (page 32)

Discounts received   (General Ledger *page 18*)

			Folio	£
	2012			
	Sept 2 S. Small		PL75	10

Discounts allowed   (General Ledger *page 17*)

	Folio	£	
2012			
Sept 2 W. Clarke	SL12	5	

W. Clarke   (Sales Ledger *page 12*)

	Folio	£			Folio	£
2012			2012			
Sept 1 Balance	b/d	100	Sept 2 Cash		CB32	95
		___		2 Discount	GL17	5
		100				100

S. Small   (Purchases Ledger *page 75*)

	Folio	£			Folio	£
2012			2012			
Sept 3 Bank	CB32	390	Sept 1 Balance		b/d	400
3 Discount	GL18	10				___
		400				400

It is the accounting custom to enter the word 'Discount' in the personal accounts without stating whether it is a discount received or a discount allowed.

 Activity 13.3   Why do you think it is accounting custom only to enter the word 'Discount' in the personal accounts?

13.8   Discounts columns in cash book

The *discounts allowed account* and the *discounts received account* are in the general ledger along with all the other revenue and expense accounts. It has already been stated that every effort should be made to avoid too many entries in the general ledger. To avoid this, we add two columns for discount in the cash book.

An extra column is added on each side of the cash book in which the amounts of discounts are entered. Discounts received are entered in the discounts column on the credit side of the cash book, and discounts allowed in the discounts column on the debit side of the cash book.

The cash book entries for the two examples so far dealt with would be:

	Cash book								(*page 32*)
	Folio	Discount	Cash	Bank		Folio	Discount	Cash	Bank
2012		£	£	£	2012		£	£	£
Sept 2 W. Clarke	SL12	5	95		Sept 3 S. Small	PL75	10		390

There is no alteration to the method of showing discounts in the personal accounts.

To make entries in the discounts accounts in the general ledger

At the end of the period:

Total of discounts column on receipts side of cash book } Enter on **debit** side of discounts allowed account.

Total of discounts column on payments side of cash book } Enter on **credit** side of discounts received account.

13.9   A worked example

2012			£
May	1	Balances brought down from April:	
		Cash balance	29
		Bank balance	654
		Accounts receivable accounts:	
		B. King	120
		N. Campbell	280
		D. Shand	40
		Accounts payable accounts:	
		U. Barrow	60
		A. Allen	440
		R. Long	100
	2	B. King pays us by cheque, having deducted 2½ per cent cash discount £3.	117
	8	We pay R. Long his account by cheque, deducting 5 per cent cash discount £5.	95
	11	We withdrew £100 cash from the bank for business use.	100
	16	N. Campbell pays us his account by cheque, deducting 2½ per cent discount £7.	273
	25	We paid office expenses in cash.	92
	28	D. Shand pays us in cash after having deducted 5 per cent cash discount.	38
	29	We pay U. Barrow by cheque less 5 per cent cash discount £3.	57
	30	We pay A. Allen by cheque less 2½ per cent cash discount £11.	429

Folio numbers have been included in the solution to make the example more realistic.

			Cash book								(page 64)
		Folio	Discount £	Cash £	Bank £			Folio	Discount £	Cash £	Bank £
2012						2012					
May 1	Balance	b/d		29	654	May 8	R. Long	PL58	5		95
2	B. King	SL13	3		117	11	Cash	¢			100
11	Bank	¢		100		25	Office	GL77		92	
16	N. Campbell	SL84	7		273		expenses				
28	D. Shand	SL91	2	38		29	U. Barrow	PL15	3		57
						30	A. Allen	PL98	11		429
						31	Balances	c/d		75	363
			12	167	1,044				19	167	1,044
Jun 1	Balances	b/d		75	363						

Sales ledger
B. King
(page 13)

2012			Folio	£	2012			Folio	£
May	1	Balance	b/d	120	May	2	Bank	CB64	117
						2	Discount	CB64	3
				120					120

N. Campbell (page 84)

2012			Folio	£	2012			Folio	£
May	1	Balance	b/d	280	May	16	Bank	CB64	273
				___		16	Discount	CB64	7
				280					280

D. Shand (page 91)

2012			Folio	£	2012			Folio	£
May	1	Balance	b/d	40	May	28	Cash	CB64	38
				___		28	Discount	CB64	2
				40					40

Purchases ledger
U. Barrow (page 15)

2012			Folio	£	2012			Folio	£
May	29	Bank	CB64	57	May	1	Balance	b/d	60
	29	Discount	CB64	3					___
				60					60

R. Long (page 58)

2012			Folio	£	2012			Folio	£
May	8	Bank	CB64	95	May	1	Balance	b/d	100
	8	Discount	CB64	5					___
				100					100

A. Allen (page 98)

2012			Folio	£	2012			Folio	£
May	30	Bank	CB64	429	May	1	Balance	b/d	440
	30	Discount	CB64	11					
				440					440

General ledger
Office expenses (page 77)

2012			Folio	£
May	25	Cash	CB64	92

Discounts received (page 88)

					2012			Folio	£
					May	31	Total for the month	CB64	19

Discounts allowed (page 89)

2012			Folio	£
May	31	Total for the month	CB64	12

Is the above method of entering discounts correct?

You can easily check:

Discounts in ledger accounts	Debits		Credits	
		£		
Discounts received	U. Barrow	3	Discounts received	£19
	R. Long	5		
	A. Allen	11		
		19		
				£
Discounts allowed	Discounts allowed £12		B. King	3
			N. Campbell	7
			D. Shand	2
				12

You can see that proper double entry has been carried out. Equal amounts, in total, have been entered on each side of the two discount accounts.

13.10 Bank overdrafts

A business may borrow money from a bank by means of a bank **overdraft**. This means that the business is allowed to pay more out of its bank account than the total amount it has deposited in the account.

Up to this point, the bank balances have all been money at the bank, so they have all been assets, i.e. debit balances. When the bank account is overdrawn, the business owes money to the bank, so the account is a liability and the balance becomes a credit one.

Taking the cash book last shown, suppose that the amount payable to A. Allen was £1,429 instead of £429. The amount in the bank account, £1,044, is exceeded by the amount withdrawn. We will take the discount for Allen as being £11. The cash book would appear as follows:

Cash book								*(page 64)*
	Discount	Cash	Bank		Discount	Cash	Bank
2012	£	£	£	2012	£	£	£
May 1 Balances b/d		29	654	May 8 R. Long	5		95
2 B. King	3		117	11 Cash			100
11 Bank		100		25 Office			
16 N. Campbell	7		273	expenses		92	
28 D. Shand	2	38		29 U. Barrow	3		57
31 Balance c/d				30 A. Allen	11		1,429
			637	31 Balance c/d		75	
	12	167	1,681		19	167	1,681
Jun 1 Balance b/d		75		Jun 1 Balance b/d			637

On a statement of financial position, a bank overdraft is included under the heading 'current liabilities'.

13.11 Bank cash books

In the United Kingdom, except for very small organisations, three-column cash books are not usually used. All receipts, whether of cash or cheques, will be banked daily. A 'petty cash book' will be used for payments of cash. As a result, there will be no need for cash columns in the cash book itself.

This move towards only recording bank transactions in the cash book is not yet evident in countries where banking systems are not as developed or as efficient as in the UK.

13.12 Multiple column cash book

In Chapter 18, you will learn how to prepare an analytical (or multiple column) petty cash book. Cash books are often prepared with multiple columns where additional columns are added for each ledger account to which many entries may be made in a period. As with columns for discount, this has the advantage of reducing the number of entries made in the accounts in the general ledger.

Learning outcomes

You should now have learnt:

1 That a cash book consists of a cash account and a bank account put together into one book.

2 How to enter up and balance a two-column cash book, i.e. one containing a debit and a credit column for the bank account, and a debit and a credit column for the cash account.

3 That the bank columns in the cash book are for cheques and any other transfers of funds that have been made into or out of the bank account.

4 That a folio column is included in the cash book so as to help trace entries made into accounts in the ledgers and so as to provide assurance that the double entries have been made.

5 That cash discounts are given to encourage people to pay their accounts within a stated time limit.

6 That 'cash discount' is the name given for discount for quick payment even where the payment was made by cheque or by direct transfer into the bank account, rather than by payment in cash.

7 That cash discounts appear in the profit and loss part of the income statement.

8 How to enter up and balance a three-column cash book, i.e. one containing a debit and a credit column for the bank account, a debit and a credit column for the cash account, and a debit and a credit column for discount.

9 That the discounts columns in the cash book make it easier to enter up the books. They act as a collection point for discounts allowed and discounts received, for which double entry into the general ledger is completed when the totals are transferred to the discount accounts in the general ledger, usually at the end of the month.

10 That a multiple column cash book is often used in order to further reduce the number of entries made in the general ledger.

11 How to add additional columns to the cash book for frequently recurring items and make the appropriate entries in them and in the general ledger.

Answers to activities

13.1   Although the cash book is a book of original entry, it is also where the cash account and bank account are recorded. In effect, it is both a book of original entry and a ledger dedicated to those two accounts. As a result, each transaction in the cash book is only posted once to another account, the first part of the entry having been made when the transaction was recorded in the cash book.

13.2   If an entry has not been filled in, i.e. if the folio column is blank against an entry, the double entry has not yet been made. As a result, looking through the entry lines in the folio columns to ensure they have all been filled in helps detect such errors quickly.

13.3   It should be quite obvious whether discount is received or allowed. And, more importantly, the double entry is with the cash book columns for discount, not with either the discount allowed account or the discount received account in the general ledger. At the end of the period (usually a month) the totals of the two discount columns in the cash book are posted to the discount allowed and discount received accounts in the general ledger.

Multiple choice questions: Set 2

Now attempt Set 2 of multiple choice questions. (Answers to all the multiple choice questions are given in Appendix 2 at the end of this book.)

Each of these multiple choice questions has four suggested answers, (A), (B), (C) and (D). You should read each question and then decide which choice is best, either (A) or (B) or (C) or (D). *Write down your answers on a separate piece of paper.* You will then be able to redo the set of questions later without having to try to ignore your answers from previous attempts.

MC21   Gross profit is

(A)   Excess of sales over cost of goods sold
(B)   Sales less purchases
(C)   Cost of goods sold + opening inventory
(D)   Net profit less expenses of the period

MC22   Net profit is calculated in the

(A)   Trading account
(B)   Profit and loss account
(C)   Trial balance
(D)   Statement of financial position

MC23   To find the value of closing inventory at the end of a period we

(A)   Do this by physically counting the inventory (i.e. stocktaking)
(B)   Look in the inventory account
(C)   Deduct opening inventory from cost of goods sold
(D)   Deduct cost of goods sold from sales

MC24   The credit entry for net profit is on the credit side of

(A)   The trading account
(B)   The profit and loss account
(C)   The drawings account
(D)   The capital account

MC25   Which of these best describes a statement of financial position?

(A)   An account proving the books balance
(B)   A record of closing entries
(C)   A listing of balances
(D)   A statement of assets

MC26   The descending order in which current assets should be shown in the statement of financial position is

(A)   Inventory, Accounts receivable, Bank, Cash
(B)   Cash, Bank, Accounts receivable, Inventory
(C)   Accounts receivable, Inventory, Bank, Cash
(D)   Inventory, Accounts receivable, Cash, Bank

MC27   Which of these best describes non-current assets?

(A)   Items bought to be used in the business
(B)   Items which will not wear out quickly
(C)   Expensive items bought for the business
(D)   Items having a long life and not bought specifically for resale

MC28   Carriage inwards is charged to the trading account because

(A)   It is an expense connected with buying goods
(B)   It should not go in the statement of financial position
(C)   It is not part of motor expenses
(D)   Carriage outwards goes in the profit and loss account

MC29   Given figures showing: Sales £8,200, Opening inventory £1,300, Closing inventory £900, Purchases £6,400, Carriage inwards £200, the cost of goods sold figure is

(A)   £6,800
(B)   £6,200
(C)   £7,000
(D)   Another figure

MC30   The costs of putting goods into a saleable condition should be charged to

(A)   The trading account
(B)   The profit and loss account
(C)   The statement of financial position
(D)   None of these

MC31   Suppliers' personal accounts are found in the

(A)   Nominal ledger
(B)   General ledger
(C)   Purchases ledger
(D)   Sales ledger

MC32   The sales day book is best described as

(A)   Part of the double entry system
(B)   Containing customers' accounts
(C)   Containing real accounts
(D)   A list of credit sales

MC33   Which of the following are personal accounts?

(*i*)   Buildings
(*ii*)   Wages
(*iii*)   Accounts receivable
(*iv*)   Accounts payable

(A)   (*i*) and (*iv*) only
(B)   (*ii*) and (*iii*) only
(C)   (*iii*) and (*iv*) only
(D)   (*ii*) and (*iv*) only

MC34   When Lee makes out a cheque for £50 and sends it to Young, then Lee is known as

(A)   The payee
(B)   The banker
(C)   The drawer
(D)   The creditor

MC35   If you want to make sure that your money will be safe if cheques sent are lost in the post, you should

(A)   Not use the postal service
(B)   Always pay by cash
(C)   Always take the money in person
(D)   Cross your cheques 'Account Payee only, Not Negotiable'

MC36   When depositing money in your current account you should always use

(A)   A cheque book
(B)   A paying-in slip
(C)   A cash book
(D)   A general ledger

MC37   A debit balance of £100 in a cash account shows that

(A)   There was £100 cash in hand
(B)   Cash has been overspent by £100
(C)   £100 was the total of cash paid out
(D)   The total of cash received was less than £100

MC38   £50 cash taken from the cash till and banked is entered

(A)   Debit cash column £50: Credit bank column £50
(B)   Debit bank column £50: Credit cash column £50
(C)   Debit cash column £50: Credit cash column £50
(D)   Debit bank column £50: Credit bank column £50

→

→ **MC39**   A credit balance of £200 on the cash columns of the cash book would mean

(A)   We have spent £200 more than we have received
(B)   We have £200 cash in hand
(C)   The bookkeeper has made a mistake
(D)   Someone has stolen £200 cash

MC40   'Posting' the transactions in bookkeeping means

(A)   Making the first entry of a double entry transaction
(B)   Entering items in a cash book
(C)   Making the second entry of a double entry transaction
(D)   Something other than the above

Review questions

13.1   Write up a two-column cash book for a pine furniture shop from the following details, and balance it off as at the end of the month:

2012
May   1   Started in business with capital in cash £5,000.
      2   Paid rent by cash £500.
      3   G. Broad lent us £6,000, paid by cheque.
      4   We paid J. Fine by cheque £900.
      5   Cash sales £400.
      7   F. Love paid us by cheque £100.
      9   We paid A. Moore in cash £150.
    11   Cash sales paid direct into the bank £300.
    15   P. Hood paid us in cash £350.
    16   We took £2,000 out of the cash till and paid it into the bank account.
    19   We repaid R. Onions £1,000 by cheque.
    22   Cash sales paid direct into the bank £600.
    26   Paid motor expenses by cheque £230.
    30   Withdrew £160 cash from the bank for business use.
    31   Paid wages in cash £420.

13.2A   Write up a two-column cash book for a second-hand bookshop from the following:

2013
Nov   1   Balance brought forward from last month: Cash £295; Bank £4,240.
      2   Cash sales £310.
      3   Took £200 out of the cash till and paid it into the bank.
      4   F. Bell paid us by cheque £194.
      5   We paid for postage stamps in cash £80.
      6   Bought office equipment by cheque £310.
      7   We paid L. Root by cheque £94.
      9   Received business rates refund by cheque £115.
    11   Withdrew £150 from the bank for business use.
    12   Paid wages in cash £400.
    13   Cash sales £430.
    14   Paid motor expenses by cheque £81.
    16   J. Bull lent us £1,500 in cash.
    20   K. Brown paid us by cheque £174.
    28   We paid general expenses in cash £35.
    30   Paid insurance by cheque £320.

13.3 A three-column cash book for a wine wholesaler is to be written up from the following details, balanced-off, and the relevant discount accounts in the general ledger shown.

2012

Mar   1   Balances brought forward: Cash £620; Bank £7,142.
      2   The following paid their accounts by cheque, in each case deducting 5 per cent cash discounts: G. Slick £260; P. Fish £320; T. Old £420 (all amounts are pre-discount).
      4   Paid rent by cheque £430.
      6   F. Black lent us £5,000 paying by cheque.
      8   We paid the following accounts by cheque in each case deducting a 2½ per cent cash discount: R. White £720; G. Green £960; L. Flip £1,600 (all amounts are pre-discount).
    10   Paid motor expenses in cash £81.
    12   J. Pie pays his account of £90, by cheque £88, deducting £2 cash discount.
    15   Paid wages in cash £580.
    18   The following paid their accounts by cheque, in each case deducting 5 per cent cash discount: A. Pony £540; B. Line & Son £700; T. Owen £520 (all amounts are pre-discount).
    21   Cash withdrawn from the bank £400 for business use.
    24   Cash drawings £200.
    25   Paid W. Peat his account of £160, by cash £155, having deducted £5 cash discount.
    29   Bought fixtures paying by cheque £720.
    31   Received commission by cheque £120.

13.4A Enter the following in the three-column cash book of an office supply shop. Balance-off the cash book at the end of the month and show the discount accounts in the general ledger.

2011

June   1   Balances brought forward: Cash £420; Bank £4,940.
      2   The following paid us by cheque, in each case deducting a 5 per cent cash discount: S. Braga £820; L. Pine £320; G. Hodd £440; M. Rae £1,040.
      3   Cash sales paid direct into the bank £740.
      5   Paid rent by cash £340.
      6   We paid the following accounts by cheque, in each case deducting 2½ per cent cash discount: M. Peters £360; G. Graham £960; F. Bell £400.
      8   Withdrew cash from the bank for business use £400.
    10   Cash sales £1,260.
    12   B. Age paid us their account of £280 by cheque less £4 cash discount.
    14   Paid wages by cash £540.
    16   We paid the following accounts by cheque: R. Todd £310 less cash discount £15; F. Dury £412 less cash discount £12.
    20   Bought fixtures by cheque £4,320.
    24   Bought lorry paying by cheque £14,300.
    29   Received £324 cheque from A. Line.
    30   Cash sales £980.
    30   Bought stationery paying by cash £56.

13.5 On 1 September, V. Duckworth, a bar manager and entrepreneur, has the following financial position relating to her activities as a corporate function organiser:

	£
Balance at bank	10,000
Accounts receivable – M. Baldwin	5,000
– A. Roberts	2,000
– G. Platt	1,000
Inventory	9,600
Accounts payable – Newton and Ridley	8,200
– J. Duckworth	400

During September the following events occur:

1 M. Baldwin settles his account after taking a cash discount of 10 per cent.
2 A. Roberts is declared bankrupt and no payments are anticipated in respect of the debt.
3 G. Platt pays in full.
4 All accounts payable are paid. Newton and Ridley had indicated that, because of the speed of payment, a 5 per cent quick settlement discount may be deducted from the payment.

Required:
(a) Use T-accounts to open a bank account and the accounts for the accounts receivable and accounts payable at 1 September.
(b) Record the above transactions for September.
(c) Balance-off the accounts at the end of the month.

13.6A At 1 September the financial position of Sara Young's business was:

	£
Cash in hand	80
Balance at bank	900
Accounts receivable: AB	200
CD	500
EF	300
Inventory	1,000
Accounts payable: GH	600
IJ	1,400

During September:

1 The three debtors settled their accounts by cheque subject to a cash discount of 4 per cent.
2 A cheque for £100 was cashed for office use.
3 GH was paid by cheque less 7.5 per cent cash discount.
4 IJ's account was settled, subject to a discount of 5 per cent, by cheque.
5 Wages of £130 were paid in cash.

Required:
(a) Open a three-column cash book and the accounts for the accounts receivable and accounts payable at 1 September.
(b) Record the above transactions for September.

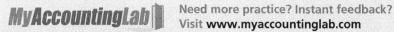

MyAccountingLab Need more practice? Instant feedback?
Visit **www.myaccountinglab.com**

Featuring unlimited practice questions, a personalised study plan that identifies the areas where you need to focus for better marks, and interactive material designed to help all kinds of learners, MyAccountingLab is a vital tool for maximising your understanding, confidence, and success. Log in at **www.myaccountinglab.com** to see why 92 per cent of students surveyed last year recommend MyAccountingLab.

14

Sales day book and sales ledger

Learning objectives

After you have studied this chapter, you should be able to:

- distinguish between a cash sale and a credit sale and between the way they are recorded in the accounting books
- explain why, when credit card payments are received at the time of sale, details of the customer are not recorded even though a debtor is created at the same time
- draw up a sales invoice
- explain why multiple copies are often made of each sales invoice
- make the appropriate entries relating to credit sales in a sales day book
- make the correct postings from the sales day book to the sales ledger and general ledger
- explain how trade discounts differ from cash discounts, both in nature and in the way they are treated in the accounting books
- describe measures that may be taken to exercise credit control over debtors

Introduction

In Chapter 11, you learnt that, rather than having only one book of original entry and only one ledger, most businesses use a set of day books (or journals) and a set of ledgers. In this chapter, you'll learn more about the sales day book (or sales journal) and the sales ledger. You'll also learn how cash and credit sales are entered in these books, and about trade discounts and how to record them.

14.1 Cash sales

As you have already learnt, when goods are paid for immediately they are described as 'cash sales', even where the payment has been made by cheque or transfer of funds from the customer's bank account into the seller's bank account. For accounting purposes, in such cases we do not need to know the names and addresses of customers nor what has been sold to them and, as a result, there is no need to enter such sales in the sales day book. **The sales day book (and all the other day books) are *only* used for credit transactions.**

Activity 14.1 Other than for accounting purposes, can you think of anything a business might want to record somewhere outside the accounting records concerning these transactions?

Credit card payments

When customers pay immediately by credit card, so far as recording details of the customer is concerned, this is treated as if it were a payment made by cash. No record is required for accounting purposes concerning the contact details of the customer. However, it is still a credit transaction and it does result in a debtor being created – the credit card company. The double entry would be a credit to the sales account and a debit to the credit card company's account in the sales ledger.

14.2 Credit sales

In all but the smallest business, most sales will be made on credit. In fact, the sales of many businesses will consist entirely of credit sales. The only major exceptions to this are Internet businesses (such as Amazon) and retailers (e.g. corner shops and supermarkets), where all sales are paid for at the time of sale.

For each credit sale, the selling business will give or send a document to the buyer showing full details of the goods sold and the prices of the goods. This document is an 'invoice'. It is known to the buyer as a 'purchase invoice' and to the seller as a **sales invoice**. The seller will keep one or more copies of each sales invoice for his or her own use.

Activity 14.2 What uses would the seller have for these copies of the sales invoice?

Exhibit 14.1 is an example of an invoice:

Exhibit 14.1

Your Purchase Order: 10/A/980	INVOICE No. 16554		J. Blake 7 Over Warehouse Leicester LE1 2AP 1 September 2013	
To: D. Poole & Co 45 Charles Street Manchester M1 5ZN				
			Per unit	Total
			£	£
21 cases McBrand Pears			20	420
5 cartons Kay's Flour			4	20
6 cases Joy's Vinegar			20	120
				560
Terms 1¼% cash discount if paid within one month				

You must not think that all invoices will look exactly like the one shown in Exhibit 14.1. Each business will have its own design. All invoices will be uniquely numbered, usually sequentially, and they will contain the names and addresses of both the supplier and the customer. In this case, the supplier is J. Blake and the customer is D. Poole. (A 'purchase order' – there's one referred to in the top left-hand corner of this sales invoice – is the record or document drawn up by the customer that the customer referred to or gave the seller when the order was placed with the seller. It is used by the buyer to check the details of the order against the invoice and against the goods delivered.)

14.3 Copies of sales invoices

As soon as the sales invoices for the goods being sold have been prepared, they are given or sent to the customer. The copies kept by the seller are created at the same time as the original.

14.4 Making entries in the sales day book

From the copy of the sales invoice, the seller enters up the transaction in the sales day book. This book is merely a list of details relating to each credit sale:

- date
- name of customer
- invoice number
- folio column
- final amount of invoice.

There is no need to show details of the goods sold in the sales day book. This can be found by looking at copy invoices.

We can now look at Exhibit 14.2, which shows page 26 of a sales day book, starting with the record of the sales invoice already shown in Exhibit 14.1. (These could have been on any page. In this example, we are assuming they have been entered on page 26 as pages 1–25 have been filled with details of earlier transactions.)

Exhibit 14.2

		Sales Day Book		(page 26)
		Invoice No.	Folio	Amount £
2013				
Sept	1 D. Poole	16554		560
	8 T. Cockburn	16555		1,640
	28 C. Carter	16556		220
	30 D. Stevens & Co	16557		1,100
				3,520

14.5 Posting credit sales to the sales ledger

Instead of having one ledger for all accounts, we now have a separate sales ledger for credit sale transactions. This was described in Chapter 11.

1 The credit sales are now posted, one by one, to the debit side of each customer's account in the sales ledger.
2 At the end of each period the total of the credit sales is posted to the credit of the sales account in the general ledger.

This is now illustrated in Exhibit 14.3.

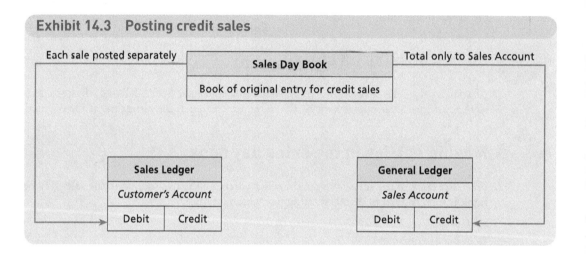

Exhibit 14.3   Posting credit sales

14.6   An example of posting credit sales

The sales day book in Exhibit 14.2 is now shown again. This time, posting is made to the sales ledger and the general ledger. Notice the completion of the folio columns with the reference numbers.

	Sales Day Book			(page 26)
		Invoice No.	Folio	Amount
2013				£
Sept	1 D. Poole	16554	SL 12	560
	8 T. Cockburn	16555	SL 39	1,640
	28 C. Carter	16556	SL 125	220
	30 D. Stevens & Co	16557	SL 249	1,100
	Transferred to Sales Account		GL 44	3,520

Sales Ledger
D. Poole *(page 12)*

2013		Folio	£	
Sept	1 Sales	SB 26	560	

T. Cockburn *(page 39)*

2013		Folio	£	
Sept	8 Sales	SB 26	1,640	

C. Carter   *(page 125)*

2013		Folio	£	
Sept 28 Sales		SB 26	220	

D. Stevens & Co   *(page 249)*

2013		Folio	£	
Sept 30 Sales		SB 26	1,100	

General Ledger
Sales   *(page 44)*

	2013		Folio	£
	Sept 30 Credit sales for		SB 26	3,520
	the month			

Before you continue you should attempt Review Question 14.1.

14.7 Trade discounts

Suppose you are the proprietor of a business. You are selling to three different kinds of customer:

1 traders who buy a lot of goods from you;
2 traders who buy only a few items from you;
3 the general public (direct).

The traders themselves have to sell the goods to the general public in their own areas. They have to make a profit to help finance their businesses, so they will want to pay you less than the retail price (i.e. the price at which the goods are sold to the general public).

The traders who buy in large quantities will not want to pay as much as those traders who buy in small quantities. You want to attract large customers like these, so you are happy to sell to these traders at a lower price than the price you charge the other customers.

This means that your selling prices are at three levels:

1 to traders buying large quantities;
2 to traders buying small quantities; and
3 to the general public.

Let's use an example to illustrate this. You sell a food mixing machine. The basic price is £200. The traders who buy in large quantities are given 25 per cent trade discount. The other traders are given 20 per cent, and the general public get no trade discount. The price paid by each type of customer would be:

		Trader 1		Trader 2	General Public
		£		£	£
Basic price		200		200	200
Less Trade discount	(25%)	(50)	(20%)	(40)	nil
Price to be paid by customer		150		160	200

You could deal with this by having three price lists, and many businesses do. However, some use trade discounts instead. This involves having only one price list but giving a **trade discount** to traders so that they are invoiced for the correct price.

Exhibit 14.4 is an example of an invoice for a food manufacturer and retailer that shows how trade discount is presented clearly and the trade discounted price easily identified. It is for the same items as were shown in Exhibit 14.1 as having been sold to D. Poole. In that example, the seller operated a different price list for each category of customer. This time the seller is R. Grant and trade discount is used to adjust the selling price to match the category of customer.

Exhibit 14.4

		R. Grant
Your Purchase Order: 11/A/G80		Higher Side
	INVOICE No. 30756	Preston PR1 2NL
		2 September 2013
To: D. Poole & Co		Tel (01703) 33122
45 Charles Street		Fax (01703) 22331
Manchester M1 5ZN		

	Per unit	Total
	£	£
21 cases McBrand Pears	25	525
5 cartons Kay's Flour	5	25
6 cases Joy's Vinegar	25	150
		700
Less 20% trade discount		(140)
		560

By comparing Exhibits 14.1 and 14.4, you can see that the amount paid by D. Poole was the same. It is simply the method of calculating it and presenting it in the exhibit that is different.

14.8 No double entry for trade discounts

As trade discount is simply a way of calculating sales prices, no entry for trade discount should be made in the double entry records, nor in the sales day book. The recording of Exhibit 14.4 in R. Grant's sales day book and D. Poole's personal account will be:

Sales Day Book			(page 87)
	Invoice No.	*Folio*	*Amount*
2013			£
Sept 2 D. Poole	30756	SL 32	560

Sales Ledger
D. Poole *(page 32)*

2013		*Folio*	£	
Sept 2 Sales		SB 87	560	

To compare with cash discounts:

- Trade discounts: *never* shown in double entry accounts, nor in the income statement.
- Cash discounts: *always* shown in double entry accounts and in the profit and loss part of the income statement.

Be very careful about this topic. Students often get confused between the treatment of trade discount and the treatment of cash discount. Remember, it is trade discount that is not entered anywhere in either the ledger accounts or the financial statements. Cash discount appears in the cash book and is always shown in the financial statements.

14.9 Manufacturer's recommended retail price

Looking at an item displayed in a shop window, you will frequently see something like the following:

50 inch HD LCD TV	
Manufacturer's Recommended Retail Price	£1,200
Less discount of 20 per cent	(240)
You pay only	£960

Very often the manufacturer's recommended retail price is a figure above what the manufacturer would expect the public to pay for its product. In the case of the TV, the manufacturer would probably have expected the public to pay around £960 for the TV.

The inflated figure used for the 'manufacturer's recommended retail price' is simply a sales gimmick. Most people like to believe they are getting a bargain. They feel happier about making a purchase like this if they are told they are getting '20 per cent discount' and pay £960 rather than being told that the price is £960 and that they cannot get any discount.

14.10 Credit control

Any organisation which sells goods on credit should keep a close check to ensure that debtors pay their accounts on time. If this is not done properly, the amount of accounts receivables can grow to a level that will make the business short of cash. Businesses that grow too short of cash will fail, no matter how profitable they may be.

The following procedures should be carried out:

1 A credit limit should be set for each debtor. Debtors should not be allowed to owe more than their credit limit. The amount of the limit will depend on the circumstances. Such things as the size of the customer's business and the amount of business done with it, as well as its past record of payments, will help guide the choice of credit limit. Credit rating agencies may be used to assess the credit worthiness of customers before credit is granted.

2 As soon as the payment date set by the seller has been reached, a check should be made to verify whether the debtor has paid the amount due. Failure to pay on time may trigger a refusal to supply any more goods to the customer until payment is received, even if the customer's credit limit has not been reached.

3 Where payment is not forthcoming, after investigation it may be necessary to take legal action to sue the customer for the debt. This will depend on the circumstances.

4 It is important that the customer is aware of what will happen if the amount due is not paid by the deadline set by the seller.

Learning outcomes

You should now have learnt:

1 That 'sales day book' and 'sales journal' are different names for the same book.

2 That cash sales are not entered in the sales day book.

3 That when credit card payments are received at the time of sale, details of the customer are not recorded even though a debtor is created at the same time.

4 That the sales day book (or sales journal) contains information relating to each credit sale made in each period.

5 That the sales day book is used for posting credit sales to the sales ledger.

6 That the total of the sales day book for the period is posted to the credit of the sales account in the general ledger.

7 How to make the appropriate entries relating to credit sales in a sales day book and make the correct postings from it to the sales ledger and general ledger.

8 How to prepare a sales invoice.

9 Why multiple copies are often made of each sales invoice.

10 That no entry is made for trade discounts in the double entry accounts.

11 That all businesses should operate a sound system of credit control over their debtors.

12 Some measures that may be taken to exercise credit control over debtors.

Answers to activities

14.1 A business may want to know the contact details of cash customers for marketing purposes. In fact, most businesses of any size would like to keep records in a database of all their cash customers for this reason. Businesses may also want to encourage cash customers to open credit accounts with the business so that they may be more likely to buy from the business in future. Also, where the goods sold are to be delivered to the customer, the customer's contact details will need to be recorded, but this will be in a record held elsewhere than in the accounting books.

14.2 Sellers keep copies of sales invoices for a number of reasons including: to prove that a sale took place; to enable the entries in the books to be correctly recorded and checked; to pass to the inventory department so that the correct goods can be selected for shipping to the customer; to pass to the delivery department, so that the correct goods will be shipped to the customer and to the correct address, and to enable the goods to be shipped accompanied by a copy of the sales invoice so that the customer can acknowledge receipt of the correct goods.

Review questions

14.1 You are to enter up the Sales Day Book from the following details. Post the items to the relevant accounts in the Sales Ledger and then show the transfer to the sales account in the General Ledger.

2012

Mar	1	Credit sales to B. Hope	£310
	3	Credit sales to T. Fine	£285
	6	Credit sales to L. Moore	£38
	10	Credit sales to B. Hope	£74
	17	Credit sales to H. Tor	£534
	19	Credit sales to J. Young	£92
	27	Credit sales to T. Most	£44
	31	Credit sales to R. Best	£112

14.2A Enter up the Sales Day Book from the following details. Post the items to the relevant accounts in the Sales Ledger and then show the transfer to the sales account in the General Ledger.

2013
Mar	1	Credit sales to I. Hood	£520
	3	Credit sales to S. Bell	£318
	5	Credit sales to J. Smart	£64
	7	Credit sales to K. Byers	£165
	16	Credit sales to T. Todd	£540
	23	Credit sales to W. Morris	£360
	30	Credit sales to F. Lock	£2,040

14.3 F. Benjamin of 10 Lower Street, Plymouth, is selling the following items at the recommended retail prices as shown: white tape £10 per roll, green felt at £4 per metre, blue cotton at £6 per sheet, black silk at £20 per dress length. He makes the following sales:

2013
May 1 To F. Gray, 3 Keswick Road, Portsmouth: 3 rolls white tape, 5 sheets blue cotton, 1 dress length black silk. Less 25 per cent trade discount.

  4 To A. Gray, 1 Shilton Road, Preston: 6 rolls white tape, 30 metres green felt. Less 33$^1/_3$ per cent trade discount.

  8 To E. Hines, 1 High Road, Malton: 1 dress length black silk. No trade discount.

  20 To M. Allen, 1 Knott Road, Southport: 10 rolls white tape, 6 sheets blue cotton, 3 dress lengths black silk, 11 metres green felt. Less 25 per cent trade discount.

  31 To B. Cooper, 1 Tops Lane, St. Andrews: 12 rolls white tape, 14 sheets blue cotton, 9 metres green felt. Less 33$^1/_3$ per cent trade discount.

You are to (a) draw up a sales invoice for each of the above sales, (b) enter them up in the Sales Day Book and post to the personal accounts, and (c) transfer the total to the sales account in the General Ledger.

14.4A J. Fisher, White House, Bolton, is selling the following items at the retail prices as shown: plastic tubing at £1 per metre, polythene sheeting at £2 per length, vinyl padding at £5 per box, foam rubber at £3 per sheet. She makes the following sales:

2012
June 1 To A. Portsmouth, 5 Rockley Road, Worthing: 22 metres plastic tubing, 6 sheets foam rubber, 4 boxes vinyl padding. Less 25 per cent trade discount.

  5 To B. Butler, 1 Wembley Road, Colwyn Bay: 50 lengths polythene sheeting, 8 boxes vinyl padding, 20 sheets foam rubber. Less 20 per cent trade discount.

  11 To A. Gate, 1 Bristol Road, Hastings: 4 metres plastic tubing, 33 lengths of polythene sheeting, 30 sheets foam rubber. Less 25 per cent trade discount.

  21 To L. Mackeson, 5 Maine Road, Bath: 29 metres plastic tubing. No trade discount is given.

  30 To M. Alison, Daley Road, Box Hill: 32 metres plastic tubing, 24 lengths polythene sheeting, 20 boxes vinyl padding. Less 33$^1/_3$ per cent trade discount.

Required:
(a) Draw up a sales invoice for each of the above sales.
(b) Enter them up in the Sales Day Book and post to the personal accounts.
(c) Transfer the total to the sales account in the General Ledger.

Purchases day book and purchases ledger

Learning objectives
....

After you have studied this chapter, you should be able to:

- make the appropriate entries relating to credit purchases in a purchases day book
- make the correct postings from the purchases day book to the purchases ledger and general ledger
- explain the differences between the processes of recording credit sales and credit purchases in the books

Introduction
....

In this chapter, you'll continue your look at the day books and ledgers by looking in more detail at the purchases day book (or purchases journal) and the purchases ledger. Having already looked at the sales side of transactions in Chapter 14, you're now going to look at them from the side of purchases. Much of what you will learn in this chapter is virtually identical to what you learnt in Chapter 14. This shouldn't come as a surprise. After all, you're looking once more at how transactions are processed in day books and ledgers and the process ought to be similar as you move from the sales side to the purchases side of similar transactions. If it weren't, accounting would be a far more complex subject than it is.

15.1 Purchases invoices

In Chapter 14, you learnt that an invoice is called a 'sales invoice' when it is entered in the books of the seller. When an invoice is entered in the books of the buyer, it is called a '**purchases invoice**'. For example, in Exhibit 14.1, the first invoice you looked at in Chapter 14,

- in the books of J Blake, the seller, it is a sales invoice; and
- in the books of D Poole, the buyer, it is a purchases invoice.

15.2 Making entries in the purchases day book

From the purchases invoices for goods bought on credit, the purchaser enters the details in the purchases day book (or purchases journal).

Activity 15.1 Think back to what you learnt about the list of items contained in the sales day book. What do you think is the list of items recorded in the purchases day book?

There is no need to show details of the goods bought in the purchases day book. This can be found by looking at the invoices themselves. Exhibit 15.1 is an example of a purchases day book.

Exhibit 15.1

Purchases Day Book			*(page 49)*
	Invoice No.	*Folio*	*Amount* £
2013			
Sept 1 J. Blake	9/101		560
8 B. Hamilton	9/102		1,380
19 C. Brown	9/103		230
30 K. Gabriel	9/104		510
			2,680

Activity 15.2 Note the entry for 1 September and compare it to the entry on the same date shown in the sales day book of J. Blake in Exhibit 14.2. What differences are there between the entries in the two day books? Why do you think these differences arise?

15.3 Posting credit purchases to the purchases ledger

We now have a separate purchases ledger. The double entry is as follows:

1 The credit purchases are posted one by one, to the credit of each supplier's account in the purchases ledger.
2 At the end of each period the total of the credit purchases is posted to the debit of the purchases account in the general ledger. This is now illustrated in Exhibit 15.2.

Exhibit 15.2 Posting credit purchases

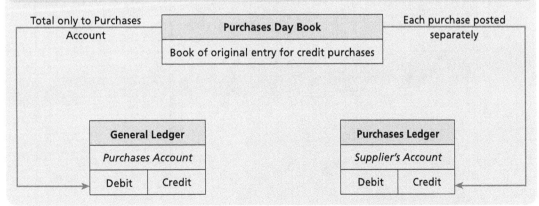

15.4 An example of posting credit purchases

The purchases day book in Exhibit 15.1 is now shown again in Exhibit 15.3 but, this time, posting is made to the purchases ledger and the general ledger. Note the completion of the folio columns indicating that the posting had been completed.

Exhibit 15.3

Purchases Day Book				(page 49)
		Invoice No.	Folio	Amount
2013				£
Sept	1 J. Blake	9/101	PL 16	560
	8 B. Hamilton	9/102	PL 29	1,380
	19 C. Brown	9/103	PL 55	230
	30 K. Gabriel	9/104	PL 89	510
Transferred to Purchases Account			GL 63	2,680

Purchases Ledger
J. Blake (page 16)

			2013			Folio	£
			Sept	1	Purchases	PB 49	560

B. Hamilton (page 29)

			2013			Folio	£
			Sept	8	Purchases	PB 49	1,380

C. Brown (page 55)

			2013			Folio	£
			Sept	19	Purchases	PB 49	230

K. Gabriel (page 89)

			2013			Folio	£
			Sept	30	Purchases	PB 49	510

General Ledger
Purchases (page 63)

2013			Folio	£			
Sept	30	Credit purchases for the month	PB 49	2,680			

Learning outcomes

You should now have learnt:

1 That 'purchases day book' and 'purchases journal' are different names for the same book.

2 That cash purchases are not entered in the purchases day book.

3 That the purchases day book is a list of all credit purchases.

4 That the purchases day book is used to post the items to the personal accounts in the purchases ledger.

5 That the total of credit purchases for the period is posted from the purchases day book to the debit of the purchases account in the general ledger.

6 How to make the appropriate entries relating to credit purchases in a purchases day book and make the correct postings from it to the purchases ledger and general ledger.

7 That the process of making entries in the books of the purchaser is very similar to that of making those in the books of the seller.

Answers to activities

15.1 Similarly to the sales day book, the purchases day book is merely a list of details relating to each credit purchase. The list of items is virtually identical to those recorded in the sales day book, the only differences being that it is the name of the supplier that is recorded, not the purchaser, and that the invoice number is replaced with the buyer's own internally generated reference number:

- date
- name of supplier
- the reference number of the invoice
- folio column
- final amount of invoice.

15.2 Apart from the name of the day books, there are two differences. Firstly, the description of the entry in each case contains the name of the other party to the transaction. This is the personal account in the respective ledger (sales or purchases) where details of the transaction will be entered. The second difference is in the entry in the Invoice Number column. In the case of the seller, Blake, the number entered in Chapter 14 was the number of the invoice that Blake gave to the invoice and is the invoice number shown on the invoice in Exhibit 14.1. In the case of the buyer, Poole, the invoice number is one Poole gave the invoice when it was received from the seller, Blake. As with the number assigned to it by the seller, the buyer also gives each purchase invoice a unique number relating to its place in the sequence of purchase invoices that the buyer has received so far in the period. '9/101' probably means 'month nine' (9), 'purchase invoice' (1) 'number one' (01).

Review questions

15.1   A. Jack has the following purchases for the month of May 2012:

2012
May   1   From D. Pope: 4 DVDs at £60 each, 3 mini hi-fi units at £240 each. Less 25 per cent trade discount.
         3   From F. Lloyd: 2 washing machines at £280 each, 5 vacuum cleaners at £80 each, 2 dishwashers at £200 each. Less 20 per cent trade discount.
       15   From B. Sankey: 1 hi-fi unit at £600, 2 washing machines at £320 each. Less 25 per cent trade discount.
       20   From J. Wilson: 6 CD/radios at £45 each. Less 33$\frac{1}{3}$ per cent trade discount.
       30   From R. Freer: 4 dishwashers at £240 each. Less 20 per cent trade discount.

Required:
(a)   Draw up a purchases invoice for each of the above purchases.
(b)   Enter up the purchases day book for the month.
(c)   Post the transactions to the suppliers' accounts.
(d)   Transfer the total to the purchases account.

15.2A   J. Glen has the following purchases for the month of June 2012:

2012
June   2   From F. Day: 2 sets golf clubs at £800 each, 5 footballs at £40 each. Less 25 per cent trade discount.
       11   From G. Smith: 6 cricket bats at £60 each, 6 ice skates at £35 each, 4 rugby balls at £30 each. Less 20 per cent trade discount.
       18   From F. Hope: 6 sets golf trophies at £90 each, 4 sets golf clubs at £900. Less 33$\frac{1}{3}$ per cent trade discount.
       25   From L. Todd: 5 cricket bats at £52 each. Less 25 per cent trade discount.
       30   From M. Moore: 8 goal posts at £80 each. Less 40 per cent trade discount.

Required:
(a)   Enter up the purchases day book for the month.
(b)   Post the items to the suppliers' accounts.
(c)   Transfer the total to the purchases account.

15.3   C. Phillips, a sole trader specialising in material for Asian clothing, has the following purchases and sales for March 2013:

Mar   1   Bought from Smith Stores: silk £40, cotton £80. All less 25 per cent trade discount.
        8   Sold to A. Grantley: lycra goods £28, woollen items £44. No trade discount.
       15   Sold to A. Henry: silk £36, lycra £144, cotton goods £120. All less 20 per cent trade discount.
       23   Bought from C. Kelly: cotton £88, lycra £52. All less 25 per cent trade discount.
       24   Sold to D. Sangster: lycra goods £42, cotton £48. Less 10 per cent trade discount.
       31   Bought from J. Hamilton: lycra goods £270. Less 33$\frac{1}{3}$ per cent trade discount.

Required:
(a)   Prepare the purchases and sales day books of C. Phillips from the above.
(b)   Post the items to the personal accounts.
(c)   Post the totals of the day books to the sales and purchases accounts.

15.4A A. Henriques has the following purchases and sales for May 2013:

2013
May 1 Sold to M. Marshall: brass goods £24, bronze items £36. Less 25 per cent trade discount.
     7 Sold to R. Richards: tin goods £70, lead items £230. Less 33$\frac{1}{3}$ per cent trade discount.
     9 Bought from C. Clarke: tin goods £400. Less 40 per cent trade discount.
    16 Bought from A. Charles: copper goods £320. Less 50 per cent trade discount.
    23 Sold to T. Young: tin goods £50, brass items £70, lead figures £80. All less 20 per cent trade discount.
    31 Bought from M. Nelson: brass figures £100. Less 50 per cent trade discount.

Required:
(*a*) Write up the sales and purchases day books.
(*b*) Post the items to the personal accounts.
(*c*) Post the totals of the day books to the sales and purchases accounts.

15.5 A. Jones has the following credit purchases and credit sales for May:

May 1 Sold to M. Marshall: brass goods £24, bronze items £36. All less 25 per cent trade discount.
        Sold to R. Richards: tin goods £70, lead items £230. All less 33$\frac{1}{3}$ per cent trade discount.
     9 Bought from C. Clarke: tin goods £400 less 40 per cent trade discount.
    16 Bought from A. Charles: copper goods £320 less 50 per cent trade discount.
    23 Sold to T. Young: tin goods £50, brass items £70, lead figures £80. All less 20 per cent trade discount.
    31 Bought from M. Nelson: brass figures £100 less 50 per cent trade discount.

Required:
(*a*) Write up sales and purchases day books.
(*b*) Post the items to the personal accounts.
(*c*) Post the totals of the day books to the sales and purchases accounts.
(*d*) What are the books of prime entry within a business and why are they so called? Illustrate your answer with suitable examples.

Returns day books

Introduction
············

In this chapter, you'll continue your look at the day books and ledgers by looking in more detail at the two day books that are used to record returns – the returns inwards day book (or returns inwards journal) and the returns outwards day book (or returns outwards journal). Having already looked at the sales side of trans-actions in Chapter 14 and the purchases side in Chapter 15, you'll find that much of what you will learn in this chapter is very similar. In fact, postings from the returns day books to the personal accounts are the mirror image of the ones you learnt to make for sales and purchases.

16.1 Returns inwards and credit notes

You know that businesses allow customers to return goods they've bought. You've probably done so yourself at some time or other. Some retail businesses give every customer the right to do so within a few days of the sale and won't ask why they are being returned. It is a means of assuring the customer that the seller believes that the goods are of good quality and will do what the customer wants. Whatever the rights of return granted by the seller, in the UK there are also legal rights of return that permit retail customers to return goods for a refund should the goods prove to have been unfit for the purpose that was intended.

Businesses that deal with trade customers may operate a similar policy, but that would be more unusual and would normally include a proviso that the customer had a justifiable and reasonable reason for returning the goods.

Activity 16.1 List as many reasons as you can think of why (a) retail customers and (b) trade customers may return goods to the seller.

Sometimes sellers may agree to keep the goods returned, even when they don't normally do so, but won't provide a full refund. Sometimes buyers will agree to keep goods they had wanted to return if the seller offers to refund some of the price they paid.

When the seller agrees to take back goods and refund the amount paid, or agrees to refund part or all of the amount the buyer paid, a document known as a **credit note** will be sent to the customer, showing the amount of the allowance given by the seller.

It is called a credit note because the customer's account will be credited with the amount of the allowance, to show the reduction in the amount owed.

Referring back to Exhibit 14.4, if D. Poole returns two of the cases of McBrand Pears, a credit note like the one shown in Exhibit 16.1 would be issued by R. Grant, the seller.

Exhibit 16.1

To: D. Poole & Co
    45 Charles Street
    Manchester M1 5ZN

R. Grant
Higher Side
Preston PR1 2NL
8 September 2013

Tel (01703) 33122
Fax (01703) 22331

CREDIT NOTE No. 9/37

	Per unit	Total
	£	£
2 cases McBrand Pears	25	50
Less 20% trade discount		(10)
		40

To stop them being mistaken for invoices, credit notes are often printed in red.

16.2 Returns inwards day book

The credit notes are listed in a returns inwards day book (or returns inwards journal). This is then used for posting the items, as follows:

1 Sales ledger: credit the amount of credit notes, one by one, to the accounts of the customers in the ledger.
2 General ledger: at the end of the period the total of the returns inwards day book is posted to the debit of the returns inwards account.

16.3 Example of a returns inwards day book

Exhibit 16.2 presents an example of a returns inwards day book showing the items to be posted to the sales ledger and the general ledger followed by the entries in the ledger accounts.

Exhibit 16.2

Returns Inwards Day Book			(page 10)
	Note No.	Folio	Amount
2013			£
Sept 8 D. Poole	9/37	SL 12	40
17 A. Brewster	9/38	SL 58	120
19 C. Vickers	9/39	SL 99	290
29 M. Nelson	9/40	SL 112	160
Transferred to Returns Inwards Account		GL 114	610

Sales Ledger
D. Poole (page 12)

	2013	Folio	£
	Sept 8 Returns inwards	RI 10	40

A. Brewster (page 58)

	2013	Folio	£
	Sept 17 Returns inwards	RI 10	120

C. Vickers (page 99)

	2013	Folio	£
	Sept 19 Returns inwards	RI 10	290

M. Nelson (page 112)

	2013	Folio	£
	Sept 29 Returns inwards	RI 10	160

General Ledger
Returns Inwards (page 114)

2013	Folio	£	
Sept 30 Returns for the month	RI 10	610	

The returns inwards day book is sometimes known as the sales returns day book, because it is goods that were sold that are being returned.

16.4 Returns outwards and debit notes

If the supplier agrees, goods bought previously may be returned. When this happens a **debit note** is sent by the customer to the supplier giving details of the goods and the reason for their return.

The credit note received from the supplier will simply be evidence of the supplier's agreement, and the amounts involved.

Also, an allowance might be given by the supplier for any faults in the goods. Here also, a debit note should be sent to the supplier. Referring back to Exhibit 16.1, Exhibit 16.3 shows an example of the debit note that Poole, the buyer, may have sent to Grant, the seller.

Exhibit 16.3

To: R. Grant Higher Side Preston PR1 2NL	D. Poole & Co 45 Charles Street Manchester M1 5ZN 7 September 2013 Tel (0161) 488 2142 Fax (0161) 488 2143	
DEBIT NOTE No. 9.22		
	Per unit	Total
2 cases McBrand Pears damaged in transit *Less* 20% trade discount	£ 25	£ 50 (10) 40

Note the differences between this debit note and the credit note in Exhibit 16.1: the names and addresses have swapped places and the document is described as 'Debit Note No. 9.22' rather than 'Credit Note No. 9/37', because Poole uses its own debit note numbering sequence. Also, the dates are different. In this case, it is assumed that Poole raised the debit note on 7 September and sent it and the goods to Grant. Grant received the goods on 8 September and raised the credit note on that date. Finally, the reason for the return of the goods is given.

16.5 Returns outwards day book

The debit notes are listed in a returns outwards day book (or returns outwards journal). This is then used for posting the items, as follows:

1 Purchases ledger: debit the amounts of debit notes, one by one, to the personal accounts of the suppliers in the ledger.
2 General ledger: at the end of the period, the total of the returns outwards day book is posted to the credit of the returns outwards account.

16.6   Example of a returns outwards day book

Exhibit 16.4 presents an example of a returns outwards day book showing the items to be posted to the purchases ledger and the general ledger followed by the entries in the ledger accounts.

Exhibit 16.4

Returns Outwards Day Book				(page 7)
		Note No.	Folio	Amount
				£
2013				
Sept	7 R. Grant	9.22	PL 29	40
	16 B. Rose	9.23	PL 46	240
	28 C. Blake	9.24	PL 55	30
	30 S. Saunders	9.25	PL 87	360
Transferred to Returns Outwards Account			GL 116	670

Purchases Ledger
R. Grant   *(page 29)*

2013		Folio	£		
Sept	7 Returns outwards	RO 7	40		

B. Rose   *(page 46)*

2013		Folio	£		
Sept	16 Returns outwards	RO 7	240		

C. Blake   *(page 55)*

2013		Folio	£		
Sept	28 Returns outwards	RO 7	30		

S. Saunders   *(page 87)*

2013		Folio	£		
Sept	30 Returns outwards	RO 7	360		

General Ledger
Returns Outwards   *(page 116)*

		2013		Folio	£
		Sept 30 Returns for the month		RO 7	670

The returns outwards day book is sometimes known as the purchases returns day book, because it is goods that were purchased that are being returned.

16.7   Double entry and returns

Exhibit 16.5 shows how the entries are made for returns inwards and returns outwards.

Exhibit 16.5 Posting returns inwards and returns outwards

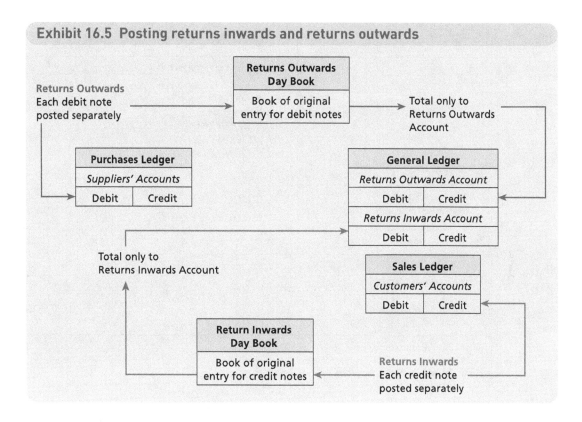

16.8   Statements

At the end of each month, a statement of account or, **'statement'**, should be sent to each debtor who owes money on the last day of the month. It is really a copy of the debtor's account in the seller's books. It should show:

1 the amount owing at the start of the month;
2 the amount of each sales invoice sent to the debtor during the month;
3 credit notes sent to the debtor in the month;
4 cash and cheques received from the debtor during the month; and, finally,
5 the amount due from the debtor at the end of the month.

Exhibit 16.6 on the next page shows an example of a statement.

Debtors will check to see if the account in their accounting records agrees with the statement. If the statement shows that they owe £520, but their records show a different amount due, they will investigate the difference in order to see whether either the statement or their records is incorrect. If they discover that there has been an error in their books, they will correct it. If they find that there is an error in the statement, they will contact the seller.

Activity 16.2 What sort of things could result in the statement and the account held in the books of the debtor showing different balances?

Exhibit 16.6

STATEMENT OF ACCOUNT

R. GRANT
Higher Side
Preston PR1 2NL
Tel (01703) 33122
Fax (01703) 22331

Accounts Dept
D. Poole & Co
45 Charles Street
Manchester M1 5ZN

Date		Details	Debit	Credit	Balance
2013			£	£	£
Sept	1	Balance b/d			880
	2	Invoice 30756	560		1,440
	8	Returns 9/37		40	1,400
	25	Bank		880	520
Sept	30	Balance owing c/d			520

All accounts due and payable within 1 month

Apart from enabling debtors to check the amount due, the statement also acts as a reminder to debtors that they owe the seller money, and shows the date by which they should make payment. Sellers who are contacted by a debtor querying a statement will benefit from having any errors identified in their records.

16.9 Sales and purchases via credit cards

Various banks, building societies and other financial institutions issue credit cards to their customers. The most common examples are Visa and MasterCard. The holder of the credit card purchases goods or services without giving cash or cheques, but simply signs a credit card voucher. The customer is given a copy and the other copy is filed by the seller. Such sales are very rarely sales to anyone other than the general public.

The seller is paid later by the credit card company for all the credit card transactions in the period since the last payment made to the seller. This payment is subject to a deduction of commission by the credit card company.

Once a month, the customer pays the credit card company for all of the payments charged to the credit card during the previous month.

As far as the purchaser is concerned, he has seen goods and has received them (or received the service he requested). In the eyes of the customer, they were paid for at the time of purchase and a loan has been granted by the credit card company in order to do so.

Once the customer has the goods, or has received the appropriate services, the customer does not become a debtor needing an entry in a sales ledger and so (as mentioned in Chapter 14), similarly to a cash sale, no ledger account is maintained for the customer. All the selling company is then interested in, from a recording point of view, is collecting the money from the credit card company.

The double entry needed is:

Sale of items via credit cards:	Dr: Credit card company
	Cr: Sales
Receipt of money from credit card company:	Dr: Bank
	Cr: Credit card company
Commission charged by credit card company:	Dr: Selling expenses
	Cr: Credit card company

Note: the commission is *not* a deduction from the selling price. It is treated in the same way as cash discounts. That is, it is a selling expense and is entered in the profit and loss account section of the income statement.

16.10 Internal check

When sales invoices are prepared, they should be very carefully checked. A system is usually set up so that each stage of the preparation of an invoice is checked by someone other than the person whose job is to send out the invoice.

 Activity 16.3 What sort of things could occur that make checking of all invoices, both those for sales and those for purchases, something that all businesses should do?

A system should, therefore, be set up whereby invoices are checked at each stage by someone other than the person who sends out the invoices or is responsible for paying them.

For purchase invoices, checks should be established, such as using a rubber stamp to stamp each incoming invoice with a mini form with spaces for ticks as each stage of the check on them is completed. The spaces in the stamp will be filled in by the people responsible for making each of the checks on the purchase invoices received, e.g.:

- one person certifying that the goods were actually received;
- a second person certifying that the goods were ordered;
- a third person certifying that the prices and calculations on the invoice are correct, and in accordance with the order originally placed and agreed;
- a fourth person certifying that the goods are in good condition and suitable for the purpose for which ordered.

Naturally, in a small business, simply because the office staff might be quite small, this cross-check may be in the hands of only one person other than the person who will pay the invoice.

A similar sort of check will be made in respect of sales invoices being sent out and on credit notes, both those being sent out and those being received.

16.11 Factoring

You've already learnt that one of the problems that many businesses face is the time taken by debtors to pay their accounts. Few businesses have so much cash available to them that they do not mind how long debtors take to pay. It is a rather surprising fact that a lot of businesses which fail do so not because the business is not making a profit, but because it has run out of cash funds. Once that happens, confidence in the business evaporates, and the business then finds that very few people will supply it with goods. It also cannot pay its employees. Closure of the business then happens fairly quickly in many cases.

As mentioned in Chapter 8, in the case of accounts receivable, the cash flow problem may be alleviated by using the services of a financial intermediary called a factor.

Factoring is a financial service designed to improve the cash flow of healthy, growing companies, enabling them to make better use of management time and the money tied up in trade credit to customers.

In essence, factors provide their clients with three closely integrated services covering sales accounting and collection; credit management, which can include protection against bad debts; and the availability of finance against sales invoices.

16.12 E&OE

On some invoices and other documents you will see 'E&OE' printed at the bottom. This abbreviation stands for 'Errors and Omissions Excepted'. Basically, this is a warning that there may possibly be errors or omissions which could mean that the figures shown could be incorrect, and that the recipient should check carefully the figures before taking any action concerning them.

Learning outcomes

You should now have learnt:

1 That 'returns inwards day book', 'returns inwards journal', 'sales returns journal' and 'sales returns day book' are different names for the same book.

2 That 'returns outwards day book', 'returns outwards journal', 'purchases returns journal' and 'purchases returns day book' are different names for the same book.

3 That goods returned by customers are all entered in a returns inwards day book.

4 That the returns inwards day book is used to post each item to the credit of the personal account of the customer in the sales ledger.

5 That the total of the returns inwards day book is debited at the end of the period to the returns inwards account in the general ledger.

6 That goods returned to suppliers are all entered in a returns outwards day book.

7 What the difference is between a credit note and a debit note.

8 That the returns outwards day book is used to debit the personal account of each supplier in the purchases ledger.

9 That the total of the returns outwards day book is credited at the end of the period to the returns outwards account in the general ledger.

10 How to make the appropriate entries relating to returns in the returns inwards and returns outwards day books and make the correct postings from them to the purchases ledger, sales ledger and general ledger.

11 That the process of making entries for returns in the books of purchasers and sellers is the mirror image of those made in their books for purchases and sales.

12 That statements are used by debtors to check the entries made in their books.

13 Of a range of causes for differences that can arise between statements and the seller's account in the debtor's purchases ledger and that such differences may not all be the result of an error.

14 How credit card transactions are recorded in the books and how commission charged to sellers by the credit card companies is treated in the income statement.

15 Why an effective system of invoice checking should be used by all businesses.

16 Why factoring is an attractive option for some businesses.

Answers to activities

16.1 In either case, the reasons why goods may be returned include:

- they were of the wrong type (e.g. the wrong model number of replacement remote control for a TV);
- the item purchased was one that was already owned by the customer (e.g. a CD);
- they were the wrong colour (e.g. paint doesn't match the existing colour);
- they were the wrong size (e.g. a pair of trousers was too tight);
- they were faulty (e.g. a computer kept crashing);
- a customer bought more than was needed (newsagents returning unsold newspapers);
- a customer changed her mind (e.g. hire purchase agreement on a DVD player);
- a customer saw the same goods elsewhere at a cheaper price;
- a customer found the goods too difficult to use (e.g. the instructions for setting up and operating a video recorder were too complicated);
- (for trade customers) a customer had returned a faulty item to them and they were now returning it to their supplier;
- items had been received in a damaged condition by the customer (e.g. fruit delivered to a supermarket);
- the seller had asked all customers to return a specific item (e.g. when an electrical good or a child's toy was found to be dangerous).

16.2 Differences could be due to a number of things having occurred, including the following:

- a purchase had been omitted from the books of either the seller or the debtor;
- a purchase had been incorrectly entered in the books of either the seller or the debtor;
- a purchase had been made at the end of the month but only entered in the books of either the seller or the debtor in the following month;
- goods returned had been entered in the books of the seller but not in the books of the debtor;
- goods returned had been incorrectly entered in the books of either the seller or the debtor;
- the debtor had entered goods as having been returned in the books when, in fact, the goods were not returned to the seller;
- a purchase had been recorded in the books of the seller in the debtor's account when it should have been entered in the account of another customer;
- a purchase had been recorded in the books of the debtor in the seller's account when it should have been entered in the account of another seller;
- a payment made to the supplier and entered in the books of the debtor had not yet been received by the seller;
- goods had been despatched by the seller and entered in the books of the seller but had not yet been received by the debtor.

16.3 If this were not done, it would be possible for someone inside a business to send out an invoice at a price less than the true price. Any difference could then be split between that person and the outside business. For example, if an invoice was sent to Ivor Twister & Co for £2,000 but the invoice clerk made it out deliberately for £200 then, if there was no cross-check, the difference of £1,800 could be split between the invoice clerk and Ivor Twister & Company.

Similarly, outside businesses could send invoices for goods which were never received by the business. This might be in collaboration with an employee within the business, but there are businesses sending false invoices which rely on the businesses receiving them being inefficient and paying for items never received. There have been cases of businesses sending invoices for such items as advertisements which have never been published. The cashier of the business receiving the invoice, if the business is an inefficient one, might possibly think that someone in the business had authorised the advertisements and would pay the bill. Besides these there are, of course, genuine errors that an invoice checking system helps to avoid.

Review questions

16.1   You are to enter up the Purchases Day Book and the Returns Outwards Day Book from the following details, then to post the items to the relevant accounts in the Purchases Ledger and to show the transfers to the General Ledger at the end of the month.

2013
May   1   Credit purchase from F. Bean £324.
       4   Credit purchases from the following: A. Clerk £216; B. Lock £322; F. Turner £64; G. Rill £130.
       7   Goods returned by us to the following: F. Bean £56; A. Clerk £28.
      10   Credit purchase from B. Lock £140.
      18   Credit purchases from the following: J. Top £230; I. Gray £310; F. Low £405; P. Able £180.
      25   Goods returned by us to the following: I. Gray £140; B. Lock £34.
      31   Credit purchases from: F. Turner £174; T. Burns £230.

16.2A   Enter up the Sales Day Book and the returns inwards day book from the following details. Then post to the customers' accounts and show the transfers to the General Ledger.

2012
June   1   Credit sales to: B. Dock £240; M. Ryan £126; G. Soul £94; F. Trip £107.
       6   Credit sales to: P. Coates £182; L. Job £203; T. Mann £99.
      10   Goods returned to us by: B. Dock £19; F. Trip £32.
      20   Credit sales to B. Uphill £1,790.
      24   Goods returned to us by L. Job £16.
      30   Credit sales to T. Kane £302.

16.3   You are to enter up the sales, purchases, returns inwards and returns outwards day books from the following details, then to post the items to the relevant accounts in the sales and purchases ledgers. The totals from the day books are then to be transferred to the accounts in the General Ledger.

2013
May   1   Credit sales: T. Thompson £56; L. Rodriguez £148; K. Barton £145.
       3   Credit purchases: P. Potter £144; H. Harris £25; B. Spencer £76.
       7   Credit sales: K. Kelly £89; N. Mendes £78; N. Lee £257.
       9   Credit purchases: B. Perkins £24; H. Harris £58; H. Miles £123.
      11   Goods returned by us to: P. Potter £12; B. Spencer £22.
      14   Goods returned to us by: T. Thompson £5; K. Barton £11; K. Kelly £14.
      17   Credit purchases: H. Harris £54; B. Perkins £65; L. Nixon £75.
      20   Goods returned by us to B. Spencer £14.
      24   Credit sales: K. Mohammed £57; K. Kelly £65; O. Green £112.
      28   Goods returned to us by N. Mendes £24.
      31   Credit sales: N. Lee £55.

16.4A You are to enter the following items in the books, post to personal accounts, and show the transfers to the General Ledger.

2013

July

1   Credit purchases from: K. Hill £380; M. Norman £500; N. Senior £106.

3   Credit sales to: E. Rigby £510; E. Phillips £246; F. Thompson £356.

5   Credit purchases from: R. Morton £200; J. Cook £180; D. Edwards £410; C. Davies £66.

8   Credit sales to: A. Green £307; H. George £250; J. Ferguson £185.

12   Returns outwards to: M. Norman £30; N. Senior £16.

14   Returns inwards from: E. Phillips £18; F. Thompson £22.

20   Credit sales to: E. Phillips £188; F. Powell £310; E. Lee £420.

24   Credit purchases from: C. Ferguson £550; K. Ennevor £900.

31   Returns inwards from: E. Phillips £27; E. Rigby £30.

31   Returns outwards to: J. Cook £13; C. Davies £11.

The journal

Learning objectives

After you have studied this chapter, you should be able to:

- explain the purpose of having a journal
- enter up the journal
- post from the journal to the ledgers
- complete opening entries for a new set of accounting books in the journal and make the appropriate entries in the ledgers
- describe and explain the accounting cycle

Introduction

In this chapter, you will learn about the book of original entry that sweeps up all the transactions that have not been entered fully in the other five books of original entry – the journal. You'll learn about the sort of transactions that are entered in the journal and how to make those entries. You'll also learn how to transfer those entries to the accounts in the ledgers. Finally, you will learn what the accounting cycle consists of and see how it links all the material you have learnt so far in this book.

17.1 Main books of original entry

We have seen in earlier chapters that most transactions are entered in one of the following books of original entry:

- cash book
- sales day book
- purchases day book
- returns inwards day book
- returns outwards day book.

These books are each devoted to a particular form of transaction. For example, all credit sales are in the sales day book. To trace any of the transactions entered in these five books would be relatively easy, as we know exactly which book of original entry would contain the information we are looking for.

17.2   The journal: the other book of original entry

The other items which do not pass through these five books are much less common, and sometimes much more complicated. It would be easy for a bookkeeper to forget the details of these transactions if they were made directly into the ledger accounts from the source documents and, if the bookkeeper left the business, it could be impossible to understand such bookkeeping entries.

 Activity 17.1   If these five books are used to record all cash and bank transactions, and all credit purchase and sales items, what are these other items that need to be recorded in a sixth book of original entry?

What is needed is a form of diary to record such transactions, before the entries are made in the double entry accounts. This book is called the **journal**. For each transaction it will contain:

- the date
- the name of the account(s) to be debited and the amount(s)
- the name of the account(s) to be credited and the amount(s)
- a description and explanation of the transaction (this is called a **narrative**)
- a folio reference to the source documents giving proof of the transaction.

The use of a journal makes fraud by bookkeepers more difficult. It also reduces the risk of entering the item once only instead of having double entry. Despite these advantages there are many businesses which do not have such a book.

17.3   Typical uses of the journal

Some of the main uses of the journal are listed below. It must not be thought that this is a complete list.

1 The purchase and sale of fixed assets on credit.
2 Writing-off bad debts.
3 The correction of errors in the ledger accounts.
4 Opening entries. These are the entries needed to open a new set of books.
5 Adjustments to any of the entries in the ledgers.

The layout of the journal is:

The Journal					
Date	Details		Folio	Dr	Cr
	The name of the account to be debited.				
	The name of the account to be credited.				
	The narrative.				

On the first line in the entry is the account to be debited. The second line gives the account to be credited. It is indented so as to make it obvious that it is the credit part of the double entry. The final line is a description of what is being done and provides a permanent record of the reason(s) for the entry.

You should remember that the journal is not a double entry account. It is a form of diary, just as are the day books you learnt about in Chapters 14 to 16. Entering an item in the journal is not the same as recording an item in an account. Once the journal entry is made, the entry in the double entry accounts can then be made.

Note for students: The vertical lines have been included above in order to illustrate how the paper within the journal may be printed. You may find it useful to rule your paper according to this layout when attempting examples and questions on this topic.

17.4   Journal entries in examination questions

If you were to ask examiners what type of bookkeeping and accounting questions are always answered badly by students they would certainly include 'questions involving journal entries'. This is not because they are difficult, but because many students seem to suffer some sort of mental block when doing such questions. The authors, who have been examiners for a large number of accounting bodies around the world, believe that this occurs because students fail to view the journal as a document containing instructions, three per transaction:

1 The account(s) to be debited.
2 The account(s) to be credited.
3 A description of the transaction.

To help you avoid this sort of problem with journal entries, you'll first of all see what the entries are in the accounts, and then be shown how to write up the journal for each of these entries. Let's now look at a few examples.

In practice, the folio reference entered in the T-accounts is often that of the other account involved in the transaction, rather than that of a journal entry. However, this is done when no journal entry has been prepared. When a journal entry has been prepared, it is always the journal entry folio reference that appears in the T-accounts.

Purchase and sale on credit of non-current assets

1 A milling machine is bought on credit from Toolmakers Ltd for £10,550 on 1 July 2012.

The transaction involves the acquisition of an asset matched by a new liability. From what you have learnt in earlier chapters, you will know that the acquisition of an asset is represented by a debit entry in the asset account. You will also know that a new liability is recorded by crediting a liability account. The double entries would be:

				Machinery				Folio	GL1
2012					£				
July	1	Toolmakers Ltd		J1	10,550				

				Toolmakers Ltd				Folio	PL55
				2012					£
				July	1	Machinery		J1	10,550

Activity 17.2   All the folio numbers have been entered in these ledger accounts. You do need to enter them at some time so that you can trace the other side of the entries, but why have they already been entered?

Now what we have to do is to record those entries in the journal. Remember, the journal is simply a kind of diary, not in account form but in ordinary written form. It says which account has to be debited, which account has to be credited, and then gives the narrative which simply describes the nature of the transaction. For the transaction above, the journal entry will appear as follows:

The Journal				*(page 1)*
Date	*Details*	*Folio*	*Dr*	*Cr*
2012 July 1	Machinery Toolmakers Ltd Purchase of milling machine on credit, Purchases invoice No 7/159	GL1 PL55	£ 10,550	£ 10,550

2 Sale of van no longer required for £800 on credit to K. Lamb on 2 July 2012.

Here again it is not difficult to work out what entries are needed in the double entry accounts. They are as follows:

K. Lamb				Folio	SL79
2012 July 2 Van	J2	£ 800			

Van				Folio	GL51
			2012 July 2 K. Lamb	J2	£ 800

The journal entry will appear as follows:

The Journal				*(page 2)*
Date	*Details*	*Folio*	*Dr*	*Cr*
2012 July 2	K. Lamb Van Sales of van no longer required. See letter ref. KL3X8g	SL79 GL51	£ 800	£ 800

Bad debts

A debt of £78 owing to us from H. Mander is written off as a bad debt on 31 August 2012.

As the debt is now of no value we have to stop showing it as an asset. This means that we will credit H. Mander to cancel it out of his account. A bad debt is an expense, and so we will debit it to a bad debts account. The double entry for this is shown as:

Bad Debts				Folio	GL16
2012 Aug 31 H. Mander	J3	£ 78			

H. Mander				Folio	SL99
			2012 Aug 31 Bad debts	J3	£ 78

The journal entry is:

The Journal				*(page 3)*
Date	*Details*	*Folio*	*Dr*	*Cr*
2012 Aug 31	Bad debts H. Mander Debt written-off as bad. See letter in file HM2X8	GL16 SL99	£ 78	£ 78

Correction of errors

This is explained in detail in Chapters 32 and 33.

However, the same procedures are followed as in the case of these other types of journal entries.

Opening entries

J. Brew, after being in business for some years without keeping proper records, now decides to keep a double entry set of books. On 1 July 2012 he establishes that his assets and liabilities are as follows:

Assets: Van £3,700; Fixtures £1,800; Inventory £4,200;
               Accounts receivable – B. Young £95, D. Blake £45; Bank £860; Cash £65.
Liabilities: Accounts payable – M. Quinn £129, C. Walters £410.

The Assets therefore total £3,700 + £1,800 + £4,200 + £95 + £45 + £860 + £65 = £10,765; and the Liabilities total £129 + £410 = £539.

The Capital consists of Assets – Liabilities, i.e. £10,765 – £539 = £10,226.

1 July 2012 will be the first day of the accounting period, as that is the date on which all the asset and liability values were established.

We start the writing up of the books on 1 July 2012. To do this we:

1   Open the journal and make the journal entries to record the opening assets, liabilities and capital.
2   Open asset accounts, one for each asset. Each opening asset is shown as a debit balance.
3   Open liability accounts, one for each liability. Each opening liability is shown as a credit balance.
4   Open an account for the capital. Show it as a credit balance.

The journal records what you are doing, and why. Exhibit 17.1 shows:

- The journal
- The opening entries in the double entry accounts.

Exhibit 17.1

Date	Details	Folio	Dr	Cr
	The Journal			*(page 5)*
2012 July 1	Van	GL1	£ 3,700	£
	Fixtures	GL2	1,800	
	Inventory	GL3	4,200	
	Accounts receivable – B. Young	SL1	95	
	D. Blake	SL2	45	
	Bank	CB1	860	
	Cash	CB1	65	
	Accounts payable – M. Quinn	PL1		129
	C. Walters	PL2		410
	Capital	GL4		10,226
	Assets and liabilities at this date entered to open the books.		10,765	10,765

General Ledger
Van
(page 1)

2012		Folio	£	
July 1	Balance	J 5	3,700	

Fixtures
(page 2)

2012		Folio	£	
July 1	Balance	J 5	1,800	

Inventory
(page 3)

2012		Folio	£	
July 1	Balance	J 5	4,200	

Capital
(page 4)

		2012		Folio	£
		July 1	Balance	J 5	10,226

Sales Ledger
B. Young
(page 1)

2012		Folio	£	
July 1	Balance	J 5	95	

D. Blake
(page 2)

2012		Folio	£	
July 1	Balance	J 5	45	

Purchases Ledger
M. Quinn
(page 1)

		2012		Folio	£
		July 1	Balance	J 5	129

C. Walters
(page 2)

		2012		Folio	£
		July 1	Balance	J 5	410

Cash Book
Cash   Bank
(page 1)

2012		Folio	Cash £	Bank £	
July 1	Balances	J 5	65	860	

Once these opening balances have been recorded in the books, the day-to-day transactions can be entered in the normal manner.

At the elementary level of examinations in bookkeeping, questions are often asked which require you to open a set of books and record the day-by-day entries for the ensuing period.

Activity 17.3   Do you think you will ever need to do this again for this business? (Hint: think about the entries to be made at the start of the next accounting period.)

Adjustments to any of the entries in the ledgers

These can be of many types and it is impossible to write out a complete list. Several examples are now shown:

1 K. Young, a debtor, owed £2,000 on 1 July 2013. He was unable to pay his account in cash, but offers a five-year-old car in full settlement of the debt. The offer is accepted on 5 July 2013.

The personal account has now been settled and needs to be credited with the £2,000. On the other hand, the business now has an extra asset, a car, resulting in the car account needing to be debited with the £2,000 value that has been placed upon the new car.

The double entry recorded in the ledgers is:

		Car		GL171

			£	
2013				
July 5 K. Young	J6		2,000	

			K. Young			SL333

2013		£	2013			£
July 1 Balance b/d		2,000	July 5 Motor car	J6		2,000

The journal entry is:

	The Journal			*(page 6)*
Date	*Details*	*Folio*	*Dr*	*Cr*
2013 July 5	Car		£	£
	K. Young	GL171 SL333	2,000	2,000
	Accepted car in full settlement of debt per letter dated 5/7/2013			

2 T. Jones is a creditor. On 10 July 2013 his business is taken over by A. Lee to whom the debt of £150 is now to be paid.

Here one creditor is just being exchanged for another one. The action needed is to cancel the amount owing to T. Jones by debiting his account, and to show it owing to Lee by opening an account for Lee and crediting it.

The entries in the ledger accounts are:

			T. Jones			SL92

2013		£	2013		£
July 10 A. Lee	J7	150	July 1 Balance b/d		150

	A. Lee		SL244

	2013		£
	July 10 T. Jones	J7	150

The journal entry is:

The Journal					(page 7)
Date	*Details*		*Folio*	*Dr*	*Cr*
2013 July 10	T. Jones		SL 92	£ 150	£
	A. Lee		SL244		150
	Transfer of indebtedness as per letter ref G/1335				

3 We had not yet paid for an office printer we bought on credit for £310 because it was not working properly when installed. On 12 July 2013 we returned it to the supplier, RS Ltd. An allowance of £310 was offered by the supplier and accepted. As a result, we no longer owe the supplier anything for the printer.

The double entry in the ledger accounts is:

			RS Ltd			PL124
2013			£	2013		£
July 12	Office machinery	J8	310	July 1 Balance b/d		310

		Office Machinery			GL288
2013		£	2013		£
July 1 Balance b/d		310	July 12 RS Ltd	J8	310

The journal entry is:

The Journal					(page 8)
Date	*Details*		*Folio*	*Dr*	*Cr*
2013 July 12	RS Ltd		PL124	£ 310	£
	Office machinery		GL288		310
	Faulty printer returned to supplier.				
	Full allowance given. See letter 10/7/2013.				

17.5 Examination guidance

Later on in your studies, especially in *Business Accounting 2*, you may find that some of the journal entries become rather more complicated than those you have seen so far. The best plan for nearly all students is to follow this advice:

1 On your examination answer paper write a heading 'Workings'. Then show the double entry accounts under that heading.
2 Now put a heading 'Answer', and show the answer in the form of the Journal, as shown in this chapter.

If the question asks for journal entries you must *not* fall into the trap of just showing the double entry accounts, as you could get no marks at all *even though your double entry records are correct*. The examiner wants to see the journal entries, and you *must* show those in your answer.

17.6 The basic accounting cycle

Now that we have covered all aspects of bookkeeping entries, we can show the whole **accounting cycle** in the form of the diagram in Exhibit 17.2.

Note that the 'accounting cycle' refers to the sequence in which data is recorded and processed until it becomes part of the financial statements at the end of the period.

Exhibit 17.2 The accounting cycle for a profit-making organisation

Source documents

Where original information is to be found

- Sales and purchases invoices
- Debit and credit notes for returns
- Bank pay-in slips and cheque counterfoils
- Receipts for cash paid out and received
- Correspondence containing other financial information

Original entry

What happens to it

Classified and then entered in books of original entry:

- The cash books*
- Sales and purchases day books
- Returns inwards and outwards day books
- The journal

Double entry

How the dual aspect of each transaction is recorded

Double entry accounts

General ledger	Sales ledger	Purchases ledger	Cash books*
Real and nominal accounts	Accounts receivable	Accounts payable	Cash book and petty cash book

(*Note: Cash books fulfil the roles both of books of original entry and double entry accounts)

Check arithmetic

Checking the arithmetical accuracy of double entry accounts

Trial balance

Profit or loss

Calculation of profit or loss for the accounting period shown in a financial statement

Income statement

Closing financial position

Financial statement showing liabilities, assets and capital at the end of the accounting period

Statement of financial positon

What are the six books of original entry?

Learning outcomes

You should now have learnt:

1 What the journal is used for.

2 That the journal is the collection place for items that do not pass fully through the other five books of original entry.

3 That there is a range of possible types of transactions that must be entered in the journal.

4 That the opening double entries made on starting a set of books for the first time are done using the journal.

5 How to make the opening entries for a new set of books in the journal and in the ledger accounts.

6 That the main parts of the accounting cycle are as follows:

(a) Collect source documents.
(b) Enter transactions in the books of original entry.
(c) Post to ledgers.
(d) Extract trial balance.
(e) Prepare the income statement.
(f) Draw up the statement of financial position.

Answers to activities

17.1 All transactions relating to non-current assets. Also, entries have to be recorded somewhere when errors in the books have to be corrected, or when any figures in the ledger accounts need to be changed. Also, any transfers involving the Capital Account, such as when funds are set aside from the Capital Account to provide resources should a building need to be repaired or replaced.

17.2 You are looking at the ledger accounts after the details have been entered in them from the journal and you always enter the folio number in the ledger account as you make each entry, not afterwards. The check that the entries has been completed is made by only entering the folio numbers *in the journal* as each entry is written in the appropriate ledger account. You could, therefore, see an entry in the journal that has no folio numbers entered against it. This would signify that the journal entry has not yet been fully recorded in the appropriate ledger accounts. As mentioned above, you should *never* see this in a ledger account as the folio number is always entered *at the same time* as the rest of the details from the journal are entered.

17.3 The need for opening entries will not occur very often. They will not be needed each year as the balances from the previous period will have been brought forward. They will only be required a second time if the business goes through a change in status, for example, if it becomes a limited company.

17.4 Cash book, sales day book, purchases day book, returns inwards day book, returns outwards day book, and the journal.

Review questions

17.1   You are to show the journal entries necessary to record the following items which occured in 2012:

(a)   May 1 Bought a van on credit from Deedon Garage for £6,000.
(b)   May 3 A debt of £100 owing from P. Knight was written off as a bad debt.
(c)   May 8 Office furniture bought by us for £600 was returned to the supplier Timewas Ltd, as it was unsuitable. Full allowance will be given to us.
(d)   May 12 We are owed £500 by R. Twig. He is declared bankrupt and we received £200 in full settlement of the debt.
(e)   May 14 We take goods costing £20 out of the business inventory without paying for them.
(f)   May 28 Some time ago we paid an insurance bill thinking that it was all in respect of the business. We now discover that £80 of the amount paid was in fact insurance of our private house.
(g)   May 28 Bought machinery for £2,400 on credit from Electrotime Ltd.

17.2A   Show the journal entries necessary to record the following items:

2013
Apr   1   Bought fixtures on credit from Bell and Co £1,153.
      4   We take goods costing £340 out of the business inventory without paying for them.
      9   £68 of the goods taken by us on 4 April is returned back into inventory by us. We do not take any money for the return of the goods.
      12 H. Cowes owes us £640. He is unable to pay his debt. We agree to take some computer equipment from him at that value and so cancel the debt.
      18 Some of the fixtures bought from Bell and Co, £42 worth, are found to be unsuitable and are returned to them for full allowance.
      24 A debt owing to us by P. Lees of £124 is written off as a bad debt.
      30 Office equipment bought on credit from Furniture Today Ltd for £1,710.

17.3   You are to open the books of F. Polk, a trader, via the journal to record the assets and liabilities, and are then to record the daily transactions for the month of May. A trial balance is to be extracted as on 31 May 2013.

2013
May   1   *Assets*: Premises £34,000; Van £5,125; Fixtures £810; Inventory £6,390; Accounts receivable: P. Mullen £140, F. Lane £310; Cash at bank £6,240; Cash in hand £560.
          Liabilities: Accounts payable: S. Hood £215, J Brown £640.
      1   Paid storage costs by cheque £40.
      2   Goods bought on credit from: S. Hood £145; D. Main £206; W. Tone £96; R. Foot £66.
      3   Goods sold on credit to: J. Wilson £112; T. Cole £164; F. Syme £208; J. Allen £91; P. White £242; F. Lane £90.
      4   Paid for motor expenses in cash £60.
      7   Cash drawings by proprietor £150.
      9   Goods sold on credit to: T. Cole £68; J. Fox £131.
      11 Goods returned to Polk by: J. Wilson £32; F. Syme £48.
      14 Bought another van on credit from Abel Motors Ltd £4,850.
      16 The following paid Polk their accounts by cheque less 5 per cent cash discount: P. Mullen; F. Lane; J. Wilson; F. Syme.
      19 Goods returned by Polk to R. Foot £6.
      22 Goods bought on credit from: L. Mole £183; W. Wright £191.
      24 The following accounts were settled by Polk by cheque less 5 per cent cash discount: S. Hood; J. Brown; R. Foot.
      27 Salaries paid by cheque £740.
      30 Paid business rates by cheque £140.
      31 Paid Abel Motors Ltd a cheque for £4,850.

The analytical petty cash book and the imprest system

Learning objectives

After you have studied this chapter, you should be able to:

- explain why many organisations use a petty cash book
- make entries in a petty cash book
- transfer the appropriate amounts from the petty cash book to the ledgers at the end of each period
- explain and operate the imprest system for petty cash
- explain why some organisations use a bank cash book
- make entries in a bank cash book

Introduction

You may remember that you learnt in Chapter 13 that there is a second type of cash book, called the **petty cash book**, which many businesses use to record small amounts paid for in cash. (It was included in the accounting cycle shown in Exhibit 17.2.) In this chapter, you'll learn of the type of items that are recorded in the petty cash book, and how to make the entries to it. You'll also learn how to transfer financial data from the petty cash book into the ledgers. Finally, you will learn about bank cash books and how they differ from the cash books you learnt about in Chapter 13.

18.1 Division of the cash book

As businesses continue to grow, some now having a commercial value in excess of that of many smaller countries, you have learnt that, for many, it has become necessary to have several books instead of just one ledger. In fact, nowadays all but the very smallest organisations use sets of ledgers and day books.

Activity 18.1 Why do we have day books? Why don't we just enter every transaction directly into the appropriate ledger accounts?

The cash book became a book of original entry so that all cash and bank transactions could be separated from the rest of the accounts in the general ledger. It is for much the same reason that many organisations use a petty cash book. Every business has a number of transactions of very small value which, were they all recorded in the cash book, would only serve to make it more difficult to identify the important transactions that businesses need to keep a close eye upon. Just like the cash book, the petty cash book is both a book of original entry and a ledger account.

The advantages of using a petty cash book can be summarised as follows:

- The task of handling and recording small cash payments can be given by the cashier (the person responsible for recording entries in the cash book) to a junior member of staff. This person is known as the 'petty cashier'. The cashier, who is a more senior and, consequently, higher paid member of staff would be saved from routine work.
- If small cash payments were entered into the main cash book, these items would then need posting one by one to the ledgers. For example, if travelling expenses were paid to staff on a daily basis, this could mean approximately 250 postings to the staff travelling expenses account during the year, i.e. 5 days per week × 50 working weeks per year. However, if a petty cash book is used, it would only be the monthly totals for each period that need posting to the general ledger. If this were done, only 12 entries would be needed in the staff travelling expenses account instead of approximately 250.

When a petty cashier makes a payment to someone, then that person will have to fill in a voucher showing exactly what the payment was for. They usually have to attach bills, e.g. for petrol, to the petty cash voucher. They would sign the voucher to certify that their expenses had been received from the petty cashier.

18.2 The imprest system

It is all very well having a petty cash book, but where does the money paid out from it come from? The **imprest system** is one where the cashier gives the petty cashier enough cash to meet the petty cash needs for the following period. Then, at the end of the period, the cashier finds out the amounts spent by the petty cashier, by looking at the entries in the petty cash book. At the same time, the petty cashier may give the petty cash vouchers to the cashier so that the entries in the petty cash book may be checked. The cashier then passes cash to the value of the amount spent on petty cash in the period to the petty cashier. In other words, the cashier tops up the amount remaining in petty cash to bring it back up to the level it was at when the period started. This process is the imprest system and this topped-up amount is known as the petty cash **float**.

Exhibit 18.1 shows an example of this method.

Exhibit 18.1

		£
Period 1	The cashier gives the petty cashier	100
	The petty cashier pays out in the period	(78)
	Petty cash now in hand	22
	The cashier now gives the petty cashier the amount spent	78
	Petty cash in hand at the end of Period 1	100
Period 2	The petty cashier pays out in the period	(84)
	Petty cash now in hand	16
	The cashier now gives the petty cashier the amount spent	84
	Petty cash in hand at the end of Period 2	100

It may be necessary to increase the petty cash float to be held at the start of each period. In the above case, if we had wanted to increase the float at the end of the second period to £120, then the cashier would have given the petty cashier an extra £20, i.e. £84 + £20 = £104.

In some small organisations, no petty cash book is kept. Instead, at the end of each period, the amount left in petty cash is reconciled (i.e. checked and verified as correct) with the receipts held by the petty cashier. The amount spent is then given to the petty cashier in order to restore the float to its agreed level. However, this is not an ideal method to adopt. Businesses need to control the uses of all their resources, including petty cash, and so virtually every organisation that operates a petty cash float maintains a petty cash book. The most common format adopted is the 'analytical petty cash book'.

18.3 Illustration of an analytical petty cash book

An analytical petty cash book is shown in Exhibit 18.2. This example shows one for a nursery school.

Exhibit 18.2

Petty Cash Book *(page 31)*

Receipts	Folio	Date	Details	Voucher No.	Total	Motor Expenses	Staff Travelling Expenses	Postage	Cleaning	Ledger Folio	Ledger Accounts
£					£	£	£	£	£		£
300	CB 19	Sept 1	Cash								
		2	Petrol	1	16	16					
		3	J. Green	2	23		23				
		3	Postage	3	12			12			
		4	D. Davies	4	32		32				
		7	Cleaning	5	11				11		
		9	Petrol	6	21	21					
		12	K. Jones	7	13		13				
		14	Petrol	8	23	23					
		15	L. Black	9	5		5				
		16	Cleaning	10	11				11		
		18	Petrol	11	22	22					
		20	Postage	12	12			12			
		22	Cleaning	13	11				11		
		24	G. Wood	14	7		7				
		27	C. Brown	15	13					PL18	13
		29	Postage	16	12			12			
					244	82	80	36	33		13
						GL	GL	GL	GL		
244	CB 22	30	Cash			17	29	44	64		
		30	Balance	c/d	300						
544					544						
300		Oct 1	Balance	b/d							

The receipts column is the debit side of the petty cash book. On giving £300 to the petty cashier on 1 September, the credit entry is made in the cash book while the debit entry is made in the petty cash book. A similar entry is made on 30 September for the £244 paid by the headteacher to the petty cashier. As this amount covers all the expenses paid by the petty cashier, the float is now restored to its earlier level of £300. The credit side is used to record all the payments made by the petty cashier.

The transactions that were recorded in the petty cash book were:

2012		Voucher number		£
Sept	1	–	The headteacher gives £300 as float to the petty cashier	
			Payments out of petty cash during September:	
	2	1	Petrol: School bus	16
	3	2	J. Green – travelling expenses of staff	23
	3	3	Postage	12
	4	4	D. Davies – travelling expenses of staff	32
	7	5	Cleaning expenses	11
	9	6	Petrol: School bus	21
	12	7	K. Jones – travelling expenses of staff	13
	14	8	Petrol: School bus	23
	15	9	L. Black – travelling expenses of staff	5
	16	10	Cleaning expenses	11
	18	11	Petrol: School bus	22
	20	12	Postage	12
	22	13	Cleaning expenses	11
	24	14	G. Wood – travelling expenses of staff	7
	27	15	Settlement of C. Brown's account in the Purchases Ledger	13
	29	16	Postage	12
	30	–	The headteacher reimburses the petty cashier the amount spent in the month.	

The process followed during the period that led to these entries appearing in the petty cash book as shown in Exhibit 18.2 is:

1 Enter the date and details of each payment. Put the amount paid in the Total column.
2 Put the same amount in the column for that type of expense.
3 At the end of each period, add up the Total column.
4 Add up each of the expense columns. The total found in step 3 should equal the total of all the expense columns. In Exhibit 18.2 this is £244.
5 Enter the amount reimbursed to make up the float in the Receipts column.
6 Balance-off the petty cash book, carrying down the petty cash in hand balance to the next period.

To complete the double entry for petty cash expenses paid:

1 The total of each expense column is debited to the appropriate expense account in the general ledger.
2 The folio number of each expense account in the general ledger is entered under the appropriate expense column in the petty cash book. (This signifies that the double entry to the ledger account has been made.)
3 The last column in the petty cash book is a Ledger column. It contains entries for items paid out of petty cash which need posting to a ledger other than the general ledger. (This might arise, for example, if a purchases ledger account was settled out of petty cash.)

Activity 18.2   Where is the other side of the double entry for all these expense postings to the ledgers recorded?

The double entries for all the items in Exhibit 18.2 are shown in Exhibit 18.3.

Exhibit 18.3

Cash Book
(Bank and Folio columns only)   *(page 19)*

			Folio	£
2012				
Sept	1	Petty cash	PCB 31	300
	30	Petty cash	PCB 31	244

General Ledger
School Bus Expenses   *(page 17)*

2012			Folio	£	
Sept	30	Petty cash	PCB 31	82	

Staff Travelling Expenses   *(page 29)*

2012			Folio	£	
Sept	30	Petty cash	PCB 31	80	

Postage   *(page 44)*

2012			Folio	£	
Sept	30	Petty cash	PCB 31	36	

Cleaning   *(page 64)*

2012			Folio	£	
Sept	30	Petty cash	PCB 31	33	

Purchases Ledger
C. Brown   *(page 18)*

2012			Folio	£	2012				£
Sept	30	Petty cash	PCB 31	13	Sept	1	Balance	b/d	13

Note how the Folio column is used to enter 'b/d'. You may have noticed previously that this is done for both 'b/d' and 'c/d' in all ledger accounts and in the cash book where contra entries are also indicated in the folio column by use of the symbol '₵'.

18.4 Bank cash book

Nowadays, many businesses have only a small number of sales that are paid for with cash. The rest of the 'cash' sales are actually paid using credit cards, cheques and direct transfers into the business bank account using debit cards (which, as you learnt in Chapter 12, are issued by UK banks and involve a customer's bank card being swiped into a special machine in the same way that credit card payments are processed). Debit cards are used in retail transactions and result in the payment being transferred immediately from the customer's bank account into the business bank account.

Organisations which have only a small number of sales for cash may use a different form of cash book from the one you learnt about in Chapter 13. If they do, they will use a petty cash book and a **bank cash book**. The bank cash book is given this name because *all* payments in cash are entered in the petty cash book, and the bank cash book contains *only* bank columns and discount columns.

In a bank cash book (it could also be done in an 'ordinary' cash book), an extra column may be added. The extra column would show the details of the cheques and direct transfers banked, with just the total of the banking being shown in the total column.

Exhibit 18.4 shows the receipts side of a bank cash book containing this extra column. The totals of the deposits made into the bank on each of the three days were £192, £381 and £1,218. The details column shows what the bankings are made up of.

Exhibit 18.4

Bank Cash Book (Receipts side)

Date 2013	Details	Discount £	Items £	Total Banked £
May 14	G. Archer	5	95	
14	P. Watts	3	57	
14	C. King		40	192
20	K. Dooley	6	114	
20	Cash Sales		55	
20	R. Jones		60	
20	P. Mackie	8	152	381
31	J. Young		19	
31	T. Broome	50	950	
31	Cash Sales		116	
31	H. Tiller	7	133	1,218

Learning outcomes

You should now have learnt:

1 That the petty cash book saves (a) the cash book and (b) the ledger accounts from containing a lot of trivial detail.

2 That the use of the petty cash book enables the cashier or a senior member of staff to delegate this type of work to a more junior member of staff.

3 That the cashier should periodically check the work performed by the petty cashier.

4 That all payments made by the petty cashier should have petty cash vouchers as evidence of proof of expense.

5 How to enter petty cash transactions into the petty cash book.

6 How to transfer the totals for each expense recorded in the petty cash book to the appropriate ledger accounts.

7 How to operate a float system for petty cash.

8 The difference between a cash book and a bank cash book.

9 Why some organisations use a bank cash book instead of a cash book.

Answers to activities

18.1 One reason why we have day books is to avoid too much detail being entered in the ledgers.

18.2 In the petty cash book. Like the cash book, the petty cash book is not only a book of original entry, it is also an account that would otherwise appear in the general ledger.

Review questions

18.1 The following is a summary of the petty cash transactions of Jockfield Ltd for May 2012.

May			£
	1	Received from Cashier £300 as petty cash float	
	2	Postage	18
	3	Travelling	12
	4	Cleaning	15
	7	Petrol for delivery van	22
	8	Travelling	25
	9	Stationery	17
	11	Cleaning	18
	14	Postage	5
	15	Travelling	8
	18	Stationery	9
	18	Cleaning	23
	20	Postage	13
	24	Delivery van 5,000 mile service	43
	26	Petrol	18
	27	Cleaning	21
	29	Postage	5
	30	Petrol	14

You are required to:
(a) Rule up a suitable petty cash book with analysis columns for expenditure on cleaning, motor expenses, postage, stationery, travelling.
(b) Enter the month's transactions.
(c) Enter the receipt of the amount necessary to restore the imprest and carry down the balance for the commencement of the following month.
(d) State how the double entry for the expenditure is completed.

(Association of Accounting Technicians)

18.2

(a) Why do some businesses keep a petty cash book as well as a cash book?
(b) Kathryn Rochford keeps her petty cash book on the imprest system, the imprest being £25. For the month of April 2013 her petty cash transactions were as follows:

Apr			£
	1	Petty cash balance	1.13
	2	Petty cashier presented vouchers to cashier and	
		obtained cash to restore the imprest	23.87
	4	Bought postage stamps	8.50
	9	Paid to Courtney Bishop, a creditor	2.35
	11	Paid bus fares	1.72
	17	Bought envelopes	0.70
	23	Received cash for personal telephone call	0.68
	26	Bought petrol	10.00

  (i) Enter the above transactions in the petty cash book and balance the petty cash book at 30 April, bringing down the balance on 1 May.
  (ii) On 1 May Kathryn Rochford received an amount of cash from the cashier to restore the imprest. Enter this transaction in the petty cash book.

(c) Open the ledger accounts to complete the double entry for the following:

  (i) The petty cash analysis columns headed *Postage and Stationery* and *Travelling Expenses*;
  (ii) The transactions dated 9 and 23 April 2013.

(Northern Examinations and Assessment Board: GCSE)

18.3A Rule up a petty cash book with analysis columns for office expenses, motor expenses, cleaning expenses and casual labour. The cash float is £600 and the amount spent is reimbursed on 30 June.

2013			£
June	1	F. Black – casual labour	18
	2	Letterheadings	41
	2	Abel Motors – motor repairs	67
	3	Cleaning materials	4
	6	Envelopes	11
	8	Petrol	22
	11	P. Lyon – casual labour	16
	12	T. Upton – cleaner	8
	12	Paper clips	3
	14	Petrol	19
	16	Adhesive tape	2
	16	Petrol	25
	21	Motor taxation	95
	22	F. Luck – casual labour	19
	23	T. Upton – cleaner	14
	24	J. Lamb – casual labour	27
	25	Copy paper	8
	26	Lively Cars – motor repairs	83
	29	Petrol	24
	30	F. Tred – casual labour	21

18.4 Fine Teas operates its petty cash account on the imprest system. It is maintained at a figure of £140, with the balance being restored to that amount on the first day of each month. At 30 April 2012 the petty cash box held £24.37 in cash.

During May 2012, the following petty cash transactions arose:

			£
May	1	Cash received to restore imprest (to be derived)	?
	1	Bus fares	0.41
	2	Stationery	2.35
	4	Bus fares	0.30
	7	Postage stamps	6.50
	7	Trade journal	0.95
	8	Bus fares	0.64
	11	Tippex	1.29
	12	Typewriter ribbons	5.42
	14	Parcel postage	3.45
	15	Paper-clips	0.42
	15	Newspapers	2.00
	16	Photocopier repair	16.80
	19	Postage stamps	1.50
	20	Drawing pins	0.38
	21	Train fare	5.40
	22	Photocopier paper	5.63
	23	Display decorations	3.07
	23	Tippex	1.14
	25	Wrapping paper	0.78
	27	String	0.61
	27	Sellotape	0.75
	27	Biro pens	0.46
	28	Stapler repair	13.66
	30	Bus fares	2.09
June	1	Cash received to restore imprest (to be derived)	?

Required:
(a)   Open and post the company's analysed petty cash book for the period 1 May to 1 June 2012 inclusive.
(b)   Balance the account at 30 May 2012.
(c)   Show the imprest reimbursement entry on June 1.

Computerised accounting systems

Learning objectives

After you have studied this chapter, you should be able to:

- explain how computerised accounting systems mimic manual accounting systems and can do everything that is done by a manual accounting system
- describe how computerised accounting systems automate most of the entries required in a manual accounting system including, in some cases, the initial entry for each transaction
- describe and explain the advantages and pitfalls of using a computerised accounting system
- explain the importance of fully integrating a computerised accounting system
- explain the importance of full compatibility between the various components of a computerised accounting system
- explain the importance of implementing adequate controls to safeguard data in a computerised accounting system
- explain the need to take great care when converting from a manual accounting system to a computerised one

Introduction

In this chapter, you'll learn about the differences between manual and computerised accounting information systems and about the benefits of using computerised accounting systems to produce output for decision-making. You will also learn of the variety of output that can be produced by a computerised information system. In addition, you will learn of the importance of integration and compatibility of all the components of a computerised accounting system and of the need to take great care when switching from a manual system to a computerised one.

23.1 Background

Most businesses, except the very smallest, now use computers to handle their accounting data. When businesses switch to computerised accounting, they soon discover that bookkeeping and accounting skills are more important than computing ones. This is because users of many computerised accounting systems have very little to learn in order to use them. As you can see from the entry screen of the *Sage Instant Accounts 2011* accounting package shown in Exhibit 23.1, the interfaces look fairly familiar – the file menu is usually in the top left, for example, and many of the icons are the same and have the same meanings across a whole range of software produced by different companies.

Exhibit 23.1

Source: *Sage Accounting System*, Sage (UK) Ltd.

Activity 23.1   Not very long ago, only the largest businesses used computers to handle their accounting data. Why do you think the situation is so different now?

The methods adopted in computer-based accounting adhere to the fundamental principles of accounting covered in this and other accounting textbooks. No matter how sophisticated and easy to use a computerised accounting system is, it will not overcome the need for bookkeeping and accounting knowledge by those in control. Imagine, for example, how anyone who does not know how to prepare journal entries could correct an error in an original entry correctly from an accounting point of view and, just as importantly, understand why it is important not to erase the original entry.

Apart from a need for knowledge of accounting principles in order to best convert a business from manual to computer-based accounting, some accounting knowledge is required to help understand the significance of many of the outputs from a computerised accounting system, just as it is required in respect of output from a manual accounting system.

Thus, computerised accounting systems do not remove the need for some accounting knowledge among those responsible for key accounting tasks or from those who use the output from the accounting systems. In fact, some accountants working in practice would tell you that they believe there is an even greater need for accounting knowledge among those who record the transactions in a computerised accounting system than among those using a manual one.

Activity 23.2   What do you think? Is there an even greater need for accounting knowledge among those that record the transactions in a computerised accounting system? Why?/Why not?

23.2 Benefits of using a computerised accounting system

As you learnt in Chapter 22, there are many benefits of using a computerised accounting system. Overall, probably the greatest benefit comes from the fact that a computerised accounting system can do the same things as a manual system, but does them better. Thus, all the features in a manual system, such as the one shown in Exhibit 23.2, can be replicated in a computerised accounting system which not only does them quicker, more accurately, and 100 per cent consistently, but can also do them more frequently *and* do other things as well.

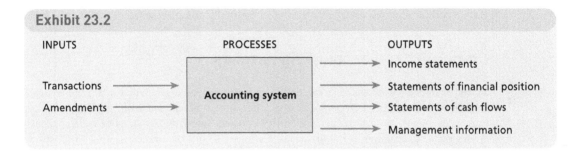

Exhibit 23.2

INPUTS	PROCESSES	OUTPUTS
		Income statements
Transactions →	**Accounting system**	Statements of financial position
Amendments →		Statements of cash flows
		Management information

Let's look at some of these benefits in more detail.

Speed and accuracy

The main aim of computerising an accounting system is to perform the processing stage electronically, much more quickly, consistently and accurately than if it were done manually. However, transactions and amendment details have to be input into the process (1) in the correct form, (2) in the correct order, and (3) in a timely manner. Although there is scope to use electronic methods of entering some of this information (e.g. EPOS systems and document scanning), it requires a good deal of initiative and an organised way of doing things in order to do so. Nevertheless, improved accuracy is one of the more obvious benefits of any kind of computerised accounting system.

Further time-saving can be achieved by immediate output of reports, such as customer statements, purchase analysis, cash and bank statements, and details about whether the business is meeting sales targets. Such reports and statements can be produced both on request and, automatically, by the computer searching through information generated and saved within the accounting system and then producing whatever report is required.

Error detection

Effective error detection improves the decision-making process. For example, a computerised accounting system should be capable of detecting when a customer appears to be running up excessive debts with the business, so offering the chance for the credit controller to take remedial action.

Another area is the need to remain within budgets. Many business expenses can get out of hand if they are not checked at regular intervals. A computerised accounting system should be capable of an activity called **exception reporting**, a process of issuing a warning message to decision-makers when something unexpected is happening: for example, when expenditure against a budget is higher than it should be. In a manual accounting system, the situation can occur that errors or unwanted transactions go unnoticed until it is too late, resulting in unnecessary costs being incurred by the business.

Enhanced reporting

For many businesses, the task of producing reports on a regular basis, such as VAT Returns, payroll processing, cash flow analysis, and financial statements, can be time-consuming, tedious and unrewarding. The use of a computerised accounting system speeds up the process to the point, in some cases, where it is done automatically thus reducing the monotony of producing lengthy reports requiring extensive preparatory analysis of data. In many cases, such as VAT Returns and payslips, businesses find that they can use computer printouts or electronic output, e.g. on computer disks, instead of having to manually complete official or standard forms.

23.3   Computerised accounting records

Many businesses now make good use of accounting packages which are readily available and have been well tested. Such packages are commonly modularised with, typically, the sales ledger, purchases ledger, general ledger, inventory control, sales invoicing, sales order processing, purchases order processing, non-current assets, payroll, bill of materials, and job costing all being offered as separate modules in their own right. When a business decides to computerise its accounting system, it acquires only the modules it needs. For example, a sole trader would have no use for a payroll module.

The various ledgers and accounts maintained in a computerised accounting system mimic those kept in a manual system. The general ledger, for example, will adhere to the basic rules of double entry bookkeeping in that each debit entry has a corresponding credit entry – if a customer is issued with an invoice, the transaction giving precise details of the invoice will be stored in the credit sales records to form part of the customer history and then the double entry is made by crediting sales accounts and debiting a debtor's account.

The difference lies in the method of entry – each transaction is entered only once (accountants refer to this as a 'single entry' system) and the software automatically completes the double entry. This has a downside, however: some computerised accounting packages will post various amounts into suspense accounts when it is unclear where postings are to be made. These require manual intervention and journal entries to remove each item from the suspense account and complete the original double entry.

(Suspense accounts are the topic of Chapter 33.)

Flexibility

The information stored in a computerised accounting system is available instantly and can be used to produce statements, ledger account details, analysis of how long debts have been outstanding, etc. immediately it is requested. For example, the computerised sales ledger will hold all details about customers. The starting point would be to enter the details concerning the customer (name, address, etc.) along with the balance brought forward from the manual system (if such a transfer is occurring; otherwise, if it is a new customer, an opening zero balance will be created automatically by the software).

All transactions relating to a customer, such as the issue of an invoice or receipt of payment, are entered into the system and automatically posted to the customer's account. Customers can, at any time, be issued with a statement of their account, and the business can always obtain an up-to-date and complete history of trading with any particular customer. The purchases ledger will operate in exactly the same way in that supplier details are held and, once entered through the purchases module, all transactions relating to individual purchasers will automatically be posted to the appropriate account.

Bank payments and receipts are a central feature of computerised accounting systems. The modules can be operated by someone with virtually no bookkeeping knowledge. For example, if an electricity bill is paid, the system will prompt for the details of the transaction that are required to process and record the double entry. The system will not assume any knowledge of double entry on the part of the individual making the entries.

Account codes

In order to use a computerised accounting system efficiently and effectively, someone with both accounting skills and a good knowledge of the business will be required to organise the accounts and ledgers in the first instance. Some of these packages are not written for specific businesses and need to be 'tailored' to the one that is going to use it. Most require businesses to define what accounts they are to have in their general ledger and how such accounts are to be grouped.

For example, accounts for non-current assets may have account references commencing with 'N', while expense accounts commence with 'E'. The package will probably have its own default set of **account codes** (the computerised equivalent of the folio references in a manual system), and it may be necessary to override the defaults in the accounting package in order to use the business's own account code list (also known as the '**chart of accounts**'). In addition, part of the setting-up of a computer system will require the tailoring of the package for certain reports such as the income statement and statement of financial position.

Knowledge of double entry

Most packages are capable of allowing businesses to set up their preferred methods for dealing with depreciation of non-current assets and regular payments of, for example, rent and rates. However, as you saw with the need to correct entries in a suspense account arising from the computer not knowing how to complete a double entry, such packages do require a good 'knowledge' of double entry so that adjustments can be made through their journal entries. For example, the computer will not overcome some errors and omissions, such as the operator mis-reading an amount on an invoice or crediting a payment to the wrong customer account. Anyone correcting these errors will require a full knowledge of the relevant part of the accounting system as well as knowledge of bookkeeping and accounting principles.

23.4 Computerised inventory control and modular integration

Automation of much of the data processing can be taken further when integrating other modules. Inventory control offers the benefit of keeping very close tabs on inventory levels. If an invoicing package is also in use, then an invoice can be generated in such a way that an operator can collect the details of the business or person to invoice from the sales ledger and details of all inventory to be invoiced from the inventory files. Once the invoice has been raised, the recorded inventory levels fall accordingly, the sales ledger is updated and the nominal entries are made by crediting sales and debiting accounts receivable control (a topic which will be covered in Chapter 31).

Sales order processing

Sales order processing allows an order to be placed into the system which can then be used at a later stage to generate an invoice. Sales order processing is important to many businesses as it gives them an indication about what inventory levels are required. Having sales orders on computer also offers the advantage of being able to monitor sales orders outstanding and so ensure that they are supplied on time to the customers. Computers can produce outstanding order reports and such things as 'picking lists' (a list of items to be taken out of storage and given or shipped to customers) very quickly.

Purchase order processing

Purchase order processing allows an operator to print an order to send off to a supplier or, in some more advanced systems, to transmit it over a direct link into the supplier's accounting system where it will be recorded and converted into an issue from inventory. The computerised purchase order system also serves the useful purpose of allowing instant access to information about what is on order. This prevents duplicate orders arising.

Modular integration

The full use of all modules in this integrated manner allows a business to access inventory details and get a complete profile on its status in terms of what is left in stock, what is on order, and what has been ordered by customers. Furthermore, most packages keep a history of inventory movements so helping the business to analyse specific inventory turnovers. When integrated in this fashion, the processing structure may be as depicted in Exhibit 23.3.

Exhibit 23.3 An integrated computerised accounting system

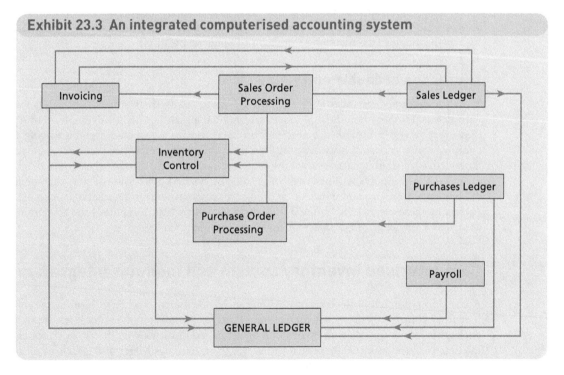

Exhibit 23.3 includes a payroll module. Businesses with a large number of employees would find this particularly useful as payroll systems require a good deal of regular processing. Again, a reasonable knowledge of payroll is required in order to set up the system in the first place.

23.5 Accounting information systems

An **accounting information system (AIS)** is the total suite of components that, together, comprise all the inputs, storage, transaction processing, collating and reporting of financial transaction data. It is, in effect, the infrastructure that supports the production and delivery of accounting information.

The objective of an accounting information system is to collect and store data about accounting transactions so as to generate meaningful output for decision-making. The combination of a shoebox containing receipts for all purchases and a cheque book being kept by the corner shopkeeper is, in itself, an accounting system, as is the set of day books and ledgers kept by the local department store and the integrated computerised accounting system of a large company.

There is no need for an AIS to be computerised in order to be described in this way. Computerisation may only have been introduced on some of the accounting tasks, such as the accounting books, the payroll system or the inventory control system. When the entire suite of accounting tasks and records is computerised, the benefits are clearly greater than when only parts of the AIS are computerised. **Most people assume you are talking about a** *fully* **computerised accounting system when you refer to an AIS and** *this is how we shall use the term in the rest of this chapter.* However, much of what follows, apart from the benefits of full integration, is also applicable to partially computerised AISs.

Full integration and compatibility

For an AIS to be fully effective, *all* the components need to be integrated with each other, otherwise information gets lost, misentered from one record to another, or duplicated (often incorrectly as each version of it is updated at different times). Major errors may ultimately arise if integration is not 100 per cent. In a computerised AIS, there is the added problem that some of the components or modules may be written for use in a different operating system and may not be immediately compatible with the other modules with which data is to be exchanged, retrieved or transferred. This was a major problem until the late 1980s, since when much of the difficulty of operating system incompatibility has been eradicated.

However, with software the problem still remains – even documents prepared on one version of word processing software may not transfer with 100 per cent accuracy to an earlier or later version of the same software, never mind to other word processing packages. The same holds for other software, such as spreadsheets and database files. Therefore, at the planning stage, it is important to ensure that all hardware and software that is to be used is 100 per cent compatible and that, where it is not, steps are taken to ensure that a workable alternative way of communicating data and information between modules is found.

 Activity 23.3 If there is not full integration of an AIS, what examples can you think of where data may need to be entered more than once and maintained in two or more different records simultaneously? What problems may result from this?

Outputs

An AIS, computerised or manual, can, of course, produce whatever reports you wish, so long as the relevant data is stored within the AIS or accessible to the AIS. Where a fully computerised AIS is clearly superior is in the range of reports it can produce virtually instantly and in the way it can be programmed to produce periodic reports precisely when they are scheduled to be available. There is no need for decision-makers to wait two weeks for the summary of the previous month's business activities – a delay that was commonplace in manual accounting systems. It is now available as soon as business closes at the end of the last day of the month.

Some of the other reports produced by most manual AISs can also take a very long time to produce. Some only take an hour or two to prepare manually. However, a computerised AIS can produce these reports in seconds, and as often as the decision-makers wish. These include aged accounts receivable reports (a list of debtors showing how much they each owe, and for how long the amounts have been outstanding); price lists; inventory levels and quantities for reordering; lists of invoices and credit notes; and audit trail information to enable errors to be traced and corrected (whereby the route a transaction took through the accounting records to the financial statements is revealed). The savings in personnel and time and, therefore, costs that can result from fully computerising the AIS cannot be understated, even for smaller businesses that wish to maximise their efficiency.

 Activity 23.4   When computers were first used in this way, many decision-makers were far from pleased. Why?

In the early days of computerised AISs, all the output was on paper. Now, much of it is electronic.

Electronic dissemination

One of the major benefits of a computerised AIS is that output generated from it need not be in hard copy. It can be visual on a computer screen, or distributed electronically on DVD, CD or floppy disk, or by direct file transfer to another computer over a LAN, WAN, intranet or extranet or the Internet.

While many organisations still require that information be passed to them on their own forms, the IT revolution of the past few years has led to many organisations being willing to accept printout generated from a computer, emailed electronic documents, or disks containing the document, instead of having their own forms completed and returned. For example, fairly standard and repetitive information generation, such as VAT receipts and payments, are common to most businesses, and the Revenue and Customs accept computer-generated VAT returns, computer-generated payroll data and computer-generated tax returns.

In fact, Revenue and Customs accepts all the following documents electronically:

- annual tax returns (income tax and corporation tax);
- starter/leaver details (forms P45, P46, P160);
- daily coding (form P6);
- PAYE return;
- annual and budget code number updates (form P9);
- pension and works number updates;
- end-of-year returns (forms P35, P38A and P14);
- expenses and benefits (form P11D);
- construction industry vouchers CIS23 and CIS25;
- tax credit notices (form TC700 series);
- student declaration (form P38s);
- student loan deductions (forms SL1 and SL2);
- VAT Return (form 100);

and electronic filing is compulsory for VAT, Corporation Tax, and PAYE.

Benefits of electronic filing of documents

Among the recognised benefits of electronic submission of documents and hence, potentially, of a computerised AIS are:

- speed;
- improved accuracy in that what is sent is what was intended to be sent;

- improved accuracy in that what is sent is received, and in the form intended;
- lower administration costs;
- greater security;
- less use of paper;
- immediate acknowledgement of receipt.

Benefits of electronic transmission of funds

Of course, if electronic submission of documents is a recent phenomenon, electronic transmission of funds has been around a good deal longer. Among the benefits attributed to it and again, potentially, to a computerised AIS are:

- certainty of payment on a specific date;
- certainty that exactly the amount due to be paid is paid;
- immediate acknowledgement of receipt;
- lower administration costs;
- lower bank charges;
- greater security.

Benefits of linking AISs

Another significant recent change brought about by computerisation of AISs is the growth in electronic data exchange between supplier and customer. Some very large companies now insist that their suppliers link their inventory systems to the customer's AIS. The customer can then interrogate the inventory records of the supplier to see if items are available and place orders directly into the supplier's AIS without any need for physical transmission of an order document. This has helped the growth of just-in-time inventory keeping by customers who, rather than holding their own inventory, simply order it from their suppliers when required.

Among the benefits attributed to linking AISs and again, potentially, to a computerised AIS are:

- speed;
- lower administration costs;
- greater awareness of the current position;
- improved control of related risks;
- greater security of a continuing relationship between the parties.

23.6 Data safeguards

In any computerised accounting system, there is a need to take adequate steps to prevent theft of data, fraudulent or malicious data manipulation and data loss.

Activity 23.5 What do you think may cause a business to lose some data that is in its accounting information system?

Prevention of data theft

Today's computers have password access controls available, both when a computer is switched-on and at access to any intranet to which the computer has access. Sometimes, these are combined into one entry of a password. However, even where that is the case, a username is typically also required. As a result, any unauthorised person attempting access needs two items of information, not just one. Software packages often also have a level of password control at the point of entry to the package.

Unfortunately, many people are careless in their selection of passwords. For example, many use the same one for everything, or use the names of their children, or their date of birth. As a result, these levels of security may not be sufficient for highly sensitive information. They are, however, an essential minimum for any business.

Prevention of fraudulent data manipulation

Many instances of this form of fraud have been detected since computers first started to be used in business. Many warehouse managers have stayed at work over lunch while everyone else has left, logged on to the computer system using the sign-in details of one of the warehouse assistants, and then cancelled items out of inventory by writing them off as defective/destroyed/imperfect. Miraculously, the cancelled items find their way back to the warehouse manager's home that same day.

In one unreported case in the UK, a retailer's warehouse manager was supplying his own customers with the company's goods for over 18 months before he was caught when the company management began to worry about a rise in scrap levels from its inventory and called in a forensic accountant. In another, a forensic accountant discovered over £10 million of fraudulent data manipulation by the financial director of a medium-sized company after it was taken over by a larger organisation.

Effective security measures do not eliminate the risk of these types of events occurring, but they do make them more difficult.

Prevention of malicious data manipulation

Disgruntled employees, such as someone who has just been sacked, are particularly well-placed to destroy the validity of data. It takes very little time to delete computer files, or enter fictitious transactions and anyone with the appropriate access to computerised data has the potential to do a lot of damage, often without anyone realising what was done for a considerable period of time.

For this form of information system risk, there needs to be a managerial action control in place to remove system access from anyone considered a potential threat. It is not an easy security threat to eliminate – who can tell how an individual may react to being sacked? However, thought should be given to how such threats may be minimised. This is one of the reasons why people are sometimes sacked and told to leave the premises immediately. This also occurs sometimes when an employee gets a job with a competitor but, in that case, it is more likely to be related to the threat of data theft rather than any risk of malicious data manipulation.

Prevention of data loss

Other than through malicious loss of data, businesses may lose data for a number of reasons including:

- corrupt data files;
- loss of passwords to data files;
- faulty storage media, such as hard drives, floppy disks, CDs, DVDs, USB sticks, and tapes;
- fire;
- flood;
- earthquake;
- acts of terrorism.

When computers started to be used in business, it did not take long for the concept of the 'backup' to develop. Companies backed-up their data very regularly, often nightly, by copying their computerised data onto a second device, such as a tape which was then stored somewhere watertight and secure, ideally at a different location.

As time passed, it was not just the large companies which used computers, and backups would be done on any appropriate media. As a result, when disaster struck, lost data could be reinstated from the latest available backup.

This system was never perfect – a backup might be done at midnight but if a hard disk failed at 3pm the next day, although data was available up to midnight the previous day, all data for that day was lost. Nevertheless, it is far easier to recreate a few hours of data than it is to create data for a month or longer.

It is essential that a backup system be implemented and observed for any computerised accounting system. The recent shift towards 'cloud computing' – data storage at an Internet site rather than on a local computer – for personal data storage may, ultimately, become the norm for business as well. Whether it does or not, the security controls put in place to ensure that adequate backup is in place need to recognise also that any data held as backup is another target for data theft, something that is often overlooked.

23.7 Issues to consider when introducing a fully computerised AIS

When you computerise an accounting system, you have some decisions to make. These include:

1 Deciding whether to mimic what you have been doing manually or start from scratch and redesign everything. For example, you may only have been using one ledger in the manual system, but may choose to use three or four in the computerised system. You may have had a two-column cash book in the manual system but decide to have a columnar cash book in the computerised system.

2 Deciding whether to buy a general accounting package 'off-the-shelf' or create one from scratch. Depending on the size of the business, creating one from scratch may be done using a spreadsheet and a database package or it may involve having computer programmers writing the entire system.

3 If you decide to buy one off-the-shelf, you need to decide how much to customise it, if at all.

4 If you decide not to customise it, or aren't able to customise parts of it, you may need to change the terminology you use when referring to parts of the accounting system. For example, you may need to refer to the Nominal Ledger rather than the General Ledger and to the Purchases Journal rather than the Purchases Day Book. For example, *Sage* uses the term 'Customers Module' rather than Sales Ledger and 'Suppliers Module' instead of a Purchases Ledger.

5 You need to decide who is going to be responsible for overseeing the project.

6 You need to decide how long you are going to allow for the new system to be developed and make plans to introduce it accordingly.

7 You need to decide who is to be trained in using it and when.

8 You need to decide how long you will run the new system in parallel with the existing manual system before you stop using the manual system.

9 You need to identify the hardware you will need and ensure that it is in place at the appropriate time.

10 You need to decide how data is to be safeguarded from theft or loss.

11 You need to identify who is going to test the new system and what data is to be used to do so.

12 You need to weigh up the costs and benefits of computerising the accounting system and decide whether it is actually worth doing it.

These are just some of the issues you need to deal with. Many more will appear as each of these questions is answered and many more will materialise as the project proceeds.

The most popular software used by small and medium-sized businesses in the UK is *Sage*. However, you should look at a range of available alternatives, such as *Pegasus*, *Quickbooks* and *Microsoft Dynamics GP*, before proceeding to purchase the package you intend using. Factors to consider obviously include price, but they also include capacity, hardware requirements, ease of use, reliability, appropriateness of the way data is entered, stored and secured, and the range and style of reports that can be produced. You also need to consider compatibility of the package with any other systems or packages you might wish to link it to if that is, in fact, a possibility in the first place. Accountants are not normally the most knowledgeable people to answer these technical questions and guidance from an IT specialist is often advisable.

Once the package is installed and fully operational, you need to monitor its effectiveness and reliability and need to have contingency plans in place should it ultimately prove to have been a mistake. (In other words, you need to ensure you can revert to the previous system if necessary.)

When you come to review your hardware or operating system with a view to upgrading it, you need to ensure that the package will continue to run without any problems when you upgrade. You also need to consider carefully before committing to an upgrade of the accounting package, in case things that used to work no longer function or need to be done in very different ways.

You also need to ensure that the data stored in the system is backed up regularly and that password or other security devices are in place in order to prevent unauthorised access to it.

Overall, you need to think the whole thing through very carefully before committing to the switch and you need to ensure you have all the controls over the system in place before it starts to be used.

Nevertheless, although great care and a lot of effort must be expended when converting to a computerised accounting system, there is no doubt that the benefits of having an appropriate one will vastly improve the quality and reliability of the accounting data and information produced.

Learning outcomes

You should now have learnt that:

1 Bookkeeping and accounting skills and knowledge are more important than computing skills and knowledge when a switch is made from a manual accounting system to a computerised accounting system.

2 The user interface of an accounting package often looks similar to those of other frequently used Windows-based software packages.

3 Computerised accounting systems can do everything a manual accounting system can do, but does them quicker, more accurately, more consistently, and with greater flexibility.

4 A considerably enhanced ability to obtain reports is available from a computerised accounting system compared to a manual accounting system.

5 The various records maintained in a computerised accounting system mimic those in a manual accounting system, though the names of some of the records may be different.

6 Acccount codes are used in computerised accounting systems instead of folio numbers.

7 Maximised integration of the various components in a computerised accounting system generates the maximum benefits.

8 Compatibility between the various components in a computerised accounting system is essential if it is to operate effectively.

9 One of the major benefits of computerised accounting systems is the ability to generate electronic output.

10 Implementing adequate controls to safeguard data is essential when accounting systems are computerised.

11 Implementing a switch to a computerised accounting system is a non-trivial task that should never be done lightly and needs to be done with the greatest of care.

Answers to activities

23.1   This question can be answered from many perspectives including:

- vastly lower relative cost of computer technology and IT in general;
- greater ease of use thanks to a graphical rather than a text-based visual interface (this only really became the norm in the mid-1990s);
- wide range of available software to choose from;
- the current high flexibility in (even off-the-shelf) software enabling customisation to suit the needs of the business;
- a vastly greater level of IT literacy;
- pressure from accountants to modernise methods and so increase control over the accounting records;
- greater financial awareness among business people generally (e.g. the enormous growth in MBA holders over the past 20 years);
- pressures from the authorities to maintain up-to-date accounting records (e.g. VAT);
- pressure from competitors (i.e. the need to keep up);
- deeper insight that can be gained by using computers and information technology to present views of the business and business opportunities virtually instantly when they could only be produced manually after weeks of effort;
- a desire to appear 'modern and up-to-date'.

23.2   Most accountants would disagree with the comment in a general sense but agree with it in the context of (a) knowing the accounts to use, (b) knowing whether an entry looks correct and, most importantly, (c) knowing how to make appropriate entries when an error has occurred.

23.3   One example would be where the inventory control system is not integrated with the Sales Ledger. A customer could return goods that were recorded in the inventory control system immediately. However, it might take a few hours, even days, for the credit entry to be made in the customer's account in the Sales Ledger. During the delay period, the customer might be refused credit because the account showed that the customer's credit limit had been reached when, in fact, the customer had no outstanding debt to the business as a result of having returned the items purchased. The customer might also be sent a statement of the account that did not show the credit entry but was accompanied by a letter demanding immediate payment as the account was now overdue. If the reverse happened and the first entry was made in the Sales Ledger, orders from other customers for the same items might be rejected because the inventory records showed a zero amount of those items in inventory when, in fact, the ones returned by the customer were in the warehouse.

Another problem of non-integration relates to customer details. If they are changed, for example by a change of address, and only entered in the Sales Ledger and not in the records maintained by the delivery department, goods ordered by the customer could be sent to the wrong address.

If the Cash Book is not fully integrated with the Sales Ledger, customers may pay their accounts but still be shown as debtors when the system is asked to print an aged list of debtors in the middle of a month. Time and effort might then be expended chasing a debt that didn't exist and, of course, the customer would not be exactly pleased either.

23.4   There were a number of issues at that time:

- The output was sometimes inaccurate, mainly due to the inexperience of the people who were keying data into the AIS, but also due to errors in programming. Also, until the late 1970s, much of the input was by punched card and cards in a batch had to be entered into the computer in the same order as they were produced. If a batch of cards was dropped before being put into the card reader that then transferred the data into the computer, all sorts of nonsense could result. This type of situation gave rise to the phrase 'garbage in, garbage out' which was often used by those who favoured traditional manual systems when explaining why computers were 'useless'. It still applies today, but for different reasons, such as the original data being incorrect or out of date.
- Many early AISs were developed by computer specialists, not accountants. They often produced reports that were less meaningful than they might have been, frequently omitting key information. The decision-makers did not know what rules had been followed in generating numbers in the reports and so would sometimes reach a decision assuming the data meant one thing

when, in fact, it meant something else. (For example, the scrap value of a non-current asset may have been ignored when calculating whether it should be used for one more year or replaced.) They also often gave everything possible to the decision-makers, resulting in huge piles of reports being received of which only a few pages were actually of any interest.

In other words, the output from early computerised AISs was often less than useful and often could not be relied upon.

23.5 Loss of data can be the result of malicious deletion, corrupt data files, faulty hardware (e.g. discs), fire, flood and other natural disasters, plus man-made events, such as acts of terrorism and wars.

Review questions

23.1 What benefits for the whole accounting system can follow from using a computer for accounting work?

23.2 Why is the need for accounting skills and knowledge important when the accounting system is computerised?

23.3 Why is the need to fully integrate a computerised accounting system so important?

23.4 What issues need to be considered when making the switch from a manual accounting system to a computerised accounting system?

Adjustments for Financial Statements 1

Capital expenditure and revenue expenditure

Learning objectives

After you have studied this chapter, you should be able to:

- distinguish between expenditure that is capital in nature and that which is revenue expenditure
- explain why some expenditure is a mixture of capital expenditure and revenue expenditure
- explain the effect on the financial statements and the profits shown there, if revenue expenditure is wrongly treated as being capital expenditure, and vice versa

Introduction

In this chapter, you'll learn about the difference between capital expenditure and revenue expenditure. You will learn how to split expenditure that is a mixture of both capital and revenue expenditure and to make the appropriate entries in the ledgers and in the financial statements. You will also learn why organisations generally prefer to treat as much expenditure as possible as capital expenditure, how to deal with loan interest relating to acquisition of a non-current asset, and how to classify and deal with the income generated when a non-current asset is sold.

24.1 Capital expenditure

Before you start this topic, you need to be aware that 'capital expenditure' has nothing to do with the owner's Capital Account. The two terms happen to start with the same first word, and they are both things that are likely to be around the business for quite a long time. While both are, in a sense, long-term investments, one made by the business, the other made by the owner, they are, by definition, two very different things.

Capital expenditure is incurred when a business spends money either to:

- buy non-current assets; or
- add to the value of an existing non-current asset.

Included in such amounts should be spending on:

- acquiring non-current assets
- bringing them into the business
- legal costs of buying buildings
- carriage inwards on machinery bought
- any other cost needed to get a non-current asset ready for use.

24.2 Revenue expenditure

Expenditure which is not spent on increasing the value of non-current assets, but is incurred in running the business on a day-to-day basis, is known as **revenue expenditure**.

The difference between revenue expenditure and capital expenditure can be seen clearly with the total cost of using a van for a business. Buying a van is an example of capital expenditure. The van will be in use for several years and is, therefore, a non-current asset.

Paying for petrol to use in the van is revenue expenditure. This is because the expenditure is used up in a short time and does not add to the value of non-current assets.

> **Activity 24.1** Why do you think a business might want to treat an item of expenditure as capital rather than as revenue? (*Hint*: where does an item of capital expenditure *not* appear in the financial statements?)

24.3 Differences between capital and revenue expenditure

The examples listed in Exhibit 24.1 demonstrate the difference in classification.

Exhibit 24.1

Expenditure	Type of Expenditure
1 Buying van	Capital
2 Petrol costs for van	Revenue
3 Repairs to van	Revenue
4 Putting extra headlights on van	Capital
5 Buying machinery	Capital
6 Electricity costs of using machinery	Revenue
7 We spent £1,500 on machinery: £1,000 was for an item (improvement) added to the machine; and £500 was for repairs	Capital £1,000 Revenue £500
8 Painting outside of new building	Capital
9 Three years later – repainting outside of the building in (8)	Revenue

You already know that revenue expenditure is chargeable to the income statement, while capital expenditure will result in increased figures for non-current assets in the statement of financial position. Getting the classification wrong affects the profits reported and the capital account and asset values in the financial statements. It is, therefore, important that this classification is correctly done.

24.4   **Capital expenditure: further analysis**

As mentioned earlier, capital expenditure not only consists of the cost of purchasing a non-current asset, but also includes other costs necessary to get the non-current asset operational.

> **Activity 24.2**   Spend a minute listing some examples of these other costs like the ones you've already learnt about.

24.5   **Joint expenditure**

Sometimes one item of expenditure will need to be divided between capital and revenue expenditure – there was an example in Exhibit 24.1 when £1,500 spent on machinery was split between capital and revenue.

Exhibit 24.2

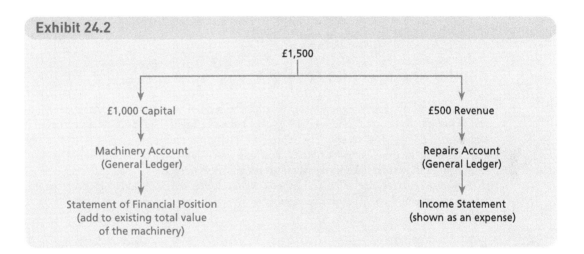

£1,500

£1,000 Capital   £500 Revenue

Machinery Account   Repairs Account
(General Ledger)   (General Ledger)

Statement of Financial Position   Income Statement
(add to existing total value   (shown as an expense)
of the machinery)

> **Activity 24.3**   A builder was engaged to tackle some work on your premises, the total bill being for £3,000. If one-third of this was for repair work and two-thirds for improvements, where should the two parts be entered in the accounting books and where would they appear in the financial statements?

24.6   **Incorrect treatment of expenditure**

If one of the following occurs:

1 capital expenditure is incorrectly treated as revenue expenditure; or
2 revenue expenditure is incorrectly treated as capital expenditure;

then both the statement of financial position figures and the income statement figures will be incorrect.

This means that the net profit figure will be incorrect and, if the expenditure affects items in the trading account part of the income statement, the gross profit figure will also be incorrect.

Activity 24.4   Can you think of an example where an item may have been treated wrongly as revenue expenditure and charged in the trading account when it should have been treated as capital expenditure?

24.7   Treatment of loan interest

If money is borrowed to finance the purchase of a non-current asset, interest will have to be paid on the loan. Most accountants would argue that the loan interest is *not* a cost of acquiring the asset, but is simply a cost of *financing* its acquisition. This meant that loan interest was revenue expenditure and *not* capital expenditure. In 1993, this changed and it because compulsory to capitalise interest incurred in *constructing* a non-current asset.

Activity 24.5   Why shouldn't the interest on the funds borrowed to finance *acquisition* of a non-current asset be included in its cost?

24.8   Capital and revenue receipts

When an item of capital expenditure is sold, the receipt is called a 'capital receipt'. Suppose a van is bought for £5,000 and sold five years later for £750. The £5,000 was treated as capital expenditure. The £750 received is treated as a capital receipt and credited to the non-current asset account in the General Ledger. (You will learn later in your studies that it is a bit more complicated than this, but this treatment is technically correct.)

'Revenue receipts' are sales and other revenue items that are added to gross profit, such as rent receivable and commissions receivable.

24.9   Finally

Students generally find this topic very difficult to grasp. Trying to remember when something should be treated as capital expenditure and when something should be treated as revenue expenditure seems just too difficult to remember correctly.

In fact, the rules are *very* simple:

1 If expenditure is *directly* incurred in bringing a non-current asset into use for the first time, it is capital expenditure.
2 If expenditure improves a non-current asset (by making it superior to what it was when it was first owned by the organisation, e.g. building an extension to a warehouse), it is capital expenditure.
3 All other expenditures are revenue expenditure.

So, faced with having to decide, ask if (1) is true in this case. If it isn't, ask if (2) is true in this case. If it isn't, it is revenue expenditure. If either (1) or (2) is true, it is capital expenditure. Try it on the items in Exhibit 24.1 – it works!

Learning outcomes

You should now have learnt:

1 How to distinguish between capital expenditure and revenue expenditure.

2 That some items are a mixture of capital expenditure and revenue expenditure, and the total outlay need to be apportioned accordingly.

3 That if capital expenditure or revenue expenditure is mistaken one for the other, then gross profit and/or net profit will be incorrectly stated, as will the capital account and non-current assets in the statement of financial position.

4 That if capital receipts or revenue receipts are mistaken one for the other, then gross profit and/or net profit will be incorrectly stated, as will the capital account and non-current assets in the statement of financial position.

Answers to activities

24.1 Capital expenditure appears in the statement of financial position whereas revenue expenditure appears in the income statement. If expenditure is treated as revenue expenditure, it reduces profit immediately by the amount spent. If it is treated as capital expenditure, there is no immediate impact upon profit. Profit is only affected when a part of the expenditure is charged against income during the time the item purchased is in use, and those charges (called 'depreciation') spread the cost of the item over a number of years. As a result, profits in the period in which the expenditure took place are lower if an item of expenditure is treated as revenue expenditure. Businesses like to show that they are being as profitable as possible, so they tend to want to treat everything possible as a capital expense. Doing this also makes the business look more wealthy as the non-current assets are at a higher value than they would have been had the expenditure been treated as revenue. (You'll learn about depreciation in Chapter 26.)

24.2 Some of the other possible additional costs are: (*a*) installation costs; (*b*) inspection and testing the asset before use; (*c*) architects' fees for building plans and for supervising construction of buildings; (*d*) demolition costs to remove something before new building can begin.

24.3 The debit entries would be Repairs £1,000 and Premises £2,000. The credit entry would be Accounts Payable 'Builder' £3,000. The £1,000 will appear, therefore, in the income statement (in the profit and loss part) as revenue expenditure. The £2,000 identified as capital expenditure will appear in the statement of financial position as part of the figure for Premises.

24.4 When goods are being manufactured from raw materials, employees will be being paid wages. Those wages will be part of the cost of the inventory of finished goods. It sometimes happens that employees do other work in periods when their normal work is not keeping them busy. Imagine some employees were moved temporarily to help build an extension to the premises – for example, by helping to build a small garage to hold the company chairman's car while he was working in his office. If their wages for that period were mistakenly included as usual in the cost of goods produced, that would be an example of capital expenditure being wrongly classified as revenue expenditure and would result in gross profit being understated.

24.5 Organisations have a number of sources of funds, only one of which is borrowing. The non-current asset could have been paid for using existing funds already held by the organisation. The funds borrowed to pay for it could just as easily have been used to buy raw materials while the funds already available for purchase of raw materials could have been used to finance the new non-current asset. How could anyone be sure that the funds borrowed were actually used to purchase it, and why should they be tied so strongly to it when other funds could have been used instead? It is a very circuitous argument but, in the end, the funds borrowed entered the pool of all the organisation's funds. Just because an amount equal to the amount borrowed was then used to pay for the non-current asset is not sufficient reason to include the interest costs in the cost of the non-current asset. The interest costs are simply part of the costs of financing all the assets of the organisation.

However, this changed in 1993 when an accounting standard was issued (IAS 23 *Borrowing costs*) that allows interest directly attributable to the construction of a tangible non-current asset to be capitalised as part of the cost of that asset. In 2007, the standard was amended making it compulsory to capitalise such borrowing costs. Note that it *does not* permit capitalisation of interest incurred on the funds used to purchase a non-current asset, only interest incurred *on the construction* of one.

Review questions

24.1

(a) What is meant by 'capital expenditure' and by 'revenue expenditure'?
(b) Some of the following items should be treated as capital and some as revenue. For each of them state which classification applies:

(i) The purchase of machinery for use in the business.
(ii) Carriage paid to bring the machinery in (i) above to the works.
(iii) Complete redecoration of the premises at a cost of £1,500.
(iv) A quarterly account for heating.
(v) The purchase of a soft drinks vending machine for the canteen with a stock of soft drinks.
(vi) Wages paid by a building contractor to his own workmen for the erection of an office in the builder's stockyard.

24.2A Indicate which of the following would be revenue items and which would be capital items in a wholesale bakery:

(a) Purchase of a new van.
(b) Purchase of replacement engine for existing van.
(c) Cost of altering interior of new van to increase carrying capacity.
(d) Cost of motor tax for new van.
(e) Cost of motor tax for existing van.
(f) Cost of painting business's name on new van.
(g) Repair and maintenance of existing van.

24.3 State the type of expenditure, capital or revenue, incurred in the following transactions:

(a) Breakdown van purchased by a garage.
(b) Repairs to a fruiterer's van.
(c) The cost of installing a new machine.
(d) Cost of hiring refrigeration plant in a butcher's shop.
(e) Twelve dozen sets of cutlery, purchased by a catering firm for a new dining-room.
(f) A motor vehicle bought for resale by a motor dealer.
(g) The cost of acquiring patent rights.

24.4A On what principles would you distinguish between capital and revenue expenditure? Illustrate your answer by reference to the following:

(a) The cost of repairs and an extension to the premises.
(b) Installation of a gas central heating boiler in place of an oil-fired central heating boiler.
(c) Small but expensive alterations to a cigarette manufacturing machine which increased the machine's output by 20 per cent.

24.5 Explain clearly the difference between capital expenditure and revenue expenditure. State which of the following you would classify as capital expenditure, giving your reasons:

(a) Cost of building extension to factory.
(b) Purchase of extra filing cabinets for sales office.
(c) Cost of repairs to accounting machine.
(d) Cost of installing reconditioned engine in delivery van.
(e) Legal fees paid in connection with factory extension.

24.6A The data which follows was extracted from the books of account of H. Kirk, an engineer, on 31 March 2012, his financial year end.

		£
(a)	Purchase of extra milling machine (includes £300 for repair of an old machine)	2,900
(b)	Rent	750
(c)	Electrical expenses (includes new wiring £600, part of premises improvement)	3,280
(d)	Carriage inwards (includes £150 carriage on new cement mixer)	1,260
(e)	Purchase of extra drilling machine	4,100

You are required to allocate each or part of the items above to either 'capital' or 'revenue' expenditure.

24.7 For the business of J. Charles, wholesale chemist, classify the following between 'capital' and 'revenue' expenditure:

(a) Purchase of an extra van.
(b) Cost of rebuilding warehouse wall which had fallen down.
(c) Building extension to the warehouse.
(d) Painting extension to warehouse when it is first built.
(e) Repainting extension to warehouse three years later than that done in (d).
(f) Carriage costs on bricks for new warehouse extension.
(g) Carriage costs on purchases.
(h) Carriage costs on sales.
(i) Legal costs of collecting debts.
(j) Legal charges on acquiring new premises for office.
(k) Fire insurance premium.
(l) Costs of erecting new machine.

24.8A For the business of H. Ward, a food merchant, classify the following between 'capital' and 'revenue' expenditure:

(a) Repairs to meat slicer.
(b) New tyre for van.
(c) Additional shop counter.
(d) Renewing signwriting on shop.
(e) Fitting partitions in shop.
(f) Roof repairs.
(g) Installing thief detection equipment.
(h) Wages of shop assistant.
(i) Carriage on returns outwards.
(j) New cash register.
(k) Repairs to office safe.
(l) Installing extra toilet.

24.9

(a) Distinguish between capital and revenue expenditure.

(b) Napa Ltd took delivery of a PC and printer on 1 July 2012, the beginning of its financial year. The list price of the equipment was £4,999 but Napa Ltd was able to negotiate a price of £4,000 with the supplier. However, the supplier charged an additional £340 to install and test the equipment. The supplier offered a 5% discount if Napa Ltd paid for the equipment and the additional installation costs within seven days. Napa Ltd was able to take advantage of this additional discount. The installation of special electrical wiring for the computer cost £110. After initial testing certain modifications costing £199 proved necessary. Staff were sent on special training courses to operate the PC and this cost £990. Napa Ltd insured the machine against fire and theft at a cost of £49 per annum. A maintenance agreement was entered into

→

with Sonoma plc. Under this agreement Sonoma plc promised to provide 24-hour breakdown cover for one year. The cost of the maintenance agreement was £350.

Required:
Calculate the acquisition cost of the PC to Napa Ltd.

(c) The following costs were also incurred by Napa Ltd during the financial year ended 30 June 2013:

   (1) Interest on loan to purchase PC.
   (2) Cost of software for use with the PC.
   (3) Cost of customising the software for use in Napa Ltd's business.
   (4) Cost of paper used by the computer printer.
   (5) Wages of computer operators.
   (6) Cost of ribbons used by the computer printer.
   (7) Cost of adding extra memory to the PC.
   (8) Cost of floppy disks used during the year.
   (9) Costs of adding a manufacturer's upgrade to the PC equipment.
   (10) Cost of adding air conditioning to the computer room.

Required:
Classify each of the above as capital expenditure or revenue expenditure.

(*Association of Accounting Technicians*)

24.10A Classify the following items as either revenue or capital expenditure:

(a) An extension to an office building costing £24,000.
(b) The cost of replacement valves on all the labelling machines in a canning factory.
(c) Repairs to the warehouse roof.
(d) Annual service costs for a courier firm's fleet of vans.
(e) Replacement of rubber tread on a printing press with a plastic one that has resulted in the useful economic life of the printing press being extended by three years.
(f) A new bicycle purchased by a newsagent for use by the newspaper delivery boy.
(g) Repairs to a refrigeration system of a meat wholesaler.
(h) Repainting of the interior of a bar/restaurant which has greatly improved the potential for finding a buyer for the bar/restaurant as a going concern.
(i) Wages paid to employees who worked on the construction of their company's new office building.

24.11 A Bloggs, a building contractor, had a wooden store shed and a brick-built office which have balances b/d in the books of £850 and £179,500 respectively. During the year, the wooden shed was pulled down at a cost of £265, and replaced by a brick building. Some of the timber from the old store shed was sold for £180 and the remainder, valued at £100, was used in making door frames, etc., for the new store. The new brick-built store was constructed by the builder's own employees, the expenditure thereon being materials (excluding timber from the old store shed) £4,750; wages £3,510; and direct expenses of £85.

At about the same time, certain repairs and alterations were carried out to the office, again using the builder's own materials, the cost of which was: wages £290 and materials £460. It was estimated that £218 of this expenditure, being mainly that incurred on providing additional windows, represented improvements, 50% of this being wages, 50% materials.

Required:
Prepare the following four ledger accounts as they would appear after giving effect to all the above matters:
(a) Wooden store shed account
(b) Office buildings account
(c) New store account
(d) Office buildings repairs account

24.12 At the beginning of the financial year on 1 April 2013, a company had a balance on plant account of £372,000 and on provision for depreciation of plant account of £205,400.

The company's policy is to provide depreciation using the reducing balance method applied to the non-current assets held at the end of the financial year at the rate of 20% per annum.

On 1 September 2013 the company sold for £13,700 some plant which it had acquired on 31 October 2009 at a cost of £36,000. Additionally, installation costs totalled £4,000. During 2011 major repairs costing £6,300 had been carried out on this plant and, in order to increase the capacity of the plant, a new motor had been fitted in December 2011 at a cost of £4,400. A further overhaul costing £2,700 had been carried out during 2012.

The company acquired new replacement plant on 30 November 2013 at a cost of £96,000, inclusive of installation charges of £7,000.

Required:
Calculate:
(a) the balance of plant at cost at 31 March 2014
(b) the provision for depreciation of plant at 31 March 2014
(c) the profit or loss on disposal of the plant.

(*Association of Chartered Certified Accountants*)

24.13A Sema plc, a company in the heavy engineering industry, carried out an expansion programme in the 2012 financial year, in order to meet a permanent increase in contracts.

The company selected a suitable site and commissioned a survey and valuation report, for which the fee was £1,500. On the basis of the report the site was acquired for £90,000.

Solicitors' fees for drawing up the contract and conveyancing were £3,000.

Fees of £8,700 were paid to the architects for preparing the building plans and overseeing the building work. This was carried out partly by the company's own workforce (at a wages cost of £11,600), using company building materials (cost £76,800), and partly by subcontractors who charged £69,400, of which £4,700 related to the demolition of an existing building on the same site.

The completed building housed two hydraulic presses.

The cost of press A was £97,000 (ex-works), payable in a single lump sum two months after installation. Sema was given a trade discount of 10% and a cash discount for prompt payment of 2%. Hire of a transporter to collect the press and to convey it to the new building was £2,900. Installation costs were £2,310, including hire of lifting gear, £1,400.

Press B would have cost £105,800 (delivered) if it had been paid in one lump sum. However, Sema opted to pay three equal annual instalments of £40,000, starting on the date of acquisition. Installation costs were £2,550, including hire of lifting gear, £1,750.

The whole of the above expenditure was financed by the issue of £500,000 7% Loan notes (on which the annual interest payable was £35,000).

Before the above acquisitions were taken into account, the balances (at cost) on the non-current asset accounts for premises and plant were £521,100 and £407,500 respectively.

Required:
(a) Using such of the above information as is relevant, post and balance the premises and plant accounts for the 2012 financial year.
(b) State, with reasons, which of the given information you have not used in your answer to (a) above.

(*Association of Chartered Certified Accountants*)

24.14 Why is the distinction between classifying something as capital expenditure and classifying it as revenue expenditure so important to the users of financial statements?

24.15A John Boggis saw a computer for sale in a local store for £1,499. This was much cheaper than he'd seen it for sale elsewhere. He needed five of these PCs and also needed the cabling to network them. Following negotiations with the retailer, he obtained the machines for a total of £7,000. However, the cost of the cabling was £300 and the supplier was going to charge £500 to install the network. If John paid the total amount due before installation, he would receive a discount of $2\frac{1}{2}$ per cent. He liked this idea and paid immediately.

Subsequently, he purchased three printers costing £125 each and software costing £350, together with CDs and other consumables costing a total of £250. The supplier gave a discount of £50 on the consumables due to the size of the order.

All of John's staff were sent on a customised training course organised by the retailer at a total cost of £500.

Required:

(a) Calculate the amount capitalised in the statement of financial position and also the amount to be charged to revenue accounts.

(b) 'Materiality' is a concept which sometimes has an effect on the capitalisation of amounts within a statement of financial position. Give examples of how this may be done.

MyAccountingLab

Need more practice? Instant feedback?
Visit **www.myaccountinglab.com**

Featuring unlimited practice questions, a personalised study plan that identifies the areas where you need to focus for better marks, and interactive material designed to help all kinds of learners, MyAccountingLab is a vital tool for maximising your understanding, confidence, and success. Log in at **www.myaccountinglab.com** to see why 92 per cent of students surveyed last year recommend MyAccountingLab.

Bad debts, allowances for doubtful debts, and provisions for discounts on accounts receivable

Learning objectives

After you have studied this chapter, you should be able to:

- explain and show how bad debts are written-off
- explain why allowances for doubtful debts are made
- make the necessary entries to record an allowance for doubtful debts in the books
- calculate and make provisions for discounts on accounts receivable
- make all the entries in the income statement and statement of financial position for bad debts, allowances for doubtful debts, and provisions for cash discount

Introduction

In this chapter, you'll learn how businesses deal with bad debts and how they provide for the possibility that other debts will not be paid. You'll learn how to record increases and decreases in the allowance for doubtful debts. Finally, you'll learn how to make and adjust provisions for cash discounts.

25.1 Bad debts

With many businesses a large proportion, if not all, of the sales are on credit. The business is therefore taking the risk that some of the customers may never pay for the goods sold to them on credit. This is a normal business risk and such **bad debts** are a normal business expense. They must be charged to the income statement as an expense when calculating the net profit or loss for the period. The other thing that needs to be done is to remove the bad debt from the asset account. Usually, this will mean closing the debtor's account.

When a debt is found to be 'bad', the asset as shown by the debt in the debtor's account is worthless. It must be eliminated from the account. If doing so reduces the balance to zero, the debtor's account is closed.

To record a bad debt, you credit the debtor's account to cancel the asset and increase the expense account by debiting it to the bad debts account.

Activity 25.1 What circumstances might lead you to write-off a debt as bad and *not* close the debtor's account?

There is a range of possible scenarios that may exist concerning a bad debt. The first two were discussed in the answer to Activity 25.1:

- the debtor may be refusing to pay one of a number of invoices;
- the debtor may be refusing to pay part of an invoice;
- the debtor may owe payment on a number of invoices and have indicated that only a proportion of the total amount due will ever be paid because the debtor's business has failed;
- the debtor's business has failed and nothing is ever likely to be received.

Whatever the reason, once a debt has been declared 'bad', the journal entry is the same. You debit the bad debt account with the amount of the bad debt and credit the debtor's account in the sales ledger to complete the double entry.

At the end of the period, the total of the bad debts account is transferred to the income statement. An example of debts being written off as bad is shown in Exhibit 25.1:

Exhibit 25.1

C. Bloom

2011			£	2011				£
Jan	8	Sales	520	Dec	31	Bad debts		520

R. Shaw

2011			£	2011				£
Feb	16	Sales	375	Aug	17	Cash		125
				Dec	31	Bad debts		250
			375					375

Bad Debts

2011			£	2011			£
Dec	31	C Bloom	520	Dec	31	Profit and loss	770
		R Shaw	250				
			770				770

Income Statement (extract) for the year ending 31 December 2011

	£
Gross profit	xxx
Less Expenses:	
Bad debts	(770)

25.2 ## Allowance for doubtful debts

Why allowances are needed

When we are drawing up our financial statements, we want to achieve the following objectives:

- to charge as an expense in the income statement for that year an amount representing debts that will never be paid;
- to show in the statement of financial position a figure for accounts receivable as close as possible to the true value of accounts receivable at the date of the statement of financial position.

Debts declared bad are usually debts that have existed for some time, perhaps even from previous accounting periods.

However, how about other debts that have not been paid by the year end? These may not have been owing for so long, in which case it will be more difficult to determine which of them will be bad debts. Nevertheless, as all businesses experience bad debts at some time, it is likely that at least some of these other debts will ultimately prove to be bad. The prudence concept – you learnt about this in Chapter 10 – says that this possibility needs to be provided for in the current period, otherwise both the accounts receivable balance reported in the statement of financial position and the profit reported in the income statement will almost certainly be overstated.

It is impossible to determine with absolute accuracy at the year end what the true amount is in respect of debtors who will never pay their accounts. So, how do you decide on the amount of a provision (i.e. an allowance) against the possibility of some of the remaining debts (after removing those which have been written off as bad) proving bad in a future period?

In order to arrive at a figure for doubtful debts, a business must first consider that some debtors will never pay any of the amount they owe, while others will pay a part of the amount owing only, leaving the remainder permanently unpaid. The estimated figure can be made:

(*a*) by looking at each debt, and deciding to what extent it will be bad;
(*b*) by estimating, on the basis of experience, what percentage of the total amount due from the remaining debtors will ultimately prove to be bad debts.

It is well known that the longer a debt is owing, the more likely it is that it will become a bad debt. Some businesses draw up an 'ageing schedule', showing how long debts have been owing. Older debtors need higher percentage estimates of bad debts than do newer debtors. The percentages chosen should reflect the actual pattern of bad debts experienced in the past. Exhibit 25.2 gives an example of an ageing schedule.

Exhibit 25.2

Ageing Schedule for Doubtful Debts			
Period debt owing	*Amount*	*Estimated percentage doubtful*	*Allowance for doubtful debts*
	£	%	£
Less than 1 month	5,000	1	50
1 month to 2 months	3,000	3	90
2 months to 3 months	800	4	32
3 months to 1 year	200	5	10
Over 1 year	160	20	32
	9,160		214

Most businesses don't go to this level of detail. Instead, they apply a percentage to the overall balance of accounts receivable (after deducting the bad debts). The percentage will be one the business has established over the years as being the most appropriate.

Now, let's look at how the allowance for doubtful debts is entered in the books.

Accounting entries for allowances for doubtful debts

The accounting entries needed for the **allowance for doubtful debts** are:

Year in which the allowance is *first* made:

1 Debit the profit and loss account with the amount of the allowance (i.e. deduct it from gross profit as an expense).
2 Credit the *Allowance for Doubtful Debts Account*.

Exhibit 25.3 shows the entries needed for the initial allowance for doubtful debts.

Exhibit 25.3

At 31 December 2011, the accounts receivable figure after deducting bad debts was £10,000. It is estimated that 2 per cent of debts (i.e. £200) will eventually prove to be bad debts, and it is decided to make a provision for these. The accounts will appear as follows:

Profit and Loss

2011		£	
Dec 31	Allowance for doubtful debts	200	

Allowance for Doubtful Debts

		2011		£
		Dec 31	Profit and loss	200

In the financial statements, the allowance is shown as follows:

Income Statement (extract) for the year ending 31 December 2011

	£
Gross profit	xxx
Less Expenses:	
Allowance for doubtful debts	(200)

Statement of Financial Position (extract) as at 31 December 2011

	£	£
Current assets		
Accounts receivable	10,000	
Less Allowance for doubtful debts	(200)	
		9,800

As shown, in the statement of financial position, the balance on the allowance for doubtful debts is deducted from the accounts receivable total.

You'll have noticed that we are using two different accounts to make the two different types of adjustments to accounts receivable. This is done in order to make it clear how much is (*a*) being written-off as bad debts, and how much is (*b*) being treated as an allowance for doubtful debts:

1 **Bad debts account:** This expense account is used when a debt is believed to be irrecoverable and is written-off.
2 **Allowance for doubtful debts account:** This account is used only for estimates of the amount of debt remaining at the year end *after the debts have been written off* that are likely to finish up as bad debts. (This account is also known as the 'allowance for *bad* debts account'.)

By charging both (1) and (2) in the income statement, we present the full picture of the amounts provided for in respect of both bad and doubtful debts. As you've already seen in Exhibits 25.1 and 25.3, these amounts are shown as deductions from the gross profit.

By showing (2) as a deduction from the figure of accounts receivable in the statement of financial position, we get a net figure, which represents a more accurate figure of the value of accounts receivable than the total of all the accounts receivable balances in the sales ledger. It may not be absolutely accurate – only time will tell which debts will turn out to be bad – but it is better than not attempting to make an estimate.

When you look at depreciation in Chapter 26, you will see that it bears similarities to the allowance for doubtful debts. Depreciation is charged as a debit to the profit and loss account and as a credit against non-current asset accounts in the ledger. It represents an estimate of how much of the overall economic usefulness of a non-current asset has been used up in each accounting period. Like the allowance for doubtful debts, it can never be completely accurate since only in several years' time, when the asset is put out of use, can it be determined whether or not the provisions made have been appropriate. Having to make estimates where absolute accuracy is impossible is a part of accounting.

> **Activity 25.2** Why do accountants have to make these allowances?

25.3 Increasing the allowance

Let us suppose that for the same business as in Exhibit 25.3, at the end of the following year, 31 December 2012, the allowance for doubtful debts needed to be increased. This was because the allowance was kept at 2 per cent, but the accounts receivable figure had risen to £12,000. An allowance of £200 had been brought forward from the *previous* year, but we now want a total allowance of £240 (i.e. 2 per cent of £12,000). All that is now needed is a provision for an extra £40. The double entry will be:

1 Debit Profit and Loss Account with the increase in the allowance (i.e. deduct it from gross profit as an expense).
2 Credit the Allowance for Doubtful Debts Account.

These entries are illustrated in Exhibit 25.4.

Exhibit 25.4

Profit and Loss

2012		£	
Dec 31	Allowance for doubtful debts	40	

Allowance for Doubtful Debts

2012			£	2012				£
Dec 31	Balance c/d		240	Jan	1	Balance b/d		200
			___	Dec	31	Profit and loss		40
			240					240
				2013				
				Jan	1	Balance b/d		240

Income Statement (extract) for the year ending 31 December 2012

	£
Gross profit	xxx
Less Expenses	
Allowance for doubtful debts (increase)	(40)

Statement of Financial Position (extract) as at 31 December 2012

Current assets	£	£
Accounts receivable	12,000	
Less Allowance for doubtful debts	(240)	
		11,760

Activity 25.3 Why do you only need to create an expense for the difference between the provisions of the two years?

25.4 **Reducing the allowance**

To reduce the allowance, you simply do the opposite to what you did to increase it. The allowance for doubtful debts has a credit balance. Therefore, to reduce it we would need a debit entry in the allowance account. The credit would be in the profit and loss account. Let's assume that at 31 December 2013, the figure for accounts receivable had fallen to £10,500 but the allowance remained at 2 per cent, i.e. £210 (2 per cent of £10,500).

As the allowance had previously been £240, it now needs to be reduced by £30. The double entry is:

1 Debit Allowance for Doubtful Debts Account.
2 Credit Profit and Loss Account (i.e. add it as a gain to gross profit).

These entries are illustrated in Exhibit 25.5.

Exhibit 25.5

Allowance for Doubtful Debts

2013			£	2013				£
Dec	31	Profit and loss	30	Jan	1	Balance b/d		240
	31	Balance c/d	210					
			240					240
				2014				
				Jan	1	Balance b/d		210

Profit and Loss

			2013			£
			Dec	31	Allowance for doubtful debts	30

Income Statement (extract) for the year ending 31 December 2013

	£
Gross profit	xxx
Add Reduction in allowance for doubtful debts	30

Statement of Financial Position (extract) as at 31 December 2013

Current assets	£	£
Accounts receivable	10,500	
Less Allowance for doubtful debts	(210)	
		10,290

You will have noticed that increases in the allowance for doubtful debts increases the total for expenses and so reduce net profit. On the other hand, a reduction in the allowance for doubtful debts will increase the gross profit.

Activity 25.4 Without looking back in your textbook, write down the double entries for (a) an increase and (b) a decrease in the allowance for doubtful debts.

Let us now look at a comprehensive example in Exhibit 25.6:

Exhibit 25.6

A business starts on 1 January 2005 and its financial year end is 31 December annually. A table of the accounts receivable, the bad debts written off and the estimated bad debts at the rate of 2 per cent of accounts receivable at the end of each year is now given. The double entry accounts and the extracts from the financial statements follow.

Year to 31 December	Bad debts written off during year	Accounts receivable at end of year (after bad debts written off)	Debts thought at end of year to be impossible to collect: 2% of accounts receivable
	£	£	£
2010	423	6,000	120 (2% of £6,000)
2011	510	7,000	140 (2% of £7,000)
2012	604	7,750	155 (2% of £7,750)
2013	610	6,500	130 (2% of £6,500)

Bad Debts

2010			£	2010			£
Dec	31	Various accounts receivable	423	Dec	31	Profit and loss	423
2011				2011			
Dec	31	Various accounts receivable	510	Dec	31	Profit and loss	510
2012				2012			
Dec	31	Various accounts receivable	604	Dec	31	Profit and loss	604
2013				2013			
Dec	31	Various accounts receivable	610	Dec	31	Profit and loss	610

Allowance for Doubtful Debts

2010			£	2010			£
Dec	31	Balance c/d	120	Dec	31	Profit and loss	120
2011				2011			
Dec	31	Balance c/d	140	Jan	1	Balance b/d	120
				Dec	31	Profit and loss	20
			140				140
2012				2012			
Dec	31	Balance c/d	155	Jan	1	Balance b/d	140
				Dec	31	Profit and loss	15
			155				155
2013				2013			
Dec	31	Profit and loss	25	Jan	1	Balance b/d	155
		Balance c/d	130				
			155				155
				2014			
				Jan	1	Balance b/d	130

→

→

Income Statements (extracts) for the years ending 31 December		
	£	£
Gross profit for 2010, 2011, 2012, 2013		xxx
2010 *Less* Expenses:		
Bad debts	423	
Allowance for doubtful debts (increase)	120	
		(543)
2011 *Less* Expenses:		
Bad debts	510	
Allowance for doubtful debts (increase)	20	
		(530)
2012 *Less* Expenses:		
Bad debts	604	
Allowance for doubtful debts (increase)	15	
		(619)
2013 *Add* Reduction in allowance for doubtful debts	25	
Less Expenses:		
Bad debts	(610)	
		(585)

Statements of Financial Position (extracts) as at 31 December		
	£	£
2010 Accounts receivable	6,000	
Less Allowance for doubtful debts	(120)	
		5,880
2011 Accounts receivable	7,000	
Less Allowance for doubtful debts	(140)	
		6,860
2012 Accounts receivable	7,750	
Less Allowance for doubtful debts	(155)	
		7,595
2013 Accounts receivable	6,500	
Less Allowance for doubtful debts	(130)	
		6,370

25.5 Bad debts recovered

Sometimes, a debt written-off in previous years is recovered. When this happens, you:

1 Reinstate the debt by making the following entries:

> *Dr* Debtor's account
>   *Cr* Bad debts recovered account

2 When payment is received from the debtor in settlement of all or part of the debt:

> *Dr* Cash/bank
>   *Cr* Debtor's account

with the amount received.

At the end of the financial year, the credit balance in the bad debts recovered account is transferred either to the bad debts account or direct to the credit side of the profit and loss account. The effect is the same, since the bad debts account will, in itself, be transferred to the profit and loss account at the end of the financial year.

 Activity 25.5 Why do you think we reinstate the debt just to cancel it out again? Why don't we simply debit the bank account and credit the bad debts recovered account?

25.6 Provisions for cash discounts on accounts receivable

Some businesses create provisions for cash discounts to be allowed on the accounts receivable outstanding at the date of the statement of financial position. This, they maintain, is quite legitimate, as the amount of accounts receivable less any allowance for doubtful debts is not the best estimate of collectable debts, owing to cash discounts which will be given to debtors if they pay within a given time. The cost of discounts, it is argued, should be charged in the period when the sales were made. While this practice is of dubious merit (as cash discount is treated as a finance charge, not as an adjustment to sales revenue), it is one used in practice by some businesses.

The procedure for dealing with this is similar to the allowance for doubtful debts. It must be borne in mind that the estimate of discounts to be allowed should be based on the net figure of accounts receivable less the allowance for doubtful debts, as it is obvious that cash discounts are not allowed on bad debts! Let's look at an example in Exhibit 25.7:

Exhibit 25.7

Year ended 31 December	Accounts receivable	Allowance for doubtful debts	Provision for cash discounts allowed
	£	£	%
2010	4,000	200	2
2011	5,000	350	2
2012	4,750	250	2

Provision for Cash Discounts on Accounts Receivable

			£				£
2010				2010			
Dec	31	Balance c/d	76	Dec	31	Profit and loss	76
2011				2011			
Dec	31	Balance c/d	93	Jan	1	Balance b/d	76
			—	Dec	31	Profit and loss	17
			93				93
2012				2012			
Dec	31	Profit and loss	3	Jan	1	Balance b/d	93
		Balance c/d	90				
			93				—
							93
				2013			
				Jan	1	Balance b/d	90

→

→

Income Statements (extracts) for the years ending 31 December

	£
Gross profits (2010, 2011 and 2012)	xxx
Less Expenses:	
(2010) Provision for cash discounts on accounts receivable	(76)
(2011) Increase in provision for cash discounts on accounts receivable	(17)
Add (2012) Reduction in provision for cash discounts on accounts receivable	3

Statements of Financial Position (extracts) as at 31 December

		£	£	£
2010	Accounts receivable		4,000	
	Less Allowance for doubtful debts	200		
	Provision for cash discounts on accounts receivable	76		
			(276)	
				3,724
2011	Accounts receivable		5,000	
	Less Allowance for doubtful debts	350		
	Provision for cash discounts on accounts receivable	93		
			(443)	
				4,557
2012	Accounts receivable		4,750	
	Less Allowance for doubtful debts	250		
	Provision for cash discounts on accounts receivable	90		
			(340)	
				4,410

Activity 25.6

Which one of the following would result from a decrease in the allowance for doubtful debts?

(a) An increase in gross profit
(b) A reduction in gross profit
(c) An increase in net profit
(d) A reduction in net profit

25.7 Finally

As with distinguishing between capital expenditure and revenue expenditure, students generally find this topic very difficult to grasp. It seems to be too difficult for some students to remember the difference between the treatment of bad debts and the treatment of allowances for doubtful debts. They also often struggle to make the correct adjustments when the allowance changes, with the most common error being that they charge all the allowance, instead of only the change, to profit and loss.

There is no shortcut to getting this right. You need to keep the difference between bad debts and allowances for doubtful debts very clearly in your mind. Learning them as two separate topics seems to help. So far as the treatment of the change in the allowance is concerned, don't try calling it 'change in the allowance for doubtful debts', you'll only get confused when you make the entry in the statement of financial position. And there is where the difficulty lies. *In the statement of financial position, the entire allowance is deducted from the figure for accounts receivable but, in the income statement, you only include the change.* Try to memorise this last sentence. It may make all the difference.

Learning outcomes

You should now have learnt:

1 That debts we are unable to collect are called bad debts.

2 That bad debts are credited to the customer's account (to cancel them) and debited to a bad debts account.

3 That allowances for doubtful debts are needed, otherwise the value of the accounts receivable in the statement of financial position will show too high a value, and could mislead anyone looking at the statement of financial position. Also, making a provision of this type allows for more accurate calculation of profits and losses.

4 That the allowance for doubtful debts is calculated *after* bad debts have been deducted from the debtor balances.

5 That the amount of the allowance for doubtful debts is based on the best estimate that can be made taking all the facts into account.

6 That an increase in the allowance for doubtful debts will create a debit entry in the profit and loss account.

7 That a reduction in the allowance for doubtful debts will create a credit entry in the profit and loss account.

8 That the allowance for doubtful debts is shown as a deduction from accounts receivable in the statement of financial position.

9 That provisions for cash discount are made in the same way as provisions for doubtful debts.

10 How to record bad debts, allowances for doubtful debts, and provisions for cash discounts in the accounting books and in the income statement and statement of financial position.

Answers to activities

25.1 Sometimes a debtor will contest an invoice and refuse to pay it while continuing to pay all other invoices. This may happen, for example, when the debtor claims that the goods were delivered damaged and you have refused to issue a credit note because you believe the goods were delivered intact. Another example occurs when the debtor is refusing to pay part of an invoice. This may happen, for example, when the customer claims not to have received all the items on the invoice. In both those circumstances, many businesses will eventually write off the debt on the disputed invoice and continue to trade with the customer.

25.2 The prudence concept which you learnt about in Chapter 10 requires it.

25.3 During the year, some debts will have been written off as bad. They will include debts from the previous year which last year's allowance for doubtful debts was intended to cover. If last year's estimate was correct, you could add this year's bad debts to the change in the allowance and the total would be the same as the total allowance you want to make this year, not just the difference between the two years' provisions. So, in effect, you've converted last year's allowance into this year's bad debts. All you need do now is adjust the balance on the allowance for doubtful debts account to make it equal to the provision you want to make against this year's closing accounts receivable balance.

25.4 (a) *Dr* Profit and loss account   *Cr* Allowance for doubtful debts account
(b) *Dr* Allowance for doubtful debts account   *Cr* Profit and loss account

Note how they are the opposite of each other.

25.5   The reason for reinstating the debt in the ledger account of the debtor is to have a detailed history of the debtor's account as a guide for granting credit in future. When a debt is written-off as bad, it is recorded in the debtor's ledger account. Therefore, when a bad debt is recovered, it should also be shown in the debtor's ledger account, so as to provide the full picture.

25.6   (c)   An increase in net profit.

Review questions

25.1   In a new business during the year ended 31 December 2013 the following debts are found to be bad, and are written-off on the dates shown:

31 May	S. Gill & Son	£600
30 September	H. Black Ltd	£400
30 November	A. Thom	£200

On 31 December 2013 the schedule of remaining accounts receivable totalling £15,000 is examined and it is decided to make an allowance for doubtful debts of £500.

You are required to show:
(a)   The Bad Debts Account, and the Allowance for Doubtful Debts Account.
(b)   The charge to the Income Statement.
(c)   The relevant extracts from the Statement of Financial Position as at 31 December 2013.

25.2   A business had always made an allowance for doubtful debts at the rate of 2 per cent of accounts receivable. On 1 January 2011 the amount for this, brought forward from the previous year, was £300.
    During the year to 31 December 2011 the bad debts written-off amounted to £700.
    On 31 December 2011 the accounts receivable balance was £17,000 and the usual allowance for doubtful debts is to be made.

You are to show:
(a)   The Bad Debts Account for the year ended 31 December 2011.
(b)   The Allowance for Doubtful Debts Account for the year.
(c)   Extract from the Income Statement for the year.
(d)   The relevant extract from the Statement of Financial Position as at 31 December 2011.

25.3   A business started trading on 1 January 2010. During the two years ended 31 December 2010 and 2011 the following debts were written off to the Bad Debts Account on the dates stated:

31 May 2010	F. Lamb	£200
31 October 2010	A. Clover	£300
31 January 2011	D. Ray	£100
30 June 2011	P. Clark	£400
31 October 2011	J. Will	£ 50

On 31 December 2010 the total accounts receivable was £55,000. It was decided to make an allowance for doubtful debts of £800.
    On 31 December 2011 the total accounts receivable was £59,000. It was decided to make an allowance for doubtful debts of £900.

You are required to show:
(i)   The Bad Debts Account and the Allowance for Doubtful Debts Account for each of the two years.
(ii)   The relevant extracts from the Statements of Financial Position as at 31 December 2010 and 2011.

25.4A   A business, which started trading on 1 January 2010, adjusted its allowance for doubtful debt at the end of each year on a percentage basis, but each year the percentage rate is adjusted in accordance with the current 'economic climate'. The following details are available for the three years ended 31 December 2010, 2011 and 2012.

	Bad debts written off year to 31 December	Accounts receivable at 31 December after bad debts written-off	Percentage allowance for doubtful debts
	£	£	
2010	1,240	41,000	4
2011	2,608	76,000	6
2012	5,424	88,000	5

You are required to show:
(a)   Bad Debts Accounts for each of the three years.
(b)   Allowance for Doubtful Debts Accounts for each of the three years.
(c)   Statement of Financial Position extracts as at 31 December 2010, 2011 and 2012.

25.5   A business which prepares its financial statements annually to 31 December suffered bad debts which were written-off:

2010   £420
2011   £310
2012   £580

The business had a balance of £400 on the Allowance for Doubtful Debts Account on 1 January 2010.
   At the end of each year, the business considered which of its debtors appeared doubtful and carried forward an allowance of:

2010   £500
2011   £600
2012   £400

Show each of the entries in the income statements and prepare the Allowance for Doubtful Debts Account for each of the three years.

25.6A

(a)   Businesses often create an allowance for doubtful debts.

   (i)   Of which concept (or convention) is this an example? Explain your answer.
   (ii)   What is the purpose of creating an allowance for doubtful debts?
   (iii) How might the amount of an allowance for doubtful debts be calculated?

(b)   On 1 January 2011 there was a balance of £500 in the an Allowance for Doubtful Debts Account, and it was decided to maintain the provision at 5% of the accounts receivable at each year end. The debtors on 31 December each year were:

	£
2011	12,000
2012	8,000
2013	8,000

Show the necessary entries for the **three** years ended 31 December 2011 to 31 December 2013 inclusive in the following:

   (i)   the Allowance for Doubtful Debts Account;
   (ii)   the Income Statements.

(c)   What is the difference between bad debts and allowance for doubtful debts?
(d)   On 1 January 2013 Warren Mair owed Jason Dalgleish £130. On 25 August 2013 Mair was declared bankrupt. A payment of 30p in the £ was received in full settlement. The remaining balance was written off as a bad debt. Write up the account of Warren Mair in Jason Dalgleish's ledger.

(Northern Examinations and Assessment Board: GCSE)

25.7 The statement of financial position as at 31 May 2010 of Forest Traders Limited included an allowance for doubtful debts of £2,300. The company's accounts for the year ended 31 May 2011 are now being prepared. The company's policy now is to relate the allowance for doubtful debts to the age of debts outstanding. The debts outstanding at 31 May 2011 and the required allowances for doubtful debts are as follows:

Debts outstanding	Amount	Allowance for doubtful debts
	£	%
Up to 1 month	24,000	1
More than 1 month and up to 2 months	10,000	2
More than 2 months and up to 3 months	8,000	4
More than 3 months	3,000	5

Customers are allowed a cash discount of $2\frac{1}{2}$% for settlement of debts within one month. It is now proposed to make a provision for discounts to be allowed in the company's accounts for the year ended 31 May 2011.

Required:
Prepare the following accounts for the year ended 31 May 2011 in the books of Forest Traders Limited to record the above transactions:

(a) Allowance for doubtful debts;
(b) Provision for discounts to be allowed on debtors.

(*Association of Accounting Technicians*)

25.8A A business makes an allowance for doubtful debts of 3% of accounts receivable, also a provision of 1% for discount on accounts receivable.

On 1 January 2011 the balances brought forward on the relevant accounts were allowance for doubtful debts £930 and provision for discounts on accounts receivable £301.

(a) Enter the balances in the appropriate accounts, using a separate Allowance for Doubtful Debts Account.

During 2011 the business incurred bad debts of £1,110 and allowed discounts of £362. On 31 December 2011 accounts receivable amounted to £42,800.

(b) Show the entries in the appropriate accounts for the year 2011, assuming that the business's accounting year ends on 31 December 2011, also income statement extracts at 31 December 2011.

25.9 J. Blane commenced business on 1 January 2009 and prepares her financial statements to 31 December every year. For the year ended 31 December 2009, bad debts written off amounted to £1,400. It was also found necessary to create an allowance for doubtful debts of £2,600.

In 2010, debts amounting to £2,200 proved bad and were written-off. J. Sweeny, whose debt of £210 was written off as bad in 2009, settled her account in full on 30 November 2010. As at 31 December 2010 total debts outstanding were £92,000. It was decided to bring the provision up to 4% of this figure on that date.

In 2011, £3,800 of debts were written-off during the year, and another recovery of £320 was made in respect of debts written-off in 2009. As at 31 December 2011, total debts outstanding were £72,000. The allowance for doubtful debts is to be changed to 5% of this figure.

You are required to show for the years 2009, 2010 and 2011, the
(a) Bad Debts Account.
(b) Bad Debts Recovered Account.
(c) Allowance for Doubtful Debts Account.
(d) Extract from the Income Statement.

25.10
(A) Explain why a provision may be made for doubtful debts.
(B) Explain the procedure to be followed when a customer whose debt has been written-off as bad subsequently pays the amount originally owing.
(C) On 1 January 2010 D. Watson had debtors of £25,000 on which he had made an allowance for doubtful debts of 3%.

During 2010,
(*i*) A. Stewart, who owed D. Watson £1,200, was declared bankrupt and a settlement of 25p in the £ was made, the balance being treated as a bad debt.
(*ii*) Other bad debts written-off during the year amounted to £2,300.

On 31 December 2010 total accounts receivable amounted to £24,300 but this requires to be adjusted as follows:

(*a*) J. Smith, a debtor owing £600, was known to be unable to pay and this amount was to be written off.
(*b*) A cheque for £200 from S. McIntosh was returned from the bank unpaid.

D. Watson maintained his allowance for doubtful debts at 3% of accounts receivable.

Required:
(1) For the financial year ended 31 December 2010, show the entries in the following accounts:
  (*i*) Allowance for doubtful debts
  (*ii*) Bad debts
(2) What is the effect on net profit of the change in the allowance for doubtful debts?

(*Scottish Qualifications Authority*)

25.11A D. Faculti started in business buying and selling law textbooks, on 1 January 2012. At the end of each of the next three years, his figures for accounts receivable, before writing-off any bad debts, were as follows:

    31 December 2012   £30,000
    31 December 2013   £38,100
    31 December 2014   £4,750

Bad debts to be written-off are as follows:

    31 December 2012   £2,100
    31 December 2013   £750

The allowance for doubtful debts in each year is 5 per cent of accounts receivable.

Required:
(*a*) Prepare Faculti's bad debts expense account and allowance for doubtful debts account for 2012, 2013 and 2014.
(*b*) The amounts due from B. Roke (£70) and H. A. Ditt (£42) became irrecoverable in 2012 and were written-off. Show the entries in the ledger accounts to record these write-offs.

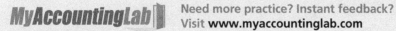

Adjustments for Financial Statements 2

Depreciation of non-current assets: nature and calculations

26.1 Nature of non-current assets

Before going any further, you need to be sure that you know what a non-current asset is.

Activity 26.1 Write down the three characteristics that distinguish non-current assets from current assets.

If you don't or didn't know how to define non-current assets, be sure that you do before going on to look at the topic of depreciation.

26.2 Depreciation of tangible non-current assets

Tangible non-current assets (i.e. long-term assets which can be touched, such as machinery, motor vehicles, fixtures and even buildings) do not last for ever. If the amount received (if any) on the disposal of a non-current asset is deducted from the cost of buying it, the value of the non-current asset can be said to have 'depreciated in value' by that amount over its period of usefulness to the business. For example, if a van was bought for £10,000 and sold five years later for £2,000 then its value has depreciated over the period of its use by £8,000.

This is the only time that depreciation can be calculated accurately. That is, you can only *estimate* what it should be each year while the non-current asset continues to be used.

26.3 Depreciation is an expense

Depreciation is that part of the original cost of a non-current asset that is consumed during its period of use by the business. It needs to be charged to the profit and loss account every year. The amount charged in a year for depreciation is based upon an estimate of how much of the overall economic usefulness of non-current assets has been used up in that accounting period. It is an expense for services consumed in the same way as expenses are incurred for items such as wages, rent or electricity. Because it is charged as an expense to the profit and loss account, depreciation reduces net profit.

For example, if a PC cost £1,200 and was expected to be used for three years, it might be estimated at the end of the first year that a third of its overall usefulness had been consumed. Depreciation would then be charged at an amount equal to one-third of the cost of the PC, i.e. £400. Profit would be reduced by £400 and the value of the PC in the statement of financial position would be reduced from £1,200 to £800.

Using an example of a van and the petrol it consumes, you can see that the only real difference between the expense of depreciation for the van and the expense of petrol incurred in order to use the van is that the petrol expense is used up in a short time, whereas the expense for use of the van is spread over several years. Both the petrol and the cost of the van are expenses of the business.

Activity 26.2 If depreciation reduces profits and reduces the value of assets and so reduces the capital account of the owner, why do businesses bother providing for depreciation?

26.4 Causes of depreciation

Physical deterioration, economic factors, time and depletion all give rise to a reduction in the value of a tangible non-current asset. Let's look at these in more detail.

Physical deterioration

1 **Wear and tear.** When a motor vehicle or machinery or fixtures and fittings are used they eventually wear out. Some last many years, others last only a few years. This is also true of buildings, although some may last for a long time.
2 **Erosion, rust, rot and decay.** Land may be eroded or wasted away by the action of wind, rain, sun and other elements of nature. Similarly, the metals in motor vehicles or machinery will rust away. Wood will rot eventually. Decay is a process which will also be present due to the elements of nature and the lack of proper attention.

Economic factors

These may be said to be the reasons for an asset being put out of use even though it is in good physical condition. The two main factors are usually **obsolescence** and **inadequacy**.

1 **Obsolescence.** This is the process of becoming out of date. For instance, over the years there has been great progress in the development of synthesisers and electronic devices used by leading commercial musicians. The old equipment will therefore have become obsolete, and much of it will have been taken out of use by such musicians.

   This does not mean that the equipment is worn out. Other people may well buy the old equipment and use it, possibly because they cannot afford to buy new up-to-date equipment.

2 **Inadequacy**. This arises when an asset is no longer used because of the growth and changes in the size of the business. For instance, a small ferryboat that is operated by a business at a coastal resort will become entirely inadequate when the resort becomes more popular. Then it will be found that it would be more efficient and economical to operate a large ferryboat, and so the smaller boat will be put out of use by the business.

In this case also it does not mean that the ferryboat is no longer in good working order, nor that it is obsolete. It may be sold to a business at a smaller resort.

Time

Obviously, time is needed for wear and tear, erosion, etc., and for obsolescence and inadequacy to take place. However, there are non-current assets to which the time factor is connected in a different way. These are assets which have a legal life fixed in terms of years.

For instance, you may agree to rent some buildings for 10 years. This is normally called a lease. When the years have passed, the lease is worth nothing to you, as it has finished. Whatever you paid for the lease is now of no value.

A similar case arises when you buy a patent so that only you are able to produce something. When the patent's time has finished it then has no value. The usual length of life of a patent is sixteen years.

Instead of using the term depreciation, the term **amortisation** is often used for these assets.

Depletion

Other assets are of wasting character, perhaps due to the extraction of raw materials from them. These materials are then either used by the business to make something else, or are sold in their raw state to other businesses. Natural resources such as mines, quarries and oil wells come under this heading. To provide for the consumption of an asset of a wasting character is called provision for **depletion**.

26.5 Land and buildings

Prior to the issue in 1977 of a UK accounting standard (SSAP 12) which focused on this topic, freehold and long leasehold properties were very rarely subject to a charge for depreciation. It was contended that, as property values tended to rise rather than fall, it was inappropriate to charge depreciation.

The accounting standard changed all that by requiring that depreciation be written off over the property's useful life, with the exception that freehold land does not normally require a provision for depreciation. This is because land normally has an unlimited useful life. Buildings do, however, eventually fall into disrepair or become obsolete and must be subject to a charge for depreciation each year.

When FRS 15 replaced SSAP 12 in 1999, it repeated these requirements. It also dealt with the problem of the distinction between the cost of freehold land and the cost of the buildings upon it, by insisting that the two elements of the cost be separated.

IASs 16 (*Property, plant and equipment*), 23 (*Borrowing costs*) and 36 (*Impairment of assets*) are the relevant international standards and they have the same requirements on these issues as FRS 15.

26.6 Appreciation

At this stage, you may be wondering what happens when non-current assets increase (appreciate) in value. The answer is that normal accounting procedure would be to ignore any such appreciation, as to bring appreciation into account would be to contravene both the historical cost concept and the prudence concept you learnt about in Chapter 10.

> Go back to Chapter 10 to refresh your understanding of the historical cost concept and the prudence concept.

However, one of the problems when SSAP 12 was introduced was that the UK was in the middle of a boom in property prices which had been going on for some time and didn't really end until the early 1990s. Businesses could see that the market value of their properties was rising. At the same time, they were being instructed (by the accounting standard) to charge their profit and loss account with depreciation that represented a fall in the value of the property over the period. Not surprisingly, this didn't seem to make any sense. To address this, IAS 16 allows non-current assets to be revalued at fair value (which is determined from market-based evidence) for land and buildings or market value (= open market value, i.e. the amount for which it could currently be sold) for plant and equipment. Depreciation is then calculated on the basis of the new value.

26.7 Provision for depreciation as an allocation of cost

Depreciation in total over the life of a non-current asset can be calculated quite simply as cost less the amount receivable when the non-current asset is put out of use by the business. This amount receivable is normally referred to as the **residual value** (or 'scrap value') of an asset. IAS 16 states that residual value should be based on prices current at the date of the statement of financial position, not at the date of original purchase. If the item is bought and sold for a lower amount within the same accounting period, then the difference in value is charged as depreciation in arriving at that period's net profit.

The difficulties start when the asset is used for more than one accounting period: an attempt has to be made to charge each period with an appropriate amount of depreciation.

Although depreciation provisions are intended to allocate the cost of a non-current asset to each accounting period in which it is in use, it does not follow that there is any truly accurate method of performing this task. All that can be said is that the cost should be allocated over the life of the non-current asset in such a way as to charge it as equitably as possible to the periods in which it is used. The difficulties involved are considerable and include:

1 Apart from a few assets, such as leases, how accurately can a business assess an asset's useful life? Even a lease may be put out of use if the leased asset has become inadequate or inappropriate (e.g. after a change in the product being sold or unexpected growth in the size of the business).

2 How is 'use' measured? A car owned by a business for two years may have been driven one year by a very careful driver and another year by a reckless driver. The standard of driving will affect the condition of the car and also the amount of cash receivable on its disposal. How should a business apportion the car's depreciation costs?

3 There are other expenses besides depreciation, such as repairs and maintenance of the non-current asset. As both of these affect the rate and amount of depreciation, should they not also affect the depreciation provision calculations?

4 How can a business possibly know the amount receivable in x years' time when an asset is put out of use?

These are only some of the difficulties. Accounting has developed some methods that can be used to calculate depreciation. However, you will see that none of them really manages to address all these issues. Nevertheless, just as with doubtful debts, making some allowance for depreciation is better than making none at all.

26.8   Non-current assets held for sale

When non-current assets are reclassified as being held for sale, they must not be depreciated.

26.9   Methods of calculating depreciation charges

The two main methods in use are the **straight line method** and the **reducing balance method**. Other methods may be used in certain cases, and some are discussed briefly in Section 26.12. Most accountants think that the straight line method is the one that is generally most suitable.

Straight line method

In this method, the number of years of use is estimated. The cost is then divided by the number of years. This gives the depreciation charge for each year.

For instance, if a van was bought for £22,000 and we thought we would keep it for four years and then sell it for £2,000 the depreciation to be charged each year would be:

$$\frac{\text{Cost (£22,000)} - \text{Estimated disposal value (£2,000)}}{\text{Number of expected years of use (4)}} = \frac{£20,000}{4}$$

= £5,000 depreciation each year for four years.

On the other hand, if we thought that after four years the van would have no disposal value, the charge for depreciation would be:

$$\frac{\text{Cost (£22,000)}}{\text{Number of expected years of use (4)}} = \frac{£22,000}{4}$$

= £5,500 depreciation each year for four years.

Reducing balance method

In this method, a fixed percentage for depreciation is deducted from the cost in the first year. In the second and later years the same percentage is taken of the reduced balance (i.e. cost *less* depreciation already charged). This method is also known as the *diminishing balance method* or the *diminishing debit balance method*.

If a machine is bought for £10,000 and depreciation is to be charged at 20 per cent, the calculations for the first three years would be as follows:

	£
Cost	10,000
First year: depreciation (20%)	(2,000)
	8,000
Second year: depreciation (20% of £8,000)	(1,600)
	6,400
Third year: depreciation (20% of £6,400)	(1,280)
Cost not yet apportioned, end of Year 3	5,120

The basic formula used to find the percentage to apply with this method is:

$$r = 1 - \sqrt[n]{\frac{s}{c}}$$

where n = the number of years

   s = the net residual value (this must be a significant amount or the answers will be absurd, since the depreciation rate would amount to nearly one)

   c = the cost of the asset

   r = the rate of depreciation to be applied.

Using as an example the figures

   n = 4 years
   s = residual value £256
   c = cost £10,000

the calculations would appear as:

$$r = 1 - \sqrt[4]{\frac{256}{£10,000}} = 1 - \frac{4}{10} = 0.6 \text{ or } 60 \text{ per cent}$$

The depreciation calculation applied to each of the four years of use would be:

	£
Cost	10,000
Year 1: Depreciation provision 60% of £10,000	(6,000)
Cost not yet apportioned, end of Year 1	4,000
Year 2: Depreciation provision 60% of £4,000	(2,400)
Cost not yet apportioned, end of Year 2	1,600
Year 3: Depreciation provision 60% of £1,600	(960)
Cost not yet apportioned, end of Year 3	640
Year 4: Depreciation provision 60% of £640	(384)
Cost not yet apportioned, end of Year 4	256

In this case, the percentage to be applied worked out conveniently to an easy to calculate figure of 60 per cent. However, the answer will often come out to several decimal places, e.g. 59.846512. When it does, normal practice is to take the nearest whole figure as a percentage to be applied. However, nowadays, this calculation is usually performed using a spreadsheet. Doing so means you don't need to worry any more about the difficulties of performing calculations using numbers with lots of decimal places. You simply build the formula into the calculation and don't need to worry about how many decimal places the depreciation rate may have. The spreadsheet will then produce the depreciation amount for each year.

Activity 26.3   What do you think you do when the *amount* of depreciation to be charged in a period is not a whole number?

   The depreciation rate percentage to be applied under this method, assuming a significant amount for residual value, is usually between two and three times greater than under the straight line method.

   The advocates of the reducing balance method usually argue that it helps to even out the total amount charged as expenses for the use of the asset each year. Provisions for depreciation are not the only costs charged. There are also the running costs. The repairs and maintenance element of running costs usually increases with age. Therefore, in order to equate total usage costs for each year of use, the depreciation provisions should fall over time, while the repairs and maintenance element increases. However, as can be seen from the figures in the example already given, the repairs and maintenance element would have to be comparatively large after the first year to bring about an equal total charge for each year of use.

To summarise, the people who favour this method say that:

In the early years A higher charge for depreciation + A lower charge for repairs and upkeep	will tend to be close to the sum of	In the later years A lower charge for depreciation + A higher charge for repairs and upkeep

26.10 Choice of method

The purpose of depreciation is to spread the total cost of a non-current asset over the periods in which it is to be used. The method chosen should be that which allocates cost to each period in accordance with the proportion of the overall economic benefit from using the non-current asset that was expended during that period.

If, therefore, the main value is to be obtained from the asset in its earliest years, it may be appropriate to use the reducing balance method, which charges more in the early years. If, on the other hand, the benefits are to be gained evenly over the years, then the straight line method would be more appropriate.

The repairs and maintenance factor also has to be taken into account. One argument supporting this was mentioned in the last section.

Exhibit 26.1 gives a comparison of the calculations using the two methods.

Exhibit 26.1

A business has just bought a machine for £8,000. It will be kept in use for four years, when it will be disposed of for an estimated amount of £500. The accountant has asked you to prepare a comparison of the amounts charged as depreciation using both methods.

For the straight line method, a figure of (£8,000 − £500) ÷ 4 = £7,500 ÷ 4 = £1,875 per annum is to be used. For the reducing balance method, a percentage figure of 50 per cent will be used.

	Method 1 Straight Line £		Method 2 Reducing Balance £
Cost	8,000		8,000
Depreciation: year 1	(1,875)	(50% of £8,000)	(4,000)
	6,125		4,000
Depreciation: year 2	(1,875)	(50% of £4,000)	(2,000)
	4,250		2,000
Depreciation: year 3	(1,875)	(50% of £2,000)	(1,000)
	2,375		1,000
Depreciation: year 4	(1,875)	(50% of £1,000)	(500)
Disposal value	500		500

This example illustrates the fact that using the reducing balance method has a much higher charge for depreciation in the early years, and lower charges in the later years.

26.11 Depreciation provisions and assets bought or sold

There are two main methods of calculating depreciation provisions for assets bought or sold during an accounting period.

1 Ignore the dates during the accounting period that the assets were bought or sold, and simply calculate a full period's depreciation on the assets in use at the end of the period. Thus, assets sold during the accounting period will have had no provision for depreciation made for that last period irrespective of how many months they were in use. Conversely, assets bought during the period will have a full period of depreciation provision calculated even though they may not have been owned throughout the whole of the period.

2 Provide for depreciation on the basis of 'one month's ownership = one month's provision for depreciation'. Fractions of months are usually ignored. This is obviously a more precise method than Method 1.

The first method is the one normally used in practice. However, for examination purposes, where the dates on which assets are bought and sold are shown, you should use Method 2. If no such dates are given then, obviously, Method 1 is the one to use, but you should indicate that you are assuming this is the method to be adopted.

26.12 Other methods of calculating depreciation

There are many more methods of calculating depreciation, some of which are used in particular industries, such as the hotel and catering industry. We'll now look briefly at five of these other methods so that you are aware of how and why they may be used.

There is no information easily available to show how many organisations are using each method. It is possible to devise one's own special method. If it brings about an equitable charge for depreciation for the organisation, then the method will be suitable.

The revaluation method

When there are a few expensive non-current assets, it is not difficult to draw up the necessary accounts for depreciation. For each item we:

(*a*) Find its cost.
(*b*) Estimate its years of use to the business.
(*c*) Calculate and provide depreciation.
(*d*) Make the adjustments when the asset is disposed of.
(*e*) Calculate profit or loss on disposal.

This is worth doing for expensive items. There are, however, many examples of non-current assets for which the calculation would not be worth doing and, in fact, may be impossible. Some businesses will have many low-cost non-current assets. Garages or engineering works will have a lot of spanners, screwdrivers and other small tools; brewers will have crates; laboratories will have many small, low-cost glass instruments.

It would be impossible to follow procedures (*a*) to (*e*) above for every screwdriver or crate. Instead the revaluation method is used.

The method is not difficult to use. An example is shown in Exhibit 26.2:

Exhibit 26.2

A business has a lot of steel containers. These are not sold but are used by the business.

	£
On 1 January 2009 the containers were valued at	3,500
During the year to 31 December containers were purchased costing	1,300
On 31 December 2009 the containers were valued at	3,800

The depreciation is calculated:

	£
Value at start of period	3,500
Add Cost of items bought during period	1,300
	4,800
Less Value at close of period	(3,800)
Depreciation for year to 31 December 2009	1,000

The depreciation figure of £1,000 will be charged as an expense. Using this approach, we can look at Exhibit 26.3, where depreciation is entered in the books for the first three years of a new business.

Exhibit 26.3

The business starts in business on 1 January 2009.

	£
In its first year it buys crates costing	800
Their estimated value at 31 December 2009	540
Crates bought in the year ended 31 December 2010	320
Estimated value of all crates in hand on 31 December 2010	530
Crates bought in the year ended 31 December 2011	590
Estimated value of all crates in hand on 31 December 2011	700

Crates

2009			£	2009			£
Dec 31	Cash (during the year)		800	Dec 31	Profit and loss		260
			___	31	Inventory c/d		540
			800				800
2010				2010			
Jan 1	Inventory b/d		540	Dec 31	Profit and loss		330
Dec 31	Cash (during the year)		320	31	Inventory c/d		530
			860				860
2011				2011			
Jan 1	Inventory b/d		530	Dec 31	Profit and loss		420
Dec 31	Cash (during the year)		590	31	Inventory c/d		700
			1,120				1,120
2012							
Jan 1	Inventory b/d		700				

Profit and Loss for the year ended 31 December

		£	
2009			
Dec 31	Use of crates	260	
2010			
Dec 31	Use of crates	330	
2011			
Dec 31	Use of crates	420	

The balance of the crates account at the end of each year is shown as a non-current asset in the statement of financial position.

Sometimes the business may make its own items such as tools or crates. In these instances the tools account or crates account should be debited with labour costs and material costs.

Revaluation is also used, for instance, by farmers for their cattle. As with other non-current assets depreciation should be provided for, but during the early life of an animal it will be appreciating in value, only to depreciate later. The task of calculating the cost of an animal becomes virtually impossible if it has been born on the farm, and reared on the farm by grazing on the pasture land and being fed on other foodstuffs, some grown on the farm and others bought by the farmer.

To get over this problem the revaluation method is used. Because of the difficulty of calculating the cost of the animals, they are valued at the price which they would fetch if sold at market. This is an exception to the general rule of assets being shown at cost price.

Depletion unit method

With non-current assets such as a quarry from which raw materials are dug out to be sold to the building industry, a different method is needed: the depletion unit method.

If a quarry was bought for £5,000 and it was expected to contain 1,000 tonnes of saleable materials, then for each tonne taken out we would depreciate it by £5, since £5,000 ÷ 1,000 = £5.

This can be shown as:

$$\frac{\text{Cost of asset}}{\text{Expected total contents in units}} \times \text{Number of units taken in period}$$

$$= \text{Depreciation for that period.}$$

Machine hour method

With a machine the depreciation provision may be based on the number of hours that the machine was operated during the period compared with the total expected running hours during the machine's life with the business. A business which bought a machine costing £2,000 having an expected running life of 1,000 hours, and no scrap value, could provide for depreciation of the machine at the rate of £2 for every hour it was operated during a particular accounting period.

Sum of the years' digits method

This method is popular in the USA but not common in the UK. It provides for higher depreciation to be charged early in the life of an asset with lower depreciation in later years.

Given an asset costing £3,000 which will be in use for five years, the calculations will be:

From purchase the asset will last for	5 years
From the second year the asset will last for	4 years
From the third year the asset will last for	3 years
From the fourth year the asset will last for	2 years
From the fifth year the asset will last for	1 year
Sum of these digits	15

	£
1st year 5/15 of £3,000 is charged =	1,000
2nd year 4/15 of £3,000 is charged =	800
3rd year 3/15 of £3,000 is charged =	600
4th year 2/15 of £3,000 is charged =	400
5th year 1/15 of £3,000 is charged =	200
	3,000

Units of output method

This method establishes the total expected units of output expected from the asset. Depreciation, based on cost less salvage value, is then calculated for the period by taking that period's units of output as a proportion of the total expected output over the life of the asset.

An instance of this could be a machine which is expected to be able to produce 10,000 widgets over its useful life. It has cost £6,000 and has an expected salvage value of £1,000. In year 1 a total of 1,500 widgets are produced, and in year 2 the production is 2,500 widgets.

The depreciation per period is calculated:

$$(\text{Cost} - \text{salvage value}) \times \left(\frac{\text{period's production}}{\text{total expected production}} \right)$$

Year 1: $£5,000 \times \dfrac{1,500}{10,000} = £750$ depreciation

Year 2: $£5,000 \times \dfrac{2,500}{10,000} = £1,250$ depreciation

Learning outcomes

You should now have learnt:

1 That depreciation is an expense of the business and has to be charged against any period during which a non-current asset has been in use.

2 That the main causes of depreciation are: physical deterioration, economic factors, the time factor and depletion.

3 How to calculate depreciation using the straight line method.

4 How to calculate depreciation using the reducing balance method.

5 How to calculate depreciation on assets bought or sold within an accounting period.

6 That there are other methods of calculating depreciation in addition to the straight line and reducing balance methods.

Answers to activities

26.1 Non-current assets are those assets of material value which are:

- of long life; and
- to be used in the business; and
- not bought with the main purpose of resale.

26.2 Firstly, financial statements must show a true and fair view of the financial performance and position of the business. If depreciation was not provided for, both non-current assets and profits would be stated in the financial statements at inflated amounts. This would only mislead the users of those financial statements and so depreciation must be charged. Secondly, IAS 16 requires that non-current assets are depreciated.

26.3 Just as with the depreciation percentage, you round it to the nearest whole number.

Review questions

26.1 A. Gill purchased a notebook PC for £1,200. It has an estimated life of four years and a scrap value of £100.

She is not certain whether she should use the straight line or the reducing balance basis for the purpose of calculating depreciation on the computer.

You are required to calculate the depreciation (to the nearest £) using both methods, showing clearly the balance remaining in the computer account at the end of each of the four years under each method. (Assume that 45 per cent per annum is to be used for the reducing balance method.)

26.2 A machine costs £8,000. It will be kept for five years, and then sold for an estimated figure of £2,400. Show the calculations of the figures for depreciation (to nearest £) for each of the five years using (a) the straight line method, (b) the reducing balance method, for this method using a depreciation rate of 20 per cent.

26.3 A car costs £12,000. It will be kept for three years, and then sold for £3,000. Calculate the depreciation for each year using (a) the reducing balance method, using a depreciation rate of 35 per cent, (b) the straight line method.

26.4A A photocopier costs £23,000. It will be kept for four years, and then traded in for £4,000. Show the calculations of the figures for depreciation for each year using (a) the straight line method, (b) the reducing balance method, for this method using a depreciation rate of 35 per cent.

26.5A A printer costs £800. It will be kept for five years and then scrapped. Show your calculations of the amount of depreciation each year if (a) the reducing balance method at a rate of 60 per cent was used, (b) the straight line method was used.

26.6A A bus is bought for £56,000. It will be used for four years, and then sold back to the supplier for £18,000. Show the depreciation calculations for each year using (a) the reducing balance method with a rate of 25 per cent, (b) the straight line method.

26.7 A company, which makes up its financial statements annually to 31 December, provides for depreciation of its machinery at the rate of 15 per cent per annum using the reducing balance method.

On 31 December 2011, the machinery consisted of three items purchased as shown:

	£
On 1 January 2009 Machine A	Cost 2,000
On 1 September 2010 Machine B	Cost 4,000
On 1 May 2011 Machine C	Cost 3,000

Required:
Your calculations showing the depreciation provision for the year 2011.

26.8 A motor vehicle which cost £12,000 was bought on credit from Trucks Ltd on 1 January 2009. Financial statements are prepared annually to 31 December and depreciation of vehicles is provided at 25 per cent per annum under the reducing balance method.

Required:
Prepare the motor vehicle account and the accumulated provision for depreciation on motor vehicles account for the first two years of the motor vehicle's working life.

26.9 Ivor Innes has supplied you with the following information:

	1 April 2010	31 March 2011
	£	£
Cash	840	700
Fixtures	7,600	7,600
Balance at bank	5,500	8,320
Inventory	17,800	19,000
Accounts receivable	8,360	4,640
Accounts payable	5,200	8,800

During the year to 31 March 2011, Ivor withdrew £11,400 from the business for private purposes. In November 2010, Ivor received a legacy of £18,000 which he paid into the business bank account.

Ivor agrees that £600 should be provided for depreciation of fixtures and £200 for doubtful debts.

Required:
Prepare a statement of financial position as at 31 March 2011 which clearly indicates the net profit or loss for the year.

26.10A On 10 August 2009 Joblot, a computer software retailer, bought a non-current asset which cost £100,000. It had an anticipated life of four years and an estimated residual value of £20,000. Due to unforeseen events in the computer industry, the asset was suddenly sold on 10 March 2012 for £45,000.

The policy of the company is to provide depreciation in full in the year of purchase and none in the year of sale.

Required:
(a) Calculate the charge for depreciation for each of the years using both the straight line method and the reducing balance method, showing clearly the net book values as at the end of each of the years.
(b) Calculate the profit or loss on the disposal of the asset under both of the above methods.
(c) Explain why assets are depreciated and provide an example where it would be more appropriate to use the straight line method and another example where it would be more appropriate to use the reducing balance method.
(d) Explain what the figures for net book value that are shown in the statement of financial position represent.

26.11A Black and Blue Ltd depreciates its forklift trucks using a reducing balance rate of 30 per cent. Its accounting year end is 30 September. On 30 September 2013, it owned four forklift trucks:

(A) Purchased on 1 January 2010 for £2,400
(B) Purchased on 1 May 2011 for £2,500
(C) Purchased on 1 October 2011 for £3,200
(D) Purchased on 1 April 2013 for £3,600

Required:
Calculate the depreciation provision for the year ending 30 September 2013.

26.12 State which depreciation method will be the most appropriate in the case of each of the following assets and why. Also, indicate to what extent obsolescence will affect each of the assets.

(a) A delivery van used by a baker.
(b) A filing cabinet.
(c) A shop held on a 20-year lease.
(d) A plastic moulding machine to manufacture a new novelty – plastic fireguards. It is expected that these will be very popular next Christmas and that sales will continue for a year or two thereafter but at a very much lower level.
(e) Machine X. This machine is used as a standby when the normal machines are being maintained. Occasionally it is used to increase capacity when there is a glut of orders. Machine X is of an old type and is inefficient compared with new machines. When used on a full-time basis, the machine should last for approximately four years.

Double entry records for depreciation

Learning objectives

After you have studied this chapter, you should be able to:

- incorporate depreciation calculations into the accounting records
- record the entries relating to disposal of non-current assets
- make depreciation entries using either a one-stage or a two-stage approach to recording depreciation

Introduction

Now that you know what depreciation is and how it may be calculated, in this chapter you'll learn how to make the appropriate entries for depreciation in the accounting books. You'll also learn how to make the appropriate period-end entries in the financial statements.

27.1 Recording depreciation

Previously, the charge for depreciation on a non-current asset was recorded in the account for that fixed asset. This is no longer done.

Activity 27.1 Why do you think this is no longer done?

Recording depreciation now involves maintaining each non-current asset at its cost in the ledger account while operating another ledger account where the depreciation to date is recorded. This account is known as the 'accumulated provision for depreciation account', often shortened to the **accumulated depreciation account** (or sometimes, confusingly, known as the 'provision for depreciation account').

Activity 27.2 Why do you think it would be confusing to call the accumulated provision for depreciation account the 'provision for depreciation account'?

Let's look at how this is done by first looking at the double entry required and then looking at how it is used in an example, shown in Exhibit 27.1.

The depreciation is posted directly into the cumulative provision for depreciation account. The double entry is:

Debit the profit and loss account
Credit the accumulated provision for depreciation account

Exhibit 27.1

A business has a financial year end of 31 December. A computer is bought for £2,000 on 1 January 2008. It is to be depreciated at the rate of 20 per cent using the reducing balance method. The records for the first three years are:

Computer

2008			£	
Jan	1	Cash	2,000	

Accumulated Provision for Depreciation: Computer

2008			£	2008			£
Dec	31	Balance c/d	400	Dec	31	Profit and loss	400
2009				2009			
Dec	31	Balance c/d	720	Jan	1	Balance b/d	400
				Dec	31	Profit and loss	320
			720				720
2010				2010			
Dec	31	Balance c/d	976	Jan	1	Balance b/d	720
				Dec	31	Profit and loss	256
			976				976
				2011			
				Jan	1	Balance b/d	976

Profit and Loss

2008			£	
Dec	31	Acc Provn for Depn: Computer	400	
2009				
Dec	31	Acc Provn for Depn: Computer	320	
2010				
Dec	31	Acc Provn for Depn: Computer	256	

Income Statement (extracts) for the years ending 31 December

		£
2008	Depreciation	400
2009	Depreciation	320
2010	Depreciation	256

Note: In this case, the depreciation for the period being entered in the income statement is being described as 'depreciation' and *not* by the name of the account it originated from (the accumulated provision for depreciation account).

Activity 27.3   What advantages are there in making this exception to the rule by using 'depreciation' rather than 'accumulated provision for depreciation' in the entry in the income statement?

Now the balance on the Computer Account is shown on the statement of financial position at the end of each year less the balance on the Accumulated Provision for Depreciation Account.

Statements of Financial Position (extracts)

	£	£
As at 31 December 2008		
Computer at cost	2,000	
Less Accumulated depreciation	(400)	
		1,600
As at 31 December 2009		
Computer at cost	2,000	
Less Accumulated depreciation	(720)	
		1,280
As at 31 December 2010		
Computer at cost	2,000	
Less Accumulated depreciation	(976)	
		1,024

27.2 The disposal of a non-current asset

Reason for accounting entries

Upon the sale of a non-current asset, we will want to remove it from our ledger accounts. This means that the cost of that asset needs to be taken out of the asset account. In addition, the accumulated depreciation on the asset which has been sold will have to be taken out of the accumulated provision. Finally, the profit and loss on sale, if any, will have to be calculated and posted to the profit and loss account.

When we charge depreciation on a non-current asset we are having to make an informed guess. We will not often guess correctly. This means that, when we dispose of an asset, the amount received for it is usually different from our estimate.

Activity 27.4 List as many things as you can think of in one minute that could cause the amount charged for depreciation to have been incorrect.

Accounting entries needed

On the sale of a non-current asset, in this example a computer, the following entries are needed:

(A) Transfer the cost price of the asset sold to an assets disposal account (in this case a computer disposals account):

> Debit computer disposals account
>   Credit computer account

(B) Transfer the depreciation already charged to the assets disposal account:

> Debit accumulated provision for depreciation: computer
>   Credit computer disposals account

(C) For the amount received on disposal:

> Debit cash book
>   Credit computer disposals account

(D) Transfer the difference (i.e. the amount needed to balance the computer disposals account) to the profit and loss account.

(i) If the computer disposals account shows a difference on the debit side (i.e. if more has been credited to the account than has been debited to it), there is a profit on the sale:

   Debit computer disposals account
      Credit profit and loss account

(ii) If the computer disposals account shows a difference on the credit side, there is a loss on sale:

   Debit profit and loss account
      Credit computer disposals account

These entries can be illustrated by looking at those needed if the computer in Exhibit 27.1 was sold on 2 January 2011. At 31 December 2010, the cost was £2,000 and a total of £976 had been written off as depreciation leaving a net book value of £2,000 – £976 = £1,024. If the computer is sold in 2011 for *more* than £1,024 a profit on sale will be made. If, on the other hand, the computer is sold for *less* than £1,024 then a loss will be incurred.

Exhibit 27.2 shows the entries needed when the computer has been sold for £1,070 and a profit of £46 on sale has, therefore, been made. Exhibit 27.3 shows the entries where the computer has been sold for £950, thus incurring a loss on sale of £74. In both cases, the sale is on 2 January 2011 and no depreciation is to be charged for the two days' ownership in 2011. (The letters in brackets refer to the accounting double entries, A–D, above.)

Exhibit 27.2 Non-current asset sold at a profit

Computer

2008			£	2011				£
Jan	1	Cash	2,000	Jan	2	Computer disposals	(A)	2,000

Accumulated Provision for Depreciation: Computer

2011				£	2011			£
Jan	2	Computer disposals	(B)	976	Jan	1	Balance b/d	976

Computer Disposals

2011				£	2011				£
Jan	2	Computer	(A)	2,000	Jan	2	Accumulated provision		
Dec	31	Profit and loss	(D)	46			for depreciation	(B)	976
						2	Cash	(C)	1,070
				2,046					2,046

Profit and Loss

				2011			£
				Dec	31	Computer disposals (gain) (D)	46

Income Statement (extract) for the year ending 31 December 2011

	£
Gross profit	xxx
Add Gain on sale of computer	46

Exhibit 27.3 Non-current asset sold at a loss

Computer

2008				£	2011				£
Jan	1	Cash		2,000	Jan	2	Computer disposals	(A)	2,000

Accumulated Provision for Depreciation: Computer

2011				£	2011			£
Jan	2	Computer disposals	(B)	976	Jan	1	Balance b/d	976

Computer Disposals

2011				£	2011				£
Jan	2	Computer	(A)	2,000	Jan	2	Accumulated provision for depreciation	(B)	976
						2	Cash	(C)	950
					Dec	31	Profit and loss	(D)	74
				2,000					2,000

Profit and Loss

2011				£	
Dec	31	Computer disposal (loss)	(D)	74	

Income Statement (extract) for the year ending 31 December 2011

	£
Gross profit	xxx
Less Loss on sale of computer	(74)

In many cases, the disposal of an asset will mean that we have sold it. This will not always be the case. For example, a car may be given up in part payment for a new car. Here the disposal value is the exchange value. If a new car costing £10,000 was to be paid for with £6,000 in cash and an allowance of £4,000 for the old car, then the disposal value of the old car is £4,000.

Similarly, a car may have been in an accident and now be worthless. If a payment is received from an insurance company, the amount of that payment will be the disposal value. If an asset is scrapped, the disposal value is that received from the sale of the scrap, which may be nil.

27.3 Change of depreciation method

It is possible to make a change in the method of calculating depreciation. This should not be done frequently, and it should only be undertaken after a thorough review. Where a change is made, if material (see Chapter 10 on materiality), the effect of the change on the figures reported should be shown as a note to the financial statements in the year of change.

Further examples

So far, the examples have deliberately been kept simple. Only one non-current asset has been shown in each case. Exhibits 27.4 and 27.5 give examples of more complicated cases.

Exhibit 27.4

A machine is bought on 1 January 2008 for £1,000 and another one on 1 October 2009 for £1,200. The first machine is sold on 30 June 2010 for £720. The business's financial year ends on 31 December. The machinery is to be depreciated at 10 per cent, using the straight line method. Machinery in existence at the end of each year is to be depreciated for a full year. No depreciation is to be charged on any machinery disposed of during the year.

Machinery

2008			£	2008			£
Jan	1	Cash	1,000	Dec	31	Balance c/d	1,000
2009				2009			
Jan	1	Balance b/d	1,000	Dec	31	Balance c/d	2,200
Oct	1	Cash	1,200				
			2,200				2,200
2010				2010			
Jan	1	Balance b/d	2,200	Jun	30	Machinery disposals	1,000
				Dec	31	Balance c/d	1,200
			2,200				2,200
2011							
Jan	1	Balance b/d	1,200				

Accumulated Provision for Depreciation: Machinery

2008			£	2008			£
Dec	31	Balance c/d	100	Dec	31	Profit and loss	100
2009				2009			
Dec	31	Balance c/d	320	Jan	1	Balance b/d	100
				Dec	31	Profit and loss	220
			320				320
2010				2010			
Jun	30	Disposals of machinery		Jan	1	Balance b/d	320
		(2 years × 10% × £1,000)	200	Dec	31	Profit and loss	120
Dec	31	Balance c/d	240				
			440				440
				2011			
				Jan	1	Balance b/d	240

Machinery Disposals

2010			£	2010			£
Jun	30	Machinery	1,000	Jun	30	Cash	720
					30	Accumulated provision for depreciation	200
				Dec	31	Profit and loss	80
			1,000				1,000

Profit and Loss (extracts)

2008			£	
Dec	31	Acc Provn for Depn: Machinery	100	
2009				
Dec	31	Acc Provn for Depn: Machinery	220	
2010				
Dec	31	Acc Provn for Depn: Machinery	120	
	31	Machinery disposals (loss)	80	

Income Statement (extracts) for the years ending 31 December

		£
Gross profit		xxx
	Less Expenses:	
2008	Provision for depreciation: Machinery	(100)
2009	Provision for depreciation: Machinery	(220)
2010	Provision for depreciation: Machinery	(120)
	Loss on machinery sold	(80)

Statement of Financial Position (extracts) as at 31 December

		£	£
2008	Machinery at cost	1,000	
	Less Accumulated depreciation	(100)	
			900
2009	Machinery at cost	2,200	
	Less Accumulated depreciation	(320)	
			1,880
2010	Machinery at cost	1,200	
	Less Accumulated depreciation	(240)	
			960

Another example can now be given. This is somewhat more complicated. Firstly, it involves a greater number of items. Secondly, the depreciation provisions are calculated on a proportionate basis, i.e. one month's depreciation for one month's ownership.

Exhibit 27.5

A business with its financial year end on 31 December buys two vans on 1 January 2004, No. 1 for £8,000 and No. 2 for £5,000. It also buys another van, No. 3, on 1 July 2006 for £9,000 and another, No. 4, on 1 October 2006 for £7,200. The first two vans are sold, No. 1 for £2,290 on 30 September 2007, and No. 2 for scrap for £50 on 30 June 2008.

Depreciation is on the straight line basis, 20 per cent per annum, ignoring scrap value in this particular case when calculating depreciation per annum. Shown below are extracts from the assets account, provision for depreciation account, disposal account, profit and loss account, and income statements for the years ending 31 December 2004, 2005, 2006, 2007 and 2008, and the statements of financial position as at those dates.

Vans

2004			£	2004			£
Jan	1	Cash	13,000	Dec	31	Balance c/d	13,000
2005				2005			
Jan	1	Balance b/d	13,000	Dec	31	Balance c/d	13,000
2006				2006			
Jan	1	Balance b/d	13,000	Dec	31	Balance c/d	29,200
July	1	Cash	9,000				
Oct	1	Cash	7,200				
			29,200				29,200
2007				2007			
Jan	1	Balance b/d	29,200	Sept	30	Disposals	8,000
				Dec	31	Balance c/d	21,200
			29,200				29,200
2008				2008			
Jan	1	Balance b/d	21,200	June	30	Disposals	5,000
				Dec	31	Balance c/d	16,200
			21,200				21,200
2009							
Jan	1	Balance b/d	16,200				

Accumulated Provision for Depreciation: Vans

2004			£	2004			£
Dec	31	Balance c/d	2,600	Dec	31	Profit and loss	2,600
2005				2005			
Dec	31	Balance c/d	5,200	Jan	1	Balance b/d	2,600
				Dec	31	Profit and loss	2,600
			5,200				5,200
2006				2006			
Dec	31	Balance c/d	9,060	Jan	1	Balance b/d	5,200
				Dec	31	Profit and loss	3,860
			9,060				9,060
2007				2007			
Sept	30	Disposals	6,000	Jan	1	Balance b/d	9,060
Dec	31	Balance c/d	8,500	Dec	31	Profit and loss	5,440
			14,500				14,500
2008				2008			
June	30	Disposals	4,500	Jan	1	Balance b/d	8,500
Dec	31	Balance c/d	7,740	Dec	31	Profit and loss	3,740
			12,240				12,240
				2009			
				Jan	1	Balance b/d	7,740

Workings – depreciation provisions		£	£
2004	20% of £13,000		2,600
2005	20% of £13,000		2,600
2006	20% of £13,000 × 12 months	2,600	
	20% of £9,000 × 6 months	900	
	20% of £7,200 × 3 months	360	
			3,860
2007	20% of £21,200 × 12 months	4,240	
	20% of £8,000 × 9 months	1,200	
			5,440
2008	20% of £16,200 × 12 months	3,240	
	20% of £5,000 × 6 months	500	
			3,740

Workings – transfers of depreciation provisions to disposal accounts

Van 1   Bought Jan 1 2004 Cost £8,000
Sold Sept 30 2007
Period of ownership $3^3/4$ years
Depreciation provisions $3^3/4 \times 20\% \times £8,000 = £6,000$

Van 2   Bought Jan 1 2004 Cost £5,000
Sold June 30 2008
Period of ownership $4^1/2$ years
Depreciation provisions $4^1/2 \times 20\% \times £5,000 = £4,500$

Disposals of Vans

2007			£	2007			£
Sept	30	Van	8,000	Sept	30	Accumulated provision	
Dec	31	Profit and loss	290			for depreciation	6,000
						Cash	2,290
			8,290				8,290
2008				2008			
Jun	30	Van	5,000	Jun	30	Accumulated provision	
						for depreciation	4,500
						Cash	50
				Dec	31	Profit and loss	450
			5,000				5,000

Profit and Loss (extracts)

2004		£				£
Dec 31	Acc Provn for Depn: Vans	2,600				
2005						
Dec 31	Acc Provn for Depn: Vans	2,600				
2006						
Dec 31	Acc Provn for Depn: Vans	3,860				
2007			2007			
Dec 31	Acc Provn for Depn: Vans	5,440	Dec 31	Disposal of Vans (Gain)		290
2008						
Dec 31	Acc Provn for Depn: Vans	3,740				
	Disposal of Vans (loss)	450				

Income Statement (extracts) for the years ending 31 December

		£	£
Gross profit (each year 2004, 2005, 2006)			xxx
	Less Expenses:		
2004	Provision for depreciation: vans		(2,600)
2005	Provision for depreciation: vans		(2,600)
2006	Provision for depreciation: vans		(3,860)
2007	Gross profit		x,xxx
	Add Profit on van sold		290
			x,xxx
	Less Expenses:		
	Provision for depreciation: vans		(5,440)
			x,xxx
2008	Gross profit		x,xxx
	Less Expenses:		
	Provision for depreciation: vans	3,740	
	Loss on van sold	450	
			(4,190)

Statements of Financial Position (extracts) as at 31 December

		£	£
2004	Vans at cost	13,000	
	Less Accumulated depreciation	(2,600)	
			10,400
2005	Vans at cost	13,000	
	Less Accumulated depreciation	(5,200)	
			7,800
2006	Vans at cost	29,200	
	Less Accumulated depreciation	(9,060)	
			20,140
2007	Vans at cost	21,200	
	Less Accumulated depreciation	(8,500)	
			12,700
2008	Vans at cost	16,200	
	Less Accumulated depreciation	(7,740)	
			8,460

27.4 Depreciation provisions and the replacement of assets

Making a provision for depreciation does not mean that money is invested somewhere to finance the replacement of the asset when it is put out of use. It is simply a bookkeeping entry, and the end result is that lower net profits are shown because the provisions have been charged to profit and loss.

It is not surprising to find that many people – especially students – who have not studied accounting misunderstand the situation. They often think that a provision is the same as money kept somewhere with which to replace the asset eventually. Never make that mistake. It may cost you a lot of marks in an exam!

A cautious owner may take out less drawings if the net profit is lower, but that is no justification for arguing that depreciation results in funds being available to replace the asset later!

27.5 Another approach

In this chapter, you've learnt how to perform the double entries necessary to record the periodic charge for depreciation. The approach you learnt about is known as the 'one-stage approach'. It was based upon the use of one double entry, a credit to the accumulated provision for depreciation account and a debit to the profit and loss account.

There is another approach which is widely used in practice. It involves using a '**provision for depreciation account**', often shortened to '**depreciation account**', as well as the 'accumulated provision for depreciation account'. At the end of the period, you calculate the depreciation for the period and make the following double entries:

1 **Debit the depreciation account**
   Credit the accumulated provision for depreciation account
2 Debit the profit and loss account
   Credit the depreciation account

Compare this two-stage approach to the one-stage approach you learnt earlier:

> Debit the profit and loss account
> Credit the accumulated provision for depreciation account

Note how the double entry you learnt earlier combines the two entries used in the two-stage approach by cancelling out the debit and credit to the depreciation account. This makes it much simpler to record the entries required, but adopting the two-stage approach has the advantage that it actually shows what has happened rather than compressing the two double entries that theory says should be used into one.

However, some accountants still prefer to keep recording the entries as simple as possible and so use only the 'accumulated provision for depreciation account' (i.e. the 'one-stage approach').

Nevertheless, you need to be aware of and able to use the two-stage approach described above, just in case you should be asked to do so by an examiner. If you are *not* asked for two accounts (a depreciation account *plus* an accumulated provision for depreciation account) you should assume that the one-stage approach is the one you are expected to use.

Note: As in Review Questions 27.7A, 27.8 and 27.9A, examiners sometimes ask for a 'depreciation' account to be shown in an answer and they do not mention an 'accumulated provision for depreciation' account. When this happens, it is usually the 'accumulated provision for depreciation' account they are looking for. That is, they expect the balance on it to be carried forward to the next period, as in the case of the one-stage method. It is the one-stage method they want you to use but they have given the account the 'wrong' name. Use the name they used ('depreciation') but treat it as if it were an 'accumulated provision for depreciation' account. When examiners want you to prepare both a 'depreciation' account and an 'accumulated provision for depreciation' account, it will be obvious from the wording of the question.

27.6   Finally

This chapter has covered all the principles involved. Obviously examiners can present their questions in their own way. In fact, in order to better test your understanding, examiners do tend to vary the way questions involving depreciation are presented. Practise all the questions in this book, including those in the exhibits, and compare them with the answers shown in full. Doing so will demonstrate the truth of this statement and prepare you better for your examination when you can be virtually guaranteed that you will need to be able to calculate and make appropriate entries for depreciation.

Learning outcomes

You should now have learnt:

1 That the method of showing depreciation in the asset account is now used only by some small organisations, and should be avoided.

2 That non-current asset accounts should show only the cost. Depreciation is credited to an accumulated provision for depreciation account.

3 That when we sell a non-current asset, we must transfer both the cost and the accumulated depreciation to a separate disposal account.

4 That it is very rare for the depreciation provided to have been accurate.

5 That a profit on the disposal of a non-current asset is transferred to the credit of the profit and loss account.

6 That a loss on the disposal of a non-current asset is transferred to the debit of the profit and loss account.

7 That there are two approaches which may be adopted when entering depreciation into the accounting books.

8 That the approach you have learnt does so in one double entry and uses one ledger account for the accumulated provision for depreciation.

9 That the other, 'two-stage', approach uses two journal entries and two ledger accounts, one for the depreciation expense and the other to record the accumulated provision for depreciation.

10 That there are a number of alternatives for the names of the depreciation accounts involved under these two approaches.

11 That the name 'provision for depreciation' is often used in place of 'accumulated provision for depreciation' in the statement of financial position account that shows the depreciation accumulated to date.

Answers to activities

27.1   It has the effect of reducing the balance shown in the ledger for the non-current asset so that, over time, it may be very much less than the original cost. This makes it difficult to identify the original cost of non-current assets and means that, in the statement of financial position, the only information that can be given is the value to which each non-current asset has been written down. Anyone looking at this information will have no way of assessing whether a non-current asset was originally very expensive (which may be relevant, for example, if it is a building) and so cannot arrive at a realistic view of what the non-current assets really comprise. Nor, especially in the case of smaller businesses, is it immediately obvious how long a non-current asset is likely to continue to be used or, in fact, whether there is actually an asset in current use – if the value has been written down to zero, it wouldn't have a balance, may have been written out of the ledger, and certainly wouldn't be included in the statement of financial position.

27.2 Use of the term 'provision for depreciation account' can be very confusing as the name of the account used to record provisions for doubtful debts is the 'allowance for doubtful debts account' and, as you know, that account is closed off at the end of the accounting period and the balance transferred to the debit side of the profit and loss account. In contrast, the balance on the 'accumulated provision for depreciation account' is shown in the statement of financial position at the year end and carried forward to the next accounting period. The two treatments could hardly be more different. It is, therefore, asking for mistakes to be made if you use the same stem, 'provision for . . .', for them both. It must be said, however, that many people do, including some examiners. So, you need to be aware that when you see an account called the 'provision for depreciation account', it is referring to the account we shall call in this book the 'accumulated provision for depreciation account'. To help you get used to this, some of the multiple choice questions and review questions at the end of this chapter use the term 'provision for depreciation account'.

27.3 Doing so makes it clear that just one period's depreciation is involved and *not* the entire accumulated depreciation to date.

27.4 We cannot be absolutely certain how long we will keep the asset in use, nor can we be certain how much the asset will be sold for when we dispose of it, or even that it will be possible to sell it at that time. We may also have chosen the wrong depreciation method causing the net book value of the asset (i.e. cost less accumulated depreciation) to have been reduced too quickly (reducing balance) or too slowly (straight line) in the event that it is disposed of earlier than expected.

Multiple choice questions: Set 3

Now attempt Set 3 of multiple choice questions. (Answers to all the multiple choice questions are given in Appendix 2 at the end of this book.)

Each of these multiple choice questions has four suggested answers, (A), (B), (C) and (D). You should read each question and then decide which choice is best, either (A) or (B) or (C) or (D). *Write down your answers on a separate piece of paper.* You will then be able to redo the set of questions later without having to try to ignore your answers.

MC41 A cash discount is best described as a reduction in the sum to be paid

(A) If payment is made within a previously agreed period
(B) If payment is made by cash, not cheque
(C) If payment is made either by cash or cheque
(D) If purchases are made for cash, not on credit

MC42 Discounts received are

(A) Deducted when we receive cash
(B) Given by us when we sell goods on credit
(C) Deducted by us when we pay our accounts
(D) None of these

MC43 The total of the 'Discounts Allowed' column in the Cash Book is posted to

(A) The debit of the Discounts Allowed account
(B) The debit of the Discounts Received account
(C) The credit of the Discounts Allowed account
(D) The credit of the Discounts Received account

MC44 Sales invoices are first entered in

(A)   The Cash Book
(B)   The Purchases Journal
(C)   The Sales Account
(D)   The Sales Journal

MC45 The total of the Sales Journal is entered on

(A)   The credit side of the Sales Account in the General Ledger
(B)   The credit side of the General Account in the Sales Ledger
(C)   The debit side of the Sales Account in the General Ledger
(D)   The debit side of the Sales Day Book

MC46 Given a purchases invoice showing five items of £80 each, less trade discount of 25 per cent and cash discount of 5 per cent, if paid within the credit period, your cheque would be made out for

(A)   £285
(B)   £280
(C)   £260
(D)   None of these

MC47 An alternative name for a Sales Journal is

(A)   Sales Invoice
(B)   Sales Day Book
(C)   Daily Sales
(D)   Sales Ledger

MC48 Entered in the Purchases Journal are

(A)   Payments to suppliers
(B)   Trade discounts
(C)   Purchases invoices
(D)   Discounts received

MC49 The total of the Purchases Journal is transferred to the

(A)   Credit side of the Purchases Account
(B)   Debit side of the Purchases Day Book
(C)   Credit side of the Purchases Book
(D)   Debit side of the Purchases Account

MC50 Credit notes issued by us will be entered in our

(A)   Sales Account
(B)   Returns Inwards Account
(C)   Returns Inwards Journal
(D)   Returns Outwards Journal

MC51 The total of the Returns Outwards Journal is transferred to

(A)   The credit side of the Returns Outwards Account
(B)   The debit side of the Returns Outwards Account
(C)   The credit side of the Returns Outwards Book
(D)   The debit side of the Purchases Returns Book

→

MC52 We originally sold 25 items at £12 each, less 33⅓ per cent trade discount. Our customer now returns 4 of them to us. What is the amount of credit note to be issued?

(A) £48
(B) £36
(C) £30
(D) £32

MC53 Depreciation is

(A) The amount spent to buy a non-current asset
(B) The salvage value of a non-current asset
(C) The part of the cost of the non-current asset consumed during its period of use by the firm
(D) The amount of money spent replacing non-current assets

MC54 A firm bought a machine for £3,200. It is to be depreciated at a rate of 25 per cent using the reducing balance method. What would be the remaining book value after two years?

(A) £1,600
(B) £2,400
(C) £1,800
(D) Some other figure

MC55 A firm bought a machine for £16,000. It is expected to be used for five years then sold for £1,000. What is the annual amount of depreciation if the straight line method is used?

(A) £3,200
(B) £3,100
(C) £3,750
(D) £3,000

MC56 At the date of the statement of financial position the balance on the Accumulated Provision for Depreciation Account is

(A) Transferred to the Depreciation account
(B) Transferred to Profit and Loss
(C) Simply deducted from the asset in the Statement of Financial Position
(D) Transferred to the Asset account

MC57 In the trial balance the balance on the Provision for Depreciation Account is

(A) Shown as a credit item
(B) Not shown, as it is part of depreciation
(C) Shown as a debit item
(D) Sometimes shown as a credit, sometimes as a debit

MC58 If an accumulated provision for depreciation account is in use then the entries for the year's depreciation would be

(A) Credit Provision for Depreciation Account, debit Profit and Loss Account
(B) Debit Asset Account, credit Profit and Loss Account
(C) Credit Asset Account, debit Provision for Depreciation Account
(D) Credit Profit and Loss Account, debit Provision for Depreciation Account

MC59 When the financial statements are prepared, the Bad Debts Account is closed by a transfer to the

(A) Statement of Financial Position
(B) Profit and Loss Account

(C)   Trading Account
(D)   Allowance for Doubtful Debts Account

MC60   An Allowance for Doubtful Debts is created

(A)   When debtors become bankrupt
(B)   When debtors cease to be in business
(C)   To provide for possible bad debts
(D)   To write-off bad debts

Review questions

27.1   A company starts in business on 1 January 2011. You are to write up the vans account and the provision for depreciation account for the year ended 31 December 2011 from the information given below. Depreciation is at the rate of 25 per cent per annum, using the basis that one complete month's ownership needs one month's depreciation.

2011   Bought two vans for £8,000 each on 1 January
       Bought one van for £9,000 on 1 September

27.2   A company starts in business on 1 January 2010, the financial year end being 31 December. You are to show:

(a)   The equipment account.
(b)   The provision for depreciation account.
(c)   The statement of financial position extracts for each of the years 2010, 2011, 2012, 2013.

The equipment bought was:

2010   1 January   1 machine costing £800
2011   1 July   2 machines costing £1,200 each
       1 October   1 machine costing £600
2012   1 April   1 machine costing £1,400

Depreciation is over 10 years, using the straight line method, machines being depreciated for the proportion of the year that they are owned.

27.3A   A company maintains its non-current assets at cost. A provision for depreciation account is used for each type of asset. Machinery is to be depreciated at the rate of 15 per cent per annum, and fixtures at the rate of 5 per cent per annum, using the reducing balance method. Depreciation is to be calculated on assets in existence at the end of each year, giving a full year's depreciation even though the asset was bought part of the way through the year. The following transactions in assets have taken place:

2012   1 January   Bought machinery £2,800, fixtures £290
       1 July   Bought fixtures £620
2013   1 October   Bought machinery £3,500
       1 December   Bought fixtures £130

The financial year end of the business is 31 December.

You are to show:
(a)   The machinery account.
(b)   The fixtures account.
(c)   The two separate provision for depreciation accounts.
(d)   The non-current assets section of the statement of financial position at the end of each year, for the years ended 31 December 2012 and 2013.

27.4 A company depreciates its plant at the rate of 25 per cent per annum, straight line method, for each month of ownership. From the following details draw up the plant account and the provision for depreciation account for each of the years 2010, 2011, 2012 and 2013.

2010	Bought plant costing £2,600 on 1 January.
	Bought plant costing £2,100 on 1 October.
2012	Bought plant costing £2,800 on 1 September.
2013	Sold plant which had been bought for £2,600 on 1 January 2010 for the sum of £810 on 31 August 2013.

You are also required to draw up the plant disposal account and the extracts from the statement of financial position as at the end of each year.

27.5 A company maintains its non-current assets at cost. Depreciation provision accounts for each asset are kept.

At 31 December 2011 the position was as follows:

	Total cost to date £	Total depreciation to date £
Machinery	94,500	28,350
Office furniture	3,200	1,280

The following additions were made during the financial year ended 31 December 2012:
Machinery £16,000, office furniture £460.
A machine bought in 2008 for £1,600 was sold for £360 during the year.
The rates of depreciation are:
Machinery 20 per cent, office furniture 10 per cent, using the straight line basis, calculated on the assets in existence at the end of each financial year irrespective of the date of purchase.

You are required to show the asset and depreciation accounts for the year ended 31 December 2012 and the statement of financial position entries at that date.

27.6 A vehicle bought on 1 January 2013 cost £16,000. Its useful economic life is estimated at four years and its trade-in value at that point is estimated as being £4,000.
During 2015 a review of the vehicle's probable useful economic life suggested that it should be retained until 1 January 2018 and its residual value should be £2,500.

Required:
What is the amount of straight line depreciation charged in the income statement in the year ending 31 December 2015 and the amount included in the statement of financial position for accumulated depreciation at that date?

27.7A

(a) What is the meaning of depreciation?
(b) Give **three** reasons why depreciation may occur.
(c) Name **two** methods of depreciation.
(d) In what way do you think the concept of consistency applies to depreciation?
(e) 'Since the calculation of depreciation is based on estimates, not facts, why bother to make the calculation?'
    Explain briefly why you think that the calculation of depreciation is based on estimates.
(f) If depreciation was omitted, what effects would this have on the final accounts?
(g) 'Some assets increase (appreciate) in value, but normal accounting procedure would be to ignore any such appreciation.'
    Explain why bringing appreciation into account would go against the prudence concept.
(h) A business whose financial year ends at 31 December purchased on 1 January 2012 a machine for £5,000. The machine was to be depreciated by ten equal instalments. On 4 January 2014 the machine was sold for £3,760.

Ignoring any depreciation in the year of sale, show the relevant entries for each of the following accounts for the years ended 31 December 2012, 2013 and 2014:

(*i*)   Machinery
(*ii*)   Provision for depreciation of machinery^{Authors' Note 1}
(*iii*)   Machinery disposals
(*iv*)   Profit and loss
(*v*)   Extracts from the income statement.^{Authors' Note 2}

(*Northern Examinations and Assessment Board: GCSE*)

Authors' Note 1: this is the accumulated provision for depreciation of machinery account.
Authors' Note 2: part (v) was not included in the original question.

27.8

(*a*) Identify the four factors which cause non-current assets to depreciate.
(*b*) Which one of these factors is the most important for each of the following assets?
    (*i*)   a gold mine;
    (*ii*)   a van;
    (*iii*)   a 50-year lease on a building;
    (*iv*)   land;
    (*v*)   a ship used to ferry passengers and vehicles across a river following the building of a bridge across the river;
    (*vi*)   a franchise to market a new computer software package in a certain country.
(*c*) The financial year of Ochre Ltd will end on 31 December 2009. At 1 January 2009 the company had in use equipment with a total accumulated cost of £135,620 which had been depreciated by a total of £81,374. During the year ended 31 December 2009 Ochre Ltd purchased new equipment costing £47,800 and sold off equipment which had originally cost £36,000, and which had been depreciated by £28,224, for £5,700. No further purchases or sales of equipment are planned for December. The policy of the company is to depreciate equipment at 40% using the diminishing balance method. A full year's depreciation is provided for on all equipment in use by the company at the end of each year.

Required:
Show the following ledger accounts for the year ended 31 December 2009:
(*i*)   the Equipment Account;
(*ii*)   the Provision for Depreciation on Equipment Account;^{Authors' Note}
(*iii*) the Assets Disposals Account.

(*Association of Accounting Technicians*)
Authors' Note: this is the accumulated provision for depreciation account.

27.9A   Mavron plc owned the following motor vehicles as at 1 April 2012:

Motor Vehicle	Date Acquired	Cost	Estimated Residual Value	Estimated Life (years)
		£	£	
AAT 101	1 October 2012	8,500	2,500	5
DJH 202	1 April 2013	12,000	2,000	8

Mavron plc's policy is to provide at the end of each financial year depreciation using the straight line method applied on a month-by-month basis on all motor vehicles used during the year.

During the financial year ended 31 March 2013 the following occurred:

(*i*)   On 30 June 2012 AAT 101 was traded in and replaced by KGC 303. The trade-in allowance was £5,000. KGC 303 cost £15,000 and the balance due (after deducting the trade-in allowance) was paid partly in cash and partly by a loan of £6,000 from Pinot Finance. KGC 303 is expected to have a residual value of £4,000 after an estimated economic life of five years.
(*ii*) The estimated remaining economic life of DJH 202 was reduced from six years to four years with no change in the estimated residual value.

→

Required:
(a) Show any Journal entries necessary to give effect to the above.
(b) Show the Journal entry necessary to record depreciation on Motor Vehicles for the year ended 31 March 2013.
(c) Reconstruct the Motor Vehicles Account and the Provision for Depreciation Account for the year ended 31 March 2013.^Authors' Note

Show the necessary calculations clearly.

(Association of Accounting Technicians)

Authors' Note: this is the accumulated provision for depreciation account.

27.10 A business buys a non-current asset for £10,000. The business estimates that the asset will be used for five years. After exactly two and a half years, however, the asset is suddenly sold for £5,000. The business always provides a full year's depreciation in the year of purchase and no depreciation in the year of disposal.

Required:
(a) Write up the relevant accounts (including disposal account but not profit and loss account) for each of Years 1, 2 and 3:
    (i) Using the straight line depreciation method (assume 20% pa);
    (ii) Using the reducing balance depreciation method (assume 40% pa).
(b) (i) What is the purpose of depreciation? In what circumstances would each of the two methods you have used be preferable?
    (ii) What is the meaning of the net figure for the non-current asset in the statement of financial position at the end of Year 2?
(c) If the asset was bought at the beginning of Year 1, but was not used at all until Year 2 (and it is confidently anticipated to last until Year 6), state under each method the appropriate depreciation charge in Year 1, and briefly justify your answer.

(Association of Chartered Certified Accountants)

27.11A Contractors Ltd was formed on 1 January 2012 and the following purchases and sales of machinery were made during the first 3 years of operations.

Date	Asset	Transaction	Price
1 January 2012	Machines 1 and 2	purchase	£40,000 each
1 October 2012	Machines 3 and 4	purchase	£15,200 each
30 June 2014	Machine 3	sale	£12,640
1 July 2014	Machine 5	purchase	£20,000

Each machine was estimated to last 10 years and to have a residual value of 5 per cent of its cost price. Depreciation was by equal instalments, and it is company policy to charge depreciation for every month an asset is owned.

Required:
(a) Calculate
    (i) the total depreciation on Machinery for each of the years 2012, 2013 and 2014;
    (ii) the profit or loss on the sale of Machine 3 in 2014.
(b) Contractors Ltd depreciates its vehicles by 30 per cent per annum using the diminishing balance method. What difference would it have made to annual reported profits over the life of a vehicle if it had decided instead to depreciate this asset by 20 per cent straight line?

(Scottish Qualifications Authority)

27.12 A friend of the family believes that depreciation provides him with a reserve to purchase new assets. His secretary has blown up his computer, but he knows he has the funds to replace it in the accumulated depreciation account. You know he is wrong and have grown tired of listening to him going on about it, but he won't listen to what you have to say. You decide to put him out of his misery by writing a letter to him about it that he may actually read before he realises that it is telling him things he does not want to hear.

Write him a letter, using fictitious names and addresses, which defines depreciation and explains why his view is incorrect.

27.13A A machine cost £40,000 on 1 January 2012. The reducing balance depreciation method is used at 25 per cent per annum. Year end is 31 December. During 2014, it was decided that a straight line method would be more appropriate. At that time, the remaining useful economic life of the machine was seven years with a residual value of £1,500.

Required:
The accumulated provision for depreciation account for the years 2012 to 2014 inclusive together with the relevant statement of financial position extract on 31 December in each of those years.

27.14 (a) A machine was bought on credit for £15,000 from the XY Manufacturing Co Ltd, on 1 October 2011. The estimated useful economic life of the machine was seven years and the estimated scrap value £1,000. The machine account is to be maintained at cost. Financial statements are prepared annually to 30 September and the straight line depreciation method is used on machines.

Required:
(a) Prepare the journal entries and ledger accounts to record the machine and its depreciation for the first two years of its working life.
(b) Illustrate how the machine would appear in the statement of financial position at 30 September 2013.

(c) The machine was sold for £7,500 cash to another manufacturer on 1 October 2014. A new replacement machine was bought on credit for £18,000 from the XY Manufacturing Co Ltd. It also has an estimated useful economic life of seven years but its estimated scrap value is £1,200.

Required:
(a) Prepare the machine account, the accumulated provision for depreciation account and the machine disposal account for the year to 30 September 2015.
(b) Repeat (a) but this time assume that the selling price of the old machine was £12,000.

27.15A Distance Limited owned three lorries at 1 April 2012:

Lorry A: purchased on 21 May 2008 for £31,200
Lorry B: purchased on 20 June 2010 for £19,600
Lorry C: purchased on 1 January 2012 for £48,800

Depreciation is charged annually at 20 per cent on cost on all vehicles in use at the end of the year.

During the year ended 31 March 2013, the following transactions occurred:

(i) 1 June 2012: Lorry B was involved in an accident and considered to be a write-off by the insurance company which paid £10,500 in settlement.
(ii) 7 June 2012: Lorry D was purchased for £32,800.
(iii) 21 August 2012: Lorry A was sold for £7,000.
(iv) 30 October 2012: Lorry E was purchased for £39,000.
(v) 6 March 2013: Lorry E was considered not to be suitable for carrying the type of goods required and was exchanged for lorry F. The value of lorry F was deemed to be £37,600.

Required:
Prepare the ledger T-accounts recording these transactions for the year ending 31 March 2013 and bring down the balances at 1 April.

27.16 XY Ltd provides for depreciation of its machinery at 20 per cent per annum on cost; it charges for a full year in the year of purchase but no provision is made in the year of sale/disposal.

Financial statements are prepared annually to 31 December.

2011
January 1   Bought machine 'A' £10,000
July 1   Bought machine 'B' £6,000.

2012
March 31   Bought machine 'C' £8,000

2013
October 7   Sold machine 'A' – proceeds £5,500
November 5   Bought machine 'D' £12,000

2014
February 4   Sold machine 'B' – proceeds £3,000
February 6   Bought machine 'B' £9,000
October 11   Exchanged machine 'D' for machinery valued at £7,000

Prepare
(a)   The machinery account for the period 1 January 2011 to 31 December 2014.
(b)   The accumulated provision for depreciation on machinery account, for the period 1 January 2011 to 31 December 2014.
(c)   The disposal of machinery accounts showing the profit/loss on sale for each year.
(d)   The statement of financial position extract for machinery at (i) 31 December 2013 and (ii) 31 December 2014.

27.17A   A company maintains its non-current assets at cost. Accumulated provision for depreciation accounts are kept for each asset.

At 31 December 2011 the position was as follows:

	Total cost to date £	Total depreciation to date £
Machinery	52,950	25,670
Office furniture	2,860	1,490

The following transactions were made in the year ended 31 December 2012:

(a)   Purchased – machinery £2,480 and office furniture £320
(b)   Sold machinery which had cost £2,800 in 2008 for £800

Depreciation is charged, on a straight line basis, at 10 per cent on machinery and at 5 per cent on office furniture on the basis of assets in use at the end of the year irrespective of the date of purchase.

Required:
Show the asset and accumulated provision for depreciation accounts for the year 31 December 2012 and the relevant statement of financial position entries at that date.

27.18   Alice Burke prepares her financial statements on 31 December each year and maintains a Plant and Equipment register at cost. She provides depreciation for the full year on non-current assets which are in use at the end of the year, and none in the year of disposal.

At 31 December 2009 the plant account balance was £180,000 and the balance on the accumulated provision for depreciation account was £70,000. Depreciation was provided on the reducing balance method at 20 per cent.

Early in 2012, an item of plant which had cost £20,000 on 1 March 2010 was sold for £14,000.

At the end of 2012, it was decided that for that and all succeeding years the straight line method of calculating depreciation should be used. It was assumed that all the plant would be sold at the end of 2015 for approximately £30,000.

Required:
Prepare the ledger accounts recording all of the above. You are not required to prepare the profit and loss account.

27.19A

(a)   The following trial balance was extracted from the books of M. Jackson on 30 April 2013. From it, and the note below it, prepare his income statement for the year ending 30 April 2013, and a statement of financial position as at that date.

	Dr	Cr
	£	£
Sales		18,614
Purchases	11,570	
Inventory 1 May 2012	3,776	
Carriage outwards	326	
Carriage inwards	234	
Returns inwards	440	
Returns outwards		355
Salaries and wages	2,447	
Motor expenses	664	
Rent	576	
Sundry expenses	1,202	
Motor vehicles	3,400	
Fixtures and fittings	600	
Accounts receivable	4,577	
Accounts payable		3,045
Cash at bank	3,876	
Cash in hand	120	
Drawings	2,050	
Capital		13,844
	35,858	35,858

Note:

Closing inventory amounted to £4,000. Depreciation is to be charged at rates of 10 per cent on cost for fixtures and fittings and 25 per cent on cost for motor vehicles. Bad debts of £800 are to be written off.

(b) Michael has indicated that he thinks that the accounts receivable amounts that have been written off will be paid eventually. He is also querying why adjustments are made in the financial statements for bad debts and depreciation. Write a short note to him, making appropriate references to accounting concepts, outlining why these adjustments are made.

27.20 On 1 April 2009 a business purchased a machine costing £112,000. The machine can be used for a total of 20,000 hours over an estimated life of 48 months. At the end of that time the machine is expected to have a trade-in value of £12,000.

The financial year of the business ends on 31 December each year. It is expected that the machine will be used for:

4,000 hours during the financial year ending 31 December 2009
5,000 hours during the financial year ending 31 December 2010
5,000 hours during the financial year ending 31 December 2011
5,000 hours during the financial year ending 31 December 2012
1,000 hours during the financial year ending 31 December 2013

Required:

(a) Calculate the annual depreciation charges on the machine on each of the following bases for each of the financial years ending on 31 December 2009, 2010, 2011, 2012 and 2013:
  (i) the straight line method applied on a month for month basis,
  (ii) the diminishing balance method at 40% per annum applied on a full year basis, and
  (iii) the units of output method.
(b) Suppose that during the financial year ended 31 December 2010 the machine was used for only 1,500 hours before being sold for £80,000 on 30 June.
  Assuming that the business has chosen to apply the straight line method on a month for month basis, show the following accounts for 2010 only:
  (i) the Machine account,
  (ii) the Provision for Depreciation – Machine account, and
  (iii) the Assets Disposals account.

(Association of Accounting Technicians)

27.21A   On 1 January 2011 a business purchased a laser printer costing £1,800. The printer has an estimated life of four years after which it will have no residual value.

It is expected that the output from the printer will be:

Year	Sheets printed
2011	35,000
2012	45,000
2013	45,000
2014	55,000
	180,000

Required:

(a)   Calculate the annual depreciation charges for 2011, 2012, 2013 and 2014 on the laser printer on the following bases:

(i)   the straight line basis,

(ii)   the diminishing balance method at 60 per cent per annum, and

(iii)   the units of output method.

Note: Your workings should be to the nearest £.

(b)   Suppose that in 2014 the laser printer were to be sold on 1 July for £200 and that the business had chosen to depreciate it at 60 per cent per annum using the diminishing balance method applied on a month for month basis.

Reconstruct the following accounts for 2014 only:

(i)   the Laser Printer account,

(ii)   the Provision for Depreciation – Laser Printer account, and

(iii)   the Assets Disposals account.

(Association of Accounting Technicians)

Adjustments for Financial Statements 3

28

Accruals and prepayments and other adjustments for financial statements

Learning objectives

After you have studied this chapter, you should be able to:

- adjust expense accounts for accruals and prepayments
- adjust revenue accounts for amounts owing
- show accruals, prepayments and revenue accounts receivable in the statement of financial position
- ascertain the amounts of expense and revenue items to be shown in the income statement after making adjustments for accruals and prepayments
- make the necessary end-of-period adjustments relating to drawings that have not yet been entered in the books
- explain what an extended trial balance is and describe what it looks like
- prepare accrual and prepayment entries to the accounts using two different methods

Introduction

In this chapter, you'll continue to learn about adjustments made to the ledger accounts at the end of a period. You'll learn how to make the appropriate entries in the accounts for outstanding balances on expense and income accounts and make the appropriate entries in the income statement and the statement of financial position.

28.1 Financial statements so far

The income statements you have looked at so far have taken the sales for a period and deducted all the expenses for that period, the result being a net profit or a net loss.

Up to this part of the book it has always been assumed that the expenses incurred belong to the period of the income statement when they took place. If the income statement for the year ending 31 December 2012 was being prepared, then the rent paid as shown in the trial balance was all treated as relating to 2012. There was no rent owing at the beginning of 2012 nor any owing at the end of 2012, nor had any rent been paid in advance relating to 2013.

This was done to make your first meeting with financial statements as straightforward as possible.

28.2   Adjustments needed

Let's look at two businesses which pay rent for buildings in Oxford. The rent for each building is £6,000 a year.

1 Business A pays £5,000 in the year. At the year end it owes £1,000 for rent.

$$\begin{aligned}\text{Rent expense used up} \;&=\; \pounds6{,}000\\\text{Rent paid for}\;&=\;\pounds5{,}000\end{aligned}$$

2 Business B pays £6,500 in the year. This figure includes £500 paid in advance for the following year.

$$\begin{aligned}\text{Rent expense used up} \;&=\; \pounds6{,}000\\\text{Rent paid for}\;&=\;\pounds6{,}500\end{aligned}$$

An income statement for 12 months needs 12 months' rent as an expense = £6,000. This means that in both 1 and 2 the double entry accounts will have to be adjusted.

> **Activity 28.1**   From your knowledge of double entry, you should be able to work out what the double entry required is in these two cases. What do you think it is? If you don't know what names to give the accounts, have a guess. (Hint: in the first case, there will be a credit balance in the statement of financial position and in the other, it will be a debit balance.)

In all the examples in this chapter the income statements are for the year ending 31 December 2011. Unless otherwise indicated, all entries in the income statement are in the profit and loss section of the statement. All mentions of 'profit and loss' refer to the ledger account of that name which is summarised in the income statement.

28.3   Accrued expenses

Assume that rent of £4,000 per year is payable at the end of every three months. The rent was paid on time in March, but this is not always the case.

Amount	Rent due	Rent paid
£1,000	31 March 2011	31 March 2011
£1,000	30 June 2011	2 July 2011
£1,000	30 September 2011	4 October 2011
£1,000	31 December 2011	5 January 2012

Rent

2011			£	
Mar	31	Cash	1,000	
Jul	2	Cash	1,000	
Oct	4	Cash	1,000	

The rent for the last quarter was paid on 5 January 2012 and so will appear in the books of the year 2012 as the result of a double entry made on that date.

The expense for 2011 is obviously £4,000 as that is the year's rent, and this is the amount needed to be transferred to the profit and loss account. But, if £4,000 was put on the credit side of the rent account (the debit being in the profit and loss account) the account would be out of balance by £1,000 because the payment due on 31 December 2011 was not made until 5 January 2012. That is, if we posted £4,000 to profit and loss on 31 December, we would have £4,000 on the credit side of the account and only £3,000 on the debit side:

Rent

2011			£	2011			£
Mar	31	Cash	1,000	Dec	31	Profit and loss	4,000
Jul	2	Cash	1,000				
Oct	4	Cash	1,000				

This cannot be right.

To make the account balance the £1,000 rent owing for 2011, but paid in 2012, must be carried down to 2012 as a credit balance because it is a liability on 31 December 2011. Instead of rent owing it could be called rent accrued or just simply an 'accrual'.

The completed account can now be shown:

Rent

2011			£	2011			£
Mar	31	Cash	1,000	Dec	31	Profit and loss	4,000
Jul	2	Cash	1,000				
Oct	4	Cash	1,000				
Dec	31	Accrued c/d	1,000				
			4,000				4,000
				2012			
				Jan	1	Accrued b/d	1,000

The balance c/d has been described as 'accrued c/d', rather than as 'balance c/d'. This is to explain what the balance is for. It is for an **accrued expense**.

28.4 Prepaid expenses

Insurance for a business is at the rate of £840 a year, starting from 1 January 2011. The business has agreed to pay this at the rate of £210 every three months. However, payments were not made at the correct times. Details were:

Amount	Insurance due	Insurance paid
£210	31 March 2011	£210 28 February 2011
£210 £210	30 June 2011 30 September 2011	£420 31 August 2011
£210	31 December 2011	£420 18 November 2011

The insurance account in the ledger for the year ended 31 December 2011 is:

Insurance

2011			£	2011			£
Feb	28	Bank	210	Dec	31	Profit and loss	840
Aug	31	Bank	420				
Nov	18	Bank	420				

The last payment of £420 is not just for 2011. It can be split as £210 for the three months to 31 December 2011 and £210 for the three months ended 31 March 2012. For a period of 12 months the cost of insurance is £840 and this is, therefore, the figure needing to be transferred to the income statement.

If £840 is posted to the debit of profit and loss at 31 December 2011, the insurance account will still have a debit balance of £210. This is a benefit paid for but not used up at the end of the period. It is an asset and needs carrying forward as such to 2012, i.e. as a debit balance. Items like this are called **prepaid expenses**, 'prepayments' or 'amounts paid in advance'.

The account can now be completed:

Insurance

2011			£	2011				£
Feb	28	Bank	210	Dec	31	Profit and loss	840
Aug	31	Bank	420		31	Prepaid c/d	210
Nov	18	Bank	420				
			1,050				1,050
2012							
Jan	1	Prepaid b/d	210				

Prepayment happens when items other than purchases are bought for use in the business, but are not fully used up in the period.

For instance, packing materials are normally not entirely used up over the period in which they are bought. There is usually an inventory of packing materials in hand at the end of the period. This is a form of prepayment and needs carrying down to the period in which it will be used.

This can be seen in the following example:

Year ended 31 December 2011:
Packing materials bought in the year = £2,200.
Inventory of packing materials in hand as at 31 December 2011 = £400.

Looking at the example, it can be seen that in 2011 the packing materials used up will have been £2,200 – £400 = £1,800. (We are assuming that there was no inventory of packing materials at the start of 2011.) We have an inventory of £400 packing materials at 31 December 2011 to be carried forward to 2012. The £400 inventory of packing materials will be carried forward as an asset balance (i.e. a debit balance) to 2012:

Packing Materials

2011			£	2011				£
Dec	31	Bank	2,200	Dec	31	Profit and loss	1,800
					31	Inventory c/d	400
			2,200				2,200
2012							
Jan	1	Inventory b/d	400				

The inventory of packing materials is *not* added to the inventory of unsold goods in hand in the statement of financial position, but is added to the other prepaid expenses in the statement of financial position.

28.5   Revenue owing at the end of period

The revenue owing for sales is already shown in the books as the debit balances on customers' accounts, i.e. accounts receivable. There may be other kinds of revenue, all of which has not been received by the end of the period, e.g. rent receivable. An example now follows.

Example

Our warehouse is larger than we need. We rent part of it to another business for £1,800 per annum. Details for the year ended 31 December were as follows:

Amount	Rent due	Rent received
£450	31 March 2011	4 April 2011
£450	30 June 2011	6 July 2011
£450	30 September 2011	9 October 2011
£450	31 December 2011	7 January 2012

The Rent Receivable Account entries for 2011 will appear as:

Rent Receivable

				£
	2011			
	Apr	4	Bank	450
	Jul	6	Bank	450
	Oct	9	Bank	450

The rent received of £450 on 7 January 2012 will be entered in the accounting records in 2012.

Any rent paid by the business would be charged as a debit to the profit and loss account. Any rent received, being the opposite, is transferred to the credit of the profit and loss account, as it is a revenue.

The amount to be transferred for 2011 is that earned for the 12 months, i.e. £1,800. The rent received account is completed by carrying down the balance owing as a debit balance to 2012. The £450 owing is an asset on 31 December 2011.

The rent receivable account can now be completed:

Rent Receivable

2011			£	2011				£
Dec	31	Profit and loss	1,800	Apr	4	Bank		450
				Jul	6	Bank		450
				Oct	9	Bank		450
				Dec	31	Accrued c/d		450
			1,800					1,800
2012								
Jan	1	Accrued b/d	450					

28.6 Expenses and revenue account balances and the statement of financial position

In all cases dealing with adjustments in the financial statements, there will still be a balance on each account after the preparation of the income statement. All such balances remaining should appear in the statement of financial position. The only question left is where and how they should be shown.

The amounts owing for expenses could be called expenses payable, expenses owing or accrued expenses. However, we'll use the term 'accruals'. They represent *very* current liabilities – they will have to be paid in the very near future.

The items prepaid could be called prepaid expenses or payments in advance, but we'll call them 'prepayments'. Similarly to accruals, they represent *very* current assets as they should be received very soon.

> **Activity 28.2**
> From your knowledge of accounting, how should all the expense account debit and credit balances appear in the statement of financial position – as one debit entry and one credit entry or as a separate entry for each item? Why?

> **Activity 28.3**
> (a) Where in the current asset sequence do you place prepayments?
> (b) Where in the current liability sequence do you place accruals?
> (c) Why?

Amounts owing for rents receivable or other revenue owing are a special case. If you look back at the T-account in Section 28.5, you'll see that they are described as 'accrued'. However, they are not accrued expenses, as they represent amounts receivable. They are, therefore, **accrued income**.

> **Activity 28.4**
> Where do you think these items of accrued income go in the statement of financial position?

The part of the statement of financial position in respect of the accounts so far seen in this chapter is therefore:

Statement of Financial Position as at 31 December 2011 (extract)

	£	£
Current assets		
Inventory	xxx	
Accounts receivable	450	
Prepayments (400 + 210)	610	
Bank	xxx	
Cash	xxx	
⋮		x,xxx
Current liabilities		
Trade accounts payable	xxx	
Accrued expenses	1,000	
		(x,xxx)

28.7 Expenses and revenue accounts covering more than one period

So far we've only looked at accounts where there were closing accruals or prepayments. In real life, you will also expect to see some opening accruals and prepayments, such as that shown in the final version of the Rent Receivable Account in Section 28.5. This is something that students are often asked to deal with in examinations as it tests their knowledge and ability to distinguish the treatment of these items at the beginning and end of a period. Typically, they may be asked to draw up an expense or revenue account for a full year which has amounts owing or prepaid at both the beginning and end of the year. We can now see how this is done.

Example A

The following details are available:

(A) On 31 December 2010, three months' rent amounting to a total of £3,000 was owing.
(B) The rent chargeable per year was £12,000.
(C) The following rent payments were made in the year 2011:
    6 January £3,000; 4 April £3,000; 7 July £3,000; 18 October £3,000.
(D) The final three months' rent for 2011 is still owing.

Now we can look at the completed rent account. The letters (A) to (D) give reference to the details above.

Rent

2011				£	2011				£
Jan	6	Bank	(C)	3,000	Jan	1	Accrued b/d	(A)	3,000
Apr	4	Bank	(C)	3,000	Dec	31	Profit and loss	(B)	12,000
Jul	7	Bank	(C)	3,000					
Oct	18	Bank	(C)	3,000					
Dec	31	Accrued c/d	(D)	3,000					
				15,000					15,000
					2012				
					Jan	1	Accrued b/d		3,000

Example B

The following details are available:

(A) On 31 December 2010, packing materials in hand amounted to £1,850.
(B) During the year to 31 December 2011, we paid £27,480 for packing materials.
(C) There was no inventory of packing materials on 31 December 2011.
(D) On 31 December 2011, we still owed £2,750 for packing materials already received and used.

The packing materials account will appear as:

Packing Materials

2011				£	2011			£
Jan	1	Inventory b/d	(A)	1,850	Dec	31	Profit and loss	32,080
Dec	31	Bank	(B)	27,480				
	31	Owing c/d	(D)	2,750				
				32,080				32,080
					2012			
					Jan	1	Owing b/d	2,750

The figure of £32,080 is the difference on the account, and is transferred to the profit and loss account.
    We can prove it is correct:

	£	£
Inventory at start of year		1,850
Add Bought and used:		
Paid for	27,480	
Still owed for	2,750	
Cost of packing materials bought and used in the year		30,230
Cost of packing materials used in the year		32,080

Example C

Where different expenses are put together in one account, it can get even more confusing. Let us look at where rent and rates are joined together. Here are the details for the year ended 31 December 2011:

(A) Rent is payable of £6,000 per annum.
(B) Rates of £4,000 per annum are payable by instalments.
(C) At 1 January 2011, rent of £1,000 had been prepaid in 2010.
(D) On 1 January 2011, rates of £400 were owed.
(E) During 2011, rent of £4,500 was paid.
(F) During 2011, rates of £5,000 were paid.
(G) On 31 December 2011, rent of £500 was owing.
(H) On 31 December 2011, rates of £600 had been prepaid.

A combined rent and rates account is to be drawn up for the year 2011 showing the transfer to profit and loss, and the balances to be carried down to 2012.

Rent and Rates

2011			£	2011			£
Jan 1	Rent prepaid b/d	(C)	1,000	Jan 1	Rates owing b/d	(D)	400
Dec 31	Bank: rent	(E)	4,500	Dec 31	Profit and loss	(A) + (B)	10,000
31	Bank: rates	(F)	5,000				
31	Rent accrued c/d	(G)	500	31	Rates prepaid c/d	(H)	600
			11,000				11,000
2012				2012			
Jan 1	Rates prepaid b/d	(H)	600	Jan 1	Rent accrued b/d	(G)	500

To enter the correct figures, you need to keep the two items separate in your own mind. This is easiest if you produce a schedule like the one we produced above for packing materials inventory. The one for rent would look like this:

	£	£
Rent due during the year		6,000
Less:		
Rent prepaid at start of year	1,000	
Rent paid during the year	4,500	
		(5,500)
Rent accrued at the end of the year		500

Activity 28.5 Prepare a similar schedule for rates.

28.8 Goods for own use

Traders will often take inventory out of their business for their own use without paying for them. There is nothing wrong about their doing this, but an entry should be made to record that this has happened. This is done by:

1 Debit drawings account, to show that the owner has taken the goods for private use.
2 Credit purchases account, to reduce cost of goods available for sale.

In the United Kingdom, an adjustment may be needed for Value Added Tax. If goods supplied to a trader's customers have VAT added to their price, then any such goods taken for own use will need such an adjustment. This is because the VAT regulations state that VAT should be added to the cost of goods taken. The double entry for the VAT content would be:

1 Debit drawings account.
2 Credit VAT account.

Adjustments may also be needed for other private items. For instance, if a trader's private insurance (e.g. insurance premiums for the contents of the trader's home) had been incorrectly charged to the business insurance account, then the correction would be:

1 Debit drawings account.
2 Credit insurance account.

28.9 Distinctions between various kinds of capital

The capital account represents the claim the owner has against the assets of the business at a point in time. That is, the amount of the business that belongs to the owner. The word **capital** is, however, often used in a specific sense. The main meanings are listed below.

Capital invested

This means the total monetary value of everything brought into the business by the owners from their outside interests. The amount of capital invested is not disturbed by the amount of profits made by the business or losses incurred.

Capital employed

Students at an early stage in their studies are often asked to define this term. In fact, for those who progress to a more advanced stage, it will be seen in *Business Accounting 2* that capital employed could have several meanings as the term is often used quite loosely. At its simplest, it is taken to mean the monetary value of the resources that are being used in the business. Thus, if all the assets were added together and the liabilities of the business deducted, the answer would be that the difference is the amount of money employed in the business. You will by now realise that this is the same as the closing balance of the capital account. It is also sometimes called 'net assets' or 'net worth'.

Working capital

This is a term for the excess of the current assets over the current liabilities of a business and is the same as '**net current assets**'.

28.10 Financial statements in the services sector

So far we have only looked at financial statements for businesses trading in some sort of goods. We drew up a trading account for some of these businesses because we wanted to identify the gross profit on goods sold.

There are, however, many businesses which do not deal in 'goods' but instead supply 'services'. This will include professional businesses such as accountants, solicitors, doctors, dentists, vets, management consultants, advertising agencies, estate agents and Internet service providers. Other examples include businesses specialising in computer repairs, window cleaning, gardening, hairdressing, chimney sweeping, piano tuning, and banks, football clubs, health clubs, gyms and leisure centres.

As they do not deal in 'goods' there is no point in their attempting to draw up trading accounts. While it is quite possible for, say, a dentist to treat depreciation on equipment, the costs of materials consumed, and the dental assistant's salary as deductions from income in order to arrive at a figure for gross profit, such information is likely to be of little benefit in terms of decision-making. They will, however, prepare an income statement (containing only the profit and loss items) and a statement of financial position.

The first item in the income statement will be the revenue which might be called 'work done', 'fees', 'charges', 'accounts rendered', 'takings', etc., depending on the nature of the organisation. Any other items of income will be added, e.g. rent receivable, and then the expenses will be listed and deducted to arrive at a net profit or net loss.

An example of the income statement of a solicitor might be as per Exhibit 28.1:

Exhibit 28.1

J. Plunkett, Solicitor
Income Statement for the year ending 31 December 2011

	£	£
Revenue:		
Fees charged		87,500
Insurance commissions		1,300
		88,800
Less Expenses:		
Wages and salaries	29,470	
Rent and rates	11,290	
Office expenses	3,140	
Motor expenses	2,115	
General expenses	1,975	
Depreciation	2,720	
		(50,710)
Net profit		38,090

Other than for the descriptions given in the revenue section, it doesn't look very different from the ones you've prepared for traders. In effect, if you can prepare an income statement for a trader, you can do so for a service organisation. You just need to remember that it will contain no trading account items and that the income will need to be appropriately described.

28.11 Extended trial balances

Instead of drafting a set of financial statements in the way shown so far in this textbook, you could prepare an 'extended trial balance', or 'worksheet'. It can be very useful when there are a large number of adjustments to be made. Professional accountants use them a lot for that very reason.

Extended trial balances are usually drawn up on specially preprinted types of stationery with suitable vertical columns printed across the page. You start with the trial balance extracted from the ledgers and then enter adjustments in the columns to the right. Columns for the trading account, income statement, and the statement of financial position then follow.

Exhibit 28.2 shows an example of the extended trial balance that could have been drawn up as an answer to Review Question 28.11. Once you have attempted the question yourself, compare your answer to the one shown in Exhibit 28.2. The gross profits and net profits are the same; it is simply the method of displaying the information that is different.

Exhibit 28.2

JOHN BROWN WORKSHEET

See Review Question 28.11

	Trial Balance		Adjustments		Trading Account		Profit and Loss Account		Balance Sheet	
	1 Dr	2 Cr	3 Dr	4 Cr	5 Dr	6 Cr	7 Dr	8 Cr	9 Dr	10 Cr
Sales		400,000				400,000				
Purchases	350,000				350,000					
Sales returns	5,000				5,000					
Purchases returns		6,200				6,200				
Inventory 1.1.2013	100,000				100,000					
Allowance for doubtful debts		800		180 (iv)						980
Wages and salaries	30,000		5,000 (ii)				35,000			
Rates	6,000			500 (iii)			5,500			
Telephone	1,000		220 (v)				1,220			
Shop fittings	40,000			4,000 (vi)					36,000	
Van	30,000			6,000 (vi)					24,000	
Accounts receivable	9,800								9,800	
Accounts payable		7,000								7,000
Bad debts	200						200			
Capital		179,000								179,000
Bank	3,000								3,000	
Drawings	18,000								18,000	
	593,000	593,000								
Inventory 31.12.2013 – Asset			120,000 (i)						120,000	
Inventory 31.12.2013 – Cost of goods sold				120,000 (i)		120,000				
Accrued expenses				5,000 (ii)						5,000
				220 (v)						220
Allowance for doubtful debts			180 (iv)				180			
Prepaid expenses			500 (iii)						500	
Depreciation shop fittings			4,000 (vi)				4,000			
Depreciation van			6,000 (vi)				6,000			
			135,900	135,900						
Gross profit (balancing figure)					71,200			71,200		
					526,200	526,200				
Net profit (balancing figure)							19,100			19,100
							71,200	71,200	211,300	211,300

If you look carefully, you will notice that all the journal entries are dealt with in one double column. That column has been split vertically in two. On the left is a sub-column for debit entries and, on the right, is a sub-column for credit entries. The reference number of each journal entry is placed to the right of each debit entry and each credit entry.

This makes it easy to detect errors in each entry, such as where a debit entry is for a different total amount than that shown in the relevant credit entry.

Activity 28.6
Why is identifying errors of this type easier when using an extended trial balance than when using a conventional manual approach to preparing the financial statements?

Sometimes, students confuse their debits and their credits and switch the entries to the accounts, the one that should have been debited being credited, and vice versa. If this happens, the trial balance and the statement of financial position will still balance, but the information contained in the statement of financial position will be incorrect. This is no different from what may occur with journal entries being processed in 'the books', rather than in an extended trial balance. However, if the extended trial balance is prepared using a spreadsheet, correcting the entries and producing correct financial statements may be done considerably faster, which is one reason why it is wise to use a spreadsheet rather than paper to prepare an extended trial balance.

Another advantage of the use of a spreadsheet relates to how easy it is to amend adjustments. If profit is too high or too low, some businessmen will seek ways of using journal entries to adjust it down or up. If their accountant has an extended trial balance on a spreadsheet, this makes such sensitivity analysis very easy. Thankfully for everyone else, there are rules and regulations governing the adjustments that can be made (Chapter 10). However, there are times when for genuinely honest reasons, tinkering with the figures in this way may be appropriate.

Activity 28.7
List three examples of situations where this may be appropriate.

If you were an accountant, the financial statements you prepare and give to the owner and to anyone else who was an interested party, such as the Inspector of Taxes or a bank, would not be in the style of an extended trial balance. Instead, having completed the extended trial balance, the figures for the trading account, income statement, and statement of financial position would be transferred to financial statements prepared using the conventional style of presentation.

To provide such special stationery in an examination is unusual, although it has been known to happen. For students to draw-up an extended trial balance from scratch could be very time-consuming. Therefore, it is very rare for examiners to ask for one to be prepared from scratch. However, the examiner may ask you something about extended trial balances (or worksheets) or provide a partially completed one to work on, if this topic is included in the syllabus. You should note, however, that nowadays spreadsheets are often used to produce financial statements in this way. If your course includes use of spreadsheets to prepare financial statements, you are more likely to be asked to prepare an extended trial balance in your examination or as part of your assessed coursework.

28.12 Definition of accounting

In Chapter 1, you were given a definition of bookkeeping as being concerned with the work of entering information into accounting records and afterwards maintaining such records properly. This definition does not need to be amended.

However, **accounting** was not fully defined in Chapter 1. It would probably not have meant much to you at that stage in your studies. The following is a commonly used definition: '*The process of identifying, measuring, and communicating economic information to permit informed judgements and decisions by users of the information.*'

28.13 An alternative way to record accruals and prepayments

After learning in Chapter 27 that there was a second commonly used way to record provisions for depreciation, it will come as no surprise to you to learn that there is a second commonly used way to record accruals and prepayments. Just as with the two-stage method of recording depreciation provisions, the alternative way to record accruals and prepayments requires that you create additional ledger accounts. You open an accruals account and a prepayments account and post any balances on expense accounts at the period end to the appropriate one of the two new accounts.

The balance carried down in an expense account under the method you learnt earlier in this chapter is described as either 'accrued c/d' or 'prepaid c/d'. Under the alternative method, there would be no balance in the expense account after the double entry to the accruals account or prepayments account. Instead, there will be a balance on these two accounts which is then entered in the statement of financial position in exactly the same way as you did under the other method.

At the start of the next period, you reverse the entry by crediting the prepayments account and debiting each of the expense accounts that had debit balances. Similarly, the accruals account is debited and the expense accounts that had credit balances are credited with the appropriate amounts.

For example, in the insurance account from Section 28.4, the entries in the insurance account were:

Insurance

2011			£	2011			£
Feb	28	Bank	210	Dec	31	Profit and loss	840
Aug	31	Bank	420				
Nov	18	Bank	420		31	Prepaid c/d	210
			1,050				1,050
2012							
Jan	1	Prepaid b/d	210				

The same information if a prepayments account were used would be entered:

Insurance

2011			£	2011			£
Feb	28	Bank	210	Dec	31	Profit and loss	840
Aug	31	Bank	420				
Nov	18	Bank	420		31	Prepayments	210
			1,050				1,050
2012							
Jan	1	Prepayments	210				

Prepayments

2011			£	2011			£
Dec	31	Insurance	<u>210</u>	Dec	31	Balance c/d	<u>210</u>
2012				2012			
Jan	1	Balance b/d	210	Jan	1	Insurance	210

In reality, it doesn't matter which of these two methods you use. Examiners will accept them both unless they specifically ask for one of them to be used. Your teacher or lecturer will know whether this is likely to happen. Follow the guidance of your teacher or lecturer and use whichever method he or she indicates is more appropriate.

In order not to confuse things by switching back and forth between the two methods, all examples of accruals and prepayments and all questions involving accruals and prepayments in the rest of this textbook will use the first method that has been covered in detail in this chapter. Should you be using the second method, as you will have seen above, it is very obvious what the equivalent entries would be when you look at examples prepared using the method adopted in this textbook.

Mnemonic

The following acronyms may help you to remember the treatment of accruals and prepayments in the statement of financial position:

PAPA and **ALLA**

		Treated as current
Prepaid	Expense	Asset
Accrued		Liability
Prepaid	Revenue	Liability
Accrued		Asset

Learning outcomes

You should now have learnt:

1 That adjustments are needed so that the expenses and income shown in the financial statements equal the expenses incurred in the period and the revenue that has arisen in the period.

2 That the balances relating to the adjustments will be shown on the statement of financial position at the end of the period as current assets and current liabilities.

3 That goods taken for the owner's own use without anything being recorded in the books will necessitate a transfer from purchases to the drawings account, plus an adjustment for VAT if appropriate.

4 How to record appropriate entries in the accounts and financial statements at the end of a period for accrued expenses, prepaid expenses, accrued income, and drawings.

5 That private expenses should not be charged as an expense in the income statement, but should be charged to the drawings account.

6 That an extended trial balance is an alternative way of arriving at the figures to be included in the financial statements.

7 That there are two common ways to prepare accruals and prepayments.

Answers to activities

28.1 Don't worry if you didn't know what names to give the accounts other than the rent account. What is important is that you thought about it and that you knew which side the entries should be in the rent account.

(a) *Dr* Rent account £1,000   *Cr* Accruals account £1,000
(b) *Dr* Prepayments account £500   *Cr* Rent account £500

Note how the two entries in the rent account are on opposite sides. The £200 rent owing at the end of the year is an expense that has not yet been entered in the books, but it must be as it relates to the current year. The £100 paid in advance for next year is not an expense of the current year, so you need to reduce the amount you have currently in the rent account so that the correct expense will be included in the income statement. The accruals account is similar to a creditor's account, but it is used for expenses unpaid at the year end. Similarly, the prepayments account is like a debtor's account, but it is used to record amounts paid for expenses in advance of the accounting period in which the benefit (i.e. what was paid for) is received.

28.2 All the debit entries should be added together and shown as one entry called 'prepayments' within current assets. Similarly, all the credit entries should be added together and shown as one entry called 'accruals' under current liabilities. This is done so as to minimise the clutter in the statement of financial position while providing enough information for anyone looking at the financial statement to be able to identify the figure for accruals and the figure for prepayments.

28.3 (a) Between accounts receivable and bank.
(b) Between accounts payable and bank overdraft.
(c) Their degree of liquidity.

28.4 They are usually added to accounts receivable. This is because these represent a regular source of income and, even though the income has nothing to do with the goods or services that form the main activity of the business, they are in every other sense another form of customer account. It makes sense, therefore, to include them in the accounts receivable balance shown in the statement of financial position.

28.5

	£
Rates due during the year	4,000
Add: Rates accrued at the start of the year	400
	4,400
Less: Rates paid during the year	(5,000)
Rates prepaid at the end of the year	(600)

28.6 Under a conventional manual approach, the journal entries will be made in the accounts in the ledger, so changing the balances as shown in that book. If the amount debited is different from the amount credited, the ledger accounts used for these entries will need to be inspected in order to discover what the error was. Looking at the note of the journal entry in the Journal is not likely to be of help. It will almost certainly show the same amounts in the debit and the credit parts of the entry. Errors in posting journal entries are usually made at the point of completion rather than at the point of origin.

With an extended trial balance, you take the balance on the ledger account before it was changed by the journal entry. You know that the balance on the ledger account is likely to be correct because your trial balance has balanced. In producing your financial statements, you do not first enter the adjustments in your ledger. First, you complete your extended trial balance. You can then make the appropriate entries in the ledger and check the resulting balances against the figures shown in the extended trial balance.

Of course, you can take a similar approach using a conventional approach and make the adjustments to your trial balance on a piece of paper before entering numbers in your financial statements. However, it will lack the neatness and internal checks that are built into the matrix of the extended trial balance.

28.7 You could list a number of situations where this may be appropriate. For example, if a businessman was unhappy with the amount set aside as an allowance for doubtful debts, he could suggest a more appropriate figure and see if it was worth making the change. Another example would be where an error was found in the accounts that required changes to be made to some of the adjustments, such as depreciation or bad debts. Despite what many people believe, businessmen do not generally adjust their accounting numbers simply to look better but they do adjust them when it is believed to be appropriate to do so. Sometimes, things come to light after an extended trial balance has been prepared that should have been included in it.

Review questions

28.1   The financial year of M. Hussey ended on 31 December 2009. Show the ledger accounts for the following items including the balance transferred to the necessary part of the financial statements, also the balances carried down to 2010:

(a)   Motor expenses: Paid in 2009 £800; Owing at 31 December 2009 £100.
(b)   Insurance: Paid in 2009 £900; Prepaid as at 31 December 2009 £70.
(c)   Stationery: Paid during 2009 £400; Owing as at 31 December 2008 £200; Owing as at 31 December 2009 £300.
(d)   Business rates: Paid during 2009 £2,000; Prepaid as at 31 December 2008 £180; Prepaid as at 31 December 2009 £160.
(e)   Hussey sublets part of the premises. He receives £1,600 during the year ended 31 December 2009. Willis, the tenant, owed Hussey £190 on 31 December 2008 and £210 on 31 December 2009.

28.2A   W. Hope's year ended on 30 June 2011. Write up the ledger accounts, showing the transfers to the financial statements and the balances carried down to the next year for the following:

(a)   Stationery: Paid for the year to 30 June 2011 £240; Inventory of stationery at 30 June 2010 £60; at 30 June 2011 £95.
(b)   General expenses: Paid for the year to 30 June 2011 £470; Owing at 30 June 2010 £32; Owing at 30 June 2011 £60.
(c)   Rent and business rates (combined account): Paid in the year to 30 June 2011 £5,410; Rent owing at 30 June 2010 £220; Rent paid in advance at 30 June 2011 £370; Business rates owing 30 June 2010 £191; Business rates owing 30 June 2011 £393.
(d)   Motor expenses: Paid in the year to 30 June 2011 £1,410; Owing as at 30 June 2010 £92; Owing as at 30 June 2011 £67.
(e)   Hope earns commission from the sales of one item. Received for the year to 30 June 2011 £1,100; Owing at 30 June 2010 £50; Owing at 30 June 2011 £82.

28.3   On 1 January 2011 the following balances, among others, stood in the books of M. Prior, a sole proprietor:

(a)   Business rates, £400 (Dr);
(b)   Packing materials, £800 (Dr).

During the year ended 31 December 2011 the information related to these two accounts is as follows:

(i)   Business rates of £3,600 were paid to cover the period 1 April 2011 to 31 March 2012;
(ii)   £6,000 was paid for packing materials bought;
(iii)   £700 was owing on 31 December 2011 in respect of packing materials bought on credit;
(iv)   Old materials amounting to £200 were sold as scrap for cash;
(v)   Closing inventory of packing materials was valued at £1,300.

You are required to write up the two accounts showing the appropriate amounts transferred to the income statement at 31 December 2011, the end of the financial year of the trader.

Note: Individual accounts are not opened for accounts payable for packing materials bought on credit.

28.4A   On 1 January 2012 the following balances, among others, stood in the books of B. Baxter:

(a)   Lighting and heating, (Dr) £192.
(b)   Insurance, (Dr) £1,410.

During the year ended 31 December 2012 the information related to these two accounts is as follows:

(*i*)   Fire insurance, £1,164 covering the year ended 31 May 2013 was paid.
(*ii*)   General insurance, £1,464 covering the year ended 31 July 2013 was paid.
(*iii*)   An insurance rebate of £82 was received on 30 June 2012.
(*iv*)   Electricity bills of £1,300 were paid.
(*v*)   An electricity bill of £162 for December 2012 was unpaid as on 31 December 2012.
(*vi*)   Oil bills of £810 were paid.
(*vii*)   Inventory of oil as on 31 December 2012 was £205.

You are required to write up the accounts for lighting and heating, and for insurance, for the year to 31 December 2012. Carry forward necessary balances to 2013.

28.5   Three of the accounts in the ledger of Charlotte Williams indicated the following balances at 1 January 2013:

Insurance paid in advance £562;
Wages outstanding £306;
Rent receivable, received in advance £36.

During 2013 Charlotte:

Paid for insurance £1,019, by bank standing order;
Paid £15,000 wages, in cash;
Received £2,600 rent, by cheque, from the tenant.

At 31 December 2013, insurance prepaid was £345. On the same day rent receivable in arrears was £105 and wages accrued amounted to £419.

(*a*)   Prepare the insurance, wages and rent receivable accounts for the year ended 31 December 2013, showing the year end transfers and the balances brought down.
(*b*)   Prepare the income statement extract showing clearly the amounts transferred from each of the above accounts for the year ending 31 December 2013.
(*c*)   Explain the effects on the financial statements of accounting for (*i*) expenses accrued and (*ii*) income received in advance at year end.
(*d*)   What are the purposes of accounting for (*i*) expenses accrued and (*ii*) income received in advance at year end?

(*Edexcel Foundation, London Examinations: GCSE*)

28.6A   The two accounts below were taken from the books of a retailer at the end of his financial year, 31 December 2010.

Insurance Account

Dr			£				Cr £
2010				2010			
Jan	1	Balance	80	Dec	31	Profit and loss	530
Jan–Dec		Bank	540		31	Balance c/d	90
			620				620
2011							
Jan	1	Balance b/d	90				

Rent Receivable Account

Dr			£				Cr £
2010				2010			
Dec	31	Profit and loss	885	Jan	1	Balance	60
	31	Balance c/d	75	Jan–Dec		Bank	900
			960				960
				2011			
				Jan	1	Balance b/d	75

Required:
Answers to the following questions.

1 What type of account is the insurance account?
2 What type of account is the rent receivable account?
3 In which subdivision of the ledger will these accounts be found?
4 Under which heading will the closing balance of the insurance account be found on the statement of financial position?
5 Under which heading will the closing balance of the rent receivable account be found on the statement of financial position?
6 In which subsidiary book (book of prime entry) will the entries transferring amounts to the profit and loss account be found?
7 Which document will be the source of information for the entry in the insurance account 'bank £540'?
8 Which document will be the source of information for the entry in the rent receivable account 'bank £900'?
9 What amount for insurance will appear in the trial balance dated 31 December 2010 prepared prior to the preparation of financial statements?
10 What amount for rent receivable will appear in the trial balance dated 31 December 2010 prepared prior to the preparation of financial statements?
11 If the adjustment in the insurance account for £90 on 31 December had been overlooked, would the net profit have been under- or overstated and by how much?
12 If the adjustment in the rent receivable account for £75 on 31 December had been overlooked, would the net profit have been under- or overstated and by how much?

(*Southern Examining Group: GCSE*)

28.7A   The owner of a small business selling and repairing cars which you patronise has just received a copy of his accounts for the current year.

He is rather baffled by some of the items and as he regards you as a financial expert, he has asked you to explain certain points of difficulty to him. This you have readily agreed to do. His questions are as follows:

(*a*) 'What is meant by the term "assets"? My mechanical knowledge and skill is an asset to the business but it does not seem to have been included.'
(*b*) 'The house I live in cost £130,000 five years ago and is now worth £360,000, but that is not included either.'
(*c*) 'What is the difference between "non-current assets" and "current assets"?'
(*d*) 'Why do amounts for "vehicles" appear under both non-current asset and current asset headings?'
(*e*) 'Why is the "bank and cash" figure in the statement of financial position different from the profit for the year shown in the income statement?'
(*f*) 'I see the income statement has been charged with depreciation on equipment, etc. I bought all these things several years ago and paid for them in cash. Does this mean that I am being charged for them again?'

Required:
Answer each of his questions in terms which he will be able to understand.

(*Association of Chartered Certified Accountants*)

28.8   The following trial balance was extracted from the books of R. Giggs at the close of business on 28 February 2010.

	Dr £	Cr £
Purchases and sales	92,800	157,165
Cash at bank	4,100	
Cash in hand	324	
Capital account 1 March 2009		11,400
Drawings	17,100	
Office furniture	2,900	
Rent	3,400	
Wages and salaries	31,400	
Discounts	820	160
Accounts receivable and accounts payable	12,316	5,245
Inventory 1 March 2009	4,120	
Allowance for doubtful debts 1 March 2009		405
Delivery van	3,750	
Van running costs	615	
Bad debts written off	730	
	174,375	174,375

Notes:
(a) Inventory 28 February 2010 £2,400.
(b) Wages and salaries accrued at 28 February 2010 £340.
(c) Rent prepaid at 28 February 2010 £230.
(d) Van running costs owing at 28 February 2010 £72.
(e) Increase the allowance for doubtful debts by £91.
(f) Provide for depreciation as follows: Office furniture £380; Delivery van £1,250.

Required:
Draw up the income statement for the year ending 28 February 2010 together with a statement of financial position as at 28 February 2010.

28.9 The trial balance for a small business at 31 August 2011 is as follows:

	£	£
Inventory 1 September 2010	8,200	
Purchases and sales	26,000	40,900
Rent	4,400	
Business rates	1,600	
Sundry expenses	340	
Motor vehicle at cost	9,000	
Accounts receivable and accounts payable	1,160	2,100
Bank	1,500	
Provision for depreciation on motor vehicle		1,200
Capital at 1 September 2010		19,700
Drawings	11,700	
	63,900	63,900

At 31 August 2011 there was:

● Inventory valued at cost prices £9,100
● Accrued rent of £400
● Prepaid business rates of £300
● The motor vehicle is to be depreciated at 20 per cent of cost

Required:
1 The adjustments to the ledger accounts for rent and business rates for the year to 31 August 2011.
2 An income statement for the year ending 31 August 2011, together with a statement of financial position as at that date.

28.10A J. Wright, a sole trader, extracted the following trial balance from his books at the close of business on 31 March 2012:

	Dr £	Cr £
Purchases and sales	61,420	127,245
Inventory 1 April 2011	7,940	
Capital 1 April 2011		25,200
Bank overdraft		2,490
Cash	140	
Discounts	2,480	62
Returns inwards	3,486	
Returns outwards		1,356
Carriage outwards	3,210	
Rent and insurance	8,870	
Allowance for doubtful debts		630
Fixtures and fittings	1,900	
Van	5,600	
Accounts receivable and accounts payable	12,418	11,400
Drawings	21,400	
Wages and salaries	39,200	
General office expenses	319	
	168,383	168,383

Notes:
(a) Inventory 31 March 2012 £6,805.
(b) Wages and salaries accrued at 31 March 2012 £3,500; Office expenses owing £16.
(c) Rent prepaid 31 March 2012 £600.
(d) Increase the allowance for doubtful debts by £110 to £740.
(e) Provide for depreciation as follows: Fixtures and fittings £190; Van £1,400.

Required:
Prepare the income statement for the year ending 31 March 2012 together with a statement of financial position as at that date.

28.11 This question also relates to extended trial balances (see Exhibit 28.2).
From the following trial balance of John Brown, store owner, prepare an income statement for the year ending 31 December 2013, and a statement of financial position as at that date, taking into consideration the adjustments shown below:

Trial Balance as at 31 December 2013

	Dr £	Cr £
Sales		400,000
Purchases	350,000	
Sales returns	5,000	
Purchases returns		6,200
Opening inventory at 1 January 2013	100,000	
Allowance for doubtful debts		800
Wages and salaries	30,000	
Rates	6,000	
Telephone	1,000	
Shop fittings at cost	40,000	
Van at cost	30,000	
Accounts receivable and accounts payable	9,800	7,000
Bad debts	200	
Capital		179,000
Bank balance	3,000	
Drawings	18,000	
	593,000	593,000

(i)   Closing inventory at 31 December 2013 £120,000.
(ii)   Accrued wages £5,000.
(iii) Rates prepaid £500.
(iv)   The allowance for doubtful debts to be increased to 10 per cent of accounts receivable.
(v)   Telephone account outstanding £220.
(vi)   Depreciate shop fittings at 10 per cent per annum, and van at 20 per cent per annum, on cost.

28.12A   The following trial balance has been extracted from the ledger of Mr Yousef, a sole trader.

Trial Balance as at 31 May 2012

	Dr £	Cr £
Sales		138,078
Purchases	82,350	
Carriage	5,144	
Drawings	7,800	
Rent, rates and insurance	6,622	
Postage and stationery	3,001	
Advertising	1,330	
Salaries and wages	26,420	
Bad debts	877	
Allowance for doubtful debts		130
Accounts receivable	12,120	
Accounts payable		6,471
Cash in hand	177	
Cash at bank	1,002	
Inventory as at 1 June 2011	11,927	
Equipment		
at cost	58,000	
accumulated depreciation		19,000
Capital		53,091
	216,770	216,770

The following additional information as at 31 May 2012 is available:

(a)   Rent is accrued by £210.
(b)   Rates have been prepaid by £880.
(c)   £2,211 of carriage represents carriage inwards on purchases.
(d)   Equipment is to be depreciated at 15% per annum using the straight line method.
(e)   The allowance for doubtful debts to be increased by £40.
(f)   Inventory at the close of business has been valued at £13,551.

Required:
Prepare an income statement for the year ending 31 May 2012 and a statement of financial position as at that date.

(*Association of Accounting Technicians*)

28.13   Mr Chai has been trading for some years as a wine merchant. The following list of balances has been extracted from his ledger as at 30 April 2010, the end of his most recent financial year.

	£
Capital	83,887
Sales	259,870
Trade accounts payable	19,840
Returns out	13,407
Allowance for doubtful debts	512
Discounts allowed	2,306
Discounts received	1,750
Purchases	135,680
Returns inwards	5,624
Carriage outwards	4,562
Drawings	18,440
Carriage inwards	11,830
Rent, rates and insurance	25,973
Heating and lighting	11,010
Postage, stationery and telephone	2,410
Advertising	5,980
Salaries and wages	38,521
Bad debts	2,008
Cash in hand	534
Cash at bank	4,440
Inventory as at 1 May 2009	15,654
Trade accounts receivable	24,500
Fixtures and fittings – at cost	120,740
Provision for depreciation on fixtures and fittings – as at 30 April 2010	63,020
Depreciation	12,074

The following additional information as at 30 April 2010 is available:

(a)   Inventory at the close of business was valued at £17,750.
(b)   Insurances have been prepaid by £1,120.
(c)   Heating and lighting is accrued by £1,360.
(d)   Rates have been prepaid by £5,435.
(e)   The allowance for doubtful debts is to be adjusted so that it is 3% of trade accounts receivable.

Required:
Prepare Mr Chai's income statement for the year ending 30 April 2010 and a statement of financial position as at that date.

(*Association of Accounting Technicians*)

The valuation of inventory

Learning objectives

After you have studied this chapter, you should be able to:

- calculate the value of inventory using three different methods
- explain why using the most appropriate method to value inventory is important
- explain what effect changing prices has on inventory valuation under each of three different methods
- explain why net realisable value is sometimes used instead of cost for inventory valuation
- adjust inventory valuations, where necessary, by a reduction to net realisable value
- explain how subjective factors influence the choice of inventory valuation method
- explain why goods purchased on 'sale or return' are not included in the buyer's inventory

Introduction

In this chapter, you will learn how to calculate the monetary value of inventory using a variety of methods. You will learn why choosing the most appropriate method of inventory valuation is important; and that a range of subjective factors can influence the choice of method, including the need to reflect how the inventory is physically used. Finally, you'll learn how to treat goods sold on 'sale or return' and about the need to adjust inventory levels identified in a stocktake (i.e. physical count of the inventory) to the level they would have been at the date of the statement of financial position.

29.1 Different valuations of inventory

Inventory is the name given to the goods for resale, work-in-progress and raw materials that are held at a point in time. The rules to follow in valuing inventory are contained in IAS 2 (*Inventories*). This is dealt with in detail in *Business Accounting 2*.

Most people assume that when a value is placed upon inventory, it is the only figure possible. This is not true.

Assume that a business has just completed its first financial year and is about to value inventory at cost price. It has dealt in only one item. A record of the transactions is now shown in Exhibit 29.1:

Exhibit 29.1

Bought		£	Sold		£
2011			2011		
January	10 at £30 each	300	May	8 for £50 each	400
April	10 at £34 each	340	November	24 for £60 each	1,440
October	20 at £40 each	800			
	40	1,440		32	1,840

A quick check by the storeman showed that there were still eight units in inventory at 31 December, which confirms what the records show above.

 Activity 29.1   What valuation do you think should be placed on the eight units of inventory? Why?

The total figure of purchases is £1,440 and sales revenue during the year was £1,840. The trading account for the first year of trading can now be completed using the closing inventory in the calculations.

Let's now look at the three most commonly used methods of valuing inventory.

29.2   First in, first out method (FIFO)

This is usually referred to as **FIFO**, from the first letters of each word. This method says that the first items to be received are the first to be issued. Using the figures in Exhibit 29.1 we can now calculate the cost of closing inventory on a FIFO basis as follows:

Date	Received	Issued	Inventory after each transaction	£	£
2011 January	10 at £30 each		10 at £30 each		300
April	10 at £34 each		10 at £30 each 10 at £34 each	300 340	640
May		8 at £30 each	2 at £30 each 10 at £34 each	60 340	400
October	20 at £40 each		2 at £30 each 10 at £34 each 20 at £40 each	60 340 800	1,200
November		2 at £30 each 10 at £34 each 12 at £40 each 24	8 at £40 each		320

Thus, the closing inventory at 31 December 2011 at cost is valued under FIFO at £320.

 Activity 29.2   Can you see another, simpler way of arriving at the same valuation under FIFO?

29.3 Last in, first out method (LIFO)

This is usually referred to as **LIFO**. As each issue of items is made they are assumed to be from the last batch received before that date. Where there is not enough left of the last batch, then the balance needed is assumed to come from the previous batch still unsold.

From the information shown in Exhibit 29.1 the calculation can now be shown.

Date	Received	Issued	Inventory after each transaction		
2011 January	10 at £30 each		10 at £30 each	£	£ 300
April	10 at £34 each		10 at £30 each 10 at £34 each	300 340	640
May		8 at £34 each	10 at £30 each 2 at £34 each	300 68	368
October	20 at £40 each		10 at £30 each 2 at £34 each 20 at £40 each	300 68 800	1,168
November		20 at £40 each 2 at £34 each 2 at £30 each 24	8 at £30 each		240

Thus, the closing inventory at 31 December 2011 at cost is valued under LIFO at £240.

Activity 29.3 Can you see another, simpler way of arriving at the same valuation under LIFO?

29.4 Average cost method (AVCO)

Using the **AVCO** method, with each receipt of goods the average cost for each item is recalculated. Further issues of goods are then at that figure, until another receipt of goods means that another recalculation is needed. From the information in Exhibit 29.1 the calculation can be shown:

Date	Received	Issued	Average cost per unit of inventory held	Number of units in inventory	Total value of inventory
2011			£		£
January	10 at £30		30	10	300
April	10 at £34		32*	20	640
May		8 at £32	32	12	384
October	20 at £40		37**	32	1,184
November		24 at £37	37	8	296

The closing inventory at 31 December 2011 is therefore valued at £296.

*In April, this is calculated as follows: inventory 10 × £30 = £300 + inventory received (10 × £34) = £340 = total £640. You then divide the 20 units in inventory into the total cost of that inventory, i.e. £640 ÷ 20 = £32.
**In October, this is calculated as follows: inventory 12 × £32 = £384 + inventory received (20 × £40) = £800 = £1,184. There are 32 units in inventory, so the average is £1,184 ÷ 32 = £37.

Note, using this approach you recalculate the average after every receipt of a batch of new inventory and then use it as the cost of the next batch sold.

 Activity 29.4   If two units had been sold in December, at what cost would they have been sold?

29.5 Inventory valuation and the calculation of profits

Using the figures from Exhibit 29.1 with inventory valuations shown by the three methods of FIFO, LIFO and AVCO, the trading account entries under each method would be:

Trading Account for the year ending 31 December 2011							
	FIFO £	LIFO £	AVCO £		FIFO £	LIFO £	AVCO £
Purchases	1,440	1,440	1,440	Sales	1,840	1,840	1,840
less Closing inventory	(320)	(240)	(296)				
Cost of goods sold	1,120	1,200	1,144				
Gross profit	720	640	696				
	1,840	1,840	1,840		1,840	1,840	1,840

Activity 29.5   Which method has produced (*a*) the highest, (*b*) the middle and (*c*) the lowest value for closing inventory? Why do you think this has occurred?

As you can see, different methods of inventory valuation result in different profits. It is, therefore, important that the method chosen is the one that is closest in its assumptions to the nature of the business.

29.6 Reduction to net realisable value

Having selected the most appropriate method to apply when determining the cost of closing inventory, you next need to consider whether that value is realistic – that is, whether it is what the inventory is *actually* worth at the end of the period. This is an example of application of the prudence concept that you learnt about in Chapter 10. Following the prudence concept, inventory should never be undervalued or overvalued.

Activity 29.6   (*a*) What happens to gross profit if closing inventory is undervalued? Why?
(*b*) What happens to gross profit if closing inventory is overvalued? Why?

To check that inventory is not overvalued, accountants calculate its **net realisable value**. This is done according to the formula:

$$\text{Saleable value (i.e. what it can be sold for)} - \text{Expenses needed before completion of sale (such as costs of delivery to the seller's shops)} = \text{Net realisable value.}$$

If the net realisable value of inventory is less than the cost of the inventory, then the figure to be used in the financial statements is net realisable value *not* cost.

A somewhat exaggerated example will illustrate why this is done. Assume that an art dealer has bought only two paintings during the financial year ended 31 December 2011. She starts off the year without any inventory, and then buys a genuine masterpiece for £6,000 and sells it later in the year for £11,500. The other is a fake, but she does not realise this when she buys it for £5,100. During the year she discovers that she made a terrible mistake and that its net realisable value is only £100. The fake remains unsold at the end of the year. The trading account part of the income statement, shown in Exhibit 29.2, would appear as (*a*) if inventory is valued at cost, and as (*b*) if inventory is valued at net realisable value.

Exhibit 29.2

Trading Account section of the Income Statement for the year ending 31 December 2011

		(a) £		(b) £
Sales		11,500		11,500
Purchases	11,100		11,100	
Less: Closing inventory	(5,100)		(100)	
		(6,000)		(11,000)
Gross profit		5,500		500

Method (*a*) ignores the fact that the dealer had a bad trading year owing to her mistake. If this method was used, then the loss on the fake would reveal itself in the following year's trading account. Method (*b*) recognises that the loss really occurred at the date of purchase rather than at the date of sale. Following the concept of prudence, accounting practice is to use method (*b*).

29.7 Inventory groups and valuation

If there is only one sort of item in inventory, calculating the lower of cost or net realisable value is easy. If we have several or many types of item in inventory, we can use one of two ways of making the calculation – by category and by item.

Exhibit 29.3

Inventory at 31 December 2011			
Item	*Different categories*	*Cost*	*Net realisable value*
		£	£
1	A	100	80
2	A	120	150
3	A	300	400
4	B	180	170
5	B	150	130
6	B	260	210
7	C	410	540
8	C	360	410
9	C	420	310
		2,300	2,400

In Exhibit 29.3, Items 1, 2 and 3 are televisions; 4, 5 and 6 are DVD recorders; and 7, 8 and 9 are games consoles. From the information given in the exhibit, we will calculate the value of the inventory using both these approaches.

(1) The category method

The same sorts of items are put together in categories. Thus, televisions are in Category A, DVDs are in Category B, and Category C is games consoles.

A calculation showing a comparison of cost valuation and net realisable value for each category is now shown.

Category	Cost	Net realisable value
A	£100 + £120 + £300 = £520	£80 + £150 + £400 = £630
B	£180 + £150 + £260 = £590	£170 + £130 + £210 = £510
C	£410 + £360 + £420 = £1,190	£540 + £410 + £310 = £1,260

The lower of cost and net realisable value is, therefore:

	£
Category A: lower of £520 or £630	= 520
Category B: lower of £590 or £510	= 510
Category C: lower of £1,190 or £1,260	= 1,190
Inventory is valued for financial statements at	2,220

(2) The item method

By this method, the lower of cost or net realisable value for each item is compared and the lowest figure taken. From Exhibit 29.3 this gives us the following valuation:

Item	Valuation
	£
1	80
2	120
3	300
4	170
5	130
6	210
7	410
8	360
9	310
	£2,090

Of these two methods, it is Method 2, the item method, that should be used. It provides a more realistic overall value for the inventory.

29.8 Some other inventory valuation bases in use

Retail businesses often estimate the cost of inventory by calculating it in the first place at selling price, and then deducting the normal margin of gross profit on such inventory. Adjustment is made for items which are to be sold at other than normal selling prices.

Where standard costing is in use, the figure of **standard cost** is frequently used. You'll learn about standard costing in *Business Accounting 2*. Standard cost is, effectively, what you would expect something to cost. When standard costing is in use, a standard cost will have been determined for purchases and it is that standard cost that would be used to value closing inventory.

'Base inventory' (often referred to as 'base stock') is a method used in industries where a minimum level of inventory is always maintained. Power station fuel supplies, for example, may fall within this classification. The base inventory is assumed to never deteriorate or be replaced and is valued at its original cost. Any other inventory is valued using a 'normal' method, such as FIFO, LIFO or AVCO.

29.9 Periodic inventory valuation

Some businesses do not keep detailed inventory records like those shown in Exhibit 29.1. Instead, they wait until the end of a period before calculating the value of their closing inventory. In this case, AVCO is based upon the total cost of inventory available for sale in the period divided by the number of units of inventory available for sale in the period. You then multiply the closing inventory by the overall average cost of the inventory to get the value of that inventory.

If you did this for the data in Exhibit 29.1 the closing inventory value at cost would be (£1,440 ÷ 40 =) £36 × 8 = £288 (rather than £296, as calculated in Section 29.4). This method is also known as the 'weighted average cost method'.

If you used FIFO or LIFO in these circumstances, FIFO gives the same answer as under the method presented earlier. LIFO, on the other hand, would become the opposite of FIFO, with all closing inventory assumed to have come from the earliest batches of purchases.

 Activity 29.7 If you have no detailed inventory records, how could you use AVCO, FIFO or LIFO?

Unless an examiner asks you to calculate them using a periodic inventory valuation basis, you should assume that you are to calculate AVCO, FIFO and LIFO in the way they were presented earlier in this chapter (i.e. on a perpetual valuation basis).

29.10 Factors affecting the inventory valuation decision

The overriding consideration applicable in all circumstances when valuing inventory is the need to give a 'true and fair view' of the state of affairs of the undertaking as at the date of the statement of financial position and of the trend of the business's trading results. There is, however, no precise definition of what constitutes a 'true and fair view' and it rests on the judgement of the persons concerned. Unfortunately, the judgement of any two persons will not always be the same in the differing circumstances of various businesses.

In fact, the only certain thing about inventory valuation is that the concept of consistency (which you learnt about in Chapter 10) should be applied, i.e. once adopted, the same basis should be used in the financial statements until some good reason occurs to change it. A reference should then be made in the notes that accompany the financial statements as to the effect of the change on the reported profits, if the amount involved is material.

Let's look briefly at some of the factors which cause a particular basis to be chosen. The list is intended to be indicative rather than comprehensive, and is merely intended as a first brief look at matters which will have to be studied in depth by those intending to make a career in accountancy.

1 **Ignorance.** The people involved may not appreciate the fact that there is more than one possible way of valuing inventory.

2 **Convenience.** The basis chosen may not be the best for the purposes of profit calculation but it may be the easiest to calculate. It must always be borne in mind that the benefits which flow from possessing information should be greater than the costs of obtaining it. The only difficulty with this is actually establishing when the benefits do exceed the cost but, in some circumstances, the decision not to adopt a given basis will be obvious.

3 **Custom.** It may be the particular method used in a certain trade or industry.

4 **Taxation.** The whole idea may be to defer the payment of tax for as long as possible. Because the inventory figures affect the calculation of profits on which the tax is based the lowest possible inventory figures may be taken to show the lowest profits up to the date of the statement of financial position. (But doing this will result in a higher profit in the following period when the inventory is sold!)

5 **The capacity to borrow money or to sell the business at the highest possible price.** The higher the inventory value, the higher will be the profits calculated and, therefore, at first sight the business looks more attractive to a buyer or lender. Either of these considerations may be more important to the owners than anything else. It may be thought that those in business are not so gullible, but all business people are not necessarily well acquainted with accounting customs. In fact, many small businesses are bought, or money is lent to them, without the expert advice of someone well versed in accounting.

6 **Remuneration purposes.** Where someone managing a business is paid in whole or in part by reference to the profits earned, then one basis may suit them better than others. They may therefore strive to have that basis used to suit their own ends. The owner, however, may try to follow another course to minimise the remuneration that he/she will have to pay out.

7 **Lack of information.** If proper inventory records have not been kept, then such bases as the average cost method or the LIFO method may not be calculable using the approaches you learnt at the start of this chapter. Of course, a lack of proper inventory records makes it very difficult to detect theft or losses of inventory. If for no other reason than to enable these factors to be controlled, proper inventory records should be kept by all trading businesses. As a result, this barrier to adopting AVCO and LIFO should not arise very often.

8 **Advice of the auditors.** Auditors are accountants who review the accounting records and the financial statements in order to report whether or not the financial statements present a true and fair view of the financial performance and financial position of a business. Many businesses use a particular basis because the auditors advised its use in the first instance. A different auditor may well advise that a different basis be used.

29.11 The conflict of aims

The list given in the previous section of some of the factors which affect decisions concerning the valuation of inventory is certainly not exhaustive, but it does illustrate the fact that valuation is usually a compromise. There is not usually only one figure which is true and fair; there may be a variety of possibilities. The desire to borrow money and, in so doing, to paint a good picture by being reasonably optimistic in valuing inventory will be tempered by the fact that this may increase the tax bill. Inventory valuation is, therefore, a compromise between the various ends which it serves.

29.12 Work-in-progress

The valuation of work-in-progress is subject to all the various criteria and methods used in valuing inventory of finished goods. Probably the cost element is more strongly pronounced than in inventory valuation, as it is very often impossible or irrelevant to say what net realisable value or replacement price would be applicable to partly finished goods. Businesses operating in industries such as those which have contracts covering several years have evolved their own methods.

The valuation of long-term contract work-in-progress is regulated by IAS 11 (*Construction contracts*) and is dealt with in *Business Accounting 2*.

29.13 Goods on sale or return

Goods received on sale or return

Sometimes goods may be received from a supplier on a **sale or return** basis. This is, for example, typically what happens when newsagents purchase newspapers. What this means is that the goods do not have to be paid for if they are not sold. If they cannot be sold, they are returned to the supplier. This means that until the goods are sold they belong to the seller, *not* the buyer.

The effect of an arrangement of this type is that there isn't a liability to pay the seller until the goods have been sold on to a customer of the buyer. If there is no liability, the buyer cannot recognise the existence of the goods held on this basis when the buyer's financial statements are being prepared at the end of the accounting period. As a result, if goods on sale or return are held by the buyer at the stocktaking date (i.e. the date when inventory is counted), they should not be included in the buyer's inventory valuation, nor in the figure for purchases.

Goods sent to customers on sale or return

If a seller sends goods to a customer on a sale or return basis, the goods will continue to belong to the seller until they are sold on by the buyer. At the end of the supplier's accounting period, any goods held on this basis by its customers should be included in the seller's inventory valuation, not in the figure for sales.

29.14 Stocktaking and the date of the statement of financial position

All but the very smallest of trading businesses need to physically check that the inventory their records tell them they have actually exists. The process of doing so is called **stocktaking**. Students often think that all the counting and valuing of inventory is done on the last day of the accounting period. This might be true in a small business, but it is often impossible in larger businesses. There may be too many items of inventory to do it that quickly.

This means that stocktaking may take place over a period of days. To convert the physical stocktake inventory levels to their actual levels at the date of the statement of financial position, adjustments must be made to the inventory levels found during the stocktake. Exhibit 29.4 gives an example of such adjustments.

Exhibit 29.4 Adjustments to inventory following stocktake

Lee Ltd has a financial year which ends on 31 December 2010. The stocktaking is not done until 8 January 2011; the items in the inventory on that date are valued at their cost of £28,850. The following information is available about transactions between 31 December 2010 and 8 January 2011:

1 Purchases since 31 December 2010 amounted to £2,370 at cost.
2 Returns inwards since 31 December 2010 were £350 at selling price.
3 Sales since 31 December 2010 amounted to £3,800 at selling price.
4 The selling price is always cost price + 25 per cent.

Lee Ltd
Computation of inventory on 31 December 2010

			£
Inventory (at cost)			28,850
Add Items now sold which were in inventory on 31 December 2010 (at cost)			
		£	
Sales		3,800	
Less Profit content (20 per cent of selling price)(Note)		(760)	
			3,040
			31,890
Less Items which were not in inventory on 31 December 2010 (at cost)			
		£	
Returns inwards		350	
Less Profit content (20 per cent of selling price)Note		(70)	
	280		
Purchases (at cost)	2,370		
			(2,650)
Inventory in hand as on 31 December 2010			29,240

Note: Inventory is valued at cost (or net realisable value), and not at selling price. As this calculation has a sales figure in it which includes profit, we must deduct the profit part to get to the cost price. This is true also for returns inwards.

The professional accounting bodies encourage the auditors of companies to be present as observers at stocktaking in order to verify that procedures were correctly followed.

29.15 Inventory levels

One of the most common mistakes found in the running of a business is that too high a level of inventory is maintained.

A considerable number of businesses that have problems with a shortage of funds will find that they can help matters by having a look at the amount of inventory they hold. It would be a very rare business indeed which, if it had not investigated the matter previously, could not manage to let parts of its inventory run down. This would stop the investment of funds in items – the unneeded inventory – that are not required.

Learning outcomes

You should now have learnt:

1 That methods of valuing inventory, such as FIFO, LIFO and AVCO, are only that – methods of *valuing* inventory. It does not mean that goods are actually sold on a FIFO or LIFO basis.

2 That because different methods of valuing inventory result in different closing inventory valuations, the amount of profit reported for a particular accounting period is affected by the method of inventory valuation adopted.

3 That using net realisable when this is lower than cost, so that profits are not overstated, is an example of the application of the prudence concept in accounting.

4 That many subjective factors may affect the choice of inventory valuation method adopted.

5 That without inventory records of quantities of items, it would be very difficult to track down theft or losses or to detect wastage of goods.

6 That without proper inventory records, it is unlikely that AVCO and LIFO can be applied in the way described at the start of this chapter.

7 That goods sold on sale or return should be included in the inventory of the seller until the buyer has sold them.

8 That stocktaking is usually done over a period of time around the end of the accounting period.

9 That the inventory levels identified at a stocktake need to be adjusted to the level they would have been at had the stocktake taken place on the date of the statement of financial position.

Answers to activities

29.1 This is not as easy a question to answer as it first appears, especially if you have never studied this topic before. Firstly, applying the historic cost convention you learnt about in Chapter 10, we should value the inventory at the cost of having it available for sale. That is, it should be valued at cost. If all purchases during the year cost the same per unit, arriving at the value to place on inventory would be trivially easy. For example, if all of the units cost £30 each, the closing value would be 8 × £30 = £240.

However, the goods in this example have been purchased at different prices. To cope with this, we look at it from the perspective of which of the goods purchased have been sold. Knowing which of them has been sold allows us to know which ones remain unsold, which will make valuing the inventory very straightforward. In this case, purchases were made at £30, £34 and £40. If all the £34 and £40 purchases have been sold, we know to use £30 as the unit cost of the stock.

Unfortunately, many businesses do not know whether they have sold all the older units before they sell the newer units. For instance, a business selling spanners may not know if the older spanners had been sold before the newer ones were sold. A petrol station doesn't know whether all the fuel it has was from one delivery or whether it is a mixture of all the deliveries received from the supplier. Accounting deals with this by selecting the method of valuation that is most likely to fairly represent the cost of the goods sold and, hence, the value of the remaining inventory.

To answer the question, you don't have enough information to decide what value to place on the eight units of inventory, but it should be based upon the best estimate you can make of the cost of those eight units.

29.2 As at least eight units were received in the last batch purchased, you can simply take the unit cost of that batch and multiply it by the units in inventory. If you are asked to show your workings for calculation of closing inventory under FIFO, this is a perfectly acceptable approach to adopt.

29.3 It's not so simple under LIFO. If you receive three batches of purchases of ten, four and six units respectively and you have ten left in inventory, there is no guarantee that they will all be from the first batch. You may have sold all ten of the first batch before the second batch was received. Alternatively, you may have sold three before the second batch of four was delivered and then sold six before the last batch of six was received and then sold one before the year end. You do have ten in inventory, but five are from the first batch received and five from the last one. There is no shortcut available for ascertaining in which batch the remaining inventory was received.

29.4 There have been no further deliveries of new inventory received so the average value of inventory is still £37.

29.5 The AVCO inventory valuation is between the values of FIFO and LIFO. FIFO has the highest value because the cost of purchases has been rising. Had they been falling, it would have been LIFO that had the greatest closing inventory value. AVCO will lie between the other two whichever way prices are moving.

29.6 (a) Gross profit will be understated if closing inventory is undervalued because the lower the value of closing inventory, the higher the cost of goods sold.
     (b) Gross profit will be overstated if closing inventory is overvalued because the higher the value of closing inventory, the lower the cost of goods sold.

29.7 It may be impossible. However, whatever the quality of your inventory records, all businesses must retain evidence of their transactions. As a result, you could have a record of what was purchased, when, from whom and for how much, but you may well have no record at all of what was sold, when, to whom or for how much – if all sales are for cash, your only record may be the till receipt for each transaction, and that frequently shows no more than the date and value of the sale.

Review questions

29.1 From the following figures calculate the closing inventory-in-trade that would be shown using (*i*) FIFO, (*ii*) LIFO, (*iii*) AVCO methods.

Bought		*Sold*	
March	200 at £20 each	December	240 for £30 each
September	100 at £22 each		

29.2 For Question 29.1 draw up the trading account part of the income statement for the year showing the gross profits that would have been reported using (*i*) FIFO, (*ii*) LIFO, (*iii*) AVCO methods.

29.3A From the following figures calculate the closing inventory-in-trade that would be shown using (*i*) FIFO, (*ii*) LIFO, (*iii*) AVCO methods on a perpetual inventory basis.

Bought		*Sold*	
January	120 at £16 each	June	125 at £22 each
April	80 at £18 each	November	210 at £25 each
October	150 at £19 each		

29.4A Draw up trading account parts of the income statement using each of the three methods from the details in Question 29.3A.

29.5 The sixth formers at the Broadway School run a tuck shop business. They began trading on 1 December 2012 and sell two types of chocolate bar, 'Break' and 'Brunch'.

Their starting capital was a £200 loan from the School Fund.
Transactions are for cash only.
Each Break costs the sixth form 16p and each Brunch costs 12p.
25% is added to the cost to determine the selling price.
Transactions during December are summarised as follows:

December 6   Bought 5 boxes, each containing 48 bars, of Break; and 3 boxes, each containing 36 bars of Brunch.
December 20   The month's sales amounted to 200 Breaks and 90 Brunches.

(a) Record the above transactions in the cash, purchases and sales accounts. All calculations must be shown.
(b) On 20 December (the final day of term) a physical stocktaking showed 34 Break and 15 Brunch in inventory. Using these figures calculate the value of the closing inventory, and enter the amount in the inventory account.
(c) Prepare a trading account for the tuck shop, calculating the gross profit/loss for the month of December 2012.^Authors' Note
(d) Calculate the number of each item that should have been in inventory. Explain why this information should be a cause for concern.

(Edexcel, London Examinations: GCSE)

Authors' Note: Examiners typically only ask for 'a trading account' in questions rather than 'the trading account section of the income statement'. If you get a question asking for 'a trading account', assume you are being asked to prepare the trading account section of the income statement unless it is obvious that the examiner wants the trading account in the ledger rather than the financial statement.

29.6 Thomas Brown and Partners, a business of practising accountants, have several clients who are retail distributors of the Allgush Paint Spray guns.

The current price list of Gushing Sprayers Limited, manufacturers, quotes the following wholesale prices for the Allgush Paint Spray guns:

Grade A distributors   £500 each
Grade B distributors   £560 each
Grade C distributors   £600 each

The current normal retail price of the Allgush Paint Spray gun is £750.

Thomas Brown and Partners are currently advising some of their clients concerning the valuation of stock in trade of Allgush Paint Spray guns.

1 Charles Gray – Grade B distributor
On 30 April 2012, 15 Allgush Paint Spray guns were in inventory, including one gun which was slightly damaged and expected to sell at half the normal retail price. Charles Gray considers that this gun should remain in inventory at cost price until it is sold.

K. Peacock, a customer of Charles Gray, was expected to purchase a spray gun on 30 April 2012, but no agreement was reached owing to the customer being involved in a road accident and expected to remain in hospital until late May 2012.

Charles Gray argues that he is entitled to regard this as a sale during the year ended 30 April 2012.

2 Jean Kim – Grade C distributor
On 31 May 2012, 22 Allgush Paint Spray guns were in inventory. Unfortunately Jean Kim's business is suffering a serious cash flow crisis. It is very doubtful that the business will survive and therefore a public auction of the inventory-in-trade is likely. Reliable sources suggest that the spray guns may be auctioned for £510 each; auction fees and expenses are expected to total £300.

Jean Kim has requested advice as to the basis upon which her inventory should be valued at 31 May 2012.

→ 3 Peter Fox – Grade A distributor

Peter Fox now considers that inventory valuations should be related to selling prices because of the growing uncertainties of the market for spray guns.

Alternatively, Peter Fox has suggested that he uses the cost prices applicable to Grade C distributors as the basis for inventory valuations – 'after all this will establish consistency with Grade C distributors'.

Required:

A brief report to each of Charles Gray, Jean Kim and Peter Fox concerning the valuation of their inventories-in-trade.

Note: Answers should include references to appropriate accounting concepts.

(Association of Accounting Technicians)

29.7A Mary Smith commenced trading on 1 September 2012 as a distributor of the Straight Cut garden lawn mower, a relatively new product which is now becoming increasingly popular.

Upon commencing trading, Mary Smith transferred £7,000 from her personal savings to open a business bank account.

Mary Smith's purchases and sales of the Straight Cut garden lawn mower during the three months ended 30 November 2012 are as follows:

2012	Bought	Sold
September	12 machines at £384 each	–
October	8 machines at £450 each	4 machines at £560 each
November	16 machines at £489 each	20 machines at £680 each

Assume all purchases are made in the first half of the month and all sales are in the second half of the month.

At the end of October 2012, Mary Smith decided to take one Straight Cut garden lawn mower out of inventory for cutting the lawn outside her showroom. It is estimated that this lawn mower will be used in Mary Smith's business for eight years and have a nil estimated residual value. Mary Smith wishes to use the straight line basis of depreciation.

Additional information:

1 Overhead expenses paid during the three months ended 30 November 2012 amounted to £1,520.
2 There were no amounts prepaid on 30 November 2012, but sales commissions payable of $2\frac{1}{2}\%$ of the gross profit on sales were accrued due on 30 November 2012.
3 Upon commencing trading, Mary Smith resigned a business appointment with a salary of £15,000 per annum.
4 Mary Smith is able to obtain interest of 10% per annum on her personal savings.
5 One of the lawn mowers not sold on 30 November 2012 has been damaged in the showroom and is to be repaired in December 2012 at a cost of £50 before being sold for an expected £400.

Note: Ignore taxation.

Required:

(a) Prepare, in as much detail as possible, Mary Smith's income statement for the quarter ending 30 November 2012 using:
   (i) the first in first out basis of inventory valuation, and
   (ii) the last in first out basis of inventory valuation.
(b) Using the results in (a) (i) above, prepare a statement comparing Mary Smith's income for the quarter ended 30 November 2012 with that for the quarter ended 31 August 2012.
(c) Give one advantage and one disadvantage of each of the bases of inventory valuations used in (a) above.

(Association of Accounting Technicians)

29.8 'The idea that inventory should be included in accounts at the lower of historical cost and net realisable value follows the prudence convention but not the consistency convention.'

Required:
(a) Do you agree with the quotation?
(b) Explain, with reasons, whether you think this idea (that inventory should be included in accounts at the lower of historical cost and net realisable value) is a useful one. Refer to at least two classes of user of financial accounting reports in your answer.

(*Association of Chartered Certified Accountants*)

29.9 After stocktaking for the year ended 31 May 2012 had taken place, the closing inventory of Cobden Ltd was aggregated to a figure of £87,612.
    During the course of the audit which followed, the undernoted facts were discovered:

(a) Some goods stored outside had been included at their normal cost price of £570. They had, however, deteriorated and would require an estimated £120 to be spent to restore them to their original condition, after which they could be sold for £800.
(b) Some goods had been damaged and were now unsaleable. They could, however, be sold for £110 as spares after repairs estimated at £40 had been carried out. They had originally cost £200.
(c) One inventory sheet had been over-added by £126 and another under-added by £72.
(d) Cobden Ltd had received goods costing £2,010 during the last week of May 2012 but, because the invoices did not arrive until June 2012, they have not been included in inventory.
(e) An inventory sheet total of £1,234 had been transferred to the summary sheet as £1,243.
(f) Invoices totalling £638 arrived during the last week of May 2012 (and were included in purchases and in accounts payable) but, because of transport delays, the goods did not arrive until late June 2012 and were not included in closing inventory.
(g) Portable generators on hire from another company at a charge of £347 were included, at this figure, in inventory.
(h) Free samples sent to Cobden Ltd by various suppliers had been included in inventory at the catalogue price of £63.
(i) Goods costing £418 sent to customers on a sale or return basis had been included in inventory by Cobden Ltd at their selling price, £602.
(j) Goods sent on a sale or return basis to Cobden Ltd had been included in inventory at the amount payable (£267) if retained. No decision to retain had been made.

Required:
Using such of the above information as is relevant, prepare a schedule amending the inventory figure as at 31 May 2012. State your reason for each amendment or for not making an amendment.

(*Association of Chartered Certified Accountants*)

29.10A Yuan Ltd has an accounting year ended 28 February 2011. Due to staff shortages, the stocktaking had not been undertaken until 9 March 2011 and the inventory valued at this date is £100,600. This value was also used in the company draft accounts for the year ended 28 February 2011 which showed a net profit of £249,600 and a current asset total of £300,000. The selling price of goods is based on cost plus 25%.
    During the company audit, the following errors were discovered:

1 Sales invoices for goods dispatched to customers during the period 1–9 March 2011 amounted to £43,838 which include carriage on sales of 5%.
2 Goods costing £14,000 were delivered to the company during the period 1–9 March 2011.
3 During the period 1–9 March 2011, returns from customers at selling price were £4,170, and returns to suppliers amounted to £850.
4 The inventory valuation of 9 March 2011 included the inventory of the company's office cleaning materials. These materials had all been bought during February 2011 at a cost of £600.

5 Inventory with a selling price of £1,650 had been borrowed by the marketing department on 27 February 2011 to be displayed at an exhibition from 28 February to 16 March. This had helped to attract orders of £27,400 for delivery in April 2011.

6 Inventory with a selling price of £800 was sent to a customer on sale or return basis on 14 February 2011. On 23 February 2011, the customer sold half of the consignment. This credit sale had not yet been recorded in Yuan Ltd's accounts for the year ended 28 February 2011. On 9 March 2011, the remaining half of the consignment had not been returned to Yuan Ltd, and the customer had not signified its acceptance.

7 On 3 March 2011, Yuan Ltd. received a batch of free samples which had been included in the inventory valuation at the list price of £20.

Required:

(a) Prepare a schedule amending the inventory figure as at 28 February 2011.

(b) Calculate the revised net profit for the year ending 28 February 2011 and the correct value of current assets at that date.

Introduction to the Financial Statements of Limited Companies

An introduction to the financial statements of limited liability companies

Learning objectives

After you have studied this chapter, you should be able to:

- explain how limited companies differ from sole traders and partnerships
- explain the differences between different classes of shares
- calculate how distributable profits available for dividends are divided between the different classes of shares
- explain the differences between shares and loan notes
- prepare the income statement for a company for internal purposes
- prepare the statement of financial position for a company for both internal and external purposes
- explain what is shown in a statement of changes in equity
- explain what an audit report is
- explain how to present goodwill in company financial statements

Introduction

In this chapter, you'll learn about the different types of companies that can exist and about the different types of long-term funds they can raise in order to finance their activities. You'll learn how to prepare the financial statements for companies and about the differences between the treatment of goodwill in company accounts and its treatment in the accounts of sole traders and partnerships.

45.1 Need for limited companies

Limited liability companies, more commonly referred to as **limited companies**, came into existence originally because of the growth in the size of businesses, and the need to have a lot of people investing in the business who would not be able to take part in its management.

Activity 45.1 Why do you think a partnership was not an appropriate form of business in this case?

The UK law governing companies, their formation and the duties relating to their members, directors, auditors and officials is largely contained in the Companies Act 2006. This Act consolidated the Companies Acts of 1985, 1989 and 2004. However much of the requirements concerning financial statements continue to be found in the 1985 Act.

45.2 Limited liability

The capital of a limited company is divided into **shares**. Shares can be of any nominal value – 10p, 25p, £1, £5, £10 or any other amount per share. To become a member of a limited company, or a **shareholder**, a person must buy one or more of the shares.

If shareholders have paid in full for their shares, their liability is limited to what they have already paid for those shares. If a company loses all its assets, all those shareholders can lose is their shares. They cannot be forced to pay anything more in respect of the company's losses.

Shareholders who have only partly paid for their shares can be forced to pay the balance owing on the shares, but nothing else.

Shareholders are therefore said to have 'limited liability' and this is why companies are known as 'limited liability' or, more usually, simply 'limited' companies. By addressing the need for investors to have limited risk of financial loss, the existence of limited liability encourages individuals to invest in these companies and makes it possible to have both a large number of owners and a large amount of capital invested in the company.

There are a few companies which have unlimited liability, but these are outside the scope of this book.

45.3 Public and private companies

In the UK, there are two main classes of company, the **public company** and the **private company**. Private companies far outnumber public companies. In the Companies Act, a public company is defined as one which fulfils the following conditions:

- Its memorandum (a document that describes the company) states that it is a public company, and that it has registered as such.
- It has an authorised share capital of at least £50,000.
- Minimum membership is one. There is no maximum.
- Its name must end with the words 'public limited company' or the abbreviation 'PLC'. It can have the Welsh equivalent ('CCC') if registered in Wales.

PLCs can, but don't have to, offer their shares for sale on the Stock Exchange. It is through the Stock Exchange that a large ownership base can be established.

A private company is usually, but not always, a smaller business, and may be formed by one or more persons. It is defined by the Act as a company which is not a public company. The main differences between a private company and a public company are that a private company

- can have an authorised capital of less than £50,000; and
- *cannot* offer its shares for subscription to the public at large, whereas public companies can.

This means that if you were to walk into a bank, or similar public place, and see a prospectus offering anyone the chance to take up shares in a company, then that company would be a public company, i.e. a PLC.

The shares that are dealt in on the Stock Exchange are all those of public limited companies. This does not mean that shares of all public companies are traded on the Stock Exchange. For various reasons, some public companies have either chosen not to, or have not been allowed to have their shares traded there. The ones whose shares are traded are known as 'quoted companies' meaning that their shares have prices quoted on the Stock Exchange. They have to comply with Stock Exchange requirements in addition to those laid down by the Companies Act and accounting standards.

Activity 45.2 Apart from not having to worry about complying with the Stock Exchange requirements, what other reasons can you think of that would explain why some PLCs do not wish to offer their shares on the Stock Market?

45.4 Directors of the company

The day-to-day business of a company is *not* carried out by the shareholders. The possession of a share normally confers voting rights on the holder, who is then able to attend general meetings of the company. At one of these general meetings, normally the **Annual General Meeting** or AGM, the shareholders vote for **directors**, these being the people who will be entrusted with the running of the business. At each AGM, the directors report on their stewardship, and this report is accompanied by a set of financial statements and other documents – the 'annual report'.

45.5 Legal status of a limited company

A limited company is said to possess a 'separate legal identity' from that of its shareholders. Put simply, this means that a company is not seen as being exactly the same as its shareholders. For instance, a company can sue one or more of its shareholders, and similarly, a shareholder can sue the company. This would not be the case if the company and its shareholders were exactly the same thing, as one cannot sue oneself. This concept is often referred to as the **veil of incorporation**.

Note: This is an extremely important concept. The most frequently cited example of the strength of the veil of incorporation is a case that went to the House of Lords in 1897. The case is known as *Saloman* v *Saloman & Co Ltd*. It involved a company formed by a Mr Saloman. The company was run by Mr Saloman in the same way as when he was operating as a sole trader. He received all the profits and made all the decisions. However, the *veil of incorporation* meant that the company was treated as completely separate from him. When the business failed owing a large amount of money, Mr Saloman did not have to pay for the business debts personally. The debts were the responsibility of the company, not of Mr Saloman. This was held to be the case even though Mr Saloman had lent some money to the company in the form of secured debentures (now called secured loan notes). This meant that any funds left in the company when it failed were first used to repay *those* loan notes (because they were 'secured' on the assets of the company) and the rest of the creditors (who were not 'secured') received nothing.

45.6 Share capital

Shareholders of a limited company obtain their reward in the form of a share of the profits, known as a **dividend**. The directors decide on the amount of profits which are placed in reserves (i.e. 'retained'). The directors then propose the payment of a certain amount of dividend from the remaining profits. It is important to note that the shareholders cannot propose a higher dividend for themselves than that already proposed by the directors. They can, however, propose that a lesser dividend should be paid, although this is very rare indeed. If the directors propose that no dividend be paid, then the shareholders are powerless to alter the decision.

The decision by the directors as to the amount proposed as dividends is a very complex one and cannot be fully discussed here. Such points as government directives to reduce dividends, the effect of taxation, the availability of bank balances to pay the dividends, the possibility of take-over bids and so on will all be taken into account.

The dividend is usually expressed as a percentage. A dividend of 10 per cent in Business A on 500,000 ordinary shares of £1 each will amount to £50,000. A dividend of 6 per cent in Business B on 200,000 ordinary shares of £2 each will amount to £24,000. A shareholder having 100 shares in each business would receive £10 from Business A and £12 from Business B.

There are two main types of shares:

1 **Preference shares.** Holders of these shares get an agreed percentage rate of dividend before the ordinary shareholders receive anything.
2 **Ordinary shares.** Holders of these shares receive the remainder of the total profits available for dividends. There is no upper limit to the amounts of dividends they can receive.

For example, if a company had 50,000 5 per cent preference shares of £1 each and 200,000 ordinary shares of £1 each, then the dividends could be payable as in Exhibit 45.1.

Exhibit 45.1

Year	1	2	3	4	5
	£	£	£	£	£
Profits appropriated for dividends	6,500	10,500	13,500	28,500	17,500
Preference dividends (5%)	2,500	2,500	2,500	2,500	2,500
Ordinary dividends	(2%)4,000	(4%)8,000	(5½%)11,000	(13%)26,000	(7½%)15,000
	6,500	10,500	13,500	28,500	17,500

The two main types of preference shares are non-cumulative preference shares and cumulative preference shares:

1 **Non-cumulative preference shares.** These can receive a dividend up to an agreed percentage each year. If the amount paid is less than the maximum agreed amount, the shortfall is lost by the shareholder. The shortfall cannot be carried forward and paid in a future year.
2 **Cumulative preference shares.** These also have an agreed maximum percentage dividend. However, any shortfall of dividend paid in a year can be carried forward. These arrears of preference dividends will have to be paid before the ordinary shareholders receive anything.

 Activity 45.3 Why do you think an investor might purchase preference shares rather than ordinary shares in a company?

Exhibit 45.2

A company has 500,000 £1 ordinary shares and 100,000 5 per cent non-cumulative preference shares of £1 each. The profits available for dividends are: year 1 £145,000, year 2 £2,000, year 3 £44,000, year 4 £118,000, year 5 £264,000. Assuming all profits are paid out in dividends, the amounts paid to each class of shareholder are:

Year	1	2	3	4	5
	£	£	£	£	£
Profits appropriated for dividends	145,000	2,000	44,000	118,000	264,000
Preference dividend (non-cumulative) (limited in Year 2)	5,000	2,000	5,000	5,000	5,000
Dividends on ordinary shares	140,000	–	39,000	113,000	259,000
	145,000	2,000	44,000	118,000	264,000

Exhibit 45.3

Assume that the preference shares in Exhibit 45.2 had been cumulative. The dividends would have been:

Year	1	2	3	4	5
	£	£	£	£	£
Profits appropriated for dividends	145,000	2,000	44,000	118,000	264,000
Preference dividend	5,000	2,000	8,000*	5,000	5,000
Dividends on ordinary shares	140,000	–	36,000	113,000	259,000
	145,000	2,000	44,000	118,000	264,000

*including arrears.

Note: This exhibit shows how much of the profit made in each year was paid out as dividend. The dividends are shown in the financial statements in the year they were paid, which may be a year later than the year in which the profit used to pay them was earned – see Section 45.12, especially Exhibit 45.5.

45.7 Share capital: different meanings

The term 'share capital' can have any of the following meanings:

1 **Authorised share capital.** Sometimes known as 'registered capital' or 'nominal capital'. This is the total of the share capital which the company is allowed to issue to shareholders.
2 **Issued share capital.** This is the total of the share capital actually issued to shareholders.

Note: Some students mix up these two terms and throw away marks in examinations as a result. In order to remember which is which, you only need to think about what the words 'authorised' and 'issued' mean.

If all of the authorised share capital has been issued, then 1 and 2 above would be the same amount.

3 **Called-up capital.** Where only part of the amount payable on each issued share has been asked for, the total amount asked for on all the issued shares is known as the called-up capital.
4 **Uncalled capital.** This is the total amount which is to be received in future relating to issued share capital, but which has not yet been asked for.
5 **Calls in arrears.** The total amount for which payment has been asked for (i.e. 'called for'), but has not yet been paid by shareholders.
6 **Paid-up capital.** This is the total of the amount of share capital which has been paid for by shareholders.

Exhibit 45.4 illustrates these different meanings.

Exhibit 45.4

1 Better Enterprises Ltd was formed with the legal right to issue 1 million shares of £1 each.
2 The company has actually issued 750,000 shares.
3 None of the shares has yet been fully paid up. So far, the company has made calls of 80p (£0.80) per share.
4 All the calls have been paid by shareholders except for £200 owing from one shareholder.

(a)	Authorised or nominal share capital is:	1	£1 million.
(b)	Issued share capital is:	2	£750,000.
(c)	Called-up share capital is:	3	750,000 × £0.80 = £600,000.
(d)	Calls in arrears amounted to:	4	£200.
(e)	Paid-up share capital is:	(c)	£600,000 less (d) £200 = £599,800.

45.8 Bonus shares

The issue of **bonus shares** would appear to be outside the scope of syllabuses at this level. However, some examinations have included a minor part of a question concerned with bonus shares. All that is needed here is a very brief explanation only, leaving further explanations for a later stage in your studies.

Bonus shares are 'free' shares issued to shareholders without their having to pay anything for them. The reserves (e.g. retained profits shown in the statement of financial position) are utilised for the purpose. Thus, if before the bonus issue there were £20,000 of issued share capital and £12,000 reserves, and a bonus issue of 1 for 4 was then made (i.e. 1 bonus share for every 4 shares already held) the bonus issue would amount to £5,000. The share capital then becomes £25,000 and the reserves become £7,000.

A fuller explanation appears in *Business Accounting 2*. An issue of bonus shares is often referred to as a **scrip issue**.

45.9 Loan notes

You will recall the note about the veil of incorporation where loan notes had been issued to the owner of company. The term **loan note** is used when a limited company receives money on loan, and a document called a loan note certificate is issued to the lender. Interest will be paid to the holder, the rate of interest being shown on the certificate. (You will sometimes see them referred to as 'debentures', 'loan stock' or 'loan capital', but the correct term is 'loan note'.)

Interest on loan notes has to be paid whether profits are made or not. They are, therefore, different from shares, where dividends depend on profits being made. A loan note may be either:

● redeemable, i.e. repayable at or by a particular date; or
● irredeemable, normally repayable only when the company is officially terminated by going into liquidation. (Also sometimes referred to as 'perpetual' loan notes.)

If dates are shown on a loan note, e.g. 2009/2016, it means that the company can redeem it in any of the years covered by the date(s) showing, in this case 2009 to 2016 inclusive.

People lending money to companies in the form of loan notes will be interested in how safe their investment will be. Some loan notes are assigned the legal right that on certain happenings the holders of the loan notes will be able to take control of specific assets, or of the whole of the assets. They can then sell the assets and recoup the amount due under their loan notes, or deal with the assets in ways specified in the deed under which the loan notes were issued. Such loan notes are said to be 'secured' against the assets – this was the case in the veil of incorporation note in Section 45.5. (The term 'mortgage' loan note is sometimes used instead of 'secured'.) Other loan notes have no prior right to control the assets under any circumstances. These are known as 'simple' or 'naked' loan notes.

Activity 45.4 Why do you think a loan note might be 'secured' rather than being designated as a 'simple' loan note? (*Hint*: think about Mr Saloman.)

45.10 Goodwill

Companies can recognise goodwill arising on acquisitions as an intangible non-current asset. However, each year they must consider whether the value it is carried at has been impaired (i.e. has fallen), when this happens, the reduction must be shown in the profit and loss section of the income statement. The rules relating to this are to be found in IFRS 3 (*Business combinations*), IAS 36 (*Impairment of assets*) and IAS 38 (*Intangible assets*).

45.11 Income statements of companies

The income statements of both private and public companies are drawn up in exactly the same way.

The trading account section of the income statement of a limited company is no different from that of a sole trader or a partnership. However, some differences may be found in the profit and loss account section. Two expenses that would be found only in company accounts are directors' remuneration and loan note interest.

Directors' remuneration

As directors exist only in companies, this type of expense is found only in company financial statements.

Directors are legally employees of the company, appointed by the shareholders. Their remuneration is charged to the profit and loss account.

Loan note interest

The interest payable for the use of the money borrowed is an expense of the company, and is payable whether profits are made or not. This means that interest on loan notes is charged as an expense in the profit and loss account. Contrast this with dividends which are dependent on profits having been made.

45.12 Statement of changes in equity

Unlike partnership income statements, following the profit and loss account section of company income statements there is no section called the 'profit and loss appropriation account'. Instead, companies produce a **statement of changes in equity**. This shows separately:

(a) the retained profit for the period;
(b) distributions of equity (e.g. dividends) and contributions of equity (e.g. share issues);
(c) a reconciliation between the opening and closing carrying amount of each component of equity (i.e. share capital and **reserves**).

Taxation is shown as a deduction when arriving at retained profits on the face of the income statement. This differs from its treatment in partnership and role trader financial statements.

Exhibit 45.5 contains an example showing the changes in equity of a new business for its first three years of trading.

Exhibit 45.5

IDC Ltd has share capital of 400,000 ordinary shares of £1 each and 200,000 5 per cent preference shares of £1 each.

● The retained profits for the first three years of business ended 31 December are: 2011, £109,670; 2012 £148,640; and 2013 £158,220.
● Transfers to reserves are made as follows: 2011 nil; 2012, general reserve, £10,000; and 2013, non-current assets replacement reserve, £22,500.
● Dividends were paid for each year on the preference shares at 5 per cent and on the ordinary shares at: 2011, 10 per cent; 2012, 12.5 per cent; 2013, 15 per cent.

IDC Ltd
Statements of changes in equity (extracts)
(1) For the year ending 31 December 2011

	£
Retained profits	109,670
Less Dividends paid: Preference 5%	10,000
Ordinary 10%	40,000
	(50,000)
Retained profits carried forward	59,670

(2) For the year ended 31 December 2012

	£	£	£
Retained profits			148,640
Add Retained profits brought forward			59,670
			244,310
Less Transfer to general reserve		10,000	
Dividends paid:			
Preference dividend of 5%	10,000		
Ordinary dividend of 12.5%	50,000		
		60,000	
			(70,000)
Retained profits carried forward			174,310

(3) For the year ended 31 December 2013

	£	£	£
Retained profits			158,220
Add Retained profits brought forward			174,310
			332,530
Less Transfer to non-current assets replacement reserve		22,500	
Dividends paid:			
Preference dividend of 5%	10,000		
Ordinary dividend of 15%	60,000		
		70,000	
			(92,500)
Retained profits carried forward			240,030

45.13 The statement of financial position

Prior to the UK Companies Act 1981, provided it disclosed the necessary information, a company could draw up its statement of financial position and income statement for publication in any way that it wished. The 1981 Act, however, stopped this, and laid down the precise details to be shown. These are unchanged in the Companies Act 2006 and the current legal requirements are largely contained in the Companies Act 1985. International standards are not specific about the layout to adopt so UK companies tend to continue to use the Companies Act layouts. We will cover this topic in more detail in *Business Accounting 2*.

Exhibits 45.6 and 45.7 present two versions of a statement of financial position. They both comply with International GAAP. Exhibit 45.6 shows more detail. The detail that is omitted from Exhibit 45.7 would be shown separately as a note. Both these statements of financial position would be prepared by companies for their own use rather than for their stakeholders, such as shareholders and creditors. Statements of financial position prepared for publication (i.e. for external users) contain much less detail and will be covered in detail in *Business Accounting 2*.

Exhibit 45.6 Greater detail for internal use

Statement of Financial Position as at 31 December 2012

		Cost	Depreciation to date (b)	Net book value
Non-current assets	(a)	£000	£000	£000
Goodwill		15,000	5,000	10,000
Buildings		15,000	6,000	9,000
Machinery		8,000	2,400	5,600
Motor vehicles		4,000	1,600	2,400
		42,000	15,000	27,000
Current assets				
Inventory			6,000	
Accounts receivable			3,000	
Bank			4,000	
				13,000
Total assets				40,000
Less Current liabilities				
Accounts payable		3,000		
Corporation tax owing		2,000		
			5,000	
Net current assets				
Non-current liabilities				
Six per cent loan notes: repayable 2014			8,000	
Total liabilities				(13,000)
Net assets				27,000
Equity				
Share capital				
Authorised 30,000 shares of £1 each	(c)			30,000
Issued 20,000 ordinary shares of £1 each, fully paid	(d)			20,000
Reserves	(e)			
Share premium	(f)		1,200	
General reserve			3,800	
Retained profits			2,000	
				7,000
Total equity	(g)			27,000

Notes:

(a) Non-current assets should normally be shown either at cost or alternatively at some other valuation. In either case, the method chosen should be clearly stated. As you will see in Exhibit 45.7, you could show the intangible non-current asset (goodwill) separately from the other non-current assets.

(b) The total depreciation from date of purchase to the date of the statement of financial position should be shown.

(c) The authorised share capital, where it is different from the issued share capital, is shown as a note.

(d) Where shares are only partly called-up, it is the amount actually called up that appears in the statement of financial position and not the full amount.

(e) Reserves consist either of those unused profits remaining in the retained profits, or those transferred to a reserve account appropriately titled, e.g. general reserve or non-current assets replacement reserve. These reserves are shown in the statement of financial position after share capital under the heading of 'Reserves'.

(f) The share premium account is credited with the difference between the nominal value of shares issued and the issue price of those shares. For example, if a share has a nominal value of £1 and it is issued at a price of £3, £2 will be credited to the share premium account and £1 will be credited to the issued share capital account.

(g) The share capital and reserves should be totalled so as to show the book value of all the shares in the company. Either the term 'shareholders' funds' or 'members' equity' is often given to the total of share capital plus reserves.

Exhibit 45.7 Less detail for internal use

Letters in brackets (A) to (G) refer to notes following the statement of financial position.

Statement of Financial Position as at 31 December 2012

		£000	£000	£000
Non-current assets				
Intangible assets	(A)			
Goodwill				10,000
Tangible assets	(B)			
Buildings			9,000	
Machinery			5,600	
Motor vehicles			2,400	
				17,000
				27,000
Current assets				
Inventory			6,000	
Accounts receivable			3,000	
Bank			4,000	
				13,000
Total assets				40,000
Current liabilities	(C)			
Accounts payable		3,000		
Corporation tax owing		2,000		
			5,000	
Total assets less current liabilities				
Non-current liabilities	(D)			
Loan notes			8,000	
Total liabilities				(13,000)
Net assets				27,000
Equity				
Called-up share capital	(E)			20,000
Share premium account	(F)			1,200
Other reserves				
General reserve				3,800
Retained profits				2,000
Total equity				27,000

Notes:
(A) Intangible assets are those not having a 'physical' existence; for instance, you can see and touch tangible assets under (B), i.e. buildings, machinery etc., but you cannot see and touch goodwill.
(B) Tangible non-current assets under a separate heading. Note that figures are shown net after depreciation. In a note accompanying the financial statements the cost and depreciation on these assets would be given.
(C) Only items payable within one year go under this heading.
(D) These loan notes are repayable in several years' time. If they had been payable within one year they would have been shown under current liabilities.
(E) An analysis of share capital will be given in supplementary notes to the statement of financial position.
(F) One reserve that is not labelled with the word 'reserve' in its title is the share premium account. (Another is retained profits.) For various reasons (discussed fully in *Business Accounting 2*) shares can be issued for more than their face (or 'nominal') value. The excess of the price at which they are issued over the nominal value of the shares is credited to a share premium account. This is then shown with the other reserves in the statement of financial position.

If you are asked in an examination to prepare a statement of financial position for internal use and choose to present a statement of financial position similar to Exhibit 45.7 you should include in a note the details from the layout as in Exhibit 45.6 that you have omitted from the statement of financial position.

In *Business Accounting 2* you will be told more about the differences between 'revenue reserves' and 'capital reserves'. The most important reason for the distinction has to do with deciding how much can be treated as being available for paying out to shareholders as dividends. 'Revenue reserves', which include the retained profits and the general reserve, can be treated as available for such dividends. 'Capital reserves', which will include revaluation reserves on property and land, and also some reserves (which you have not yet met) which have to be created to meet some legal statutory requirement, cannot be treated as available for payment of dividends.

A term which sometimes appears in examinations is that of 'fungible assets'. Fungible assets are assets which are substantially indistinguishable one from another.

Now, let's prepare two more statements of financial position and an income statement for internal use.

A fully worked example

Exhibit 45.8

The following trial balance is extracted from the books of F W Ltd as on 31 December 2011.

Trial balance as on 31 December 2011

	Dr £	Cr £
10% preference share capital		200,000
Ordinary share capital		700,000
10% loan notes (repayable 2015)		300,000
Goodwill at cost	255,000	
Buildings at cost	1,050,000	
Equipment at cost	120,000	
Motor vehicles at cost	172,000	
Provision for depreciation: buildings 1.1.2011		100,000
Provision for depreciation: equipment 1.1.2011		24,000
Provision for depreciation: motor vehicles 1.1.2011		51,600
Inventory 1.1.2011	84,912	
Sales		1,022,000
Purchases	439,100	
Carriage inwards	6,200	
Salaries and wages	192,400	
Directors' remuneration	123,000	
Motor expenses	3,120	
Business rates and insurances	8,690	
General expenses	5,600	
Loan note interest	15,000	
Accounts receivable	186,100	
Accounts payable		113,700
Bank	8,390	
General reserve		50,000
Share premium account		100,000
Interim ordinary dividend paid	35,000	
Retained profits 31.12.2010		43,212
	2,704,512	2,704,512

The following adjustments are needed:

(i)   Inventory at 31.12.2011 was £91,413.
(ii)   Depreciate buildings £10,000; motor vehicles £18,000; equipment £12,000.
(iii) Accrue loan note interest £15,000.
(iv)   Provide for preference dividend £20,000 and final ordinary dividend of 10 per cent.
(v)   Transfer £10,000 to general reserve.
(vi)   Write-off goodwill impairment of £30,000.
(vii) Authorised share capital is £200,000 in preference shares and £1 million in ordinary shares.
(viii) Provide for corporation tax £50,000.

The financial statements are shown below. First, there's an income statement for internal use. (The income statement for publication is greatly summarised and we will cover that topic in *Business Accounting 2*.) We then show two versions of the internal statement of financial position.

(a) Income statement **for internal use only,** not for publication.

F. W. Ltd
Income Statement for the year ending 31 December 2011

		£	£
Revenue			1,022,000
Less Cost of goods sold:			
Opening inventory		84,912	
Add Purchases		439,100	
Add Carriage inwards		6,200	
		530,212	
Less Closing inventory		(91,413)	
			(438,799)
Gross profit			583,201
Less Expenses:			
Salaries and wages		192,400	
Motor expenses		3,120	
Business rates and insurances		8,690	
General expenses		5,600	
Directors' remuneration	(A)	123,000	
Loan note interest	(B)	30,000	
Goodwill impairment		30,000	
Depreciation: Buildings		10,000	
Equipment		12,000	
Motor vehicles		18,000	
			(432,810)
Profit for the year before taxation			150,391
Less Corporation tax			(50,000)
Retained profits			100,391
Note			
Ordinary share dividends paid	(C)	35,000	

Notes:
(A) Directors' remuneration is shown as an expense in the income statement.
(B) Loan note interest is an expense to be shown in the income statement.
(C) The final dividend of 10 per cent is based on the issued ordinary share capital and *not* on the authorised ordinary share capital. It is, therefore, £70,000. However, both it and the preference dividend of £20,000 should only be included as notes to the income statement. They should not be treated as current liabilities and should not appear in any financial statement. As only the interim ordinary dividend was paid during the year, this is the only one of these three dividend items that will appear in the statement of changes in equity.

→ **(b)** Statement of financial position in greater detail for internal use.

Statement of Financial Position as at 31 December 2011

	Cost	Depreciation to date	Net book value
Non-current assets	£	£	£
Goodwill	255,000	30,000	225,000
Buildings	1,050,000	110,000	940,000
Equipment	120,000	36,000	84,000
Motor vehicles	172,000	69,600	102,400
	1,597,000	245,600	1,351,400
Current assets			
Inventory		91,413	
Accounts receivable		186,100	
Bank		8,390	
			285,903
Total assets			1,637,303
Current liabilities			
Accounts payable	113,700		
Loan note interest accrued	15,000		
Taxation	50,000		
		(178,700)	
Non-current liabilities			
10% loan notes		300,000	
Total liabilities			(478,700)
Net assets			1,158,603

	Authorised	Issued
Equity		
Share Capital	£	£
Preference shares	200,000	200,000
Ordinary shares	1,000,000	700,000
	1,200,000	900,000
Reserves		
Share premium	100,000	
General reserve	60,000	
Retained profits	98,603	
		258,603
Total equity		1,158,603

The proposed dividends should be shown in a note.

Note that the difference between the two statements of financial position is solely that of detail. You should use whichever layout is more appropriate.

(c) Statement of financial position in less detail for internal use.

F. W. Ltd
Statement of Financial Position as at 31 December 2011

		£	£	£
Non-current assets				
Intangible assets				
Goodwill				225,000
Tangible assets	(A)			
Buildings			940,000	
Equipment			84,000	
Motor vehicles			102,400	
				1,126,400
				1,351,400
Current assets				
Inventory			91,413	
Accounts receivable			186,100	
Bank			8,390	
				285,903
Total assets				1,637,303
Current liabilities				
Accounts payable		113,700		
Loan note interest accrued		15,000		
Taxation		50,000		
			178,700	
Non-current liabilities				
10% Loan notes			300,000	
				(478,700)
Total liabilities				1,158,603
Net assets				
Equity	(B)			
Called-up share capital	(C)			900,000
Share premium account				100,000
Other reserves				
General reserve				60,000
Retained profits				98,603
Total equity				1,158,603

The proposed dividends should be shown in a note.

(A) Notes to be given in an appendix as to cost, acquisitions and sales in the year and depreciation.

(B) Reserves consist either of those unused profits remaining in the appropriation account, or those transferred to a reserve account appropriately titled, e.g. general reserve, non-current assets replacement reserve, etc.

  The closing balance of retained profits from the statement of changes in equity (not prepared for this example) is shown under reserves. These are profits not already appropriated, and therefore 'reserved' for future use.

(C) The authorised share capital, where it is different from the issued share capital, is shown as a note. Notice that the total figure of £1,200,000 for authorised capital is not included when adding up the statement of financial position sides. Only the issued capital amounts are included in statement of financial position totals.

45.14   True and fair view

When the financial statements of a company are published no one, neither the directors nor the auditors, ever states that 'the financial statements are correct'. This is because in preparing company financial statements many subjective estimates and judgements affect the figures. The valuation of inventory, or the estimates of depreciation, cannot be said to be 'correct', just as it is impossible to say that the allowance for doubtful debts is 'correct'. Only time will tell whether these estimates and judgements will turn out to have been 'correct'.

The expression that is used is that the financial statements give a **true and fair view** of the financial position and financial performance of the company.

45.15   IFRS 5 Non-current assets held for sale and discontinued operations

Accounting is not a static subject. Changes occur over the years as they are seen to be necessary, and also get general agreement as to their usefulness. Since the introduction of accounting standards over thirty years ago, the number of changes that practitioners and students have had to learn has increased at a very fast rate.

Suppose that you are considering the affairs of a business over the years. The business has not changed significantly, there have been no acquisitions, no discontinued operations, no fundamental reorganisation or restructuring of the business. In these circumstances, when comparing the financial statements over the years, you are comparing like with like, subject to the problem of the effects of inflation or deflation.

On the other hand, suppose that it has been decided to sell some non-current assets or to discontinue some of the operations of the business. When trying to see what the future might hold for the company, simply basing your opinions on what has happened in the past could be very misleading.

To help you to distinguish the past and the future, and to give you some idea as to what changes have occurred, IFRS 5 requires that:

- non-current assets held for sale are shown at the lower of carrying amount and fair value less selling costs;
- non-current assets held for sale are presented separately on the face of the statement of financial position after current assets;
- non-current assets held for sale are not depreciated;
- gains or losses on the remeasurement of a non-current asset held for sale should be included in profit or loss from continuing operations;
- the results of discontinued operations are shown separately on the face of the income statement after the figure for profit for the period from continuing operations.

45.16   IAS 1 and financial statements

IAS 1 (*Presentation of financial statements*) was revised and reissued in 2007. In the revised standard, the balance sheet was renamed the 'statement of financial position' (though use of the term 'balance sheet' is still permitted). It also changed the title of the 'cash flow statement' to 'statement of cash flows'. It also introduced a new primary statement: the statement of comprehensive income. It states that there are four primary statements:

- a statement of financial position;
- a statement of comprehensive income;
- a statement of changes in equity;
- a statement of cash flows.

When a separate income statement is also presented, it is presented immediately before the statement of comprehensive income. In that case, the statement of comprehensive income starts with the profit or loss identified in the income statement. The difference in approach is cosmetic and the option to show a separate income statement simply enables continuation of use of the term 'income statement'.

As a minimum, **the statement of comprehensive income** must include line items presenting:

(a) revenue;
(b) finance costs;
(c) share of profits or losses of associates and joint ventures accounted for using the equity method;
(d) tax;
(e) the total of post-tax profit or loss on discontinued operations *plus* the post-tax gain or loss recognised on the measurement to fair value less costs to sell or on the disposal of the assets or disposal group(s) constituting the discontinued operations;
(f) profit or loss;
(g) each component of other comprehensive income classified by nature excluding amounts in (h);
(h) share of the other comprehensive income of associates and joint ventures accounted for using the entity method;
(i) total comprehensive income.

If a separate income statement is presented, it will contain items (a) to (f). Other comprehensive income comprises items that are not recognised in profit or loss, such as:

- changes in revaluation surplus;
- gains or losses arising from translating the financial statements of a foreign operation;
- gains and losses on remeasuring available-for-sale financial assets.

Total comprehensive income is the change in equity during a period other than those changes resulting from transactions with owners (i.e. holders of equity) in their capacity as owners (e.g. dividend payments).

The statement of changes in equity presents:

(a) total comprehensive income;
(b) the amounts of transactions with owners in their capacity as owners;
(c) for each component of equity, a reconciliation between the opening and closing carrying amount.

Either in the statement of changes in equity or in a note, the amount of dividend distributed to owners during the period must be shown, along with the related amount per share.

IAS 1 is covered in greater detail in *Business Accounting 2*. In this book we are simply explaining some of its requirements. The overall effect is that financial statements prepared for publication (i.e. for external users) are very different from those produced for internal use. You will not be required to prepare either a statement of comprehensive income in this book.

45.17 The Audit Report

The Companies Act requires that all companies other than dormant companies (i.e. companies that have not traded during the year) and small private companies be audited every year. ('Small' is currently defined as having a turnover of not more than £5.6 million and a statement of financial position total (of assets) of not more than £2.8 million.)

The auditors are appointed each year by the shareholders at the company annual general meeting (AGM). The auditors complete the report after examining the books and accounts and, in the report, they must say whether or not they agree that the accounts give a true and fair view. The report is presented to the shareholders at the same time as the financial statements are presented to them at the AGM.

In preparing the audit report, the auditor must consider whether

- the accounts have been prepared in accordance with the Companies Act;
- the statement of financial position shows a true and fair view of the state of the company's affairs at the end of the period and the income statement shows a true and fair view of the results for the period;
- proper accounting records have been kept and proper returns received from parts of the company not visited by the auditor;
- the accounts are in agreement with the accounting records;
- the directors' report is consistent with the accounts.

While smaller companies are exempt from the requirement to have their financial statements audited, they may still do so, if they wish.

Organisations that are not required to have their financial statements audited, such as sole traders, partnerships, clubs and societies, can still have their accounts audited. In this case, the audit is described as a *non-statutory audit*.

A qualified audit report indicates that the auditor is not satisfied that the financial statements present a true and fair view. When a company receives a qualified audit report, it acts as a signal to all stakeholders that something may be amiss. As such, it is a vitally important safeguard of the interests of the shareholders.

Contrary to what most of the public think, auditors do not guarantee to discover any fraud that may have occurred. That is not what the audit is for. Following such financial scandals as Enron, the Maxwell affair, BCCI bank, Polly Peck and Barlow Clowes there has been pressure exerted upon the accounting profession to reconsider its position regarding the discovery of fraud when auditing the financial statements of a company.

Learning outcomes

You should now have learnt:

1 That limited companies exist because of the disadvantages and constraints arising from partnerships.

2 That a fully paid-up shareholder's liability is limited to the shares he or she holds in the company. Shareholders cannot then be asked to pay any other company debt from their private resources.

3 The difference between public and private companies.

4 That there are far more private companies than public companies.

5 The difference between a PLC and a company that is not a PLC.

6 That a limited company has a 'separate legal entity' from that of its members.

7 The difference between ordinary shares and preference shares.

8 How dividends are calculated.

9 The difference between shares and loan notes.

10 The contents of and purpose of a company's appropriation account.

11 That directors' remuneration is charged to the profit and loss account section of the income statement.

12 That loan note interest is charged to the profit and loss account section of the income statement.

13 That taxation is shown in the income statement.

14 That transfers to reserves and dividends are shown in the statement of changes in equity.

15 How to prepare company income statements for internal purposes.

16 How to prepare company statements of financial position for internal purposes.

17 How IAS 1 governs the preparation of financial statements prepared for publication.

18 That financial statements for publication differ greatly from those prepared for internal use.

Answers to activities

45.1 Partnerships were not suitable for such businesses because:

- normally they cannot have more than 20 partners, not counting limited partners;
- if a partnership business fails, partners could lose part, or all, of their private assets to pay the debts of the business.

Limited companies do not have restrictions on the number of owners. Nor do the owners of limited companies generally run the risk of losing everything they own if the company fails.

45.2 There may be any number of explanations, including:

- they may not want a wide ownership base;
- they may feel that the costs of doing so are prohibitive;
- they may feel that there would not be sufficient demand for the shares to make it worthwhile;
- the directors may be concerned that it would make it easier for the company to be taken over;
- they may wish to wait until the Stock Market is at a higher level, i.e. they may wish to wait until they can maximise the amount they can sell the shares for when they first offer them for sale on the Stock Market;
- the Stock Market may be very volatile, making choosing a price at which to sell the shares very difficult – if the company gets it wrong, they may not sell all the shares they wanted to sell or they may not receive as much for each share as they could have done had they waited for the Stock Market to stabilise.

45.3 There is less risk for the investor. The annual preference dividend is known and it will be paid before any funds left over are used to pay a dividend on the ordinary shares. Even when an ordinary dividend is paid, it is not known in advance how much this will be, as it depends on how profitable the business has been over the financial period. It could be more than the preference dividend (which is normally the case) or it could be less. Although the preference dividend will often be at a lower rate than an ordinary dividend (i.e. a preference shareholder will receive less of a dividend for the same investment as an ordinary shareholder) the reduced risk results in some people preferring to purchase preference shares.

45.4 The lender may require it or the company may offer secured loan note status in order to attract funds at a more favourable rate of interest.

Multiple choice questions: Set 5

Now attempt Set 5 of multiple choice questions. (Answers to all the multiple choice questions are given in Appendix 2 at the end of this book.)

Each of these multiple choice questions has four suggested answers, (A), (B), (C) and (D). You should read each question and then decide which choice is best, either (A) or (B) or (C) or (D). *Write down your answers on a separate piece of paper.* You will then be able to redo the set of questions later without having to try to ignore your answers.

MC81 Given opening accounts receivable of £11,500, Sales £48,000 and receipts from debtors £45,000, the closing accounts receivable total should be

(A) £8,500
(B) £14,500
(C) £83,500
(D) £18,500

MC82 In a Sales Ledger Control Account the Bad Debts written off should be shown in the account

(A) As a debit
(B) As a credit
(C) Both as a debit and as a credit
(D) As a balance carried down

MC83 If cost price is £90 and selling price is £120, then

(*i*) Mark-up is 25 per cent
(*ii*) Margin is 33$\frac{1}{3}$ per cent
(*iii*) Margin is 25 per cent
(*iv*) Mark-up is 33$\frac{1}{3}$ per cent

(A) (*i*) and (*ii*)
(B) (*i*) and (*iii*)
(C) (*iii*) and (*iv*)
(D) (*ii*) and (*iv*)

MC84 Given cost of goods sold £16,000 and margin of 20 per cent, then sales figure is

(A) £20,160
(B) £13,600
(C) £21,000
(D) £20,000

MC85 If opening inventory is £3,000, closing inventory £5,000, sales £40,000 and margin 20 per cent, then inventory turnover is

(A) 8 times
(B) 7$\frac{1}{2}$ times
(C) 5 times
(D) 6 times

MC86 If accounts payable at 1 January 2012 were £2,500, accounts payable at 31 December 2012 £4,200 and payments to creditors £32,000, then purchases for 2012 are

(A) £30,300
(B) £33,700
(C) £31,600
(D) £38,700

MC87 Given opening capital of £16,500; closing capital as £11,350; and drawings of £3,300, then

(A) Loss for the year was £1,850
(B) Profit for the year was £1,850
(C) Loss for the year was £8,450
(D) Profit for the year was £8,450

MC88 A Receipts and Payments Account is one

(A) Which is accompanied by a statement of financial position
(B) In which the profit is calculated
(C) In which the opening and closing cash balances are shown
(D) In which the surplus of income over expenditure is calculated

MC89 Prime cost includes

(*i*) Direct labour
(*ii*) Factory overhead expenses
(*iii*) Raw materials consumed
(*iv*) Direct expenses

(A) (*i*), (*ii*) and (*iii*)
(B) (*ii*), (*iii*) and (*iv*)
(C) (*i*), (*iii*) and (*iv*)
(D) (*i*), (*ii*) and (*iv*)

MC90 Which of the following should be charged in the Income Statement?

(A) Office rent
(B) Work-in-progress
(C) Direct materials
(D) Carriage on raw materials

MC91 In the Manufacturing Account is calculated

(A) The production costs paid in the year
(B) The total cost of goods produced
(C) The production cost of goods completed in the period
(D) The gross profit on goods sold

MC92 The recommended method of departmental accounts is

(A) To allocate expenses in proportion to sales
(B) To charge against each department its controllable costs
(C) To allocate expenses in proportion to purchases
(D) To charge against each department its uncontrollable costs

MC93 Where there is no partnership agreement then profits and losses

(A) Must be shared in the same proportion as capitals
(B) Must be shared equally
(C) Must be shared equally after adjusting for interest on capital
(D) None of these

MC94 If it is required to maintain fixed capitals then the partners' shares of profits must be

(A) Debited to capital accounts
(B) Credited to capital accounts
(C) Debited to partners' current accounts
(D) Credited to partners' current accounts

→

→

MC95   You are to buy an existing business which has assets valued at Buildings £50,000, Motor vehicles £15,000, Fixtures £5,000 and Inventory £40,000. You are to pay £140,000 for the business. This means that

(A)   You are paying £40,000 for Goodwill
(B)   Buildings are costing you £30,000 more than their value
(C)   You are paying £30,000 for Goodwill
(D)   You have made an arithmetical mistake

MC96   Assets can be revalued in a partnership change because

(A)   The law insists upon it
(B)   It helps prevent injustice to some partners
(C)   Inflation affects all values
(D)   The depreciation charged on them needs to be reversed

MC97   Any loss on revaluation is

(A)   Credited to old partners in old profit-sharing ratios
(B)   Credited to new partners in new profit-sharing ratios
(C)   Debited to old partners in old profit-sharing ratios
(D)   Debited to new partners in new profit-sharing ratios

MC98   In a limited company which of the following is shown in the statement of changes in equity?

(*i*)   Loan note interest
(*ii*)   Dividends paid
(*iii*)   Transfers to reserves
(*iv*)   Directors' remuneration

(A)   (*i*) and (*ii*)
(B)   (*ii*) and (*iii*)
(C)   (*i*) and (*iv*)
(D)   (*ii*) and (*iv*)

MC99   The Issued Capital of a company is

(A)   Always the same as the Authorised Capital
(B)   The same as Preference Share Capital
(C)   Equal to the reserves of the company
(D)   None of the above

MC100   A company wishes to pay out all available profits as dividends. Net profit is £26,600. There are 20,000 8% Preference shares of £1 each, and 50,000 Ordinary shares of £1 each. £5,000 is to be transferred to General Reserve. What Ordinary dividends are to be paid, in percentage terms?

(A)   20 per cent
(B)   40 per cent
(C)   10 per cent
(D)   60 per cent

Review questions

45.1   Flyer Ltd started in business on 1 April 2011. Its issued share capital was 200,000 ordinary shares of £1 each and 100,000 5 per cent preference shares of £1 each. The following information is available:

● Its net profits for the first two years of business were: 2011/12 £90,200; 2012/13 £84,600.
● Preference dividends were paid for each of these years, whilst ordinary dividends were proposed as 2011/12 8 per cent and 2012/13 6 per cent.
● Transfers to general reserve took place: 2011/12 £20,000; 2012/13 £15,000.

Draw up a statement of changes in equity for each of the years ending 31 March 2012 and 2013.

45.2   Trainsign Ltd has an authorised capital of £500,000, consisting of 350,000 ordinary shares of £1 each and 150,000 7 per cent preference shares of £1 each. Of these, 260,000 ordinary shares and 90,000 preference shares had been issued when the company first started trading. The following information is available:

● The company has a financial year end of 31 December. The first three years of business resulted in net profit as follows: 2011 £62,400; 2012 £81,900; 2013 £114,190.
● Dividends were paid each year on the preference shares. Dividends on the ordinary shares were proposed as follows: 2011 6 per cent; 2012 8 per cent; 2013 12 per cent.
● Transfers to reserves were: general reserve 2011 £10,000, 2012 £18,000, and foreign exchange reserve 2013 £15,000.

You are to show the statement of changes in equity for each of the years 2011, 2012 and 2013.

45.3   A statement of financial position is to be drawn up from the following information as at 30 September 2011:

	£
Issued share capital: ordinary shares £1 each	200,000
Authorised share capital: ordinary shares of £1 each	500,000
6 per cent loan notes (repayable 30 September 2015)	40,000
Buildings at cost	330,000
Motor vehicles at cost	74,000
Fixtures at cost	9,200
Retained profits	32,000
Non-current assets replacement reserve	30,000
Inventory	21,400
Accounts receivable	10,300
General reserve	50,000
Accounts payable	13,700
Depreciation to date: Buildings	40,000
Motor vehicles	41,000
Fixtures	5,100
Bank (balancing figure for you to ascertain)	?

45.4   The following balances remained in the ledger of OK Ltd after preparation of the income statement for the year ending 31 March 2012

	£000
Inventory	52
Accounts receivable	24
Ordinary share capital	100
8% preference share capital	50
Accounts payable	37
Balance at bank	14
General reserve	30
Retained profits 2011	27
Net profit for the year to 31 March 2012	29
Non-current assets at cost, less depreciation	167

The directors propose:
(*i*)   a transfer to general reserve of £10,000;
(*ii*)   payment of the preference dividend and a 12% dividend on the ordinary shares (Dividends relating to 2011 were paid in March 2012 at the same rates.).

Required:
(*a*)   Prepare a statement of changes in equity for the year ended 31 March 2012.
(*b*)   Prepare a statement of financial position as at 31 March 2012, showing clearly the ordinary shareholders' equity, the total shareholders' funds and the working capital.

45.5A   Developing Ltd has an authorised capital of 50,000, 10% preference shares of £1 each and 200,000 ordinary shares of 50p each. After preparation of the income statement for 2013, the following balances remained in the ledger:

	£000
Share capital: fully paid-up:	
Preference	30
Ordinary	80
Loan notes	20
Share premium account	4
General reserve	7
Retained profits 2012	3
Net profit for 2013	27
Non-current assets	140
Current assets	50
Accounts payable	19

The directors recommend:
(*i*)   that £10,000 be transferred to general reserve,
(*ii*)   payment of the preference dividend,
(*iii*) an ordinary dividend of 15%.

Required:
Prepare a statement of changes in equity for 2013 and a statement of financial position as at 31 December 2013.

45.6   Select Ltd is registered with an authorised capital of 300,000 ordinary shares of £1. The following trial balance was extracted from the books of the company on 31 March 2012, after the preparation of the trading account:

	Dr £	Cr £
Ordinary share capital, fully paid		200,000
Land and buildings at cost	170,000	
Sundry accounts receivable	38,300	
Furniture and fittings at cost	80,000	
VAT	3,800	
Sundry accounts payable		25,000
Inventory at 31 March 2012	42,000	
Bank	12,000	
Trading account: gross profit		98,050
Office salaries and expenses	25,000	
Accumulated provision for depreciation on furniture and fittings		32,000
Share premium account		20,000
Advertising and selling expenses	5,000	
Bad debts	250	
Allowance for doubtful debts		600
Retained profits		12,000
Directors' fees	11,300	
	387,650	387,650

Required:
Prepare the profit and loss account section of the income statement and a statement of changes in equity for of the company for the year ending 31 March 2012, and statement of financial position as at that date, after taking into account the following adjustments:

(*i*)   The allowance for doubtful debtors is to be adjusted to £700.
(*ii*) Depreciation is to be provided in respect of furniture and fittings at 10% per annum on cost.
(*iii*) £25,000 is to be transferred from profit and loss to general reserve.
(*iv*) Provide for a proposed dividend on share capital at 10%.

Present the statement of financial position in a form which shows the shareholders' equity and the working capital.

45.7A

	£000
Non-current assets, at cost	160
Inventory	40
Bank overdraft	30
Ordinary share capital	100
Accounts payable	45
Retained profits	22
Accumulated depreciation	50
Accounts receivable	47

Required:
(*a*) From the above information, prepare the statement of financial position of Budgie Limited indicating clearly the shareholders' funds and working capital.
(*b*) Comment on the capital position disclosed by the statement of financial position you have prepared.

45.8 The trial balance extracted from the books of Tailor Times Ltd at 31 December 2012 was as follows:

	£	£
Share capital		200,000
Retained profits 31 December 2011		27,500
Freehold premises at cost	271,000	
Provision for depreciation on freehold premises at 31 December 2011		54,000
Machinery at cost	84,000	
Provision for depreciation on machinery account as at 31 December 2011		21,000
Purchases	563,700	
Sales		925,300
General expenses	14,600	
Wages and salaries	179,400	
Business rates	6,100	
Electricity	4,800	
Bad debts	1,400	
Allowance for doubtful debts at 31 December 2011		1,200
Accounts receivable	74,200	
Accounts payable		68,300
Inventory at 31 December 2011	81,900	
Bank balance	16,200	
	1,297,300	1,297,300

You are given the following additional information:

(*i*)   The authorised and issued share capital is divided into 400,000 ordinary shares of 50p each.
(*ii*)   Inventory at 31 December 2012, £94,300.
(*iii*)   Wages and salaries due at 31 December 2012 amounted to £1,800.
(*iv*)   Business rates paid in advance at 31 December 2012 amounted to £700.
(*v*)   A dividend of £20,000 is proposed for 2012.
(*vi*)   The allowance for doubtful debts is to be increased to £1,500.
(*vii*)   A depreciation charge is to be made on freehold premises of £25,000 and machinery at the rate of 25 per cent per annum on cost.

Required:
An income statement for 2012 and a statement of financial position as at 31 December 2012.

45.9A   The following is the trial balance of Tully Ltd as on 31 December 2013:

	Dr £	Cr £
Share capital issued: ordinary shares 20p		375,000
Accounts receivable and accounts payable	169,600	74,900
Inventory 31 December 2012	81,300	
Bank	17,900	
Premises at cost	265,000	
Machinery at cost	109,100	
Motor vehicles at cost	34,700	
Depreciation provisions at 31.12.2012:		
Premises		60,000
Machinery		41,400
Motor vehicles		18,200
Sales		975,600
Purchases	623,800	
Motor expenses	4,300	
Repairs to machinery	3,600	
Sundry expenses	2,900	
Wages and salaries	241,500	
Directors' remuneration	82,600	
Retained profits as at 31.12.2012		31,200
General reserve		60,000
	1,636,300	1,636,300

Given the following information, you are to draw up an income statement for the year ending 31 December 2013, and a statement of financial position as at that date:

(*i*)   Authorised share capital: £500,000 in ordinary shares of 20p.
(*ii*)   Inventory at 31 December 2013 £102,400.
(*iii*)   Motor expenses owing £280.
(*iv*)   Ordinary dividend proposed of 5 per cent.
(*v*)   Transfer £7,500 to general reserve.
(*vi*)   Provide for depreciation: motor vehicles and machinery 20% on cost; premises 5% on cost.

45.10   You are to draw up an income statement for the year ending 31 December 2011, and a statement of financial position as at that date from the following trial balance and details of Partido Ltd:

	Dr	Cr
	£	£
Bank	8,100	
Accounts receivable	321,219	
Accounts payable		237,516
Inventory at 31 December 2010	290,114	
Buildings at cost	800,000	
Equipment at cost	320,000	
Retained profits as at 31 December 2010		136,204
General reserve		120,000
Foreign exchange reserve		20,000
Authorised and issued share capital		800,000
Purchases	810,613	
Sales		1,606,086
Carriage inwards	2,390	
Carriage outwards	13,410	
Salaries	384,500	
Business rates	14,800	
Office expenses	9,100	
Sundry expenses	2,360	
Provisions for depreciation at 31 December 2010:		
Buildings		80,000
Equipment		96,000
Directors' remuneration	119,200	
	3,095,806	3,095,806

Notes at 31 December 2011:

(*i*) Inventory £317,426.
(*ii*) Business rates owing £1,700; Office expenses owing £245.
(*iii*) Dividend of 15 per cent proposed.
(*iv*) Transfers to reserves: General £70,000; Foreign exchange £30,000.
(*v*) Depreciation on cost: Buildings 5 per cent; Equipment 15 per cent.

45.11A Here is the trial balance of Falta Ltd as at 30 April 2012:

	Dr	Cr
	£	£
Share capital: authorised and issued		200,000
Inventory as at 30 April 2011	102,994	
Accounts receivable	227,219	
Accounts payable		54,818
8% loan notes		40,000
Non-current assets replacement reserve		30,000
General reserve		15,000
Retained profits as at 30 April 2011		12,411
Loan note interest	1,600	
Equipment at cost	225,000	
Motor vehicles at cost	57,200	
Bank	4,973	
Cash	62	
Sales		880,426
Purchases	419,211	
Returns inwards	18,400	
Carriage inwards	1,452	
Wages and salaries	123,289	
Rent, business rates and insurance	16,240	
Discounts allowed	3,415	
Directors' remuneration	82,400	
Provision for depreciation at 30 April 2011:		
Equipment		32,600
Motor vehicles		18,200
	1,283,455	1,283,455

→

Given the following information as at 30 April 2012, draw up an income statement and statement of financial position for the year to that date:

(*i*)   Inventory £111,317.

(*ii*) The share capital consisted of 300,000 ordinary shares of 50p each and 50,000 12 per cent preference shares of £1 each. The dividend on the preference shares was proposed to be paid as well as a dividend of 18 per cent on the ordinary shares.

(*iii*) Accrued: rent £802; Directors' remuneration £6,000.

(*iv*) Loan note interest ½ year's interest owing.

(*v*)   Depreciation on cost: Equipment 20 per cent; Motor vehicles 25 per cent.

(*vi*) Transfers to reserves: General reserve £5,000; Non-current assets replacement reserve £10,000.

45.12 Burden PLC has an authorised capital of 500,000 ordinary shares of £0.50 each.

(*a*) At the end of its financial year, 31 May 2012, the following balances appeared in the company's books:

	£
Issued capital: 400,000 shares fully paid	200,000
Freehold land and buildings at cost	320,000
Inventory	17,800
10% loan notes	30,000
Trade accounts receivable	6,840
Trade accounts payable	28,500
Expenses prepaid	760
Share premium	25,000
General reserve	20,000
Expenses outstanding	430
Retained profits balance (1 June 2011)	16,200
Bank overdrawn	3,700
Fixtures, fittings and equipment at cost	54,000
provision for depreciation	17,500

The company's income statement had been prepared and revealed a net profit of £58,070. However, this figure and certain balances shown above needed adjustment in view of the following details which had not been recorded in the company's books.

(*i*)   It appeared that a trade debtor who owed £300 would not be able to pay. It was decided to write his account off as a bad debt.

(*ii*) An examination of the company's inventory on 31 May 2012 revealed that some items shown in the accounts at a cost of £1,800 had deteriorated and had a resale value of only £1,100.

(*iii*) At the end of the financial year some equipment which had cost £3,600 and which had a net book value of £800 had been sold for £1,300. A cheque for this amount had been received on 31 May 2012.

Required:

1 A statement which shows the changes which should be made to the net profit of £58,070 in view of these unrecorded details.

(*b*) The directors proposed to pay a final dividend of 10% and to transfer £50,000 to general reserve on 31 May 2012.

Required:

For Burden PLC (taking account of *all* the available information)

2 A statement of changes in equity for the year ended 31 May 2012.

3 Two *extracts* from the company's statement of financial position as at 31 May 2012, showing in detail:

   (*i*) the current assets, current liabilities and working capital

   (*ii*) the items which make up the shareholders' funds.

(c) The directors are concerned about the company's liquidity position.

   Required:
   4 **THREE** transactions which will increase the company's working capital. State which statement of financial position items will change as a result of each transaction and whether
   the item will increase or decrease in value.

(Southern Examining Group: GCSE)

45.13A The accountant of Fiddles PLC has begun preparing financial statements but the work is
not yet complete. At this stage the items included in the trial balance are as follows:

	£000
Land	100
Buildings	120
Plant and machinery	170
Depreciation provision	120
Share capital	100
Retained profits brought forward	200
Accounts receivable	200
Accounts payable	110
Inventory	190
Operating profit	80
Loan notes (16%)	180
Allowance for doubtful debts	3
Bank balance (asset)	12
Suspense	1

Notes (*i*) to (*vii*) below are to be taken into account:

(*i*) The accounts receivable control account figure, which is used in the trial balance, does not
   agree with the total of the accounts receivable ledger. A contra of £5,000 has been entered
   correctly in the individual ledger accounts but has been entered on the wrong side of both
   control accounts.
      A batch total of sales of £12,345 had been entered in the double entry system as £13,345,
   although individual ledger account entries for these sales were correct. The balance of £4,000
   on sales returns account has inadvertently been omitted from the trial balance, though correctly entered in the ledger records.

(*ii*) A standing order received from a regular customer for £2,000, and bank charges of £1,000,
   have been completely omitted from the records.

(*iii*) A debtor for £1,000 is to be written off. The allowance for doubtful debts balance is to be
   adjusted to 1% of accounts receivable.

(*iv*) The opening inventory figure had been overstated by £1,000 and the closing inventory figure
   had been understated by £2,000.

(*v*) Any remaining balance on suspense account should be treated as purchases if a debit balance
   and as sales if a credit balance.

(*vi*) The loan notes were issued three months before the year end. No entries have been made as
   regards interest.

(*vii*) A dividend of 10% of share capital is to be proposed.

Required:
(a) Prepare journal entries to cover items in notes (*i*) to (*v*) above. You are NOT to open any new
   accounts and may use only those accounts included in the trial balance as given.
(b) Prepare financial statements for internal use in good order within the limits of the available
   information. For presentation purposes all the items arising from notes (*i*) to (*vii*) above
   should be regarded as material.

(Association of Chartered Certified Accountants)

45.14 'The historical cost convention looks backwards but the going concern convention looks forwards.'

Required:
(a) Explain clearly what is meant by:
    (i)   the historical cost convention;
    (ii) the going concern convention.
(b) Does traditional financial accounting, using the historical cost convention, make the going concern convention unnecessary? Explain your answer fully.
(c) Which do you think a shareholder is likely to find more useful – a report on the past or an estimate of the future? Why?

(*Association of Chartered Certified Accountants*)

45.15 The chairman of a public limited company has written his annual report to the shareholders, extracts of which are quoted below.

Extract 1
'In May 2012, in order to provide a basis for more efficient operations, we acquired PAG Warehousing and Transport Ltd. The agreed valuation of the net tangible assets acquired was £1.4 million. The purchase consideration, £1.7 million, was satisfied by an issue of 6.4 million equity shares, of £0.25 per share, to PAG's shareholders. These shares do not rank for dividend until 2013.'

Extract 2
'As a measure of confidence in our ability to expand operations in 2013 and 2014, and to provide the necessary financial base, we issued £0.5 million 8% Redeemable Loan Stock, 2007/2013, 20 million 6% £1 Redeemable Preference Shares and 4 million £1 equity shares. The opportunity was also taken to redeem the whole of the 5 million 11% £1 Redeemable Preference Shares.'

Required:
Answer the following questions on the above extracts.

Extract 1
(a) What does the difference of £0.3 million between the purchase consideration (£1.7m) and the net tangible assets value (£1.4m) represent?
(b) What does the difference of £0.1 million between the purchase consideration (£1.7m) and the nominal value of the equity shares (£1.6m) represent?
(c) What is the meaning of the term 'equity shares'?
(d) What is the meaning of the phrase 'do not rank for dividend'?

Extract 2
(e) In the description of the loan note issue, what is the significance of
    (i)   8%?
    (ii) 2007/2013?
(f) In the description of the preference share issue, what is the significance of
    (i)   6%?
    (ii) Redeemable?
(g) What is the most likely explanation for the company to have redeemed existing preference shares but at the same time to have issued others?
(h) What effect will these structural changes have had on the gearing of the company?^Authors' Note
(j) Contrast the accounting treatment in the company's income statement of the interest due on the loan notes with dividends proposed on the equity shares.
(k) Explain the reasons for the different treatments you have outlined in your answer to (j) above.

(*Association of Chartered Certified Accountants*)

Authors' Note: Part (h) of the question is covered in the text in Section 47.4.

45.16 The directors of the company by which you are employed as an accountant have received the forecast income statement for 2012 which disclosed a net profit for the year of £36,000.

This is considered to be an unacceptably low figure and a working party has been set up to investigate ways and means of improving the forecast profit.

The following suggestions have been put forward by various members of the working party:

(a) 'Every six months we deduct income tax of £10,000 from the loan note interest and pay it over to the HM Revenue & Customs. If we withhold these payments, the company's profit will be increased considerably.'

(b) 'I see that in the three months August to October 2012 we have forecast a total amount of £40,000 for repainting the exterior of the company's premises. If, instead, we charge this amount as capital expenditure, the company's profit will be increased by £40,000.'

(c) 'In November 2012, the replacement of a machine is forecast. The proceeds from the sale of the old machinery should be credited to profit and loss account.'

(d) 'There is a credit balance of £86,000 on general reserve account. We can transfer some of this to the income statement to increase the 2012 profit.'

(e) 'The company's £1 ordinary shares, which were originally issued at £1 per share, currently have a market value of £1.60 per share and this price is likely to be maintained. We can credit the surplus £0.60 per share to the 2012 profit and loss account.'

(f) 'The company's premises were bought many years ago for £68,000, but following the rise in property values, they are now worth at least £300,000. This enhancement in value can be utilised to increase the 2012 profit.'

You are required, as the accounting member of the working party, to comment on the feasibility of each of the above suggestions for increasing the 2012 forecast profit.

(*Association of Chartered Certified Accountants*)

45.17 Explain what you understand by the accounting term 'loan notes' and indicate the circumstances under which a loan note issue would or would not be an appropriate form of financing.

(*Scottish Qualifications Authority*)

The Financial Statements
of Limited Companies

The increase and reduction of the share capital of limited companies

Learning objectives

After you have studied this chapter, you should be able to:

- explain the various ways in which a limited company may alter its share capital
- describe the difference between a bonus issue and a rights issue of shares
- explain why a company may introduce a scheme for the reduction of its capital
- describe the effect upon the balance sheet of bonus issues, rights issues and schemes for the reduction of capital

Introduction

Sometimes companies need to alter their issued share capital. In this chapter, you'll learn about the alternatives available. You'll learn about the difference between scrip issues and rights issues and how to record the appropriate ledger account entries when either occurs. You will also learn that the nominal value of share capital can be reduced, and how to do so.

10.1 Alteration of capital

A limited company may, if authorised by its Articles, and if the correct legal formalities are observed, alter its share capital in any of the following ways:

1 Increase its share capital by issuing new shares, e.g. increase authorised share capital from £500,000 to £1 million and then issue more shares.
2 Consolidate and divide all or any of its share capital into shares of a larger nominal value than its existing shares, for instance convert 500,000 ordinary shares of £1 each into 100,000 ordinary shares of £5 each.
3 Subdivide all, or any, of its shares into shares of smaller denominations, e.g. convert 1 million ordinary shares of £1 each into 2 million ordinary shares of £0.50 each, or 4 million ordinary shares of 25p each.
4 Cancel shares which have not been taken up. This is known as 'diminution of capital', and is not to be confused with 'reduction of capital', described later in the chapter. Thus, a company with an authorised share capital of £200,000 and an issued share capital of £175,000 can alter its share capital to authorised share capital of £175,000 and issued share capital of £175,000.
5 Redenominate shares from a fixed nominal value in one currency (e.g. £) to a fixed nominal value in another currency (e.g. €).

Activity 10.1   Why do you think a company would wish to change its share capital?

10.2   Bonus shares

Bonus shares are shares issued to existing shareholders free of charge. An alternative name often used is **scrip issue**.

If the Articles give the power, and the requisite legal formalities are observed, the following may be applied in the issuing of bonus shares:

1 the retained profits;
2 any other revenue reserve;
3 any capital reserve, e.g. share premium.

This thus comprises all of the reserves.

The reason why this should ever be needed can be illustrated by taking the somewhat exaggerated example shown in Exhibit 10.1:

Exhibit 10.1

When Better Price Ltd started in business 50 years ago, it issued 10,000 ordinary shares of £1 each and deposited £10,000 in the bank. The company has constantly retained a proportion of its profits to finance its operations, thus diverting them from being used for cash dividend purposes. This has preserved an appropriate level of working capital.

The firm's balance sheet as at 31 December 2007 is shown as:

Better Price Ltd
Balance Sheet as at 31 December 2007
(before bonus shares are issued)

	£
Non-current assets	150,000
Current assets	220,000
Total assets	370,000
Current liabilities	(70,000)
Net assets	300,000
Share capital	10,000
Reserves (including retained profits)	290,000
	300,000

If an annual profit of £45,000 was being earned (i.e. 15% on capital employed) and £10,000 were paid annually as cash dividends, then the dividend declared each year would be 100% (i.e. a dividend of £10,000 on shares with a nominal value of £10,000).

It is obvious that the dividends and the share capital are out of step with one another. Employees and trade unions could start complaining due to a lack of accounting knowledge (or even misuse of it) because they believe that the company is making unduly excessive profits. Customers may also be deluded into thinking that they are being charged excessive prices. Even though this could be demonstrated not to be true because of the prices charged by competitors, they may still have the feeling that they are somehow being duped.

In fact, an efficient company in this industry may only be achieving 'average' rewards for the risks it has taken if it is making a profit of 15% on capital employed. The figure of 100% for the dividend is due to the very misleading convention in accounting in the UK of calculating dividends in relationship to the nominal amount of the share capital, rather than the capital employed.

If it is felt that £80,000 of the reserves could not be used for dividend purposes, due to the fact that the net assets should remain at a minimum of £90,000, made up of non-current assets £80,000 and working capital of £10,000, then besides the £10,000 share capital which cannot be returned to the shareholders there are also £80,000 of reserves which cannot be rationally returned to them. Instead of this £80,000 being called reserves, it might as well be called capital, as it is needed by the business on a permanent basis.

To remedy this position, as well as some other less obvious needs, the concept of bonus shares was developed. The reserves are made non-returnable to the shareholders by being converted into share capital. Each holder of one ordinary share of £1 each will receive eight bonus shares (in the shape of eight ordinary shares) of £1 each. The balance sheet, if the bonus shares had been issued immediately, would be:

Better Price Ltd
Balance sheet as at 31 December 2007
(after bonus shares are issued)

	£
Non-current assets	150,000
Current assets	220,000
Total assets	370,000
Current liabilities	(70,000)
Net assets	300,000
Share capital (£10,000 + £80,000)	90,000
Reserves (£290,000 − £80,000)	210,000
	300,000

When the annual dividends of £10,000 are declared in the future, they will represent:

$$\frac{£10,000}{£90,000} \times \frac{100}{1} = \text{a dividend of } 11.1\%$$

This will cause fewer problems in the minds of employees, trade unions and customers.

Of course the issue of bonus shares may be seen by any of the interested parties to be some form of excessive generosity on the part of the company. To give eight shares of £1 each free for one previously owned may be seen as unfair by employees and their trade unions. In fact, the shareholders have gained nothing. Before the bonus issue there were 10,000 shareholders who owned between them £300,000 of net assets. Therefore, assuming for this purpose that the book 'value' is the same as any other 'value', each share was worth £30. After the bonus issue, each shareholder has nine shares for every one share held before. If a shareholder had owned one share only, he now owns nine shares. He is therefore, the owner of $^9/_{90,000}$ of the company. The 'value' of the net assets is £300,000, and he owns $^9/_{90,000}$ of them, so his shares are worth £30. This is exactly the same 'value' as that applying before the bonus issue was made.

It would be useful, in addition, to refer to other matters for comparison. Anyone who had owned a £1 share 50 years ago, then worth £1, would now have nine £1 shares. A new house of a certain type 50 years ago might have cost £x; it may now cost £9x. Price inflation affects different items in different ways. The cost of a bottle of beer may now be y times greater than it was 50 years ago, a loaf of bread may cost z times more, and so on. But, at least the shareholders now have some tangible increase in the nominal value of their investment. Of course, the company has brought a lot of trouble on itself by waiting so many years to capitalise its reserves. It should have been done in several stages over the years.

This is a very simplified example, but it is a situation many companies have had to face. There is, also, no doubt that a misunderstanding of accounting and financial matters has caused a great deal of unnecessary friction in the past and will probably still do so in the future. Yet another very common misunderstanding is the assumption that the asset balance sheet values equal the amount they could be sold for. Thus, a profit of £100,000 when the book value of the net assets is £200,000 may appear to be excessive yet, if the realisable value of the net assets were used, the net worth of the company may be £2 million, making a profit of £100,000 appear perhaps a little low, rather than appearing excessive.

The accounting entries when bonus shares are issued are to debit the reserve accounts utilised, and to credit a bonus account. The shares are then issued and the entry required to record this is to credit the share capital account and to debit the bonus account. The journal entries in our example would be:

The Journal

	Dr	Cr
	£	£
Reserve account(s) (show each account separately)	80,000	
Bonus account		80,000
Transfer of an amount equal to the bonus payable in fully paid shares		
Bonus account	80,000	
Share capital account		80,000
Allotment and issue of 80,000 shares of £1 each, in satisfaction of the bonus declared		

10.3 Rights issue

You learnt in Chapter 5 that a company can also increase its issued share capital by making a **rights issue**. This is the issue of shares to existing shareholders at a price lower than the ruling market price of the shares. You will remember that the price is lower so as to compensate for the reduction in value of shares held previously.

The price at which the shares of a profitable company are quoted on the Stock Exchange is usually higher than the nominal value of the shares. For instance, the market price of the shares of a company might be quoted at £2.50 while the nominal value per share is only £1.00. If the company has 800,000 shares of £1 each and declares a rights issue of one for every eight held at a price of £1.50 per share, it is obvious that it will be cheaper for the existing shareholders to buy the rights issue at this price instead of buying the same shares in the open market for £2.50 per share. Assume that all the rights issue were taken up, then the number of shares taken up will be 100,000 (i.e. 800,000 ÷ 8), and the amount paid for them will be £150,000. The journal entries will be:

The Journal

	Dr	Cr
	£	£
Cash	150,000	
Share capital		100,000
Share premium		50,000
Being the rights issue of one for every eight shares held at a price of £1.50 nominal value being £1.00		

As the nominal value of each share is £1.00 while £1.50 was paid, the extra 50p constitutes a share premium to the company.

Notice also that the market value of the shares will be reduced or 'diluted' by the rights issue, as was the case for bonus shares. Before the rights issue there were 800,000 shares at a price of £2.50, giving a market capitalisation of £2 million. After the rights issue there are 900,000 shares and the assets have increased by £150,000. The market value may now be £2.39 [(£2 million + £150,000)/900,000], although the precise market price after the rights issue will be influenced by the information given surrounding the sale about the future prospects of the company and may not be exactly the £2.39 calculated above.

10.4 Reduction of capital

Where capital is not represented by assets

Any scheme for the reduction of capital needs to go through legal formalities via the shareholders and other interested parties, and must receive the consent of the court.

Capital reduction means that the share capital – all of it if there is only one class such as ordinary shares, or all or part of it if there is more than one class of shares – has been subjected to a lessening of its nominal value, or of the called-up part of the nominal value. Thus:

(a) a £4 share might be converted into a £3 share;
(b) a £5 share might be converted into a £1 share;
(c) a £3 share, £2 called up, might be converted into a £1 share fully paid up;
(d) a £5 share, £3 called up, might be converted into a £3 share £1 called up;

plus any other variations.

Why should such action be necessary? The reasons are rather like the issue of bonus shares in reverse. However, in this case, the share capital has fallen out of line with the assets, in that the share capital is not fully represented by assets. For example, Robert Ltd may have a balance sheet as follows:

Robert Ltd
Balance Sheet as at 31 December 2007

	£
Net assets	300,000
Equity	
100,000 ordinary shares of £5 each, fully paid	500,000
Less Retained profits (debit balance)	(200,000)
	300,000

The net assets are shown at £300,000, and it is felt that the book value represents a true and fair view of their actual value. The company will almost certainly be precluded from paying dividends until the debit balance of retained profits has been eradicated and replaced with a credit balance. If profits remaining after taxation are now running at the rate of £30,000 per annum, it will be seven years before a dividend can be paid. One reason for buying shares is to provide income (although there may well enter another reason, such as capital appreciation). Consequently, the denial of income to the shareholders for this period of time could seriously affect the company.

A solution would be to cancel, i.e. reduce, the capital which was no longer represented by assets. In this case, £200,000 of the share capital can lay no claim to any assets. The share capital should therefore be reduced by £200,000. This is done by converting the shares into £3 shares fully paid instead of £5 shares. The balance sheet would become:

Robert Ltd
Balance Sheet as at 31 December 2007

	£
Net assets	300,000
	300,000
Ordinary share capital	300,000
	300,000

Now that there is no debit balance of retained profits, the £30,000 available profit next year can be distributed as dividends.

Of course, the Robert Ltd example has been simplified to make what is being explained easier to understand. Often, both preference and ordinary shareholders are involved. Sometimes, loan-note holders as well. Even creditors occasionally sacrifice part of the amount owing to them, the idea being that the increase in working capital so generated will help the business to achieve prosperity, in which case the creditors hope to once again enjoy the profitable contact that they used to have with the company.

Capital reduction schemes are matters for negotiation between the various interested parties. For instance, preference shareholders may be quite content for the nominal value of their shares to be reduced if the rate of interest they receive is increased accordingly. As with any negotiation, the various parties will put forward their points of view and discussions will take place until a compromise solution is arrived at. When the court's sanction has been obtained, the accounting entries are:

1 For amounts written off assets:
    Dr Capital reduction account
        Cr Various asset accounts

2 For reduction in liabilities (e.g. creditors):
    Dr Liability accounts
        Cr Capital reduction account

3 The reduction in the share capital:
    Dr Share capital accounts (each type)
        Cr Capital reduction account

4 If a credit balance now exists on the capital reduction account:
    Dr Capital reduction account (to close)
        Cr Capital reserve

It is unlikely that there would ever be a debit balance on the capital reduction account, as the court would rarely agree to any scheme which would bring this about.

Capital reduction schemes for private companies are used less frequently now than previously, thanks to companies having been granted the right to purchase their own shares.

Where some of the assets are no longer needed

Where some of the assets are no longer needed, probably due to a contraction in a company's activities, it may find itself with a surplus of liquid assets. Subject to the legal formalities being observed, in this case the reduction of capital is effected by returning cash to the shareholders, i.e.:

1 *Dr* Share capital account (with amount returnable)
        Cr Sundry shareholders

2 *Dr* Sundry shareholders
        Cr Bank (amount actually paid)

Such a scheme could be objected to by the creditors if it affected their interests.

Learning outcomes

You should now have learnt:

1 That a limited company may alter its share capital if it is authorised to do so by its Articles of Association.

2 Alterations to share capital can be made by a limited company:
   (a) issuing new shares;
   (b) consolidating all or any of its share capital into shares of a higher nominal value;
   (c) subdividing all or any of its share capital into shares of a lower nominal value;
   (d) cancelling shares that have not been 'taken up' – the difference between the 'authorised share capital' and the 'issued share capital';
   (e) redenominating shares into a different currency.

3 Some reasons why companies change their share capital.

4 That where share capital is overvalued in relation to assets, a capital reduction scheme may be adopted in order to bring the share capital into line with the underlying asset value of the business as reported in the balance sheet.

Answer to activity

10.1 As you will see later in this chapter, there are many possible reasons. It may be that the nominal value of the share capital is significantly understated compared with current earnings. An increase in nominal share capital would help redress this imbalance and make things like earnings per share more intuitively meaningful. Alternatively, it may be that large reserves have been built up and the company wishes to increase the amount of its share capital by converting the reserves into shares. Another possibility is that the share price has risen significantly since the shares were first quoted on the Stock Exchange and it now appears unreasonably high relative to comparable shares. By splitting each share into a number of shares of a lower nominal value, the share price can be brought back to an appropriate level. Don't forget, companies can both increase and reduce the nominal value of their share capital.

Review questions

10.1 The Merton Manufacturing Co Ltd has been in business for many years making fitted furniture and chairs. During 2004 and 2005 substantial losses have been sustained on the manufacture of chairs and the directors have decided to concentrate on the fitted furniture side of the business which is expected to produce a profit of at least £22,500 per annum before interest charges and taxation. A capital reduction scheme has been proposed under which:

(i)   a new ordinary share of 50p nominal value will be created;
(ii)   the £1 ordinary shares will be written off and the shareholders will be offered one new ordinary share for every six old shares held;
(iii)   the £1 6% redeemable preference shares will be cancelled and the holders will be offered for every three existing preference shares one new ordinary share;
(iv)   the existing 11½% loan note will be exchanged for a new loan note yielding 8% at a rate of two old loan notes for three new loan notes. In addition, existing loan-note holders will be offered one new ordinary share for every £4 of the old loan note held;

(*v*)   existing reserves will be written off;

(*vi*)   goodwill is totally impaired and to be written off;

(*vii*)   any remaining balance of write-off which is necessary is to be achieved by writing down plant and equipment; and

(*viii*)   existing ordinary shareholders will be invited to subscribe for two fully paid new ordinary shares at par for every three old shares held.

The balance sheet of the Merton Manufacturing Co Ltd immediately prior to the capital reduction is as follows:

	£	£
Non-current intangible assets		
Goodwill		50,000
Non-current tangible assets		
Freehold land and buildings at cost		95,000
Plant and equipment at cost	275,000	
Less Depreciation to date	(89,500)	
		185,500
		330,500
Current assets		
Inventory	25,000	
Accounts receivable	50,000	
		75,000
Total assets		405,500
Current liabilities		
Accounts payable	63,500	
Bank overdraft	15,850	
	79,350	
Non-current liabilities		
11½% loan note, secured on the freehold		
land and buildings	100,000	
Total liabilities		179,350
Net assets		226,150
Equity		
£1 ordinary shares fully paid		90,000
6% £1 redeemable preference shares fully paid		150,000
Share premium account		25,000
Retained profits		(38,850)
		226,150

On liquidation, freehold land and buildings are expected to produce £120,000; plant and equipment £40,000; inventory £15,000; and accounts receivable £45,000. Goodwill has no value.

There are no termination costs associated with ceasing the manufacture of chairs.

Required:

(*a*) Assuming that the necessary approval is obtained and that the new share issue is successful, produce a balance sheet of the company showing the position immediately after the scheme has been put into effect.

(*b*) Show the effect of the scheme on the expected earnings of the old shareholders.

(*c*) Indicate the points which a preference shareholder should take into account before voting on the scheme.

Corporation tax may be taken at 33⅓%.

(*Association of Chartered Certified Accountants*)

10.2   Deflation Ltd, which had experienced trading difficulties, decided to reorganise its finances. On 31 December 2005 a final trial balance extracted from the books showed the following position:

	£	£
Share capital, authorised and issued:		
150,000 6% cumulative preference shares of £1 each		150,000
200,000 ordinary shares of £1 each		200,000
Share premium account		40,000
Retained profits	114,375	
Preliminary expenses	7,250	
Goodwill (at cost)	55,000	
Trade accounts payable		43,500
Accounts receivable	31,200	
Bank overdraft		51,000
Leasehold property (at cost)	80,000	
(provision for depreciation)		30,000
Plant and machinery (at cost)	210,000	
(provision for depreciation)		62,500
Inventory	79,175	
	577,000	577,000

Approval of the Court was obtained for the following scheme for reduction of capital:

1 The preference shares to be reduced to £0.75 per share.
2 The ordinary shares to be reduced to £0.125 per share.
3 One £0.125 ordinary share to be issued for each £1 of gross preference dividend arrears; the preference dividend had not been paid for three years.
4 The balance on share premium account to be utilised.
5 Plant and machinery to be written down to £75,000.
6 The retained profits, and all intangible assets, to be written off.

At the same time as the resolution to reduce capital was passed, another resolution was approved restoring the total authorised capital to £350,000, consisting of 150,000 6% cumulative preference shares of £0.75 each and the balance in ordinary shares of £0.125 each. As soon as the above resolutions had been passed, 500,000 ordinary shares were issued at par, for cash, payable in full upon application.

You are required:
(a) to show the journal entries necessary to record the above transactions in the company's books; and
(b) to prepare a balance sheet of the company, after completion of the scheme.

(*Institute of Chartered Accountants*)

10.3 On 31 March 2002, the following was the balance sheet of Quality Yarns Ltd:

Balance Sheet

	£	£
Non-current assets		
Goodwill and trade marks as valued	280,000	
Plant and machinery (at cost *less* depreciation)	320,000	
Furniture and fittings (at cost *less* depreciation)	8,400	
		608,400
Current assets		
Inventory	190,200	
Sundry accounts receivable	74,600	
Cash	300	
		265,100
Total assets		873,500
Current liabilities		
Sundry accounts payable	33,200	
Bank overdraft	44,400	
		(77,600)
Net assets		795,900
Equity		
Authorised capital		
200,000 6% preference shares of £1 each	200,000	
3 million ordinary shares of 50p each	1,500,000	
	1,700,000	
Issued and fully paid capital		
100,000 6% preference shares of £1 each		100,000
1,750,000 ordinary shares of 50p each		875,000
		975,000
Capital reserve	60,000	
Less: Retained profits	(239,100)	(179,100)
		795,900

The following scheme of capital reduction was sanctioned by the Court and agreed by the shareholders:

(a) Preference shares were to be reduced to 80p each.
(b) Ordinary shares were to be reduced to 25p each.
(c) The capital reserve was to be eliminated.
(d) The reduced shares of both classes were to be consolidated into new ordinary shares of £1 each.
(e) An issue of £300,000 5% loan notes at par was to be made to provide fresh working capital.
(f) The sum written off the issued capital of the company and the capital reserve to be used to write off the debit balance of retained profits and to reduce non-current assets by the following amounts:

Goodwill and trade marks	£250,000
Plant and machinery	£22,200
Furniture and fittings	£4,400

(g) The bank overdraft was to be paid off out of the proceeds of the loan notes which were duly issued and paid in full.

A further resolution was passed to reduce the authorised capital of the company to 1,750,000 ordinary shares of £1 each.

Required:
Prepare journal entries (cash transactions to be journalised) to give effect to the above scheme and draw up the balance sheet of the company after completion of the scheme.

10.4A   The balance sheet of Tatters Ltd on 31 December 2008 was as follows:

Balance Sheet

	£	£
Goodwill		50,000
Non-current assets		190,000
		240,000
Current assets		
Inventory	21,000	
Work in progress	3,000	
Accounts receivable	25,000	
Bank	18,000	
		67,000
Capital expenses		
Formation expenses		3,000
Total assets		310,000
Current liabilities: accounts payable	30,000	
Non-current liabilities: 5% loan notes	60,000	
Total liabilities		(90,000)
		220,000
Equity		
Issued share capital		
200,000 ordinary shares of £1 each		200,000
100,000 4% cumulative preference shares of £1 each		100,000
		300,000
Retained profits		(80,000)
		220,000

The dividend on the preference shares is £12,000 in arrears. A scheme of reconstruction was accepted by all parties and was completed on 1 January 2009.

A new company was formed, Rags Ltd, with an authorised share capital of £250,000, consisting of 250,000 ordinary shares of £1 each. This company took over all the assets of Tatters Ltd. The purchase consideration was satisfied partly in cash and partly by the issue, at par, of shares and 6% loan notes by the new company in accordance with the following arrangements:

1 The creditors of the old company received, in settlement of each £10 due to them, £6 in cash and four fully paid ordinary shares in the new company.
2 The holders of preference shares in the old company received nine fully paid ordinary shares in the new company to every ten preference shares in the old company and four fully paid ordinary shares in the new company for every £5 of arrears of dividend.
3 The ordinary shareholders in the old company received one fully paid share in the new company for every four ordinary shares in the old company.
4 The holders of 5% loan notes in the old company received £50 in cash and £50 of 6% loan notes issued at par for every £100 loan notes held in the old company.
5 The balance of the authorised capital of the new company was issued at par for cash and was fully paid on 1 January 2009.
6 Goodwill was eliminated, the inventory was valued at £15,000 and the other current assets were brought into the new company's books at the amounts at which they appeared in the old company's balance sheet. The balance of the purchase consideration represented the agreed value of the non-current assets.

You are required to show:
(a) the closing entries in the realisation account and the sundry shareholders account in the books of Tatters Ltd;

(b) your calculation of:
  (i) the purchase consideration for the assets, and
  (ii) the agreed value of the non-current assets;
(c) the summarised balance sheet of Rags Ltd as on 1 January 2009.

10.5A The ledger balances of Tick Tick Ltd at 31 March 2011 were as follows:

	£
Freehold premises	90,000
Plant	300,000
Inventory	82,000
Accounts receivable	96,000
Development expenditure*	110,000
Cash at bank	11,000
Retained profits (debit balance)	121,000
250,000 8% preference shares of £1 each	250,000
500,000 ordinary shares of £1 each	500,000
Accounts payable	60,000

A capital reduction scheme has been sanctioned under which the 250,000 preference shares are to be reduced to 80p each, fully paid; and the 500,000 ordinary shares are to be reduced to 20p each, fully paid.

Development expenditure and the debit balance of retained profits are to be written off, the balance remaining being used to reduce the book value of the plant.

Required:
Prepare the journal entries recording the reduction scheme and the balance sheet as it would appear immediately after the reduction. Narrations are not required in connection with journal entries.

*Development expenditure is a non-current asset. (See Chapter 11.)

11

Accounting standards and related documents

Learning objectives

After you have studied this chapter, you should be able to:

● explain the measures being taken by the International Accounting Standards Board to develop a framework for the preparation and presentation of financial statements

● describe the full range of international accounting standards currently in issue and their aims and objectives

Introduction

In this chapter, you'll learn about the background to the formation of the International Accounting Standards Board and of the range of international accounting standards and international financial reporting standards currently in force.

11.1 Why do we need accounting standards?

Accounting is used in every kind of business and organisation from large multinational organisations to your local shop, from sole traders to companies. It can cover an unlimited range of activities as different as breweries, charities, churches, dentists, doctors, lawyers, mines, oil wells, betting shops, banks, cinemas, circuses, funeral undertakers, farms, waste disposal, deepsea diving, airlines, estate agents and so on.

Let's assume that you have received a copy of the published financial statements of a company. You want to be sure that you can rely on the methods it selected to calculate its revenues, expenditures and balance sheet values. Without this assurance you would not be able to have any faith at all in the figures, and could not sensibly take any decision concerning your relationship with the company.

It is the same for all investors. People invest in organisations of all types and they would all like to have faith and trust in the figures reported in their financial statements. But this diversity of type of business, and also of size, means that, while general principles can be laid down, detailed regulations that it would make sense to apply to one company would be wholly inappropriate for another company. It is, quite simply, impossible to provide 100% assurance of the validity of the financial statements of every conceivable organisation through the creation of a single set of rules and procedures. There has to be some flexibility within the rules laid down.

If it isn't feasible to produce a set of all-encompassing regulations, why bother with rules at all? To understand why there was a move to regulation, we need to look back to what happened in the 1960s.

11.2 The background in the UK

In the late 1960s there was a general outcry that the methods used by different businesses were showing vastly different profits on similar data. In the UK, a controversy had arisen following the takeover of AEI Ltd by GEC Ltd. In fighting the takeover bid made by GEC, the AEI directors had produced a forecast, in the tenth month of their financial year, that the profit before tax for the year would be £10 million. After the takeover, the financial statements of AEI for that same year showed a loss of £4.5 million. The difference was attributed to there being £5 million of 'matters substantially of fact' and £9.5 million of 'adjustments which remain matters substantially of judgement'.

The financial pages of the national press started demanding action, calling for the accounting profession to lay down consistent principles for businesses to follow.

In December 1969, the Institute of Chartered Accountants in England and Wales issued a *Statement of Intent on Accounting Standards in the 1970s*. The Institute set up the Accounting Standards Steering Committee in 1970. Over the following six years, it was joined by the five other UK and Irish accountancy bodies and, in 1976, the committee became the Accounting Standards Committee (ASC). The six accountancy bodies formed the Consultative Committee of Accountancy Bodies (CCAB).

Prior to the issue of any accounting standard by the ASC, a great deal of preparatory work was done and an exposure draft (ED) was issued and copies were sent to those with a special interest in the topic for comment. The journals of the CCAB (i.e. the official magazines of each of the six accountancy bodies) also gave full details of the exposure drafts. After the period allowed for consultation ended, it was seen to be desirable, and an accounting standard on the topic was issued. The Standards issued by the ASC were called Statements of Standard Accounting Practice (SSAPs).

Because the ASC had to obtain approval from its six professional accountancy body members, it did not appear to be as decisive and independent as was desired. In 1990, a new body, the Accounting Standards Board (ASB), took over the functions of the ASC. The ASB is more independent of the accounting bodies and can issue its recommendations, known as financial reporting standards (FRSs), without approval from any other body. The ASB adopted the SSAPs in force but many have since been replaced by FRSs (of which 27 were inforce in December 2007) and, by December 2007, only 7 SSAPs remained in force. As with the ASC, the ASB issues exposure drafts – FREDs – on which comments are invited prior to the issue of a new standard.

In 1997, the ASB issued a third category of standard – the Financial Reporting Standard for Smaller Entities (FRSSE). SSAPs and FRSs had generally been developed with the larger company in mind. The FRSSE was the ASB's response to the view that smaller companies should not have to apply all the cumbersome rules contained in the SSAPs and FRSs. It is, in effect, a collection of some of the rules from virtually all the other accounting standards. Small companies can choose whether or not to apply the FRSSE or, as seems unlikely, continue to apply all the other accounting standards.

In addition to the FRSs and the FRSSE, the ASB also issues Urgent Issues Task Force Abstracts (UITFs). These are issued in response to an urgent need to regulate something pending the issue of a new or amended FRS. They have the same status as an FRS but, due to the perceived urgent need for them to be issued, no exposure drafts are issued.

While there is no general law compelling observation of the standards, accounting standards have had statutory recognition since the Companies Act 1989. As a result, apart from entities exempted from certain standards or sections within standards – SSAPs 13 (*Research and development*) and 25 (*Segmental reporting*), and FRS 1 (*Cash flow statements*), for example, all contain exemption clauses based on company size – accounting standards must be complied with by all entities that are reporting under UK GAAP when preparing financial statements intended to present a 'true and fair view'. The Companies Acts state that failure to comply with the requirements of an accounting standard must be explained in the financial statements.

Historically, the main method of ensuring compliance with the standards by their members has always been through each professional body's own disciplinary procedures on their members.

The ASB felt this was insufficient – such measures only seek to control individual accountants, not the organisations they work for. As a result, it created a Review Panel with power to prosecute companies under civil law where their financial statements contain a major breach of the standards.

In 2005, all European companies listed on a stock exchange were required to switch from UK GAAP to International GAAP when preparing consolidated financial statements. All other companies were given the option of doing so, and many have. While there is currently no equivalent of the FRSSE in force, the IASB is currently considering introducing one, a situation that may delay the switch for some companies. Nevertheless, it is likely that in a few years' time all UK companies will be reporting using International GAAP.

So far as UK and Irish standards are concerned, the ASB has been at pains to ensure that most of the provisions of the relevant international standards are incorporated in existing SSAPs and FRSs, the difference in the information required or in the manner of its presentation is often minimal. To this end, each FRS indicates the level of compliance with the relevant international standard(s), making it easier for companies to determine the potential impact on their financial statements should they adopt international standards instead of SSAPs and FRSs.

> **Activity 11.1**   Why do you think many UK and Irish companies are switching voluntarily to international accounting standards?

This book deals in outline with all international accounting standards issued and still in force up to December 2007. It does not deal with all the many detailed points contained in the standards and exposure drafts. It would be a far larger book if this was attempted. You will find similar details and coverage of UK GAAP in *Business Accounting UK GAAP*. Students at the later stages of their professional examinations will need to get full copies of all standards and study them thoroughly. There are many web-based resources which provide the latest details on international standards. For example, **www.iasplus.com** contains summaries of all extant international standards.

The remainder of this chapter deals with all the current international accounting standards and related documents which are not covered in detail elsewhere in this book.

The next section presents an overview of the history of international accounting standards.

11.3 International accounting standards

The Accounting Standards Board issues accounting standards for adoption in the UK and Ireland. Other countries also have their own accounting standards boards – for example, the FASB (Financial Accounting Standards Board) operates in the USA and Australia has the AASB (Australian Accounting Standards Board). However, many smaller countries could not justify the creation of their own accounting standards but needed some form of regulation over the financial statements produced. This led, in 1973, to the setting up of the International Accounting Standards Committee (IASC). The IASC was replaced in 2001 by the International Accounting Standards Board (IASB). At that time, like the ASB, the IASB adopted all the International Accounting Standards (IASs) that the IASC had issued. All new standards issued by the IASB are called International Financial Reporting Standards (IFRSs).

The work of the IASB is overseen by 22 trustees, six from Europe, six from North America, and six from Asia/Pacific. The remaining four trustees can be from anywhere so long as geographical balance is retained. The IASB has 12 full-time members and two part-time members. Its members must also reflect an appropriate balance of auditors, financial statement preparers, users of financial statements and academics.

When the IASC was founded, it had no formal authority and the IASs were entirely voluntary and initially intended for use in countries that did not have their own accounting standards or which had considerable logistical difficulty in establishing and maintaining the infrastructure necessary to sustain a national accounting standards board.

Apart from providing standards for use in countries that do not issue their own accounting standards, the need today for the IASB is mainly due to:

1 The considerable growth in international investment, which means it is desirable to have similar methods the world over so that investment decisions are based on more compatible information.
2 The growth in multinational firms which have to produce financial statements covering a large number of countries. Standardisation between countries makes the accounting work easier, and reduces costs.
3 It is desirable that the activities and efforts of the various national standard-setting bodies be harmonised.

Let's look at the principles that underpin accounting standards.

11.4 The Framework for the Preparation and Presentation of Financial Statements

The Framework for the Preparation and Presentation of Financial Statements was issued in 1989. It is split into seven main sections:

1 the objective of financial statements;
2 underlying assumptions;
3 qualitative characteristics of financial statements;
4 the elements of financial statements;
5 recognition of the elements of financial statements;
6 measurement of the elements of financial statements;
7 concepts of capital and capital maintenance.

1 The objective of financial statements

The objective of financial statements is to provide information about the financial position, performance and changes in financial position of an entity that is useful to a wide range of users in making economic decisions.

2 Underlying assumptions

In order to meet their objectives, financial statements are prepared on the accrual basis of accounting and on the assumption that an entity is a going concern and will continue in operation for the foreseeable future.

3 Qualitative characteristics of financial statements

Qualitative characteristics are the attributes that make the information provided in financial statements useful to users. The four principal qualitative characteristics are **understandability**, **relevance**, **reliability** and **comparability**.

Understandability

An essential quality of the information provided in financial statements is that it is readily understandable by users. Information about complex matters that should be included because of its relevance to the economic decision-making needs of users should not be excluded merely because it may be too difficult for certain users to understand.

Relevance

To be useful, information must be relevant to the decision-making needs of users. Information is relevant when it influences the economic decisions of users by helping them evaluate past, present or future events or confirming, or correcting, their past evaluations. Other aspects of information must be considered when considering the relevance of information:

(i) **Materiality** is crucial to relevance: information is material if its omission or misstatement could influence the economic decisions of users taken on the basis of the financial statements. It depends on the size of the item or error judged in the particular circumstances of its omission or misstatement. Thus, materiality provides a threshold or cut-off point rather than being a primary qualitative characteristic which information must have if it is to be useful.

(ii) **Reliability** exists when information is free from material error and bias and can be depended upon by users to represent faithfully that which it either purports to represent or could reasonably be expected to represent.

(iii) **Faithful representation** exists when information represents faithfully the transactions and other events it either purports to represent or could reasonably be expected to represent.

(iv) **Substance over form** must be applied, in that transactions and other events that information purports to represent must be accounted for and presented in accordance with their substance and economic reality and not merely their legal form.

(v) **Neutrality**, i.e. a lack of bias must be a characteristic of the information presented. Much of the information presented in financial statements is determined by the person preparing those statements. This often entails taking decisions concerning what to include and what to exclude – for example, what allowance to make for doubtful debts. Any such accounting estimates must be neutral, neither understated nor overstated.

(vi) **Prudence** is related to neutrality. Prudence is the inclusion of a degree of caution in the exercise of the judgements needed in making the estimates required under conditions of uncertainty, such that assets or income are not overstated and liabilities or expenses are not understated.

(vii) **Completeness** of the information in financial statements must be achieved within the bounds of materiality and cost if that information is to be reliable. An omission can cause information to be false or misleading and thus unreliable and deficient in terms of its relevance.

Comparability

To enable users to identify trends in its financial position and performance the measurement and display of the financial effect of like transactions and other events must be carried out in a consistent way throughout an entity and over time. To this end, financial statements must also show corresponding information for the preceding period.

Constraints on relevant and reliable information

There are four such constraints:

(a) **Timeliness**: if there is undue delay in the reporting of information it may lose its relevance but information presented too soon may be too uncertain to be reliable. In achieving a balance between relevance and reliability, the overriding consideration is how best to satisfy the economic decision-making needs of users.

(b) **Balance between benefit and cost**: the benefits derived from information should exceed the cost of providing it. This constraint is pervasive throughout accounting and is often raised as an issue to consider before embarking upon obtaining information that is difficult to obtain.

(c) **Balance between qualitative characteristics**: in practice, a trade-off between qualitative characteristics is often necessary. Any such trade-off should meet the objective of financial statements.

(d) **True and fair view/fair presentation**: the application of the principal qualitative characteristics and of appropriate accounting standards normally results in financial statements that convey what is generally understood as a true and fair view of, or as presenting fairly such information.

A useful diagram (Exhibit 11.1) illustrating the qualitative characteristics of accounting information was included by the ASB in an early draft of its equivalent of the IASB Principles (upon which it was based):

Exhibit 11.1 The qualitative characteristics of accounting information

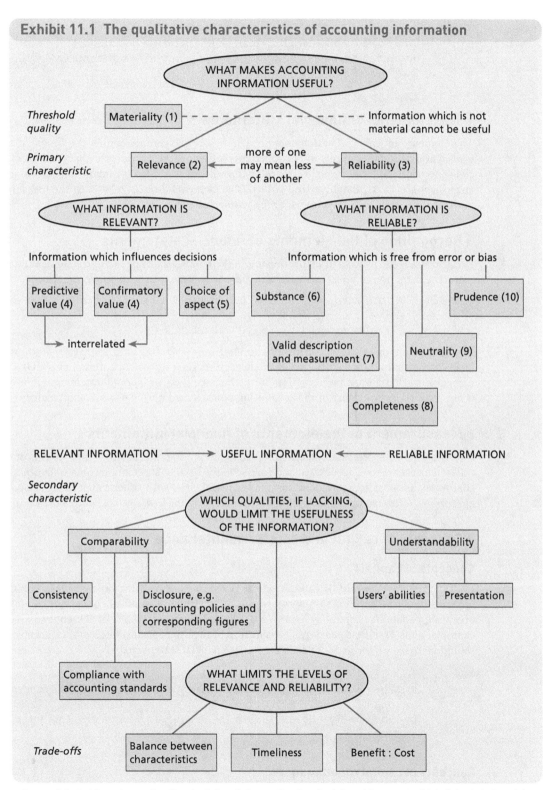

Why do you think there is such an emphasis on the qualitative aspects of information in the *Framework for the Preparation and Presentation of Financial Statements*?

4 The elements of financial statements

The elements of financial statements are the broad classes into which the financial effects of transactions and other events are grouped (according to their economic characteristics) in financial statements. The elements directly related to the measurement of financial position in the balance sheet are assets, liabilities and equity. The elements directly related to the measurement of performance in the income statement are income and expenses.

5 Recognition of the elements of financial statements

Recognition is the process of incorporating in the balance sheet or income statement an item that meets the definition of an element and satisfies the following criteria for recognition:

- it is probable that any future economic benefit associated with the item will flow to or from the entity; and
- it has a cost or value that can be measured with reliability.

Recognition involves the depiction of the item in words and by a monetary amount and the inclusion of that amount in the balance sheet or income statement totals. Items that satisfy the recognition criteria must be recognised in the balance sheet or income statement. Failure to do so is not rectified by disclosure of the accounting policies used nor by notes or explanatory material.

6 Measurement of the elements of financial statements

Measurement is the process of determining the monetary amounts at which the elements of the financial statements are to be recognised and carried in the balance sheet and income statement. The most commonly adopted measurement basis is historical cost, with other bases being adopted where appropriate – for example, the valuing of inventories at the lower of cost and net realisable value.

7 Concepts of capital and capital maintenance

Concepts of capital

Under a **financial concept of capital** (which is the one adopted by most entities), capital is synonymous with the net assets or equity of the entity. Under a **physical concept of capital**, such as operating capability, capital is regarded as the productive capacity of the entity based on, for example, units of output per day. The selection of the appropriate concept of capital by an entity should be based on the needs of the users of its financial statements.

(a) When would it be appropriate for an entity to adopt a financial concept of capital?
(b) When would it be appropriate for an entity to adopt a physical concept of capital?

Concepts of capital maintenance

These provide the link between the concepts of capital and the concepts of profit by providing the point of reference by which profit is measured. Only inflows of assets in excess of amounts needed to maintain capital may be regarded as profit and therefore as a return on capital. Hence, profit or loss is the residual amount that remains after expenses have been deducted from income.

The two concepts of capital give rise to two concepts of capital maintenance:

(a) *Financial capital maintenance*: a profit is earned only if the financial amount of the net assets at the end of the period exceeds the financial amount of net assets at the beginning of the period, after excluding any distributions to, and contributions from, owners during the period.

(b) *Physical capital maintenance*: a profit is earned only if the physical productive capacity (or operating capability) of the entity (or the resources or funds needed to achieve that capacity) at the end of the period exceeds the physical productive capacity at the beginning of the period, after excluding any distributions to, and contributions from, owners during the period.

We'll now look at each of the current international accounting standards, in number order. However, because it underpins every other international accounting standard, we'll start by looking at IAS 8 (*Accounting policies, changes in accounting estimates and errors*).

11.5 IAS 8 Accounting policies, changes in accounting estimates and errors

Users of financial statements issued by organisations want to analyse and evaluate the figures contained within them. They cannot do this effectively unless they know which accounting policies have been used when preparing such statements.

Accounting policies

These are defined in IAS 8 as:

> *the specific principles, bases, conventions, rules and practices applied by an entity in preparing and presenting financial statements.*

In other words, accounting policies define the processes whereby relevant and reliable information about the transactions, other events and conditions to which they apply are reflected in the financial statements. The accounting policies selected should enable the financial statements to give a true and fair view.

When selecting an accounting policy, its appropriateness should be considered in the context of producing information that is:

(a) relevant to the economic decision-making needs of users; and
(b) reliable, in that the financial statements:
    (i) represent faithfully the financial position, financial performance and cash flows of the entity;
    (ii) reflect the economic substance of transactions, other events and conditions, and not merely the legal form;
    (iii) are neutral, i.e. free from bias;
    (iv) are prudent;
    (v) are complete in all material aspects.

Changes in estimates

The use of estimates is an essential part of the preparation of financial statements and does not undermine their reliability. Business is full of uncertainty and any items in financial statements must be estimated. Making an estimate involves judgements based on the latest available, reliable information. For example, estimates may be required of:

(*a*) doubtful debts;
(*b*) obsolescence of inventory;
(*c*) the fair value of financial assets or financial liabilities;
(*d*) the useful lives of, or expected pattern of consumption of the future economic benefits embodied in, depreciable assets; and
(*e*) warranty obligations.

An estimate may need to be revised if changes occur in the circumstances upon which it was based or as a result of new information or more experience. By its nature, the revision of an estimate does not relate to prior periods and is not the correction of an error.

A change in the measurement basis applied is a change in an accounting policy, and is not a change in an accounting estimate. When it is difficult to distinguish a change in an accounting policy from a change in an accounting estimate, the change is treated as a change in an accounting estimate.

The effect of a change in an accounting estimate is recognised by including it in profit or loss in:

(*i*)   the period of the change, if the change affects that period only; or
(*ii*) the period of the change and future periods, if the change affects both.

Errors

Errors can arise in respect of the recognition, measurement, presentation or disclosure of elements of financial statements. Financial statements do not comply with accounting standards if they contain errors made intentionally to achieve a particular presentation of an entity's financial position, financial performance or cash flows. Errors are sometimes not discovered until a subsequent period. When an error is found in a subsequent period, the error must be corrected in the comparative information presented in the financial statements for that subsequent period.

Corrections of errors are *not* changes in acounting estimates. Accounting estimates are approximations that may need revision as additional information becomes known. For example, the gain or loss recognised on the outcome of a contingency is not the correction of an error.

11.6 IAS 1 Presentation of financial statements

IAS 1 prescribes the basis for presentation of general purpose financial statements to ensure comparability both with the entity's financial statements of previous periods and with the financial statements of other entities. It sets out the overall requirements for the presentation of financial statements, guidelines for their structure and minimum requirements for their content.

Purpose of financial statements

The standard states that:

> *financial statements are a structured representation of the financial position and financial performance of an entity. The objective of financial statements is to provide information about the financial position, financial performance and cash flows of an entity that is useful to a wide range of users in making economic decisions. Financial statements also show the results of the management's stewardship of the resources entrusted to it. To meet this objective, financial statements provide information about an entity's:*
>
> *(a) assets;*
> *(b) liabilities;*

(c) *equity;*
(d) *income and expenses, including gains and losses;*
(e) *contributions by and distributions to owners in their capacity as owners; and*
(f) *cash flows.*

This information, along with other information in the notes, assists users of financial statements in predicting the entity's future cash flows and, in particular, their timing and certainty.

A complete set of financial statements

There are seven components to a complete set of financial statements that entities can produce (six, if the income statement information is included within the statement of comprehensive income), all of which must be given equal prominence:

(a) A **statement of financial position** (i.e. a balance sheet) as at the end of the period.
(b) An **income statement** (if shown separately from the statement of comprehensive income) which should show *as a minimum* line items for:
   1 revenue;
   2 finance costs;
   3 share of the profit or loss of associates and joint ventures accounted for using the equity method;
   4 tax expense;
   5 a single amount comprising the total of:
      (*i*) the post-tax profit or loss of discontinued operations; and
      (*ii*) the post-tax gain or loss recognised on the measurement to fair value less costs to sell or on the disposal of the assets or disposal group(s) constituting the discontinued operation;
   6 profit or loss.
(c) A **statement of comprehensive income** which, if no separate income statement is prepared, includes the items that would otherwise appear in the income statement plus:
   6 the profit or loss (as shown in the income statement);
   7 each component of other comprehensive income (i.e. items of income and expense that are not recognised in profit and loss) classified by nature. These include:
      ● changes in revaluation surplus (IAS 16 *Property, plant and equipment* and IAS 38 *Intangible assets*);
      ● actuarial gains and losses on defined benefit plans recognised in accordance with paragraph 93A of IAS 19 Employee benefits;
      ● gains and losses arising from translating the financial statements of a foreign operation (IAS 21 Effects of changes in foreign exchange rates);
      ● gains and losses on remeasuring available-for-sale financial assets (IAS 39 Financial instruments: recognition and measurement);
      ● the effective portion of gains and losses on hedging instruments in a cash flow hedge (IAS 39);
   8 share of the other comprehensive income of associates and joint ventures accounted for using the equity method; and
   9 total comprehensive income.

If no income statement is prepared, the statement of comprehensive income must contain *as a minimum* all nine items listed above.

(d) A **statement of changes in equity.**
(e) A **statement of cash flows.**
(f) **Notes,** comprising a summary of significant accounting policies and other explanatory information. As a minimum, the notes must include information about:

- accounting policies followed;
- the judgements that management has made in the process of applying the entity's accounting policies that have the most significant effect on the amounts recognised in the financial statements; and
- the key assumptions concerning the future, and other key sources of estimation uncertainty, that have a significant risk of causing a material adjustment to the carrying amounts of assets and liabilities within the next financial year.

Preparation of the seventh component to a complete set of financial statements obviously depends upon circumstances and is unlikely to be prepared very frequently:

(g) A **statement of financial position** as at the beginning of the earliest comparative period when an entity applies an accounting policy retrospectively or makes a retrospective restatement of items in its financial statements, or when it reclassifies items in its financial statements.

The Statement of Financial Position (balance sheet)

IAS 1 does not prescribe the order or format in which items are presented. However, *as a minimum* the statement of financial position should include the following line items:

(a) property, plant and equipment;
(b) investment property;
(c) intangible assets;
(d) financial assets (excluding amounts shown under (e), (h) and (i));
(e) investments accounted for using the equity method;
(f) biological assets;
(g) inventories;
(h) trade and other receivables;
(i) cash and cash equivalents;
(j) the total of assets classified as held for sale and assets included in disposal groups classified as held for sale in accordance with IFRS 5 Non-current assets held for sale and discontinued operations;
(k) trade and other payables;
(l) provisions;
(m) financial liabilities (excluding amounts shown under (k) and (l));
(n) liabilities and assets for current tax, as defined in IAS 12 Income taxes;
(o) deferred tax liabilities and deferred tax assets, as defined in IAS 12;
(p) liabilities included in disposal groups classified as held for sale in accordance with IFRS 5;
(q) minority interest, presented within equity; and
(r) issued capital and reserves attributable to owners of the parent.

The Statement of Changes in Equity

This statement must show the following four items:

(i)   total comprehensive income for the period, showing separately the total amounts attributable to owners of the parent and to minority interest;
(ii) for each component of equity, the effects of retrospective application or retrospective restatement recognised in accordance with IAS 8 (Accounting policies);
(iii) the amounts of transactions with owners in their capacity as owners, showing separately contributions by and distributions to owners; and
(iv) for each component of equity, a reconciliation between the carrying amount at the beginning and the end of the period, separately disclosing each change.

In addition, the amount of dividends recognised as distributions to owners during the period and the related amount per share must be shown, either in the statement or as a note.

The titles of financial statements

Entities are permitted to use whatever title they wish for each financial statement, so long as it is clear what the statement is presenting.

Comparative information

Two versions of each financial statement must be prepared, one for the current period and one for the preceding period. This is usually done by including additional columns in the financial statements for the preceding period amounts.

11.7 IAS 2 Inventories

Due to the many varying kinds of businesses and conditions in companies, there simply cannot be one system of valuation for inventories. All that the standard can do is to narrow down the different methods that could be used.

Inventories

Inventories should be stated at the total of the lower of cost and net realisable value. The same cost formula must be used for all inventory of a similar nature and use to the entity. Profit should not be recognised in advance, but immediate account should be made for anticipated losses.

In the balance sheet (or in the notes), stocks should be sub-classified so as to indicate the amounts held in each of the main categories: raw materials and consumables; work in progress; finished goods and goods for resale; and payments on account.

Net realisable value consists of the expected selling price less any expenses necessary to sell the product. This may be below cost because of obsolescence, deterioration or falling selling prices. Replacement cost may be used if it is the best available measure of net realisable value.

Cost is defined as: *'all costs of purchase, conversion and other costs incurred in bringing the inventories to their present location and condition'*.

Cost of purchase comprises purchase price including import duties and other irrecoverable taxes, transport and handling costs and any other directly attributable costs, less trade discounts, rebates and subsidies.

Cost of conversion comprises:

(a) costs which are specifically attributable to units of production, i.e. direct labour, direct expenses and subcontracted work;
(b) systematically allocated fixed and variable production overheads.

Other costs comprise any other expenditure attributable to bringing the product or service to its present location and condition.

Fixed production overheads are allocated on the basis of the normal capacity of the production facilities expected to be achieved on average over a number of periods under normal circumstances. Obviously, neither selling nor administrative overheads should be included in cost.

Notice that abnormal costs should not be included, as they should not have the effect of increasing inventory valuation; and neither should storage costs.

The last in, first out (LIFO) method should not be used for valuation of inventory, as it does not provide an up-to-date valuation.

The financial statements should disclose:

(a) the accounting policies adopted in measuring inventories, including the cost formula used;
(b) the total carrying amount of inventories and the carrying amount in classifications appropriate to the entity;
(c) the carrying amount of inventories carried at fair value less costs to sell;
(d) the amount of inventories recognised as an expense during the period;
(e) the amount of any write-down of inventories recognised as an expense in the period;
(f) the amount of any reversal of any write-down that is recognised as a reduction in the amount of inventories recognised as expense in the period;
(g) the circumstances or events that led to the reversal of a write-down of inventories; and
(h) the carrying amount of inventories pledged as security for liabilities.

Information about the carrying amounts held in different classifications of inventories and the extent of the changes in these assets is useful to financial statement users. Common classifications of inventories are merchandise, production supplies, materials, work in progress and finished goods. The inventories of a service provider may be described as work in progress.

11.8 IAS 7 Statement of cash flows

This accounting standard is covered in Chapter 15.

11.9 IAS 8 Accounting policies, changes in accounting estimates and errors

This accounting standard was covered in Section 11.5.

11.10 IAS 10 Events after the reporting period

Obviously, any event which occurred during a financial period will be taken into account when the financial statements were prepared. Generally, once financial statements have been approved and authorised for issue, it becomes impossible to alter them. However, during the period between the balance sheet date and the date when the financial statements are authorised for issue, events may arise which throw some light upon the valuation of assets or amounts of liabilities in those financial statements. IAS 10 directs its attention to such events during this period.

To clarify the period involved, entities must report the date on which their financial statements were authorised for issue. For companies, this *is not* the date when they are presented to the shareholders at the AGM. Rather, it is the date on which the directors authorised the financial statements to be issued.

Two terms are of particular importance in applying the requirements of IAS 10: 'adjusting events' and 'non-adjusting events'.

Adjusting events

These are events which provide evidence of conditions that existed at the balance sheet date for which the entity shall adjust the amounts recognised in its financial statements or recognise items that were not previously recognised. Examples include:

- The settlement after the balance sheet date of a court case that confirms the liability of the entity at the balance sheet date.
- The discovery after the balance sheet date of errors or frauds which show that the financial statements were incorrect.
- Information received after the balance sheet date that indicates that the value of an asset was impaired (i.e. less than previously believed) at the balance sheet date. This could arise in many ways, for example:

    (a) **Non-current assets.** The subsequent determination of the purchase price or of the proceeds of sale of assets purchased or sold before the year end.

    (b) **Property.** A valuation which provides evidence of a permanent diminution in value.

    (c) **Investments.** The receipt of a copy of the financial statements or other information in respect of an unlisted company which provides evidence of a permanent diminution in the value of a long-term investment.

    (d) **Inventories of raw materials, goods for resale and work in progress:**

    (i) the receipt of proceeds of sales after the balance sheet date or other evidence concerning the net realisable value of stocks;

    (ii) the receipt of evidence that the previous estimate of accrued profit on a long-term contract was materially inaccurate.

    (e) **Debtors.** The renegotiation of amounts owing by debtors, or the insolvency of a debtor.

Non-adjusting events

These are events which arise after the balance sheet date and concern conditions which did not exist at that time. Consequently they do not result in changes in amounts in financial statements. They may, however, be of such materiality that their disclosure is required by way of notes to ensure that the financial statements are not misleading. Such disclosure should describe the nature of the event and an estimate of its financial effect (or a statement that it is not possible to do so).

Examples of non-adjusting events given in IAS 10 which may require disclosure include:

- a decline in market value of investments between the balance sheet date and the date when the financial statements are authorised for issue;
- a major business combination after the balance sheet date or disposing of a major subsidiary;
- announcing a plan to discontinue an operation, disposing of assets or settling liabilities attributable to a discontinuing operation or entering into binding agreements to sell such assets or settle such liabilities;
- major purchases and disposals of assets, or expropriation of major assets by government;
- the destruction of a major production plant by a fire after the balance sheet date;
- announcing, or commencing the implementation of, a major restructuring;
- major ordinary share transactions and potential ordinary share transactions after the balance sheet date;
- abnormally large changes after the balance sheet date in asset prices or foreign exchange rates;
- changes in tax rates or tax laws enacted or announced after the balance sheet date that have a significant effect on current and deferred tax assets and liabilities;
- entering into significant commitments or contingent liabilities, for example, by issuing significant guarantees;
- commencing major litigation arising solely out of events that occurred after the balance sheet date.

The standard makes it clear that dividends proposed or declared after the balance sheet date are not to be treated as a liability in the balance sheet. Rather they are to be disclosed in a note to the financial statements.

11.11 IAS 11 Construction contracts

Chapter 3 deals with this topic.

11.12 IAS 12 Income taxes

The standard prescribes the treatment of tax on income in the financial statements. It distinguishes between two categories of tax:

1 **Current tax**. This refers to the amount of tax payable on taxable profits for the period. Income tax payable for current and prior periods is recognised as a liability. Income tax refundable is recognised as an asset.
2 **Deferred tax**. This relates to the difference between the carrying amount of assets and liabilities in the balance sheet and the tax base (i.e. the amount that will be deductible for tax purposes against any taxable economic benefits that will flow to an entity when it recovers the carrying amount) of those assets and liabilities.

For example, a machine cost £15,000 and has a carrying amount of £10,000. Tax depreciation in the form of capital allowances, to date, is £9,000. The tax rate is 25%. The tax base is £6,000 (i.e. cost minus tax depreciation = £15,000 – £9,000). To recover the carrying amount (of £10,000), the entity must earn that amount, i.e. £10,000 but will only be able to deduct additional tax depreciation of £6,000 (= the tax base or the so far unclaimed element of the original cost). The entity must recognise the deferred tax liability of £10,000 (i.e. £10,000 – £6,000 = £4,000 @ 25%).

A deferred tax liability must be recognised in full. A deferred tax asset is recognised only to the extent that it is probable that a tax benefit will be realised in the future.

Deferred tax is measured at the tax rate expected to apply when it is realised (asset) or settled (liability).

Deferred tax is a non-current item in the balance sheet.

Both the taxation charge for the current period and the deferred tax charged to the current period are shown on the face of the income statement.

11.13 IAS 16 Property, plant and equipment

This IAS applies to all tangible non-current assets except investment properties, biological assets related to agricultural activity (IAS 41), exploration and evaluation assets (IFRS 6), and non-current assets held for sale (IFRS 5).

The standard provides a number of definitions:

Carrying amount: the amount at which an asset is recognised after deducting any accumulated depreciation and accumulated impairment losses.
Cost: the amount of cash or cash equivalents paid or the fair value of the other consideration given to acquire an asset at the time of its acquisition or construction or, where applicable, the amount attributed to that asset when initially recognised in accordance with the specific requirements of other IFRSs. Cost includes amounts incurred subsequently to add to, replace part of, or service an asset.
Depreciable amount: the cost of an asset, or other amount substituted for cost, less its residual value.
Depreciation: the systematic allocation of the depreciable amount of an asset over its useful life.

Entity-specific value: the present value of the cash flows an entity expects to arise from the continuing use of an asset and from its disposal at the end of its useful life or expects to incur when settling a liability.

Fair value: the amount for which an asset could be exchanged between knowledgeable, willing parties in an arm's-length transaction.

An impairment loss: the amount by which the carrying amount of an asset exceeds its recoverable amount.

Property, plant and equipment: tangible items that: (*i*) are held for use in the production or supply of goods or services, for rental to others, or for administrative purposes; and (*ii*) are expected to be used during more than one period.

Recoverable amount: the higher of an assets net selling price and its value in use.

The **residual value** of an asset: the estimated amount that an entity would *currently* obtain from disposal of the asset, after deducting the estimated costs of disposal, if the asset were already of the age and in the condition expected at the end of its useful life.

Useful life is:
(*a*) the period over which an asset is expected to be available for use by an entity; or
(*b*) the number of production or similar units expected to be obtained from the asset by an entity.

Depreciation should be provided in respect of all tangible non-current assets which have a finite useful life other than those excluded by other IASs and IFRSs. It should be provided by allocating the cost (or revalued amount) less net realisable value over the periods expected to benefit from the use of the asset being depreciated. Depreciation begins when an asset is available for use. No depreciation method is prescribed, but the method selected should be that which produces the most appropriate allocation of depreciation to each period in relation to the benefit being received in that period through use of the asset. In doing so, it should reflect the pattern in which the asset's future economic benefits are expected to be consumed by the entity. The depreciation should be recognised in profit or loss, not against reserves.

When the useful life of an asset is longer than 50 years, no depreciation need be charged.

Useful lives and residual values should be reviewed at least at the end of each reporting period. If expectations differ from previous estimates, the changes are accounted for as changes in accounting estimates in accordance with IAS 8 (Accounting policies, changes in accounting estimates and errors).

The depreciation method may be changed only if there is a change in the expected pattern of consumption of those future economic benefits embodied in the asset, i.e. only when to do so will give a fairer presentation of the results and of the financial position. A change in depreciation method does not constitute a change in accounting policy. Where a change of method occurs, the effect, if material, should be shown as a note attached to the financial statements, as required by IAS 8.

Asset measurement after recognition

An entity shall choose either the cost model or the revaluation model as its accounting policy and shall apply that policy to an entire class of property, plant and equipment.

Cost model

After recognition as an asset, an item of property, plant and equipment shall be carried at its cost less any accumulated depreciation and any accumulated impairment losses.

Revaluation model

After recognition as an asset, an item of property, plant and equipment whose fair value can be measured reliably shall be carried at a revalued amount, being its fair value at the date of the revaluation less any subsequent accumulated depreciation and subsequent accumulated impairment losses. Revaluations shall be made with sufficient regularity to ensure that the carrying amount does not differ materially from that which would be determined using fair value at the balance sheet date.

The fair value of land and buildings is usually determined from market-based evidence by appraisal that is normally undertaken by professionally qualified valuers. The fair value of items of plant and equipment is usually their market value determined by appraisal.

If an item of property, plant and equipment is revalued, the entire class of property, plant and equipment to which that asset belongs must be revalued.

If an asset's carrying amount is increased as a result of a revaluation, the increase shall be credited directly to equity under the heading of revaluation surplus. However, the increase shall be recognised in profit or loss to the extent that it reverses a revaluation decrease of the same asset previously recognised in profit or loss.

If an asset's carrying amount is decreased as a result of a revaluation, the decrease shall be recognised in profit or loss. However, the decrease shall be debited directly to equity under the heading of revaluation surplus to the extent of any credit balance existing in the revaluation surplus in respect of that asset.

Land and buildings

Land and buildings are separable assets and are accounted for separately, even when they are acquired together. With some exceptions, such as quarries and sites used for landfill, land has an unlimited useful life and therefore is not depreciated. Buildings have a limited useful life and therefore are depreciable assets. An increase in the value of the land on which a building stands does not affect the determination of the depreciable amount of the building.

Disclosure

The financial statements shall disclose, for each class of property, plant and equipment:

(a) the measurement bases used for determining the gross carrying amount;
(b) the depreciation methods used;
(c) the useful lives or the depreciation rates used;
(d) the gross carrying amount and the accumulated depreciation (aggregated with accumulated impairment losses) at the beginning and end of the period; and
(e) a reconciliation of the carrying amount at the beginning and end of the period showing:
  (i)   additions;
  (ii) assets classified as held for sale or included in a disposal group classified as held for sale in accordance with IFRS 5 and other disposals;
  (iii) acquisitions through business combinations;
(f) increases or decreases resulting from revaluations and from impairment losses recognised or reversed directly in equity in accordance with IAS 36;
(g) impairment losses recignised in profit or loss in accordance with IAS 36;
(h) impairment losses reversed in profit or loss in accordance with IAS 36;
(i) depreciation;
(j) the net exchange differences arising on the translation of the financial statements from the functional currency into a different presentation currency, including the translation of a foreign operation into the presentation currency of the reporting entity; and
(k) other changes.

11.14 IAS 17 Leases

Details of IAS 17 were given in Chapter 2.

11.15 IAS 18 Revenue

Revenue is measured at the fair value of the consideration received or receivable. Revenue from sale of goods is recognised when:

(*a*) significant risks and rewards of ownership are transferred to the buyer;
(*b*) the seller has no continuing managerial involvement or control over the goods;
(*c*) the amount of revenue can be measured reliably;
(*d*) it is probable that economic benefits will flow to the seller (i.e. the seller will be paid);
(*e*) the costs of the transaction can be measured reliably.

Revenue from services is recognised when (*c*), (*d*), and (*e*) are satisfied plus the stage of completion of the transaction can be measured reliably. If the outcome cannot be measured reliably, revenue can only be recognised to the extent that the expenditures recognised are recoverable.

11.16 IAS 19 Employee benefits

This standard prescribes how to account for and how to disclose employee benefits. There are four categories of employee benefit:

(*i*) short-term employee benefits, such as wages, salaries, National Insurance contributions, paid annual leave, paid sick leave, profit-sharing, bonuses, medical care, cars, housing, and free goods or services. These must be recognised when the employee has performed the work for which the benefit is to be paid;
(*ii*) post employment benefits, for example, pensions;
(*iii*) other long-term employee benefits, such as long-service leave or sabbatical leave, long-term disability benefits;
(*iv*) termination benefits.

Categories (*ii*), (*iii*), and (*iv*) have more complex rules for recognition that lie outside the scope of this book. Students wishing to find out more on this topic should consult IAS 19.

11.17 IAS 20 Accounting for government grants and disclosure of government assistance

Many different types of grant are or have been obtainable from government departments. Where these relate to revenue expenditure, e.g. subsidies on wages, they should be credited to revenue in the period when the revenue is incurred. The principle is that the grants should be recognised in profit and loss so as to match the expenditure to which they are intended to contribute. This is done by either including such grants as 'other income' or by deducting them from the related expenditure.

Where there are grants relating to capital expenditure, they should be recognised as income over the periods necessary to match them with the related costs which they are intended to compensate, on a systematic basis. This is achieved by treating the amount of the grant as a deferred income, a portion of which is credited to profit and loss annually, over the life of the asset, on a basis consistent with depreciation. The amount of the deferred credit should, if material, be shown separately. It should not be shown as part of shareholders' funds.

The same effect as treating the grant as deferred income could be achieved by crediting the grant to the asset account and depreciating only the net balance of the cost of the asset over its lifetime (depreciation is thus reduced by the grant). However, while this is permitted under IAS 20, it is prohibited by the Companies Act.

11.18 IAS 21 The effects of changes in foreign exchange rates

This standard is discussed in Chapter 1, Section 1.14.

11.19 IAS 23 Borrowing costs

Borrowing costs comprise of interest and other costs incurred on funds borrowed. Borrowing costs are recognised as an expense when incurred. However, borrowing costs that are directly attributable to the acquisition, construction or production of a 'qualifying asset' (i.e. an asset that necessarily takes a substantial period of time to get ready for its intended use or sale) may be capitalised.

11.20 IAS 24 Related party disclosures

This standard prescribes the disclosures to be made when related parties exist or when transactions have occurred and/or balances exist with related parties. A related party transaction is a transfer of resources, services, or obligations between related parties, whether or not a price is charged.

A party is related to an entity if:

(a) directly, or indirectly through one or more intermediaries, the party:
    (i) controls, is controlled by, or is under common control with, the entity (this includes parents, subsidiaries and fellow subsidiaries);
    (ii) has an interest in the entity that gives it significant influence over the entity; or
    (iii) has joint control over the entity;
(b) the party is an associate (as defined in IAS 28 Investments in associates) of the entity;
(c) the party is a joint venture in which the entity is a venturer (see IAS 31 Interests in joint ventures);
(d) the party is a member of the key management personnel of the entity or its parent;
(e) the party is a close member of the family of any individual referred to in (a) or (d);
(f) the party is an entity that is controlled, jointly controlled or significantly influenced by, or for which significant voting power in such entity resides with, directly or indirectly, any individual referred to in (d) or (e); or
(g) the party is a post-employment benefit plan for the benefit of employees of the entity, or of any entity that is a related party of the entity.

11.21 IAS 26 Accounting and reporting by retirement benefit plans

This standard specifies the disclosures to make in the financial statements of retirement benefit plans. A retirement benefit plan is an arrangement where an entity provides benefits for employees on or after termination of service (e.g. after they retire). There are two types:

● **Defined contribution plans** – amounts to be paid as retirement benefits are determined by contributions to a fund plus the earnings from the investment of the fund. In this case, the financial statements should contain a statement of net assets available for benefits and a description of the funding policy.
● **Defined benefit plans** – amounts to be paid as retirement benefits are determined by a formula usually based on employee earnings and/or years of service. In this case, the financial statements should contain either:

(*a*) a statement that shows:
  (*i*) the net assets available for benefits;
  (*ii*) the actuarial present value of promised retirement benefits, distinguishing between vested benefits and non-vested benefits; and
  (*iii*) the resulting excess or deficit; or
(*b*) a statement of net assets available for benefits including either:
  (*iv*) a note disclosing the actuarial present value of promised retirement benefits, distinguishing between vested benefits and non-vested benefits; or
  (*v*) a reference to this information in an accompanying actuarial report.

If an actuarial valuation has not been prepared at the date of the financial statements, the most recent valuation shall be used as a base and the date of the valuation disclosed.

11.22 IAS 27 Consolidated and separate financial statements

This standard is discussed in Chapter 26.

11.23 IAS 28 Investments in associates

This standard is discussed in Chapter 26.

11.24 IAS 29 Financial reporting in hyperinflationary economies

The results of an entity whose functional currency is the currency of a hyperinflationary economy must be restated in terms of the measuring unit current at the balance sheet date (i.e. the currency value at that date) before being translated into a different presentation currency. Comparative figures for prior periods are also restated into the measuring unit at the current balance sheet date. Balance sheet amounts not already expressed in terms of the measuring unit current at the balance sheet date are restated by applying a general price index. Any gain or loss as a result on the net monetary position must be included in net income and separately disclosed.

11.25 IAS 31 Interests in joint ventures

This standard is covered in Chapter 26.

11.26 IAS 32 Financial instruments: disclosure and presentation

A financial instrument is any contract that gives rise to a financial asset of one entity and a financial liability or equity instrument of another entity. Each financial instrument must be classified as either a financial liability or as an equity instrument. It is an equity instrument if, and only if, both the following conditions are met:

1 The instrument includes no contractual obligation:
  (*a*) to deliver cash or another financial asset to another entity; or
  (*b*) to exchange financial assets or financial liabilities with another entity under conditions that are potentially unfavourable to the issuer.
2 If the instrument will or may be settled in the issuer's own equity instruments, it is:

(*a*) a non-derivative that includes no contractual obligation for the issuer to deliver a variable number of its own equity instruments; or

(*b*) a derivative that will be settled by the issuer exchanging a fixed amount of cash or another financial asset for a fixed number of its own equity instruments. For this purpose, the issuer's own equity instruments do not include instruments that are themselves contracts for the future receipt or delivery of the issuer's own equity instruments.

If it does not meet these conditions, it is a financial liability.

An example of a type of financial instrument that you have encountered many times in *Business Accounting 1* and *2* is preference shares. They may be either financial liabilities or equity instruments. If they are not redeemable and dividends are at the discretion of the issuer, they are equity instruments and are included in equity in the balance sheet. In contrast, where they are redeemable for fixed or determinable amounts at a fixed or determinable future date, or where the holder has the option to redeem them, they are classified as a financial liability and included in liabilities in the balance sheet. This issue is currently under review by the IASB.

11.27 IAS 33 Earnings per share

The objective of earnings per share (EPS) information is to provide a measure of the interests of each ordinary share of a parent entity in the performance of the entity over the reporting period. Basic earnings per share is a widely used stock market measure. The IAS tries to bring about a consistent method to aid comparability and reduce misunderstandings.

Under IAS 33, entities must calculate basic earnings per share amounts for profit or loss attributable to ordinary equity holders of the parent entity and, if presented, profit or loss from continuing operations attributable to those equity holders. Basic earnings per share is calculated by dividing profit or loss attributable to ordinary equity holders of the parent entity (the numerator) by the weighted average number of ordinary shares outstanding (the denominator) during the period.

When there are potential ordinary shares (for example if share options are exercised) they are treated as dilutive when, and only when, their conversion to ordinary shares would decrease earnings per share or increase loss per share from continuing operations. When there are dilutive ordinary shares, a diluted earnings per share must also be calculated.

Entities must present on the face of the income statement basic and, where applicable, diluted earnings per share for profit or loss from continuing operations attributable to the ordinary equity holders of the parent entity and for profit or loss attributable to the ordinary equity holders of the parent entity for the period for each class of ordinary shares that has a different right to share in profit for the period. Basic and diluted earnings per share must be presented with equal prominence for all periods presented.

The standard prescribes how to adjust the average number of shares when events occur to change the number of ordinary shares, such as bonus issues, share splits, and share consolidations. Students taking examinations which cover IAS 33 in detail should read the actual standard.

	£	£
Basic EPS is calculated as follows:		
Profit on continuing activities after taxation		XXX
Less: Minority interest (see chapters on group financial statements)[Note]	XXX	
Preference dividends	XXX	
		(XXX)
Profit available to equity shareholders		XXX

$$EPS = \frac{Profit\ available\ to\ equity\ shareholders}{Number\ of\ ordinary\ shares} = EPS\ in\ pence$$

Note: You will see later that minority interests exist only where the entity controls another entity which is partly owned by outsiders.

11.28 IAS 34 Interim financial reporting

Companies listed on the Stock Exchange are required to produce half-year interim reports. The Listing Rules stipulate the minimum requirements for the report. IAS 34 also defines the minimum requirements and entities must comply with them, whether or not they are subject to the Listing Rules.

Among the requirements are:

- comparative amounts for the balance sheet at the end of the previous full financial year must be disclosed;
- quarterly interim reports must contain figures (except for the balance sheet) for the cumulative period to date and for the corresponding period of the preceding year;
- minimum content of an interim financial report is a condensed balance sheet, condensed income statement, condensed statement of cash flows, condensed statement of changes in equity, plus notes;
- notes in interim reports are primarily an explanation of the events and changes that are significant to an understanding of the changes in financial position and performance of the entity since the last reporting date;
- accounting policies should be consistent with those applied in the annual financial statements unless a change in accounting policy is to be made in the next annual report, in which case the new accounting policy can be adopted in the interim report;
- basic and diluted earnings per share must be presented on the face of the income statement;
- consolidated interim financial statements must be produced if the last annual report was prepared on a consolidated basis.

11.29 IAS 36 Impairment of assets

This standard prescribes the procedures to be applied by an entity to ensure that its assets are carried at no more than their recoverable amount. An asset is carried at more than its recoverable amount if its 'carrying amount' exceeds the amount to be recovered through use or sale of the asset. (**Carrying amount** is the amount at which an asset is recognised after deducting any accumulated depreciation and accumulated impairment losses thereon.) If this is the case, the asset is described as impaired and IAS 36 requires the entity to recognise an impairment loss. The standard also specifies when an entity should reverse an impairment loss and the disclosures to make.

Other standards applicable to some types of assets contain requirements for recognising and measuring certain assets. As a result, IAS 36 does not apply to:

(a) inventories (IAS 2 Inventories);
(b) assets arising from construction contracts (IAS 11 Construction contracts);
(c) deferred tax assets (IAS 12 Income taxes);
(d) assets arising form employee benefits (IAS 19 Employee benefits);
(e) assets classified as held for sale (or included in a disposal group that is classified as held for sale) (IFRS 5 Non-current assets held for sale and discontinued operations);
(f) financial assets that are within the scope of IAS 39 Financial instruments: recognition and measurement;
(g) investment property that is measured at fair value (IAS 40 Investment property);
(h) biological assets related to agricultural activity that are measured at fair value less estimated point-of-sale costs (IAS 41 Agriculture);
(i) deferred acquisition costs, and intangible assets, arising from an insurer's contractual rights under insurance contracts within the scope of IFRS 4 Insurance contracts.

IAS 36 applies to financial assets classified as:

- subsidiaries, as defined in IAS 27 Consolidated and separate financial statements;
- associates, as defined in IAS 28 Investments in associates; and
- joint ventures, as defined in IAS 31 Interests in joint ventures

and to assets that are carried at revalued amount (i.e. fair value) in accordance with other standards (e.g. the revaluation model in IAS 16 Property, plant and equipment).

Identifying whether a revalued asset may be impaired depends on the basis used to determine fair value:

(a) if the asset's fair value is its market value, the only difference between the asset's fair value and its fair value less costs to sell is the cost of disposal:

  (i) if the disposal costs are negligible, the recoverable amount of the revalued asset is necessarily close to, or greater than, its revalued amount (i.e. fair value). In this case, it is unlikely that the revalued asset is impaired and recoverable amount need not be estimated.

  (ii) if the disposal costs are not negligible, the fair value less costs to sell of the revalued asset is necessarily less than its fair value. Therefore, the revalued asset will be impaired if its value in use is less than its revalued amount (i.e. fair value). In this case, after the revaluation requirements have been applied, an entity applies IAS 36 to determine whether the asset may be impaired.

(b) if the asset's fair value is determined on a basis other than its market value, its revalued amount (i.e. fair value) may be greater or lower than its recoverable amount. Hence, after the revaluation requirements have been applied, an entity applies IAS 36 to determine whether the asset may be impaired.

Impairment review

Entities must assess at each reporting date whether there is any indication that an asset may be impaired. If there is, the recoverable amount of the asset must be estimated. Irrespective of whether there is any indication of impairment, entities must also:

(a) test goodwill acquired in a business combination for impairment annually; and

(b) annually test intangible assets with indefinite useful lives and intangible assets not yet available for use for impairment by comparing their carrying amounts with their recoverable amounts. This impairment test may be performed at any time during an annual period, provided it is performed at the same time every year. Different intangible assets may be tested for impairment at different times. If an intangible asset was initially recognised during a period, it must be tested for impairment before the end of that period.

In assessing whether there is any indication that an asset may be impaired, entities should consider *at least* the following indicators of impairment:

(i) During the period, has an asset's market value declined significantly more than would be expected as a result of the passage of time or normal use?

(ii) Have significant changes with an adverse effect on the entity occurred during the period, or take place in the near future, in the technological, market, economic or legal environment in which the entity operates or in the market to which an asset is dedicated?

(iii) Have market interest rates or other market rates of return on investments increased during the period, and are those increases likely to affect the discount rate used in calculating an asset's value in use and decrease the asset's recoverable amount materially?

(iv) Is the carrying amount of the net assets of the entity more than its market capitalisation?

(v) Is evidence available of obsolescence or physical damage of an asset?

(*vi*) Have significant changes with an adverse effect on the entity taken place during the period, or are expected to take place in the near future, in the extent to which, or manner in which, an asset is used or is expected to be used? (These changes include the asset becoming idle, plans to discontinue or restructure the operation to which an asset belongs, plans to dispose of an asset before the previously expected date, and reassessing the useful life of an asset as finite rather than indefinite.)

(*vii*) Is evidence available from internal reporting that indicates that the economic performance of an asset is, or will be, worse than expected?

Recognition of impairment losses

The carrying amount of the asset must be reduced to its recoverable amount if, and only if, the recoverable amount of an asset is less than its carrying amount. **That reduction is an impairment loss.**

Non-revalued assets – an impairment loss on a non-revalued asset is recognised in profit or loss.

Revalued assets – an impairment loss on a revalued asset is recognised directly against any revaluation surplus for the asset to the extent that the impairment loss does not exceed the amount in the revaluation surplus for that same asset.

When the amount estimated for an impairment loss is greater than the carrying amount of the asset to which it relates, an entity shall recognise a liability if, and only if, required by another standard.

After the recognition of an impairment loss, the depreciation or amortisation charge for the asset must be adjusted in future periods to allocate the asset's revised carrying amount, less any residual value, on a systematic basis over its remaining useful life.

Goodwill

Allocating goodwill to cash-generating units

A *cash-generating unit* is, 'the smallest identifiable group of assets that generates cash inflows that are largely independent of the cash inflows from other assets or groups of assets'. For the purposes of impairment review, goodwill acquired in a business combination is allocated to each of the acquirer's cash-generating units, or groups of cash-generating units expected to benefit from the combination, irrespective of whether other assets or liabilities of the acquiree are assigned to those units or groups of units. Each unit or group of units to which the goodwill is allocated must:

(*i*) represent the lowest level within the entity at which the goodwill is monitored for internal management purposes; and

(*ii*) not be larger than an operating segment determined in accordance with IFRS 8 Operating segments.

A cash-generating unit to which goodwill has been allocated must be tested for impairment both annually and whenever there is an 'indication that the unit may be impaired, by comparing the carrying amount of the unit, including the goodwill, with the recoverable amount of the unit. If the carrying amount of the unit exceeds the recoverable amount of the unit, the entity must recognise the impairment loss by allocating it to reduce the carrying amount of the assets of the unit (group of units) in the order:

(*a*) to reduce the carrying amount of any goodwill allocated to the cash-generating unit (group of units);

(*b*) to the other assets of the unit (group of units) pro rata on the basis of the carrying amount of each asset in the unit (group of units).

In doing so, the carrying amount of an asset must not be reduced below the highest of:

- its fair value less costs to sell;
- its value in use; and
- zero.

The amount of the impairment loss that would otherwise have been allocated to the asset shall be allocated pro rata to the other assets of the unit or group of units.

Reversing an impairment loss for goodwill

An impairment loss recognised for goodwill can not be reversed, as it is likely to be an increase in internally generated goodwill which IAS 38 (Intangible assets) prohibits from recognition.

Reversing an impairment loss of assets other than goodwill

If it appears that an impairment loss recognised for an asset other than goodwill may no longer exist or may have decreased, this may indicate that the remaining useful life, the depreciation (or amortisation) method or the residual value may need to be reviewed and adjusted in accordance with the standard applicable to the asset, even if this means that no impairment loss is reversed for the asset. When this is not the case, an impairment loss recognised in prior periods for an asset other than goodwill is reversed if, and only if, there has been a change in the estimates used to determine the asset's recoverable amount since the last impairment loss was recognised. If so, the carrying amount of the asset must be increased to its recoverable amount. **That increase is a reversal of an impairment loss.**

However, the increased carrying amount of an asset other than goodwill attributable to a reversal of an impairment loss can not exceed the carrying amount that would have been determined (net of amortisation or depreciation) had no impairment loss been recognised for the asset in prior years. **When it does, the excess is a revaluation.**

A reversal of an impairment loss for an asset other than goodwill is recognised immediately in profit or loss. However, if the asset is carried at a revalued amount it is treated as a revaluation increase and credited directly to equity under the heading revaluation surplus *unless* the impairment loss was previously recognised in profit or loss, in which case a reversal of that impairment loss is also recognised in profit or loss.

Reversal of an impairment loss for cash-generating units

Reversals of this type must be allocated to the assets of the unit, except for goodwill, pro rata with the carrying amounts of those assets. These increases in carrying amounts are treated in the same way as reversals of impairment losses for individual assets. The carrying amount of an asset can not be increased above the lower of:

(*i*) its recoverable amount; and
(*ii*) the carrying amount that would have been determined (net of amortisation or depreciation) had no impairment loss been recognised for the asset in prior periods.

Any excess reversal that would otherwise have been allocated to that asset must be allocated pro rata to the other assets of the unit, except for goodwill.

11.30 IAS 37 Provisions, contingent liabilities and contingent assets

IAS 37 defines a provision as: '*a liability that is of uncertain timing or amount*'.

A provision should be recognised only when it is probable that a transfer of economic benefits will have to occur and a reasonable estimate can be made of the amount involved.

A contingent liability is:

either a possible obligation arising from past events whose existence will be confirmed only by the occurrence of one or more uncertain future events not wholly within the entity's control; or a present obligation that arises from past events but is not recognised because it is not probable that a transfer of economic benefits will be required to settle the obligation or because the amount of the obligation cannot be measured with sufficient reliability.

A contingent asset is:

a possible asset arising from past events whose existence will be confirmed only by the occurrence of one or more uncertain events not wholly within the entity's control.

Neither contingent liabilities nor contingent assets should be recognised. Contingent liabilities should be disclosed unless the possibility of an outflow of resources embodying economic benefits is remote. Contingent assets should only be disclosed where an inflow of economic benefits is probable.

11.31   IAS 38 Intangible assets

Entities frequently expend resources, or incur liabilities, on the acquisition, development, maintenance or enhancement of intangible resources. An *intangible asset* is an identifiable non-monetary asset without physical substance, such as the results of expenditure on advertising and on training; and research and development activities. As with all assets, an intangible asset must be identifiable, the entity must have control over it, and future economic benefits must be expected to flow to the entity as a result of its existence. An intangible asset will be recognised if, and only if it is probable that the expected future economic benefits that are attributable to the asset will flow to the entity and the cost of the asset can be measured reliably.

For example, an intangible asset held under a finance lease (*see* Chapter 2) is accounted for using the rules of this standard, as are rights under licensing agreements for items such as motion picture films, video recordings, plays, manuscripts, patents and copyrights.

The accounting treatment of some intangible assets is dealt with in other standards and is not subject to the rules of IAS 38. These intangible assets include:

- intangible assets held by an entity for sale in the ordinary course of business (IAS 2 Inventories and IAS 11 Construction contracts);
- deferred tax assets (IAS 12 Income taxes);
- leases that are within the scope of IAS 17 Leases;
- assets arising from employee benefits (IAS 19 Employee benefits);
- financial assets as defined in IAS 32 Financial instruments: disclosure and presentation, the recognition and measurement of some of which are covered by IAS 27 Consolidated and separate financial statements, IAS 28 Investments in associates and IAS 31 Interests in joint ventures;
- goodwill acquired in a business combination (IFRS 3 Business combinations);
- deferred acquisition costs, and intangible assets, arising from an insurer's contractual rights under insurance contracts within the scope of IFRS 4 Insurance contracts. IFRS 4 sets out specific disclosure requirements for those deferred acquisition costs but not for those intangible assets. Therefore, the disclosure requirements in this standard apply to those intangible assets;
- non-current intangible assets classified as held for sale (or included in a disposal group that is classified as held for sale) in accordance with IFRS 5 Non-current assets held for sale and discontinued operations;
- the recognition and measurement of exploration and evaluation assets (IFRS 6 Exploration for and evaluation of mineral resources).

Also excluded from the scope of IAS 38 is expenditure on the development and extraction of, minerals, oil, natural gas and similar non-regenerative resources.

One form of asset that has caused considerable problems over the years is expenditure on research and development.

Research and development

Research and development activities involve the development of knowledge. Therefore, although these activities may result in an asset with physical substance (e.g. a prototype), the physical element of the asset is secondary to its intangible component – the knowledge embodied within it.

Research is original and planned investigation undertaken with the prospect of gaining new scientific or technical knowledge and understanding. No intangible asset arising from research (or from the research phase of an internal project) shall be recognised. Expenditure on research (or on the research phase of an internal project) shall be recognised as an expense when it is incurred.

Development is the application of research findings or other knowledge to a plan or design for the production of new or substantially improved materials, devices, products, processes, systems or services before the start of commercial production or use. An intangible asset arising from development (or from the development phase of an internal project) shall be recognised if, and only if, an entity can demonstrate all of the following:

(*i*) the technical feasibility of completing the intangible asset so that it will be available for use or sale;

(*ii*) its intention to complete the intangible asset and use or sell it;

(*iii*) its ability to use or sell the intangible asset;

(*iv*) how the intangible asset will generate probable future economic benefits. Among other things, the entity can demonstrate the existence of a market for the output of the intangible asset or the intangible asset itself or, if it is to be used internally, the usefulness of the intangible asset;

(*v*) the availability of adequate technical, financial and other resources to complete the development and to use or sell the intangible asset;

(*vi*) its ability to measure reliably the expenditure attributable to the intangible asset during its development.

Apart from defining what can be considered to be an intangible asset, IAS 38 also specifies how to measure that carrying amount of intangible assets and states the specified disclosures to be made about intangible assets in the financial statements.

Measurement

As with all assets, intangible assets are initially measured at cost comprising:

(*a*) purchase price, including import duties and non-refundable purchase taxes, after deducting trade discounts and rebates; and

(*b*) any directly attributable cost of preparing the asset for its intended use, for example, costs of employee benefits (as defined in IAS 19) arising directly from bringing the asset to its working condition; professional fees arising directly from bringing the asset to its working condition; and costs of testing whether the asset is functioning properly.

Expenditures that are not part of the cost of an intangible asset include:

(*i*) costs of introducing a new product or service (including costs of advertising and promotional activities);

(*ii*) costs of conducting business in a new location or with a new class of customer (including costs of staff training); and

(*iii*) administration and other general overhead costs.

Different treatments are adopted depending upon whether an intangible asset has a finite or an indefinite useful life.

Intangible assets with finite useful lives

As with tangible non-current assets, the depreciable amount of an intangible asset with a finite useful life must be allocated on a systematic basis over its useful life. Amortisation begins when the asset is available for use, i.e. when it is in the location and condition necessary for it to be capable of operating in the manner intended by management. Amortisation ceases at the earlier of the date that the asset is classified as held for sale (or included in a disposal group that is classified as held for sale) in accordance with IFRS 5 and the date that the asset is derecognised.

The amortisation method used must reflect the pattern in which the asset's future economic benefits are expected to be consumed by the entity. If that pattern cannot be determined reliably, the straight line method shall be used.

The amortisation charge for each period is recognised in profit or loss unless IAS 38 *or another standard* permits or requires it to be included in the carrying amount of another asset. For example, the amortisation of intangible assets used in a production process is included in the carrying amount of inventories (see IAS 2 Inventories).

A variety of amortisation methods can be used to allocate the depreciable amount of an asset on a systematic basis over its useful life, including straight line, reducing balance, and unit of production. The method used is selected on the basis of the expected pattern of consumption of the expected future economic benefits embodied in the asset and is applied consistently from period to period, unless there is a change in the expected pattern of consumption of those future economic benefits. There is rarely, if ever, persuasive evidence to support an amortisation method for intangible assets with finite useful lives that results in a lower amount of accumulated amortisation than under the straight line method, such as would occur if an inverted version of the reducing balance method were used.

The amortisation period and the amortisation method for an intangible asset with a finite useful life must be reviewed at least at each financial year-end. If the expected useful life of the asset is different from previous estimates, the amortisation period must be changed accordingly. If there has been a change in the expected pattern of consumption of the future economic benefits embodied in the asset, the amortisation method should be changed to reflect the changed pattern. Such changes are treated as changes in accounting estimates in accordance with IAS 8.

Intangible assets with indefinite useful lives

If an intangible asset is assessed as having an indefinite useful life, the carrying amount of that asset and the reasons supporting the indefinite useful life assessment must be disclosed. Such an asset should not be amortised *but* its useful life should be reviewed each reporting period to determine whether events and circumstance continue to support an indefinite useful life assessment for that asset. If they do not, the change in the useful life assessment from indefinite to finite should be accounted for as a change in accounting estimates in accordance with IAS 8.

Impairment review of intangible assets

In accordance with IAS 36, an entity is required to test an intangible asset with an indefinite useful life for impairment by comparing its recoverable amount with its carrying amount:

(*a*) annually; and
(*b*) whenever there is an indication that the intangible asset may be impaired.

Retirements and disposals

An intangible asset is derecognised on disposal; or when no future economic benefits are expected from its use or disposal. The gain or loss arising from the derecognition of an intangible asset is determined as the difference between the net disposal proceeds, if any, and the carrying amount of the asset. It is recognised in profit or loss when the asset is derecognised (unless IAS 17 requires otherwise on a sale and leaseback). Gains are *not* classified as revenue.

Amortisation of an intangible asset with a finite useful life does not cease when the intangible asset is no longer used, unless the asset has been fully depreciated or is classified as held for sale (or included in a disposal group that is classified as held for sale) as under IFRS 5.

Disclosure

An entity must disclose the following for each class of intangible assets, distinguishing between internally generated intangible assets and other intangible assets:

(*a*) whether the useful lives are indefinite or finite and, if finite, the useful lives or the amortisation rates used;

(*b*) the amortisation methods used for intangible assets with finite useful lives;

(*c*) the gross carrying amount and any accumulated amortisation (aggregated with accumulated impairment losses) at the beginning and end of the period;

(*d*) the line item(s) of the income statement in which any amortisation of intangible assets is included;

(*e*) a reconciliation of the carrying amount at the beginning and end of the period showing:

    (*i*)   additions, indicating separately those from internal development, those acquired separately, and those acquired through business combinations;

    (*ii*)   assets classified as held for sale or included in a disposal group classified as held for sale in accordance with IFRS 5 and other disposals;

    (*iii*) increases or decreases during the period resulting from revaluations and from impairment losses recognised or reversed directly in equity in accordance with IAS 36;

    (*iv*) impairment losses recognised in profit or loss during the period in accordance with IAS 36;

    (*v*)   impairment losses reversed in profit or loss during the period in accordance with IAS 36;

    (*vi*) any amortisation recognised during the period;

    (*vii*) net exchange differences arising on the translation of the financial statements into the presentation currency, and on the translation of a foreign operation into the presentation currency of the entity; and

    (*viii*) other changes in the carrying amount during the period.

Entities must also disclose:

- for intangible assets assessed as having an indefinite useful life, the carrying amount of each asset and the reasons supporting the assessment of an indefinite useful life including a description of the factors that played a significant role in determining that the asset has an indefinite useful life;
- a description, the carrying amount and remaining amortisation period of any individual intangible asset that is material to the entity's financial statements;
- for intangible assets acquired by way of a government grant and initially recognised at fair value:
  - the fair value initially recognised for these assets;
  - their carrying amount; and
  - whether they are measured after recognition under the cost model or the revaluation model;
- the existence and carrying amounts of intangible assets whose title is restricted and the carrying amounts of intangible assets pledged as security for liabilities;
- the amount of contractual commitments for the acquisition of intangible assets.

Intangible assets measured after recognition using the revaluation model

If intangible assets are accounted for at revalued amounts, an entity shall disclose the following:

- by class of intangible assets:
  - the effective date of the revaluation;
  - the carrying amount of revalued intangible assets; and
  - the carrying amount that would have been recognised had the revalued class of intangible assets been measured after recognition;
- the amount of the revaluation surplus that relates to intangible assets at the beginning and end of the period, indicating the changes during the period and any restrictions on the distribution of the balance to shareholders; and
- the methods and significant assumptions applied in estimating the assets' fair values.

Research and development expenditure

The aggregate amount of research and development expenditure recognised as an expense during the period must be disclosed.

Other information that may be disclosed

Entities are encouraged to disclose the following information:

(a) a description of any fully amortised intangible asset that is still in use; and
(b) a brief description of significant intangible assets controlled by the entity but not recognised as assets because they did not meet the recognition criteria in this standard or because they were acquired or generated before the version of IAS 38 Intangible assets issued in 1998 (which this version replaced in 2004) was effective.

11.32   IAS 39 Financial instruments: recognition and measurement

The definition of a financial instrument is extremely wide and includes cash, debt, and equity investments, loans, trade receivable and payables, certain provisions, and derivatives. IAS 39 covers the recognition, measurement and derecognition of financial instruments, along with rules on hedge accounting (relating to attempts to offset risk). IAS 39 is possibly the most complex of all standards and is beyond the scope of this book.

11.33   IAS 40 Investment property

Investment property is property (land or a building – or part of a building – or both) held (by the owner or by the lessee under a finance lease) to earn rentals or for capital appreciation or both, rather than for:

(a) use in the production or supply of goods or services or for administrative purposes; or
(b) sale in the ordinary course of business. Investment property is initially recognised at cost. A decision must then be made as to which of two methods are to be adopted thereafter:
  - Cost less accumulated depreciation and any accumulated impairment losses, as per IAS 16 Property, plant and equipment; or
  - Fair value, i.e. the price at which the property could be exchanged between knowledgeable, willing parties in an arm's length transaction. Movements in fair value are recognised immediately in profit or loss.

All investment properties of an entity must be accounted for on the same basis and the method adopted must be disclosed.

A change from one method to the other is made only if the change results in a more appropriate presentation. Whereas under the revaluation model, increases in carrying amount above a cost-based measure are recognised as revaluation surplus, under the fair value model all changes in fair value are recognised in profit or loss. Investment properties held under an operating lease must be accounted for by the lessee using the fair value model.

Students often overlook the fact that investment property can be land. The standard offers the following examples of investment property:

- land held for long-term capital appreciation rather than for short-term sale in the ordinary course of business;
- land held for a currently undetermined future use (if an entity has not determined that it will use the land as owner-occupied property or for short-term sale in the ordinary course of business, the land is regarded as held for capital appreciation);
- a building owned by the entity (or held by the entity under a finance lease) and leased out under one or more operating leases;
- a building that is vacant but is held to be leased out under one or more operating leases.

Gains or losses arising from the retirement or disposal of investment property are equal to the difference between the net disposal proceeds and the carrying amount of the asset and are recognised in profit or loss (unless IAS 17 requires otherwise on a sale and leaseback) in the period of the retirement or disposal.

11.34 IAS 41 Agriculture

IAS 41 prescribes the accounting treatment, financial statement presentation, and disclosures related to agricultural activity, a matter not covered in other standards. Agricultural activity is the '*management by an entity of the biological transformation of living animals or plants (biological assets) for sale, into agricultural produce, or into additional biological assets*'. IAS 41 is applied to agricultural produce (i.e. the harvested product of the entity's biological assets) only at the point of harvest. Thereafter, IAS 2 Inventories or another applicable standard is applied. The standard does not apply to:

(*a*) land related to agricultural activity (see IAS 16 Property, plant and equipment and IAS 40 Investment property); and

(*b*) intangible assets related to agricultural activity (see IAS 38 Intangible assets).

Agricultural produce harvested from an entity's biological assets is measured at its fair value less estimated point-of-sale costs at the point of harvest. Gains or losses arising on initial recognition at fair value less point of sale costs and from a change in fair value less point of sale costs is included in profit or loss. Unconditional government grants related to biological assets are recognised as income when the grant becomes receivable. Conditional government grants are not recognised until the conditions attaching to them are met.

11.35 IFRS 1 The first-time adoption of international reporting standards

IFRS 1 applies to entities the first time they switch to International GAAP. Entities must comply with each IFRS effective at the reporting date of their first IFRS financial statements. The main requirement is that in the opening IFRS balance sheet it prepares as a starting point for its accounting under IFRSs, an entity must:

(*i*) recognise all assets and liabilities whose recognition is required by IFRSs;

(*ii*) not recognise items as assets or liabilities if IFRSs do not permit such recognition;

(*iii*) reclassify items that it recognised under previous GAAP as one type of asset, liability or component of equity, but are a different type of asset, liability or component of equity under IFRSs; and

(*iv*) apply IFRSs in measuring all recognised assets and liabilities.

The IFRS gives limited exemptions from these requirements in specified areas where the cost of complying with them would be likely to exceed the benefits to users of financial statements. The IFRS also prohibits retrospective application of IFRSs in some areas, particularly where retrospective application would require judgements by management about past conditions after the outcome of a particular transaction is already known.

The IFRS requires disclosures that explain how the transition from previous GAAP to IFRSs affected the entity's reported financial position, financial performance and cash flows.

11.36 IFRS 2 Share-based payment

Under IFRS 2, share-based payments must be recognised as an expense, measured at fair value which should be based on market prices and should take into account the terms and conditions upon which the instruments were granted. The standard gives the accounting treatment to be adopted and disclosures to be made by entities making such payments.

IFRS 2 identifies three types of share-based payment transaction:

(a) equity-settled share-based payment transactions. These are transactions in which the entity receives goods or services as consideration for equity instruments of the entity;

(b) cash-settled share-based payment transactions. These are transactions in which the entity acquires goods or services by incurring liabilities to the supplier of those goods or services for amounts that are based on the price (or value) of the entity's equity instruments;

(c) transactions in which the entity receives or acquires goods or services and the terms of the arrangement provide one or other of the parties to the transaction with a choice as to whether the transaction is settled in cash or by issuing equity instruments.

Examples of share-based payments include:

(a) all types of executive share option and share purchase plans and employee share option and share purchase schemes, including Save-As-You-Earn (SAYE) plans and similar arrangements;

(b) arrangements such as share appreciation rights, where a cash payment is made, the amount of which depends on the share price; and

(c) transactions with suppliers of goods or non-employee services that involve share-based payments being made in exchange for those goods or services.

11.37 IFRS 3 Business combinations

This standard is covered in Chapter 25. Among the topics it deals with is goodwill. Purchased positive goodwill should be capitalised. It must not be amortised but should be checked for impairment annually. Any impairment should be written off to profit or loss and cannot be reinstated. Negative goodwill must be eliminated immediately by reviewing and amending the fair values of the net assets acquired and, if necessary, recognising the gain in profit or loss.

11.38 IFRS 4: Insurance contracts

IFRS 4 applies to all insurance contracts (including reinsurance contracts) that an entity issues and to reinsurance contracts that it holds, except for specified contracts covered by other IFRSs. It does not apply to other assets and liabilities of an insurer, such as financial assets and financial liabilities within the scope of IAS 39 Financial instruments: recognition and measurement. Furthermore, it does not address accounting by policyholders.

This IFRS does not address other aspects of accounting by insurers, such as accounting for financial assets held by insurers and financial liabilities issued by insurers (IAS 32 Financial instruments: presentation, IAS 39 Financial instruments: recognition and measurement and IFRS 7 Financial instruments: disclosures).

An entity shall not apply this IFRS to:

(a) product warranties issued directly by a manufacturer, dealer or retailer (IAS 18 Revenue and IAS 37 Provisions, contingent liabilities and contingent assets);

(b) employers' assets and liabilities under employee benefit plans (IAS 19 Employee benefits and IFRS 2 Share-based payment) and retirement benefit obligations reported by defined benefit retirement plans (IAS 26 Accounting and reporting by retirement benefit plans);

(c) contractual rights or contractual obligations that are contingent on the future use of, or right to use, a non-financial item (for example, some licence fees, royalties, contingent lease payments and similar items), as well as a lessee's residual value guarantee embedded in a finance lease (IAS 17 Leases, IAS 18 Revenue and IAS 38 Intangible assets);

(d) financial guarantee contracts unless the issuer has previously asserted explicitly that it regards such contracts as insurance contracts and has used accounting applicable to insurance contracts, in which case the issuer may elect to apply either IAS 39, IAS 32 and IFRS 7 or this Standard to such financial guarantee contracts. The issuer may make that election contract by contract, but the election for each contract is irrevocable;

(e) contingent consideration payable or receivable in a business combination (IFRS 3 Business combinations);

(f) direct insurance contracts that the entity holds (i.e. direct insurance contracts in which the entity is the *policyholder*). However, a *cedant* shall apply this IFRS to reinsurance contracts that it holds.

An insurer may change its accounting policies for insurance contracts if, and only if, the change makes the financial statements more relevant to the economic decision-making needs of users and no less reliable, or more reliable and no less relevant to those needs. An insurer shall judge relevance and reliability by the criteria in IAS 8 (Accounting policies, changes in accounting estimates and errors).

The IFRS specifies the financial reporting for *insurance contracts* by any entity that issues such contracts (described in this IFRS as an *insurer*) and requires:

(i) limited improvements to accounting by insurers for insurance contracts;

(ii) disclosure that identifies and explains the amounts in an insurer's financial statements arising from insurance contracts and helps users of those financial statements understand the amount, timing and uncertainty of future cash flows from insurance contracts.

11.39 IFRS 5 Non-current assets held for sale and discontinued operations

Non-current assets are assets that include amounts expected to be recovered more than 12 months after the balance sheet date. IFRS 5 requires that a non-current asset (or disposal group) be classified as held for sale if its carrying amount will be recovered principally through a sale transaction rather than through continuing use. Assets or disposal groups that are classified as held for sale are carried at the lower of carrying amount and fair value less costs to sell, are not depreciated, are presented separately on the balance sheet, and their results are disclosed separately in the income statement.

A 'component of an entity' comprises operations and cash flows that can be clearly distinguished, operationally and for financial reporting purposes, from the rest of the entity, i.e. a cash-generating unit or a group of cash-generating units. A 'discontinued operation' is a component of an entity that either has been disposed of, or is classified as held for sale, and:

- represents a separate major line of business or geographical area of operations;
- is part of a single co-ordinated plan to dispose of a separate major line of business or geographical area of operations; or
- is a subsidiary acquired exclusively with a view to resale.

The results of discontinued operations are shown separately on the face of the income statement in the form of a single line comprising the total of (*a*) the post-tax profit/loss from discontinued operations, plus (*b*) the post-tax gain/loss recognised in the measurement of the fair value less costs to sell or on the disposal of the assets of the discontinued operations.

Sometimes an entity disposes of a group of assets, possibly with some directly associated liabilities, in a single transaction. Such a disposal group may be a group of *cash-generating units*, a single cash-generating unit, or part of a cash-generating unit. The disposal group may include any assets and any liabilities of the entity, including current assets, current liabilities and assets excluded from the measurement requirements of IFRS 5. If a non-current asset within the scope of the measurement requirements of IFRS 5 is part of a disposal group, the measurement requirements of IFRS 5 apply to the group as a whole, so that the group is measured at the lower of its carrying amount and fair value less costs to sell.

The classification and presentation requirements of this IFRS apply to all recognised non-current assets and to all *disposal groups* of an entity. The measurement requirements of IFRS 5 apply to all recognised non-current assets and disposal groups except:

- deferred tax assets (IAS 12 Income taxes);
- assets arising from employee benefits (IAS 19 Employee benefits);
- financial assets within the scope of IAS 39 Financial instruments: recognition and measurement;
- non-current assets that are accounted for in accordance with the fair value model in IAS 40 Investment property;
- non-current assets that are measured at fair value less estimated point-of-sale costs in accordance with IAS 41 Agriculture;
- contractual rights under insurance contracts as defined in IFRS 4 Insurance contracts.

Assets classified as non-current in accordance with IAS 1 Presentation of financial statements should not be reclassified as *current assets* until they meet the criteria to be classified as held for sale in accordance with IFRS 5. Assets of a class that an entity would normally regard as non-current that are acquired exclusively with a view to resale shall not be classified as current unless they meet the criteria to be classified as held for sale in accordance with IFRS 5.

An entity must present and disclose information that enables users of the financial statements to evaluate the financial effects of discontinued operations and disposals of non-current assets (or disposal groups).

11.40 IFRS 6 Exploration for and evaluation of mineral resources

IFRS 6 specifies the financial reporting for the exploration for and evaluation of mineral resources. The IFRS requires exploration and evaluation assets to be measured at cost and requires entities that recognise exploration and evaluation assets to assess such assets for impairment and measure any impairment in accordance with IAS 36 Impairment of assets. It also requires the disclosures that identify and explain the amounts in the entity's financial statements arising from the exploration for and evaluation of mineral resources and help users of those financial statements understand the amount, timing and certainty of future cash flows from any exploration and evaluation assets recognised.

The IFRS:

(*a*) permits an entity to develop an accounting policy for exploration and evaluation assets without specifically considering the requirements of paragraphs 11 and 12 of IAS 8 Accounting polices, changes in accounting estimates and errors. Thus, an entity adopting IFRS 6 may continue to use the accounting policies applied immediately before adopting the IFRS. This includes continuing to use recognition and measurement practices that are part of those accounting policies;

(b) requires entities recognising exploration and evaluation assets to perform an impairment test on those assets when facts and circumstances suggest that the carrying amount of the assets may exceed their recoverable amount;

(c) varies the recognition of impairment from that in IAS 36 but measures the impairment in accordance with IAS 36 once the impairment is identified.

Entities must apply IFRS 6 to exploration and evaluation expenditures that they incur. However, the IFRS does not address other aspects of accounting by entities engaged in the exploration for and evaluation of mineral resources.

Entities must not apply the IFRS to expenditures incurred:

(i) before the exploration for and evaluation of mineral resources, such as expenditures incurred before the entity has obtained the legal rights to explore a specific area; or

(ii) after the technical feasibility and commercial viability of extracting a mineral resource are demonstrable.

Entities must determine an accounting policy specifying which expenditures are recognised as exploration and evaluation assets and apply the policy consistently. In making this determination, entities must consider the degree to which the expenditure can be associated with finding specific mineral resources.

Examples of expenditures that might be included in the initial measurement of exploration and evaluation assets include:

- acquisition of rights to explore;
- topographical, geological, geochemical and geophysical studies;
- exploratory drilling;
- trenching;
- sampling; and
- activities in relation to evaluating the technical feasibility and commercial viability of extracting a mineral resource.

Expenditures related to the development of mineral resources are not exploration and evaluation assets. The *Framework* and IAS 38 Intangible assets provide guidance on the recognition of assets arising from development.

In accordance with IAS 37 Provisions, contingent liabilities and contingent assets an entity recognises any obligations for removal and restoration that are incurred during a particular period as a consequence of having undertaken the exploration for and evaluation of mineral resources.

After recognition, an entity must apply either the cost model or the revaluation model to the exploration and evaluation assets. If the revaluation model is applied (either the model in IAS 16 Property, plant and equipment or the model in IAS 38), it must be consistent with the classification of the assets.

An entity may change its accounting policies for exploration and evaluation expenditures if the change makes the financial statements more relevant to the economic decision-making needs of users and no less reliable, or more reliable and no less relevant to those needs. An entity must judge relevance and reliability using the criteria in IAS 8.

Classification of exploration and evaluation assets

An entity must classify exploration and evaluation assets as tangible or intangible according to the nature of the assets acquired and apply the classification consistently.

Some exploration and evaluation assets are treated as intangible (e.g. drilling rights). Others are tangible (e.g. vehicles and drilling rigs). To the extent that a tangible asset is consumed in developing an intangible asset, the amount reflecting that consumption is part of the cost of the intangible asset. However, using a tangible asset to develop an intangible asset does not change a tangible asset into an intangible asset.

Reclassification of exploration and evaluation assets

When the technical feasibility and commercial viability of extracting a mineral resource are demonstrable, an asset previously classified as an exploration and evaluation asset loses its classification. Exploration and evaluation assets must be assessed for impairment, and any impairment loss recognised, before reclassification.

Exploration and evaluation assets should be assessed for impairment when facts and circumstances suggest that the carrying amount of an exploration and evaluation asset may exceed its recoverable amount. When facts and circumstances confirm that this is the case, an entity must measure, present and disclose any resulting impairment loss in accordance with IAS 36.

Disclosure

Entities must disclose:

(a) their accounting policies for exploration and evaluation expenditures including the recognition of exploration and evaluation assets;
(b) the amounts of assets, liabilities, income and expense and operating and investing cash flows arising from the exploration for and evaluation of mineral resources.

In doing so, entities should treat exploration and evaluation assets as a separate class of assets and make the disclosures required by either IAS 16 or IAS 38 consistent with how the assets are classified.

11.41 IFRS 7 Financial instruments: disclosures

IFRS 7 complements the principles for recognising, measuring and presenting financial assets and financial liabilities in IAS 32 Financial instruments: disclosure and presentation and IAS 39 Financial instruments: recognition and measurement. It regulates the disclosures that must be made in the financial statements of entities with financial instruments. These disclosures are intended to enable users to evaluate:

(i) the significance of financial instruments for the entity's financial position and performance; and
(ii) the nature and extent of risks arising from financial instruments to which the entity is exposed during the period and at the reporting date, and how the entity manages those risks.

As with IAS 39, IFRS 7 is beyond the scope of this book.

11.42 IFRS 8 Operating segments

IFRS 8 requires an entity to disclose information that enables users of its financial statements to evaluate the nature and financial effects of the business activities in which it engages and the economic environments in which it operates. In order to do so, the financial and descriptive information reported under the standard must be allocated across appropriate segments of the business called 'operating segments'. An operating segment is a component of an entity that engages in business activities from which it may earn revenues and incur expenses and about which separate financial information is available that is evaluated regularly by the chief operating decision-maker in deciding how to allocate resources and in assessing performance.

An entity must report separately information about each operating segment that meets any of the following quantitative thresholds:

(*i*) its reported revenue, including both sales to external customers and inter-segment sales or transfers, is 10% or more of the combined revenue, internal and external, of all operating segments;

(*ii*) the absolute amount of its reported profit or loss is 10% or more of the greater, in absolute amount, of (*a*) the combined reported profit of all operating segments that did not report a loss, and (*b*) the combined reported loss of all operating segments that reported a loss.

(*iii*) its assets are 10% or more of the combined assets of all operating segments.

Operating segments that do not meet any of the quantitative thresholds may be separately disclosed if management believes that information about the segment would be useful to users of the financial statements.

Operating segments that have similar economic characteristics can be aggregated and reported as one segment. When operating segments are considered to be too immaterial to be reported separately, they are combined and reported in an 'all other segments' category. The segments that remain after any aggregation are known as 'reportable segments'. It is these segments that the standard requires entities to report upon in both their annual financial statements and interim financial reports. IFRS 8 also sets out requirements for related disclosures about products and services, geographical areas and major customers.

The IFRS requires an entity to report operating segment profit or loss and segment assets, segment liabilities, and particular income and expense items if they are regularly provided to the chief operating decision-maker. It requires reconciliations of total reportable segment revenues, total profit or loss, total assets, liabilities and other amounts disclosed for reportable segments to corresponding amounts in the entity's financial statements.

Information must also be reported concerning the revenues derived from its products or services (or groups of similar products and services), about the countries in which it earns revenues and holds assets, and about major customers. However, the IFRS does not require an entity to report information that is not prepared for internal use if the necessary information is not available and the cost to develop it would be excessive.

The IFRS also requires an entity to give descriptive information about the way the operating segments were determined, the products and services provided by the segments, differences between the measurements used in reporting segment information and those used in the entity's financial statements, and changes in the measurement of segment amounts from period to period.

Unlike other IFRSs, IFRS 8 only applies to separate or consolidated financial statements of entities listed or seeking listing on a stock exchange for its debt or equity instruments. However, if a financial report contains both the consolidated financial statements of a parent that is within the scope of IFRS 8 as well as the parent's separate financial statements, segment information is required only in the consolidated financial statements.

Entities must also disclose the following general information:

(*i*) the factors used to identify the entity's reportable segments, including the basis of organisation (e.g. whether management has chosen to organise the entity around differences in products and services, geographical areas, regulatory environments, or a combination of factors and whether operating segments have been aggregated); and

(*ii*) the types of products and services from which each reportable segment derives its revenues.

Information on the latest developments in international standards can be found at the IASB website: **www.iasb.org**

Learning outcomes

You should now have learnt:

1 That accounting standards have statutory recognition and must, therefore, be complied with when preparing financial statements intended to present a true and fair view.

2 That the *Framework for the Preparation and Presentation of Financial Statements* provides details of the concepts that underpin accounting standards.

3 That as of December 2007, there were 37 international accounting standards (29 IASs and 8 IFRSs) in force.

4 About the main requirements of a range of accounting standards.

Answers to activities

11.1 Apart from the legal requirement that certain companies switch to international standards, international accounting standards are becoming increasingly adopted across the world. At the same time, there is an increasing internationalisation of business and a need for greater international uniformity in the regulations underpinning the preparation of company financial statements, particularly for multinational companies.

11.2 Most non-accountants assume that the information in financial statements is accurate, correct and free of bias. They believe this to be the case because they assume that all such information is based on firm facts – for example, what something cost is shown in the invoice and confirmed by the amount paid for it as shown in the bank statement. They do not realise that many of the figures shown are based on estimates and subject to the subjective interpretation of a situation by the person preparing the financial statements. They are unaware that accountants have many choices to make, so much so that it is unlikely that two accountants would ever produce identical financial statements for any but the smallest of organisations.

By placing an emphasis on the qualitative aspects of information, the *Statement of Principles* seeks to restrict diversity in the range of options open to the preparers of financial statements and so guide them towards a more uniform interpretation of the options available to them, thereby increasing the level of faith that users of those statements may have in the information they contain.

11.3 (From the *Framework*, paragraph 103) A financial concept of capital should be adopted if the users of financial statements are primarily concerned with the maintenance of nominal invested capital or the purchasing power of invested capital. If, however, the main concern of users is with the operating capability of the entity, a physical concept of capital should be used. The concept chosen indicates the goal to be attained in determining profit, even though there may be some measurement difficulties in making the concept operational.

Review questions

11.1 In preparing its accounts for the year to 31 May 2007, Whiting plc had been faced with a number of accounting problems, the details of which were as follows:

(*i*) The company had closed down its entire American operations which represented a significant part of Whiting plc's business.

(*ii*) The corporation tax for the year to 31 May 2006 had been over-provided by £5,000.

(*iii*) Land and buildings had been revalued at an amount well in excess of the historic cost (note: the current value is to be adjusted in the financial statements).

(*iv*) A trade debtor had gone into liquidation owing Whiting plc an amount equivalent to 20% of Whiting's turnover for the year. It is highly unlikely that any of this debt will ever be repaid.

(v) During the year, the company changed its method of valuing inventory. If the same method had been adopted in the previous year, the profits for that year would have been considerably less than had previously been reported.

Required:
Being careful to give your reasons, explain how each of the above matters should be treated in the financial statements of Whiting plc for the year to 31 May 2007 if the company follows the requirements of IAS 1 and IFRS 5.

(*Association of Accounting Technicians*)

11.2 The directors are preparing the published accounts of Dorman plc for the year to 31 October 2005. The following information is provided for certain of the items which are to be included in the final accounts.

(i)   *Inventories of raw material, monolite:*

	£
Cost	26,500
Replacement cost	48,100

(ii)   *Inventory of finished goods:*

	Paramite £	Paraton £
Direct costs	72,600	10,200
Proportion of fixed factory overhead	15,300	4,600
Proportion of selling expenses	6,870	1,800
Net realisable value	123,500	9,520

(iii) *Plant and machinery.* An item of plant was shown in the 2004 accounts at a net book value of £90,000 (£160,000 cost less accumulated depreciation £70,000). The plant was purchased on 1 November 2002 and has been depreciated at 25% reducing balance. The directors now consider the straight line basis to be more appropriate: they have estimated that at 1 November 2004 the plant had a remaining useful life of six years and will possess zero residual value at the end of that period.

(iv)   *Freehold property.* The company purchased a freehold property for £250,000 11 years ago, and it is estimated that the land element was worth £50,000 at that date.
        The company has never charged depreciation on the property but the directors now feel that it should have done so; the building is expected to have a total useful life of 40 years.

(v)   *Research expenditure* incurred in an attempt to discover a substitute for raw materials currently purchased from a politically sensitive area of the world amounted to £17,500 during the year.

(vi)   *Development expenditure* on Tercil, which is nearly ready for production, amounted to £30,000. Demand for Tercil is expected significantly to exceed supply for at least the next four years.

(vii) *Accident.* On 1 December 2005 there was a fire in the warehouse which damaged inventory, other than the items referred to in (i) and (ii) above. The book value of the damaged inventory was £92,000. The company has discovered that it was underinsured and only expects to recover £71,000 from the insurers.

(viii) *Investments.* Dorman purchased 30,000 ordinary shares in Lilleshall Ltd on 1 November 2004 for £96,000, and immediately succeeded in appointing two of its directors to Lilleshall's board. The issued share capital of Lilleshall consists of 100,000 ordinary shares of £1 each. The profits of Lilleshall for the year to 31 October 2005 amounted to £40,000. (Ignore taxation.)

Required:
Explain how each of the above items should be dealt with in the published financial statements of Dorman plc.

(*Institute of Chartered Secretaries and Administrators*)

11.3A In preparing the published financial statements of a company, briefly state the significant accounting/disclosure requirements you would have in mind in ensuring that the financial statements comply with best accounting practice as embodied in accounting standards and the Companies Act 2006 concerning:

(a) Value added tax.
(b) Earnings per share.
(c) The disclosure requirements of each major class of depreciable assets.
(d) Research expenditure.
(e) Capital-based grants relating to fixed assets.
(f) Goodwill on consolidation.
(g) The disclosure requirements relating to generally accepted fundamental accounting concepts.
(h) The accounts of a subsidiary undertaking having similar activities to that of the parent undertaking.

(*Association of Accounting Technicians*)

11.4A Oldfield Enterprises Limited was formed on 1 January 2005 to manufacture and sell a new type of lawn mower. The bookkeeping staff of the company have produced monthly figures for the first 10 months to 31 October 2005 and from these figures together with estimates for the remaining two months, Barry Lamb, the managing director, has drawn up a forecast profit and loss account for the year to 31 December 2005 and a balance sheet as at that date.

These statements together with the notes are submitted to the board for comment. During the board meeting discussion centres on the treatment given to the various assets. The various opinions are summarised by Barry Lamb who brings them, with the draft accounts, to you as the company's financial adviser.

Oldfield Enterprises Ltd
Draft Income Statement (extract) for the year ending 31 December 2005

	£000	£000
Revenue		3,000
Cost of sales		1,750
Gross profit		1,250
Administration overheads	350	
Selling and distribution overheads	530	
		880
Net profit before taxation		370

Draft Balance Sheet at 31 December 2005

Non-current assets – tangible	Cost £000	Depreciation and amortisation £000	Net £000
Leasehold land and buildings	375	125	250
Freehold land and buildings	350	–	350
Plant and machinery	1,312	197	1,115
	2,037	322	1,715
Non-current assets – intangible			
Research and development			375
Current assets			
Inventory		375	
Accounts receivable		780	
			1,155
Total assets			3,245
Current liabilities			
Accounts payable	250	250	
Bank overdraft	125	125	
			375
Net assets			2,870
Equity			
Share capital			2,500
Retained profits			370
			2,870

Notes:
(a) Administration overheads include £50,000 written off research and development.
(b) The lease is for 15 years and cost £75,000. Buildings have been put up on the leasehold land at a cost of £300,000. Plant and machinery has been depreciated at 15%. Both depreciation and amortisation are included in cost of sales.

Opinions put forward
Leasehold land and buildings:
The works director thinks that although the lease provides for a rent review after three years the buildings have a 50-year life. The buildings should therefore be depreciated over 50 years and the cost of the lease should be amortised over the period of the lease.

The managing director thinks that because of the rent review clause the whole of the cost should be depreciated over three years.

The sales director thinks it is a good idea to charge as much as the profits will allow in order to reduce the tax bill.

Freehold land and buildings:
The works director thinks that as the value of the property is going up with inflation no depreciation is necessary.

The sales director's opinion is the same as for leasehold property.

The managing director states that he has heard that if a property is always kept in good repair no depreciation is necessary. This should apply in the case of his company.

Plant and machinery:
The managing director agrees with the 15% for depreciation and proposes to use the reducing balance method.

The works director wants to charge 25% straight line.

Research and development:
The total spent in the year will be £425,000. Of this £250,000 is for research into the cutting characteristics of different types of grass, £100,000 is for the development of an improved drive system for lawn mowers and £75,000 is for market research to determine the ideal lawn mower characteristics for the average garden.

The managing director thinks that a small amount should be charged as an expense each year.

The works director wants to write off all the market research and 'all this nonsense of the cutting characteristics of grass'.

The sales director thinks that, as the company has only just started, all research and development expenditure relates to future sales so all this year's expenditure should be carried forward.

Inventory:
Both the managing director and the works director are of the opinion that inventory should be shown at prime cost.

The sales director's view is that inventory should be shown at sales price as the inventory is virtually all sold within a very short period.

Required:
(a) You are asked to comment on each opinion stating what factors should be taken into account to determine suitable depreciation and write-off amounts.
(b) Indicate what amounts should, in your opinion, be charged to profit or loss and show the adjusted profit produced by your recommendations, stating clearly any assumptions you may make.

(*Association of Chartered Certified Accountants*)

11.5   The accountant of Hook, Line and Sinker, a partnership of seven people, has asked your advice in dealing with the following items in the partnership accounts for the year to 31 May 2007.

(a) (i) Included in invoices prepared and dated in June 2007 were £60,000 of goods despatched during the second half of May 2007.
    (ii) Inventory of components at 31 May 2007 includes parts no longer used in production. These components originally cost £50,000 but have been written down for purposes of the accounts to £25,000. Scrap value of these items is estimated to be £1,000. Another user has expressed interest in buying these parts for £40,000.

(b) After May 2007 a customer who accounts for 50% of Hook, Line and Sinker sales suffered a serious fire which has disrupted his organisation. Payments for supplies are becoming slow and Hook, Line and Sinker sales for the current year are likely to be substantially lower than previously. This customer owed £80,000 to Hook, Line and Sinker at 31 May 2007

(c) During the year to 31 May, Hook, Line and Sinker commenced a new advertising campaign using television and expensive magazine advertising for the first time. Sales during the year were not much higher than previous years as the partners consider that the effects of advertising will be seen in future years.

Expenditure on advertising during the year is made up of:

	£
Television	50,000
Advertisements in magazines	60,000
Advertisements in local papers	25,000

All the expenditure has been treated as expense in the accounts but the partners wish to carry forward three-quarters of the television and magazine costs as it is expected that this cost will benefit future years' profits and because this year's profits will compare unfavourably with previous years if all the expenditure is charged in the accounts.

(d) Three projects for the construction of sinkers have the following cost and revenue characteristics:

	Project A	Project B	Project C
Degree of completion	75%	50%	15%
	£	£	£
Direct costs to date	30,000	25,000	6,000
Sales price of complete project	55,000	50,000	57,500
Overheads allocated to date	4,000	2,000	500
Costs to complete – Direct	10,000	25,000	40,000
– Overheads	2,000	2,000	3,000

No profits or losses have been included in the accounts.

(e) After considerable discussion with management, the sales of a newly developed special purpose hook have been given the following probabilities:

First year of production

Sales	Probability
£	
15,000	0.2
30,000	0.5
40,000	0.3

Second year of production

Increase over first year	Probability
£	
10,000	0.1
20,000	0.5
30,000	0.4

Second year sales may be assumed independent of first year levels.
Cost–volume–profit analysis shows that the breakeven point is £50,000.

Production of the special purpose hook started prior to the end of the accounting year and inventory of the finished product are included at cost amounting to £20,000. It has been decided that if there is less than 0.7 probability of breakeven being reached in the second year then inventory should be written down by 25%.

(f) During the year it was discovered that some inventory sheets had been omitted from the calculations at the previous year end. The effect is that opening inventory for the current year, shown as £35,000, should be £42,000. No adjustment has yet been made.

Required:
Discuss the treatment of each item with reference to relevant accounting standards and accounting concepts and conventions. Recommend the appropriate treatment for each item showing the profit effect of each recommendation made.

(*Association of Chartered Certified Accountants*)

11.6   The chief accountant of Uncertain Ltd is not sure of the appropriate accounting treatment for a number of events occurring during the year 2005/6.

(*i*)   A significant number of employees have been made redundant, giving rise to redundancy payments of £100,000 which have been included in manufacturing cost of sales.

(*ii*)   One of Uncertain Ltd's three factories has been closed down. Closure costs amounted to £575,000. This amount has been deducted from reserves in the balance sheet.

(*iii*)   The directors have changed the basis of charging depreciation on delivery vehicles. The difference between the old and new methods amounts to £258,800. This has been treated as a charge in accounting policy and the comparative figures have been adjusted accordingly.

(*iv*)   During October 2006 a fire occurred in one of the remaining factories belonging to Uncertain Ltd and caused an estimated £350,000 of additional expenses. This amount has been included in manufacturing cost of sales.

(*v*)   It was discovered on 31 October 2006 that a customer was unable to pay his debt to the company of £125,000. The £125,000 was made up of sales in the period July to September 2006. No adjustment has been made in the draft accounts for this item.

Uncertain Ltd
Draft Income Statement for the year ending 30 September 2006

	£	£
Revenue		5,450,490
Manufacturing cost of sales		3,284,500
Gross profit		2,165,990
Administration expenses	785,420	
Selling expenses	629,800	
		(1,415,220)
		750,770
Corporation tax (50%)		(375,385)
Profit for the period		375,385

Required:

(a)   Write a report to the chief accountant of Uncertain Ltd with suggestions for appropriate treatment for each of the items (*i*) to (*v*), with explanations for your proposals.

(b)   Amend the draft income statement to take account of your proposals.

(*Association of Chartered Certified Accountants*)

11.7   With reference to IAS 10 *Events after the reporting period* and IAS 37 *Provisions, contingent liabilities and contingent assets*:

(a)   define the following terms:
  (*i*)   post-balance sheet events
  (*ii*)   adjusting events
  (*iii*)   non-adjusting events
  (*iv*)   contingent asset/liability;
(b)   give FOUR examples of adjusting events, and FOUR examples of non-adjusting events; and
(c)   state how
  (*i*)   a material contingent liability, and
  (*ii*)   material contingent assets should be accounted for in financial statements.

The financial statements of limited companies: income statements, related statements and notes

Learning objectives
....

After you have studied this chapter, you should be able to:

- explain how to present financial information under International GAAP in an Income Statement, Statement of Comprehensive Income and Statement of Changes in Equity
- describe the differences between the format of the income statement for publication and the format generally adopted for internal use
- state how the Companies Act 2006 defines company size

Introduction
....

In this chapter, you'll learn about the way in which international accounting standards and, in particular, IAS 1 (*Presentation of financial statements*) govern the presentation of information relating to income and changes in equity for a period in published company financial statements.

12.1 Background

When a company draws up its own financial statements, purely for internal use by directors and the management, it can adopt any format it wishes. It can, for example, switch the order of items in the balance sheet, combine items that are never combined when official formats are used, and use its own terminology in place of normal accounting terminology. There are no rules which must be followed when preparing accounting information for internal use. Drawing up an income statement and balance sheet for a company's own use is not, therefore, necessarily the same as drawing up such financial statements for other purposes.

If an organisation wishes to charge something in the trading account that, in theory, ought to be charged to profit and loss, there is nothing to prevent it from doing so. On the other hand, students sitting an exam and accountants preparing financial statements for publication must base their work on accounting theory and accounting rules and regulations, *not* on the internal reporting practices of an organisation.

When it comes to publication, prior to 1981, UK companies had considerable freedom in how and what information was presented, but when financial statements are prepared under

International GAAP for publication, i.e. when the financial statements are to be sent to the shareholders or to the Registrar of Companies, the information to be shown and the information to prepare are laid down in IASs and IFRSs and in the *Framework for the Preparation and Presentation of Financial Statements*.

> **Activity 12.1**   What do you think the advantages of companies having to follow set rules in this case may be?

A Statement of Comprehensive Income must be prepared under International GAAP. This statement may incorporate the Income Statement, or simply contain items not included in the Income Statement. As custom in the UK has always been to prepare an Income Statement, we'll adopt that approach and discuss the Statement of Comprehensive Income in Section 12.9.

12.2   Financial statement formats

International GAAP permits two approaches for presentation of items in the income statement: by function or by nature. In the UK, there is little difference in the presentation of information in the income statement under International GAAP compared with UK GAAP. So far as the balance sheet is concerned, the difference is far greater. Under International GAAP, assets are presented together in the order non-current then current (or in order of liquidity) and liabilities are then presented typically in the order current then non-current. Finally, there is a section for equity. Alternatively, equity may precede non-current and current liabilities.

We are going to approach this topic, first, by presenting you with an income statement produced for use within a company (an 'internal' income statement) which can easily be adapted to cover publication requirements under International GAAP. (We will deal with balance sheets in Chapter 13.)

Despite freedom to do otherwise, most companies base the format of their internal financial statements on those required for published financial statements.

> **Activity 12.2**   The reason for taking this approach ought to be fairly obvious. What do you think it is?

All companies, even the smallest, that adopt International GAAP must produce financial statements for their shareholders that adhere to its requirements. 'Small' and 'medium-sized' companies can, however, file summarised financial statements with the Registrar of Companies, but they must still prepare a full set of financial statements for their shareholders. In addition, listed companies may send their shareholders summary financial statements in place of the full version, but each shareholder has the right to request a full version, and many do.

The Companies Act 2006 definition of 'small-' and 'medium-sized' companies is that, for the financial year in question and the previous year, the company is defined as 'small-' or 'medium-sized' if it lies within the limits of at least two of the following three criteria:

	Small	Medium-sized
Turnover not more than	£5.6 million	£22.8 million
Balance sheet total not more than	£2.8 million	£11.4 million
Employees not more than	50	250

12.3 Items to be presented on the face of the Income Statement for publication

The following is the minimum information that must be shown on the face of the Income Statement:

1 Revenue.
2 Finance costs.
3 Share of the profits or losses of associates and joint ventures accounted for using the equity method (see Chapter 26).
4 Taxation expenses.
5 Post-tax profit or loss of discontinued operations plus the post-tax gain or loss recognised on the measurements to fair value less cost to sell of the assets or disposal groups constituting the discontinued operation.
6 Profit or loss for the period.

An analysis of total expenses must be shown either on the face of the Income Statement or in the notes on the basis of either the nature or function of the expenses (see Section 12.6).

Earnings per share must be shown at the foot of the statement (see Section 11.27).

Additional items can be shown when it is relevant to an understanding of the company's financial performance. (It is this flexibility that results in there being little difference between an income statement prepared under International GAAP and one prepared under UK GAAP.)

In addition, in the case of consolidated income statements, profit or loss for the period should be shown as allocated between minority interests and equity holders. For example, if profit for the period were £165,000 and there was a 10% minority shareholding in the group, lines would be inserted below the profit for the period line as follows:

Attributable to:	£
Owners of the parent	148,500
Minority interest	16,500
	165,000

12.4 Income statement for internal use

Exhibit 12.1 shows an income statement drawn up for internal use. As mentioned earlier, there are no statutory rules concerning how financial statements are prepared for internal use. However, as you learnt in Activity 12.2, if the internal financial statements were drawn up in a completely different fashion from those needed for publication, quite a lot of work might be needed in order to reassemble the figures into an income statement for publication.

Exhibit 12.1 Income statement for internal use

Block plc
Income Statement for the year ending 31 December 2006

	£000	£000	£000
Revenue			800
Less Cost of sales:			
Inventory 1 January 2006		100	
Add Purchases		525	
		625	
Less Inventory 31 December 2006		(125)	
			(500)
Gross profit			300
Distribution costs			
Salaries and wages	30		
Motor vehicle costs: Distribution	20		
General distribution expenses	5		
Depreciation: Motors	3		
Machinery	2		
		60	
Administrative expenses			
Salaries and wages	25		
Motor vehicle costs: Administration	2		
General administration expenses	7		
Auditors' remuneration	2		
Depreciation: Motors	3		
Machinery	1		
		40	
			(100)
			200
Other operating income			30
Operating profit			230
Finance income			
Income from shares in group entities		20	
Income from associates and joint ventures		10	
Income from shares from non-related companies		5	
Other interest receivable		15	
			50
			280
Finance costs			
Amounts written off investments		4	
Interest payable			
Loans repayable within five years	10		
Loans repayable in ten years	6		
		16	
			(20)
Profit before taxation			260
Taxation			(95)
Profit for the year			165
Retained profits brought forward from last year			60
			225
Transfer to general reserve		40	
Ordinary dividend paid		100	
			(140)
Retained profits carried forward to next year			85

In Exhibit 12.1, the internal income statement has been prepared using a format which makes it easy to get the figures for the published income statement. Examination questions on this topic sometimes ask for both (*a*) internal and (*b*) published financial statements. You should find things are easier if the internal and published financial statements follow a similar format.

12.5 Income statement for publication

Exhibit 12.2 redrafts Exhibit 12.1 into a form suitable for publication under International GAAP. You will see that one difference between the two exhibits is that the detail between each entry has been removed. Such detail could, of course, be included as notes to the published financial statement. The other main difference is that none of the lines after the profit for the year line appear in an income statement for publication.

Exhibit 12.2 Income statement for publication complying with International GAAP

Block plc
Income Statement for the year ending 31 December 2006

	£000	£000
Revenue		800
Cost of sales		(500)
Gross profit		300
Distribution costs	60	
Administrative expenses	40	
		(100)
		200
Other operating income		30
Operating profit		230
Finance income		
Income from shares in group entities	20	
Income from associates and joint ventures	10	
Income from other non-current asset investments	5	
Other interest receivable and similar income	15	
		50
		280
Finance costs		
Amounts written off investments	4	
Interest payable	16	
		(20)
Profit before taxation		260
Taxation		(95)
Profit for the year		165

Attributable to:	£000
Owners of the parent	148.5
Minority interest	16.5
	165.0

Earnings per share 25p

Note: Appropriations of profits should either be shown in the notes or in the separate Statement of Changes in Equity.

When internal financial statements are prepared in the format shown in Exhibit 12.1, they could be published just as they are excluding the lines after 'profit for the year'. International GAAP does not force companies to publish financial statements as detailed as the one shown in

Exhibit 12.1. Rather, it states the *minimum* information which must be disclosed. A company can show more than the minimum if it wants to but companies usually prefer to do so in notes to the financial statement, or, as noted above, in a separate statement.

> **Activity 12.3**   Why would most companies *not* want to publish detailed financial statements?

12.6   Classification of expenses by nature or function

The items on the face of the income statement below revenue should be analysed using a classification based on either their nature or their function. This should be done either on the face of the income statement (which is encouraged by IAS 1) or in the notes. Traditionally, this is done by function showing, for example:

(*a*) cost of sales
(*b*) gross profit
(*c*) other income
(*d*) distribution costs
(*e*) administration expenses
(*f*) other expenses.

This is the approach that was taken in Exhibit 12.2. This information should include depreciation and amortisation expenses and employee benefit costs (i.e. pension costs).

When analysed using a classification by nature, the analysis may comprise:

(*a*) other income
(*b*) changes in inventory of finished goods and work in progress
(*c*) raw materials and consumables used
(*d*) employee benefit costs
(*e*) depreciation and amortisation expense
(*f*) other expenses.

12.7   Other disclosure required in the notes

The list of possible items is lengthy and beyond the scope of this book. However, the most commonly encountered at this level include:

● research and development expenditure recognised as an expense during the period;
● foreign-exchange differences recognised in profit or loss;
● impairment losses and reversal of impairment losses recognised during the period for each class of asset;
● the amount of intangible asset amortisation for each class of intangible asset recognised during the period, plus where it is included in the income statement;
● income, expenses, gains, and losses resulting from financial assets and financial liabilities;
● the major components of the taxation expense;
● the amount of each significant category of revenue recognised during the period including:
  (*i*)   sale of goods
  (*ii*)   rendering of services
  (*iii*) interest
  (*iv*)   royalties
  (*v*)   dividends;
● the nature and amount of any change in accounting estimate that has an effect in the current or a future period.

For UK companies, the Companies Act requires further disclosure in the notes of:

1. Interest on bank loans, overdrafts and other loans:
   (a) repayable within five years from the end of the accounting period;
   (b) finally repayable after five years from the end of the accounting period.
2. Amounts set aside for redemption of share capital and for redemption of loans.
3. Rents from land, if material.
4. Costs of hire of plant and machinery.
5. Auditors' remuneration, including expenses.

There is also more information required to be disclosed in the notes by a number of accounting standards. These were mainly covered in Chapter 11; and some are covered in Chapters 13–26.

12.8 Allocation of expenses

It will be obvious under which heading most expenses will be shown, whether they are:

(a) cost of sales;
(b) distribution costs; or
(c) administrative expenses.

However, as these terms are not defined, some items are not so easy to allocate with certainty. Some companies may choose one heading for a particular item, while others will choose another. For example:

1. **Discounts received.** These are for prompt payment of amounts owing by us. Where they are for payments to suppliers of goods they could be regarded either as a reduction in the cost of goods or, alternatively, as a financial recompense, i.e. the reward for paying money on time. If regarded in the first way they would be deducted from cost of sales, whereas the alternative approach would be to deduct them from administrative expenses. However, these discounts are also deducted when paying bills in respect of distribution costs or administrative expenses, and it would also be necessary to deduct from these headings if the cost of sales deduction approach is used. As this raises complications in the original recording of discounts received, it would be more suitable in this book if all cash discounts received are deducted in arriving at the figure of administrative expenses.
2. **Discounts allowed.** To be consistent in dealing with discounts, this should be included in administrative expenses.
3. **Bad debts.** These could be regarded as an expense connected with sales: after all, they are sales which are not paid for. The other point of view is that for a debt to become bad, at least part of the blame must be because the proper administrative procedures in checking on customers' creditworthiness has not been thorough enough. In this book bad debts will be treated as being part of administrative expenses.

12.9 Statement of Comprehensive Income

As mentioned in Section 12.1, under IAS 1 the Income Statement may either be shown as a separate primary financial statement or as part of a primary statement called a Statement of Comprehensive Income. When a separate income statement is prepared, the Statement of Comprehensive Income comprises:

(a) profit or loss for the period (as shown in the income statement);
(b) each component of other comprehensive income classified by nature;
(c) share of the other comprehensive income of associates and joint ventures accounted for using the equity method (see Chapter 26);
(d) total comprehensive income;

Exhibit 12.3 An example of a Statement of Comprehensive Income

Block plc
Statement of Comprehensive Income for the year ending 31 December 2006

	£000	£000
Revenue		800
Cost of sales		(500)
Gross profit		300
Distribution costs	60	
Administrative expenses	40	
		(100)
		200
Other operating income		30
Operating profit		230
Finance income:		
Income from shares in group entities	20	
Income from interest in associates and joint ventures	10	
Income from non-current asset investments	5	
Other interest receivable and similar income	15	
		50
		280
Finance costs:		
Amount written off investments	4	
Interest payable	16	
		(20)
Profit before taxation		260
Taxation		(95)
Profit for the year		165

Other comprehensive income		
Changes in revaluation surplus	20	
Actuarial loss on defined benefit plans	(30)	
Gains from translation of financial statements of foreign operations	15	
Losses from remeasuring available-for-sale financial assets	(25)	
Gains on hedging instruments	5	
		(15)
Total comprehensive income		150

Profit attributable to:	£000
Owners of the parent	148.5
Minority interest	16.5
	165.0

Total comprehensive income attributable to:	
Owners of the parent	135
Minority interest	15
	150

Earnings per share 25p

Note: Taxation on each item of other comprehensive income would be shown as a note. (The figures shown above are net of taxation.)

and in the notes the total comprehensive income for the period is disclosed attributable to (*i*) minority interests; and (*ii*) owners of the parent.

The items disclosed may be shown either net of taxation or before tax with a separate line showing the taxation amount. If the net approach is adopted, the tax on each item must be shown separately in a note.

Other comprehensive income comprises items of income and expense (including reclassification adjustments, i.e. the amounts reclassified to profit or loss in the current period that were recognised in other comprehensive income in the current or previous periods) that are not recognised in profit or loss such as:

(*a*) changes in revaluation surplus (see IAS 16 and IAS 38);
(*b*) actuarial gains and losses on defined benefit (pension) plans (see IAS 19);
(*c*) gains and losses arising from the translation of the financial statements of foreign operations (see IAS 21);
(*d*) gains and losses arising from remeasuring available-for-sale financial assets (see IAS 39);
(*e*) the effective portion of gains and losses on hedging instruments in a cash flow hedge (see IAS 39).

Total comprehensive income (i.e. that shown in the income statement plus other comprehensive income) represents the change in equity during a period resulting from transactions and other events, other than those changes resulting from transactions with owners in their capacity as owners.

Exhibit 12.3 shows a Statement of Comprehensive Income which includes the information that could have been shown separately in an income statement. The income statement shown previously in Exhibit 12.2 forms the first part.

12.10 Other statements and notes required by IAS 1

Three further primary statements are required by IAS 1:

1 Statement of Changes in Equity

This statement should disclose:

(*a*) profit or loss for the period;
(*b*) each item of income or expense for the period that is recognised directly in equity and the total of such items (e.g. revaluation of non-current assets and currency translation differences);
(*c*) total income and expense for the period (i.e. (*a*) plus (*b*)) showing separately between that part attributable to parent equity holders and to minority interests;
(*d*) the effects of changes in accounting policies and correction of errors for each component of equity;
(*e*) transactions with equity holders:
    (*i*) issues of share capital;
    (*ii*) purchase of own shares;
    (*iii*) contracts that will be settled by the entity receiving or delivering a fixed number of its own equity instruments in exchange for a fixed amount of cash or another financial asset;
(*f*) transaction costs relating to the issue of share capital deducted from shareholders' equity;
(*g*) dividends and other distributions to owners;
(*h*) a reconciliation between the opening and closing amount for the following:
    (*i*) each class of share capital;
    (*ii*) share premium;
    (*iii*) own shares (treasury shares);
    (*iv*) each reserve including revaluation reserves; hedging reserves; foreign exchange translation reserves; current or deferred tax on items taken directly to or transferred from equity; equity settled share-based payment transactions;
    (*v*) retained earnings;
(*i*) the equity conversion element of convertible debt.

As an alternative, a Statement of Recognised Income and Expense may be prepared. It comprises of items (a) to (d). Items (e) to (i) must then be disclosed in the notes.

A large number of disclosures must also be made, including the number of each class of share authorised and issued and its par value.

Exhibit 12.4 presents an example of a Statement of Changes in Equity:

Exhibit 12.4 An example of a Statement of Changes in Equity

| | Attributable to Equity Holders of the Company | | | | | | |
	Share capital	Share premium	Other reserves	Retained earnings	Total	Minority interest	Total equity
Balance at 1.1.2008	50,000	30,000	10,000	140,000	230,000	1,000	231,000
Cash flow hedges, net of tax			(5)		(5)		(5)
Currency translation differences			(90)		(90)	(20)	(110)
Net expense recognised directly into equity			(95)		(95)	(20)	(115)
Profit for the year				45,000	45,000	4,000	49,000
Total recognised income and expense for 2008			(95)	45,000	44,905	3,980	48,885
Proceeds from shares issued	10,000	20,000			30,000		30,000
Dividend relating to 2007				(32,000)	(32,000)	(700)	(32,700)
	10,000	20,000		(32,000)	(2,000)	(700)	(2,700)
Balance at 31.12.2008	60,000	50,000	9,905	153,000	272,905	4,280	277,185

2 Balance sheet (or Statement of Financial Position)

This topic is covered in Chapter 13.

3 Statement of Cash Flows

This topic is covered in Chapter 15.

Learning outcomes

You should now have learnt:

1 How to present financial information under International GAAP in income statements, statements of comprehensive income, and statements of changes in equity.

2 There are prescribed formats for the preparation of published financial statements.

3 Financial statements prepared for internal use need not comply with these formats but are often based upon them.

4 How the Companies Act 2006 defines company size.

Answers to activities

12.1 Combined with the regulations enshrined in accounting standards that govern how data will be processed and selected for inclusion as information in the financial statements, the standardisation brought about by the Companies Act 1981 makes meaningful comparison between the financial statements of different companies feasible.

12.2 For the same reason that many small companies use the percentage rates provided by the tax rules relating to capital allowances when setting their depreciation rates – it saves them redoing the calculation – many small companies use the format for publication as the basis for their internal financial statements, adding more detail when they feel it is appropriate to do so.

12.3 Because doing so may give their competitors information which would lead to the company losing some of its competitive advantage.

Review questions

12.1 From the following selected balances of Filo plc as at 31 March 2005 draw up (*i*) a detailed income statement for internal use, and (*ii*) an income statement for publication.

	£
Retained profits as at 31 March 2004	102,000
Inventory 1 April 2004	84,000
Purchases	1,462,000
Revenue	2,456,000
Returns inwards	108,000
Returns outwards	37,000
Carriage inwards	14,700
Wages and salaries (*see* Note (*b*))	136,000
Rent and business rates (*see* Note (*c*))	14,000
General distribution expenses	28,000
General administrative expenses	24,000
Discounts allowed	36,000
Bad debts	5,000
Loan note interest	12,000
Motor expenses (*see* Note (*d*))	16,000
Interest received on bank deposit	6,000
Income from associates and joint ventures	3,000
Motor vehicles at cost: Administrative	54,000
Distribution	92,000
Equipment at cost: Administrative	15,000
Distribution	12,000
Royalties receivable	4,000
Dividends paid	120,000

Notes:
(a) Inventory at 31 March 2005 £102,000.
(b) Wages and salaries are to be apportioned: Distribution costs $1/4$, Administrative expenses $3/4$.
(c) Rent and business rates are to be apportioned: Distribution costs 55%, Administrative expenses 45%.
(d) Apportion motor expenses in the proportions 2:3 between distribution costs and administrative expenses.
(e) Depreciate motor vehicles 20% and equipment 10% on cost.
(f) Accrue auditors' remuneration of £11,000.
(g) Accrue corporation tax for the year on ordinary activity profits £364,000.
(h) A sum of £20,000 is to be transferred to general reserve.

12.2   From the following selected balances of State plc as at 31 December 2008, prepare (*i*) a detailed income statement for the year ended 31 December 2008 for internal use and (*ii*) an income statement for the same period for publication.

	£
Inventory 1 January 2008	140,000
Revenue	1,860,000
Purchases	1,140,000
Carriage inwards	8,000
Returns inwards	9,000
Returns outwards	5,000
Discounts allowed	11,000
Discounts received	14,000
Wages (putting goods into saleable condition)	88,000
Salaries and wages: Sales and distribution staff	62,000
Salaries and wages: Administrative staff	74,000
Motor expenses (*see* Note (*c*))	24,000
Rent and business rates (*see* Note (*d*))	28,000
Investments in associates (market value £74,000)	100,000
Income from associates	5,000
General distribution expenses	12,000
General administrative expenses	6,000
Bad debts	2,000
Interest from government securities	3,000
Haulage costs: Distribution	4,000
Loan note interest payable	2,000
Retained profits 31 December 2007	94,000
Motor vehicles at cost: Distribution and sales	60,000
Administrative	26,000
Plant and machinery at cost: Distribution and sales	50,000
Administrative	30,000
Production	60,000
Directors' remuneration	36,000
Dividends paid	60,000

Notes:
(*a*) The production department puts goods bought into a saleable condition.
(*b*) Inventory at 31 December 2008 £160,000.
(*c*) Apportion motor expenses: distribution $^3/_4$, administrative $^1/_4$.
(*d*) Apportion rent and business rates: distribution 40%, administrative 60%.
(*e*) Write £26,000 off the value of investments in undertakings in which the company has a participating interest.
(*f*) Depreciate motor vehicles 25% on cost, plant and machinery 15% on cost.
(*g*) Accrue auditors' remuneration £14,000.
(*h*) Accrue corporation tax on ordinary activity profits £104,000.
(*i*) A sum of £25,000 is to be transferred to loan note redemption reserve.

12.3 The following information has been extracted from the books of account of Rufford plc for the year to 31 March 2006:

	Dr £000	Cr £000
Administration expenses	97	
Deferred taxation		24
Depreciation on office machinery (for the year to 31 March 2006)	8	
Depreciation on delivery vans (for the year to 31 March 2006)	19	
Distribution costs	33	
Dividends received (from a UK listed company on 31 July 2005)		14
Factory closure expenses (closed on 1 April 2005)	12	
Interest payable on bank overdraft (repayable within five years)	6	
Interim dividend (paid on 30 September 2005)	21	
Interest receivable		25
Purchases	401	
Retained profit at 31 March 2005		160
Revenue (net of VAT)		642
Inventory at 1 April 2005	60	

Additional information:

1 Administrative expenses include the following items:

	£000
Auditors' remuneration	20
Directors' emoluments	45
Travelling expenses	1
Research expenditure	11
Hire of plant and machinery	12

2 It is assumed that the following tax rates are applicable for the year to 31 March 2006:

Corporation tax	50%
Income tax	30%

3 There was an overprovision for corporation tax of £3,000 relating to the year to 31 March 2005.

4 Corporation tax payable for the year to 31 March 2006 (based on the profits for that year) is estimated to be £38,000. The company, in addition, intends to transfer a further £9,000 to its deferred taxation account.

5 A final dividend of £42,000 for the year to 31 March 2006 is expected to be paid on 2 June 2006.

6 Inventory at 31 March 2006 was valued at £71,000.

7 As a result of a change in accounting policy, a prior period charge of £15,000 (net of tax) is to be made.

8 The company's share capital consists of 420,000 ordinary shares of £1 each. There are no preference shares, and no change had been made to the company's issued share capital for some years.

Required:

(a) In so far as the information permits, prepare the company's published income statement for the year to 31 March 2006 in the vertical format in accordance with the relevant accounting standards.

(NB: A statement of the company's accounting policies is not required.)

(b) Prepare balance sheet extracts in order to illustrate the balances still remaining in the following accounts at 31 March 2006:

(i) corporation tax;

(ii) proposed dividend; and

(iii) deferred taxation.

(NB: A detailed balance sheet is not required.)

(*Association of Accounting Technicians*)

→

12.4A   From the following balances in the books of Breaker plc you are to draw up (i) a detailed income statement for the year ending 31 March 2004 for internal use, and (ii) an income statement for publication:

	£
Plant and machinery, at cost (*see* Note (*c*))	105,000
Bank interest receivable	3,000
Discounts allowed	7,000
Discounts received	6,000
Hire of motor vehicles: Sales and distribution	14,000
Hire of motor vehicles: Administrative	5,000
Licence fees receivable	13,000
General distribution expenses	26,000
General administrative expenses	19,000
Wages and salaries: Sales and distribution	177,000
Administrative	98,000
Directors' remuneration	41,000
Motor expenses (*see* Note (*e*))	11,000
Ordinary dividend paid	80,000
Inventory 31 March 2003	208,000
Revenue	1,450,000
Purchases	700,000
Returns outwards	22,000
Returns inwards	29,000
Retained profits as at 31 March 2003	88,000

Notes:
(*a*) Inventory at 31 March 2004 £230,000.
(*b*) Accrue auditor's remuneration £8,000.
(*c*) Of the plant and machinery, £70,000 is distributive in nature, while £35,000 is for administration.
(*d*) Depreciate plant and machinery 25% on cost.
(*e*) Of the motor expenses, $^4/_5$ are for sales and distribution and $^1/_5$ for administration.
(*f*) Corporation tax on ordinary profits is estimated at £143,000.
(*g*) A sum of £25,000 is to be transferred to general reserve.

12.5A The following balances have been extracted from the books of Mitchell plc on 31 July 2002. From them draw up (*i*) a detailed income statement for internal use, for the year ending 31 July 2002, also (*ii*) an income statement for publication for the year to that date.

	£
Purchases	1,310,000
Revenue	1,790,000
Returns inwards	29,000
Returns outwards	57,000
Carriage inwards	10,000
Wages – productive	109,000
Discounts allowed	11,000
Discounts received	15,000
Inventory 31 July 2001	317,000
Wages and salaries: Sales and distribution	41,000
Wages and salaries: Administrative	62,000
Motor expenses: Sales and distribution	26,000
Motor expenses: Administrative	8,000
General distribution expenses	7,000
General administrative expenses	6,000
Rent and business rates (*see* Note (*c*))	17,000
Directors' remuneration	35,000
Retained profits 31 July 2001	141,000
Advertising	19,000
Bad debts	3,000
Hire of plant and machinery (*see* Note (*b*))	14,000
Motor vehicles at cost: Sales and distribution	45,000
Administrative	18,000
Plant and machinery: Distribution	13,000
Loan note interest payable	7,000
Income from shares in group entities	8,000
Income from associates and joint ventures	5,000
Preference dividend paid	20,000
Profit on disposal of investments	14,000
Tax on profit on disposal of investments	3,000
Ordinary dividend paid	110,000

Notes:
(*a*) Inventory at 31 July 2002 £303,000.
(*b*) The hire of plant and machinery is to be apportioned: productive £12,000, administrative £2,000.
(*c*) Rent and business rates to be apportioned: distribution $^3/_4$, administrative $^1/_4$.
(*d*) Motors are to be depreciated at $33^1/_3$% on cost; plant and machinery to be depreciated at 10% on cost.
(*e*) Auditors' remuneration of £15,000 to be accrued.
(*f*) Corporation tax on profit from ordinary activities for the year is estimated at £29,000, excluding tax on disposal of investments.
(*g*) Transfer £50,000 to general reserve.

12.6A   Bunker plc is a trading company; it does not carry out *any* manufacturing operations. The following information has been extracted from the books of account for the year to 31 March 2010:

	£000
Auditors' remuneration	30
Corporation tax: based on the accounting profit for the year to 31 March 2010	7,200
overprovision for the year to 31 March 2009	200
United Kingdom corporation tax relief on	
overseas operations: closure costs	30
Delivery expenses	1,200
Dividends: final (proposed – to be paid 1 August 2010)	200
interim (paid on 1 October 2009)	100
Non-current assets at cost:	
Delivery vans	200
Office cars	40
Stores plant and equipment	5,000
Investment income (amount received from listed companies)	1,600
Office expenses	800
Overseas operations: closure costs of entire operations on 1 April 2009	350
Purchases (net of value added tax)	24,000
Revenue (net of value added tax)	35,000
Inventory at cost:	
at 1 April 2009	5,000
at 31 March 2010	6,000
Storeroom costs	1,000
Wages and salaries:	
Delivery staff	700
Directors' emoluments	300
Office staff	100
Storeroom staff	400

Additional information:

1 Depreciation policy:
   Depreciation is provided at the following annual rates on a straight line basis: delivery vans 20%; office cars 7.5%; stores plant and equipment 10%.
2 The following taxation rates may be assumed:
   corporation tax 35%; income tax 25%; value added tax 15%.
3 The investment income arises from investments held in non-current asset investments.
4 It has been decided to transfer an amount of £150,000 to the deferred taxation account.
5 There were 1,000,000 ordinary shares of £1 each in issue during the year to 31 March 2010. There were no preference shares in issue.

Required:
In so far as the information permits, prepare Bunker plc's published income statement for the year ending 31 March 2010 in accordance with the minimum requirements of the related accounting standards.

Note: A statement of accounting policies is NOT required, but where appropriate, other formal notes SHOULD be attached to your income statement. Detailed workings should also be submitted with your answer.

(*Association of Accounting Technicians*)

The financial statements of limited companies: balance sheets

Learning objectives

After you have studied this chapter, you should be able to:

- describe commonly used formats that may be used when preparing balance sheets for external reporting purposes
- describe the differences between the formats used for publication and formats generally adopted for internal use
- describe the exemption of some 'small' companies from having their financial statements audited
- describe the exemptions available to small and medium-sized companies in respect of filing modified financial statements
- describe the option available to public limited companies to send members a summary financial statement

Introduction

In this chapter, you'll learn about the format of balance sheets prepared for publication under International GAAP. You will also be reminded of the fundamental accounting concepts that you covered in *Business Accounting 1* and introduced to the rules relating to the preparation of modified financial statements for small and medium-sized companies.

13.1 The title 'Balance Sheet'

'Balance sheet' is the traditional name for what IAS 1 calls a 'Statement of Financial Position'. We'll continue to use the traditional name – it is likely to be many years before the IAS 1 title becomes commonplace, if it ever does. Besides which, IAS 1 itself states that any title can be used so long as it does not mislead the users of the statements. However, **you need to be aware of the IAS 1 title: examiners could and may use it at any time.**

13.2 Balance sheet contents

A balance sheet presents a summary of the financial position of an entity at a point in time. Companies prepare balance sheets for publication at the end of each financial year (i.e. at the end of each 12-month period in which they operate). They must also prepare six-monthly interim balance sheets if listed on a stock exchange.

A company is generally free to use its judgement concerning how to present the information in its balance sheet and what to include in it and what to include in the notes that accompany it. However, at a minimum, it must present the following on the face of the balance sheet:

- Assets
  Non-current (a) property, plant and equipment;
  (b) investment property;
  (c) intangible assets (see Section 13.4);
  (d) financial assets (see Section 13.6);
  (e) investments accounted for using the equity method;
  (f) biological assets;
  (g) deferred tax assets (see IAS 12, Chapter 11);
  Current   (h) inventories;
  (i) current tax assets (see IAS 12, Chapter 11);
  (j) trade and other receivables;
  (k) cash and cash equivalents (see Section 13.5);
  Other   (l) (the total of) assets classified as held for sale and assets included in disposal groups classified as held for sale (see IFRS 5, Chapter 11).
- Liabilities (a) trade and other payables;
  (b) provisions;
  (c) financial liabilities (excluding amounts included in (a) and (b));
  (d) liabilities for current tax (see IAS 12, Chapter 11);
  (e) deferred tax liabilities (see IAS 12, Chapter 11);
  (f) liabilities included in disposal groups classified as held for sale (see IFRS, Chapter 11).
- Equity   (a) issued capital (see Section 13.3);
  (b) reserves attributable to owners of the parent;
  (c) minority interest.

The standard does not prescribe the order or format in which the items are presented. However, a company should normally group assets and liabilities on a current and non-current basis using 12 months after the reporting period to distinguish between the two categories.

Activity 13.1 Why does the above list not split the liabilities into non-current and current?

13.3 Balance sheet disclosure

Companies can show as much detail as they wish on the face of the balance sheet. However, single-line entries are typically used for each of the items listed in Section 13.2, and the detail is shown in the notes.

Subject to materiality, the disclosure would, for example, disaggregate the line entry for:

(a) property, plant and equipment;
(b) receivables into trade receivables, receivables from related parties, prepayments, and other amounts;
(c) inventories into sub-categories such as finished goods, raw materials, and work in progress;
(d) provisions into provisions for employee benefits and other provisions;
(e) equity capital into various classes of equity and separating share premium from other reserves.

For each class of share capital, the following must be disclosed:

(i)   the number of shares authorised;
(ii) the number of shares issued and fully paid;

(*iii*) the number of shares issued but not fully paid;

(*iv*) the par (or nominal) value per share;

(*v*) a reconciliation between the opening and closing number of shares in issue;

(*vi*) any rights, preferences, and restrictions, including restrictions on the distribution of dividends and the repayment of capital;

(*vii*) shares in the entity held by the entity or by its subsidiaries or associates;

(*viii*) shares reserved for issue under options and contracts for the sale of shares, including terms and amounts.

For each reserve, the nature and purpose must be disclosed.

13.4 Goodwill

Goodwill is included in intangible assets and is tested annually for impairment. Any impairment identified should be charged to profit or loss and can not be reversed. Goodwill is not amortised (depreciated). Internally generated goodwill is never recognised. Negative goodwill is eliminated immediately by adjusting the fair values of the net assets acquired and recognising any remaining negative goodwill immediately as a gain in profit or loss.

13.5 Cash equivalents

These are short-term investments that are readily convertible to a known amount of cash within a short period from the date of acquisition. The maximum qualifying period is generally taken to be three months.

13.6 Financial assets

These comprise cash; a contractual right to receive cash or another financial asset; a contractual right to exchange financial assets or liabilities with another entity; or an equity instrument of another entity.

Such assets fall into one of four categories:

(*a*) held at fair value through profit or loss – i.e. financial assets acquired to generate a short-term profit (these assets are carried at fair value with gains or losses reported in income);

(*b*) held to maturity (these assets are carried at amortised cost);

(*c*) loans and receivables (the assets are carried at amortised cost);

(*d*) available for sale (these assets are carried at fair value with gains or losses reported in equity).

13.7 Dividends proposed

Dividends proposed and unpaid at the period end are not liabilities and do not appear either on the face of the balance sheet or in the notes to the balance sheet. They are disclosed in the notes to the Income Statement.

13.8 Interest accrued on loan notes

Such interest which is unpaid at the period end is a current liability and appears on the face of the balance sheet.

13.9 Fundamental accounting principles

The following accounting principles (or 'valuation rules' as they are called in the Fourth Directive of the EU) must be followed when preparing company financial statements:

1 A company is presumed to be a going concern.
2 Accounting policies must be applied consistently from year to year.
3 The prudence concept must be followed.
4 The accruals concept must be observed.
5 Each component item of assets and liabilities must be valued separately. As an instance of this, if a company has five different types of inventory, each type must be valued separately at the lower of cost and net realisable value, rather than be valued on an aggregate basis.
6 Amounts in respect of items representing assets or income may *not* be set off against items representing liabilities or expenditure. Thus an amount owing on a hire purchase contract cannot be deducted from the value of the asset in the balance sheet.

13.10 True and fair view

If complying with the requirements of International GAAP would cause the financial statements not to be 'true and fair' then the directors must set aside such requirements. This is unlikely to arise and should not be done without real justification.

13.11 Layout of the balance sheet for internal use

As mentioned in Section 13.2, companies have considerable freedom in how they present information in their balance sheet. Balance sheets for internal use (Exhibit 13.1) are typically far more detailed than those prepared for publication and are normally in a form similar to those shown in Chapter 45 of *Business Accounting 1*:

Exhibit 13.1 A balance sheet for internal use

Balance Sheet as at 31 December 2008

	Cost (£)	Depreciation to date (£)	Net book value (£)
Non-current assets			
Goodwill	255,000	30,000	225,000
Buildings	1,050,000	110,000	940,000
Equipment	120,000	36,000	84,000
Motor vehicles	172,000	69,600	102,400
	1,597,000	245,600	1,351,400
Current assets			
Inventory		91,413	
Accounts receivable		186,100	
Bank		8,390	
			285,903
Total assets			1,637,303
Current liabilities			
Accounts payable		113,700	
Loan note interest accrued		15,000	
Taxation		50,000	
		178,700	
Non-current liabilities			
10% loan notes		300,000	
Total liabilities			(478,700)
Net assets			1,158,603

Equity		
Share capital	Authorised	Issued
Preference shares	200,000	200,000
Ordinary shares	1,000,000	700,000
	1,200,000	900,000
Reserves		
Share premium	100,000	
General reserve	60,000	
Retained profits	98,603	
		258,603
Total equity		1,158,603

Note: The presentation of goodwill is contrary to that required by International GAAP. This is permissable for balance sheets prepared for internal use. As you will see in Exhibit 13.2, in a balance sheet prepared for publication, the treatment must comply with International GAAP.

 Activity 13.2 Why do you think companies might ignore the requirements of International GAAP in this case?

13.12 Layout of the balance sheet for publication under International GAAP

Exhibit 13.2 shows the same information as Exhibit 13.1 but in a form that complies with International GAAP.

Exhibit 13.2 A balance sheet for publication

Balance Sheet as at 31 December 2008

	£	£
Non-current assets		
Property, plant and equipment		1,126,400
Intangible assets		225,000
		1,351,400
Current assets		
Inventory	91,413	
Trade and other receivables	186,100	
Cash and cash equivalents	8,390	
		285,903
Total assets		1,637,303
Current liabilities		
Trade and other payables	113,700	
Financial liabilities	15,000	
Liability for current tax	50,000	
	178,700	
Non-current liabilities		
Financial liabilities	300,000	
Total liabilities		(478,700)
Net assets		1,158,603
Equity		
Issued capital		900,000
Reserves		258,603
Total equity		1,158,603

→

Notes: 1 This is the minimum presentation required. All detail for each line will appear as a note to the balance sheet.

      2 The IAS terminology for the lines has been used. This is less informative for many companies which, rather than explaining in the notes for example that non-current financial liabilities comprise of 10% loan notes would use that term on the face of the balance sheet rather than 'non-current financial liabilities'. Exhibit 13.3 shows the same information as Exhibit 13.2 but with more informative line descriptors. Such presentation is equally permissible under International GAAP.

Exhibit 13.3 A balance sheet for publication using alternative line descriptors

Balance Sheet as at 31 December 2008

	£	£
Non-current assets		
Property, plant and equipment		1,126,400
Goodwill		225,000
		1,351,400
Current assets		
Inventory	91,413	
Accounts receivable	186,100	
Bank	8,390	
		285,903
Total assets		1,637,303
Current liabilities		
Accounts payable	113,700	
Loan note interest accrued	15,000	
Taxation	50,000	
	178,700	
Non-current liabilities		
10% loan notes	300,000	
Total liabilities		(478,700)
Net assets		1,158,603
Equity		
Share capital		900,000
Reserves		258,603
Total equity		1,158,603

Note: This layout is probably more appropriate at your stage of studies. Do not forget to include notes expanding the detail where appropriate – in this case notes would be needed for this purpose for property, plant and equipment; share capital; and reserves. You are free, however, simply to replace these single-line items with the expanded details on the face of the balance sheet. Unless otherwise indicated, examiners would need to award full marks for either approach, i.e. detailed, or single-line entries plus relevant expanding notes.

13.13 Small and medium-sized company reporting requirements

In the UK, small and medium-sized companies (for a definition, *see* Section 12.2) do not have to file a full set of financial statements with the Registrar of Companies. If they wish, they can send a full set of financial statements, but what they *have* to file is a minimum of 'modified financial statements'. They still have to send a full set to their own shareholders who request them – the modified financial statements refer only to those filed with the Registrar.

In addition, there is no audit requirement for small companies with a turnover of not more than £5.6 million and a balance sheet total of not more than £2.8 million, unless 10% or more of shareholders sign a formal notice requesting an audit and lodge this at the registered office.

 Activity 13.3   Why do you think these small companies are exempted from having their financial statements audited?

13.14   Modified financial statements of small companies

1 Neither an income statement nor a directors' report has to be filed with the Registrar.
2 A balance sheet has to be filed.

13.15   Modified financial statements of medium-sized companies

1 The income statement can begin with the figure of gross profit or loss.
2 The analyses of revenue and profit normally required as notes to the financial statements need not be given.
3 The balance sheet must be filed.

Note: Illustrative examples of published company financial statements including notes required are at the end of Chapter 14.

13.16   Summary financial statements

A public limited company (plc) may send a summary financial statement to members in place of the full statements, but any member who requests the full statements must be sent them. The summary statement must:

(*a*) state that it is only a summary of information in the company's financial statements and the directors' report;
(*b*) contain a statement by the company's auditors of their opinion as to whether the summary financial statement is consistent with those financial statements and that reports and complies with the requirements of the section in the Companies Act (CA 2006, Section 427 (unquoted company) or 428 (quoted company)) that permits the distribution of this summary financial statement and the regulations made under it;
(*c*) state whether the auditors' report on the financial statements was unqualified or qualified, and if it was qualified set out the report in full together with any further material needed to understand the qualification;
(*d*) state whether the auditors' report on the annual accounts contained a statement under either:
  (*i*) CA 2006 Section 498(2)(a) or (b) – accounting records or returns inadequate or financial statements not agreeing with records or returns; or
  (*ii*) CA 2006 Section 498(3) – failure to obtain necessary information and explanations and, if so, set out the statement in full.

 Activity 13.4   Why do you think companies are allowed to send their shareholders summary financial statements rather than the full statements?

13.17 Website publication

A quoted company must make its annual accounts and reports available on a website.

> ### Learning outcomes
>
> **You should now have learnt:**
>
> **1** There are minimum requirements for the preparation of published balance sheets.
>
> **2** Balance sheets for internal use need not comply with these requirements.
>
> **3** Accounting standards must be complied with when preparing financial statements intended to present a true and fair view.
>
> **4** Some small companies are exempted from having their financial statements audited.
>
> **5** Small and medium-sized companies may file modified financial statements with the Registrar if they wish.
>
> **6** Public limited companies may send a summary financial statement to members in place of the full statements, but any member who requests the full statements must be sent them.

Answers to activities

13.1 Some of the liabilities, for example, financial liabilities maybe either current (e.g. interest accrued) or non-current (e.g. loan notes).

13.2 When a balance sheet is prepared for internal use, it is the company's management that will use it. They may wish to know, for example, how much of goodwill has been impaired and that information is easier to see on the face of the balance sheet rather than by comparing the current balance sheet with the one prepared when the goodwill was first recognised.

13.3 Having financial statements audited is estimated as costing an average of £1,200. While this appears a small amount of money, it can be relatively expensive for small companies, particularly when they are newly formed and are making little or no profit. However, although this is a good reason for such companies not incurring the expense of having an audit, as the sole reason for not having an audit it goes against the principles upon which the need for an audit was based. A far more realistic explanation is that errors and misleading items in the financial statements of small companies have far less of an impact than in the case of larger organisations and, on a purely cost/benefit basis, it is unlikely that the costs of having an audit will be sufficiently offset by any amendments or clarifications that an audit may bring.

13.4 Many shareholders are not accountants and have no understanding of many of the items in full financial statements. Rather than sending them information they will not understand, shareholders may be sent simplified information containing those parts of the financial statements that they are both more likely to understand and more likely to be interested in having. This saves the companies (and their shareholders) money which, in itself, is a good thing. It also increases the possibility that shareholders will actually look at the financial statements.

Review questions

13.1 The following balances remained in the books of Polk Ltd on 31 March 2004, *after* the income statement had been drawn up. You are to draft the balance sheet as at 31 March 2004 in accordance with the relevant accounting standards.

	Dr £	Cr £
Ordinary share capital: £1 shares		250,000
Preference share capital: 50p shares		100,000
Calls account (ordinary shares)	1,000	
Development costs	32,000	
Goodwill	104,000	
Land and buildings – at cost	250,000	
Plant and machinery – at cost	75,000	
Provision for depreciation: Buildings		20,000
Provision for depreciation: Plant and machinery		30,000
Shares in undertakings in which the company has a participating interest	70,000	
Inventory: Raw materials	6,000	
Inventory: Finished goods	36,000	
Accounts receivable: Trade	24,000	
Amounts owed by associate entities	10,000	
Prepayments	2,000	
Loan notes (*see* Note 1)		50,000
Bank overdraft (repayable on demand)		16,000
Accounts payable: Trade (payable within one year)		17,000
Bills payable (*see* Note 2)		4,000
Share premium		50,000
Capital redemption reserve		10,000
General reserve		20,000
Retained profits		43,000
	610,000	610,000

Notes:

1 Of the loan notes, £20,000 is repayable in five months' time, while the other £30,000 is repayable in four years' time.

2 Of the bills payable, £3,000 is in respect of a bill to be paid in eight months' time and £1,000 for a bill payable in 14 months' time.

3 The depreciation charged for the year was: Buildings £5,000, Plant and machinery £7,500.

→ **13.2** After the income statement and statement of changes in equity have been prepared for the year ending 30 April 2007, the following balances remain in the books of Tickers plc. Prepare a balance sheet in accordance with the relevant accounting standards.

	£	£
Ordinary share capital		100,000
Share premium		60,000
Revaluation reserve		23,000
General reserve		30,000
Foreign exchange reserve		7,000
Retained profits		35,000
Patents, trade marks and licences	6,000	
Goodwill	42,000	
Land and buildings	280,000	
Provision for depreciation: Land and buildings		80,000
Plant and machinery	90,000	
Provision for depreciation: Plant and machinery		47,000
Inventory of raw materials: 30 April 2007	24,000	
Work in progress: 30 April 2007	9,000	
Finished goods: 30 April 2007	21,000	
Accounts receivable: Trade	84,000	
Accounts receivable: Other	3,000	
Prepayments and accrued income	2,000	
Loan notes (redeemable in 6 months' time)		50,000
Loan notes (redeemable in 4½ years' time)		40,000
Bank overdraft (repayable in 3 months)		3,000
Trade accounts payable (payable in next 12 months)		26,000
Trade accounts payable (payable after 12 months)		2,000
Bills of exchange (payable within 12 months)		5,000
Corporation tax (payable in 9 months' time)		38,000
National insurance (payable in next month)		1,000
Pensions contribution owing		8,000
Deferred taxation		6,000
	561,000	561,000

13.3 The following trial balance has been extracted from the books of Baganza plc as at 30 September 2007:

	£000	£000
Administrative expenses	400	
Called up share capital (1,200,000 ordinary shares of £1 each)		1,200
Cash at bank and in hand	60	
Corporation tax (overpayment for the year to 30 September 2006)		20
Deferred taxation (at 1 October 2006)		460
Distribution costs	600	
Dividends received (on 31 March 2007)		249
Freehold property:		
at cost	2,700	
accumulated depreciation (at 1 October 2006)		260
Interim dividend (paid in June 2007)	36	
Investments in United Kingdom companies	2,000	
Plant and machinery:		
at cost	5,200	
accumulated depreciation (at 1 October 2006)		3,600
Purchases	16,000	
Research expenditure	75	
Retained profits (at 1 October 2006)		2,022
Inventory (at 1 October 2006)	2,300	
Trade accounts payable		2,900
Trade accounts receivable	2,700	
Turnover		21,360
	£32,071	£32,071

Additional information:
1 The inventory at 30 September 2007 was valued at £3,600,000.
2 Depreciation for the year to 30 September 2007 is to be charged on the historic cost of the non-current assets as follows:
    Freehold property: 5%
    Plant and machinery: 15%
3 The basic rate of income tax is assumed to be 27%.
4 The directors propose a final dividend of 60p per share.
5 The company was incorporated in 2000.
6 Corporation tax based on the profits for the year at a rate of 35% is estimated to be £850,000.
7 A transfer of £40,000 is to be made to the deferred taxation account.

Required:
In so far as the information permits, prepare Baganza plc's income statement for the year ending 30 September 2007, and a balance sheet as at that date in accordance with the appropriate accounting standards.
    However, formal notes to the accounts are not required, although detailed workings should be submitted with your answer, which should include your calculation of earnings per share.

(*Association of Accounting Technicians*)

13.4A   The trial balance of Jeremina plc as at 31 March 2002 is as follows:

	Dr £	Cr £
Preference share capital: 50p shares		200,000
Ordinary share capital: £1 shares		300,000
General reserve		25,000
Exchange reserve		15,000
Retained profits as on 31 March 2001		21,000
Inventory 31 March 2001	184,000	
Sales		1,320,000
Returns inwards	34,000	
Purchases	620,000	
Carriage inwards	6,000	
Wages (putting goods into a saleable condition)	104,000	
Wages: Warehouse staff	40,000	
Wages and salaries: Sales staff	67,000	
Wages and salaries: Administrative staff	59,000	
Motor expenses (see Note (ii))	29,000	
General distribution expenses	17,000	
General administrative expenses	12,000	
Loan note interest	2,000	
Royalties receivable		5,000
Directors' remuneration	84,000	
Bad debts	10,000	
Discounts allowed	14,000	
Discounts received		11,000
Plant and machinery at cost (see Note (iii))	240,000	
Provision for depreciation: Plant and machinery (see Note (iv))		72,000
Motor vehicles at cost (see Note (ii))	120,000	
Provision for depreciation: Motors (see Note (iv))		48,000
Goodwill	200,000	
Development costs	24,000	
Trade accounts receivable	188,000	
Trade accounts payable		45,000
Bank overdraft (repayable on demand)		7,000
Bills of exchange payable (all due within one year)		7,000
Loan notes (redeemable in three years' time)		30,000
Preference dividend	12,000	
Ordinary dividend	40,000	
	2,106,000	2,106,000

Notes:
(i)   Inventory of finished goods on 31 March 2002 £163,000.
(ii)   Motor expenses and depreciation on motors to be apportioned: Distribution ⁴/₅, Administrative ¹/₅.
(iii)   Plant and machinery depreciation to be apportioned: Cost of sales ⁷/₁₀, Distribution ¹/₅, Administrative ¹/₁₀.
(iv)   Depreciate the following non-current assets on cost: Motor vehicles 20%, Plant and machinery 15%.
(v)   Accrue corporation tax on profits of the year £38,000. This is payable on 31 December 2002.

You are to draw up:
(a) a detailed income statement for the year ending 31 March 2002 for internal use, and
(b) an income statement for publication, also a balance sheet as at 31 March 2002.

13.5A You are presented with the following information relating to Plott plc for the year to 31 March 2011:

	£000
Bank overdraft	500
Called-up share capital (issued and fully paid)	2,100
Corporation tax (based on the profit for the year to 31 March 2011)	900
Accounts payable	300
Accounts receivable	200
Deferred taxation (credit)	80
Non-current assets: at cost	3,800
accumulated depreciation (at 31 March 2011)	1,400
Non-current asset investments: at cost	100
Retained profits (at 1 April 2010: credit)	1,200
Proposed dividend	420
Retained profit (for the year to 31 March 2011)	585
Share premium account	315
Inventory: at cost (at 31 March 2011)	400
Trade accounts payable	2,000
Trade accounts receivable	5,300

Additional information:

1 The above information has been obtained after the compilation of the company's income statement for the year ending 31 March 2001.

2 Details of non-current assets for the year to 31 March 2011 are as follows:

	£000
(a) At cost	
At 1 April 2010	3,400
Additions	600
Disposals	200
(b) Accumulated depreciation	
At 1 April 2010	1,200
Additions	500
Disposals	300

3 The market value of the non-current asset investments at 31 March 2011 was £110,000. There were no purchases or sales of non-current asset investments during the year.

4 Inventories comprise finished goods. The replacement cost of these goods is similar to the value indicated in the balance sheet.

5 Assume that the basic rate of income tax is 25%.

6 The authorised share capital of the company consists of 2,500,000 ordinary shares of £1 each.

Required:

In so far as the information permits, prepare Plott plc's balance sheet as at 31 March 2011 in accordance with the *minimum* requirements of the relevant accounting standards.

Notes:

1 Where appropriate, formal notes must be attached to your balance sheet; and

2 Detailed working should be submitted with your answer.

(*Association of Accounting Technicians*)

→ **13.6A** The following information has been extracted from the books of Quire plc as at 30 September 2011.

	£000	£000
Bank overdraft		2,400
Called-up share capital (ordinary shares of £1 each)		4,000
Deferred taxation		200
Delivery expenses	2,800	
Non-current assets: at cost	3,500	
accumulated depreciation (at 1 October 2010)		1,100
Loan notes held	100	
Loan note interest (net)		40
Interest payable	400	
Interim dividend paid	60	
Office expenses	3,000	
Other creditors		180
Other debtors	160	
Retained profits (at 1 October 2010)		820
Purchases	12,000	
Sales		19,000
Inventory (at 1 October 2010)	500	
Trade accounts payable		100
Trade accounts receivable	5,320	
	£27,840	£27,840

The following additional information is to be taken into account:

1 Inventory at 30 September 2011 was valued at £400,000.
2 All items in the above trial balance are shown net of value added tax.
3 At 30 September 2011, £130,000 was outstanding for office expenses, and £50,000 had been paid in advance for delivery van licences.
4 Depreciation at a rate of 50% is to be charged on the historic cost of the tangible non-current assets using the reducing balance method: it is to be apportioned as follows:

	%
Cost of sales	60
Distribution	30
Administration	10
	100

There were no purchases or sales of non-current assets during the year to 30 September 2011.
5 The following rates of taxation are to be assumed:

	%
Corporation tax	35
Income tax	25
Value added tax	17.5

The corporation tax payable based on the profits for the year to 30 September 2011 has been estimated at £80,000.
6 A transfer of £60,000 is to be made from the deferred taxation account.
7 The directors propose to pay a final ordinary dividend of 3p per share.

Required:
In so far as the information permits, prepare Quire plc's income statement for the year ending 30 September 2011, and a balance sheet as at that date in accordance with the requirements of the relevant accounting standards.

Note: Formal notes to the accounts are NOT required, but detailed workings should be submitted with your answer.

(*Association of Accounting Technicians*)

13.7A The following trial balance has been extracted from the books of Patt plc as at 31 March 2010:

	Dr £000	Cr £000
Bank overdraft		25
Called-up share capital (ordinary shares of £1 each)		1,440
Accounts payable		55
Accounts receivable	50	
Non-current assets: at cost	300	
accumulated depreciation (at 1 April 2009)		120
Marketing expenses	100	
Office expenses	200	
Retained profits (at 1 April 2009)		200
Production expenses	2,230	
Purchases (net of VAT)	3,700	
Sales (amounts invoiced, net of VAT)		7,000
Inventory (at 1 April 2009)	130	
Trade accounts payable		160
Trade accounts receivable	2,290	
	£9,000	£9,000

Additional information:

1 Following the preparation of the above trial balance, the following additional matters need to be taken into account:

(*a*) inventory at 31 March 2010 was valued at £170,000;

(*b*) at 31 March 2010, £20,000 was owing for office expenses, and £15,000 had been paid in advance for marketing expenses;

(*c*) a customer had gone into liquidation owing the company £290,000; the company does not expect to recover any of this debt;

(*d*) the company decides to set up an allowance for doubtful debts amounting to 5% of the outstanding trade accounts receivable as at the end of each financial year; and

(*e*) depreciation is to be charged on the non-current assets at a rate of 20% on cost; it is to be apportioned as follows:

	%
Marketing	20
Office	10
Production	70
	100

Note: There were no acquisitions or disposals of non-current assets during the year to 31 March 2010.

2 Corporation tax (based on the accounting profit for the year at a rate of 35%) is estimated to be £160,000. The basic rate of income tax is assumed to be 25%.

3 The directors are to recommend the payment of a dividend of 10p per ordinary share.

Required:

In so far as the information permits, prepare Patt plc's income statement for the year ending 31 March 2010, and a balance sheet as at that date in accordance with the relevant accounting standards.

Notes:

(*i*) Where appropriate, formal notes should be attached to your income statement and balance sheet. However, a statement of accounting policies is NOT required.

(*ii*) Detailed workings should also be submitted with your solution. They should be clearly designated as such, and they must not form part of your formal notes.

(*Association of Accounting Technicians*)

Interpretation of Financial Statements 1

Introduction to accounting ratios

Learning objectives

After you have studied this chapter, you should be able to:

- calculate some basic accounting ratios
- use accounting ratios to calculate missing figures in financial statements
- offer some explanations for changes in these ratios over time

Introduction

In this chapter, you'll learn about the relationship between mark-up and margin and how to use the relationship between them and sales revenue and gross profit to find figures that are missing in the trading account. You will also learn how to calculate the inventory turnover ratio and some explanations for why these ratios change over time.

34.1 The need for accounting ratios

We will see in, Chapter 47, that accounting ratios are used to enable us to analyse and interpret accounting statements.

This chapter has been inserted at this point in the book simply so that you will be able to deal with the material in Chapter 35 which includes the drawing up of financial statements from incomplete records. The ratios described in this chapter will be sufficient for you to deduce the data needed to make the incomplete records into a complete set of records, so that you can then prepare the financial statements. Without the use of such accounting ratios, the construction of financial statements from incomplete records would often be impossible.

Activity 34.1 What do you think is meant by the term 'incomplete records'?

34.2 Mark-up and margin

The purchase cost, gross profit and selling price of goods or services may be shown as:

> Cost Price + Gross Profit = Selling Price

When shown as a fraction or percentage of the *cost price*, the gross profit is known as the **mark-up**.

When shown as a fraction or percentage of the *selling price*, gross profit is known as the **margin**. We can calculate mark-up and margin using this example:

$$\text{Cost Price} + \text{Gross Profit} = \text{Selling Price}$$
$$\text{£4} \quad + \quad \text{£1} \quad = \text{£5}$$

$\text{Mark-up} = \dfrac{\text{Gross Profit}}{\text{Cost Price}}$ as a fraction, or if required as a percentage, multiply by 100:

$$\frac{£1}{£4} = \frac{1}{4}, \quad \text{or } \frac{1}{4} \times 100 = 25 \text{ per cent.}$$

$\text{Margin} = \dfrac{\text{Gross Profit}}{\text{Selling Price}}$ as a fraction, or if required as a percentage, multiply by 100:

$$\frac{£1}{£5} = \frac{1}{5}, \quad \text{or } \frac{1}{5} \times 100 = 20 \text{ per cent.}$$

Activity 34.2 Can you see a simple rule connecting mark-up to margin?

34.3 Calculating missing figures

Now we can use these ratios to complete trading accounts where some of the figures are missing. In all the examples in this chapter, we shall:

● assume that all the inventory in a business has the same rate of mark-up; and
● ignore wastages and theft of inventory.

Example 1

The following figures are for the year 2011:

	£
Inventory 1.1.2011	400
Inventory 31.12.2011	600
Purchases	5,200

A uniform rate of mark-up of 20 per cent is applied.

Required: find the gross profit and the sales figures.

Firstly, you prepare the trading account section of the income statement with the various missing figures shown as blank (or highlighted with a highlight pen, or with '?' inserted where the missing number should go):

Trading Account section of the Income Statement for the year ending 31 December 2011

	£	£
Sales		?
Less Cost of goods sold:		
Inventory 1.1.2011	400	
Add Purchases	5,200	
	5,600	
Less Inventory 31.12.2011	(600)	
		(5,000)
Gross profit		?

Answer:

It is known that:	Cost of goods sold + Gross profit	= Sales
and you know that you can use		
mark-up to find the profit, because:	Cost of goods sold + Percentage mark-up	= Sales
So:	£5,000 + 20%	= Sales
and Sales =	£5,000 + £1,000	= £6,000

The trading account section of the income statement can be completed by inserting the Gross Profit £1,000 and £6,000 for Sales.

Trading Account section of the Income Statement for the year ending 31 December 2011

	£	£
Sales		6,000
Less Cost of goods sold:		
Inventory 1.1.2011	400	
Add Purchases	5,200	
	5,600	
Less Inventory 31.12.2011	(600)	
		(5,000)
Gross profit		1,000

Example 2

Another business has the following figures for 2012:

	£
Inventory 1.1.2012	500
Inventory 31.12.2012	800
Sales	6,400

A uniform rate of margin of 25 per cent is in use.

Required: find the gross profit and the figure for purchases.

Trading Account section of the Income Statement for the year ending 31 December 2012

	£	£
Sales		6,400
Less Cost of goods sold:		
Inventory 1.1.2012	500	
Add Purchases	?	
	?	
Less Inventory 31.12.2012	800	?
Gross profit		?

Answer:	Cost of goods sold + Gross profit = Sales	
Moving items about:	Sales	− Gross profit = Cost of goods sold
	Sales	− 25% margin = Cost of goods sold
	£6,400	− £1,600 = £4,800

Now the following figures are known:

		£	£
Sales			6,400
Less Cost of goods sold:			
Inventory 1.1.2012		500	
Add Purchases	(1)	?	
	(2)	?	
Less Inventory 31.12.2012		(800)	
			(4,800)
Gross profit			1,600

The two missing figures are found by normal arithmetical deduction:

(2) less £800	= £4,800
Therefore (2)	= £5,600
So that: £500 opening inventory + (1)	= £5,600
Therefore (1)	= £5,100

The completed trading account section of the income statement can now be shown:

Trading Account section of the Income Statement for the year ending 31 December 2012

	£	£
Sales		6,400
Less Cost of goods sold:		
Inventory 1.1.2012	500	
Add Purchases	5,100	
	5,600	
Less Inventory 31.12.2012	(800)	
		(4,800)
Gross profit		1,600

This technique is found very useful by retail stores when estimating the amount to be bought if a certain sales target is to be achieved. Alternatively, inventory levels or sales figures can be estimated given information as to purchases and opening inventory figures.

34.4 The relationship between mark-up and margin

As you learnt in Activity 34.2, both of these figures refer to the same gross profit, but express it as a fraction or a percentage of different figures. This connection through gross profit means that if you know one of the two (*mark-up* or *margin*) you will be able to determine the other.

You learnt a simple definition of this relationship in Activity 34.2. Now we'll take it further so that you can use the relationship in any situation.

If the mark-up is known, to find the margin take the same numerator to be numerator of the margin, then for the denominator of the margin take the total of the mark-up's denominator plus the numerator. For example:

Mark-up		Margin
$\dfrac{1}{4}$	$\dfrac{1}{4+1} =$	$\dfrac{1}{5}$
$\dfrac{2}{11}$	$\dfrac{2}{11+2} =$	$\dfrac{2}{13}$

If the margin is known, to find the mark-up take the same numerator to be the numerator of the mark-up, then for the denominator of the mark-up take the figure of the margin's denominator less the numerator:

Margin		Mark-up
$\dfrac{1}{6}$	$\dfrac{1}{6-1} =$	$\dfrac{1}{5}$
$\dfrac{3}{13}$	$\dfrac{3}{13-3} =$	$\dfrac{3}{10}$

Be sure that you learn this relationship. It is very often required in examinations.

34.5   Manager's commission

Managers of businesses are very often remunerated by a basic salary plus a percentage of profits. It is quite common to find the percentage expressed not as a percentage of profits before such commission has been deducted, but as a percentage of the amount remaining after deduction of the commission.

For example, assume that profits before the manager's commission was deducted amounted to £8,400 and that the manager was entitled to 5% of the profits remaining after the commission was deducted. If 5% of £8,400 was taken, this amounts to £420, and the profits remaining would amount to £7,980. However, 5% of £7,980 amounts to £399 so that the answer of £420 is wrong.

The formula to be used to arrive at the correct answer is:

$$\frac{\text{Percentage commission}}{100 + \text{Percentage commission}} \times \text{Profit before commission}$$

In the above problem this would be used as follows:

$$\frac{5}{100 + 5} \times £8,400 = £400 \text{ manager's commission.}$$

The profits remaining are £8,000 and as £400 represents 5% of it the answer is verified.

 Activity 34.3   The same approach is taken when you want to know the VAT included in a bill you've paid. Assuming a VAT rate of 17.5%, what is the VAT when the total bill is £235?

34.6   Commonly used accounting ratios

There are some ratios that are in common use for the purpose of comparing one period's results with those of a previous period. Two of those most in use are the ratio of gross profit to sales, and the rate of **inventory turnover** (also known as 'stockturn').

Gross profit as percentage of sales

The basic formula is:

$$\frac{\text{Gross profit}}{\text{Sales}} \times \frac{100}{1} = \text{Gross profit as percentage of sales}$$

This represents the amount of gross profit for every £100 of sales revenue. If the answer turned out to be 15%, this would mean that for every £100 of sales revenue £15 gross profit was made before any expenses were paid.

This ratio is used as a test of the profitability of the sales. Just because sales revenue has increased does not, of itself, mean that gross profit will increase.

 Activity 34.4   Spend a minute thinking about this and then write down why you think gross profit won't always increase if sales revenue increases.

Exhibit 34.1 illustrates this.

Exhibit 34.1

Trading account sections of the income statements for the years ending 31 December 2009 and 2010

	£	2009 £	£	2010 £
Sales		7,000		8,000
Less Cost of goods sold:				
Opening inventory	500		900	
Add Purchases	6,000		7,200	
	6,500		8,100	
Less Closing inventory	(900)		(1,100)	
		(5,600)		(7,000)
Gross profit		1,400		1,000

In the year 2009 the gross profit as a percentage of sales was

$$\frac{1,400}{7,000} \times \frac{100}{1} = 20\%$$

In the year 2010 it became

$$\frac{1,000}{8,000} \times \frac{100}{1} = 12\frac{1}{2}\%$$

Sales had increased but, as the gross profit percentage had fallen by a relatively greater amount, the gross profit has fallen. There can be many reasons for such a fall in the gross profit percentage, including:

1 Perhaps the goods being sold have cost more, but the selling price of the goods has not risen to the same extent.
2 There may have been a greater wastage or theft of goods.
3 There could be a difference in how much has been sold of each sort of goods, called the sales mix, between the two years, with different kinds of goods carrying different rates of gross profit per £100 of sales.
4 Perhaps in order to increase sales, reductions have been made in the selling price of goods.

(The last reason was used in the answer to Activity 34.4, but any of these possible causes could have been used instead.) These are only some of the possible reasons for the decrease. The idea of calculating the ratio is to show that the profitability per £100 of sales has changed. The business would then try to find out why and how such a change has taken place.

As the figure of sales revenue less returns inwards is also known as 'turnover', the ratio is sometimes referred to as 'gross profit percentage on turnover'. However, the most frequently used names for it are 'gross profit on sales' and 'gross margin'.

Inventory turnover

If we always kept just £100 of inventory at cost which, when we sold it, would always sell for £125, and we sold this amount eight times in a year, we would make 8 × £25 = £200 gross profit. The quicker we sell our inventory (we could say the quicker we turn over our inventory) the more the profit we will make, if our gross profit percentage stays the same.

To check on how quickly we are turning over our inventory we can use the formula:

$$\frac{\text{Cost of goods sold}}{\text{Average inventory}} = \text{Number of times inventory is turned over within a period}$$

Activity 34.5 Spend a minute thinking about this and then write down why you think it might be useful to know how many times we turn over our inventory in a period.

It would be best if the average inventory held could be calculated by valuing the inventory quite a few times each year, then dividing the totals of the figures obtained by the number of valuations. For instance, monthly inventory figures could be added up and then divided by twelve. This would provide a far more meaningful figure for 'average' inventory. However, it is quite common, especially in examinations or in cases where no other information is available, to calculate the average inventory by using the figures for the opening inventory plus the closing inventory divided by two. Using the figures in Exhibit 34.1 we can calculate the inventory turnover for 2009 and 2010:

$$2009 \qquad \frac{5,600}{(500 + 900) \div 2} = 8 \text{ times per year}$$

$$2010 \qquad \frac{7,000}{(900 + 1,100) \div 2} = 7 \text{ times per year}$$

Instead of saying that the inventory turnover is so many times per year, we could say on average how long we keep inventory before we sell it. We do this by the formula:

To express it in months: $12 \div \text{Inventory turnover} = x \text{ months}$
To express it in days: $365 \div \text{Inventory turnover} = x \text{ days}$

From Exhibit 34.1:

	2009	*2010*
In months	$\dfrac{12}{8} = 1.5 \text{ months}$	$\dfrac{12}{7} = 1.7 \text{ months}$
In days	$\dfrac{365}{8} = 45.6 \text{ days}$	$\dfrac{365}{7} = 52.1 \text{ days}$

All the above figures are rounded to one decimal place.

When the rate of inventory turnover is falling it can be due to such causes as a slowing down of sales activity, or to keeping a higher amount of inventory than is really necessary. The ratio does not prove anything by itself, it merely prompts enquiries as to why it should be changing.

Current ratio

This ratio is current assets:current liabilities and indicates whether there are sufficient relatively liquid (i.e. convertible cash) assets to meet short-term debts when due. It is discussed in greater detail in Chapter 47.

This chapter has introduced ratios so as to help you understand the material in the next chapter.

In Chapter 47, we will return again to ratios, and cover the topic with a more advanced and detailed survey of what a range of ratios can be used for.

Learning outcomes

You should now have learnt:

1 That accounting ratios can be used to deduce missing figures, given certain assumptions.

2 That if the mark-up is known, the margin can easily be calculated.

3 That if the margin is known, the mark-up can easily be calculated.

4 How to calculate the gross profit on sales and inventory turnover ratios.

5 What may cause these ratios to change over time.

Answers to activities

34.1 Incomplete records exist where a business does not keep detailed accounting records. Perhaps it only operates a cash book, maybe not even that. In these circumstances, accountants have to construct the records that would have existed had a proper set of books been maintained, so that they can then prepare the financial statements. This involves working through invoices, receipts and bank records, plus any records the business has actually kept, and trying to identify and record what actually occurred during the period. Because of the logical relationships that exist between many of the items in financial statements, and because of the unambiguous rule of double entry, ratios defining the relationship between various items can be used to assist in this investigation. So, for example, if you know what inventory was held at the start, what was purchased and what inventory is left at the end, you can easily work out what was sold.

34.2 If you take mark-up and add one to the denominator (the bottom part of the fraction), you get the margin. This is *always* the case when the numerator (the top line) is 1.

34.3 As you will remember from Chapter 19 (p. 223), you use the same formula but replace both the '5s' in the example with '17.5' and 'Profit before commission' with the total amount of the bill:

$$\frac{17.5}{100 + 17.5} \times £235 = £35$$

This is a *very* useful formula to know. You would be wise to remember it.

34.4 Gross profit may increase at the same rate as sales revenue because demand absorbed more units at the original price. This is normally the case if you make relatively small increases in the volume offered for sale when demand is currently exceeding supply. However, when sales volume increases, it is often partly because selling price has been reduced. Even though total sales volume has increased, sales revenue per unit is less than previously and so gross profit as a percentage of sales revenue will be lower than previously. Unless enough additional units are sold to recover the profit lost as a result of cutting the selling price, total gross profit will fall, not increase.

When a business is in trouble and cutting selling prices to try to make more profits by selling more units, it can often look as if it is doing much better if you only look at the sales revenue and gross profit figures. However, when you calculate the gross profit as a percentage of sales (i.e. the gross margin) and compare it with the previous gross margin, you can see that the business is possibly doing less well than before in terms of overall profitability.

34.5 It is useful to know as you can compare how quickly inventory is turning over now compared to the past. If it is turning over more slowly now (i.e. less times in a period than before), inventory levels may have grown higher, which may mean that the costs of holding inventory have risen. This rise in inventory levels may be due to our now buying more inventory every time we place an order – perhaps suppliers are offering discounts for larger orders. This may be good, or it may be bad. You need to investigate the situation and find out. Hence, checking the trend in inventory turnover alerts you to the possibility that costs may be rising and that they may exceed any savings being made. You can also check your rate of inventory turnover with those of your competitors, enabling you to detect whether your ordering and storing practices are significantly different from theirs. If they are, you would then investigate what is happening so as to ensure that you are not wasting resources unnecessarily.

Review questions

34.1 V. Fraga is a trader who sells all of his goods at 30% above cost. His books give the following information at 31 December 2013:

	£
Inventory 1 January 2013	20,000
Inventory 31 December 2013	27,000
Sales for year	160,000

You are required to:
(a) Ascertain cost of goods sold.
(b) Show the value of purchases during the year.
(c) Calculate the profit made by Fraga.

Show your answer in the form of the trading account section of an income statement.

34.2A R. Jack gives you the following information as at 31 March 2014:

	£
Inventory 1 April 2013	14,000
Purchases	82,000

Jack's mark-up is 40% on 'cost of goods sold'. His average inventory during the year was £17,000. Draw up an income statement for the year ending 31 March 2014.

(a) Calculate the closing inventory as at 31 March 2014.
(b) State the total amount of profit and loss expenditure Jack must not exceed if he is to maintain a *net* profit on sales of 8%.

34.3 I. Fail's business has a rate of inventory turnover of 10 times per year. Average inventory is £14,000. Mark-up is 40%. Expenses are 60% of gross profit.

You are to calculate:
(a) Cost of goods sold.
(b) Gross profit.
(c) Turnover.
(d) Total expenses.
(e) Net profit.

34.4A The following figures relate to the retail business of A. Bell for the month of July 2012. Goods which are on sale fall into two categories, X and Y.

	Category X	Category Y
Sales to the public at manufacturer's recommended list price	£9,000	£24,000
Trade discount allowed to retailers	15%	18%
Total expenses as a percentage of sales	14%	14%
Annual rate of inventory turnover	10	16

You are to calculate for each category of goods:
(a) Cost of goods sold.
(b) Gross profit.
(c) Total expenses.
(d) Net profit.
(e) Average inventory at cost, assuming that sales are distributed evenly over the year, and that each month is of the same length.

→

34.5 The following trading account is extracted from the income statement for the year ending 31 December 2011 and is given to you by the owner of the business, M. Pole:

	£	£
Sales		271,400
Less Cost of goods sold:		
Opening inventory	34,000	
Add Purchases	237,000	
	271,000	
Less Closing inventory	(41,000)	
		(230,000)
Gross profit		41,400

Pole says that normally he adds 20% to the cost of goods to fix the sales price. However, this year there were some arithmetical errors in these calculations.

(a) Calculate what his sales would have been if he had not made any errors.
(b) Given that his expenses remain constant at 9% of his sales, calculate his net profit for the year 2011.
(c) Work out the rate of inventory turnover for 2011.
(d) He thinks that next year he can increase his mark-up to 25%, selling goods which will cost him £260,000. If he does not make any more errors in calculating selling prices, you are to calculate the expected gross and net profits for 2012.

34.6A   **Trading Account for the year ending 31 December 2012**

	£		£
Inventory 1 January 2012	3,000	Sales	60,000
Purchases	47,000		
	50,000		
Inventory 31 December 2012	(4,500)		
Cost of sales	45,500		
Gross profit	14,500		
	60,000		60,000

R. Sheldon presents you with the trading account set out above.[Authors' note] He always calculates his selling price by adding 33⅓% of cost on to the cost price.

(a) If he has adhered strictly to the statement above, what should be the percentage of gross profit to sales?
(b) Calculate his actual percentage of gross profit to sales.
(c) Give two reasons for the difference between the figures you have calculated above.
(d) His suppliers are proposing to increase their prices by 5%, but R. Sheldon considers that he would be unwise to increase his selling price. To obtain some impression of the effect on gross profit if his costs should be increased by 5% he asks you to reconstruct his trading account to show the gross profit if the increase had applied from 1 January 2012.
(e) Using the figures given in the trading account at the beginning of the question, calculate R. Sheldon's rate of inventory turnover.
(f) R. Sheldon's expenses amount to 10% of his sales. Calculate his net profit for the year ending 31 December 2012.
(g) If all expenses remained unchanged, but suppliers of inventory increased their prices by 5% as in (d) above, calculate the percentage reduction in the amount of net profit which R. Sheldon's accounts would have shown.

(Edexcel, London Examinations: GCSE)

Authors' note: The trading account shown in the question has been prepared in an unconventional way. It is, in effect, a different form of presentation of the trading account section of the income statement. Do not, yourself, ever use this format when preparing an income statement.

34.7 L. Mann started business with £5,000 in the bank on 1 April. The business transactions during the month were as follows:

(*i*)   Took £300 out of the bank for petty cash
(*ii*)   Bought a second-hand van and paid by cheque £3,500
(*iii*)   Bought goods on credit from A. Supplier for £2,500
(*iv*)   Sold goods for cash for £300
(*v*)   Sold goods on credit for £1,000 to B. Safe
(*vi*)   Returned faulty goods to A. Supplier £500
(*vii*)   Paid sundry expenses of £50 in cash
(*viii*) Paid the rent of £500 by cheque
(*ix*)   Withdrew cash drawings of £500

Inventory at cost at 30 April was £1,250.

Required:
(*a*)   Prepare the ledger accounts recording the transactions.
(*b*)   Prepare the trial balance at 30 April.
(*c*)   Prepare an income statement for the month ending 30 April.
(*d*)   Prepare a statement of financial position as at 30 April.
(*e*)   Calculate the percentages of:
    (*i*)   gross profit to sales
    (*ii*) net profit to opening capital.
(*f*)   Comment on:
    (*i*)   the relationship between drawings and net profit and why it is important that Mann keeps an eye on it
    (*ii*) working capital.

34.8A Arthur deals in bicycles. His business position at 1 October was as follows:

Capital £3,369
Inventory £306 (3 × Model A bicycles @ £54 and 3 × Model B @ £48)
Balance at bank £3,063

Having established good relations with his supplier he is able to obtain bicycles on one month's credit. He kept notes of all transactions during October which he then summarised as follows:

(*i*)   Purchased on credit from Mr Raleigh: 12 Model A at £54 and 10 Model B at £48. Total purchase £1,128.
(*ii*)   Sales for cash were: 11 Model A at £81 and 8 Model B at £72.
(*iii*) Paid rent by cheque £60, advertising £66 and miscellaneous expenses £12.
(*iv*)   Drawings were £150.

Arthur's valuation of the closing inventory was £456 as at 31 October.

Required:
(*a*)   Prepare a statement showing the bank transactions during October.
(*b*)   Check the closing inventory valuation.
(*c*)   Prepare a statement showing the gross profit and net profit for October and calculate the percentages of gross profit to sales and net profit to sales.
(*d*)   Prepare an income statement for the month of October together with a statement of financial position as at 31 October.
(*e*)   Prepare a statement to show where the profit for the month has gone.

34.9 The following information is available for the years 2010, 2011 and 2012:

	2010	2011	2012
	£	£	£
Opening inventory	10,000	20,000	28,000
Purchases	70,000	86,000	77,000
	80,000	106,000	105,000
Less Closing inventory	(20,000)	(28,000)	(23,000)
Cost of sales	60,000	78,000	82,000
Sales	90,000	125,000	120,000
Gross profit	30,000	47,000	38,000

The inventory valuations used above at the end of 2010 and at the end of 2011 were inaccurate. The inventory at 31 December 2010 had been under-valued by £1,000, whilst that at 31 December 2011 had been over-valued by £3,000.

Required:
(a) Give the corrected figures of gross profit for each of the years affected by the errors in inventory valuation.
(b) Using the figures in the revised trading accounts, calculate for each year:
  (i) the percentage of gross profit to sales, and
  (ii) the rate of turnover of inventory.

An introduction to the analysis and interpretation of accounting statements

Learning objectives

After you have studied this chapter, you should be able to:

● explain how the use of ratios can help in analysing the profitability, liquidity, efficiency and capital structure of businesses

● calculate the main accounting ratios

● interpret the results of calculating accounting ratios

● explain the advantages and disadvantages of the gearing of an organisation being high or low

● explain how the proportion of costs that are fixed and variable impacts profit at different levels of activity

● explain the relevance of IAS 1 and IAS 8, and accounting standards in general, to the preparation of financial statements

Introduction

In this chapter, you'll learn how to calculate and interpret the most commonly used accounting ratios. You'll learn how to assess an organisation's profitability, liquidity, efficiency, and capital structure using ratio analysis. In addition, you'll learn more about IAS 1 (*Presentation of financial statements*) and IAS 8 (*Accounting policies, changes in accounting estimates and errors*), of their importance, and of the importance of accounting standards in general to the preparation of financial statements.

47.1 The need for ratios

Without ratios, financial statements would be largely uninformative to all but the very skilled. With ratios, financial statements can be interpreted and usefully applied to satisfy the needs of the reader.

For example, let's take the performance of four companies, all dealing in the same type of goods:

	Gross profit	Sales
	£	£
Company *A*	200,000	848,000
Company *B*	300,000	1,252,000
Company *C*	500,000	1,927,500
Company *D*	350,000	1,468,400

Suppose you want to know which company gets the 'best' profit. Simply inspecting these figures and trying to decide which performance was the best, and which was the worst, is virtually impossible. To bring the same basis of comparison to each company we need some form of common measure. As you have already seen in Chapter 34, one measure commonly used is a ratio – the gross margin, i.e. the amount of gross profit on sales as a percentage. Applying this to these four companies, we find that their margins are:

	%
Company A	23.58
Company B	23.96
Company C	25.94
Company D	23.84

On this basis, Company C with a gross margin of 25.94% or, in other words, £25.94 gross profit per £100 sales, has performed better than the other companies.

47.2   How to use ratios

You can only sensibly compare like with like. There is not much point, for example, in comparing the gross profit percentage of a wholesale chemist with that of a restaurant.

Similarly, figures are only comparable if they have been built up on a similar basis. The sales figures of Company X, which treats items as sales *only when cash is received*, **cannot** be properly compared with those of Company Z, which treats items as sales *as soon as they are invoiced*.

Another instance of this could be that of inventory turnover, which you learnt about in Chapter 34. Let's compare two companies, Company K and Company L. They are both toy shops so would seem to be comparable. Both companies have annual sales revenue of £400,000. However, the average inventory of K is £50,000 whilst that of L is £20,000. Cost of sales for both companies is £200,000, so their inventory turnover ratios are:

$$\frac{\text{Cost of sales}}{\text{Average inventory}} \qquad \frac{K}{\frac{200,000}{50,000}} = 4 \qquad \frac{L}{\frac{200,000}{20,000}} = 10$$

It looks as though L has managed to turn its inventory over ten times during the year compared with K, four times. Is this true? Well, it depends. Let's imagine that K had a financial year end of 30 November, just before Christmas, so toy inventory would be extremely high; that L had a year end of 31 January when, following the Christmas sales, its inventory had dropped to the year's lowest level; and that at 30 November both this year and last year L also had inventory valued at £50,000. Can you see how the difference in the timing of the year end can affect this ratio significantly?

Ratios therefore need *very* careful handling. They are extremely useful if used and interpreted appropriately, and very misleading otherwise.

47.3   Users of ratios

As you know, there are a great many parties interested in analysing financial statements, including shareholders, lenders, customers, suppliers, employees, government agencies and competitors. Yet, in many respects, they will be interested in different things. There is not, therefore, any definitive, all-encompassing list of points for analysis that would be useful to all these stakeholder groups.

Nevertheless, it is possible to construct a series of ratios that together will provide all of them with something that they will find relevant and from which they can investigate further if necessary.

Ratio analysis is a first step in financially assessing an entity. It removes some of the mystique surrounding the financial statements and makes it easier to pinpoint items which it would be interesting to investigate further.

Exhibit 47.1 shows some categories of ratios and indicates some of the stakeholder groups that would be interested in them.

Exhibit 47.1

Ratio category	Examples of interested groups
Profitability	Shareholders, management, employees, creditors, competitors, potential investors
Liquidity	Shareholders, suppliers, creditors, competitors
Efficiency	Shareholders, potential purchasers, competitors
Shareholder	Shareholders, potential investors
Capital structure	Shareholders, lenders, creditors, potential investors

As you will see, some ratios belong in more than one of these categories.

47.4 Categories of ratio

Profitability ratios

1 Return on capital employed (ROCE)

This is one of the most important profitability ratios, as it encompasses all the other ratios, and because an adequate return on capital employed is why people invest their money in a business in the first place.

(a) Sole proprietors
In this chapter, we will use the average of the capital account as the figure for capital employed, i.e. (opening balance + closing balance) ÷ 2.

In Businesses *C* and *D* in Exhibit 47.2, both businesses have made the same amount of net profit, but the capitals employed are different.

Exhibit 47.2

Statements of Financial Position

	C	D
	£	£
Non-current assets + Current assets – Current liabilities	100,000	160,000
Capital accounts		
Opening balance	80,000	140,000
Add Net profit	36,000	36,000
	116,000	176,000
Less Drawings	(16,000)	(16,000)
	100,000	160,000

$$\boxed{\text{Return on capital employed (ROCE)} = \frac{\text{Net profit}}{\text{Capital employed}} \times 100}$$

therefore,

$$\overset{C}{\underset{(80{,}000 + 100{,}000) \div 2}{\underline{36{,}000}}} \times \frac{100}{1} = 40\% \qquad\qquad \overset{D}{\underset{(140{,}000 + 160{,}000) \div 2}{\underline{36{,}000}}} \times \frac{100}{1} = 24\%$$

The ratio illustrates that what is important is not simply how much profit has been made but how well the capital has been employed. Business C has made far better use of its capital, achieving a return of £40 net profit for every £100 invested, whereas D has received only a net profit of £24 per £100.

(b) Limited companies
There is no universally agreed definition of return on capital employed for companies. The main ones used are:

(i)   return on capital employed sourced from ordinary shareholders;
(ii) return on capital employed sourced from all long-term suppliers of capital.

Let's now look at each of these:

(i)   In a limited company this is known as **Return on Owners' Equity (ROOE)** or, more commonly, **Return on Shareholders' Funds (ROSF)**. From now on, we shall use the second of these terms, 'Return on Shareholders' Funds', but you will need to remember that when you see 'Return on Owners' Equity', it is the same as ROSF.
    The 'Return' is the net profit for the period. The term 'Shareholders' Funds' means the book value of all things in the statement of financial position that describe the owners' capital and reserves. 'Owners' are the holders of the **ordinary** share capital. This is calculated: Ordinary Share Capital + all Reserves including Retained Profits.
(ii) This is often known simply as 'Return on Capital Employed' (ROCE). The word 'Return' in this case means net profit + any preference share dividends + loan notes and long-term loan interest. The word 'Capital' means Ordinary Share Capital + Reserves including Retained Profits + Preference Shares + Loan notes and Long-term Loans.

Given the following statements of financial position and income statements of two companies, P Ltd and Q Ltd, the calculations of ROSF and ROCE can be attempted:

Statements of Financial Position as at 31 December

	P Ltd	P Ltd	Q Ltd	Q Ltd
	£	£	£	£
	2008	*2009*	*2008*	*2009*
Non-current assets	520,000	560,000	840,000	930,000
Net current assets	280,000	340,000	160,000	270,000
	800,000	900,000	1,000,000	1,200,000
10% loan notes	–	–	(120,000)	(120,000)
	800,000	900,000	880,000	1,080,000
Share capital (ordinary)	300,000	300,000	500,000	500,000
Reserves	500,000	600,000	380,000	580,000
	800,000	900,000	880,000	1,080,000

Income Statements for the year ending 31 December 2009 (extracts)

	P Ltd £	Q Ltd £
Net profit	220,000	380,000
Dividends	(120,000)	(180,000)
	100,000	200,000

Return on Shareholders' Funds (ROSF)

P Ltd	Q Ltd
$\dfrac{220,000}{(800,000 + 900,000) \div 2} \times \dfrac{100}{1} = 25.9\%$	$\dfrac{380,000}{(880,000 + 1,080,000) \div 2} \times \dfrac{100}{1} = 38.8\%$

Return on Capital Employed (ROCE)

	P Ltd	Q Ltd
Same as ROSF[Note 1] = 25.9%		$\dfrac{380,000 + 12,000^{\text{Note 2}}}{(1,000,000 + 1,200,000) \div 2} \times \dfrac{100}{1} = 35.6\%$

Note 1: The return on capital employed by all long-term sources of capital (in *Q Ltd's* case, the shareholders' funds and the debentures) is the same as the ROSF in the case of *P Ltd*, as it has no debentures.

Note 2: The loan note interest (i.e. 10% of £120,000 = £12,000) must be added back, as it was an expense in calculating the £380,000 net profit.

2 Gross profit as a percentage of sales

The formula is:

$$\boxed{\dfrac{\text{Gross profit}}{\text{Sales}} \times 100}$$

Go back to Chapter 34 to refresh your understanding of gross profit as a percentage of sales.

3 Net profit as a percentage of sales

The formula is:

$$\boxed{\dfrac{\text{Net profit}}{\text{Sales}} \times 100}$$

Liquidity ratios

You saw earlier in this section that the ratio called 'return on capital employed' is used to provide an overall picture of profitability. It cannot always be assumed, however, that profitability is everything that is desirable. It must be stressed that accounting is used, not just to calculate profitability, but also to provide information that indicates whether or not the business will be able to pay its creditors, expenses, loans falling due, etc. at the correct times. Failure to ensure that these payments are covered effectively could mean that the business would have to be closed down. Being able to pay one's debts as they fall due is known as being 'liquid'.

It is also essential that a business is aware if a customer or borrower is at risk of not repaying the amount due. New customers are usually vetted prior to being allowed to trade on credit rather than by cash. For private individuals, there are credit rating agencies with extensive records of the credit histories of many individuals. For a small fee, a company can receive a report indicating whether a new customer might be a credit risk. Similarly, information can be purchased concerning companies that indicates their solvency, i.e. whether they are liable to be bad credit risks.

The difference between these two sources of information is that, while the information on private individuals is based on their previous credit record, that of the companies is generally based on a ratio analysis of their financial statements.

When it comes to the liquidity of a business, both its own ability to pay its debts when due and the ability of its debtors to pay the amount they owe to the business are of great importance. Ratio analysis that focuses upon liquidity (or solvency) of the business generally starts with a look at two ratios (**liquidity ratios**) that are affected most by these two aspects of liquidity, the **current ratio** and the **acid test ratio**.

1 Current ratio

This compares assets which will become liquid within approximately 12 months (i.e. total current assets) with liabilities which will be due for payment in the same period (i.e. total current liabilities) and is intended to indicate whether there are sufficient short-term assets to meet the short-term liabilities.

$$\text{Current ratio} = \frac{\text{Current assets}}{\text{Current liabilities}}$$

When calculated, the ratio may be expressed as either a ratio to 1, with current liabilities being set to 1, or as a 'number of times', representing the relative size of the amount of total current assets compared with total current liabilities.

With *all* ratios, once you have performed the calculation, you need to decide what it tells you. To do so, there is no point in using a universal guide, such as *'the ratio should always lie between 1:1 and 2:1'*. Any such guidance is at best useless and at worst misleading. Instead, you need to consider the result in its context.

For example:

- What is the norm in this industrial sector? (For example, retailers are often below 1:1.)
- Is this company significantly above or below that norm?
- If so, can this be justified after an analysis of the nature of these assets and liabilities, and of the reasons for the amounts of each held?

You need to contextualise *every* ratio you calculate when you are trying to understand what the result means, not just this one.

2 Acid test ratio

This shows that, provided creditors and debtors are paid at approximately the same time, a view might be made as to whether the business has sufficient liquid resources to meet its current liabilities.

$$\text{Acid test ratio} = \frac{\text{Current assets} - \text{inventory}}{\text{Current liabilities}}$$

 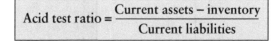 **Activity 47.1**   What is the difference between the formulae for the current ratio and the acid test ratio?

Exhibit 47.3 shows how two businesses may have similar profitability, yet their liquidity positions may be quite different.

Exhibit 47.3

	E		F	
	£	£	£	£
Non-current assets		40,000		70,000
Current assets				
Inventory	30,000		50,000	
Accounts receivable	45,000		9,000	
Bank	15,000		1,000	
		90,000		60,000
Total assets		130,000		130,000
Current liabilities: accounts payable		(30,000)		(30,000)
Net assets		100,000		100,000
Capital				
Opening capital		80,000		80,000
Add Net profit		36,000		36,000
		116,000		116,000
Less Drawings		(16,000)		(16,000)
		100,000		100,000

Note: Sales for both *E* and *F* amounted to £144,000. Gross profits for *E* and *F* were identical at £48,000.

Profitability is the same for both businesses. However, there is a vast difference in the liquidity of the two businesses.

Current ratios

$$E = \frac{90,000}{30,000} = 3$$

$$F = \frac{60,000}{30,000} = 2$$

This looks adequate on the face of it, but let's look at the acid test ratio:

Acid test ratios

$$E = \frac{60,000}{30,000} = 2$$

$$F = \frac{10,000}{30,000} = 0.33$$

This reveals that *F* may be in trouble, as it will probably find it difficult to pay its current liabilities on time. **No matter how profitable a business is, unless it is adequately liquid it may fail.**

However, although a business should be adequately liquid, it is possible for it to have too high a current ratio or acid test ratio. If too many resources are being held as current assets, it would make these two ratios appear healthy, but those resources could have been used more profitably – you don't get any interest on inventory! Too high a balance in a current account at the bank also means that resources are being wasted.

Activity 47.2 Why is inventory omitted from the acid test ratio?

Efficiency ratios

1 Inventory turnover

Inventory turnover measures how efficient a business is at maintaining an appropriate level of inventory. When it is not being as efficient as it used to be, or is being less efficient than its competitors, this may indicate that control over inventory levels is being undermined.

A reduction in inventory turnover can mean that the business is slowing down. Inventory may be piling up and not being sold. This could lead to a liquidity crisis, as money may be being taken out of the bank simply to increase inventory which is not then sold quickly enough.

Note: In this chapter, we are classifying inventory turnover as an efficiency ratio. It is often also classified as a liquidity ratio.

For Exhibit 47.3 the cost of sales for each company was £144,000 − £48,000 = £96,000. If opening inventory had been E £34,000 and F £46,000 then, using the average of the opening and closing inventory, the inventory turnovers would have been:

	E	F
Cost of sales	$\dfrac{96,000}{(34,000+30,000)\div 2}$	$\dfrac{96,000}{(46,000+50,000)\div 2}$
Average inventory	$=\dfrac{96,000}{32,000}=3$ times	$=\dfrac{96,000}{48,000}=2$ times

It appears that *F*'s inventory may be too high, perhaps because it is having difficulty selling it compared with *E*. Or perhaps it is *E* that has a problem obtaining enough inventory. Either way, further investigation is needed.

2 Accounts receivable/sales ratio

The resources tied up in accounts receivable is an important ratio subject. Money tied up unnecessarily in accounts receivable is unproductive money. In the example in Exhibit 47.3 the **accounts receivable/sales ratio** can be calculated for the two companies as:

	E	F
Accounts receivable/sales	$45,000/144,000 = 1 : 3.2$	$9,000/144,000 = 1 : 16$

This relationship is often translated into the length of time a debtor takes to pay:

E	F
$365 \times \dfrac{1}{3.2} = 114$ days	$365 \times \dfrac{1}{16} = 22.8$ days

Why Company *E* should have allowed so much time for its debtors to pay is a matter for investigation. Possibly the company was finding it harder to sell goods, and to sell at all was eventually forced to sell to customers on long credit terms. It could well be that *E* has no proper credit control system, whereas *F* has an extremely efficient one.

When the ratio is deteriorating (i.e. it is rising) this may signal liquidity problems.

Note: In this chapter, we are classifying accounts receivable/sales as an efficiency ratio. Like inventory turnover, it is often also classified as a '*liquidity ratio*', as it can reveal both efficiency and liquidity issues. The next ratio, accounts payable/purchases, also provides this double aspect view.

3 Accounts payable/purchases ratio

Assuming that purchases for *E* amounted to £92,000 and for *F* £100,000 then the **accounts payable/purchases ratio** can be calculated for each as:

	E	F
Accounts payable/purchases	30,000/92,000 = 1:3.07	30,000/100,000 = 1:3.3

This also is often translated into the length of time we take to pay our creditors. This turns out to be:

$$E \qquad\qquad F$$

$$365 \times \frac{1}{3.07} = 119 \text{ days} \qquad\qquad 365 \times \frac{1}{3.3} = 110 \text{ days}$$

Shareholder ratios

These will include the following ratios. Note that 'price' means the price of the shares on the Stock Exchange.

1 Earnings per share (EPS)

The formula is:

$$\text{Earnings per share} = \frac{\text{Net profit after interest and tax and preference dividends}}{\text{Number of ordinary shares issued}}$$

This gives the shareholder (or prospective shareholder) a chance to compare one year's earnings with another in terms easily understood. Many people consider EPS to be *the* most important ratio that can be calculated from the financial statements.

2 Price/earnings ratio (P/E)

The formula is:

$$\text{Price/earnings ratio} = \frac{\text{Market price per share}}{\text{Earnings per share}}$$

This puts the price into context as a multiple of the earnings. The greater the P/E ratio, the greater the demand for the shares.

3 Dividend yield

This is found by the formula:

$$\text{Dividend yield} = \frac{\text{Gross dividend per share}}{\text{Market price per share}}$$

This measures the real rate of return by comparing the dividend paid to the market price of a share.

4 Dividend cover

This is found by the formula:

$$\text{Dividend cover} = \frac{\text{Net profit after tax and preference dividends}}{\text{Ordinary dividends paid and proposed}}$$

This gives the shareholder some idea as to the proportion that the ordinary dividends bear to the amount available for distribution to ordinary shareholders. Usually, the dividend is described as being so many times covered by profits made. If, therefore, the dividend is said to be *three times covered*, it means that one-third of the available profits is being distributed as dividends.

Capital structure ratios

Gearing

The relationship of equity shares (ordinary shares) to other forms of long-term financing (long-term loans plus preference shares) can be extremely important. Analysts are, therefore, keen to ascertain a ratio to express this relationship.

There is more than one way of calculating **gearing**. The most widely used method is as follows:

$$\frac{\text{Long-term loans} + \text{Preference shares}}{\text{Ordinary share capital} + \text{Reserves} + \text{Preference shares} + \text{Long-term liabilities}} \times 100$$

This formula is sometimes abbreviated to:

$$\frac{\text{Prior charge capital}}{\text{Total capital}} \times 100$$

which is exactly the same.

Long-term loans include loan notes. Total capital includes preference shares and ordinary shares, all the reserves and long-term loans.

Let's look at the calculations of the gearing of two small companies, *A Ltd* and *B Ltd* in Exhibit 47.4. Both have been trading for five years.

Exhibit 47.4

Year 5: items per statement of financial position	A Ltd £	B Ltd £
10% loan notes	20,000	200,000
10% preference shares	40,000	100,000
Ordinary shares	200,000	40,000
Reserves	140,000	60,000
	400,000	400,000

Gearing ratios:

$$A\ Ltd: \quad \frac{20,000 + 40,000}{20,000 + 40,000 + 200,000 + 140,000} \times \frac{100}{1} = 15\% \text{ (low gearing)}$$

$$B\ Ltd: \quad \frac{200,000 + 100,000}{200,000 + 100,000 + 40,000 + 60,000} \times \frac{100}{1} = 75\% \text{ (high gearing)}$$

Now let us look at how dividends are affected, given the same level of profits made before payment of loan note interest and preference dividends. All the profits made in these years are to be distributed.

A Ltd: Low gearing		Year 6	Year 7	Year 8	Year 9
		£	£	£	£
Profits before deducting the following:		40,000	30,000	60,000	80,000
Loan note interest	2,000				
Preference dividend	4,000				
		(6,000)	(6,000)	(6,000)	(6,000)
Profits left for ordinary dividend		34,000	24,000	54,000	74,000
Rate of ordinary dividend		17%	12%	27%	37%
B Ltd: High gearing		Year 6	Year 7	Year 8	Year 9
		£	£	£	£
Profits before deducting the following:		40,000	30,000	60,000	80,000
Loan note interest	20,000				
Preference dividend	10,000				
		(30,000)	(30,000)	(30,000)	(30,000)
Profits left for ordinary dividend		10,000	–	30,000	50,000
Rate of ordinary dividend		25%	–	75%	125%

A company with a high percentage gearing ratio is said to be *high geared*, whereas one with a low percentage gearing is said to be *low geared*. As you can see from the above example, the proportionate effect gearing has upon ordinary shareholders is far greater in a high geared company, ranging from 0 to 125 per cent dividend for B Ltd, whilst the range of ordinary dividends for A Ltd varied far less and lay between 17 and 37 per cent.

A high rate of debt (i.e. long-term loans and preference shares) means that in bad times very little might be left over for ordinary shareholders after payment of interest on the debt items and also preference dividends. In good times, however, the ordinary shareholders will enjoy a far higher return than in a low geared company.

This means that people investing in ordinary shares in a high geared company are taking a far greater risk with their money than if they had invested instead in a low geared company. It would have only required a drop of profits of £5,000 in Year 6 for B Ltd to find that there would be no ordinary dividends at all for Years 6 and 7. Such a drop in Year 6 for A Ltd would still have allowed a dividend of 12 per cent for both of Years 6 and 7. Investors therefore who are prepared to risk their money in the hope of large dividends would have chosen B Ltd, whilst those who wanted to cut down on their risk and be more certain about receiving dividends would choose A Ltd.

Changing the gearing of a company

The management might decide that for various reasons it would like to change the gearing of the company. It can do this as follows:

To reduce gearing	*To increase gearing*
1 By issuing new ordinary shares	1 By issuing loan notes
2 By redeeming loan notes	2 By buying back ordinary shares in issue
3 By retaining profits	3 By issuing new preference shares

Such changes will be influenced by what kinds of investors the company wishes to attract. A highly geared company will attract risk-taking buyers of ordinary shares, whilst a low geared company will be more attractive to potential ordinary shareholders who wish to minimise risk.

Other ratios

There are a large number of other ratios which could be used, far more than can be mentioned in a textbook such as this. It will depend on the type of company, exactly which ratios are the most important and it is difficult to generalise too much.

Different users of the financial statements will want to use the ratio analysis which is of vital concern to them. If we can take as an example a bank which lends money to a company, it will want to ensure two things:

(a) that the company will be able to pay interest on the loan as it falls due; *and*
(b) that it will be able to repay the loan on the agreed date.

The bank is therefore interested in:

(a) short-term liquidity, concerning payment of loan interest; and
(b) long-term solvency for eventual repayment of the loan.

Possible ratios for each of these could be:

(a) *Short-term liquidity ratios*, mainly the *acid test ratio* and the *current ratio*, already described.
(b) *Long-term solvency ratios*, which might include:
  (i) *Operating profit/loan interest.* This indicates how much of the profits are taken up by paying loan interest. Too great a proportion would mean that the company was borrowing more than was sensible, as a small fall in profits could mean the company operating at a loss with the consequent effect upon long-term solvency.
  (ii) *Total external liabilities/shareholders' funds.* This ratio measures how much financing is done via share capital and retained profits, and how much is from external sources. Too high a proportion of external liabilities could bring about long-term solvency problems if the company's profit-making capacity falls by a relatively small amount, as outside liabilities still have to be met.
  (iii) *Shareholders' funds/total assets (excluding intangibles).* This highlights the proportion of assets financed by the company's own funds. Large falls in this ratio will tend to show a difficulty with long-term solvency. Similarly, investors will want to see ratios suitable for their purposes, which are not the same as those for the bank. These will not only be used on a single company comparison, but probably with the average of the same type of ratios for other companies in the same industry.

47.5   The investor: choosing between shares and loan notes

The choice of an investor will always be related to the amount of acceptable risk. We can list the possible investments under the headings of risk.

Lowest risk

Loan note holders have their interest paid to them whether or not profits are made. This contrasts with shares, both preference and ordinary, where there have to be profits available for distribution as dividends.

In addition, should there be insufficient cash funds available to pay loan note interest, many loan notes give their holders the right to sell off some or all of the assets of the company, and to recoup the amount of their loan notes before anyone else has a claim. Such an investment does not have as much security as, say, government stocks, but it certainly ranks above the shares of that same company.

Medium risk

Preference shareholders have their dividends paid after the loan note interest has been paid, but before the ordinary shareholders. They still are dependent upon profits being available for distribution. If they are of the cumulative variety then any shortfall can be carried forward to future years and paid before any ordinary dividends are taken.

Highest risk

Ordinary shareholders have the highest risk. They must give way to both loan note holders and to preference shareholders for interest and dividends. However, should the remaining profits for distribution be very high then they may get a high return on their money.

47.6 Trend figures

In examinations, a student is often given just one year's accounting figures and asked to comment on them. Obviously, lack of space on an examination paper may preclude several years' figures being given; also, the student lacks the time to prepare a comprehensive survey of several years' financial statements.

In real life, however, it would be extremely stupid for anyone to base decisions on just one year's financial statements, if more information was available. What is important for a business is not just what, say, accounting ratios are for one year, but what the trend has been.

Given two similar types of businesses G and H, both having existed for five years, if both of them had exactly the same ratios in Year 5, are they both equally desirable as investments? Given one year's accounts it may appear so, but if one had all the five years' figures it may not give the same picture, as Exhibit 47.5 illustrates.

Exhibit 47.5

	Years					
		1	2	3	4	5 (current)
Gross profit as % of sales	G	40	38	36	35	34
	H	30	32	33	33	34
Net profit as % of sales	G	15	13	12	12	11
	H	10	10	10	11	11
Net profit as % of capital employed	G	13	12	11	11	10
	H	8	8	9	9	10
Current ratio	G	3	2.8	2.6	2.3	2.0
	H	1.5	1.7	1.9	1.0	2.0

From these figures G appears to be the worse investment for the future, as the trend appears to be downwards. If the trend for G is continued it could be in a very dangerous financial situation in a year or two. Business H, on the other hand, is strengthening its position all the time.

Of course, it would be ridiculous to assert that H will continue on an upward trend. One would have to know more about the business to be able to judge whether or not that could be true.

However, given all other desirable information, trend figures would be an extra important indicator.

47.7 Fixed and variable costs

Some costs will remain constant whether activity increases or falls, at least within a given range of change of activity. These costs are called **fixed costs**. An example of this would be the rent of a shop which would remain at the same figure whether sales increased 10 per cent or fell 10 per cent. The same would remain true of such things as rates, fire insurance and so on.

Wages of shop assistants could also remain constant in such a case. If, for instance, the shop employed two assistants, then it would probably keep the same two assistants, on the same wages, whether sales increased or fell by 10 per cent.

Of course, such fixed costs can only be viewed as fixed in the short term. If sales doubled, then the business might well need a larger shop or more assistants. A larger shop would also certainly mean higher rates, higher fire insurance and so on, and with more assistants the total wage bill would be larger.

Variable costs, on the other hand, will change with swings in activity. Suppose that wrapping materials are used in the shop, then an increase in sales of 10 per cent should see 10 per cent more wrapping materials used. Similarly an increase of 10 per cent of sales, if all sales are despatched by parcel post, should see delivery charges increase by 10 per cent.

Some costs could be part fixed and part variable. Suppose that because of an increase in sales of 10 per cent, telephone calls made increased by 10 per cent. With telephone bills the cost is often in two parts, one for the rent of the phone line and the second part corresponding to the actual number of calls made. The rental charge would not change in such a case, and therefore this part of telephone expense would be 'fixed' whereas the calls part of the cost could increase by 10 per cent.

This means that the effect of a percentage change in activity could result in a greater or lesser percentage change in net profit, because the fixed costs (within that range of activity) may not alter.

Exhibit 47.6 shows the change in net profit in Business A, which has a low proportion of its expenses as 'fixed' costs, and in Business B, in which the 'fixed' costs are a relatively high proportion of its expenses.

Exhibit 47.6

Business A

	£	£	(a) If sales fell 10% £	£	(b) If sales rose 10% £	£
Sales		500,000		450,000		550,000
Less Cost of goods sold		(300,000)		(270,000)		(330,000)
Gross profit		200,000		180,000		220,000
Less Expenses:						
Fixed	30,000		30,000		30,000	
Variable	130,000		117,000		143,000	
		(160,000)		(147,000)		(173,000)
Net profit		40,000		33,000		47,000

Business B

	£	£	(a) If sales fell 10% £	£	(b) If sales rose 10% £	£
Sales		500,000		450,000		550,000
Less Cost of goods sold		(300,000)		(270,000)		(330,000)
Gross profit		200,000		180,000		220,000
Less Expenses:						
Fixed	120,000		120,000		120,000	
Variable	40,000		36,000		44,000	
		(160,000)		(156,000)		(164,000)
Net profit		40,000		24,000		56,000

The comparison of percentage changes in net profit therefore works out as follows:

	Business A	Business B
Decrease of 10% sales:		

$$\frac{\text{Reduction in profit}}{\text{Original profit}} \times \frac{100}{1} \qquad \frac{7,000}{40,000} \times \frac{100}{1} = 17.5\% \qquad \frac{16,000}{40,000} \times \frac{100}{1} = 40\%$$

Increase of 10% sales:

$$\frac{\text{Increase in profit}}{\text{Original profit}} \times \frac{100}{1} \qquad \frac{7,000}{40,000} \times \frac{100}{1} = 17.5\% \qquad \frac{16,000}{40,000} \times \frac{100}{1} = 40\%$$

You can see that a change in activity in Business *B*, which has a higher fixed expense content, results in greater percentage changes in profit: 40% in *B* compared with 17.5% in *A*.

47.8 Limitations of accounting statements

Financial statements are only partial information. They show, in financial terms, what has happened *in the past*. This is better than having no information at all, but much more information is needed to fully understand the present situation.

First, it is impossible to sensibly compare two businesses which are completely unlike one another solely by looking at their financial statements. To compare a supermarket's figures with those of a chemical factory would be rather pointless. It would be like comparing a lion with a lizard.

Second, there are a whole lot of factors that the past-focused financial statements do not disclose. The desire to keep to the money measurement concept, and the desire to be objective, both dealt with in Chapter 10, exclude a great deal of desirable information.

> **Go back to Chapter 10 to refresh your understanding of the money measurement concept and objectivity.**

Some typical desirable information can be listed but, beware, the list is indicative rather than exhaustive.

(*a*) What are the future plans of the business? Without knowing this, making an investment in a business would be sheer guesswork.
(*b*) Has the firm got good quality staff?
(*c*) Is the business situated in a location desirable for such a business? A shipbuilding business situated a long way up a river which was becoming unnavigable, to use an extreme example, could soon be in trouble.
(*d*) What is its position as compared with its competitors? A business manufacturing a single product, which has a foreign competitor which has just invented a much improved product which will capture the whole market, is obviously in for a bad time.
(*e*) Will future government regulations affect it? Suppose that a business which is an importer of goods from Country X, which is outside the EU, finds that the EU is to ban all imports from Country X?
(*f*) Is its plant and machinery obsolete? If so, the business may not have sufficient funds to be able to replace it.
(*g*) Is the business of a high-risk type or in a relatively stable industry?
(*h*) Has the business got good customers? A business selling largely to Country Y, which is getting into trouble because of shortage of foreign exchange, could soon lose most of its trade. Also if one customer was responsible for, say, 60 per cent of sales, then the loss of that one customer would be calamitous.
(*i*) Has the business got good suppliers of its needs? A business in wholesaling could, for example, be forced to close down if manufacturers decided to sell direct to the general public.
(*j*) Problems concerned with the effects of distortion of accounting figures caused by inflation (or deflation).

You can see that the list would have to be an extremely long one if it was intended to cover all possibilities.

47.9 IAS 1: *Presentation of financial statements*

The way in which accounting information is presented in financial statement is governed by IAS 1. It lays down the statements that must be produced and what they contain. It will be covered in detail in *Business Accounting 2*. Some aspects were covered briefly in Section 45.16.

47.10 IAS 8: *Accounting policies, changes in accounting estimates and errors*

Users of financial statements issued by organisations want to analyse and evaluate the figures contained within them. They cannot do this effectively unless they know which accounting policies have been used when preparing such statements.

Accounting policies

Accounting policies are defined in IAS 8 as:

> *the specific principles, bases, conventions, rules and practices applied by an entity in preparing and presenting financial statements.*

Accounting policies, therefore, define the processes whereby transactions and other events are reflected in the financial statements. The accounting policies selected should enable the financial statements to give a true and fair view and should be consistent with accounting standards and with relevant legislation.

When selecting an accounting policy, its appropriateness should be considered in the context of four characteristics that financial information must possess:

- **Relevance** – Does it produce information that is useful for assessing stewardship and for making economic decisions?
- **Reliability** – Does it reflect the substance of the transaction and other events that have occurred? Is it free of bias, i.e. neutral? Is it free of material error? If produced under uncertainty, has prudence been exercised?
- **Comparability** – Can it be compared with similar information about the entity for some other period or point in time?
- **Understandability** – Is it capable of being understood by users who have a reasonable knowledge of business and economic activities and accounting?

The financial information must also reflect economic reality and be neutral, prudent and complete. In addition, accounting policies must be applied consistently to 'similar transactions, events and conditions'.

Changes to accounting policies

Changes can only be made if required by a standard or if they result in reliable and more relevant information. Where the change is voluntary, it must be applied retrospectively and items restated.

Estimation techniques

Estimation techniques are the methods adopted in order to arrive at estimated monetary amounts for items that appear in the financial statements. Changes in accounting estimates relate to the carrying amount of an asset or liability or the amount of the periodic consumption of an asset. Where a change in an accounting estimate gives rise to changes in assets or liabilities, or relates to an item of equity, it is recognised by adjusting the carrying amount of the asset, liability or equity item in the period in which the change of estimate occurred.

Activity 47.3 From your knowledge of accounting, what do you think these methods may include? Think about this for a minute and then write down as many examples of estimation techniques as you can think of.

Examples of accounting policies

- The treatment of gains and losses on disposals of non-current assets – they could be applied to adjust the depreciation charge for the period, or they may appear as separate items in the financial statements.
- The classification of overheads in the financial statements – for example, some indirect costs may be included in the trading account section of the income statement, or they may be included in administration costs in the profit and loss account section of the income statement.
- The treatment of interest costs incurred in connection with the construction of non-current assets – these could be charged to profit and loss as a finance cost, or they could be capitalised and added to the other costs of creating the fixed assets (this is permitted by the relevant accounting standard).

Identifying whether an accounting policy has changed

This is done by considering whether any of three aspects have changed:

- **Recognition** – some items may be recognised in more than one way. For example, expenditure on developing new products may be recognised either as a profit and loss expense or as an asset in the statement of financial position.
- **Presentation** – how something is presented in the financial statements. For example, where certain indirect costs appear in the profit and loss account.
- **Measurement basis** – the monetary aspects of the items in the financial statements, such as the basis of valuation of inventory, say FIFO or LIFO.

If any of these three aspects have changed, this represents a change in accounting policy. If they haven't, something else has occurred, for example, the estimation technique in use. If depreciation was changed from straight line to reducing balance this would be **a change in estimation technique**, not a change in accounting policy. On the other hand, a decision to switch from valuing stock using FIFO to LIFO would constitute **a change in accounting policy** as the measurement basis would have changed.

47.11 Further thoughts on concepts and conventions

In Chapter 10, you were introduced to the concepts and conventions used in accounting. Since then, further chapters have consolidated your knowledge on specific points.

In recent years there has been a considerable change in the style of examinations in accounting at all levels. At one time nearly every examination question was purely computational, requiring you to prepare financial statements, draft journal entries, extract a trial balance and so on. Now, *in addition* to all that (which is still important) there are quite a lot of questions asking such things as:

- Why do we do it?
- What does it mean?
- How does it relate to the concepts and conventions of accounting?

Such questions depend very much on the interests and ingenuity of examiners. They like to set questions worded to find out those who can understand and interpret financial information, and eliminate those who cannot and simply try to repeat information learned by rote.

The examiners will often draw on knowledge from any part of the syllabus. It is therefore impossible for a student (or an author) to guess exactly how examiners will select questions and how they will word them.

An example of this is where the examiner could ask you to show how different concepts contradict one another. Someone who has just read about the concepts, and memorised them, could not answer this unless they had thought further about it. **Think about whether or not you could have answered that question before you read further.**

One instance is the use of the concept of consistency. Basically it says that one should keep to the same method of entering an item each year. Yet if the net realisable value of stock is less than cost, then the normal method of showing it at cost should be abandoned and the net realisable value used instead. Thus, at the end of one period, inventory may be shown at cost and at the end of the next period it will be shown at net realisable value. In this case the concept of prudence has overridden the concept of consistency.

Another instance of this is the practice of calculating profit based on sales whether they have been paid for or not. If the prudence concept were taken to extremes, then profit would only be calculated on a sale when the sale had been paid for. Instead, the realisation concept has overridden the prudence concept so you recognise a sale when it is reasonably certain that it will be paid for.

Review questions 47.11 to 47.20 are typical examination questions which obviously relate to concepts and conventions, and to a general understanding of the subject.

47.12 Some other accounting standards

As well as the accounting standards that you have read about in this book, there are some other standards which may appear in your examinations. We will cover them briefly here.

IAS 38: *Intangible assets*

Money spent on research and development presents a problem for accountants. You could argue that:

● Such costs are incurred so that profits can be earned in the future, and should therefore be carried forward to those future periods.
● Just because you have incurred such costs, you cannot be certain about future profitability occurring. It should therefore be written off as an expense in the period when the costs are incurred.

The costs can be divided between:

● **Research.** This is carried out to advance knowledge or application of knowledge.

Examples include:

● searching for new knowledge;
● search for revaluation of and final selection of applications of research findings or other knowledge;
● search for alternative materials, devices, products, processes, systems or services;
● formulation, design, evaluation and final selection of possible alternatives for new and improved materials, devices, products, processes, systems or services.

● **Development.** Work undertaken to develop research that creates an asset that will generate probable future economic benefits.

IAS 38 requires that all research expenditure must be recognised as an expense when it is incurred. However, development costs, subject to satisfying technical and commercial feasibility being confirmed, may be capitalised as an intangible asset and carried forward to future periods.

IAS 10: *Events after the date of the statement of financial position*

The statement of financial position is supposed to reflect the financial position of an organisation at the date of the statement of financial position. However, between the date of the statement of financial position and the date when the financial statements are authorised for issue, events may occur which mean that the financial statements will need to be amended.

The events can be divided between:

- **Adjusting events.** When these exist, the financial statements must be amended. Examples would include settlement of a court case, information indicating that an asset was impaired at the date of the statement of financial position, and the discovery of fraud or errors which show that the financial statements are incorrect.
- **Non-adjusting events.** These do not lead to amendments to the financial statements, but they may be shown as notes accompanying the financial statements. Examples would include changes in the market value of investments and dividends proposed.

IAS 37: *Provisions, contingent liabilities and contingent assets*

A provision may be defined as:

a liability of uncertain timing or amount.

A provision should only be recognised when an entity has a present obligation as a result of a past event *and* it is probable that an outflow of resources embodying economic benefits will have to occur *and* a reasonable estimate can be made of the amount involved.

A contingent liability may be defined as:

either a possible obligation arising from past events whose existence will be confirmed only by the occurrence of one or more uncertain future events not wholly within the entity's control; or a present obligation that arises from past events but is not recognised because it is not probable that an outflow of resources embodying economic benefits will be required to settle the obligation or the amount of the obligation cannot be measured with sufficient reliability.

An example of this could be where a legal action is being carried on, but the case has not yet been decided. For instance, a company may have been sued for £10 million damages, but the case is not yet over. The company may or may not have to pay the damages, but the case is so complex that it has no way of knowing.

A contingent asset may be defined as:

a possible asset arising from past events whose existence will be confirmed only by the occurrence or non-occurrence of one or more uncertain events not wholly within the entity's control.

Neither contingent liabilities nor contingent assets should be recognised. This is consistent with the prudence concept. A contingent liability should be disclosed.

Small and medium-sized entities and accounting standards

More than 95 per cent of all companies are small or medium sized. The UK has had an FRSSE (Financial Reporting Standard for Smaller Entities) for many years. It provides a simplified version of the body of UK accounting standards and is for use by 'smaller entities', i.e. small companies and other organisations that would be classified as 'small' if they were companies. In 2009, the IASB issued an IFRS for small and medium-sized entities. It reduces disclosure requirements and simplifies recognition and measurement requirements and is only 15 per cent of the length of the extant body of international standards.

Learning outcomes

You should now have learnt:

1 That comparing the trends to see if the ratios are getting better or worse as each period passes is essential for proper control. Prompt action needs to be taken where the trend in a ratio is deteriorating.

2 The importance of interpreting ratios in their context: that is, against those of other similar businesses or against the same ratios calculated for the same organisation using data from other time periods.

3 That a business must be both profitable *and* sufficiently liquid to be successful. One factor without the other can lead to serious trouble.

4 That careful credit control to ensure that the accounts receivable/sales ratio is not too high is usually essential to the well-being of any business.

5 That gearing affects the risk factor for ordinary share investors. High gearing means greater risk whilst low gearing means lower risks.

6 How to calculate and interpret the most commonly used ratios.

7 The relevance of ratio analysis to an assessment of liquidity, efficiency, profitability and capital structure.

8 That the relative amounts of fixed and variable costs can affect profit significantly when there are swings in business activity.

9 The importance of IAS 1 and IAS 8, and accounting standards in general, to the preparation of financial statements.

Answers to activities

47.1 The only difference in the items involved between the two ratios is that the acid test (or 'quick') ratio does not include inventory. Otherwise, it is identical to the current ratio, comparing current assets *other than inventory* to current liabilities.

47.2 Inventory is omitted as it is considered to be relatively illiquid, because, depending on prevailing and future market forces, it may be impossible it to convert it to cash in a relatively short time.

47.3 All depreciation methods and methods used to estimate doubtful debts are the main ones we have encountered so far in this book. However, we've also looked at asset revaluation, another aspect of accounting for which the methods adopted in arriving at the valuation would be considered estimation techniques. Basically, any method used to arrive at an *estimated* figure shown in the financial statements is an estimation technique. So, to answer the question fully, you need to make a list of all those items that appear in financial statements that are estimates. The methods used to arrive at the value used for those figures are all estimation techniques. This would include, for example, the method used in order to arrive at the proportion of an electricity bill spanning the period end that belongs in the period for which the financial statements are being prepared. More obviously estimates may be required for bad debts, inventory obsolescence, and the useful lives or consumption pattern of non-current assets.

Review questions

47.1 Calculate the inventory turnover ratio if average inventory is £40,000 and cost of sales is £280,000.

47.2 Calculate return on capital employed for a sole proprietor whose net profit was £60,000 and whose capital employed was £200,000.

47.3 Calculate gross profit as a percentage of sales if gross profit was £70,000 and sales were £400,000.

47.4 Calculate net profit as a percentage of sales if net profit was £45,000 and sales were £400,000.

47.5 (a) Calculate the current ratio if current assets are £50,000 and current liabilities are £30,000.
(b) If inventory is £28,000, what is the acid test ratio?

47.6 (a) If accounts receivable are £50,000 and sales are £250,000, what is the accounts receivable/sales ratio?
(b) How many days does the average debtor take to pay?

47.7 (a) If accounts payable are £40,000 and purchases are £240,000, what is the accounts payable/purchases ratio?
(b) How many days does the business take on average to pay its creditors?

47.8 From the following information, calculate:
(a) Earnings per share;
(b) Price/earnings ratio;
(c) Dividend yield; and
(d) Dividend cover.

(i) Net profit after interest and tax and preference dividends = £300,000.
(ii) Number of ordinary shares issued = 500,000.
(iii) Market price per share = £4.20.
(iv) Gross divided per share = 20p.
(v) Interest = £10,000.
(vi) Ordinary dividends paid and proposed = £120,000.

47.9 If prior charge capital = £30,000 and total capital = £210,000, what is the gearing?

47.10 You are to study the following financial statements for two furniture stores and then answer the questions which follow.

Financial Statements

	X		Y	
	£	£	£	£
Income Statements				
Sales		555,000		750,000
Less Cost of goods sold				
Opening inventory	100,000		80,000	
Add Purchases	200,000		320,000	
	300,000		400,000	
Less Closing inventory	(60,000)	(240,000)	(70,000)	(330,000)
Gross profit		315,000		420,000
Less Depreciation	5,000		15,000	
Wages, salaries and commission	165,000		220,000	
Other expenses	45,000	(215,000)	35,000	(270,000)
Net profit		100,000		150,000
Statements of financial position				
Non-current assets				
Equipment at cost	50,000		100,000	
Less Depreciation to date	(40,000)	10,000	(30,000)	70,000
Current assets				
Inventory	60,000		70,000	
Accounts receivable	125,000		100,000	
Bank	25,000	210,000	12,500	182,500
Total assets		220,000		252,500
Current liabilities				
Accounts payable		(104,000)		(100,500)
Net assets		116,000		152,000
Financed by:				
Capitals				
Balance at start of year		76,000		72,000
Add Net profit		100,000		150,000
		176,000		222,000
Less Drawings		(60,000)		(70,000)
Total capital		116,000		152,000

Required:

(a) Calculate the following ratios for each business:

(i)   gross profit as percentage of sales;

(ii)   net profit as percentage of sales;

(iii) expenses as percentage of sales;

(iv) inventory turnover;

(v)   rate of return of net profit on capital employed (use the average of the capital account for this purpose);

(vi) current ratio;

(vii) acid test ratio;

(viii) accounts receivable/sales ratio;

(ix) accounts payable/purchases ratio.

(b) Drawing upon all your knowledge of accounting, comment upon the differences and similarities of the accounting ratios for A and B. Which business seems to be the most efficient? Give possible reasons.

47.11A Study the following financial statements of two companies and then answer the questions which follow. Both companies are stores selling carpets and other floorcoverings. The values shown are in £000s.

	Spreadlight Ltd		Easylawn Ltd	
	£000	£000	£000	£000
Income Statements				
Sales		2,500		1,600
Less Cost of goods sold				
Opening inventory	190		110	
Add Purchases	2,100		1,220	
	2,290		1,330	
Less Closing inventory	(220)		(160)	
		(2,070)		(1,170)
Gross profit		430		430
Less Expenses				
Wages and salaries	180		130	
Directors' remuneration	70		120	
Other expenses	14		10	
		(264)		(260)
Net profit		166		170
Statements of financial position				
Non-current assets				
Equipment at cost	200		50	
Less Depreciation to date	(80)		(20)	
		120		30
Vans	64		48	
Less Depreciation to date	(26)		(16)	
		38		32
		158		62
Current assets				
Inventory	220		160	
Accounts receivable	104		29	
Bank	75		10	
		399		199
Total assets		557		261
Less Current liabilities				
Accounts payable		(189)		(38)
Net assets		368		223
Equity				
Issued share capital		200		100
Reserves				
General reserve	68		35	
Retained profits	100		88	
		168		123
Total equity		368		223

Notes:
Spreadlight paid a dividend of £140,000 during the year and transferred £30,000 to a general reserve of the year end. Easylawn paid a dividend of £112,000 during the year and transferred £30,000 to a general reserve of the year end. The retained profits brought forward at the start of the year were: Spreadlight £104,000; Easylawn £60,000.

Required:

(a) Calculate the following ratios for both Spreadlight Ltd and Easylawn Ltd:

(i) gross profit as percentage of sales;	(vi) current ratio;
(ii) net profit as percentage of sales;	(vii) acid test ratio;
(iii) expenses as percentage of sales;	(viii) accounts receivable/sales ratio;
(iv) inventory turnover;	(ix) accounts payable/purchases ratio.
(v) rate of return of net profit on capital employed (for the purpose of this question only, take capital as being total of share capitals + reserves at the date of the statement of financial position);	

(b) Comment briefly on the comparison of each ratio as between the two companies. State which company appears to be the most efficient, giving what you consider to be possible reasons.

47.12 Durham Limited had an authorised capital of £200,000 divided into 100,000 ordinary shares of £1 each and 200,000 8 per cent preference shares of 50p each. The following balances remained in the accounts of the company after the income statement had been prepared for the year ending 30 April 2012.

	Debit £	Credit £
Premises at cost	86,000	
General reserve		4,000
Ordinary shares: fully paid		100,000
8% Preference shares: fully paid		50,000
Electricity		100
Cash at bank	13,100	
Retained profits 1 May 2011		14,500
Accounts receivable and accounts payable	20,000	12,900
Net profit (year ending 30 April 2012)		16,500
Machinery and plant at cost	60,000	
Provision for depreciation on machinery and plant		40,000
Inventory	60,000	
Allowance for doubtful debts		4,000
Insurance	900	
Preference share dividend paid	2,000	
	242,000	242,000

The Directors have recommended:
  a transfer of £5,000 to general reserve;
  an ordinary dividend of £0.15p per share; and that the
  unpaid preference share dividend be paid.

(a) Prepare an appropriate extract from the statement of changes in equity for year ending 30 April 2012.

(b) Prepare the statement of financial position as at 30 April 2012, in a form which shows clearly the **working capital** and the **shareholders' funds**.

(c) Identify and calculate:
   (i) one ratio indicating the firm's profitability;
   (ii) two ratios indicating the firm's liquidity position.

(d) Make use of your calculations in (c) above to comment on the firm's financial position.

(e) Name two points of comparison which are not available from the information above in this question but which could make your comments in (d) above more meaningful.

(Edexcel Foundation, London Examinations: GCSE)

47.13 The summarised accounts of Hope (Eternal Springs) Ltd for the years 2011 and 2012 are given below.

Income Statements for the years ending 31 December

	2011		2012	
	£000	£000	£000	£000
Sales		200		280
Less Cost of sales		(150)		(210)
Gross profit		50		70
Less				
Administration expenses	38		46	
Loan note interest	–		4	
		(38)		(50)
Net profit		12		20

Statements of Financial Position as at 31 December

	2011		2012	
	£000	£000	£000	£000
Non-current assets at cost *less* depreciation		110		140
Current assets				
Inventory	20		30	
Accounts receivable	25		28	
Bank	–		5	
		45		63
Total assets		155		203
Current liabilities				
Accounts payable	15		12	
Bank	10		–	
	25		12	
Non-current liabilities				
8% loan notes	–		50	
Total liabilities		(25)		(62)
Net assets		130		141
Equity				
Ordinary share capital		100		100
Retained profits		30		41
Total equity		130		141

Inventory at 1 January 2011 was £50,000.

Required:
(a) Calculate the following ratios for 2011 and 2012:
    (i)   Gross profit: Sales
    (ii) Inventory turnover
    (iii) Net profit: Sales
    (iv) Quick ('acid test')
    (v) Working capital
    (vi) Net profit: Capital employed
(b) State the possible reasons for and significance of any changes in the ratios shown by your calculations.

(Midland Examining Group: GCSE)

47.14A The following figures are for AB Engineering Supplies Ltd at 31 December 2012:

	£000	£000
Turnover		160
Gross profit		40
Average inventory at cost price		10
Expenses		8
Non-current assets		108
Current assets		
Inventory	10	
Accounts receivable	8	
Bank	2	
		20
		128
Current liabilities		(10)
		118
Capital		118

(a) Calculate:
  (i) gross profit as a percentage of the sales;
  (ii) rate of inventory turnover;
  (iii) net profit as a percentage of sales;
  (iv) net profit as a percentage of total capital employed (non-current assets plus current assets);
  (v) current ratio;
  (vi) quick asset (acid test) ratio.

(b) The following figures are for another firm in the same line of business, CD Engineering Services Ltd, for the year ending 31 December 2012.

	CD Engineering Services Ltd
Gross profit as a percentage of the sales	25%
Rate of inventory turnover	9
Net profit as a percentage of sales	10%
Net profit as a percentage of total capital employed	12½%
Current ratio	1 : 1
Quick asset (acid test) ratio	0.5 : 1

Compare your results in (a) with those given for CD Engineering Services Ltd.

As a result of your comparison, say which you think was the more successful business during 2009, giving your reasons.

(*Northern Examinations and Assessment Board: GCSE*)

47.15A   Galloway Ltd has an authorised capital of 250,000 ordinary shares of £1 each.

(a)   At the end of its financial year, 30 April 2013, the following balances remained in the company's books after preparation of the income statement.

	£
Motor vehicles:	
at cost	38,400
provision for depreciation	16,300
Net profit for year	36,600
Freehold premises at cost	190,000
Inventory in trade	32,124
Share capital: 200,000 ordinary shares of £1 each, fully paid	200,000
Insurance prepaid	280
Retained profits brought forward	3,950
Wages and salaries due	774
General reserve	24,000
Trade accounts payable	3,847
Trade accounts receivable	4,782
8% loan notes	15,000
Rent receivable outstanding	175
Bank overdraft	1,830
Furniture and equipment:	
at cost	44,000
provision for depreciation	7,460

The directors have proposed

(i)   the transfer of £5,000 to the general reserve
(ii)   a final dividend on the ordinary shares of 12.5%.

(b)   Galloway Ltd's directors are making an assessment of the company's performance for the year. They are concerned by a decline in both profitability and liquidity despite an increase in turnover.

Required:
1   THREE significant differences between ordinary shares and debentures.
2   For Galloway Ltd
   (i)   a profit and loss appropriation account for the year ending 30 April 2013
   (ii)   a statement of financial position as at 30 April 2013 in a form which shows clearly:
     total shareholders' funds
     working capital.
3   Concerning the company's performance
   (i)   Name ONE ratio which could be used to assess profitability.
   (ii)   State TWO possible reasons why the profitability ratio may have declined despite increased turnover.
   (iii)   Name ONE ratio, other than working capital ratio, which could be used to assess liquidity.
   (iv)   Give FOUR suggestions as to how working capital could be increased during the year ahead.

(*Southern Examining Group: GCSE*)

47.16   The trading inventory of Joan Street, retailer, has been reduced during the year ending 31 March 2011 by £6,000 from its commencing figure of £21,000.

A number of financial ratios and related statistics have been compiled relating to the business of Joan Street for the year ending 31 March 2011. These are shown below alongside comparative figures for a number of retailers who are members of the trade association to which Joan Street belongs:

	Joan Street %	Trade association %
Net profit as % net capital employed [Authors' Note]	15	16
$\dfrac{\text{Net profit}}{\text{Sales}}$	9	8
$\dfrac{\text{Sales}}{\text{Net capital employed}}$	$166^2/_3$	200
$\dfrac{\text{Non-current assets}}{\text{Sales}}$	45	35
Working capital ratio:		
$\dfrac{\text{Current assets}}{\text{Current liabilities}}$	400	$287^1/_2$
Acid test ratio:		
$\dfrac{\text{Bank + Accounts receivable}}{\text{Current liabilities}}$	275	$187^1/_2$
$\dfrac{\text{Gross profit}}{\text{Sales}}$	25	26
Accounts receivable collection period:		
$\dfrac{\text{Accounts receivable} \times 365}{\text{Sales}}$	$36^1/_2$ days	$32^{17}/_{20}$ days
Inventory turnover (based on average inventory for the year)	10 times	8 times

Joan Street has supplied all the capital for her business and has had no drawings from the business during the year ending 31 March 2011.

Required:
(a) Prepare the income statement for the year ending 31 March 2011 and statement of financial position as at that date of Joan Street in as much detail as possible.
(b) Identify two aspects of Joan Street's results for the year ending 31 March 2011 which compare favourably with the trade association's figures and identify two aspects which compare unfavourably.
(c) Outline two drawbacks of the type of comparison used in this question.

(*Association of Accounting Technicians*)

Authors' Note: take the closing figure at 31 March 2011.

47.17A Harold Smart, who is a small manufacturer trading as Space Age Projects, is very pleased with his recently completed financial results which show that a planned 20 per cent increase in turnover has been achieved in the last accounting year.

The summarised results relating to the last three financial years are as follows:

Year ended 30 September		2011	2012	2013
		£	£	£
Sales		90,000	100,000	120,000
Cost of sales		(74,000)	(75,000)	(92,000)
Gross profit		16,000	25,000	28,000
Administrative overheads		(3,000)	(5,000)	(6,000)
Net profit		13,000	20,000	22,000

As at 30 September	2010	2011	2012	2013
	£	£	£	£
Non-current assets:				
At cost	155,000	165,000	190,000	206,000
Provision for depreciation	(42,000)	(45,000)	(49,000)	(53,000)
	113,000	120,000	141,000	153,000
Current assets:				
Inventory	3,000	4,000	7,000	30,000
Accounts receivable	14,000	19,000	15,000	10,000
Balance at bank	2,000	1,000	3,000	–
	19,000	24,000	25,000	40,000
Current liabilities:				
Accounts payable	5,000	4,000	6,000	9,000
Bank overdraft	–	–	–	2,000
	5,000	4,000	6,000	11,000

Since 30 September 2010, Harold Smart has not taken any drawings from the business.

Harold Smart has been invited recently to invest £150,000 for a five-year fixed term in government loan stock earning interest at 12½ per cent per annum.

Note: Taxation is to be ignored.

Notwithstanding his response to these financial results, Harold Smart is a very cautious person and therefore has asked a financial consultant for a report.

Required:
(a) A schedule of six accounting ratios or measures of resource utilisation covering each of the three years ended 30 September 2013 of Space Age Projects.
(b) As financial consultant prepare a report to Harold Smart on the financial results of Space Age Projects given above including comments on the alternative future actions that he might take.

Note: Reports should utilise the information given in answers to part (a) of this question.

(*Association of Accounting Technicians*)

47.18 Business A and Business B are both engaged in retailing, but seem to take a different approach to this trade according to the information available. This information consists of a table of ratios, shown below:

Ratio	Business A	Business B
Current ratio	2 : 1	1.5 : 1
Quick assets (acid test) ratio	1.7 : 1	0.7 : 1
Return on capital employed (ROCE)	20%	17%
Return on shareholders' funds (ROSF)	30%	18%
Accounts receivable turnover	63 days	21 days
Accounts payable turnover	50 days	45 days
Gross profit percentage	40%	15%
Net profit percentage	10%	10%
Inventory turnover	52 days	25 days

→

Required:
(a) Explain briefly how each ratio is calculated.
(b) Describe what this information indicates about the differences in approach between the two businesses. If one of them prides itself on personal service and one of them on competitive prices, which do you think is which and why?

(Association of Chartered Certified Accountants)

47.19A You are given summarised information about two firms in the same line of business, A and B, as follows.

Statements of financial position at 30 June	A £000	A £000	B £000	B £000
Land		80		260
Buildings	120		200	
Less: Depreciation	(40)		–	
		80		200
Plant	90		150	
Less: Depreciation	(70)		(40)	
		20		110
		180		570
Inventory	80		100	
Accounts receivable	100		90	
Bank	–		10	
		180		200
		360		770
Accounts payable	110		120	
Bank	50		–	
Loan (10% p.a.)	160	(260)	120	(250)
	100	100	130	520
Capital at start of year		100		300
Add: Profit for year		30		100
		130		400
Less: Drawings		(30)		(40)
		100		360
Land revaluation		–		160
		100		520
Sales		1,000		3,000
Cost of sales		400		2,000

Required:
(a) Produce a table of eight ratios calculated for both businesses.
(b) Write a report briefly outlining the strengths and weaknesses of the two businesses. Include comment on any major areas where the simple use of the figures could be misleading.

(Association of Chartered Certified Accountants)

47.20 The following letter has been received from a client. 'I gave my bank manager those audited accounts you prepared for last year. But he says he needs more information before he will agree to increase my overdraft. What could he possibly want to know that he can't get from those accounts? If they are not good enough why bother to prepare them?'

Required:
Outline the major points which should be included in a reply to this letter.

(Association of Chartered Certified Accountants)

47.21   An acquaintance of yours, H. Gee, has recently set up in business for the first time as a general dealer.

The majority of his sales will be on credit to trade buyers but he will sell some goods to the public for cash.

He is not sure at which point of the business cycle he can regard his cash and credit sales to have taken place.

After seeking guidance on this matter from his friends, he is thoroughly confused by the conflicting advice he has received. Samples of the advice he has been given include:

The sale takes place when:

(*i*)   'you have bought goods which you know you should be able to sell easily';
(*ii*)   'the customer places the order';
(*iii*) 'you deliver the goods to the customer';
(*iv*)   'you invoice the goods to the customer';
(*v*)   'the customer pays for the goods';
(*vi*)   'the customer's cheque has been cleared by the bank'.

He now asks you to clarify the position for him.

Required:
(*a*)   Write notes for Gee, setting out, in as easily understood a manner as possible, the accounting conventions and principles which should generally be followed when recognising sales revenue.
(*b*)   Examine each of the statements (*i*) to (*vi*) above and advise Gee (stating your reasons) whether the method advocated is appropriate to the particular circumstances of his business.

(*Association of Chartered Certified Accountants*)

47.22   The annual final accounts of businesses are normally prepared on the assumption that the business is a going concern.

Required:
Explain and give a simple illustration of:

(*a*)   the effect of this convention on the figures which appear in those final accounts.
(*b*)   the implications for the final accounts figures if this convention were deemed to be inoperative.

(*Association of Chartered Certified Accountants*)

47.23   One of the well known accounting concepts is that of materiality.

Required:
(*a*)   Explain what is meant by this concept.
(*b*)   State and explain three types of situation to which this concept might be applicable.
(*c*)   State and explain two specific difficulties in applying this concept.

(*Association of Chartered Certified Accountants*)

47.24   State three classes of people, other than managers and owners, who are likely to need to use financial accounting information. Discuss whether you think their requirements are compatible.

(*Association of Chartered Certified Accountants*)

→ **47.25** A business produces a standard manufactured product. The stages of the production and sale of the product may be summarised as follows:

Stage	A	B	C	D
Activity	Raw material	WIP-I	WIP-II	Finished product
	£	£	£	£
Costs to date	100	120	150	170
Net realisable value	80	130	190	300
Stage	E	F	G	H
Activity	For sale	Sale agreed	Delivered	Paid for
	£	£	£	£
Costs to date	170	170	180	180
Net realisable value	300	300	300	300

Required:
(a) What general rule do accountants apply when deciding when to recognise revenue on any particular transaction?
(b) Apply this rule to the above situation. State and explain the stage at which you think revenue will be recognised by accountants.
(c) How much would the gross profit on a unit of this product be? Why?
(d) Suggest arguments in favour of delaying the recognition of revenue until Stage H.
(e) Suggest arguments in favour of recognising revenue in appropriate successive amounts at Stages B, C and D.

(Association of Chartered Certified Accountants)

47.26
(a) In accounting practice a distinction is drawn between the terms 'reserves' and 'provisions' and between 'accrued expenses' and 'accounts payable'.

Required:
Briefly define each of the four terms quoted and explain the effect of each on the preparation of accounts.

(b) While preparing the final accounts for year ending 30 September 2012, the accountant of Lanep Lighting Ltd had to deal with the following matters:
  (i)   the exterior of the company's premises was being repaired. The contractors had started work in August but were unlikely to finish before the end of November 2012. The total cost would not be known until after completion. Cost of work carried out to 30 September 2012 was estimated at £21,000;
  (ii) the company rented a sales showroom from Commercial Properties plc at a rental of £6,000 per annum payable half yearly in arrears on 1 August and 1 February;
  (iii) on 3 October 2012 an invoice was received for £2,500 less a trade discount of 30 per cent, from Lucifer Ltd for goods for resale supplied during September 2012;
  (iv) the directors of Lanep Lighting Ltd have decided that an annual amount of £5,000 should be set aside, starting with year ending 30 September 2012, for the purpose of plant replacement.

Required:
State the accounting treatment which should be accorded to each of the above matters in the Lanep Lighting Ltd income statement for year ending 30 September 2012 and statement of financial position at that date.

(Association of Chartered Certified Accountants)

47.27 Bradwich plc is a medium-sized engineering company whose shares are listed on a major Stock Exchange.
   It has recently applied to its bankers for a 7-year loan of £500,000 to finance a modernisation and expansion programme.

Mr Whitehall, a recently retired civil servant, is contemplating investing £10,000 of his lump sum pension in the company's ordinary shares in order to provide both an income during his retirement and a legacy to his grandchildren after his death.

The bank and Mr Whitehall have each acquired copies of the company's most recent annual report and accounts.

Required:
(a) State, separately for each of the two parties, those aspects of the company's performance and financial position which would be of particular interest and relevance to their respective interests.
(b) State, separately for each of the two parties, the formula of four ratios which would assist in measuring or assessing the matters raised in your answer to (a).

(*Association of Chartered Certified Accountants*)

47.28 Explain what you understand by the accounting term 'capital gearing', showing clearly the benefits of, and the potential problems associated with high gearing.

(*Scottish Qualifications Authority*)

47.29A What benefits can result through the use of ratios and what limitations should be imposed on any conclusions drawn from their use?

MyAccountingLab Need more practice? Instant feedback?
Visit **www.myaccountinglab.com**

Featuring unlimited practice questions, a personalised study plan that identifies the areas where you need to focus for better marks, and interactive material designed to help all kinds of learners, MyAccountingLab is a vital tool for maximising your understanding, confidence, and success. Log in at **www.myaccountinglab.com** to see why 92 per cent of students surveyed last year recommend MyAccountingLab.

Interpretation of Financial Statements 2

Accounting ratios

After you have studied this chapter, you should be able to:

● describe various groups of accounting ratios, where they would be used, why they would be of interest, and to whom they would be of interest

● calculate a number of commonly used accounting ratios

● describe some of the difficulties that may arise in the calculation and interpretation of accounting ratios

● describe the dangers of overtrading and how ratio analysis can be used to detect it

Introduction
....

This chapter revises what you learnt in *Business Accounting 1* concerning ratios and introduces some that are more commonly used. You will also learn about one of the main causes of small business failure, overtrading, and of how ratios can be used to minimise the risk of its occurring undetected.

27.1 Background

Without ratios, financial statements would be largely uninformative to all but the very skilled. By using ratios, financial statements can be interpreted and usefully applied to satisfy the needs of the reader, whether skilled or not.

The subject of accounting ratios and their use when analysing financial statements was introduced in *Business Accounting 1*. This chapter takes that material forward, re-examining it for reinforcement, and then developing it so as to increase the depth of your knowledge and understanding.

Information can be defined as 'data organised for a purpose'. Information in financial statements is organised to enable users of the financial statements to draw conclusions concerning the financial well-being and performance of the reporting entity. In the case of the financial statements of companies, independent auditors review the manner in which the data has been presented and provide a filter mechanism attesting to the reliability of the information presented.

For partnerships and sole traders, there is generally no such independent review. However, as the financial statements are generally subject to review by the tax authorities, there is some justification in assuming that they are a reasonable reflection of reality and, in fact, many are prepared by qualified accountants who are governed by the ethical standards of their professional body and so, while not required to do so by the business involved will, nevertheless, strive to produce financial statements that represent a 'true and fair view' of the performance and financial position of the business.

Yet, being 'reasonably assured' of the reliability of such financial statements is not generally sufficient for tax authorities. As a result, they often review the financial statements of partnerships and sole traders to determine whether there may be cause to doubt their reliability. One of the key instruments at their disposal is ratios, and they use ratio analysis to compare those found in the entity under review with those typically existing in that sector of the economy. Hence, through ratio analysis, factors characteristics and deviations from the norm can be identified that would not otherwise be apparent.

Activity 27.1 What sort of 'deviations from the norm' do you think they may be looking for?

As you learnt in *Business Accounting 1*, ratio analysis can also be used to review trends and compare entities with each other. A number of financial analysis organisations specialise in this service, providing detailed ratio analysis of the financial statements of plcs to anyone who subscribes to their service, thereby enabling analysts to see, at a glance, how one company is performing, or how its financial structure compares with that of others of a similar nature.

This is fine for analysts, academic researchers and business competitors who can afford the services of such an organisation. However, there are a vast number of other stakeholders interested in analysing financial statements, including shareholders, lenders, customers, suppliers, employees and government agencies, not all of whom would either want this information, nor wish to pay for it. In many cases, each stakeholder group will be interested in different things, and so there is no definitive, all-encompassing list of points for analysis that would be useful to all the groups even if some organisation endeavoured to do so.

Nevertheless, it is possible to construct a series of ratios that together will provide all these groups with something that they will find relevant, and from which they can choose to investigate further, if necessary.

Ratio analysis is, therefore, a first step in assessing the performance and financial position of an entity. It removes some of the mystique surrounding the financial statements and makes it easier to pinpoint items which would be interesting to investigate further.

Exhibit 27.1 shows some categories of ratios and indicates some of the groups that would be interested in them. You will recall a similar list in *Business Accounting 1*. However, note that the term 'solvency' has been substituted for 'liquidity' in the list here. 'Solvency' is a broader term and more clearly indicative of precisely what we are trying to identify when we consider the ratios that fall within its group. Despite 'solvency' being the more appropriate term, many examiners use the term 'liquidity' when referring to this group of ratios.

Exhibit 27.1

Ratio category	Examples of interested groups
Profitability	Shareholders, management, employees, creditors, competitors, potential investors
Solvency	Shareholders, suppliers, creditors, competitors
Efficiency	Shareholders, potential purchasers, competitors
Shareholder	Shareholders, potential investors
Capital structure	Shareholders, lenders, creditors, potential investors

Let's now revise the main features of each category of ratios.

27.2 Profitability

These measures indicate whether the company is performing satisfactorily. They are used, among other things, to measure the performance of management, to identify whether a company may be a worthwhile investment opportunity, and to determine a company's performance relative to its competitors.

There are a large number of these ratios. You will recall that we covered three in *Business Accounting 1 – gross profit : sales; net profit after tax: sales*; and *return on capital employed*. We shall review them once more and add some others that are commonly used.

Gross profit : Sales

If gross profit is £120,000 and sales are £480,000, the ratio would be 25%. (This should not be confused with the gross margin : cost of sales ratio which compares the gross profit to the cost of goods sold which, in this case, would have a value of 33.33%.) This ratio is also called '*gross profit : revenue*'.

Net profit after tax : Sales

If net profit is £38,400 and sales are £480,000, the ratio would be 8%. It indicates how much safety there is in the price, i.e. current prices could be reduced by up to 8% without causing the company to make a loss. Of course, it is much more complex than this. As any student of economics knows only too well, if a commodity's price falls, generally demand for it rises. This could result in costs increasing (if unexpected demand has to be met in a hurry) or falling (as bulk discounts become available that were not previously obtainable owing to the lower level of demand). Nevertheless, as a general guide, it is a sensible indicator of safety, as well as an indicator of success.

While a high value for this ratio may suggest successful performance, it is not always the case. It is possible for selling prices to be so high that demand is reduced causing overall profitability to be significantly lower than it could be were a lower price being used. In this circumstance, the ratio would produce a high percentage, but performance would certainly not be as good as it ought to have been.

This ratio is also called, '*net profit after tax : revenue*'.

Return on capital employed

An adequate return on capital employed is what many investors seek and is, therefore, one of the main reasons why people invest their money in a business in the first place. As a result, this is an extremely important ratio. First, let's remind ourselves of what we learnt in *Business Accounting 1*.

(i) Sole traders

In this chapter, we will use the average of the capital account as the figure for capital employed, i.e. (opening balance + closing balance) ÷ 2.

In businesses *C* and *D* in Exhibit 27.2 the same amount of net profit has been made, but the capitals employed are different.

Exhibit 27.2

Balance Sheets

	C	D
	£	£
Non-current + Current assets – Current liabilities	10,000	16,000
Capital accounts		
Opening balance	8,000	14,000
Add Net profit	3,600	3,600
	11,600	17,600
Less Drawings	(1,600)	(1,600)
	10,000	16,000

Return on capital employed (ROCE) is:

$$\text{ROCE} = \frac{\text{Net Profit}}{\text{Capital employed}} \times 100$$

therefore

C	D
$\dfrac{3,600}{(8,000 + 10,000) \div 2} \times \dfrac{100}{1} = 40\%$	$\dfrac{3,600}{(14,000 + 16,000) \div 2} \times \dfrac{100}{1} = 24\%$

The ratio illustrates that what is important is not simply how much profit has been made but how well the capital has been employed. Business C has made far better use of its capital, achieving a return of £40 net profit for every £100 invested, whereas D has received only a net profit of £24 per £100.

(ii) Limited companies

There is no universally agreed definition of **capital employed** for companies. The main ones used are:

(a) return on capital employed by ordinary shareholders;
(b) return on capital employed by all long-term suppliers of capital.

Let's now look at each of these:

(a) In a limited company this is known as 'return on owners' equity' (ROOE) or, more commonly, 'return on shareholders' funds' (ROSF).

From now on, we shall use the second of these terms, 'return on shareholders' funds', but you will need to remember that when you see 'return on owners' equity', it is the same as ROSF.

The word 'return' is the net profit for the period. The term 'shareholders' funds' means the book value of all things in the balance sheet that describe the owners' capital and reserves. As the 'owners' are the holders of the *ordinary* share capital, shareholders funds = ordinary share capital + all reserves.

(b) This is often known as 'return on capital employed' (ROCE). The word 'return' in this case means net profit + any preference share dividends + loan note and long-term loan interest. The word 'capital' means ordinary share capital + reserves + preference shares + loan notes and other long-term loans.

Now, let's calculate ROSF and ROCE for P Ltd and Q Ltd. Q Ltd has issued loan notes, so its ROSF and ROCE will not be the same. P Ltd's capital employed is sourced solely from shareholders' funds, so its ROSF and ROCE will be identical.

Balance Sheets as at 31 December

	P Ltd		Q Ltd	
	£	£	£	£
	2008	*2009*	*2008*	*2009*
Non-current assets	5,200	5,600	8,400	9,300
Net current assets	2,800	3,400	1,600	2,700
	8,000	9,000	10,000	12,000
10% loan notes	–	–	(1,200)	(1,200)
	8,000	9,000	8,800	10,800
Share capital (ordinary)	3,000	3,000	5,000	5,000
Reserves	5,000	6,000	3,800	5,800
	8,000	9,000	8,800	10,800

Changes in Equity for years to 31 December 2009

	P Ltd	Q Ltd
	£	£
Net profit	2,200	3,800
Dividends	(1,200)	(1,800)
	1,000	2,000

Return on Shareholders' Funds (ROSF)

P Ltd

$$\frac{2,200}{(8,000 + 9,000) \div 2} \times \frac{100}{1} = 25.9\%$$

Q Ltd

$$\frac{3,800}{(8,800 + 10,800) \div 2} \times \frac{100}{1} = 38.8\%$$

Return on Capital Employed (ROCE)

P Ltd

Same as ROSF[Note 1] = 25.9%

Q Ltd

$$\frac{3,800 + 120^{[\text{Note 2}]}}{(10,000 + 12,000) \div 2} \times \frac{100}{1} = 35.6\%$$

Note 1: The return on capital employed by all long-term sources of capital (in Q Ltd's case, the shareholders' funds and the loan notes) is the same as the ROSF in the case of P Ltd, as it has no loan notes.

Note 2: The loan note interest (i.e. 10% of £1,200 = £120) must be added back, as it was an expense in calculating the £3,800 net profit.

To summarise: return on capital employed is one of the more awkward ratios to deal with. Unlike, for example, the current ratio, there is no widely agreed definition for ROCE – even the ones given here are but examples of how it may be defined. Hence, care must be taken when comparing this ratio as calculated for one company and as reported by another 'so as to confirm that like is being compared with like'. Using the services of financial analysis organisations which use the same formulae to calculate the ratios of all the companies they consider is one way around this difficulty. Another is to ensure that the formula used by the companies with which comparison is being made is known and, where necessary, the ratio result is recalculated in order to bring it into line with the internally calculated ratio.

Note: A problem you face as a student is that you will never be quite sure what an examiner wants if the exam paper refers to this ratio. You should always write down the formula you are using on your exam script.

To avoid confusion, unless otherwise indicated by, for example, the examiner, for companies use the definition of ROCE given above. The ratio compares the profit earned (usually *before* interest and tax) to the funds used to generate that return (often the total of shareholders' funds at the beginning of the accounting period plus long-term payables). If the profit before interest and tax was £40,000 and the opening capital employed shown in the balance sheet was £800,000 the return on capital employed would be 5%.

In theory, the higher the ratio, the more profitably the resources of the company have been used.

Return on share capital

In theory, the higher this ratio is, the more profitably the shareholders' investment in the company has been used. It is often used to compare a company's performance across accounting periods, rather than to make comparisons with the ROSC of other companies. As with ROCE, there are a number of different ways in which return on share capital may be calculated. One is to compare profit on ordinary activities before tax with share capital and reserves. For example, if profit on ordinary activities before tax was £40,000 and the share capital and reserves at the start of the accounting period were £720,000 the return on share capital (ROSC) would be 5.56%.

Net profit after tax : Total assets

Net profit after tax is compared with the total of all non-current assets, plus working capital (i.e. current assets less current liabilities). If working capital is £20,000 and all non-current assets total £820,000, total assets are £840,000. If net profit after tax is £30,000, the ratio is £30,000/£840,000, i.e. 3.57%.

There are problems with the validity of this ratio: it is really concerned with the operating profit generated by the net assets. However, some items of expenditure, e.g. interest on loan notes, will have been charged against the profit in arriving at the figure for profit after tax. Strictly speaking, these other payments to investors and creditors ought to be excluded from this ratio and so should be added back to arrive at the profit figure used in the ratio, otherwise the profit may be significantly understated, giving a less healthy view than would be appropriate to present.

In addition, intangible assets, such as goodwill, are included in the value of total assets used in the ratio. Many would argue that this is inappropriate, as there is not an agreed view on how such assets should be valued.

These issues result in variations of this ratio being used – some add back expenditure, some exclude all intangible assets, some don't – which may not be apparent if only the ratio result is available. As a result, intercompany comparisons may be misleading.

Net operating profit : Operating assets

This is an alternative to the *net profit after tax : total assets* ratio. It takes the net profit before interest, taxes and dividends, and before inclusion of any investment income. This is then compared with the assets other than intangibles and investments outside the company. Working capital would be included, but bank overdrafts would be excluded from the current liabilities on the basis that they are not generally short term in nature. Assume that net operating profit before interest, tax and dividends is £36,000 and tangible fixed assets excluding investments made outside the company are £600,000, working capital is £20,000 and there is a bank overdraft of £5,000. The ratio is:

$$\frac{£36,000}{£625,000} = 5.76\%$$

27.3 **Solvency**

Being solvent means having sufficient resources to meet your debts when due. Your resources must be sufficiently liquid to do so, hence the frequent use of the term 'liquidity' when referring to this group of ratios. As you learnt in *Business Accounting 1*, the solvency of individuals is often performed through credit checks undertaken by credit rating agencies. Many lenders, such as banks, use a checklist of questions concerning financial status before they will lend or grant credit to a private individual. For companies, information can be purchased that indicates their solvency, i.e. whether they are liable to be bad credit risks. Such information is usually based, at least in part, upon ratio analysis of their financial statements.

When it comes to the solvency of a business, both its own ability to pay its debts when due *and* the ability of its debtors to pay the amount they owe to the business are of great importance. Ratio analysis that focuses upon solvency (or liquidity) of the business generally starts with a look at two ratios that are affected most by these two aspects of liquidity: the **current ratio** and the **acid test ratio**.

Current ratio

The **current ratio** compares total current assets to total current liabilities and indicates whether there are sufficient short-term assets to pay the short-term liabilities. This ratio is so sector-dependent that it would be and is inappropriate to suggest a ratio result that may be seen generally as being the 'norm'. Consequently, no such guidance will be given here. Rather, a set of issues to consider are offered below:

1 What is the norm in this industrial sector?
2 Is this company significantly above or below that norm?
3 If so, can this be justified after an analysis of the nature of these assets and liabilities, and of the reasons for the amounts of each held?

The ratio may be expressed as either a ratio to 1, with current liabilities being set to 1, or as a 'number of times', representing the relative size of the amount of total current assets compared with total current liabilities.

Example

If total current assets are £40,000 and total current liabilities are £20,000, the current ratio could be expressed as either:

$$£40,000 : £20,000 = 2 : 1$$

or as:

$$\frac{£40,000}{£20,000} = 2 \text{ times}$$

Acid test ratio

As with the current ratio, there is no point in suggesting a norm for the ratio result to expect. The only difference in the items involved between the two ratios is that the acid test ratio (or 'quick' ratio) does not include inventory. Otherwise, it is identical to the current ratio, comparing current assets, excluding inventory, with current liabilities. Inventory is omitted as it is considered to be relatively illiquid, because it depends upon prevailing and future market forces and may be impossible to convert to cash in a relatively short time.

Many companies operate with acid test ratios below 1:1; that is, they have insufficient liquid assets to meet their short-term liabilities. The great majority of companies in this situation have no problem paying their creditors when due. Consideration of a simple example should explain how this is possible.

> **Activity 27.2**
>
> The only difference between the current and acid test ratios is that inventory is omitted from the acid test ratio. Why is it appropriate to remove inventory from the analysis?

Example

> If total current assets, including inventory of £22,000 are worth £40,000 and total current liabilities stand at £20,000, the acid test ratio will be £18,000 : £20,000 = 0.9 : 1 (or 0.9 times). This means that at the balance sheet date, had all current liabilities been due for payment, it would not have been possible to do so without converting some other assets (e.g. inventory, or some non-current assets) into cash even though it would be unlikely that they could be converted quickly into cash without offering a discount on their true value. In other words, the company would have had to pay a premium in order to meet its obligations, clearly something it would not be able to do indefinitely.

However, the reality is generally that the current liabilities shown in the balance sheet are due for payment at varying times over the coming financial period and some, for example a bank overdraft, may not in reality ever be likely to be subject to a demand for swift repayment.

The current assets, on the other hand, are within the control of the company and can be adjusted in their timing to match the due dates for payment to creditors. They can be renewed many times before one or other of the current liabilities is due for payment. For example, account receivables may be on a 10-day cycle while trade account payables are only paid after 90 days' credit has expired. Clearly, in this case, cash receipts from nine times the balance sheet account receivables figure could be received and available to meet the trade account payables figure shown in the balance sheet when it falls due.

As with the current ratio, the acid test ratio should be compared with the norms for the industrial sector, and then the underlying assets and liabilities should be considered to determine whether there is any cause for concern in the result obtained.

> **Activity 27.3**
>
> If inventory is removed from the analysis when calculating the acid test ratio, why isn't the figure for accounts receivable also removed? Accounts receivable can be just as difficult to turn into cash.

27.4 Efficiency ratios

Profitability is affected by the way that the assets of a business are used. If plant and machinery are used for only a few hours a day, the business is probably failing to utilise these assets efficiently. This may be because there is limited demand for the product produced. It could be due to the business restricting supply to maximise profitability per item produced. On the other hand, it could be that there is a shortage of skilled labour and that there is no one to operate the plant and machinery the rest of the time. Alternatively, it could be that the plant and machinery is unreliable, breaking down a lot, and that the limited level of use is a precautionary measure designed to ensure that production targets are met.

In common with all accounting ratios, it is important that the results of efficiency ratio computations are not treated as definitively good or bad. They must be investigated further through consideration both of the underlying variables in the ratios, and of the broader context of the business and its relation to the industrial sector in which it operates.

Efficiency ratios include:

Asset turnover

Asset turnover is a measure of how effectively the assets are being used to generate sales. It is one of the ratios that would be considered when interpreting the results of profitability ratio analyses like ROCE, but is of sufficient importance to be calculated and analysed irrespective of its relevance to other ratios. The calculation involves dividing revenue by total assets less current liabilities.

As a general guide, where a company's asset turnover is significantly lower than that of its competitors, it suggests there may be overinvestment in assets which could, in turn, make the company vulnerable to takeover by a company interested in selling off any surplus assets while otherwise retaining the business in its current form. However, considerable care must be taken when interpreting this ratio: the assets may be much newer than those of other companies; the company may use a lower rate of depreciation than its competitors; or the company may purchase its plant and machinery, whereas the industry norm is to lease them. On the other side of the ratio, the result may be high because, for example, selling prices are being suppressed in order to maximise volume.

Inventory turnover

Included in virtually every case where accounting ratios are being calculated, inventory turnover measures the number of times (approximately) that inventory is replenished in an accounting period. If average inventory is £100,000 and cost of goods sold is £800,000, the inventory turnover ratio would be 8 times. The ratio can also be expressed as a number of days – the number of days inventory held. In this example, 365 would be divided by 8 producing a result of 45.6 days.

There are two major difficulties in computing the inventory turnover ratio: if cost of goods sold is not available, it is tempting to use revenue instead. This should not be done. Revenue is expressed at selling prices; inventory is expressed at cost price. Use of revenue instead of cost of goods sold in the equation will not be comparing like with like.

In addition, there are at least three possible inventory values that could be used: opening, closing and the average of these figures. The average figure is the more commonly used, but use of any of the three can be justified.

Whichever approach is taken, the result will, at best, be a crude estimate. Due to seasonality of the business, inventory as shown in the balance sheet may not be representative of the 'normal' level of inventory. However, it is still useful for comparing trends over time and should be used mainly for that purpose. The result it produces needs to be handled with care. A rising inventory turnover may indicate greater efficiency; or it may be an indicator that inventory is being run down and that there may be problems in meeting demand in future. A falling inventory turnover may indicate lower efficiency, perhaps with a build-up of obsolete inventory; or it could indicate that higher inventory volumes are being held because inventory purchasing has become more efficient and the higher inventory levels are financially beneficial for the company. In addition, it is important not to overlook that any change in the ratio may have nothing to do with inventory but, instead, may be due to changes in factors relating to the sales for the period.

(This ratio is also known as '*stock turnover*' and as '*stockturn*'.)

Accounts receivable days

Accounts receivable days indicates how efficient the company is at controlling its accounts receivable. If accounts receivable are £50,000 and sales £800,000, debtors are taking, on average, 22.8 days credit, i.e.

$$\frac{£50,000}{£800,000} \times 365 = 22.8$$

Strictly speaking, the two figures are not comparable. Accounts receivable include the VAT on sales; the figure for revenue excludes VAT. However, the adjustment is not difficult to make if required for clarity.

As with inventory, the amount shown in the balance sheet for accounts receivable may not be representative of the 'normal' level of accounts receivable. Nevertheless, this is generally a useful ratio to calculate and comparison with that of other companies in the same industrial sector may be very interesting. However, as with inventory turnover, its strength lies in trend analysis between periods. (The ratio is also known as '*debtor days*'.)

Accounts payable days

The accounts payable days ratio indicates one aspect of how the company uses short-term financing to fund its activities, and further investigation will reveal whether or not the result found is due to efficiency. It is calculated by dividing accounts payable by purchases, and multiplying the result by 365. The purchases figure is not usually available in published financial statements, the cost of sales amount being used in its place. As with inventory turnover and accounts receivable days, its strength lies in trend analysis between periods. (The ratio is also known as '*creditor days*'.)

27.5   Shareholder ratios

Shareholder ratios are those most commonly used by anyone interested in an investment in a company. They indicate how well a company is performing in relation to the price of its shares and other related items including dividends and the number of shares in issue. The ratios usually calculated are described below.

Dividend yield

Dividend yield measures the real rate of return by comparing the dividend paid to the market price of a share. It is calculated as:

$$\frac{\text{Gross dividend per share}}{\text{Market price per share}}$$

Earnings per share (EPS)

EPS is the most frequently used of all the accounting ratios and is generally felt to give the best view of performance. It indicates how much of a company's profit can be attributed to each ordinary share in the company. IAS 33 *Earnings per share* provides the formula to be used when calculating this ratio:

$$\frac{\text{Net profit or loss attributable to ordinary shareholders}}{\text{The weighted average number of ordinary shares outstanding during the period}}$$

Dividend cover

Dividend cover compares the amount of profit earned per ordinary share with the amount of dividend paid, thereby showing the proportion of profits that could have been distributed and where. It differs from EPS only in having a different denominator. The formula is:

$$\frac{\text{Net profit or loss attributable to ordinary shareholders}}{\text{Net dividend on ordinary shares}}$$

Price earnings (P/E) ratio

The P/E ratio relates the earnings per share to the market price of the shares. It is calculated as:

$$\frac{\text{Market price}}{\text{Earnings per share}}$$

and is a useful indicator of how the stock market assesses the company. It is also very useful when a company proposes an issue of new shares, in that it enables potential investors to better assess whether the expected future earnings make the share a worthwhile investment.

27.6 Capital structure

There are a number of ratios that can be used to assess the way in which a company finances its activities. One, accounts payable days, was referred to in the last section. The ratios discussed in this section differ in that they are longer-term in nature, being concerned more with the strategic rather than with the operational level of corporate decision-making. Some of the more commonly analysed ratios of this type are described below.

Net worth : Total assets

This ratio indicates the proportion of non-current and current assets that are financed by net worth (the total of shareholders' funds, i.e. share capital plus reserves). If non-current assets are shown at a value of £500,000; current assets £100,000; and net worth is £300,000 then 50% of total assets are financed by shareholders' funds. As with many accounting ratios, it is the trend in this ratio between periods that is important.

Non-current assets : Net worth

This ratio focuses on the longer-term aspects of the net worth: total assets ratio. By matching long-term investment with long-term finance it is possible to determine whether borrowing has been used to finance some long-term investment in assets. Where this has occurred, there may be a problem when the borrowing is to be repaid (as the non-current assets it used to acquire cannot be readily converted into cash). Again, this ratio is of most use when the trend over time is analysed.

Non-current assets : Net worth + long-term liabilities

This ratio focuses on whether sufficient long-term finance has been obtained to meet the investment in non-current assets.

Debt ratio

This ratio compares the total debts to total assets and is concerned with whether the company has sufficient assets to meet all its liabilities when due. For example, if total liabilities are £150,000 and total assets are £600,000, the debts represent 25% of total assets. Whether this is good or bad will, as with all accounting ratios, depend upon the norm for the industrial sector in which the company operates and on the underlying items within the figures included in the ratio.

Capital gearing ratio

This ratio provides the proportion of a company's total capital that has a prior claim to profits over those of ordinary shareholders. Prior claim (or prior charge) capital includes loan notes, other long-term loans, and preference share capital and is any capital carrying a right to a fixed return. Total capital includes ordinary share capital and reserves, preference shares and non-current liabilities.

Debt : Equity ratio

This is the ratio of prior charge capital to ordinary share capital and reserves.

Borrowing : Net worth

This ratio indicates the proportion that borrowing represents of a company's net worth. If long-term liabilities are £100,000 and current liabilities are £50,000, then total borrowing is £150,000. If net worth is £300,000, the ratio is 1 : 2, or 50%.

This and the debt : equity ratio indicate the degree of risk to investors in ordinary shares in a company. The higher these ratios are, the greater the possibility of risk to ordinary shareholders – both in respect of expectations of future dividends (especially in times of depressed performance where much of the profits may be paid to the holders of prior charge capital), and from the threat of liquidation should there be a slump in performance that leads to a failure to meet payments to holders of prior charge capital. Whether these risks may be relevant can be investigated by reference to the next ratio.

Interest cover

This ratio shows whether enough profits are being earned to meet interest payments when due. It is calculated by dividing profit before interest and tax by the interest charges. Thus, the interest cover is 20 times if profit before interest and tax is £400,000 and the total interest charges are £20,000. In this case, there would be little cause for immediate concern that there was any risk of the company's failing to meet its interest charges when due. However, just because a company is making profits does not guarantee that there will be sufficient cash available to make the interest charge payments when due.

27.7 Overtrading

A very high proportion of new businesses fail within the first two years of trading. This can occur because there was insufficient demand for the goods or services provided, because of poor management, or for any of a number of other reasons of which possibly the most common to arise is **overtrading**. However, unlike the other common causes of business failure, overtrading often arises when a business is performing profitably. Furthermore, overtrading can just as easily affect established businesses as new businesses.

Overtrading occurs when poor control over working capital results in there being insufficient liquid funds to meet the demands of creditors. As the cash dries up, so do the sources of supply of raw materials and other essential inputs – suppliers will not continue to supply a business that fails to settle its bills when due. Overtrading is generally the result of sales growth being at too fast a rate in relation to the level of trade accounts receivable, trade accounts payable and inventory.

Take an example where, over a 12-month period, profits increased by 20%; revenue doubled from £1 million to £2 million; trade accounts receivable doubled from £80,000 to £160,000; trade accounts payable quadrupled from £60,000 to £240,000; inventory quadrupled from £50,000 to £200,000; and the bank balance moved from positive £20,000 to an overdraft of

£80,000. No changes occurred during the period in long-term financing of the business, though £100,000 was spent on some new equipment needed as a result of the expansion.

Working capital was 2.5 : 1; now it is 1.125 : 1 and the acid test ratio is now 0.5 : 1 from 1.67 : 1. Liquidity appears to have deteriorated significantly (but may have been high previously compared with other businesses in the same sector). Accounts receivable days are unchanged (as the ratio of revenue to accounts receivable is unaltered). However, accounts payable days have probably doubled (subject to a slight reduction due to some cheaper purchasing costs as a result of the higher volumes involved). If the bank overdraft is currently at its limit, the business would be unable to meet any requests from creditors for immediate payment, never mind pay wages and other regular expenses.

This situation can be addressed by raising long-term finance, or by cutting back on the expansion – clearly, the first option is likely to be the more acceptable one to the owners of the business.

Signals suggesting overtrading include:

(*a*) significant increases in the volume of good sold;
(*b*) lower profit margins;
(*c*) deteriorating accounts receivable, accounts payable, and inventory turnover;
(*d*) increasing reliance on short-term finance.

27.8 Summary of ratios

Profitability

Gross profit : Revenue

$$\frac{\text{Gross profit}}{\text{Sales}}$$

Net profit after tax : Revenue

$$\frac{\text{Net profit after tax}}{\text{Sales}}$$

Return on capital employed

$$\frac{\text{Profit before interest and tax}}{\text{Total assets} - \text{Current liabilities}}$$

Return on share capital

$$\frac{\text{Profit before tax}}{\text{Share capital} + \text{Reserves}}$$

Net profit after tax : Total assets

$$\frac{\text{Net profit after tax}}{\text{Non-current assets} + \text{Working capital}}$$

Net operating profit : Operating assets

$$\frac{\text{Net profit before interest, tax, dividends, and investment income}}{\text{Tangible non-current assets} - \text{Outside investments} + \text{Working capital} + \text{Bank overdraft}}$$

Solvency

Current ratio

$$\frac{\text{Current assets}}{\text{Current liabilities}}$$

Acid test ratio

$$\frac{\text{Current assets} - \text{Inventory}}{\text{Current liabilities}}$$

Efficiency

Asset turnover

$$\frac{\text{Revenue}}{\text{Total assets} - \text{Current liabilities}}$$

Inventory turnover	$\dfrac{\text{Cost of goods sold}}{\text{Average inventory}}$
Accounts receivable days	$\dfrac{\text{Accounts receivable}}{\text{Revenue}} \times 365$
Accounts payable days	$\dfrac{\text{Accounts payable}}{\text{Purchases}} \times 365$

Shareholder ratios

Dividend yield	$\dfrac{\text{Gross dividend per share}}{\text{Market price per share}}$
Earnings per share	$\dfrac{\text{Net profit or loss attributable to ordinary shareholders}}{\text{Weighted average number of ordinary shares outstanding during the period}}$
Dividend cover	$\dfrac{\text{Net profit or loss attributable to ordinary shareholders}}{\text{Net dividend on ordinary shares}}$
Price/earnings ratio	$\dfrac{\text{Market price}}{\text{Earnings per share}}$

Capital structure

Net worth : Total assets	$\dfrac{\text{Shareholders' funds}}{\text{Total assets}}$
Non-current assets : Net worth	$\dfrac{\text{Fixed assets}}{\text{Shareholders' funds}}$
Non-current assets : Net worth + long-term liabilities	$\dfrac{\text{Fixed assets}}{\text{Shareholders' funds} + \text{Long-term liabilities}}$
Debt ratio	$\dfrac{\text{Total liabilities}}{\text{Total assets}}$
Capital gearing ratio	$\dfrac{\text{Prior charge capital}}{\text{Total capital}}$
Debt : Equity ratio	$\dfrac{\text{Prior charge capital}}{\text{Ordinary share capital and reserves}}$
Borrowing : Net worth	$\dfrac{\text{Total borrowing}}{\text{Shareholders' funds}}$
Interest cover	$\dfrac{\text{Profit before interest and tax}}{\text{Interest charges}}$

Note: If you wish to read more about the topic of ratios, there are many worthwhile books available, such as Ciaran Walsh's *Key Management Ratios*, published by FT Prentice Hall. However, don't forget that there is no 'correct' formula for many of the financial ratios you have learnt about in this chapter. If you do read further on this topic *do not* make changes to these formulae. These are generally accepted formulae and ones your examiners will recognise.

Learning outcomes

You should now have learnt:

1 There are many different categories of accounting ratios and many different ratios within each category.

2 Ratios that are of interest to one group of readers of financial statements may not be of interest to another.

3 Ratios may be used to review reliability of financial statements.

4 Ratios may be used to review trends between periods for the same company.

5 Ratios may be used to compare a company to others in the same industrial sector.

6 Some ratios are in wide use for which there is no agreed 'correct' formula to calculate them. This makes comparison between analysis reported elsewhere of limited value unless the formula used can be identified.

7 The ratios derived can be misleading if taken at face value. It is essential that they are placed in context and that interpretation goes beyond a superficial comparison to general norms.

8 Used casually, accounting ratios can mislead and result in poor quality decision-making.

9 Used carefully, accounting ratios can provide pointers towards areas of interest in an entity, and provide a far more complete picture of an entity than that given by the financial statements.

10 Overtrading can be financially disastrous for a business and ratios can be used to help detect it.

Answers to activities

27.1 Lower levels of gross profit than the industry norm, which might indicate goods were being taken out of the business for the owner's own use but not being recorded as drawings. Alternatively, lower levels of gross profit than the industry norm may indicate sales for cash were not all being recorded. Revenue and Customs use ratios to detect anything that might indicate the possibility that a proprietor is understating the profit earned.

27.2 Inventory is sometimes very difficult to convert into cash, particularly at the value placed upon it in the balance sheet. Because it can be difficult to generate liquid funds through the sale of inventory, it is inappropriate to consider it when looking at the issue of whether an organisation is able to pay its debts quickly.

27.3 Accounts receivable can be very difficult to turn into cash. However, there are three aspects of accounts receivable that make them less problematic than inventory in this context. Firstly, specialist financial agencies called 'factors' will take over debts in many instances in exchange for a percentage of the amount owing. Through this medium, organisations can convert some of their accounts receivable into cash quickly and at relatively little cost. Secondly, accounts receivable can be pursued through the courts. Thus, when an organisation urgently needs money owing from accounts receivable that is already overdue, it can threaten legal action, thereby accelerating the receipt of the money due. Finally, most debtors do eventually pay their debts; inventory may never be sold.

In the context of the cash it will generate, inventory is usually sold at above the value placed upon it in the balance sheet while, apart from overestimation of doubtful debts, accounts receivable never realise more than the value shown for them in the balance sheet. However, so far as the acid test ratio is concerned, the key difference is that money owing by debtors will generally be received more quickly than money tied up in inventory.

Review questions

27.1   Five categories of accounting ratios were described in this chapter. What are they?

27.2A   Why should different groups of people be interested in different categories of accounting ratios?

27.3   Describe two ratios from each of the five groups of ratios, including how to calculate them.

27.4A   What is the purpose in using each of the following ratios:

(a) current ratio
(b) net profit after tax : revenue
(c) asset turnover
(d) interest cover
(e) dividend cover?

27.5   If you wished to assess the efficiency of a company, which of these ratios would you use:

(a) inventory turnover
(b) interest cover
(c) return on capital employed
(d) acid test ratio
(e) dividend yield?

27.6A   A company has capital of 1 million ordinary shares of £1 each. It pays a dividend of 6% of its profits after tax of £480,000 on sales of £4 million. The market price of the shares is £2.40. What is the:

(a) net profit after tax : revenue
(b) dividend yield
(c) earnings per share
(d) price earnings ratio?

27.7   In respect of each of the following events, select all the effects resulting from that event that are shown in the list of effects:

(i) a bad debt written off;
(ii) an increase in the bank overdraft;
(iii) a purchase of six months' inventory;
(iv) payment of all amounts due to trade accounts payable that had been outstanding for longer than 90 days;
(v) an offer of 5% discount to all customers who settle their accounts within two weeks.

Effects
(a) increased current ratio
(b) reduced current ratio
(c) increased acid test ratio
(d) reduced acid test ratio.

27.8A Using the following balance sheet and profit and loss accounts, calculate and comment on ten accounting ratios (ignore taxation):

Balance Sheet as at 31 March 2006 (£000)

Non-current assets		
Equipment at cost		600
Less Depreciation to date		(200)
		400
Current assets		
Inventory	300	
Accounts receivable	60	
Bank	–	
		360
Total assets		760
Current liabilities		
Accounts payable	160	
Dividends payable	12	
Bank overdraft	168	
	340	
Non-current liabilities		
5% Loan notes	(100)	
		(440)
Net assets		320
Equity		
Share capital – ordinary shares of 50p each		250
Reserves		
General reserve		40
Retained profits		30
		320

Income Statement for period ending 31 March 2006 (£000)

Revenue		2,000
Less Cost of goods sold		
Opening inventory	250	
Add Purchases	1,450	
	1,700	
Less Closing inventory	(300)	
		(1,400)
Gross profit		600
Less Depreciation	80	
Other expenses	477	
		(557)
Operating profit		43
Loan note interest		(5)
Profit for the year		38

Note: The Statement of Changes in Equity shows that retained profits at 1 April 2005 were £24,000; that £20,000 has been transferred from retained profit to the general reserve; and that a dividend of £12,000 was paid during the year. (The balance sheet reflects these items.)

27.9 Study the following financial statements for two very similar privately owned department stores which each comprise of one store in the city centre of a major UK city and then answer the questions which follow.

Summary of Financial Statements

Balance Sheets	A £000s	A £000s	B £000s	B £000s
Non-current assets				
Building at cost	300		440	
Less Depreciation to date	(255)		(220)	
		45		220
Equipment at cost	140		180	
Less Depreciation to date	(119)		(90)	
		21		90
		66		310
Current assets				
Inventory	200		240	
Accounts receivable	205		140	
Bank	4		2	
		409		382
Total assets		475		692
Current liabilities				
Accounts payable		(245)		(252)
Net assets		230		440
Financed by:				
Capital accounts				
Balance at start of year		240		430
Add Net profit		60		90
		300		520
Less Drawings		(70)		(80)
		230		440
Income Statements				
Revenue		1,800		2,700
Less: Cost of goods sold				
Opening inventory	300		280	
Add Purchases	1,300		2,250	
	1,600		2,530	
Less Closing inventory	(200)		(240)	
		(1,400)		(2,290)
Gross profit		400		410
Less Depreciation	22		40	
Other expenses	318		280	
		(340)		(320)
Net profit		60		90

Required:
(a) Calculate the following ratios:
    (i)   gross profit as % of revenue;
    (ii)   net profit as % of revenue;
    (iii) expenses as % of revenue;
    (iv) inventory turnover;
    (v)   rate of return of net profit on capital employed (use the average of the capital account for this purpose);
    (vi) current ratio;
    (vii) acid test ratio;
    (viii) accounts receivable : revenue ratio;
    (ix) accounts payable : purchases ratio.
(b) Drawing upon all your knowledge of accounting, comment upon the differences and similarities of the accounting ratios for A and B. Which business seems to be the most efficient? Justify your opinion.

27.10A Study the following financial statements of two companies and then answer the questions which follow. Both companies are stores selling carpets and other floor coverings; each company has a single store in the same 10-year old custom-built shopping complex located on the outskirts of a major UK city.

Income Statements

	R Ltd		T Ltd	
	£000s	£000s	£000s	£000s
Revenue		2,000		1,400
Less Cost of goods sold				
Opening inventory	440		144	
Add Purchases	1,550		996	
	1,990		1,140	
Less Closing inventory	(490)		(240)	
		(1,500)		(900)
Gross profit		500		500
Less Expenses				
Depreciation	27		14	
Wages and salaries	180		160	
Directors' remuneration	210		210	
Other expenses	23		16	
		(440)		(400)
Net profit		60		100

Note: The Statement of Changes in Equity shows that retained profits at the start of the year were £60,000 (R Ltd) and £20,000 (T Ltd); that dividends paid during the year were £50,000 (R Ltd) and £40,000 (T Ltd); and that both companies made transfers from retained profit to general reserve at the end of the year: £20,000 (R Ltd) and £20,000 (T Ltd).

	R Ltd		T Ltd	
Balance Sheets				
	£000s	£000s	£000s	£000s
Non-current assets				
Building at cost	300		100	
Less Depreciation to date	(150)		(50)	
		150		50
Equipment at cost	60		30	
Less Depreciation to date	(40)		(20)	
		20		10
Motor vans	40		35	
Less Depreciation to date	(16)		(14)	
		24		21
		194		81
Current assets				
Inventory	490		240	
Accounts receivable	680		320	
Bank	80		127	
		1,250		687
Total assets		1,444		768
Current liabilities				
Accounts payable		(324)		(90)
Net assets		1,120		678
Equity				
Issued share capital		1,000		500
Reserves				
General reserve	70		120	
Retained profits	50		58	
		120		178
		1,120		678

Required:

(a) Calculate the following ratios for each of R Ltd and T Ltd:
  (i)   gross profit as % of revenue;
  (ii)   net profit as % of revenue;
  (iii) expenses as % of revenue;
  (iv) inventory turnover;
  (v)   rate of return of net profit on capital employed
       (for the purpose of this question only, take capital as being total of share capitals +
       reserves at the balance sheet date);
  (vi) current ratio;
  (vii) acid test ratio;
  (viii) accounts receivable : revenue ratio;
  (ix) accounts payable : purchases ratio.

(b) Comment briefly on the comparison of each ratio as between the two companies. State which
   company appears to be the more efficient, giving what you consider to be possible reasons.

27.11 The directors of L Ltd appointed a new sales manager towards the end of 2002. This manager devised a plan to increase revenue and profit by means of a reduction in selling price and
extended credit terms to customers. This involved considerable investment in new machinery early
in 2003 in order to meet the demand which the change in sales policy had created.

The financial statements for the years ended 31 December 2002 and 2003 are shown below. The sales manager has argued that the new policy has been a resounding success because revenue and, more importantly, profits have increased dramatically.

Income Statements

	2003	2002
	£000	£000
Revenue	2,800	900
Cost of sales	(1,680)	(360)
Gross profit	1,120	540
Selling expenses	(270)	(150)
Bad debts	(140)	(18)
Depreciation	(208)	(58)
Interest	(192)	(12)
Net profit	310	302

Balance sheets

	2003		2002	
	£000	£000	£000	£000
Non-current assets				
Factory		441		450
Machinery		1,791		490
		2,232		940
Current assets				
Inventory	238		30	
Accounts receivable	583		83	
Bank	–		12	
		821		125
Total assets		3,053		1,065
Current liabilities				
Accounts payable	175		36	
Bank	11		–	
	186		36	
Non-current liabilities				
Borrowings	1,600		100	
		(1,786)		(136)
		1,267		929
Equity				
Share capital		328		300
Retained profits		939		629
		1,267		929

Note: The balance on the retained profits reserve at the end of 2002 was £327,000.

(a) **You are required to** explain whether you believe that the performance for the year ended 31 December 2003 and the financial position at that date have improved as a result of the new policies adopted by the company. You should support your answer with appropriate ratios.

(b) All of L Ltd's sales are on credit. The finance director has asked you to calculate the immediate financial impact of reducing the credit period offered to customers. Calculate the amount of cash which would be released if the company could impose a collection period of 45 days.

(*Chartered Institute of Management Accountants*)

Interpretation of financial statements

Learning objectives

After you have studied this chapter, you should be able to:

- explain the importance of trend analysis when analysing financial statements
- explain that there is no such thing as a generally 'good' or 'bad' value for any ratio
- describe the need to compare like with like if attempting to assess the quality of the result found from ratio analysis
- explain the pyramid of ratios that can be used in order to enhance the view obtained from ratio analysis
- explain that different groups of users of financial statements have access to different sources of information that may help in developing an understanding of and explanation for the results of ratio analysis

Introduction

In this chapter, you'll learn more about ratio analysis and how to use it effectively. You'll revisit how to perform comparisons between organisations and the need for effective and appropriate comparators if valid and worthwhile conclusions are to be made. You'll also learn about the interlinked relationships between ratios and look in greater detail at return on capital employed.

28.1 Background

When shareholders receive the financial statements of the company they have invested in, many simply look to see whether the business has made a profit, and then put the document away. (This is one reason why the introduction of an option to send shareholders abbreviated financial statements, rather than the far more costly to produce full set of financial statements, was introduced a few years ago.) They are aware of only one thing – that the company made a profit of £x. They do not know if it was a 'good' profit. Nor do they know whether it was any different from the profit earned in previous years. (Even if they had noticed the previous period's profit figure in the comparative column, they would be unaware of the equivalent figures for the periods that preceded it.) In addition, they would have no perception of how the performance compared with that of other companies operating in the same sector.

As explained in the previous chapter, ratio analysis can be used to assess company performance and financial position. However, as you learnt in *Business Accounting 1*, such analysis is relatively useless unless a similar task is undertaken on the financial figures for previous periods, so providing a view of the changes that have occurred over time. Trend analysis of this type is very important in the interpretation of financial statements, for it is only then that the position found can be truly placed in context and statements made concerning whether things are improving, etc.

Of similar importance if financial statements are to be usefully interpreted is comparison of the position shown with that of other companies operating in the same sector, both now and over a period of time.

28.2 Sector relevance

Analysis and interpretation of any phenomenon is all very well if conducted in isolation from the rest of the world. However, it can be of only limited use without comparators with which to develop an understanding of what is being examined. Even when this is done, it is important that the comparators are valid – there is not much point in comparing the performance of a Rolls-Royce with that of a bicycle. Like must be compared with like. Racing bike to racing bike, mountain bike to mountain bike, Premier League football team to Premier League football team, and so on. **For companies, the easiest way to ensure that like is being compared with like is to compare companies that operate in the same business sector.**

The importance of ensuring that any comparison undertaken between companies involves companies in the same sector can best be illustrated through an extreme example: that of the contrast between service companies and manufacturing companies.

Stating the obvious, a firm of consultants which advises its clients on marketing strategies will have far fewer tangible assets than a company with the same revenue and the same capital employed which manufactures forklift trucks. The firm of consultants will need premises, but these could easily be rented ready for use, whereas a manufacturing company would need to make major adjustments to the premises before using them. In addition, the firm of consultants would need very little in the way of machinery, possibly just some computer equipment and office equipment.

In comparison, the manufacturing company would need a great deal of machinery as well as lorries and various types of buildings, and so on. The manufacturing firm would also have inventory of materials and unsold forklift trucks. The consultancy would not have any inventory.

 Activity 28.1 What effect would these types of differences have on the ratios of the two businesses?

With wider use and increasing levels of personal ownership of PCs with broadband internet access, an increasing number of employees are working from home, especially in the service sector. This trend is set to continue with a resultant reduction in the need for many service industry organisations to maintain offices of the size required in the past.

All of this has an effect on the ratios of performance calculated from the financial statements of manufacturers and service industry firms. The figure of return on capital employed for a service firm, simply because of the far lower amount of tangible assets needed, may appear to be quite high. For a manufacturing firm the opposite may well be the case.

If this distinction between these completely different types of organisation is understood, then the interpreter of the financial statements is able to judge them appropriately. Failure to understand the distinction will bring forth some very strange conclusions.

28.3 Trend analysis

Looking internally at one organisation, sensible comparisons can clearly be made between the situation it was in at various points in time.

Activity 28.2 What two key things does an inward-looking analysis of this type NOT tell you? (*Hint*: think about the overall context.)

In *Business Accounting 1*, an example was shown of two companies, G and H. The example is now reintroduced and further developed. Exhibit 28.1 presents four ratios derived from the financial statements of G over this and the previous four years.

Exhibit 28.1

	Year:	1	2	3	4	5 (*now*)
Gross profit as % of revenue		40	38	36	35	34
Net profit as % of revenue		15	13	12	12	11
Net profit as % of capital employed		13	12	11	11	10
Current ratio		3.0	2.8	2.6	2.3	2.0

All other thing being equal, you would expect it more likely that all four of these ratios would rise over time. However, it is clear that they are all decreasing, but there is no other information available which might clarify whether or not this should be cause for concern. For example, the industry may be becoming more competitive, causing margins to shrink, and the falling current ratio may be due to an increase in efficiency over the control of working capital.

A company with this trend of figures could provide an explanation for the decline in margins and for the reduction in liquidity in its annual report. A reader of the financial statements could then decide to accept the explanation and put the calculations away. However, there is no guarantee that an explanation of this kind actually indicates a beneficial situation, irrespective of whether or not it is accurate.

In order to gain a better understanding of the analysis, comparison with other comparable companies in the same sector is needed. Exhibit 28.2 presents the information from Exhibit 28.1 for company G plus information on another company of a similar size operating in the same sector, company H.

Exhibit 28.2

				Years		
		1	2	3	4	5 (current)
Gross profit as % of revenue	G	40	38	36	35	34
	H	30	32	33	33	34
Net profit as % of revenue	G	15	13	12	12	11
	H	10	10	10	11	11
Net profit as % of capital employed	G	13	12	11	11	10
	H	8	8	9	9	10
Current ratio	G	3.0	2.8	2.6	2.3	2.0
	H	1.5	1.7	1.9	1.0	2.0

This form of presentation can be difficult to digest and interpret. As an alternative, these results may be compared through graphs, as shown by the example in Exhibit 28.3 which compares the trend in gross profit as a percentage of revenue of the two companies. (Note that the vertical axis does not show the percentage below 30 as there is no percentage below that amount in Exhibit 28.2. Omitting the lower figures on the graph in these circumstances allows for a more informative display of the information.)

Exhibit 28.3 The trend of gross profit as a percentage of revenue

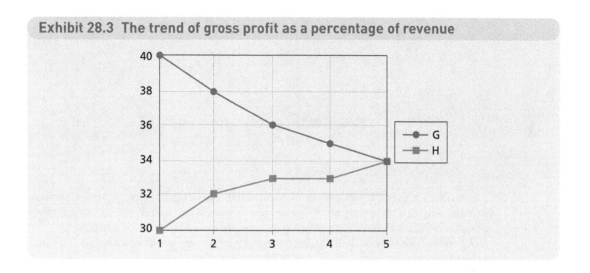

Now, you should see the importance of placing trends in context. The companies have identical ratios for the current period – does that make them equally desirable as investments? Given one year's financial statements it appears so, but the five-year trend analysis reveals a different picture.

From these figures, G appears to be the worse investment for the future, as the trend for it appears to be downwards, while that of H is upwards. It suggests that the explanation made earlier for the falling margins may not be valid. If the trend for G is continued it could be in a very dangerous financial situation in a year or two's time. H, on the other hand, is strengthening its position all the time.

While it would be ridiculous to state without reservation that H will continue on an upward trend, or that G will continue downwards, a consistent trend of this type does suggest that the situation may well continue into the foreseeable future. It is certainly cause for further investigation.

28.4 Comparisons over time

As shown in the previous section, one of the best ways of using ratios is to compare them with the ratios for the same organisation in respect of previous years. Take another example, the net profit percentage of a company for the past six years, including the current year 2008:

	2003	2004	2005	2006	2007	2008 (now)
Net profit %	5.4	5.2	4.7	4.8	4.8	4.5

This could be presented in a graph as shown in Exhibit 28.4:

Exhibit 28.4

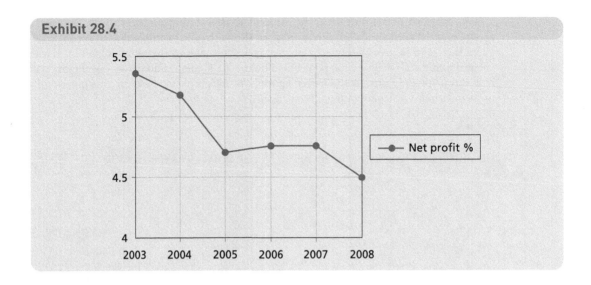

It is obvious that there is a long-term decline in the net profit percentage. This prompts us to examine why this should be so. Without measuring against past years our understanding of the direction in which the business seems to be heading would be much diminished.

We would not only look at the long-term changes in net profit percentages, but also compare similar long-term figures in relation to other aspects of the business.

Of course, other factors outside an organisation, particularly changes in the economy may make the interpretation of trends an extremely complex process. For example, the use of the historical cost accounting concept during periods of high inflation can make effective comparison of monetary amounts over time very problematic.

28.5   Comparisons with other businesses

We've already looked at some of the benefits of undertaking comparisons with other businesses in Section 28.3. Now, we'll consider it in more detail. No one can say in isolation that a business is very profitable. A business may have made an average net profit over the last few years of £6 million which, to most people, may seem profitable. On the other hand, if businesses of a similar size in the same industry are making £20 million a year, then the business making £6 million a year cannot be said to be very profitable.

Ideally, we would like to be able to compare the results of one business with those of similar businesses in the same industry. Then, and only then, would we be able to judge how well, or how badly, that business was doing.

The size of a business can have an important effect upon ratios. Just as we would not try to compare a chemist's shop with a building firm, it would also be wrong to judge a small independent supermarket against Sainsbury's, which owns hundreds of supermarkets.

Interfirm comparisons are also sometimes misleading because of the different accounting treatment of various items, and the location and ages of assets. Some industries have, however, set up interfirm comparisons with guidelines to the companies to ensure that the figures have been constructed using the same bases so that the information is comparable. The information does not disclose data which can be traced to any one firm, ensuring that full confidentiality is observed.

The information available may take the form shown in Exhibit 28.5:

Exhibit 28.5 Published ratios for the widget industry (extract)

	Solvency		Efficiency			
	Current	Acid test	Asset T/O	Inventory T/O	Debtor days	Creditor days
2006	2.4	0.7	5.4	8.2	56.4	80.4
2007	2.2	0.8	5.7	9.3	52.6	66.8

The equivalent figures for the company being assessed can then be tabulated alongside the industry figures to enable comparisons to be made, as in Exhibit 28.6.

Exhibit 28.6

	Company ratios		Industry ratios	
	2006	2007	2006	2007
Current ratio	2.9	2.8	2.4	2.2
Acid test ratio	0.5	0.6	0.7	0.8
Asset turnover	5.2	5.3	5.4	5.7
Inventory turnover	4.4	4.7	8.2	9.3
Accounts receivable days	65.9	65.2	56.4	52.6
Accounts payable days	58.3	56.8	80.4	66.8

The financial status of the company is now much clearer. What appeared to be a situation of improving liquidity and efficiency is now shown to be an increasingly poorer liquidity and efficiency position compared with the industry as a whole.

However, it should be borne in mind that the industry figures probably include many companies that are either much larger or much smaller than the company being assessed. To obtain a more complete picture, information is needed concerning companies of a similar size, such as in the comparison between G and H earlier in this chapter (see Section 28.3). This information may be available from the source of the interfirm comparison. If not, other sources would need to be used, for example the published financial statements of appropriate companies.

The other information missing from the above comparison is data from previous periods. While not so relevant to the current position, it can be useful in explaining why a situation has developed, and in determining whether the current position is likely to persist.

 Activity 28.3 When an organisation operates in more than one sector, how do you identify other appropriate organisations with which to make comparisons?

28.6 Pyramid of ratios

Once ratios have been analysed and compared, explanations must be sought for the results obtained. Sometimes it will be obvious why a certain result was obtained – for example, if a company has moved from traditional stock-keeping to a just-in-time system during the period, its stock turnover will bear no resemblance to that which it had in the previous period.

For those inside the company – its directors and management – the management accounting records are available to assist in finding explanations, as are the company's staff. Outsiders – shareholders, analysts, lenders, suppliers, customers, etc. – do not have access to all this internal information (though some of these user groups will have access to more internal information than others – banks, for example, can usually obtain copies of a company's confidential internal accounting information upon request). They must, instead, fall back upon other sources of information, such as newspaper reports and industry publications.

One source of additional information available to everyone is a result of the fact that most ratios can be further subdivided into secondary ratios which, themselves, can also be subdivided, so building into a **pyramid of ratios**. By following through the pyramid of a given ratio, the source of the original ratio can often be isolated, enabling a far more focused investigation than would otherwise be possible.

For example, one of the most important ratios is the return on the capital employed (ROCE). This ratio has not happened by itself. If the ratio of net profit to revenue had not been a particular figure and the ratio of revenue to capital employed had not been a particular figure, then the ROCE would not have turned out to be the figure that it is.

Thus, the ROCE comes about as a result of all the other ratios which have underpinned it. It is the final summation of all that has happened in the various aspects of the business. The ROCE pyramid of ratios is shown in Exhibit 28.7:

Exhibit 28.7

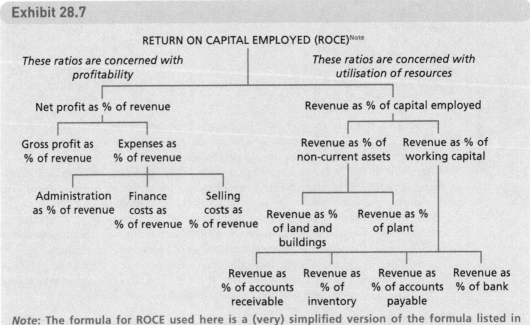

RETURN ON CAPITAL EMPLOYED (ROCE)[Note]

These ratios are concerned with profitability

These ratios are concerned with utilisation of resources

Net profit as % of revenue

Revenue as % of capital employed

Gross profit as % of revenue — Expenses as % of revenue

Revenue as % of non-current assets — Revenue as % of working capital

Administration as % of revenue — Finance costs as % of revenue — Selling costs as % of revenue

Revenue as % of land and buildings — Revenue as % of plant

Revenue as % of accounts receivable — Revenue as % of inventory — Revenue as % of accounts payable — Revenue as % of bank

Note: The formula for ROCE used here is a (very) simplified version of the formula listed in Section 27.8. Nevertheless, to all intents and purposes, it is the same formula.

By itself, the pyramid of ratios does not tell you everything. It comes into full effect when compared with similar ratios from previous years, or with similar pyramids of ratios in respect of other businesses. If the ROCE has been falling over the past year, a study of the pyramid of ratios for each of the previous two years may enable you to pinpoint exactly where the changes have been made to bring about the worsening position. Investigation of these matters may then give you some indication of the action to take.

28.7 Return on capital employed: company policy

The pyramid of ratios in Exhibit 28.7 illustrates the interdependence of each ratio. This can be examined in greater detail by investigating the policies of two companies to achieve their desired return on capital employed.

The first part of the pyramid tells us that the ROCE is dependent on both net profit as a percentage of revenue and also revenue as a percentage of capital employed. This means that:

$$ROCE = \frac{Net\ profit}{Capital\ employed}$$

which by splitting the equation between profitability ratios and resource utilisation ratios means also that:

$$ROCE = \frac{Net\ profit}{Revenue} \times \frac{Revenue}{Capital\ employed}$$

This interrelationship of the subsidiary ratios can be illustrated through an example. At the same time, it can be seen that the result of computing a primary ratio is dependent upon the items comprising it; and that there is no guarantee that a value of x will be 'good', and y 'bad'. Whether the result obtained is 'good' or 'bad' depends on the underlying factors that give rise to the result obtained (what, for example, is the company's policy on depreciation and replacement of assets, as this can significantly affect the ROCE?), the sector in which the business operates and its relative size. Without knowledge of these items, comparison of the ratio analysis of two companies is likely to be misleading at best.

Two companies, both in the grocery business, may decide to aim for the same ROCE of 10%. This can be achieved in completely different ways by the two companies.

A Ltd is a large company operating a supermarket. It seeks to attract customers by offering low prices and makes a net profit of only 1.25% on sales. Its revenue for the year is £8,000,000 on which its net profit is £100,000. Its capital employed is £1,000,000. The ROCE is, therefore, 10% (i.e. £100,000 net profit on capital employed of £1,000,000). This can also be expressed as:

$$ROCE = \frac{Net\ profit}{Revenue} \times \frac{Revenue}{Capital\ employed}$$

$$= \frac{£100,000}{£8,000,000} \times \frac{£8,000,000}{£1,000,000}$$

$$= 10\%$$

B Ltd by comparison is a small local retailer. It seeks a higher margin per £100 sales, but because of higher prices it will achieve a lower volume of business. It makes a net profit of 5% on sales. Its revenue for the year amounts to £200,000 on which it makes a net profit of £10,000. The capital employed is £100,000. The ROCE is therefore 10% (i.e. £10,000 on capital employed of £100,000). This can also be expressed as:

$$ROCE = \frac{Net\ profit}{Revenue} \times \frac{Revenue}{Capital\ employed}$$

$$= \frac{£10,000}{£200,000} \times \frac{£200,000}{£100,000}$$

$$= 10\%$$

It can be seen that two companies, despite different sizes of business and operating different pricing policies, can have the same ROCE.

Learning outcomes

You should now have learnt:

1 Ratios on their own are frequently misleading – they should not be considered in isolation from similar computations:
   (a) in previous periods; and/or
   (b) on similar-sized firms in the same sector.

2 The items in the financial statements are affected by company policy – for example, the rate of depreciation to use, and the policy of asset replacement; the policies adopted, therefore, directly affect the ratio analysis.

3 Companies of very different size and in very different sectors can have the same ratio results despite their being different in every respect.

4 The importance and impact of size, sector and company policies upon ratios mean that there is no such thing as a 'good' or 'bad' value that can be treated as a yardstick for any ratio.

5 All ratios are part of one or more pyramids of ratios.

6 When the results of ratio analysis are being investigated further, the relevant pyramid of ratios can be analysed in order to pinpoint the element giving rise to the situation being investigated.

Answers to activities

28.1 The service business will probably have a lower current ratio – it has no inventory. Its accounts payable days are probably near zero. Its return on capital employed is probably much higher. Its asset turnover may be extremely high – it may not have very many non-current assets. Overall, trying to draw any sensible conclusions by comparing the ratios of these two businesses will be a waste of time.

28.2 It won't tell you whether the organisation is or was in a good position relative to its competitors or other organisations in the same sector. Nor will it tell you if changes in the ratios are actually moving in the appropriate direction for the sector in which the organisation operates.

28.3 In this case, you can try to identify other organisations with a similar range of activities. However, it would probably be more beneficial to separate out the data relating to each type of activity and then compare the reduced data against appropriate comparators.

Advice

Ratio analysis is a topic that causes more marks to be thrown away in exams than probably every other topic combined. No other accounting topic is as concerned with understanding rather than knowledge, and examiners increasingly expect you to be able to demonstrate understanding rather than simply your ability to prepare the financial statements or calculate the ratios.

There is no one set pattern to the questions, which depend upon the examiner's ingenuity and background experience. The usual shortcomings in the answers handed in by examinees, particularly on questions relating to this topic but also on questions in other areas, can be listed as follows:

1 Not following the instructions as laid down. If the question says 'list the' then the examiner expects a list as an answer, 'Discuss the' means exactly that, 'Write a report' needs a report as the answer, and so on. You will lose a lot of marks for not giving the examiner exactly what has been asked for.

2 Very often all the ratios etc. are calculated, but then the candidate does not offer any comments even though they have been asked for. *Make certain you cover this part of the question in an appropriate amount of detail.*

3 Even where students have written something about the ratios, they often repeat what the calculations are and offer nothing else, e.g. 'you can see that the gross profit ratio has increased from 18 to 20%' and the answer has finished there. The examiner can already see from your calculations that the gross profit percentage has increased, and wants you to write about *why* it might have increased, what conclusions, if any, can be arrived at, or what further information may be needed to discover why it has changed.

4 Remember that when the examiner asks you 'what other information you would like to have' about a firm when trying to interpret the financial statements so as to give advice to someone then, ideally, you would like to know more about the plans for the future of the business, how it compares with others in the same industry, whether or not there are going to be changes in the management and so on. We should not limit ourselves to information about the past, we really need to know as much about the future as we possibly can.

5 Do not restrict your examination answers to what you have read in a textbook. Keep your eyes and ears open as you go shopping, visit factories, work, buy petrol at the filling station, go to the theatre, and so on. Reading a 'quality' newspaper helps, as there are quite a lot of items about business. Bring all of this sort of knowledge and experience into your answers. You will impress the examiners. They are extremely bored reading regurgitations of textbook learning with nothing added.

6 Quite a few questions will concern the type of business of which you will have first-hand experience, so you can introduce personal knowledge into your answer. A typical instance would be comparing two grocery businesses. One would be a large supermarket and the other would be a small corner shop. The policies of the two firms would be quite different. The supermarket would have decided on a policy of attracting new customers by lowering sales margins and yet boosting ROCE. The corner shop might have a policy of high margins, but remain open on Sundays and late at nights, and thus be a 'convenience shop', i.e. customers might well go there when other shops are closed or are too far away to be worth the extra cost in petrol, etc. when compared with the extra cost of shopping at the corner shop.

7 Last, but not least, *show your workings*. If you make a mistake in your calculations and do not show your workings you cannot be awarded any credit for a partially incorrect calculation. Consider how much longer it takes to show the detail contained in Section 28.7 above, rather than simply the result of the calculation – maybe 30 seconds. *Now consider whether you would rather spend five minutes in an exam showing the workings of ten ratio calculations, or six months studying to retake the exam you failed because you made a mistake in two of your calculations and lost five marks because the examiner could not tell why you got the answer wrong.*

Review questions

28.1 Adrian Frampton was considering the purchase of one of two businesses. However, Frampton had only been provided with limited information about the businesses, as follows:

Summarised Financial Information for the year ended 31 December 2009

Information	Business X	Business Y
Cost of goods sold	£400,000	£600,000
Administrative expenses	£50,000	£60,000
Average inventory at cost	£40,000	£50,000
Working capital as at 31 December 2009	£90,000	£250,000
Selling and distribution expenses	£15,000	£35,000
Proprietor's capital at 1 January 2009	£200,000	£350,000
Gross profit percentage mark-up on cost	20	25

Additional information:

1 Average inventory had been calculated by using the year's opening and closing inventories. Subsequently it was discovered that Business Y had overvalued its inventory on 31 December 2009 by £10,000.

2 Business X's administrative expenses included a payment for rent of £15,000 which covered a three-year period to 31 December 2011.

3 A sum of £2,500 was included in the administrative expenses of Business Y in respect of a holiday taken by the owner and his family.

4 Cash drawings for the year ended 31 December 2009 were:

	£
Business X	20,000
Business Y	25,000

5 The owners of the businesses had stipulated the following prices for their businesses:

	£
Business X	190,000
Business Y	400,000

Required:

(a) Based on the information available prepare comparative income statements for the year ending 31 December 2009.

(b) Using the information provided and the accounting statements prepared in (a), calculate relevant accounting ratios in order to give Frampton a basis for assessing the performances of the two businesses. Comment on the results.

(c) What additional information is needed in order to assess more accurately
  (i) the liquidity of the businesses;
  (ii) the future prospects of the businesses?

(AQA (Associated Examining Board): GCE A-level)

28.2 Three companies have the capital structures shown below.

Company	A	B	C
	£000	£000	£000
Ordinary shares	600	400	50
12% loan notes	–	200	550
	600	600	600

The return on capital employed was 20% for each firm in 2006, and in 2007 was 10%. Corporation tax in both years was assumed to be 55%, and loan note interest is an allowable expense against corporation tax.

(a) Calculate the percentage return on the shareholders' capital for each company for 2006 and 2007. Assume that all profits are distributed.

(b) Use your answer to explain the merits and the dangers of high gearing.

(Edexcel: University of London GCE A-level)

28.3A Martha is the accountant of a trading business. During the past year she produced interim accounts for the six months ended 30 November 2005, and draft final accounts for the year ended 31 May 2006, as follows:

	Interim accounts £	Draft final accounts £
Revenue (all on credit terms)	140,000	336,000
Cost of sales (Note 1)	42,000	112,000
Gross profit	98,000	224,000
Less Expenses	56,000	168,000
Net profit	42,000	56,000
Non-current assets	70,000	63,000
Current assets (Note 2)	42,000	71,000
Current liabilities (Note 3)	(22,000)	(30,000)
	90,000	104,000
Share capital	30,000	30,000
Retained earnings	60,000	74,000
	90,000	104,000

Notes:
1 Average inventory was £14,000 during the first six months.
2 Current assets were:

	30 Nov 2005	31 May 2006
	£	£
Inventory	16,000	25,000
Accounts receivable	24,000	28,000
Bank	2,000	18,000
	42,000	71,000

3 Current liabilities consisted entirely of trade accounts payable.

Martha informs you that the business leased additional premises from 1 December 2005, and that sales arising therefrom totalled £70,000 for the six months to 31 May 2006, with an average mark-up on cost prices of 150% being made on those goods.

Expenses relating to these additional premises totalled £21,000 for the period. Two-fifths of the closing inventory of the business was located at these premises.

Prepare a report, using appropriate accounting ratios, to explain the changes in the financial situation of the business during the year ended 31 May 2006.

(Edexcel: University of London GCE A-level)

28.4 John Jones is considering purchasing shares in one of two companies and has extracted the following information from the balance sheet of each company.

	Company A Plc	Company B Plc
	£000	£000
Authorised share capital		
£1 ordinary shares	600	1,000
8% £1 preference shares	400	
Issued share capital		
£1 ordinary shares	300	800
8% £1 preference shares	200	
Reserves		
Share premium	300	400
Retained earnings	400	200
Non-current liabilities: loan notes		
10% loan notes (2010)		200
12% loan notes (2016)	400	

Required:
(a) Define the term 'gearing' stating clearly what is meant by a low gearing ratio.
(b) Calculate the gearing factor for each company.
(c) Explain to John Jones the significance of gearing to an ordinary shareholder in each of the companies above.
(d) Assuming for each company a trading profit of £200,000 before interest and an ordinary dividend of 15% show the movement on retained earnings for a year for each company. You should ignore taxation.

(AQA (Associated Examining Board): GCE A-level)

28.5A The following are extracted from the balance sheets as at 31 March 2004 and 31 March 2005 of Glebe Ltd:

	31 March 2004		31 March 2005	
	£	£	£	£
Current assets				
Inventory	20,000		25,000	
Trade accounts receivable	10,000		17,000	
Cash	5,000		3,000	
		35,000		45,000
Current liabilities				
Trade accounts payable	12,000		16,000	
Bank overdraft	7,000		34,000	
		(19,000)		(50,000)
		16,000		(5,000)

Required:
(a) Calculate for each of the two years two ratios that indicate the liquidity position of the company.
(b) (i) From the information given, give reasons for the changes which have occurred in the working capital.
     (ii) What other information regarding the current assets and current liabilities would you consider necessary to assess the ability of the business to continue in operation?
(c) Discuss any other information available from a balance sheet that may affect an assessment of the liquidity of a business.

(AQA (Associated Examining Board): GCE A-level)

28.6 Colin Black is considering investing a substantial sum in the ordinary shares of Jacks Ltd. Having some accounting knowledge he has extracted the following information from the accounts for the last two financial years.

	As at 31 March 2008	As at 31 March 2009
	£	£
Issued share capital		
£1 ordinary shares, fully paid	100,000	150,000
Reserves		
Share premium	10,000	60,000
Retained earnings	140,000	160,000
Loan capital		
10% loan notes 2015–2016	40,000	40,000

	For year ended 31 March 2008	For year ended 31 March 2009
	£	£
Net profit after tax	60,000	70,000

Because he was disappointed with the result he obtained when he calculated the return on the equity capital employed, Colin Black has asked for your advice.

Required:
(a) Calculate the figures which prompted Colin Black's reaction.
(b) Prepare a memorandum to Colin Black pointing out other information to be considered when comparing the return on equity capital employed over two years as a basis for his investment decision.
(c) Explain why a company builds up and maintains reserves.

(AQA (Associated Examining Board): GCE A-level)

28.7A   The following information has been extracted from the accounts of Witton Way Ltd:

Income Statement for the year ending 30 April

	2005 £000	2006 £000
Revenue (all credit sales)	7,650	11,500
Less Cost of sales	(5,800)	(9,430)
Gross profit	1,850	2,070
Other expenses	(150)	(170)
Loan interest	(50)	(350)
Profit before taxation	1,650	1,550
Taxation	(600)	(550)
Profit after taxation	1,050	1,000

Note: Dividends paid in 2006 were £300,000 (2005: £300,000).

Balance Sheet at 30 April

	2005 £000	2006 £000
Non-current assets		
Tangible assets	10,050	11,350
Current assets		
Inventory	1,500	2,450
Trade accounts receivable	1,200	3,800
Cash	900	50
	3,600	6,300
Total assets	13,650	17,650
Current liabilities: accounts payable	(2,400)	(2,700)
Non-current liabilities		
Loans and other borrowings	(350)	(3,350)
Total liabilities	(2,750)	(6,050)
Net assets	10,900	11,600
Equity		
Called-up share capital	5,900	5,900
Retained profits	5,000	5,700
	10,900	11,600

Additional information:
During the year to 30 April 2006, the company tried to stimulate sales by reducing the selling price of its products and by offering more generous credit terms to its customers.

Required:
(a) Calculate six accounting ratios specifying the basis of your calculations for each of the two years to 30 April 2005 and 2006 respectively which will enable you to examine the company's progress during 2006.
(b) From the information available to you, including the ratios calculated in part (a) of the question, comment upon the company's results for the year to 30 April 2006 under the heads of 'profitability', 'liquidity', 'efficiency' and 'shareholders' interests'.
(c) State what additional information you would require in order to assess the company's attempts to stimulate sales during the year to 30 April 2006.

(*Association of Accounting Technicians*)

28.8 You are presented with the following information for three quite separate and independent companies:

Summarised Balance Sheets at 31 March 2007

	Chan plc £000	Ling plc £000	Wong plc £000
Total assets *less* current liabilities	600	600	700
Non-current liabilities			
10% loan	–	–	(100)
	£600	£600	£600
Capital and reserves:			
Called-up share capital			
Ordinary shares of £1 each	500	300	200
10% cumulative preference shares of £1 each	–	200	300
Retained profits	100	100	100
	£600	£600	£600

Additional information:

1 The operating profit before interest and tax for the year to 31 March 2008 earned by each of the three companies was £300,000.
2 The effective rate of corporation tax for all three companies for the year to 31 March 2008 is 30%. This rate is to be used in calculating each company's tax payable on ordinary profit.
3 An ordinary dividend of 20p for the year to 31 March 2008 was paid by all three companies, as were the preference dividends.
4 The market prices per ordinary share at 31 March 2008 were as follows:

	£
Chan plc	8.40
Ling plc	9.50
Wong plc	10.38

5 There were no changes in the share capital structure or in long-term loans of any of the companies during the year to 31 March 2008.

Required:

(a) In so far as the information permits, prepare the income statement for each of the three companies (in columnar format) for the year ending 31 March 2008 (formal notes to the accounts are not required).
(b) Show the change in retained profits for each company over the year.
(c) Calculate the following accounting ratios for each company:
  (i) earnings per share;
  (ii) price earnings; and
  (iii) gearing (taken as total borrowings (preference share capital and long-term loans) to ordinary shareholders' funds).
(d) Using the gearing ratios calculated in answering part (c) of the question, briefly examine the importance of gearing if you were thinking of investing in some ordinary shares in one of the three companies assuming that the profits of the three companies were fluctuating.

(Association of Accounting Technicians)

28.9A The chairman of a family business has been examining the following summary of the accounts of the company since it began three years ago.

Balance Sheet (at 30 June) £000

	2004 Actual		2005 Actual		2006 Actual	
Freehold land and buildings		150		150		150
Plant	150		150		450	
Less Depreciation	(15)		(30)		(75)	
		135		120		375
		285		270		525
Inventory: goods and work in progress	20		45		85	
Accounts receivable	33		101		124	
Bank and cash	10	63	15	161	–	209
		348		431		734
Accounts payable	20		80		35	
Taxation	4		17		6	
Overdraft	–		–		25	
		24		97		66
Loan	–		–		200	
Deferred tax	7		9		23	
		7		9		223
		(31)		(106)		(289)
Net assets		317		325		445
Ordinary share capital (£1 shares)		300		300		400
General reserve		17		25		45
		317		325		445

Income Statement (for year ending 30 June) £000

	2004 Actual		2005 Actual		2006 Actual	
Revenue		260		265		510
Trading profit		53		50		137
Depreciation	15		15		45	
Loan interest	–		–		30	
		(15)		(15)		(75)
Net profit		38		35		62
Taxation		(11)		(15)		(15)
Net profit after tax		27		20		47
Dividends proposed		10		12		14

The company's products are popular in the locality and in the first two years sales could have been higher if there had been extra machine capacity available.

On 1 January 2006, additional share and loan capital was obtained which enabled extra machinery to be purchased. This gave an immediate increase in sales and profits.

Although 2005/06 showed the best yet results, the chairman is not very happy; the accountant has suggested that a dividend should not be proposed this year (2006) because of the overdraft. The accountant has proposed, however, that the directors consider a dividend of £14,000 (£2,000 up on last year).

Naturally, the chairman is displeased and wants some explanations from the accountant regarding the figures in the accounts. He specifically asks:

(i) Why, if profits are the best ever and considering the company has obtained extra capital during the year, has the company gone into overdraft? Can there really be a profit if there is no cash left in the bank to pay a dividend next year?

(ii) Why is the freehold still valued at the same price as in 2004? The real value seems to be about £225,000. Why is this real value not in the balance sheet?

Required:
Write a report to the chairman:

(a) commenting on the state and progress of the business as disclosed by the accounts and the above information, supporting your analysis by appropriate key accounting ratios; and

(b) giving reasoned answers, in the context of recognised accounting law, rules and practices, to each of the questions raised by the chairman.

(*Institute of Chartered Secretaries and Administrators*)

28.10   The following information is provided for Bessemer Ltd which operates in an industry subject to marked variations in consumer demand.

	£000
(i) Shareholders' equity at 30 September 2005:	
Issued ordinary shares of £1 each fully paid	5,000
Retained profits	1,650
	6,650

There were no loans outstanding at the balance sheet date.

	£000
(ii) Income statement extracts: year to 30 September 2005:	
Net profit before tax	900
Less Corporation tax	270
	630

(iii) Changes in retained profits: year ending 30 September 2005:	
Retained profit at 1 October 2004	1,620
Dividends paid during year ending 30 September 2005	(600)
	1,020
Profit after tax for year ending 30 September 2005	630
Retained profit at 30 September 2005	1,650

(iv) The directors are planning to expand output. This will require an additional investment of £2,000,000 which may be financed either by issuing 1,000,000 ordinary shares each with a nominal value of £1, or by raising a 12% loan note.

(v) Forecast profits before interest charges, if any, for the year to 30 September:

	£000
2006	1,800
2007	500
2008	2,200

A corporation tax rate of 30% on reported profit before tax may be assumed; the directors plan to pay out the entire post-tax profit as dividends.

Required:

(a) The forecast dividends for each of the next three years and year-end balance sheet extracts, so far as the information permits, assuming that the expansion is financed by:
   (i) issuing additional shares; or
   (ii) issuing loan notes.

(b) Calculate the forecast return on shareholders' equity, for each of the next three years, under the alternative methods for financing the planned expansion.

(c) An assessment of the merits and demerits of the alternative methods of finance based on the calculations made under (a) and (b) and any other relevant methods of comparison.

(*Institute of Chartered Secretaries and Administrators*)

28.11A An investor is considering the purchase of shares in either AA plc or BB plc whose latest accounts are summarised below. Both companies carry on similar manufacturing activities with similar selling prices and costs of materials, labour and services.

Balance Sheets at 30 September 2007 (£000)

	AA plc		BB plc	
Freehold property at revaluation 2007		2,400		–
Plant, machinery and equipment:				
at cost	1,800		1,800	
depreciation	1,200	600	400	1,400
Goodwill		–		800
		3,000		2,200
Inventory: finished goods		400		200
work in progress		300		100
Accounts receivable		800		500
Bank deposit		–		400
Total assets		4,500		3,400
Current liabilities				
Accounts payable	600		900	
Overdraft	200		–	
	800		900	
Non-current liabilities	1,400		1,000	
Total liabilities		(2,200)		(1,900)
Net assets		2,300		1,500
Equity				
Ordinary £1 shares		1,000		500
Reserves		1,300		1,000
		2,300		1,500

Income Statements – Year ending 30 September 2007 (£000)

	AA plc	BB plc
Revenue	2,500	2,500
Operating profit	400	600
Depreciation – plant, machinery and equipment	(180)	(180)
	220	420
Finance income: Bank interest	–	100
	220	520
Finance costs: Interest	(150)	(160)
	70	360
Taxation	(20)	(90)
Profit for the year	50	270
Note:		
Dividend proposed	40	130
Price/earnings ratio	30	5
Market value of share	£1.50	£2.70

Required:
(a) write a report to the investor, giving an appraisal of the results and state of each business; and
(b) advise the investor whether, in your opinion, the price/earnings ratios and market price of the shares can be justified in the light of the figures in the accounts, giving your reasons.

(*Institute of Chartered Secretaries and Administrators*)

→

28.12 The following are the summarised accounts for B Limited, a company with an accounting year ending on 30 September.

Summarised Balance Sheets for	2005/6		2006/7	
	£000	£000	£000	£000
Tangible non-current assets – at cost				
Less Depreciation		4,995		12,700
Current assets:				
Inventory	40,145		50,455	
Accounts receivable	40,210		43,370	
Cash at bank	12,092		5,790	
		92,447		99,615
Total assets		97,442		112,315
Current liabilities				
Trade accounts payable	34,389		39,215	
Taxation	2,473		3,260	
	36,862		42,475	
Long-term liabilities				
10% loan notes 2006/2009	19,840		19,840	
Total liabilities		(56,702)		(62,315)
Net assets		40,740		50,000
Equity				
Called-up share capital of £0.25 per share		9,920		9,920
Retained profits		30,820		40,080
Shareholders' funds		40,740		50,000

Summarised Income Statements for	2005/6	2006/7
	£000	£000
Revenue	486,300	583,900
Operating profit	17,238	20,670
Interest payable	(1,984)	(1,984)
Profit before taxation	15,254	18,686
Taxation	(5,734)	(7,026)
Profit for the year	9,520	11,660
Notes:		
1 Retained profit brought forward:	23,540	30,820
2 Dividends paid during the year were:	2,240	2,400

You are required to:

(a) calculate, for each year, two ratios for each of the following user groups, which are of particular significance to them: (i) shareholders; (ii) trade accounts payable; (iii) internal management;

(b) make brief comments upon the changes, between the two years, in the ratios calculated in (a) above.

(*Chartered Institute of Management Accountants*)

28.13A The following are the financial statements of D Limited, a wholesaling company, for the year ended 31 December:

Income Statements	2004 £000	2004 £000	2005 £000	2005 £000
Revenue – credit sales	2,200		2,640	
cash sales	200		160	
		2,400		2,800
Cost of sales		(1,872)		(2,212)
Gross profit		528		588
Distribution costs		(278)		(300)
Administration expenses		(112)		(114)
Operating profit		138		174
Interest payable		–		(32)
Profit before tax		138		142

Balance Sheets as at 31 December	2004 £000	2004 £000	2005 £000	2005 £000
Tangible non-current assets		220		286
Current assets: Inventory	544		660	
Accounts receivable	384		644	
Cash at bank	8		110	
		936		1,414
Total assets		1,156		1,700
Current liabilities:				
Trade accounts payable	256		338	
Non-current liabilities				
Loan notes	–		320	
		(256)		(658)
Shareholder's funds		900		1,042

The following information should be taken into consideration.

1 You may assume that:
    (i)   the range of products sold by D Limited remained unchanged over the two years;
    (ii) the company managed to acquire its products in 2005 at the same prices as it acquired them for in 2004;
    (iii) the effects of any inflationary aspects have been taken into account in the figures.
2 Ignore taxation.
3 All calculations must be shown to one decimal place.

You are required, using the information above, to assess and comment briefly on the company, from the point of view of:
(a) profitability;
(b) liquidity.

(*Chartered Institute of Management Accountants*)

28.14 G plc is a holding company with subsidiaries that have diversified interests. G plc's board of directors is interested in the group acquiring a subsidiary in the machine tool manufacturing sector. Two companies have been identified as potential acquisitions, A Ltd and B Ltd. Summaries of both these companies' accounts are shown below:

Income Statements for the year ending 30 April 2008

	A Ltd £000	B Ltd £000
Revenue	985	560
Cost of goods sold		
Opening inventory	150	145
Materials	255	136
Labour	160	125
Factory overheads	205	111
Depreciation	35	20
Closing inventory	(155)	(140)
	650	397
Gross profit	335	163
Selling and administration expenses	(124)	(75)
Interest	(35)	(10)
Profit before taxation	176	78
Taxation	(65)	(25)
Profit for the year	111	53

Balance Sheets at 30 April 2008

	A Ltd £000	A Ltd £000	B Ltd £000	B Ltd £000
Non-current assets		765		410
Current assets				
Inventory	155		140	
Accounts receivable	170		395	
Bank	50	375	45	580
Total assets		1,140		990
Current liabilities				
Trade accounts payable	235		300	
Other	130		125	
	365		425	
Non-current liabilities				
Loan notes	220		70	
Total liabilities		585		495
Net assets		555		495
Share capital		450		440
Retained profits		105		55
		555		495

You are required to prepare a report for the board of G plc assessing the financial performance and position of A Ltd and B Ltd. Your report should be prepared in the context of G plc's interests in these two companies and should be illustrated with financial ratios where appropriate. You should state any assumptions you make as well as any limitations of your analysis.

(*Chartered Institute of Management Accountants*)

28.15A J plc supplies and fits car tyres, exhaust pipes and other components. The company has branches throughout the country. Roughly 60% of sales are for cash (retail sales). The remainder are credit sales made to car hire companies and large organisations with fleets of company cars (business sales). Business sales tend to be more profitable than retail and the company is keen to expand in this area. There is, however, considerable competition. Branch managers are responsible for obtaining business customers and have some discretion over terms of trade and discounts.

The company's computerised accounting system has recently produced the following report for the manager of the Eastown branch for the six months ended 30 September 2004:

	Eastown Branch	Average for all branches
Return on capital employed	22%	16%
Gross profit	38%	45%
Selling and promotion costs/revenue	9%	6%
Wages/revenue	19%	14%
Accounts receivable turnover (based on credit sales only)	63 days	52 days
Inventory turnover	37 days	49 days

The Eastown branch manager has only recently been appointed and is unsure whether his branch appears well managed. He has asked for your advice.

You are required to compare the performance of the Eastown branch with the average for all branches. Suggest reasons for the differences you identify.

(*Chartered Institute of Management Accountants*)

28.16A Company managers are aware that the readers of financial statements often use accounting ratios to evaluate their performance. **Explain** how this could lead to decisions which are against the company's best interests.

(*Chartered Institute of Management Accountants*)

You can find a range of additional self-test questions, as well as material to help you with your studies, on the website that accompanies this book at **www.pearsoned.co.uk/wood**

Corporate Governance

Social accounting

31.1 Background

Over time, the objective of financial statements has changed. In addition to reporting to shareholders of the company, directors are aware of a wide range of other user groups who are interested in accounting information. These user groups include employees of the company and, more controversially, the public at large. The controversy arises when considering whether or not organisations are responsible for 'social actions', that is actions which do not have purely financial implications.

31.2 Costs and measurement

One of the problems associated with actions of this type is the difficulty of identifying costs and measuring the effects of (often intangible) factors that contribute to the 'value' of an organisation. It is obvious that employee loyalty and commitment to quality performance increase this value, but how are such intangibles to be measured using objective and verifiable techniques?

> **Activity 31.1** How would you value employee loyalty?

Some of the input costs of 'social' activities can be evaluated reasonably accurately. Providing 'social' information required under the Companies Act 2006 is not particularly difficult – it requires information regarding employees to be presented in the financial statements, including numbers of employees, wages and salaries data, and details regarding the company's policy on disabled persons. Also, even where 'social' actions are required by legislation, they can often be costed reasonably accurately. For example, there are a large number of European Union direct-ives which have been implemented in the UK relating to social and environmental policies, including the monitoring and control of air and water pollution.

The costs of complying with these disclosure requirements and operational control measures can be high and, as the number of regulations increases, these costs will become a basic and essen-tial part of financial statements. It will become increasingly important that not only the costs are reported, but also the benefits, and this is where the difficulties arise – how can the benefits of controlling pollution from a factory be evaluated? Indeed, should an attempt be made to evalu-ate them at all? Would they be better reported in qualitative or non-financial quantitative terms?

As soon as a company seeks to incorporate social criteria alongside other, more traditional performance measures, problems of objectivity, comparability and usefulness arise. For example, social criteria for a paper manufacturer may include environmental issues concerning reforesta-tion; and an oil extraction company would include the environmentally safe disposal of oil rigs at the end of their useful economic lives among its social criteria.

However, issues of this type become problematical when viewed using conventional capital appraisal techniques. Not only may the measurable financial payback be so long as to be im-material – as in the case of an environmental project such as reforestation – it may be virtually non-existent, as in the case of the disposal of obsolete oil rigs. Assessment of issues of this type require different techniques from those traditionally used, and organisations' accounting information systems will need to take this into account, not just in terms of using more qualitat-ive value criteria, but also in selecting the information which is sought in order to assist in the decision-making process.

31.3 The pressure for social actions and social accounting

Despite the existence of many environmental laws, much of the pressure for social actions comes from pressure groups like Greenpeace. These groups can have an enormous impact upon an organisation's profitability, in ways that governments have singularly failed to do. For example, an air pollution law may concentrate on monitoring the quality of air around a factory, rather than on measuring emissions from the factory, making it far more difficult to enforce action against the factory, as it can always argue that another factory is the cause of any pollution found. Also, powerful cartels can influence legislation to create enormous delays in introducing socially responsible legislative controls. On the other hand, a pressure group can stop demand for a company's products, make it difficult for it to send its products to its customers, and may give it so much negative publicity that it can find its public image materially and irreversibly altered in a very short time.

While pressure groups are not a new phenomenon, their power is now far greater than it has ever been. Organisations need to be aware of the social, particularly the environmental, issues inherent in and/or related to their activities, and must be in a position to assess how best to approach these issues. They can only do so if they identify all the variables, both quantitative and qualitative, and both the inputs (costs) and the outputs (effects) of these variables, and deter-mine methods with which to determine what actions to take.

Social accounting is concerned with how to report upon the application of the social policies adopted by an organisation, and upon how they have impacted upon the organisation and its environment. An organisation that does so effectively will not only be providing user groups with rich information from which to form a view concerning its social ethos, it will also be enhancing its ability to take decisions appropriate for its own longer-term survival and prosperity.

31.4   Corporate social reporting

The reporting of the social effects of a company's activities became an issue in the UK in the 1970s. The reporting of non-financial information usually takes the form of narrative disclosure, sometimes supported by a statistical summary. As much social reporting is non-mandatory, comparison with other companies is difficult, if not pointless and misleading. This is partially due to a positive bias in what is reported – most companies tend to report only 'good news' in their social reports. It is also due to the lack of standards governing what to include and how to present social reports.

Environmental issues have been firmly on the political agenda since the early 1980s and large corporations have responded to public demands for more information about 'green issues'. Oil companies, in particular, produce a notable amount of additional information in their annual reports. This environmental information usually includes details about the company's waste disposal practices, attitudes towards pollution and natural resource depletion, as well as the overall corporate environmental policy. However, many continue to avoid any non-mandatory social reporting, and many instances have been reported of organisations claiming to be socially responsible, when they were, in fact, anything but.

In 2003, the UK government announced that all listed companies would need to include an Operating and Financial Review in their annual reports from January 2005. In November 2005, this statutory requirement was removed, with effect from January 2006. While this false start set back the move towards a greater amount of CSR in the UK, it is unlikely to be long before CSR becomes a formal part of the annual report: the pressure for CSR is now too strong for it to be ignored. The latest move in the direction in the UK is the requirement that UK listed companies prepare an Enhanced Business Review from October 2008.

31.5   Types of social accounting

Social accounting can be divided into five general areas:

(*a*) national social income accounting;
(*b*) social auditing;
(*c*) financial social accounting in profit-oriented organisations;
(*d*) managerial social accounting in profit-oriented organisations;
(*e*) financial and/or managerial social accounting for non-profit organisations.

31.6   National social income accounting

National social income accounts have now been in existence for many years. The measure of the nation's productivity recorded in the accounts – basically in sales terms – gives an income called the gross national product, usually referred to as GNP.

To an outsider, an increase in GNP would seem to indicate a betterment or progress in the state of affairs existing in the country. This is not necessarily so. The following example illustrates this point.

A new chemical factory is built in a town. Fumes are emitted during production which cause houses in the surrounding areas to suffer destruction of paintwork and rotting woodwork, and it also causes extensive corrosion of bodywork on motor vehicles in the neighbourhood. In addition it also affects the health of the people living nearby. An increase in GNP results because the profit elements in the above add to GNP. These profit elements include:

● to construction companies and suppliers of building materials: profit made on construction of plant;

- to house paint dealers and paint manufacturers, painters and decorators, joiners and carpenters: profit made on all work effected in extra painting, woodwork, etc.;
- to garages and car paint manufacturers: profit made on all extra work needed on motor vehicles;
- to chemists and medical requirement manufacturers: profit made on dealing with effects on residents' health, because of extra medical purchases, etc.

However, in real terms one can hardly say that there has been progress. Obviously, the quality of life has been seriously undermined for many people.

As national income accounts do not record the 'social' well-being of a country, other national measures have been proposed. The one most often mentioned is a system of 'social indicators'. These measure social progress in such ways as:

- national life expectancies
- living conditions
- levels of disease
- nutritional levels
- amount of crime
- road deaths.

Thus, if national life expectancies rose, or road deaths per 100,000 people decreased, there could be said to be social progress, while the converse would apply were the opposite signals found to be occurring.

The main difficulty with this approach is that (given present knowledge and techniques) it cannot be measured in monetary terms. Because of this, the national social income accounts cannot be adjusted to take account of social indicators. On the level of an individual organisation, however, social indicators similar to the above are used in Planning, Programming, Budgeting Systems (PPBS). This will be discussed in more detail in Section 31.10.

31.7 Social auditing

While national social accounting would measure national social progress, many individuals and organisations are interested in their own social progress. This form of social progress is usually called 'social responsibility'.

To identify activities to be measured, a 'social audit' is required, investigating:

(*a*) which of their activities contribute to, or detract from, being socially responsible;
(*b*) measurement of those activities;
(*c*) a report on the results disclosed by the investigation.

An example of this might be to discover how the organisation had performed in respect of such matters as:

- employment of women
- employment of disabled people
- occupational safety
- occupational health
- benefits at pensionable age
- air pollution
- water pollution
- charitable activities
- help to developing countries.

Social audits may be carried out by an organisation's own staff or by external auditors. The reports may be for internal use only or for general publication.

31.8   Financial social accounting in profit-oriented organisations

Financial social accounting is an extension to normal financial accounting. The objective may either be to show how the social actions have affected financial performance, or otherwise to put a social value on the financial statements of the organisations. The two main types of financial social accounting envisaged to date are those of human resource accounting and how the organisation has responded to governmental or professional bodies' regulations concerning environmental matters.

Human resource accounting

One of the main limitations of 'normal' financial accounting is the lack of any inclusion of the 'value' of the workforce to an organisation. The value may be determined by:

(a) capitalising recruitment and training costs of employees and apportioning value over employees' period of employment; or

(b) calculating the 'replacement cost' of the workforce and taking this as the value of human resources; or

(c) extending either of the above to include the organisation's suppliers and customers.

It is contended that such measurements have the benefits that (1) financial statements are more complete, and (2) managerial decisions can be made with a fuller understanding of their implications.

For instance, suppose that a short-term drop in demand for a firm's goods led to a manufacturer laying off part of the workforce. This might mean higher profits in the short term, because of wages and salaries saved. In the long term, it could do irreparable damage, as recruitment could then be made difficult, or because of the effect on the morale of the rest of the workforce, or changes in attitudes of suppliers and customers.

Compliance costs of statutory/professional requirements

As the effects of organisations upon societies are more widely recognised there will be more and more regulations with which to comply. The costs of compliance will obviously then become a basic and essential part of financial statements.

31.9   Managerial social accounting in profit-oriented organisations

All that has been described has an effect upon the information systems of an organisation. They will have to be established on an ongoing basis, rather than be based purely on adjustments such as those made to the financial accounts at the year end.

The information will be used to affect the day-to-day decisions needed to run the organisation.

Activity 31.2   Why is an ongoing information system required in order to do this?

31.10   Financial and/or managerial social accounting for non-profit organisations

As profit is not a measure in these organisations it can be difficult to measure how well they are performing. Two approaches to measurement have been used, **planning, programming, budgeting systems (PPBS)** and **social programme measurement**.

Both of these approaches can be said to be part of what politicians in recent years have called 'value for money'. The general attitude is that while there may be a need for all sorts of social programmes, including health, there is a great need for ensuring that money is not wasted in doing this. The demand is that we should ensure that we get 'value for money' in that the outputs from such schemes should be worth the amount of money expended in carrying them out.

Planning, programming, budgeting systems (PPBS)

It has been said that in the past there was a great deal of confusion between planning and budgeting. Annual budgeting takes a short-term financial view. Planning, on the other hand, should be long term and also be concerned with strategic thinking.

PPBS enables management of non-profit organisations to make decisions on a better informed basis about the allocation of resources to achieve their overall objectives. PPBS works in four stages:

1 Review organisational objectives.
2 Identify programmes to achieve objectives.
3 Identify and evaluate alternative ways of achieving each specific programme.
4 On the basis of cost/benefit principles, select appropriate programme.

PPBS necessitates the drawing up of a long-term corporate plan. This shows the objectives which the organisation is aiming to achieve. Such objectives may not be in accord with the existing organisational structure.

For instance, suppose that the objective of a local government authority, such as a city, is the care of the elderly. This could include providing:

- services to help them keep fit
- medical services when they are ill
- old people's housing
- sheltered accommodation
- recreational facilities
- educational facilities.

These services will usually be provided by separate departments, e.g. housing, welfare, education. PPBS relates the total costs to the care of the elderly, rather than to individual departmental budgets.

Management is therefore forced by PPBS to identify exactly which services or activities should be provided, otherwise the worthiness of the programme could not be evaluated. PPBS also provides information which enables management to assess the effectiveness of their plans, such as giving them a base to decide whether, for every thousand pounds, they are giving as good a service as possible.

As the structure of the programme will not match up with the structure of the organisation, e.g. the services provided will cut across departmental borders, a specific individual must be made responsible for controlling and supervising the programme.

Social programme measurement

The idea that governmental social programmes should be measured effectively is, as yet, in its infancy.

A government auditor would determine whether the agency had complied with the relevant laws, and had exercised adequate cost controls. The auditor would determine whether or not the results expected were being achieved and whether there were alternatives to the programmes at a lower cost.

There should be cost/benefit analyses to show that the benefits are worth the costs they incur. However, the benefit side of the analysis is often very difficult to measure. How, for instance, do you measure the benefits of not dumping a particular substance or an obsolete oil rig into the sea?

As a consequence, most social programmes do not measure results (benefits). Instead they measure 'outputs', e.g. how many prosecutions for dumping waste: a high number of prosecutions is 'good', a low number 'bad'. This is hardly a rational way of assessing results, and quite a lot of research is going into better methods of audit.

31.11   Conflict between shareholders' interests and social considerations

Obviously, an organisation has to come to a compromise about how far it should look after the interests of its shareholders and how far it should bother about social considerations. For instance, a company could treat its employees so well in terms of pay, pensions and welfare that the extra costs would mean very low profits or even losses.

On the other hand, there must be instances where, no matter what the effects on profits, the expenses just have to be incurred. If the company has a chemical plant which could easily explode, causing widespread destruction and danger to people, then there cannot be any justification for not spending the money either to keep the plant safe or to demolish it. The full severity of the law must bear down on transgressors of the law in such cases of wilful neglect.

All the facts of the particular case must be brought into account. Let us look at a typical case where the answer may seem obvious, but perhaps there may be other factors which may make the answer not so obvious. Workers in underdeveloped countries are usually paid far lower wages than those in the developed countries. What happens if a large multinational company pays its workers in a given country three or four times as much as home-based companies? Immediately everyone wants to work for the multinational company, which can afford high wages, and leave the home-based companies which cannot. Is that sensible? What chance is there for the development of the country's own home-based industries if the outside companies constantly take all the best brains and most able people?

In such a case it would probably make more sense for the multinational company to pay wages more in keeping with the particular economy, and to help that country in other ways such as by improving the health care generally for all, better education for all, and so on. Obviously, a topic such as this will engender discussions and arguments for some considerable time.

31.12   Reports from companies

Companies, mainly those based in the USA, have begun to declare their philosophy towards such matters as the environment. This is usually included in the annual reports which accompany their financial statements.

For example, a company may have decided to have the following 10 principles of environmental policy:

1 To comply with both governmental and community standards of environmental excellence.
2 To use only materials and packaging selected to be good for the health of consumers, and for the safety and quality of the environment.
3 To keep energy use per unit of output down to a low level.
4 To minimise waste.
5 To get to as low a level as possible the discharge of pollutants.
6 To use other firms which have shown commitment to environmental excellence.
7 To research fully the ecological effect of the company's products and packaging.
8 To carry on business operations in an open, honest and co-operative manner.

9 To make certain that on the board of directors there would be scientifically knowledgeable directors, and ensure that they were regularly provided with environmental reports.

10 To ensure that all the above principles are fully observed and that challenges posed by the environment are vigorously and effectively pursued.

Learning outcomes

You should now have learnt:

1 To whom organisations are responsible is a controversial area, and there is no exact definition of 'social accounting'.

2 That social indicators measure social progress, but as yet, given their inability to measure progress in monetary terms, they cannot be incorporated into social income accounts.

3 That a social audit will test the social responsibility of an organisation, including compliance with regulations, for example legislation relating to employees.

4 If an organisation wishes to take account of social and environmental factors, these items need to be incorporated into its accounting information system.

5 That there is a conflict between shareholders' interests, for example profit maximisation, and social considerations.

6 That corporate social reporting is the reporting of a company's activities and how they are related to social, including environmental, issues.

7 That there are five areas into which social accounting can be divided:
   (a) national social income accounting;
   (b) social auditing;
   (c) financial social accounting in profit-oriented organisations;
   (d) managerial social accounting in profit-oriented organisations;
   (e) financial and/or managerial social accounting for non-profit organisations.

8 That social accounting is as yet in its infancy. There is obviously a great difficulty in trying to put money values on the various aspects of being better off or worse off. There are also problems connected with exactly what 'better off' and 'worse off' mean. One person's worsening in some way may be someone else's betterment.

Answers to activities

31.1 There isn't a correct answer to this question but there are examples of values being placed on employee loyalty, for example, clocks for 25 years' service, gold watches for 50 years' service, etc. But, do acts like this actually place a value on employee loyalty? Hardly – what is the cost per year of a clock costing £25 that is presented to an employee for 25 years' loyal service to the organisation: £1 per year. Professional footballers who stay longer than the norm with one club are entitled to a testimonial match where all the proceeds are given to the loyal player. Similar schemes also exist in cricket though, in cricket, it is usually a 'benefit year' where lots of events are held for the benefit of an individual player. Yet, there have been cases where footballers have ended up out-of-pocket because the gifts they gave all the players who took part in the testimonial match (they don't get paid) and other expenses were greater than the income from the game – hardly a case of loyalty being rewarded.

Clearly, organisations don't tend to put a value on loyalty in such a way as to reward the loyal individual directly. They also cannot include a figure for employee loyalty in the balance sheet as an asset. However, when a business is sold, employee loyalty is one of the factors that will be taken into account when deciding what the business is worth.

Just about the only way a business can recognise loyalty and endeavour to give it a value is to publicise it. This can be done through the media (tv, radio, newspapers, internet, etc.). It can also be done in the annual report, the document containing all the financial statements and accompanying reports that is sent to shareholders each year. The share price may rise slightly as a result but, even if it does, it is hardly the same as the company placing a value on the loyalty of its employees.

31.2 Being socially aware means that you monitor constantly the extent to which you are achieving your social-related goals. You can't simply check once a year whether you are putting too much pollution in the local river or whether your employees are being loyal and are happy, or whether your supplies are coming from companies that do not employ child labour. If an organisation becomes socially aware and adopts social accounting, its information system needs to be amended to reflect the change. It is not necessarily the case that its accounting information system will be affected – that depends upon whether the company's social policies are to be reported by the company along with its financial information.

Review questions

31.1 Describe how an increase in gross national product may not have a positive effect on the well-being of the country.

31.2 What types of measure could be used to measure social well-being? What difficulties would be discovered in trying to use accounting in measuring these?

31.3 What aspects of an organisation's activities could be measured in a social audit?

31.4 Describe how there could be conflicts between short-term and long-term benefits.

31.5 Describe how PPBS may conflict with departmental budgets.

31.6A Review a set of company financial statements for social disclosures. Consider the usefulness of such disclosures to different user groups.

31.7 Why has the traditional model of income measurement failed to account for the impact of business activities on the environment?

(*Association of Chartered Certified Accountants*)

You can find a range of additional self-test questions, as well as material to help you with your studies, on the website that accompanies this book at **www.pearsoned.co.uk/wood**

32

Corporate governance

Learning objectives

After you have studied this chapter, you should be able to:

- explain why it is important for companies to adopt sound practices of corporate governance
- describe the background to the development of the *Combined Code on Corporate Governance*
- outline the nature of the contents of the *Combined Code on Corporate Governance*

Introduction

In this chapter, you'll learn about the increasingly important issue of **corporate governance**, of the background to the development of a code on corporate governance that UK listed companies must follow and on which they must report their compliance annually and of the nature of its contents.

32.1 The importance of corporate governance

Corporate governance has been defined as 'the exercise of power over and responsibility for corporate entities'. It is concerned with the manner in which directors carry out their stewardship responsibilities. If the directors of a company are failing to act in the interests of the shareholders, they are not performing the role to which they were appointed. Where this occurs, the shareholders need to be aware of it and take the steps necessary to ensure the directors do perform their role properly.

However, it is all very well saying this should happen. In the absence of any regulation that must be adhered to, it can take a long time for it to become clear to a company's shareholders that the directors are acting inappropriately. To this end, a set of guidelines has been developed over the last decade – the *Combined Code on Corporate Governance*.

More information on why corporate governance is important can be found in a briefing paper prepared by the ICAEW: *Briefing 03.02 Corporate governance: why should companies care?* It is available at **www.icaew.co.uk/index.cfm?route=111160**

32.2 The *Combined Code*

In 2003, in response to continuing public concerns about the actions and motivation of some company directors who appeared to have their own interests at heart, rather than those of the shareholders they were appointed to represent, a revised version of a document called the *Combined Code on*

Corporate Governance was published by the Financial Reporting Council. The latest version is the *Combined Code 2006*. It is available at **www.frc.org.uk/corporate/combinedcode.cfm**

The *Combined Code* contains a set of guidelines which can be used to determine whether directors have adequately performed their primary task of corporate stewardship. That is, whether the directors have carried out their duties adequately and in an appropriate manner, and in the best interests of the shareholders that they represent.

32.3 The policing of effective corporate governance

The *Combined Code* is a voluntary *code of conduct* for the directors of all UK limited companies. It is neither a legally enforceable code nor has it the status of an accounting standard. However, compliance with the *Combined Code* is required by the listing rules of the Stock Exchange. As a result, when a company is listed on a UK Stock Exchange, the Directors' Report (which is included in the annual report of all UK companies) must include a statement indicating the extent to which requirements of the *Combined Code* have been observed. Along with the financial statements and notes, the Directors' Report is subject to review by a company's external auditors, thus minimising the possibility of spurious claims being made by the directors.

> **Activity 32.1** If corporate governance is so important, why do you think unlisted companies are not required to apply the *Combined Code*?

32.4 The development of the *Combined Code*

The development of the *Combined Code* began with the *Cadbury Report*. This was the report of a Committee set up in May 1991 by the Financial Reporting Council, the London Stock Exchange and the accountancy profession, under the chairmanship of Sir Adrian Cadbury, to consider the financial aspects of corporate governance. The *Cadbury Report* was published in December 1992.

Its main recommendation was that the boards of all the listed companies registered in the UK should comply with a code of practice and state in their financial accounts whether or not they have complied with it, identifying any areas of non-compliance. It also stated that non-executive directors should be appointed for specified terms and re-appointment should not be automatic, that such directors should be selected through a formal process and that both their selection and their appointment should be a matter for the board as a whole.

This was followed by the establishment of a committee chaired by Sir Richard Greenbury. The committee's main remit was to look into various aspects of directors' remuneration. The *Greenbury Report* was published in July 1995 and it recommended a Code of Best Practice based on the fundamental principles of accountability, transparency, and linkage of rewards to performance.

The *Cadbury Report* and the *Greenbury Report* were then reviewed together and the report on this review, *The Committee on Corporate Governance – Final Report* (often referred to as the *Hampel Report*) was published in January 1998. This report led to the first version of the *Combined Code* being published in June 1998.

Using that version as a starting point, the current version of the *Combined Code* was developed with reference to the *Turnbull Report on Internal Control* (2002–03), the *Smith Guidance on Audit Committees* (2003) and the *Higgs Report on Reviewing the Role and Effectiveness of non-Executive Directors* (2003) and contains elements of all three reports within it.

32.5 Justification for a *Combined Code*

Following the issue of the latest version of the *Combined Code* in 2003, the need for such a code was confirmed in a report called *Enterprise Governance: Getting the Balance Right*, prepared by the Professional Accountants in Business Committee of the International Federation of Accountants (IFAC) and was published by IFAC in 2004. It looked at 27 corporate case studies – 11 outstandingly successful companies and 16 companies that had failed. It found evidence of clear failures in corporate governance in the recent well known cases, including Enron, Worldcom and Vivendi. The report can be found at **www.ifac.org/MediaCenter/files/ EnterpriseGovernance.pdf**

The study analysed information for each company including:

- whether the role of the chairman and chief executive was split;
- how long the chairman, chief executive and financial director had been in place and where they had been recruited from;
- the executive remuneration package;
- the composition and background of the board;
- information about mergers and acquisitions;
- strategy development and implementation;
- the use of complex financial engineering techniques.

Corporate governance – key failure factors

High on the list of the key failure factors identified by the study was the culture and tone at the top level of the company. By their own poor example and failure to uphold high ethical standards, senior managers allowed a culture to flourish in which secrecy, rule-breaking and fraudulent behaviour became acceptable. Many examples were found of dominant, charismatic chief executives who went unchallenged by senior executives and board directors.

The study found that strategic factors were more important than good corporate governance. This confirmed what many commentators and business analysts had always felt to be the case – while poor corporate governance can ruin a company, good corporate governance cannot, on its own, ensure success.

32.6 The content of the *Combined Code*

The *Combined Code* comprises of two sections and three schedules:
Section 1: Companies
    A: Directors
    B: Remuneration
    C: Accountability and Audit
    D: Relations with Shareholders
Section 2: Institutional Shareholders
    E: Institutional Shareholders
Schedule A: Provisions on the design of performance related remuneration
Schedule B: Guidance on liability of non-executive directors: care, skill and diligence
Schedule C: Disclosure of corporate governance arrangements

It contains a set of main and supporting principles and all listed companies have to report on how it applies to them. The form and content of this report are not prescribed, it being felt that companies should be free to explain their governance policies in the light of the principles, including any special circumstances which have led to a particular approach being adopted.

As you can see from the outline contents of the *Combined Code*, it also contains a set of provisions. Listed companies must either confirm they have complied with these provisions, or provide an explanation where they have not done so. However, companies outside the FTSE 350 (i.e. those companies that are not among the 350 largest companies) are exempt from some of the provisions.

Schedule C of the *Combined Code* contains guidance which suggests ways of applying the relevant principles and of complying with the relevant provisions on internal control (C.2 and part of C.3 in the Code); and on the provisions concerning audit committees and auditors (C.3 of the Code).

At times, the text of the *Combined Code* lacks the precision of, for instance, an accounting standard. For example, the main principle in Section 1 concerning directors states that 'Every company should be headed by an effective board, which is collectively responsible for the success of the company.' What precisely is meant by 'effective' is a matter of interpretation based on the detailed contents of the *Combined Code*.

The supporting principles concerning directors in Section 1 are similarly broadly presented:

'The board's role is to provide entrepreneurial leadership of the company within a framework of prudent and effective controls which enables risk to be assessed and managed. The board should set the company's strategic aims, ensure that the necessary financial and human resources are in place for the company to meet its objectives and review management performance. The board should set the company's values and standards and ensure that its obligations to its shareholders and others are understood and met'.

'All directors must take decisions objectively in the interests of the company'.

'As part of their role as members of a unitary board, non-executive directors should constructively challenge and help develop proposals on strategy. Non-executive directors should scrutinise the performance of management in meeting agreed goals and objectives and monitor the reporting of performance. They should satisfy themselves on the integrity of financial information and that financial controls and systems of risk management are robust and defensible. They are responsible for determining appropriate levels of remuneration of executive directors and have a prime role in appointing, and where necessary removing, executive directors, and in succession planning.'

While this may appear less likely to be effective than the heavily defined terminology of accounting standards, the nature of what is being dealt with in the *Combined Code* lends itself to this approach and there is no doubt that it is proving an effective instrument in improving corporate governance in the UK.

The full text of the *Combined Code* contains a list of related URLs which anyone wishing to look further into this topic would be well advised consulting.

Learning outcomes

You should now have learnt:

1 Why it is important for companies to adopt sound practices of corporate governance.

2 About the background to the development of the *Combined Code on Corporate Governance*.

3 About the nature of the content of the *Combined Code on Corporate Governance*.

Answer to activity

32.1 The *Combined Code* has been imposed upon listed companies following high profile incidences of financial irregularities that resulted in heightened public concerns about financial reporting, accounting procedures and the remuneration of directors. Unlisted companies are, by definition, much smaller enterprises where, typically, the directors own the majority, if not all the shares of the company. Many of these companies are exempt from an annual audit and, in the case of those that are externally audited, the only people likely to be affected by poor corporate governance are those same people who are failing in the performance of their stewardship role. Consequently, it makes little sense to require unlisted companies to apply the *Combined Code*.

Review questions

32.1 Define corporate governance.

32.2 If the *Combined Code* is a *voluntary* code of conduct for the directors of all UK limited companies, why is it that all listed UK companies must report annually on their compliance with it?

32.3 Briefly describe the development of the *Combined Code* from 1991 to the present day.

32.4 Briefly describe the main and supporting principles relating to directors contained in the *Combined Code*.

You can find a range of additional self-test questions, as well as material to help you with your studies, on the website that accompanies this book at **www.pearsoned.co.uk/wood**

Statements of Cash Flows 1

Statements of cash flows

Learning objectives
....

After you have studied this chapter, you should be able to:

- draw up a statement of cash flows for any type of organisation
- explain how statements of cash flows can give a different view of a business to that simply concerned with profits
- describe the contents of International Accounting Standard 7 (IAS 7) and the format to be used when preparing statements of cash flows using IAS 7
- describe some of the uses that can be made of statements of cash flows

Introduction
....

In this chapter, you'll learn about statements of cash flows, how to prepare them, and the requirements of IAS 7 (*Statement of cash flows*), the accounting standard that regulates their preparation.

39.1 The importance of cash

Imagine that you were the sole proprietor of a small newsagent shop and you were asked which would you prefer:

(a) your shop makes a net profit of £30,000 this year and, at the year end, all your £10,000 of assets are invested in inventory and you owe your suppliers £10,000;

(b) your shop makes a net profit of £8,000 this year but you have £5,000 in cash, £2,000 in inventory, no debtors and no liabilities at the year end.

What would you reply?

It sounds like a stupid question. Here's another: Imagine that you were the sole proprietor of an advertising agency and that you have no employees. Which would you prefer:

(c) your business makes a net profit of £30,000 this year and, at the year end, all your £10,000 of assets are amounts owed by clients and you owe £10,000 to your trade creditors;

(d) you make a net profit of £8,000 this year but you have £5,000 in cash, £2,000 is owed to you by clients, and you have no liabilities.

You are in business because you want to make a profit, aren't you? But, is (a) the sensible answer to the first question, or (c) a sensible answer to the second? Probably not. If you have no cash, how will you pay your creditors?

This is a problem faced by many small businesses and is the main cause of between 20 and 30 per cent failing in their first 12 months of trading. It does not improve very much for those that survive their first year. While two-thirds survive for two years, under half survive for four years. On average, more than 10 per cent of small businesses fail every year in the UK.

More than half of all small business failures are due to a shortage of cash, yet, a study of UK small businesses in 2010 found that:

- 29 per cent of owners were too busy to find the time to keep a close eye on their financial position;
- checks on the credit worthiness of new customers (something that is very easy and cheap to do) are not done by two-thirds and three-quarters undertake no credit check when existing customers ask for an increase in the level of their credit.

The importance of cash for any business cannot be understated. In almost all cases, the appropriate answer to select to the questions at the start of this section are (b) and (d). It is better to have enough cash to pay your creditors, particularly in the early years of a business. As businesses mature, they can relax their need for cash to some extent, but they must always be vigilant and must always have the means to raise cash when required.

If all your assets are in inventory, you may find it very difficult to raise sufficient cash to meet the needs of your creditors. Selling inventory at cost is not good for profits. Selling inventory at below cost is disastrous if done excessively. All businesses do it occasionally, none that survive do it other than in order to get rid of unsalable goods. Similarly, getting money from your debtors is not something that tends to occur quickly, especially if they think you may be having problems raising cash.

 Activity 39.1   Why might the fact you are having difficulty raising cash make some debtors take longer to pay you what they owe?

This book deals mainly with how to enter transactions in the accounting records of a business; and in how to determine the financial position of a business at a point in time (statement of financial position) and the profit of a business over a period of time (income statement). It does not focus upon cash. However, it would be wrong to learn how to record everything and produce financial statements of this type in ignorance of the importance of cash.

Exhibit 39.1 presents an example of one of a series of simulations from the MyAccountingLab website for this book. When you access the site, you will find that you can control the flow of cash along all the conduits in the diagram and see the impact that doing so has upon the levels of inventory, accounts receivable, accounts payable, profits, and funds in the bank (cash).

Exhibit 39.1

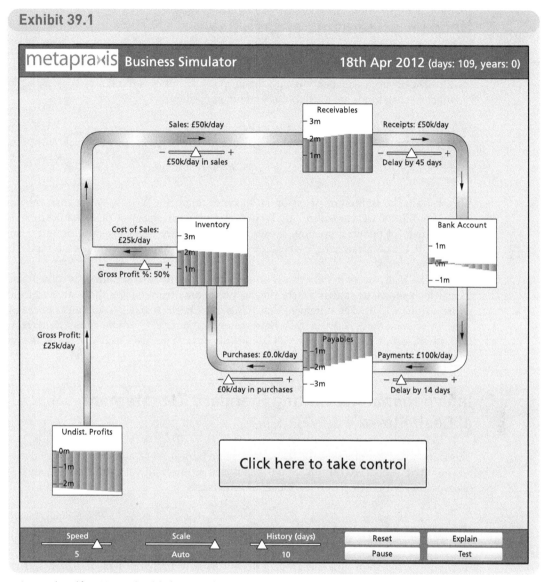

Source: adapted from Metapraxis, original source Bittlestone, R., *Financial Management for Business: Cracking the Hidden Code* (www.fm-fb.com).

These simulations show you just how important cash management is. They will help you to see how the sources and uses of cash interact and may help you to understand why a historical document like the **statement of cash flows,** the subject of this chapter, is considered an essential component of a business's set of financial statements.

In *Business Accounting 2*, you will learn about the tools used by accountants to assist managers manage the cash of their businesses. For now, we shall concentrate upon reporting how cash has been used which, in the absence of any other information, may indicate how it will be used in future. At the very least, when used in conjunction with an income statement and a statement of financial position, a statement of cash flows may highlight issues relating to use of cash that may merit attention or of the need for changes to the cash management policy of the business.

Firstly, we shall look at why it is considered necessary to prepare statements of cash flows.

39.2 Need for statements of cash flows

For any business it is important to ensure that:

- sufficient profits are made to finance the business activities; and that
- sufficient cash funds are available as and when needed.

> **Activity 39.2** What do you think is meant by 'cash' in this context? (*Hint*: which are the truly liquid assets?)

We ascertain the amount of profits in an income statement. We also show what the assets, capital and liabilities are at a given date by drawing up a statement of financial position. Although the statement of financial position shows the cash balance (see the definition in the solution to Activity 39.1) at a given date, it does not show us how we have used our cash funds during the accounting period.

What we really need, to help throw some light on to the cash situation, is some form of statement which shows us exactly where the cash has come from during the year, and exactly what we have done with it. The statement that fulfils these needs is called a statement of cash flows.

It is also sometimes called a 'cash flow statement' but IAS1 recommends use of 'statement of cash flows' so this is the term we will use in this book. You need to be aware of the alternative title in case your examiner uses it.

39.3 International Accounting Standard 7: Statement of Cash Flows

This standard, as its title suggests, concerns the preparation of statements of cash flows.

The International Accounting Standards Board requires all companies to include a statement of cash flows with their published financial statements.

39.4 Businesses other than companies

Although partnerships and sole traders do not have to prepare them, statements of cash flows can be of considerable use to all organisations.

IAS 7 prescribes a format for statements of cash flows. An example is shown later in Exhibit 39.7. This is suitable for a company but, obviously, there are factors concerning partnerships and sole traders which do not occur in companies. It will be of help to students if the statements of cash flows for sole traders and partnerships are fashioned to be as similar to those for companies as is possible. Consequently, the layouts for statements of cash flows of sole traders and partnerships in this book will follow the style of layout presented in IAS 7.

39.5 Profit and liquidity are *not* directly related

Many people think that if we are making profits then there should be no shortage of cash. As you have learnt earlier in this book, this is not necessarily so. Let's look at a few instances where, although reasonable profits are being made by each of the following businesses, they could find themselves short of cash, maybe not now, but at some time in the future.

- A sole trader is making £40,000 a year profits. However, his drawings have been over £60,000 a year for some time.
- A company has been over-generous with credit terms to debtors, and last year extended the time in which debtors could pay from one month to three months. In addition it has taken on quite a few extra customers who are not creditworthy and such sales may result in bad debts in the future.
- A partnership whose products will not be on the market for quite a long time has invested in some very expensive machinery. A lot of money has been spent now, but no income will result in the near future.

In all of these cases, each of the businesses could easily run out of cash. In fact many businesses fail and are wound up because of cash shortages, despite adequate profits being made. Statements of cash flows can help to signal the development of such problems.

 Activity 39.3 Can you think of any more examples? Spend a minute thinking about this and then write down any you come up with.

39.6 Where from: where to

Basically a statement of cash flows shows where the cash resources came from, and where they have gone to. Exhibit 39.2 shows details of such cash flows.

Exhibit 39.2

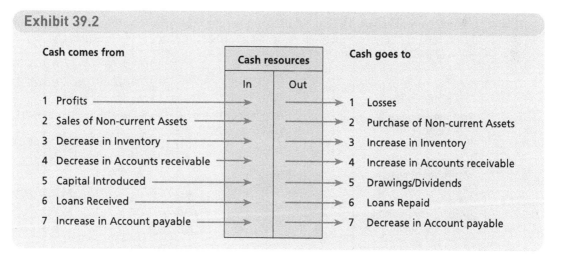

These can be explained as follow:

1 Profits bring a flow of cash into the business. Losses take cash out of it.
2 The cash received from sales of non-current assets comes into the business. A purchase of non-current assets takes it out.
3 Reducing inventory in the normal course of business means turning it into cash. An increase in inventory ties up cash funds.
4 A reduction in accounts receivable means that the extra amount paid comes into the business as cash. Letting accounts receivable increase stops that extra amount of cash coming in.
5 An increase in a sole proprietor's capital, or issues of shares in a company, brings cash in. Drawings or dividends take it out.

6 Loans received bring in cash, while their repayment reduces cash.
7 An increase in accounts payable keeps the extra cash in the business. A decrease in accounts payable means that the extra payments take cash out.

If, therefore, we take the cash (and bank) balances at the start of a financial period, and adjust it for cash flows in and out during the financial period, then we should arrive at the cash (and bank) balances at the end of the period. This can be shown as:

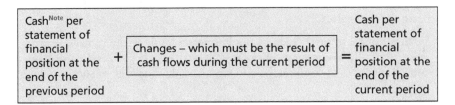

Note: 'Cash' in this context includes amounts held in bank accounts. We don't usually refer to 'cash and bank', but simply to 'cash'.

39.7 Construction of a statement of cash flows

We will first of all look at a couple of examples of statements of cash flows drawn up for sole trader businesses, as this will make it easier to understand the process of preparing one before we go on to look at a more complicated example of a limited company's statement of cash flows in Exhibit 39.8.

First, we will start with Exhibit 39.3 and use it to construct Exhibit 39.4, a statement of cash flows using the (indirect method) format prescribed by IAS 7. (We'll explain what is meant by 'indirect method' in Section 39.12.)

Exhibit 39.3

The following are the statements of financial position of T. Holmes as at 31 December 2012 and 31 December 2013:

	31.12.2012		31.12.2013	
	£	£	£	£
Non-current assets				
Premises at cost		25,000		28,800
Current assets				
Inventory	12,500		12,850	
Accounts receivable	21,650		23,140	
Cash and bank balances	4,300		5,620	
		38,450		41,610
Total assets		63,450		70,410
Current liabilities				
Accounts payable		(11,350)		(11,120)
		52,100		59,290
Net assets				
Capital				
Opening balances b/d		52,660		52,100
Add Net profit for year		16,550		25,440
		69,210		77,540
Less Drawings		(17,110)		(18,250)
Total capital		52,100		59,290

Note: For simplicity, no depreciation has been charged.

Exhibit 39.4

T. Holmes
Statement of Cash Flows for the year ending 31 December 2013

	£
Net cash flow from operating activities (see Note 1)	23,370
Investing activities	
Payment to acquire extra premises	(3,800)
Financing activities	
Drawings	(18,250)
Increase in cash	1,320

Notes:

1 Reconciliation of net profit to net cash inflow:

	£	£
Net profit		25,440
Less cash used for:		
Increase in inventory	350	
Increase in accounts receivable	1,490	
Decrease in accounts payable	230	
		(2,070)
Net cash flow from operating activities		23,370

2 Analysis of changes in cash during the year:

	£
Balance at 1 January 2013	4,300
Net cash inflow	1,320
Balance at 31 December 2013	5,620

39.8 Note on the use of brackets

As you know, in accounting it is customary to show a figure in brackets if it is a minus figure. This would be deducted from the other figures to arrive at the total of the column. These are seen very frequently in statements of cash flows. For example, instead of bringing out a sub-total of the deductions, Note 1 accompanying Exhibit 39.4 would normally be shown as:

	£
Net profit	25,440
Increase in inventory	(350)
Increase in accounts receivable	(1,490)
Decrease in accounts payable	(230)
Net cash flow from operating activities	23,370

39.9 Adjustments needed to net profit

You saw in the statement of cash flows in Exhibit 39.4 that when net profit is included as a source of cash funds, the net profit figure has to be adjusted to take account of items included which do not involve a movement of cash *in the period covered by the statement of cash flows.* The most common examples are depreciation, allowances for doubtful debts, and book profits and losses on the sale or disposal of non-current assets.

Depreciation

For example, suppose we bought equipment costing £3,000 in the year ended 31 December 2012. It is depreciated at £1,000 per annum for three years and then scrapped, disposal value being nil. This would result in the following:

		Years to 31 December		
		2012	2013	2014
		£	£	£
(i)	Item involving flow of cash:			
	Cost of equipment (as this is purchase of an asset this is not part of the net profit calculation)	3,000		
(ii)	Net profit before depreciation	12,000	13,000	15,000
(iii)	Items not involving flow of cash:			
	Depreciation	(1,000)	(1,000)	(1,000)
(iv)	Net profit after depreciation	11,000	13,000	14,000

Now the question arises as to which of figures (i) to (iv) are the ones to be used in statements of cash flows. Let's consider items (i) to (iv):

(i) A payment of £3,000 is made to buy equipment. This *does* involve a flow of cash and should therefore be included in the statement of cash flows for 2012.

(ii) Net profit before depreciation. This brings cash flowing into the business and therefore *should* be shown in statements of cash flows.

(iii) Depreciation does not involve a flow of cash. It is represented by a bookkeeping entry:
   Debit profit and loss: Credit provision for depreciation.
   As this does not involve any outflow of cash, it *should not* be shown in a statement of cash flows.

(iv) Net profit after depreciation. Depreciation does not involve cash flow, and therefore (ii) is the net profit we need to include in the statement of cash flows.

In most examination questions (ii) will not be shown. As we will show you, the figure for net profit before depreciation is calculated in the statement of cash flows itself.

Allowances for doubtful debts

An allowance for doubtful debts is similar to a provision for depreciation. The cash flow occurs when a debt is paid, *not* when provisions are made in case there may be bad debts in the future. As a result, when preparing the statement of cash flows, you need to add back to net profit any increase in the allowance for doubtful debts or deduct from net profit any decrease in the allowance for doubtful debts.

If an examination question gives you the net profits *after* an allowance for doubtful debts, then the allowance has to be added back to exclude it from the profit calculations.

 Activity 39.4   What about bad debts? Should you make similar adjustments in the cash flow statement for them? Why/why not?

Book profit/loss on sales of non-current assets

If a non-current asset with a book value (after depreciation) of £5,000 is sold for £6,400 cash, the flow of cash is £6,400. The fact that there has been a book profit of £1,400 does not provide any more cash above the figure of £6,400. Similarly, the sale of an asset with a book value of £3,000 for £2,200 cash produces a flow of cash of £2,200. **Book profits and losses of this type need to be eliminated by adjusting the net profit when preparing the statement of cash flows.**

39.10 Example of adjustments

As the net profit figure in accounts is:

(*i*)   *after* adjustments for depreciation;
(*ii*) *after* adjustment to allowances for doubtful debts; and
(*iii*) *after* book profits/losses on sales of non-current assets;

net profit needs to be adjusted in statements of cash flows for these three events. However, the adjustments are only for depreciation in *that period*, and for non-current asset book profits/losses for *that period*. No adjustments are needed with reference to previous periods. Exhibit 39.5 shows examples of three businesses.

Exhibit 39.5

	Business A £	Business B £	Business C £
Depreciation for the year	2,690	4,120	6,640
Increase in allowance for doubtful debts	540	360	
Decrease in allowance for doubtful debts			200
Book loss on sale of non-current assets	1,200		490
Book profit on sale of non-current assets		750	
Net profit after the above items are included	16,270	21,390	32,410
Reconciliation of net profit to net cash inflow	£	£	£
Net profit	16,270	21,390	32,410
Adjustment for items not involving the movement of cash:			
Depreciation	2,690	4,120	6,640
Book profit on sale of non-current assets		(750)	
Book loss on sale of non-current assets	1,200		490
Increase in allowance for doubtful debts	540	360	
Decrease in allowance for doubtful debts			(200)
Net cash flow from operating activities	20,700	25,120	39,340

You will notice that the items in brackets, i.e. **(750)** and **(200)**, had been credits in the income statements and need to be deducted, while the other items were debits and need to be added back.

39.11 **A comprehensive example**

Exhibit 39.6

The statements of financial position of R. Lester are as follows:

	31.12.2013			31.12.2014		
	£	£	£	£	£	£
Non-current assets						
Equipment at cost		28,500			26,100	
Less Depreciation to date		(11,450)			(13,010)	
		17,050			13,090	
Current assets						
Inventory		18,570			16,250	
Accounts receivable	8,470			14,190		
Less Allowance for doubtful debts	(420)			(800)		
		8,050			13,390	
Cash and bank balances		4,060			3,700	
			30,680			33,340
Total assets			47,730			46,430
Current liabilities						
Accounts payable		4,140			5,730	
Non-current liability						
Loan from J. Gorsey		10,000			4,000	
			(14,140)			(9,730)
Total liabilities			33,590			36,700
Net assets						
Capital						
Opening balances b/d		35,760			33,590	
Add Net profit		10,240			11,070	
Add Cash introduced		–			600	
		46,000			45,260	
Less Drawings		(12,410)			(8,560)	
Total capital		33,590			36,700	

Note: Equipment with a book value of £1,350 was sold for £900. Depreciation of equipment during the year was £2,610.

The (indirect method) cash flow statement will be as follows:

Exhibit 39.7

R. Lester
Statement of Cash Flows for the year ending 31 December 2014

	£	£
Net cash flow from operating activities (see Note 1)		12,700
Investing activities		
Receipts from sale of non-current assets		900
Financing activities		
Capital introduced	600	
Loan repaid to J. Gorsey	(6,000)	
Drawings	(8,560)	
		(13,960)
Decrease in cash		(360)

Notes:
1 Reconciliation of net profit to net cash inflow:

	£
Net profit	11,070
Depreciation	2,610
Loss on sale of non-current assets	450
Increase in allowance for doubtful debts	380
Decrease in inventory	2,320
Increase in accounts payable	1,590
Increase in accounts receivable	(5,720)
Net cash flow from operating activities	12,700

2 Analysis of changes in cash during the year:

	£
Balance at 1 January 2014	4,060
Net cash inflow	(360)
Balance at 31 December 2014	3,700

39.12 Companies and statements of cash flows

We have already stated that companies must publish a statement of cash flows for each accounting period. Students whose level of studies terminates with the conclusion of *Business Accounting 1* will not normally need to know more than has already been explained in this chapter. However, some will need to know the basic layout given in IAS 7.

There are two approaches available under the standard: the 'direct' method, which shows the operating cash receipts and payments summing to the net cash flow from operating activities – in effect, it summarises the cash book; and the 'indirect' method, which (as you've seen already) identifies the net cash flow via a reconciliation to operating profit. As the reconciliation has also to be shown when the direct method is used, it is hardly surprising that the indirect method is the more commonly adopted one. Although the IASB recommend use of the direct method, the indirect method is permitted because the cost of producing the data required for the direct method is likely to be greater than the benefit of doing so, in most cases. The direct method is too advanced for this book and is dealt with in *Business Accounting 2*.

As you've already seen, IAS 7 requires that cash flows be shown under only three categories of activity: operating; investing; and financing. (This is how it was presented in Exhibits 39.4 and 39.7.)

IAS 7 defines cash flows to include cash equivalents: 'short-term, highly liquid investments that are readily convertible to known amounts of cash and which are subject to an insignificant risk of changes in values'.

You have already been introduced to the basic layout of the indirect method in Exhibits 39.4 and 39.7. Exhibit 39.8 shows another example using the indirect method, this time for a company.

Exhibit 39.8 Format for an IAS 7 Statement of Cash Flows (indirect method)

X Limited
Statement of Cash Flows for the year ending 31 December 2013

	£000	£000
Cash flows from operating activities		
Operating profit before taxation	XXX	
Adjustments for:		
Depreciation	XXX	
(Profit)/Loss on sale of tangible non-current assets	XXX	
Operating cash flows before movements in working capital		XXX
(Increase)/Decrease in inventory	XXX	
(Increase)/Decrease in accounts receivable	XXX	
Increase/(Decrease) in accounts payable	XXX	
		XXX
Cash generated by operations		XXX
Tax paid	(XXX)	
Interest paid	(XXX)	
		(XXX)
Net cash from/(used in) operating activities		XXX
Cash flows from investing activities		
Dividends from joint ventures	XXX	
Dividends from associates	XXX	
Interest received	XXX	
Payments to acquire intangible non-current assets	(XXX)	
Payments to acquire tangible non-current assets	(XXX)	
Receipts from sales of tangible non-current assets	XXX	
Purchase of subsidiary undertaking	(XXX)	
Sale of business	XXX	
Net cash from/(used in) investing activities		(XXX)
Cash flows from financing activities		
Ordinary dividends paid	(XXX)	
Preference dividends paid	(XXX)	
Issue of ordinary share capital	XXX	
Repurchase of loan note	(XXX)	
Expenses paid in connection with share issues	(XXX)	
Net cash from/(used in) financing activities		XXX
Net Increase/(decrease) in cash and cash equivalents		XXX
Cash and cash equivalents at beginning of year		XXX
Cash and cash equivalents at end of year		XXX

Note: The inclusion of the reconciliation of operating profit to net cash from/(used in) operating activities at the start of the statement of cash flows in Exhibit 39.8 rather than as a note follows the approach given in the Appendix to IAS 7.

39.13 Uses of statements of cash flows

Statements of cash flows have many uses other than the legal need for some companies to prepare them. Cases where a business might find them useful in helping to answer their queries include:

(a) A small businessman wants to know why he now has an overdraft. He started off the year with money in the bank, he has made profits, and yet he now has a bank overdraft.
(b) Another businessman wants to know why the bank balance has risen even though the business is losing money.
(c) The partners in a business have put in additional capital during the year. Even so, the bank balance has fallen dramatically. They want an explanation as to how this has happened.

A study of the other financial statements themselves would not provide the information they needed. However, a study of the statement of cash flows in each case will reveal the answers to their questions.

Besides the answers to such specific queries, statements of cash flows should also help businesses to assess the following:

- the cash flows which the business may be able to generate in the future;
- how far the business will be able to meet future commitments, e.g. tax due, loan repayments, interest payments, contracts that could possibly lose quite a lot of money;
- how far future share issues may be needed, or additional capital in the case of sole traders or partnerships;
- a valuation of the business.

Learning outcomes

You should now have learnt:

1 Why statements of cash flows provide useful information for decision-making.
2 A range of sources and applications of cash.
3 How to adjust net profit for non-cash items to find the net cash flow from operating activities.
4 How to prepare a statement of cash flows as defined by IAS 7.
5 How to present the net cash flow from operating activities using the indirect method.
6 Some of the uses that can be made of statements of cash flows.

Answers to activities

39.1 When people believe that a business is trying to raise cash quickly, they may assume that the business is finding it difficult to pay its creditors. If so, this is a sign that the business may fail. Some debtors may believe that they will not have to pay their debt to the business if that happens. As a result, they will delay paying their debts to the business for as long as possible.

39.2 Liquidity is the key. Nowadays, something is generally considered as sufficiently liquid to be described as 'cash' in this context if it can definitely be turned into cash within three months. Not only does **cash** in this sense include the obvious – cash balances and bank balances – it also includes funds invested in **cash equivalents**. These cash equivalents consist of the temporary investments of cash not required at present by the business, such as funds put on short-term deposit with a bank. Such investments must be readily convertible into cash, or available as cash.

This is an important definition and is one you should memorise if cash flow statements are examinable under the syllabus of your course.

39.3 Other examples include:

- The bank overdraft has been growing steadily and is now greater than the amount owed by debtors.
- A major supplier is experiencing cash flow problems and is threatening not to provide any further goods unless all bills are paid within five working days. Your business has no other sources of supply for these goods and the bank has indicated that it will not advance any further loans or increase the overdraft facility.
- A seriously dangerous defect has been identified in the sole product manufactured by the business. This could lead to all items sold in the last year having to be replaced with newly produced replacements. The faulty items cannot be repaired. The business has already borrowed as much as it is allowed by the bank.

39.4 A bad debt that is written-off represents an expense that *does not* involve a flow of cash during the period. A debt becomes cash when paid, and only does so at the time payment is received. In writing-off the debt, you are saying that cash will not be received and have written off the debt to the profit and loss account. In theory, you need to adjust both the profit (by adding it back) and the change in the debtor balance. *However, these adjustments cancel each other out, so you need do nothing when preparing the statement of cash flows.*

Review questions

39.1 The statements of financial position of A. Vantuira, a sole trader, for two successive years are shown below. You are required to draw up a statement of cash flows for the year ending 31 December 2012 using the IAS 7 layout.

Statements of Financial Position as at 31 December

	2011		2012	
	£	£	£	£
Non-current assets				
Land and premises (cost £160,000)		140,000		138,000
Plant and equipment				
(cost £24,000)		22,000		–
(cost £30,000)		–		26,000
		162,000		164,000
Current Assets				
Inventory	9,000		7,000	
Trade accounts receivable	18,000		13,000	
Bank	–		8,000	
		27,000		28,000
Total assets		189,000		192,000
Current Liabilities				
Trade accounts payable	21,000		14,000	
Bank overdraft	17,000		–	
	38,000		14,000	
Non-current liabilities				
Loan (repayable December 2014)	–		25,000	
Total liabilities		(38,000)		(39,000)
Net assets		151,000		153,000
Capital account:				
Balance at 1 January		137,000		151,000
Add Net profit for the year		42,000		26,000
		179,000		177,000
Less Drawings		(28,000)		(24,000)
		151,000		153,000

39.2A

Gerry Peace
Statements of Financial Position as at 31 December

	2012		2013	
	£	£	£	£
Non-current assets				
Buildings		50,000		50,000
Fixtures *less* Depreciation		1,800		2,000
Van *less* Depreciation		3,920		7,400
		55,720		59,400
Current assets				
Inventory	5,600		12,400	
Trade accounts receivable	6,400		8,200	
Bank	900		–	
Cash	220		200	
		13,120		20,800
Total assets		68,840		80,200
Current liabilities				
Accounts payable	6,300		3,006	
Bank overdraft	–		94	
	6,300		3,100	
Non-current liabilities				
Loan (repayable in 10 years' time)	10,000		15,000	
Total liabilities		(16,300)		(18,100)
Net assets		52,540		62,100
Capital account:				
Balance at 1 January		37,040		52,540
Add Net profit for the year		35,200		21,160
Cash introduced		–		10,000
		72,240		83,700
Less Drawings		(19,700)		(21,600)
Total capital		52,540		62,100

Draw up a statement of cash flows for Gerry Peace for the year ending 31 December 2013 using the IAS 7 layout. You are told that fixtures bought in 2003 cost £400, whilst a van was bought for £5,500.

39.3 Malcolm Phillips is a sole trader who prepares his financial statements annually to 30 April. His summarised statements of financial position for the last two years are shown below.

Statements of Financial Position as at 30 April

	2011 £	2011 £	2012 £	2012 £
Non-current assets		15,500		18,500
Less Provision for depreciation		(1,500)		(1,700)
		14,000		16,800
Current assets				
Inventory	3,100		5,900	
Trade accounts receivable	3,900		3,400	
Bank	1,500		–	
		8,500		9,300
Total assets		22,500		26,100
Current liabilities				
Trade accounts payable	2,000		2,200	
Bank overdraft	–		900	
Total liabilities		(2,000)		(3,100)
Net assets		20,500		23,000
Capital account:				
Balance at 1 May		20,000		20,500
Add Net profit for the year		7,000		8,500
Additional capital introduced		–		2,000
		27,000		31,000
Less Drawings		(6,500)		(8,000)
Total capital		20,500		23,000

Malcolm is surprised to see that he now has an overdraft, in spite of making a profit and bringing in additional capital during the year.

Questions:
(a) Draw up a suitable financial statement which will explain to Malcolm how his overdraft has arisen.
(b) The following further information relates to the year ended 30 April 2012.

	£
Sales (all on credit)	30,000
Cost of sales	22,500

Calculate Malcolm's
(i)   gross profit margin
(ii) rate of inventory turnover.

(*Midland Examining Group: GCSE*)

39.4 From the following details you are to draft a statement of cash flows for D. Duncan for the year ending 31 December 2011, using the IAS 7 layout.

D. Duncan
Income Statement for the year ending 31 December 2011

	£	£
Gross profit		44,700
Add Discounts received	410	
Profit on sale of van	620	1,030
		45,730
Less Expenses		
Motor expenses	1,940	
Wages	17,200	
General expenses	830	
Bad debts	520	
Increase in allowance for doubtful debts	200	
Depreciation: Van	1,800	22,490
		23,240

Statements of Financial Position as at 31 December

	2010		2011	
	£	£	£	£
Non-current assets				
Vans at cost		15,400		8,200
Less Depreciation to date		(5,300)		(3,100)
		10,100		5,100
Current assets				
Inventory	18,600		24,000	
Accounts receivable *less* allowance*	8,200		6,900	
Bank	410		720	
		27,210		31,620
Total assets		37,310		36,720
Current liabilities				
Accounts payable	5,900		7,200	
Non-current liability				
Loan from J. Fry	10,000		7,500	
Total liabilities		(15,900)		(14,700)
Net assets		21,410		22,020
Capital				
Opening balance b/d		17,210		21,410
Add Net profit		21,200		23,240
		38,410		44,650
Less Drawings		(17,000)		(22,630)
Total capital		21,410		22,020

*Accounts receivable 2010 £8,800 – allowance £600.
 Accounts receivable 2011 £7,700 – allowance £800.
Note: A van was sold for £3,820 during 2005. No new vans were purchased during the year.

39.5A You are required to draw up a statement of cash flows for K. Rock for the year ending 30 June 2013 from the following information using the IAS 7 layout.

K. Rock
Income Statement for the year ending 30 June 2013

	£	£
Gross profit		155,030
Add Reduction in allowance for doubtful debts		200
		155,230
Less Expenses:		
Wages and salaries	61,400	
General trading expenses	15,200	
Equipment running costs	8,140	
Motor vehicle expenses	6,390	
Depreciation: Motor vehicles	5,200	
Equipment	6,300	
Loss on sale of equipment	1,600	
		(104,230)
Net profit		51,000

Statements of Financial Position as at 30 June

	2012		2013	
	£	£	£	£
Non-current assets				
Equipment at cost	40,400		30,800	
Less Depreciation to date	(24,600)		(20,600)	
		15,800		10,200
Motor vehicles at cost	28,300		28,300	
Less Depreciation to date	(9,200)		(14,400)	
		19,100		13,900
		34,900		24,100
Current assets				
Inventory	41,700		44,600	
Accounts receivable *less* allowance*	21,200		19,800	
Bank	12,600		28,100	
		75,500		92,500
Total assets		110,400		116,600
Current liabilities				
Accounts payable	14,300		17,500	
Non-current liability				
Loan from T Pine	20,000		10,000	
Total liabilities		(34,300)		(27,500)
Net assets		76,100		89,100
Capital				
Opening balance		65,600		76,100
Add Net profit		42,500		51,000
		108,100		127,100
Less Drawings		(32,000)		(38,000)
Total capital		76,100		89,100

*Accounts receivable 2008 £22,100 – allowance £900.
  Accounts receivable 2009 £20,500 – allowance £700.
Note: Equipment was sold for £15,800. Equipment costing £18,100 was purchased during the year.

Statements of Cash Flows 2

Statements of cash flows

Learning objectives

After you have studied this chapter, you should be able to:

- explain the purpose of cash flow information
- explain the difference between cash flow and profit
- explain the requirements of IAS 7
- prepare a statement of cash flows for a company following the format given in IAS 7 using the indirect method
- prepare a statement of cash flows for a company following the format given in IAS 7 using the direct method

Introduction

In this chapter, you'll build on what you learnt in Chapter 39 of *Business Accounting 1* relating to statements of cash flows. You will be reminded of the layout of a statement of cash flows prepared on the basis of IAS 7 using the direct method and will learn how to prepare a statement of cash flows using both the direct method and the indirect method.

15.1 Background

Business Accounting 1 introduced statements of cash flows and this chapter moves on to consider in more detail the accounting standard relating to these statements – IAS 7 *Statement of cash flows*.

IAS 7 requires that a statement of cash flows be prepared according to prescribed formats for all companies. The standard requires that the statement be included as a primary statement within the financial statements, i.e. it has the same status as the statement of comprehensive income and the balance sheet.

15.2 IAS 7: Standard headings

The objective of IAS 7 requires the provision of information about the historic changes in cash and cash equivalents of an entity by means of a statement of cash flows which classifies cash flows during the period from operating, investing and financing activities. For this reason, the statement must show the flows of cash and cash equivalents for the period under the headings:

1 operating activities
2 investing activities
3 financing activities.

The headings should appear in that order and the statement should include a total for each heading. Operating cash flows can be presented by either the *direct* method (showing the relevant constituent cash flows) or the *indirect* method (calculating operating cash flows by adjustment to the operating profit reported in the profit and loss account).

The standard indicates in which section various items are to be located and these are described in Sections 15.4 to 15.6. Further guidance concerning where items appear in the statement can be seen in the examples presented later in this chapter.

At the foot of the statement, the net change in cash and cash equivalents is identified. This is then added to the opening cash and cash equivalent balance to produce the cash and cash equivalents balance at the end of the period.

15.3 Cash flow

'Cash flow' is defined in paragraph 6 of IAS 7 as 'inflows and outflows of cash and cash equivalents'. Anything that falls outside this definition is not a cash flow and should not appear in the statement (though it could appear in the notes).

'Cash' is defined as 'cash on hand and demand deposits repayable on demand with any qualifying financial institution, less overdrafts from any qualifying financial institution repayable on demand'.

'Demand deposits' are deposits that can be withdrawn at any time without notice and without penalty or if a maturity or period of notice of not more than 24 hours or one working day has been agreed.

'Cash equivalents' are defined as short-term, highly liquid investments that are readily convertible to known amounts of cash and which are subject to an insignificant risk of changes in value.

Activity 15.1 Imagine you are running a business and you have £500,000 that you won't need for three months. How will you invest it?

15.4 Operating activities and cash flows

Operating activities are the principal revenue-producing activities of the entity and other activities that are not investing or financing activities. The net cash flow from operating activities represents the net increase or decrease in cash resulting from the operations shown in the income statement in arriving at operating profit.

The reconciliation between operating profit and net cash flow from operating activities for the period should disclose separately the changes during the period in inventory, accounts receivable, and accounts payable related to operating activities; other non-cash items, e.g. depreciation; and other items for which the cash effects are investing or financing cash flows.

In addition, cash flows from taxes on income should be disclosed separately under operating activities unless they can be attributed to specific financing or investing activities.

Also, interest and dividends must be disclosed separately under any of the three categories, so long as the same treatment is adopted from period to period.

In the statement of cash flows, **operating cash flows** may be shown using either the indirect method or the direct method. Using the **indirect method**, it would be laid out in a manner similar to that shown in Exhibit 15.1.

IAS 7 requires that in a statement of cash flows prepared using the indirect method a reconciliation be shown between the net cash flow from operating activities and the operating profit as shown in the income statement.

Exhibit 15.1

	£
Operating profit	12,000
Depreciation charges	500
Loss on sale of tangible non-current assets	10
Increase in inventories	(200)
Increase in accounts receivable	(100)
Increase in accounts payable	300
Net cash inflow from operating activities	12,510

The direct method would produce an analysis in the cash flow statement similar to that shown in Exhibit 15.2.

Exhibit 15.2

	£
Operating activities	
Cash received from customers	120,000
Cash payments to suppliers	(40,000)
Cash paid to and on behalf of employees	(60,000)
Other cash payments	(7,490)
Net cash inflow from operating activities	12,510

As you can see, both methods produce the same figure for net cash flow from operating activities. However, it is generally easier for an entity to adopt the indirect method – the figures are readily available from the income statement and balance sheet. The direct method, on the other hand, requires that the Cash Book is analysed. Despite there being much more work involved in preparing it, the IASB recommends use of the direct method when the potential benefits to users outweigh the costs of doing so – it does help provide a far clearer view of cash flow than the bookkeeping adjustments to profit that are undertaken under the indirect method.

Note: In an examination, if sufficient information on cash flows is provided for you to adopt the *direct* method, you should assume that is the approach to take.

15.5 Investing activities

These are activities involving the acquisition and disposal of non-current assets and other investments not included in cash equivalents. Examples include:

- cash payments to acquire property, plant and equipment;
- cash payments to acquire intangible non-current assets;
- cash receipts from sale of non-current assets;
- cash payments to acquire equity or debt instruments (such as loan notes) of other entities;
- cash payments to acquire an interest in a joint venture;
- cash receipts from sales of equity or debt instruments of other entities;
- cash receipts from sale of an interest in a joint venture;
- cash advances and loans made to other parties;
- cash receipts from repayments of advances and loans made to other parties.

15.6 Financing activities

These are activities that result in changes in the size and composition of the contributed equity and borrowings of the entity. Their disclosure is useful in predicting claims on future cash flows by providers of capital to the entity. Examples include:

- cash proceeds from issuing shares or other equity instruments;
- cash payments to owners to acquire or redeem the entity's shares;
- cash proceeds from issuing loan notes, bonds, mortgages and other short- or long-term borrowings;
- cash repayments of amounts borrowed;
- cash payments by a lessee for the reduction of the outstanding liability relating to a finance lease.

15.7 Foreign subsidiary cash flows

Under IAS 7, foreign subsidiary cash flows must be translated at the exchange rates prevailing at the dates of the cash flows (or an appropriate weighted average if this is infeasible).

15.8 Examples of statements of cash flows

Exhibit 15.3 presents a statement of cash flows using the indirect method.

Exhibit 15.3 Format for an IAS 7 indirect method statement of cash flows

X Limited
Statement of Cash Flows for the year ending 31 December 2007

	£000	£000
Cash flows from operating activities		
Operating profit before taxation	XXX	
Adjustments for:		
Depreciation	XXX	
(Profit)/Loss on sale of tangible non-current assets	XXX	
Operating cash flows before movements in working capital		XXX
(Increase)/Decrease in inventories	XXX	
(Increase)/Decrease in accounts receivable	XXX	
Increase/(Decrease) in accounts payable	XXX	
		XXX
Cash generated by operations		XXX
Tax paid	(XXX)	
Interest paid	(XXX)	
		(XXX)
Net cash from/(used in) operating activities		XXX
Cash flows from investing activities		
Dividends from joint ventures	XXX	
Dividends from associates	XXX	
Interest received	XXX	
Payments to acquire intangible non-current assets	(XXX)	
Payments to acquire tangible non-current assets	(XXX)	
Receipts from sales of tangible non-current assets	XXX	
Purchase of subsidiary undertaking	(XXX)	
Sale of business	XXX	
Net cash from/(used in) investing activities		(XXX)
Cash flows from financing activities		
Ordinary dividends paid	(XXX)	
Preference dividends paid	(XXX)	
Issue of ordinary share capital	XXX	
Repurchase of loan note	(XXX)	
Expenses paid in connection with share issues	(XXX)	
Net cash from/(used in) financing activities		XXX
Net increase/(decrease) in cash and cash equivalents		XXX
Cash and cash equivalents at beginning of year		XXX
Cash and cash equivalents at end of year		XXX

Note: The inclusion of the reconciliation of operating profit to net cash from/(used in) operating activities at the start of the statement of cash flows in Exhibit 15.3 follows the approach given in the Appendix to IAS 7. It is part of the IAS 7-based indirect method statement of cash flows.

The layout using the direct method is shown in Exhibit 15.4. Note that the only difference between it and the indirect method presentation is the content of the operating activities section.

Exhibit 15.4 Format for an IAS 7 direct method statement of cash flows

X Limited
Statement of Cash Flows for the year ending 31 December 2007

	£000	£000
Cash flows from operating activities		
Cash receipts from customers	XXX	
Cash paid to suppliers and employees	(XXX)	
Cash generated from operations	XXX	
Interest paid	(XXX)	
Tax paid	(XXX)	
Net cash from/(used in) operating activities		XXX
Cash flows from investing activities		
Dividends from joint ventures	XXX	
Dividends from associates	XXX	
Interest received	XXX	
Payments to acquire intangible non-current assets	(XXX)	
Payments to acquire tangible non-current assets	(XXX)	
Receipts from sales of tangible non-current assets	XXX	
Purchase of subsidiary undertaking	(XXX)	
Sale of business	XXX	
Net cash from/(used in) investing activities		(XXX)
Cash flows from financing activities		
Ordinary dividends paid	(XXX)	
Preference dividends paid	(XXX)	
Issue of ordinary share capital	XXX	
Repurchase of loan note	(XXX)	
Expenses paid in connection with share issues	(XXX)	
Net cash from/(used in) financing activities		XXX
Net increase/(decrease) in cash and cash equivalents		XXX
Cash and cash equivalents at beginning of year		XXX
Cash and cash equivalents at end of year		XXX

Activity 15.2   When the items needed for the additional information required by the direct method are so easy to identify from the Cash Book, why do you think most companies prefer to use the indirect method?

Learning outcomes

You should now have learnt:

1 The objective of IAS 7 is to require entities to provide information about the historical changes in their cash and cash equivalents in the form of a statement of cash flows which classifies cash flows during the period from operating, investing and financing activities.

2 This aids comparison between entities.

3 The IAS 7-based statement of cash flows must show the flows of cash for the period under the three headings:
   1 operating activities
   2 investing activities
   3 financing activities.

4 The headings in the statement of cash flows should be in that order and the statement should include a total for each heading.

5 Cash flow is inflows and outflows of cash and cash equivalents.

6 Operating activities are the principal revenue-producing activities of the entity and other activities that are not investing or financing activities.

7 Under IAS 7, operating cash flows can be shown using either the *indirect* method or the *direct* method.

8 The IASB recommends that companies applying IAS 7 use the *direct* method.

9 How to prepare a statement of cash flows under IAS 7 under both the indirect and direct methods.

Answers to activities

15.1 Possible short-term investments include term deposits (e.g. 30-, 60- or 90-day deposit accounts all of which are considered to be cash equivalents under IAS 7), government stock (e.g. Treasury stock) and corporate bonds (e.g. loan stock issued by companies).

15.2 In principle, the direct method is very easy to calculate. You just add up all the cash inflows and outflows relating to trading activities shown in the Cash Book. However, in practice, the volume of cash flows generated by any but the smallest business means that this can be a difficult and time-consuming task. It is not surprising that very few companies adopt this approach.

Review questions

15.1 List the three headings in the statement of cash flows, as required by IAS 7.

15.2A Give an example of the information to be included under each of the headings in an IAS 7-based statement of cash flows and indicate why this information might be useful.

15.3 Prepare a statement of cash flows for Lee Ltd for the year ended 31 December 2004 as required under IAS 7 using the direct method. The income statement, balance sheet and cash account for Lee Ltd for the year 2004 are given below:

→

Income Statement for the year ending 31 December 2004

	£	£
Sales		6,500
Less Cost of goods sold		(3,000)
		3,500
Less Expenses		
Wages	2,000	
Other costs	600	
Depreciation	500	
Interest	100	
		(3,200)
Profit for the year		300

Note: During the year, dividends of £50 were paid.

Balance Sheet as at 31 December

	2004		2003	
	£	£	£	£
Non-current assets at cost		4,500		3,800
Less Accumulated depreciation		2,300		1,800
Net book value		2,200		2,000
Current assets				
Inventory	400		500	
Trade accounts receivable	150		200	
Cash	200		100	
		750		800
Total assets		2,950		2,800
Current liabilities				
Trade accounts payable	325		300	
Accrued wages	25		50	
	350		350	
Non-current liabilities				
Loan notes	900		1,000	
Total liabilities		1,250		1,350
Net assets		1,700		1,450
Equity				
Ordinary share capital		1,000		1,000
Retained profits		700		450
		1,700		1,450

Cash Account for 2004

	£		£
Opening balance	100	Wages	2,025
Cash from customers	6,550	Other expenses	600
		Cash paid to suppliers	2,875
		Interest paid	100
		Cash purchase of non-current assets	700
		Cash paid to loan note holders	100
		Dividend paid	50
		Closing balance	200
	6,650		6,650

15.4A The balance sheets and additional information relating to Pennylane Ltd are given below. Prepare a statement of cash flows for Pennylane Ltd for the year ending 31 December 2003 as required under IAS 7 using the indirect method.

Pennylane Ltd
Balance Sheets as at 31 December

	2003 £000	2002 £000
Non-current assets		
Tangible assets	400	325
Intangible assets	230	180
Investments	–	25
	630	530
Current assets		
Inventory	120	104
Accounts receivable	400	295
90-day deposit	50	–
Cash in hand	10	4
	580	403
Total assets	1,210	933
Current liabilities		
Trade accounts payable	122	108
Bank overdraft	188	185
Taxation	120	110
	430	403
Non-current liabilities		
Long-term loan	100	–
Deferred tax	80	60
	180	60
Total liabilities	610	463
Net assets	600	470
Equity		
Share capital (£1 ordinary shares)	200	150
Share premium	160	150
Revaluation reserve	100	90
Retained profits	140	80
	600	470

Additional information:
(a) During the year interest of £75,000 was paid, and interest of £25,000 was received.
(b) The following information relates to tangible non-current assets.

At 31 December	2003 £000	2002 £000
Cost	740	615
Accumulated depreciation	(340)	(290)
Net book value	400	325

(c) The proceeds of the sale of non-current asset investments were £30,000.
(d) Plant, with an original cost of £90,000 and a net book value of £50,000 was sold for £37,000.
(e) Tax paid to Revenue and Customs during 2003 amounted to £110,000.
(f) Dividends of £80,000 were paid during 2003.

15.5   State the purposes of a statement of cash flows.

(*Association of Chartered Certified Accountants*)

15.6   The following information has been extracted from the books of Nimmo Limited for the year to 31 December 2009:

Income Statement extracts for the year ending 31 December

	2009	2008
	£000	£000
Profit before taxation	20,400	9,500
Taxation	(5,200)	(3,200)
Profit for the year	15,200	6,300

	2009	2008
Note: Dividends paid		
Preference	100	100
Ordinary	8,000	4,000
	8,100	4,100

Balance Sheets at 31 December

	2009	2008
	£000	£000
Non-current assets		
Plant, machinery and equipment, at cost	23,900	17,600
Less Accumulated depreciation	10,750	9,500
	13,150	8,100
Current assets		
Inventory	9,000	2,000
Trade accounts receivable	26,700	8,600
Prepayments	400	300
Cash at bank and in hand	–	600
	36,100	11,500
Total assets	49,250	19,600
Current liabilities		
Bank overdraft	16,200	–
Trade accounts payable	10,000	6,000
Accruals	1,000	800
Taxation	5,200	3,200
	32,400	10,000
Non-current liabilities		
15% loan notes	750	600
Total liabilities	33,150	10,600
Net assets	16,100	9,000
Equity		
Ordinary shares of £1 each	5,000	5,000
10% preference shares of £1 each	1,000	1,000
Retained profits	10,100	3,000
	16,100	9,000

Additional information:
1 The directors are extremely concerned about the large bank overdraft as at 31 December 2009 and they attribute this mainly to the increase in trade accounts receivable as a result of alleged poor credit control.

2 During the year to 31 December 2009, non-current assets originally costing £5,500,000 were sold for £1,000,000. The accumulated depreciation on these assets as at 31 December 2008 was £3,800,000.

Required:
Prepare a statement of cash flows using the IAS 7 indirect method for the year to 31 December 2009.

15.7   The following summarised balance sheets relate to Track Limited:

Balance Sheets at 30 June

	2011	2010
	£000	£000
Non-current assets at cost	650	500
Less Accumulated depreciation	300	200
	350	300
Investments at cost	50	200
	400	500
Current assets		
Inventory	700	400
Accounts receivable	1,550	1,350
Cash and bank	–	100
	2,250	1,850
Total assets	2,650	2,350
Current liabilities		
Bank overdraft	60	–
Accounts payable	920	800
Taxation	190	230
Total liabilities	1,170	1,030
Net assets	1,480	1,320
Equity		
Called-up share capital (£1 ordinary shares)	750	500
Share premium account	200	150
Retained profits	530	670
	1,480	1,320

Additional information:
1 During the year to 30 June 2011, some non-current assets originally costing £25,000 had been sold for £20,000 in cash. The accumulated depreciation on these non-current assets at 30 June 2010 amounted to £10,000. Similarly, some of the investments originally costing £150,000 had been sold for cash at their book value.
2 The taxation balances disclosed in the above balance sheets represent the actual amounts agreed with the Revenue and Customs. All taxes were paid on their due dates. Advance corporation tax may be ignored.
3 A dividend of £130,000 was paid during the year to 30 June 2011.
4 During the year to 30 June 2011, the company made a 1-for-2 rights issue of 250 ordinary £1 shares at 120p per share.

Required:
Prepare Track Ltd's statement of cash flows for the year to 30 June 2011 in accordance with the requirements of IAS 7 using the indirect method.

(Association of Accounting Technicians)

15.8A The accountant of a private company has been able to get the use of a computer to produce the spreadsheets shown below but as yet the computer lacks a program to print out final accounts. The accountant nevertheless expects to use the spreadsheet data to reconstruct a summary income statement and a statement of cash flows for the year ending 30 April 2006.

Movements of Assets during the year 2005/06 (£000)

	Balance sheet value last year	Depreciation or amortisation for year	Additions during year	Sales during year	Other changes	Balance sheet value this year
Goodwill	–	–	40	–	–	40
Property	760	(36)	–	–	–	724
Plant and vehicles	540	(84)	420	(60)	–	816
Inventories	230	–	–	–	24	254
Accounts receivable	254	–	–	–	76	330
Bank and cash	50	–	–	–	14	64
	1,834	(120)	460	(60)	114	2,228

Movement of Liabilities and Reserves during the year 2005/06 (£000)

	Balance sheet value last year	New capital issued	Payments during year	Transfers to reserves and for provisions	Other changes	Balance sheet value this year
Ordinary shares (£1 each)	1,060	440	–	–	–	1,500
Deferred taxation	36	–	–	176	–	212
General reserve	152	–	–	32	–	184
Accounts payable	136	–	–	–	24	160
Provision for corporation tax	450	–	(450)	172	–	172
	1,834	440	(450)	380	24	2,228

Notes:
(*i*) Proceeds of £40,000 were received from the sale of plant and vehicles.
(*ii*) During the year the company redeemed 10,000 of its £1 ordinary shares for £125,000 wholly out of distributable profits and this transaction has not been included in the spreadsheets.

Required:
(*a*) Reconstruct the income statement for the year ending 30 April 2006.
(*b*) Prepare a statement of cash flows for the year ending 30 April 2006.

Authors' note: Prepare the statement of cash flows under the rules of IAS 7.

(*Institute of Chartered Secretaries and Administrators*)

15.9   You are presented with the following forecast information relating to Baker Limited for the nine months to 30 September 2007.

Forecast income statements (abridged) for the three quarters ending 30 September 2007:

	March 2007 £000	June 2007 £000	Sept 2007 £000
Sales	250	300	350
Cost of goods sold	(200)	(240)	(280)
Gross profit	50	60	70
Depreciation	(3)	(20)	(4)
Administration, selling and distribution expenses	(37)	(40)	(42)
Forecast net profit	£10	–	£24

Forecast balances at	31 Dec 2006 £000	31 March 2007 £000	30 June 2007 £000	30 Sept 2007 £000
Debit balances				
Tangible non-current assets at cost	360	240	480	480
90-day deposit at cost	15	5	5	10
Inventory at cost	40	30	40	55
Trade accounts receivable	50	65	75	80
Cash at bank and in hand	80	–	–	–
Credit balances				
Loan notes (10%)	–	–	–	50
Trade accounts payable	80	120	140	150
Taxation	8	–	–	–

Additional information:

1 Sales of tangible non-current assets in March 2007 were expected to realise £12,000 in cash.

2 Administration, selling and distribution expenses were expected to be settled in cash during the month in which they were incurred.

3 Baker Limited includes as liquid resources term deposits of less than one year.

4 The directors have proposed that a dividend of £15,000 be paid on 28 February 2007.

Required:

(*a*) Calculate Baker Limited's forecast net cash position at 31 March, 30 June and 30 September 2007 respectively.

(*b*) Prepare a forecast statement of cash flows for the nine months ending 30 September 2007.

Authors' note: **Prepare the forecast statement of cash flows under the rules of IAS 7.**

(*Association of Accounting Technicians*)

15.10A   The following information has been extracted from the draft financial information of V Ltd:

Income Statement for the year ending 31 December 2003

	£000	£000
Revenue		495
Raw materials consumed	(49)	
Staff costs	(37)	
Depreciation	(74)	
Loss on disposal	(4)	
		(164)
Operating profit		331
Interest payable		(23)
Profit before tax		308
Taxation		(87)
Profit for the year		221

Note: Dividend paid = £52,000

Balance Sheets

	31 December 2003		31 December 2002	
	£000	£000	£000	£000
Non-current assets (see below)		1,145		957
Current assets				
Inventory	19		16	
Trade accounts receivable	38		29	
Bank	31		37	
		88		82
Total assets		1,233		1,039
Current liabilities				
Trade accounts payable	12		17	
Taxation	100		81	
	112		98	
Non-current liabilities				
Long-term loans	70		320	
Total liabilities		182		418
Net assets		1,051		621
Equity				
Share capital		182		152
Share premium		141		80
Revaluation reserve		170		–
Retained profits		558		389
		1,051		621

	Land & buildings £000	Machinery £000	Fixtures & fittings £000	Total £000
Non-current assets				
Cost or valuation:				
At 31 December 2002	830	470	197	1,497
Additions	–	43	55	98
Disposals	–	(18)	–	(18)
Adjustment on revaluation	70	–	–	70
At 31 December 2003	900	495	252	1,647
Depreciation				
At 31 December 2002	(90)	(270)	(180)	(540)
Charge for year	(10)	(56)	(8)	(74)
Disposals	–	12	–	12
Adjustment on revaluation	100	–	–	100
At 31 December 2003	0	(314)	(188)	(502)
Net book value				
At 31 December 2003	900	181	64	1,145
At 31 December 2002	740	200	17	957

(a) **You are required to** prepare a statement of cash flows for V Ltd for the year ended 31 December 2003 in accordance with the requirements of IAS 7.

(b) It has been suggested that the management of long-term profitability is more important than short-term cash flow. Explain why this might be so.

(*Chartered Institute of Management Accountants*)

Bank Reconciliations and Control Accounts

Bank reconciliation statements

Learning objectives
....

After you have studied this chapter, you should be able to:
- explain why bank reconciliations are prepared
- reconcile cash book balances with bank statement balances
- reconcile ledger accounts to suppliers' statements
- make the necessary entries in the accounts for dishonoured cheques

Introduction
....

In this chapter, you'll learn how to prepare a bank reconciliation statement and why you need to do this when a bank statement is received from the bank. You will also learn how to deal with dishonoured cheques in the ledger accounts.

30.1 Completing entries in the cash book

In the books of a business, funds paid into and out of the bank are entered into the bank columns of the cash book. At the same time, the bank will also be recording the flows of funds into and out of the business bank account.

If all the items entered in the cash book were the same as those entered in the records held by the bank, the balance on the business bank account as shown in the cash book and the balance on the account as shown by the bank's records would be the same.

Unfortunately, it isn't usually that simple, particularly in the case of a current account. There may be items paid into or out of the business bank account which have not been recorded in the cash book. And there may be items entered in the cash book that have not yet been entered in the bank's records of the account. To see if any of these things have happened, the cash book entries need to be compared to the record of the account held by the bank. Banks usually send a copy of that record, called a **bank statement**, to their customers on a regular basis, but a bank statement can be requested by a customer of the bank at any time.

Bank statements should *always* be checked against the cash book entries! (And you would be wise to do so yourself with your own bank account.)

Activity 30.1 What might cause the two balances to be different? Spend two minutes making a list.

Let's look at an example of a cash book and a bank statement in Exhibit 30.1:

Exhibit 30.1

Cash Book (bank columns only: *before* balancing on 31.12.2011)

2011			£	2011				£
Dec	1	Balance b/d	✔ 250	Dec	5	J. Gordon	✔	65
	20	P. Thomas	✔ 100		27	K. Hughes	✔	175
	28	D. Jones	✔ 190					

Bank Statement

				Withdrawals £	Deposits £	Balance £
2011						
Dec	1	Balance b/d	✔			250
	8	10625[Note]	✔	65		185
	21	Deposit	✔		100	285
	28	Deposit	✔		190	475
	29	10626[Note]	✔	175		300
	30	Bank Giro credit: P. Smith			70	370
	31	Bank charges		50		320

Note: 10625 and 10626 refer to the serial numbers on the cheques paid out.

It is now clear that the two items not shown in our cash book are:

Bank Giro credit: P. Smith	£70
Bank charges	£50

P. Smith had paid £70 but, instead of sending a cheque, he paid the money by bank giro credit transfer direct into the business bank account. The business did not know of this until it received the bank statement.

The other item was in respect of bank charges. The bank has charged £50 for keeping the bank account and all the work connected with it. Instead of sending an invoice, the bank has simply taken the money out of the bank account.

 Activity 30.2 What sensible rule does this give you relating to when you should balance-off the bank account in the cash book at the end of the accounting period?

As we have now identified the items missing from the cash book, we can now complete writing it up by entering the two items we have identified:

Cash Book (bank columns only: *after* balancing on 31.12.2011)

2011			£	2011			£
Dec	1	Balance b/d	250	Dec	5	J. Gordon	65
	20	P. Thomas	100		27	K. Hughes	175
	28	D. Jones	190		31	Bank charges	50
	30	P. Smith	70		31	Balance c/d	320
			610				610
2012							
Jan	1	Balance b/d	320				

Both the bank statement and cash book closing balances are now shown as being £320.

30.2 Where closing balances differ

Although a cash book may be kept up to date by a business, it obviously cannot alter the bank's own records. Even after writing up entries in the cash book, there may still be a difference between the cash book balance and the balance on the bank statement. Exhibit 30.2 shows such a case.

Exhibit 30.2

Cash Book (after being completed to date)

2012		£	2012		£
Jan	1 Balance b/d	320	Jan	10 C. Morgan	110
	16 R. Lomas	160		20 M. McCarthy	90
	24 V. Verity	140		28 Cheshire CC rates	180
	31 J. Soames	470		30 M. Peck	200
	31 R. Johnson	90		31 Balance c/d	600
		1,180			1,180
Feb	1 Balance b/d	600			

Bank Statement

2012		Withdrawals £	Deposits £	Balance £
Jan	1 Balance b/d			320
	12 10627	110		210
	16 Deposit		160	370
	23 10628	90		280
	24 Deposit		140	420
	28 Direct debit: Cheshire CC	180		240
	31 Bank Giro credit: R. Johnson		90	330

 Activity 30.3 Try to identify which items are causing the two balances to be different even after the bank statement has been checked against the cash book and the necessary additional entries have been made in the cash book. (*Hint*: there are two items involved.)

You can see that two items are in the cash book but are not shown on the bank statement. These are:

(i) A cheque had been paid to M. Peck on January 30. He deposited it in his bank on January 31 but his bank didn't collect the money from the business's bank until February 2. This is known as an **unpresented cheque**.

(ii) Although a cheque for £470 was received from J. Soames on January 31 and the business deposited it with the bank on that date, the bank did not receive the funds from Soames' bank until February. This is known as a 'bank lodgement not yet credited' to the business bank account.

The cash book balance on January 31 was £600, whereas the bank statement shows a balance of £330. To prove that although the balances are different they can be 'reconciled' (i.e. made to agree) with each other, a **bank reconciliation statement** is prepared. It will either start with the bank statement balance and then reconcile it to the cash book balance, or it will start with the cash book balance and then reconcile it to the bank statement balance. If the second approach is adopted, it would appear as:

Bank Reconciliation Statement as at 31 December 2011

		£
Balance as per cash book		600
Add Unpresented cheque	(i)	200
		800
Less Bank lodgement not on statement	(ii)	(470)
Balance per bank statement		330

If the two balances cannot be reconciled then there will be an error somewhere. This will have to be located and then corrected.

This reconciliation technique is also used when dealing with other statements drawn up outside the firm: for example, when reconciling purchase ledger accounts to suppliers' statements.

30.3 The bank balance in the statement of financial position

The balance to be shown in the statement of financial position is that per the cash book after it has been written up to date. In Exhibit 30.2, the statement of financial position figure would be £600.

This is an important point, and one that students often get wrong! The bank reconciliation shown in the last section is simply verifying that you know why there is a difference between the two balances. It is *not* calculating what the bank account figure in the statement of financial position should be because it starts with the balance in the cash book *after* adjusting it for items revealed in the bank statement.

30.4 An alternative approach to bank reconciliations

In order to avoid the confusion that may arise concerning what figure to include in the statement of financial position, many accountants use a slightly different form of bank reconciliation. In this approach, you take the balance as shown on the bank statement and the balance in the cash book *before* making any adjustments that are identified when it is compared to the bank statement. You then reconcile each of them in turn to arrive at the balance that should appear in the statement of financial position.

Having completed the reconciliation, you then update the cash book so that it balances at the correct amount, i.e. the amount that will be shown in the statement of financial position. An example is shown in Exhibit 30.3.

Exhibit 30.3

Cash Book (bank columns only: *before* balancing on 31.12.2011)

2011			£	2011			£
Dec	1	Balance b/d ✔	160	Dec	8	V. O'Connor ✔	115
	12	D. Tyrrall ✔	80		21	G. Francis ✔	35
	23	P. McCarthy ✔	130		31	D. Barnes	25
	31	S. Aisbitt	72				

Bank Statement

			Withdrawals £	Deposits £	Balance £
2011					
Dec	1	Balance b/d	✔		160
	11	24621	✔	115	45
	14	Deposit	✔	80	125
	23	24622	✔	35	90
	29	Deposit	✔	130	220
	30	Bank Giro credit: A. Parkinson		24	244
	31	Bank charges	40		204

You can see that the following are missing from the cash book:

(*a*) A bank giro credit of £24 made on December 30 by A. Parkinson.
(*b*) Bank charges of £40.

And you can see that the following are missing from the bank statement:

(*c*) A cheque paid to D. Barnes for £25 on December 31 has not yet been presented.
(*d*) A bank lodgement has not yet been credited – the cheque for £72 received from S. Aisbitt on 31 December.

The bank reconciliation statement would be:

Bank Reconciliation Statement as at 31 December 2011

		£
Balance as per cash book		267
Add Bank giro credit not yet entered	(*a*)	24
		291
Less Bank lodgement not on statement of financial position	(*b*)	(40)
Balance in statement of financial position		251
Add Cheque not yet presented	(*c*)	25
		276
Less Bank lodgement not on statement	(*d*)	(72)
Balance per bank statement		204

When you have adjustments to make to both the cash book and the bank account balances in order to reconcile them, this form of bank reconciliation statement is more useful than one that simply shows that you know why their balances are different (which is all the bank reconciliation statement in Section 30.2 shows).

An alternative approach that is often used in practice is to start with the balance as per the cash book and adjust it to arrive at the balance per the statement of financial position (i.e. the same as in the first half of the bank reconciliation statement shown above). You then have a second section that starts with the balance as per the bank statement and adjust it to once again arrive at the balance per the statement of financial position. Either of these two approaches is perfectly acceptable and both provide the same information.

30.5   Other terms used in banking

1 **Standing Orders.** A firm can instruct its bank to pay regular amounts of money at stated dates to persons or firms. For instance, you may ask your bank to pay £200 a month to a building society to repay a mortgage.

2 **Direct Debits.** These are payments which have to be made, such as gas bills, electricity bills, telephone bills, rates and insurance premiums. Instead of asking the bank to pay the money, as with standing orders, you give permission to the creditor to obtain the money directly from your bank account. This is particularly useful if the amounts payable may vary from time to time, as it is the creditor who changes the payments, not you. With standing orders, if the amount is ever to be changed, *you* have to inform the bank. With direct debits it is *the creditor* who informs the bank.

Just as with anything else omitted from the cash book, items of these types need to be included in the reconciliation and entered in the cash book before balancing it off at the end of the period.

30.6 Bank overdrafts

The adjustment needed to reconcile a bank overdraft according to the firm's books (shown by a credit balance in the cash book) with that shown in the bank's records are the same as those needed when the account is not overdrawn.

Exhibit 30.4 is of a cash book and a bank statement both showing an overdraft. Only the cheque for G. Cumberbatch (A) £106 and the cheque paid to J. Kelly (B) £63 need adjusting. Work through the reconciliation statement and then read the note after it. Because the balance shown by the cash book is correct (and, therefore, the balance that will appear in the statement of financial position), you can use the form of bank reconciliation statement shown in Section 30.2.

Exhibit 30.4

Cash Book

2011			£	2011				£
Dec	5	I. Howe	308	Dec	1	Balance b/d		709
	24	L. Mason	120		9	P. Davies		140
	29	K. King	124		27	J. Kelly	(B)	63
	31	G. Cumberbatch (A)	106		29	United Trust		77
	31	Balance c/d	380		31	Bank charges		49
			1,038					1,038

Bank Statement

			Dr	Cr	Balance
2011			£	£	£
Dec	1	Balance b/d			709 O/D
	5	Cheque		308	401 O/D
	14	P. Davies	140		541 O/D
	24	Cheque		120	421 O/D
	29	K. King: Credit transfer		124	297 O/D
	29	United Trust: Standing order	77		374 O/D
	31	Bank charges	49		423 O/D

Note: An overdraft is often shown with the letters 'O/D' following the amount. Alternatively, some banks use 'Dr' and 'Cr' after every balance entry to indicate whether the account is overdrawn.

 Activity 30.4 Will the bank statement show 'Dr' or 'Cr' if an account is overdrawn?

Bank Reconciliation Statement as at 31 December 2011

	£
Overdraft as per cash book	(380)
Add Unpresented cheque	63
	(317)
Less Bank lodgement not on bank statement	(106)
Overdraft per bank statement	(423)

Note: You may find it confusing looking at this bank reconciliation statement because the opening entry is an overdraft, i.e. a negative number. However, the adjusting entries are the same as those you make when it is positive:

	£
Balance/overdraft per cash book	xxxx
Adjustments	
Unpresented cheque	Plus
Bank lodgement not on bank statement	Less
Balance/overdraft per bank statement	xxxx

30.7 Dishonoured cheques

When a cheque is received from a customer and paid into the bank, it is recorded on the debit side of the cash book. It is also shown on the bank statement as a deposit increasing the balance on the account. However, at a later date it may be found that the customer's bank will not pay the amount due on the cheque. The customer's bank has failed to 'honour' the cheque. The cheque is described as a **dishonoured cheque**.

There are several possible reasons for this. Imagine that K. King paid a business with a cheque for £5,000 on 20 May 2012. The business deposits it at the bank but, a few days later, the bank contacts the business and informs it that the cheque has been dishonoured. Typical reasons are:

1 King had put £5,000 in figures on the cheque, but had written it in words as 'five thousand *five hundred* pounds'. A new cheque correctly completed will need to be provided by King.
2 Normally cheques are considered *stale* six months after the date on the cheque. In other words, banks will not honour cheques that are more than six months old. If King had put the year 2008 on the cheque instead of 2012, then King's bank would dishonour the cheque and King would need to be asked for a correctly dated replacement.
3 King simply did not have sufficient funds in her bank account. Suppose she had previously a balance of only £2,000 and yet she has made out a cheque for £5,000. Her bank has not allowed her an overdraft in order to honour the cheque. As a result, the cheque has been dishonoured. The bank inform the business that this has happened and the business would have to contact King, explain what has happened and ask for valid payment of the account.

In all of these cases, the bank would record the original entry in its records as being reversed. This is shown on the bank statement, for example, by the entry 'dishonoured cheque £5,000'. The business then makes the equivalent credit entry in the cash book while, at the same time, debiting King's account by the same amount.

When King originally paid the £5,000 the accounts in the ledger and cash book would have appeared as:

K. King

2012			£	2012			£
May	1	Balance b/d	5,000	May	20	Bank	5,000

Bank Account

2012		£	
May	20	K. King	5,000

After recording the dishonoured cheque, the accounts would be:

K. King

2012			£	2012			£
May	1	Balance b/d	5,000	May	20	Bank	5,000
May	25	Bank: cheque dishonoured	5,000				

Bank Account

2012			£	2012			£
May	20	K. King	5,000	May	25	K. King: cheque dishonoured	5,000

In other words, King is once again shown as owing the business £5,000.

Learning outcomes

You should now have learnt:

1 Why it is important to perform a bank reconciliation when a bank statement is received.

2 That a bank reconciliation statement should show whether or not errors have been made either in the bank columns of the cash book or on the bank statement.

3 That a bank reconciliation statement can be prepared either before or after updating the cash book with items omitted from it that are shown on the bank statement.

4 That a bank reconciliation statement prepared after updating the cash book with items omitted from it that are shown on the bank statement shows that you know why the bank statement balance is different from that shown in the cash book and statement of financial position.

5 That a bank reconciliation statement prepared before updating the cash book with items omitted from it that are shown on the bank statement is reconciled from cash book to statement of financial position amount and then to the bank statement. It shows the amount to be entered in the statement of financial position and also shows that you know why the bank statement balance is different from the balances shown in the cash book and in the statement of financial position.

6 That in the case of bank overdrafts, the reconciliation statement adjustments are the same as those shown when there is a positive bank balance, but the opening and closing balances are negative.

7 How to prepare a bank reconciliation statement *after* updating the cash book with items omitted from it that are shown on the bank statement.

8 How to prepare a bank reconciliation statement *before* updating the cash book with items omitted from it that are shown on the bank statement.

9 Why cheques may be dishonoured and what the effect is upon the bank balance.

10 How to make the appropriate entries to the accounts when a cheque is dishonoured.

Answers to activities

30.1 There is quite a long list of possible causes, including:

- a business may take a day or two to deposit some cheques that it has already entered in the cash book;
- a cheque may take a few days to be entered in the account of the business held at the bank after it is deposited (because the bank won't recognise the amount received until a few days later, in case there is a problem with it);
- bank interest paid and bank charges often aren't known by a business until a bank statement is received;
- bank interest received won't be known by a business until it receives a bank statement;
- standing orders may not be written up in the cash book of the business until they are identified on the bank statement;
- the amount of a direct debit is sometimes not known and so should not be entered in the cash book until it is confirmed how much was paid out of the bank account;
- customers may pay their accounts by direct transfer from their bank account or by paying cash directly into the business bank account and the business may only learn of their having done so some time later;
- there may have been an error made in the cash book entries;
- the bank may have made an error in operating the account, such as adding funds to it instead of to the account of the person depositing the funds;
- a cheque paid into the bank may have 'bounced' (i.e. there were insufficient funds in the writer of the cheque's bank account to make the payment).

30.2 It is wise to wait until receiving the bank statement before balancing-off the bank account in the cash book at the end of the accounting period. In a manual accounting system, if a cash book is balanced on a regular basis, balancing-off is usually done at the end of the time period selected and any additional entries are recorded along with the other entries made in the following day, week, month or quarter. However, at the end of the accounting year, the balancing-off is often done in pencil (so that financial statements can be drafted) and then done in ink after any missing entries and corrections of errors have been entered following receipt of the bank statement.

30.3 M. Peck £200 and J. Soames £470.

30.4 'Dr' indicates an overdraft. The customer is a debtor of the bank. In the customer's statement of financial position, the overdraft is included in the current liabilities, indicating that the bank is a creditor. Always remember that a bank is looking at the relationship from the opposite side to the view seen by the customer.

Review questions

30.1 From the following, draw up a bank reconciliation statement from details as on 31 December 2012:

	£
Cash at bank as per bank column of the cash book	3,000
Unpresented cheques	800
Cheques received and paid into the bank, but not yet entered on the bank statement	600
Credit transfers entered as banked on the bank statement but not entered in the cash book	300
Cash at bank as per bank statement	3,500

30.2A Draw up a bank reconciliation statement, after writing the cash book up to date, ascertaining the balance on the bank statement, from the following as on 31 March 2012:

	£
Cash at bank as per bank column of the cash book (Dr)	2,740
Bankings made but not yet entered on bank statement	410
Bank charges on bank statement but not yet in cash book	32
Unpresented cheques W. Shute	131
Standing order to Giffy Ltd entered on bank statement, but not in cash book	93
Credit transfer from B. Barnes entered on bank statement, but not yet in cash book	201

30.3 The following are extracts from the cash book and the bank statement of F. Perry.

You are required to:
(a) Write the cash book up to date, and state the new balance as on 31 December 2012, and
(b) Draw up a bank reconciliation statement as on 31 December 2012.

Cash Book

2012	Dr	£	2012	Cr	£
Dec 1	Balance b/d	3,419	Dec 8	B. Young	462
7	F. Lamb	101	15	F. Gray	21
22	G. Brock	44	28	T. Errant	209
31	W. Terry	319	31	Balance c/d	3,437
31	S. Miller	246			
		4,129			4,129

Bank Statement

2012		Dr £	Cr £	Balance £
Dec 1	Balance b/d			3,419
7	Cheque		101	3,520
11	B. Young	462		3,058
20	F. Gray	21		3,037
22	Cheque		44	3,081
31	Credit transfer: T. Morris		93	3,174
31	Bank charges	47		3,127

30.4A The bank columns in the cash book for June 2012 and the bank statement for that month for D. Hogan are as follows:

Cash Book

2012	Dr	£	2012	Cr	£
Jun 1	Balance b/d	1,410	Jun 5	L. Holmes	180
7	J. May	62	12	J. Rebus	519
16	T. Wilson	75	16	T. Silver	41
28	F. Slack	224	29	Blister Disco	22
30	G. Baker	582	30	Balance c/d	1,591
		2,353			2,353

Bank Statement

2012		Dr £	Cr £	Balance £
Jun 1	Balance b/d			1,410
7	Cheque		62	1,472
8	F. Lane	180		1,292
16	Cheque		75	1,367
17	J. Rebus	519		848
18	T. Silver	41		807
28	Cheque		224	1,031
29	SLM standing order	52		979
30	Flynn: trader's credit		64	1,043
30	Bank charges	43		1,000

You are required to:
(a) Write the cash book up to date to take the above into account, and then
(b) Draw up a bank reconciliation statement as on 30 June 2012.

30.5 Read the following and answer the questions below.

On 31 December 2011 the bank column of C. Tench's cash book showed a debit balance of £1,500.
   The monthly bank statement written up to 31 December 2011 showed a credit balance of £2,950.
   On checking the cash book with the bank statement it was discovered that the following transactions had not been entered in the cash book:

   Dividends of £240 had been paid directly to the bank.
   A credit transfer – HM Revenue & Customs VAT refund of £260 – had been collected by the bank.
   Bank charges £30.
   A direct debit of £70 for the RAC subscription had been paid by the bank.
   A standing order of £200 for C. Tench's loan repayment had been paid by the bank.
   C. Tench's deposit account balance of £1,400 was transferred into his bank current account.

A further check revealed the following items:

Two cheques drawn in favour of T. Cod £250 and F. Haddock £290 had been entered in the cash book but had not been presented for payment.
Cash and cheques amounting to £690 had been paid into the bank on 31 December 2011 but were not credited by the bank until 2 January 2012.

(a) Starting with the debit balance of £1,500, bring the cash book (bank columns) up to date and then balance the bank account.
(b) Prepare a bank reconciliation statement as at 31 December 2011.

(Midland Examining Group: GCSE)

30.6A In the draft accounts for the year ended 31 October 2012 of Thomas P. Lee, garage proprietor, the balance at bank according to the cash book was £894.68 in hand.

Subsequently the following discoveries were made:

(1) Cheque number 176276 dated 3 September 2012 for £310.84 in favour of G. Lowe Limited has been correctly recorded in the bank statement, but included in the cash book payments as £301.84.
(2) Bank commission charged of £169.56 and bank interest charged of £109.10 have been entered in the bank statement on 23 October 2012, but not included in the cash book.
(3) The recently received bank statement shows that a cheque for £29.31 received from T. Andrews and credited in the bank statements on 9 October 2012 has now been dishonoured and debited in the bank statement on 26 October 2012. The only entry in the cash book for this cheque records its receipt on 8 October 2012.
(4) Cheque number 177145 for £15.10 has been recorded twice as a credit in the cash book.
(5) Amounts received in the last few days of October 2012 totalling £1,895.60 and recorded in the cash book have not been included in the bank statements until 2 November 2012.
(6) Cheques paid according to the cash book during October 2012 and totalling £395.80 were not presented for payment to the bank until November 2012.
(7) Traders' credits totalling £210.10 have been credited in the bank statement on 26 October 2012, but not yet recorded in the cash book.
(8) A standing order payment of £15.00 on 17 October 2012 to Countryside Publications has been recorded in the bank statement but is not mentioned in the cash book.

Required:
(a) Prepare a computation of the balance at bank to be included in Thomas P. Lee's statement of financial position as at 31 October 2012.

(b)   Prepare a bank reconciliation statement as at 31 October 2012 for Thomas P. Lee.

(c)   Briefly explain why it is necessary to prepare bank reconciliation statements at accounting year ends.

(*Association of Accounting Technicians*)

30.7   The bank statement for R. Hood for the month of March 2012 is:

2012		Dr £	Cr £	Balance £
Mar	1 Balance			4,200 O/D
	8 T. MacLeod	184		4,384 O/D
	16 Cheque		292	4,092 O/D
	20 W. Milne	160		4,252 O/D
	21 Cheque		369	3,883 O/D
	31 G. Frank: trader's credit		88	3,795 O/D
	31 TYF: standing order	32		3,827 O/D
	31 Bank charges	19		3,846 O/D

The cash book for March 2012 is:

2012	Dr	£	2012	Cr	£
Mar 16	G. Philip	292	Mar 1	Balance b/d	4,200
21	J. Forker	369	6	T. MacLeod	184
31	S. O'Hare	192	30	W. Milne	160
31	Balance c/d	4,195	30	S. Porter	504
		5,048			5,048

You are required to:

(a)   Write the cash book up to date, and

(b)   Draw up a bank reconciliation statement as on 31 March 2012.

30.8A   The following is the cash book (bank columns) of F. King for December 2013:

2013	Dr	£	2013	Cr	£
Dec 6	P. Pan	230	Dec 1	Balance b/d	1,900
20	C. Hook	265	10	J. Lamb	304
31	W. Britten	325	19	P. Wilson	261
31	Balance c/d	1,682	29	K. Coull	37
		2,502			2,502

The bank statement for the month is:

2013		Dr £	Cr £	Balance £
Dec	1 Balance			1,900 O/D
	6 Cheque		230	1,670 O/D
	13 J. Lamb	304		1,974 O/D
	20 Cheque		265	1,709 O/D
	22 P. Wilson	261		1,970 O/D
	30 Tox: standing order	94		2,064 O/D
	31 F. Ray: trader's credit		102	1,962 O/D
	31 Bank charges	72		2,034 O/D

You are required to:

(a)   Write the cash book up to date to take the necessary items into account, and

(b)   Draw up a bank reconciliation statement as on 31 December 2013.

30.9 The following is a summary of a cash book as presented by George Ltd for the month of October:

	£		£
Receipts	1,469	Balance b/d	761
Balance c/d	554	Payments	1,262
	2,023		2,023

All receipts are banked and all payments are made by cheque.

On investigation you discover:

(1)   Bank charges of £136 entered on the bank statement have not been entered in the cash book.
(2)   Cheques drawn amounting to £267 had not been presented to the bank for payment.
(3)   Cheques received totalling £762 had been entered in the cash book and paid into the bank, but had not been credited by the bank until 3 November.
(4)   A cheque for £22 for sundries had been entered in the cash book as a receipt instead of as a payment.
(5)   A cheque received from K. Jones for £80 had been returned by the bank and marked 'No funds available'. No adjustment has been made in the cash book.
(6)   A standing order for a business rates instalment of £150 on 30 October had not been entered in the cash book.
(7)   All dividends received are credited directly to the bank account. During October amounts totalling £62 were credited by the bank but no entries were made in the cash book.
(8)   A cheque drawn for £66 for stationery had been incorrectly entered in the cash book as £60.
(9)   The balance brought forward in the cash book should have been £711, not £761.

Required:
(a)   Show the adjustments required in the cash book.
(b)   Prepare a bank reconciliation statement as at 31 October.

Control accounts

Learning objectives

After you have studied this chapter, you should be able to:

- explain why control accounts can be useful
- draw up sales ledger control accounts
- draw up purchases ledger control accounts
- reconcile the purchases ledger and the sales ledger with their respective control accounts

Introduction

In this chapter, you'll learn about the benefits of using control accounts in manual accounting systems and the process involved in both preparing control accounts and reconciling them to the ledgers.

31.1 The benefits of accounting controls

In any but the smallest business, the accounting information system (which you read about in Chapter 23) is set up so as to include controls that help ensure that errors are minimised and that nothing occurs that shouldn't, such as the cashier embezzling funds. One of the tasks undertaken by auditors is to check the various controls that are in place to ensure they are working satisfactorily and one of the things they will look out for is segregation of duties. So, for example, the same person will not both invoice customers and act as cashier when payment is received and, if someone claims reimbursement of an expense, it will be authorised for payment by someone else. Another form of control you've already learnt about involves whether or not customers are allowed to purchase goods on credit.

All these controls are 'organisational'. That is, they do not directly impose controls over the accounting data, nor do they ensure that accounting entries are correct. One control measure that does these things was covered in Chapter 30 – the process of bank reconciliation. In this chapter, we'll look at another type of accounting control which is used mainly in manual accounting systems, **control accounts**.

When all the accounts were kept in one ledger, a trial balance could be drawn up as a test of the arithmetical accuracy of the accounts. If the trial balance totals disagree, the books of a small business could easily and quickly be checked so as to find the errors. Of course, as you know, even when the totals do agree, certain types of error may still have occurred, the nature of which makes it impossible for them to be detected in this way. Nevertheless, using a trial balance ensures that all the double entries appear, at least, to have been recorded correctly.

Activity 31.1 How do you find errors of the types that a trial balance cannot detect?

When a business has grown and the accounting work has been so divided up that there are several ledgers, any errors could be very difficult to find if a trial balance was the only device used to try to detect errors. Every item in every ledger may need to be checked just to find one error that caused the trial balance not to balance. What is required is a type of trial balance for each ledger, and this requirement is met by control accounts. A control account is a summary account that enables you to see at a glance whether the general ledger balance for the ledger to which that control account belongs agrees with the total of all the individual accounts held within that ledger.

If you use control accounts, only the ledgers where the control accounts do not balance need detailed checking to find errors.

31.2   Principle of control accounts

The principle on which the control account is based is simple and is as follows: if the opening balance of an account is known, together with information of the additions and deductions entered in the account, the closing balance can be calculated.

Applying this to a complete ledger, the total of opening balances together with the additions and deductions during the period should give the total of closing balances. This can be illustrated by reference to a sales ledger for entries for a month.

	£
Total of opening balances, 1 January 2012	3,000
Add Total of entries which have increased the balances	9,500
	12,500
Less Total of entries which have reduced the balances	(8,000)
Total of closing balances should be	4,500

Because totals are used, control accounts are sometimes known as 'total accounts'. Thus, a control account for a sales ledger could be known as either a '**sales ledger control account**' or as a '**total accounts receivable account**'.

Similarly, a control account for a purchases ledger could be known either as a '**purchases ledger control account**' or as a '**total accounts payable account**'.

A control account is a memorandum account. It is not part of the double entry system. It will be prepared either in the general ledger or in the ledger to which it relates, i.e. the purchases ledger or the sales ledger.

A control account looks like any other T-account:

Sales Ledger Control

2012			£	2012			£
Jan	1	Balances b/d	x,xxx	Jan	31	Returns Inwards Day Book (total of all goods returned from debtors in the period)	xxx
	31	Sales day book (total of sales invoiced in the period)	xx,xxx		31	Cash book (total of all cash received from debtors in the period)	x,xxx
					31	Cash book (total of all cheques received from debtors in the period)	xx,xxx
					31	Balances c/d	x,xxx
			xx,xxx				xx,xxx

31.3 Information for control accounts

Exhibits 31.1 and 31.2 list the sources of information used to draw up control accounts.

Exhibit 31.1

Sales Ledger Control	Source
1 Opening accounts receivable	List of debtor balances drawn up at the end of the previous period
2 Credit sales	Total from the Sales Day Book
3 Returns inwards	Total of the Returns Inwards Day Book
4 Cheques received	Cash Book: bank column on received side. List extracted or the total of a special column for cheques which has been included in the Cash Book
5 Cash received	Cash Book: cash column on received side. List extracted or the total of a special column for cash which has been included in the Cash Book
6 Discounts allowed	Total of discounts allowed column in the Cash Book
7 Closing accounts receivable	List of debtor balances drawn up at the end of the period

Exhibit 31.2

Purchases Ledger Control	Source
1 Opening accounts payable	List of creditor balances drawn up at the end of the previous period
2 Credit purchases	Total from Purchases Day Book
3 Returns outwards	Total of Returns Outwards Day Book
4 Cheques paid	Cash Book: bank column on payments side. List extracted or total of a special column for cheques which has been included in the Cash Book
5 Cash paid	Cash Book: cash column on payments side. List extracted or total of a special column for cash which has been included in the Cash Book
6 Discounts received	Total of discounts received column in the Cash Book
7 Closing accounts payable	List of creditor balances drawn up at the end of the period

31.4 Form of control accounts

As shown in Section 31.2, control accounts kept in the general ledger are normally prepared in the same form as an account, with the totals of the debit entries in the ledger on the left-hand side of the control account, and the totals of the various credit entries in the ledger on the right-hand side.

The process is very straightforward. Take the sales ledger as an example. The first two steps are identical to those you learnt in Chapters 13 and 14.

1 Individual amounts received from debtors are transferred from the cash book into the personal accounts in the sales ledger. (The double entry is completed automatically in the normal way, because the cash book is, in itself, a ledger account.)
2 Individual invoice amounts are transferred from the sales day book into the personal accounts in the sales ledger. (You would complete the double entry in the normal way, by crediting the sales account.)
3 The sales ledger control account would open each period with the total of the accounts receivable balances at the start of the period.
4 Then, post the total of the returns inwards day book to the credit side of the sales ledger control account. **(This is new.)**
5 At the end of the period, you post the totals of all the payments from debtors received during the period from the cash book to the credit side of the sales ledger control account. **(This is new.)**
6 This is followed by posting to the debit side of the sales ledger control account the totals of all new sales during the period shown in the sales day book. **(This is new.)**
7 Balance-off the control account.
8 Check whether the balance on the control account is equal to the total of all the accounts receivable balances in the sales ledger.

If the balance is not the same as the total of all the balances in the sales ledger, there is an error either in the totals entered in the control account from the books of original entry or, more likely, somewhere in the sales ledger.

Note: You do *not* enter the total of the balances from the sales ledger in the control account. Instead, you balance-off the control account and check whether the balance c/d is the same as the total of all the individual balances in the sales ledger.

Activity 31.2 If you look at these eight steps, you can see that the first three are those you learnt to do earlier in the book, so you know that the other part of the double entry has been completed in the normal way. However, what about the double entries for (4), (5) and (6)? What is the other side of the double entry in each case?

Exhibit 31.3 shows an example of a sales ledger control account for a sales ledger in which all the entries are arithmetically correct and the totals transferred from the books of original entry are correct.

Exhibit 31.3

	£
Sales Ledger Control Account data:	
Accounts receivable balances on 1 January 2012	1,894
Total credit sales for the month	10,290
Cheques received from customers in the month	7,284
Cash received from customers in the month	1,236
Returns inwards from customers during the month	296
Accounts receivable balances on 31 January as extracted from the Sales Ledger	3,368

Sales Ledger Control

2012			£	2012				£
Jan	1	Balances b/d	1,894	Jan	31	Bank		7,284
	31	Sales	10,290		31	Cash		1,236
					31	Returns inwards		296
					31	Balances c/d		3,368
			12,184					12,184

We have proved the ledger to be arithmetically correct, because the control account balances with the amount equalling the total of the balances extracted from the sales ledger.

Like a trial balance, if the totals of a control account are not equal and the entries made to it were correct (i.e. the amounts transferred to it from the books of original entry have been corrrectly summed), this shows that there is an error somewhere in the ledger.

Exhibit 31.4 shows an example where an error is found to exist in a purchases ledger. The ledger will have to be checked in detail, the error found, and the control account then corrected.

Exhibit 31.4

	£
Purchases Ledger Control Account data:	
Accounts payable balances on 1 January 2012	3,890
Cheques paid to suppliers during the month	3,620
Returns outwards to suppliers in the month	95
Bought from suppliers in the month	4,936
Accounts payable balances on 31 January as extracted from the Purchases Ledger	5,151

Purchases Ledger Control

2012			£	2012			£
Jan	31	Bank	3,620	Jan	1	Balances b/d	3,890
	31	Returns outwards	95		31	Purchases	4,936
	31	Balances c/d	5,151				
			8,866 (Note)				8,826 (Note)

Note: Providing all the totals transferred into the Purchases Ledger Control Account from the books of original entry were correct, there is a £40 difference between the debit and credit entries in the Purchases Ledger.

We will have to check the purchases ledger in detail to find the error. A double line has not yet been drawn under the totals. We will do this (known as 'ruling off the account') when the error has been found and the totals corrected.

Note: You need to be sure that the totals transferred from the books of original entry were correct before assuming that an out-of-balance control account means that the ledger is incorrect.

31.5   Other advantages of control accounts in a manual accounting system

Control accounts are usually only maintained in a manual accounting system. They are not normally maintained in a computerised accounting system.

Control accounts have merits other than that of locating errors. When used, control accounts are normally under the charge of a responsible official, and fraud is made more difficult because transfers made (in an effort) to disguise frauds will have to pass the scrutiny of this person.

The balances on the control account can always be taken to equal accounts receivable and accounts payable without waiting for an extraction of individual balances. Management control is thereby aided, for the speed at which information is obtained is one of the prerequisites of efficient control.

31.6   Other sources of information for control accounts

With a large organisation there may well be more than one sales ledger or purchases ledger. The accounts in the sales ledgers may be divided up in ways such as:

- alphabetically: thus we may have three sales sub-ledgers split A–F, G–O and P–Z;
- geographically: this could be split: Europe, Far East, Africa, Asia, Australia, North America and South America.

For each of these sub-ledgers we must have a separate control account. An example of a columnar sales day book is shown as Exhibit 31.5:

Exhibit 31.5

Columnar Sales Day Book

Date	Details	Total		Ledgers	
			A–F	G–O	P–Z
2012		£	£	£	£
Feb 1	J. Archer	58	58		
3	G. Gaunt	103		103	
4	T. Brown	116	116		
8	C. Dunn	205	205		
10	A. Smith	16			16
12	P. Smith	114			114
15	D. Owen	88		88	
18	B. Blake	17	17		
22	T. Green	1,396		1,396	
27	C. Males	48		48	
		2,161	396	1,635	130

The total of the A–F column will be the total sales figures for the Sales Ledger A–F control account, the total of the G–O column for the G–O control account, and so on.

A similar form of analysis can be used in the purchases day book, the returns inwards day book, the returns outwards day book and the cash book. The *totals* necessary for each of the control accounts can be obtained from the appropriate columns in these books.

Other items, such as bad debts written off or transfers from one ledger to another, will be recorded in the Journal.

31.7   Other transfers

Transfers to bad debt accounts will have to be recorded in the sales ledger control account as they involve entries in the sales ledger.

Similarly, a contra account, whereby the same entity is both a supplier and a customer, and inter-indebtedness is set off, will also need to be entered in the control accounts. An example of this follows:

(A) The business has sold A. Hughes £600 goods.
(B) Hughes has supplied the business with £880 goods.
(C) The £600 owing by Hughes is set off against £880 owing to him.
(D) This leaves £280 owing to Hughes.

Sales Ledger
A. Hughes

		£			
Sales	(A)	600			

Purchases Ledger
A. Hughes

					£
			Purchases	(B)	880

The set-off now takes place following the preparation of a journal entry in the Journal:

Sales Ledger
A. Hughes

		£			£
Sales	(A)	600	Set-off: Purchases ledger	(C)	600

Purchases Ledger
A. Hughes

		£			£
Set-off: Sales ledger	(C)	600	Purchases	(B)	880
Balance c/d	(D)	280			
		880			880
			Balance b/d	(D)	280

The set-off will be posted from the Journal to the credit side of the sales ledger control account and to the debit side of the purchases ledger control account.

31.8   A more complicated example

Exhibit 31.6 shows a worked example of a more complicated control account.

You will see that there are sometimes credit balances in the sales ledger as well as debit balances. Suppose for instance we sold £500 goods to W. Young, he then paid in full for them, and then afterwards he returned £40 goods to us. This would leave a credit balance of £40 on the account, whereas usually the balances in the sales ledger are debit balances.

Exhibit 31.6

2012			£
Aug	1	Sales ledger – debit balances	3,816
	1	Sales ledger – credit balances	22
	31	Transactions for the month:	
		Cash received	104
		Cheques received	6,239
		Sales	7,090
		Bad debts written off	306
		Discounts allowed	298
		Returns inwards	664
		Cash refunded to a customer who had overpaid his account	37
		Dishonoured cheques	29
		Interest charged by us on overdue debt	50
		At the end of the month:	
		Sales ledger – debit balances	3,429
		Sales ledger – credit balances	40

Sales Ledger Control Account

2012			£	2012			£
Aug	1	Balances b/d	3,816	Aug	1	Balances b/d	22
	31	Sales	7,090		31	Cash	104
		Cash refunded	37			Bank	6,239
		Bank: dishonoured cheques	29			Bad debts	306
		Interest on debt	50			Discounts allowed	298
		Balances c/d	40			Returns inwards	664
						Balances c/d	3,429
			11,062				11,062

Note that you do *not* set off the debit and credit balances in the Sales Ledger.

31.9 Control accounts as part of a double entry system

Many students find control accounts confusing. This is because, as shown in Section 31.4, the existence of a control account requires extra entries to be made in the accounts over and above those that would be made were a control account not being used.

What you need to realise is that the double entry belongs to the original entries in the accounts. For example, if a debtor pays the amount due on his account, you credit the account of the debtor and debit the bank account. No entry is made in the sales ledger control account at this stage. As a result, the double entry is the same irrespective of whether or not there is a control account.

When an entry is made to the control account, it includes all movements on the personal accounts, not just the amount in the single debtor example above. There may be payments from 5 debtors or 50 or 500 included in the amount posted to the control account. And, the posting is from the Cash Book for payments received from debtors; and from the Sales Day Book for sales to debtors. It is not from the individual debtor accounts.

It is at this point that confusion sets in – where is the second part of this 'double entry'? The answer is: there isn't one. The posting to the control account is not part of a double entry. Think of it as equivalent of posting each receipt from each debtor to the debtor's account and then writing the total cash received from all the debtors on a piece of paper. The control account is that 'piece of paper'. It is a note, a helpful piece of information.

If the control account is kept in the subsidiary ledger – the Sales Ledger in this example – all it shows is the total of all the amounts received from debtors, the total of all credit sales to debtors, plus the opening balance. You can then take these three numbers and discover the closing balance on your Sales Ledger:

Opening Balance + Credit Sales to Debtors – Amounts received from Debtors

When preparing a trial balance, you can include that balance rather than all the individual debtor account balances.

If the control account is kept in the General Ledger, it is considered to be part of the double entry system **because the General Ledger will balance without any need to include balances on accounts held in subsidiary ledgers.**

 Activity 31.3 Why may some people consider this to be incorrect? That is, why is the fact that the control account is kept in the General Ledger *not* enough to justify saying that the control account is part of the double entry system?

This is not strictly correct. Yet, organisations that operate control accounts for their subsidiary ledgers often keep them in the General Ledger and view them as an integral part of the double entry system. When a trial balance is extracted, it is always the balances on the control accounts that are used rather than the balances on all the individual personal accounts.

When this is the case, the Sales Ledger and the Purchases Ledger are described as 'memorandum books' lying outside the double entry system.

This is technically incorrect but, when control accounts are kept in the General Ledger, it is 'normal' practice to describe the subsidiary ledgers in this way. **You need to be aware of this and to use the terminology in this way because it is what your examiners expect.**

In organisations where the control accounts are kept in the subsidiary ledgers, the control accounts are *not* considered to be part of the double entry system. In this case, the control account is normally described as a 'memorandum entry' in the individual subsidiary ledgers. The individual personal accounts in those subsidiary entries *are* considered to be part of the double entry system; and the subsidiary ledgers *are not* considered to be memorandum books.

Despite this difference in terminology, the same entries are made to control accounts kept in a General Ledger as are made to control accounts kept in subsidiary ledgers. In addition, it is the balance on the control account that is used in a trial balance, irrespective of whether it is kept in the General Ledger or in a subsidiary ledger.

In brief, it does not matter where a control account is kept. It is compiled in the same way and it is used in the same way. The artificial distinction concerning its place inside or outside the double entry system attributed to it depending upon the ledger in which it appears developed through custom and practice over many centuries. Control accounts are not part of a double entry system because the entries within them are not made using double entry principles. If you remember this point, you should find it relatively easy to understand the principles of control accounts.

Finally, do not confuse control accounts, which are used in order to operate subsidiary ledgers more efficiently, with wage control accounts (Chapter 21), which are used to maintain an element of control over the amounts paid relating to wages and salaries. Control accounts relate to subsidiary ledgers. Wages control accounts relate solely to wages and salaries. The two items both contain the word, 'control' in their title, but that is the only thing they have in common.

31.10 Self-balancing ledgers and adjustment accounts

Because ledgers which have a control account system are proved to be correct as far as the double entry is concerned they used to be called 'self-balancing ledgers'. The control accounts were often called 'adjustment accounts'. These terms are very rarely used nowadays, but you should remember them in case an examiner uses them.

31.11 Reconciliation of control accounts

Errors and omissions can occur when entering information into the accounting records. We have seen in Chapter 30 how these are identified and used to reconcile differences between the bank account and the bank statement balances. When a ledger control account is not in balance, it indicates that something has gone wrong with the entries made to the accounting records. This leads to an investigation which (hopefully) reveals the cause(s). Then, in order to verify whether the identified item(s) caused the failure to balance the control account, a reconciliation is carried out.

Exhibit 31.7 shows an example of a **purchases ledger control account reconciliation**. It takes the original control account balance and adjusts it to arrive at an amended balance which should equal the revised total of the source amounts that, together, equal the control account balance.

It can be seen that the general approach is similar to that adopted for bank reconciliation statements. However, as each control account may be constructed using information from a number of sources (see Section 31.3) the extent of the investigation to identify the cause of the control account imbalance is likely to be far greater than that undertaken when performing a bank reconciliation.

Exhibit 31.7

An example of a Purchases Ledger Control Account Reconciliation

	£
Original purchases ledger control account balance	xxx
Add Invoice omitted from control account, but entered in Purchases Ledger	xxx
Supplier balance excluded from Purchases Ledger total because the account had been included in the Sales Ledger by mistake	xxx
Credit sale posted in error to the debit of a Purchases Ledger account instead of the debit of an account in the Sales Ledger	xxx
Undercasting error in calculation of total end of period creditors' balances	xxx
	xxx
Less Customer account with a credit balance included in the Purchases Ledger that should have been included in the Sales Ledger	(xxx)
Return inwards posted in error to the credit of a Purchases Ledger account instead of the credit of an account in the Sales Ledger	(xxx)
Credit note entered in error in the Returns Outwards Day Book as £223 instead of £332	(xxx)
Revised purchases ledger control account balance obtained from revised source amounts	xxx

31.12 A cautionary note

Students often get the following wrong: only credit purchases are recorded in a Purchases Ledger control account. Also, in Sales Ledger control accounts, do not include cash sales or allowances for doubtful debts.

31.13 **Finally**

Control accounts are used in manual accounting systems. Most computerised accounting systems automatically provide all the benefits of using control accounts without the necessity of actually maintaining them. This is because computerised accounting systems automatically ensure that all double entries are completed, so ensuring that all the ledgers balance. Of course, errors can still arise, such as a posting made to the wrong ledger account, but not of the type that control accounts can detect.

> **Learning outcomes**
> ....
>
> **You should now have learnt:**
>
> **1** How to prepare control accounts.
>
> **2** How to prepare a control account reconciliation.
>
> **3** That control accounts enable errors to be traced down to the ledger that does not balance. Thus there will be no need to check all the books in full to find an error.
>
> **4** That transfers between sales and purchases ledgers should be prepared in the journal and shown in the control accounts.
>
> **5** That control accounts for most businesses are outside the double entry system and are kept as memorandum accounts in the general ledger or in the individual ledgers.
>
> **6** That control accounts of large organisations may be part of the double entry system, which means that the sales ledger and purchases ledger are treated as memorandum books outside the double entry system. The entries to such control accounts are the same as for control accounts that lie outside the double entry system.
>
> **7** That control accounts are normally only used in manual accounting systems.

Answers to activities

31.1 These errors tend to be detected either as the result of someone drawing attention to an entry that appears to be incorrect or as the result of sample checking of the entries that have been made in the accounting books. A debtor may, for example, question whether the amount on an invoice is correctly summed or suggest that one of the invoices listed in the debtor's monthly statement had nothing to do with the debtor. One of the tasks that auditors carry out involves checking a sample of the transactions during a period so as to determine the level of errors within the entries made relating to them. If the level of error detected is considered material, a more extensive check will be carried out.

31.2 (4) The other side of this double entry was to the debit of the returns inwards account.
      (5) The other side of the double entry was done earlier at the time when the individual amounts received from debtors were posted as credits to the individual debtor accounts in the sales ledger. That is, *the other side of this double entry was all the debit entries to the cash book* (see Chapter 13). The posting of each receipt as a credit to the individual debtor accounts done in step (1) is actually a memorandum entry and does not form part of the double entry system. So, in effect, the sales ledger has been taken out of the double entry system and is now a memorandum book. *To summarise, step (5) is actually the credit side of the double entry whose debit side is all the debit entries in the cash book.*

(6) The other side of the double entry was done earlier at the time when each sale was posted from the sales day book to the individual accounts receivable accounts in the sales ledger. That is, *the other side of this double entry was the credit entry made when the total of the sales shown in the sales day book was posted to the sales account in the general ledger* (see Chapter 14). The posting of each sale as a debit to the individual accounts receivable accounts done in step (2) is actually a memorandum entry and does not form part of the double entry system. *To summarise, step (6) is actually the debit side of the double entry whose credit side is all the credit entries in the sales account.*

31.3 The double entry system involves the entry of financial transactions into accounts using the principle of at least one debit entry for every credit entry, and vice versa. Entries into control accounts are supplementary one-sided entries for which there is no debit to match the credit or credit to match the debit. They are simply summary statements constructed in the form of an account.

The balance they produce does reflect the balance on the subsidiary ledger to which they relate, but only because the totals of all the entries into the subsidiary ledgers have been calculated and inserted into the control accounts. They are not, and never could be, 'part of the double entry system'. However, for simplicity, when control accounts are kept in the General Ledger, they are referred to in this (incorrect) way.

Review questions

31.1 You are required to prepare a sales ledger control account from the following information for the month of November:

2010				£
Nov	1	Sales ledger balances		24,000
		Totals for November:		
			Sales day book	14,000
			Returns inwards day book	1,000
			Cheques and cash received from customers	18,000
			Discounts allowed	500
	30	Sales ledger balances		18,500

31.2A You are required to prepare a purchases ledger control account from the following information for the month of April. The balance of the account is to be taken as the amount of accounts payable as on 30 April.

2011				£
April	1	Purchases ledger balances		11,241
		Totals for April:		
			Purchases day book	6,100
			Returns outwards day book	246
			Cheques paid to suppliers	8,300
			Discounts received from suppliers	749
	30	Purchases ledger balances		?

31.3 Prepare a sales ledger control account from the following information:

2012			£
March	1	Debit balances	12,000
		Totals for March:	
		Sales day book	9,000
		Cash and cheques received from debtors	11,000
		Discounts allowed	1,000
		Debit balances in the sales ledger set off against credit	
		balances in the purchases ledger	100
	31	Debit balances	?
		Credit balances	50

31.4A   Prepare a sales ledger control account from the following information for October 2012, carrying down the balance at 31 October:

2012				£
Oct	1	Sales ledger balances		28,409
	31	Sales day book		26,617
		Bad debts written off		342
		Cheques received from debtors		24,293
		Discounts allowed		416
		Cheques dishonoured		120
		Returns inwards		924
		Set-offs against balances in purchases ledger		319

31.5   The trial balance of Outsize Books Ltd revealed a difference in the books. In order that the error(s) could be located it was decided to prepare purchases and sales ledger control accounts.

From the following information prepare the control accounts and show where an error may have been made:

2011			£
Jan	1	Purchases ledger balances	19,420
		Sales ledger balances	28,227
		Totals for the year 2011	
		Purchases journal	210,416
		Sales journal	305,824
		Returns outwards journal	1,452
		Returns inwards journal	3,618
		Cheques paid to suppliers	205,419
		Petty cash paid to suppliers	62
		Cheques and cash received from customers	287,317
		Discounts allowed	4,102
		Discounts received	1,721
		Balances on the sales ledger set off against balances in the purchases ledger	640
Dec	31	The list of balances from the purchases ledger shows a total of £20,210 and that from the sales ledger a total of £38,374	

31.6   From the following figures, compile accounts receivable ledger and accounts payable ledger control accounts for the month, and ascertain what the net balances of the respective ledgers should be on 31 January 2013.

Balances on 1 January 2013	£
Accounts receivable ledger – Dr	46,462
Cr	245
Accounts payable ledger – Dr	1,472
Cr	25,465

Total for the month to 31 January 2013	£
Purchases	76,474
Sales	126,024
Purchase returns	2,154
Accounts receivable settled by contra accounts with accounts payable	455
Bad debt written off	1,253
Discounts and allowances to customers	746
Cash received from customers	120,464
Cash discount received	1,942
Cash paid to creditors	70,476
Cash paid to customers	52

31.7A

	£
Sales ledger balances, 1 July 2012 – Debit	20,040
– Credit	56
Purchases ledger balances, 1 July 2012 – Debit	12
– Credit	14,860
Activities during the half-year to 31 December 2012:	
Payments to trade accounts payable	93,685
Cheques from credit customers	119,930
Purchases on credit	95,580
Sales on credit	124,600
Bad debts written off	204
Discounts allowed	3,480
Discounts received	2,850
Returns inwards	1,063
Returns outwards	240
Sales ledger credit balances at 31 December 2012	37
Purchases ledger debit balances at 31 December 2012	26

During the half-year, debit balances in the sales ledger, amounting to £438, were transferred to the purchases ledger.

Required:
Prepare the sales ledger control account and the purchases ledger control account for the half-year to 31 December 2012.

31.8A   The following extracts have been taken from the subsidiary books of the business owned by D. Jenkinson for the month of April 2013.

Purchases Day Book

			£
Apr	3	W. Allen	480
	7	J. Morris	270
	17	T. Sage	410
	24	F. Wilding	650

Returns Outwards Day Book

			£
Apr	14	W. Allen	50
	29	T. Sage	80

Cash Book (Credit side)

			Discounts received £	Bank £
Apr	9	T. Sage	30	690
	18	F. Wilding	5	195
	24	J. Morris	31	389
	27	W. Allen	18	322

Journal

			£	£
Apr	30	Creditor W. Allen	180	
		Debtor W. Allen		180
		being transfer		
		from sales ledger		
		to purchases ledger		

It should be noted that the balances in the accounts of D. Jenkinson's suppliers on 1 April 2013 were as follows:

	£
W. Allen	360
J. Morris	140
T. Sage	720
F. Wilding	310

Required:
(a)   The name of the source document which will have been used for making entries in the
    (i)   purchases day book
    (ii)   returns outwards day book.

(b)   The name of **two** subsidiary books (other than those shown in the extracts above) which could form part of D. Jenkinson's accounting system. In the case of **one** of the subsidiary books chosen, explain its purpose.

(c)   The account of T. Sage in D. Jenkinson's purchases ledger for the month of April 2013. (The account should be balanced at the end of the month.)

(d)   D. Jenkinson's purchases ledger control account for the month of April 2013. (The account should be balanced at the end of the month.)

(e)   Advice for D. Jenkinson on **two** ways in which he might find the purchases ledger control account useful.

(*Southern Examining Group: GCSE*)

31.9   The financial year of The Better Trading Company ended on 30 November 2010. You have been asked to prepare a Total Accounts Receivable Account and a Total Accounts Payable Account in order to produce end-of-year figures for Accounts Receivable and Accounts Payable for the draft final accounts.

You are able to obtain the following information for the financial year from the books of original entry:

	£
Sales – cash	344,890
– credit	268,187
Purchases – cash	14,440
– credit	496,600
Total receipts from customers	600,570
Total payments to suppliers	503,970
Discounts allowed (all to credit customers)	5,520
Discounts received (all from credit suppliers)	3,510
Refunds given to cash customers	5,070
Balance in the sales ledger set off against balance in the purchases ledger	70
Bad debts written off	780
Increase in the allowance for doubtful debts	90
Credit notes issued to credit customers	4,140
Credit notes received from credit suppliers	1,480

According to the audited financial statements for the previous year accounts receivable and accounts payable as at 1 December 2009 were £26,555 and £43,450 respectively.

Required:
Draw up the relevant Total Accounts entering end-of-year totals for accounts receivable and accounts payable.

(*Association of Accounting Technicians*)

31.10

(a)   Why are many accounting systems designed with a purchases ledger (accounts payable ledger) control account, as well as with a purchases ledger (accounts payable ledger)?

(b)   The following errors have been discovered:
   (i)   An invoice for £654 has been entered in the purchases day book as £456;
   (ii) A prompt payment discount of £100 from a creditor had been completely omitted from the accounting records;
   (iii) Purchases of £250 had been entered on the wrong side of a supplier's account in the purchases ledger;
   (iv) No entry had been made to record an agreement to contra an amount owed to X of £600 against an amount owed by X of £400;
   (v)   A credit note for £60 had been entered as if it was an invoice.
   State the numerical effect on the purchases ledger control account balance of correcting each of these items (treating each item separately).

(c) Information technology and computerised systems are rapidly increasing in importance in data recording. Do you consider that this trend will eventually remove the need for control accounts to be incorporated in the design of accounting systems? Explain your answer briefly.

(*Association of Chartered Certified Accountants*)

31.11 Control Accounts are used mainly for accounts receivable and accounts payable. Explain:

(*a*) why it may be appropriate to use control accounts;
(*b*) the advantages of using them.

 Need more practice? Instant feedback?
Visit **www.myaccountinglab.com**

Featuring unlimited practice questions, a personalised study plan that identifies the areas where you need to focus for better marks, and interactive material designed to help all kinds of learners, MyAccountingLab is a vital tool for maximising your understanding, confidence, and success. Log in at **www.myaccountinglab.com** to see why 92 per cent of students surveyed last year recommend MyAccountingLab.

Correction of Errors and Suspense Accounts

Errors not affecting the balancing of the trial balance

Learning objectives
. . . .

After you have studied this chapter, you should be able to:

● correct errors which are not revealed by a trial balance
● distinguish between the different kinds of errors that may arise

Introduction
. . . .

In this chapter, you'll learn how to identify and correct a range of errors that can arise when financial transactions are entered in the ledger accounts.

32.1 Types of error

In Chapter 6 it was seen that if we followed the rules

● every debit entry needs a corresponding credit entry;
● every credit entry needs a corresponding debit entry;

and entered transactions in our ledgers using these rules then, when we extracted the trial balance, the totals of the two columns would be the same, i.e. it would 'balance'.

Suppose we correctly entered cash sales £70 to the debit of the Cash Book, but did not enter the £70 to the credit of the sales account. If this were the only error in the books, the trial balance totals would differ by £70. However, there are certain kinds of error which would not affect the agreement of the trial balance totals, and we will now consider these:

1 **Errors of omission** – where a transaction is completely omitted from the books. If we sold £90 goods to J. Brewer, but did not enter it in either the sales account or Brewer's personal account, the trial balance would still 'balance'.
2 **Errors of commission** – this type of error occurs when the correct amount is entered but in the wrong account, e.g. where a sale of £11 to C. Green is entered in the account of K. Green.
3 **Errors of principle** – where an item is entered in the wrong class of account, e.g. if purchase of a fixed asset, such as a van, is debited to an expenses account, such as motor expenses account.
4 **Compensating errors** – where errors cancel each other out. If the sales account was added up to be £10 too much and the purchases account was also added up to be £10 too much, then these two errors would cancel out in the trial balance. This is because the totals of both the debit side and the credit side of the trial balance will be overstated by £10.

5 **Errors of original entry** – where the original figure is incorrect, yet double entry is correctly done using the incorrect figure. For example, where a sale should have totalled £150 but an error is made in calculating the total on the sales invoice. If it were calculated as £130, and £130 were credited as sales and £130 were debited to the personal account of the customer, the trial balance would still balance.

6 **Complete reversal of entries** – where the correct accounts are used but each item is shown on the wrong side of the account. Suppose we had paid a cheque to D. Williams for £200, the double entry of which should be debit D. Williams £200, credit Bank £200. In error it is entered as debit Bank £200, credit D. Williams £200. The trial balance totals will still agree.

7 **Transposition errors** – where the wrong sequence of the individual characters within a number was entered (for example, £142 entered instead of £124). This is a common type of error and is very difficult to spot when the error has occurred in both the debit and the credit entries, as the trial balance would still balance. It is, however, more common for this error to occur on one side of the double entry only. When it does, it is easier to find.

32.2 Correction of errors

Most errors are found after the date on which they are made. When we correct errors, we should not do so by crossing out items, tearing out accounts and throwing them away, or using chemicals to make the writing disappear.

 Activity 32.1 In which book should all the correcting double entries first be entered?

We make corrections to double entry accounts by preparing journal entries. We should:

1 prepare the corrections by means of journal entries; then
2 post the journal entries to the appropriate ledger accounts.

1 Error of omission

A sale of £59 worth of goods to E. George has been completely omitted from the books. We must correct this by entering the sale in the books. The journal entry for the correction is:*

The Journal

	Dr	Cr
	£	£
E. George	59	
Sales		59

Correction of omission of Sales Invoice Number . . . from sales journal

*Note: in all these examples, the folio column has been omitted so as to make the example clearer.

2 Error of commission

A purchase £44 worth of goods from C. Simons on 4 September was entered in error in C. Simpson's account. The error was found on 30 September. To correct this, it must be cancelled out of C. Simpson's account and entered where it should be (in C. Simons' account). The journal entry will be:

The Journal

	Dr	Cr
	£	£
C. Simpson	44	
C. Simons		44
Purchase Invoice Number . . . entered in wrong personal account, now corrected		

The entries in the ledger accounts would be:

C. Simpson

	£			£
Sept 30 C. Simons (error corrected)	44	Sept 4 Purchases		44

C. Simons

		£
	Sept 30 Purchases (error corrected)	44

3 Error of principle

The purchase of a machine for £200 is debited to the purchases account instead of being debited to a machinery account. We therefore cancel the item out of the purchases account by crediting that account. It is then entered where it should be by debiting the machinery account.

The Journal

	Dr	Cr
	£	£
Machinery	200	
Purchases		200
Correction of error: purchase of fixed asset debited to purchases account		

4 Compensating error

In the cash book, the amount of cash sales transferred to the sales account was overstated by £20 and the amount transferred to the wages account was also overstated by £20. The trial balance therefore still balances.

The Journal

	Dr	Cr
	£	£
Sales	20	
Wages		20
Correction of two overcasts of £20 posted from the cash book to the sales account and the wages account which compensated for each other		

5 Error of original entry

A sale of £38 to A. Smailes was entered in the books as £28. The other £10 must be entered:

The Journal

	Dr	Cr
	£	£
A. Smailes	10	
Sales		10

Correction of error whereby sales were understated by £10

6 Complete reversal of entries

A payment of cash of £16 to M. Dickson was entered on the receipts side of the Cash Book in error and credited to M. Dickson's account. This is somewhat more difficult to adjust. First must come the amount needed to cancel the error, then comes the actual entry itself. Because of this, the correcting entry is double the actual amount first recorded. We can now look at why this is so.

We should have had:

Cash

			£
		M. Dickson	16

M. Dickson

	£		
Cash	16		

This was entered wrongly as:

Cash

	£		
M. Dickson	16		

M. Dickson

			£
		Cash	16

We can now see that we have to enter double the original amount to correct the error.

Cash

	£		£
M. Dickson	16	M. Dickson (error corrected)	32

M. Dickson

	£		£
Cash (error corrected)	32	M. Dickson	16

Overall, when corrected, the £16 debit and £32 credit in the cash account means there is a net credit of £16. Similarly, Dickson's account shows £32 debit and £16 credit, a net debit of £16. As the final (net) answer is the same as what should have been entered originally, the error is now corrected.

The Journal entry appears:

The Journal

	Dr	Cr
	£	£
M. Dickson	32	
Cash		32

Payment of cash £16 debited to cash and credited to
M. Dickson in error on . . . Error now corrected

7 Transposition error

A credit purchase from P. Maclaran costing £56 was entered in the books as £65. The £9 error needs to be removed.

The Journal

	Dr	Cr
	£	£
P. Maclaran	9	
Purchases		9

Correction of error whereby purchases were overstated by £9

32.3 Casting

You will sometimes notice the use of the term **casting**, which means adding up. **Overcasting** means incorrectly adding up a column of figures to give an answer which is greater than it should be. **Undercasting** means incorrectly adding up a column of figures to give an answer which is less than it should be.

> **Mnemonic**
>
> The following acronym may help you to remember which types of errors do not affect the balancing of a trial balance:
>
> POOR CC
> P – Principle
> O – Omission
> O – Original entry
> R – Reversal
>
> C – Compensating
> C – Commission

> ## Learning outcomes
> ····················
> You should now have learnt:
> 1 How to describe each of a range of possible errors that can be made when recording financial transactions in the accounts that will not be detected by producing a trial balance.
> 2 How to identify and correct each of these types of errors.
> 3 That when errors are found, they should be amended by using proper double entry procedures.
> 4 That all corrections of errors should take place via the Journal, where entries are first recorded before being posted to the appropriate ledger accounts.

Answer to activity

32.1   The Journal.

Review questions

32.1   Give an example of each of the different types of error which are *not* revealed by a trial balance.

32.2   Show the journal entries necessary to correct the following errors:

(a)   A sale of goods for £412 to T. More had been entered in T. Mone's account.
(b)   The purchase of a machine on credit from J. Frank for £619 had been completely omitted from our books.
(c)   The purchase of a computer for £550 had been entered in error in the Office Expenses account.
(d)   A sale of £120 to B. Wood had been entered in the books, both debit and credit, as £102.
(e)   Commission received £164 had been entered in error in the Sales account.
(f)   A receipt of cash from T. Blair £68 had been entered on the credit side of the cash book and the debit side of T. Blair's account.
(g)   A purchase of goods for £372 had been entered in error on the debit side of the Drawings account.
(h)   Discounts Allowed £48 had been entered in error on the debit side of the Discounts Received account.

32.3A   Show the journal entries needed to correct the following errors:

(a)   Purchases £1,410 on credit from A. Ray had been entered in B. Roy's account.
(b)   A cheque of £94 paid for printing had been entered in the cash column of the cash book instead of in the bank column.
(c)   Sale of goods £734 on credit to D. Rolls had been entered in error in D. Rollo's account.
(d)   Purchase of goods on credit L. Hand £819 entered in the correct accounts in error as £891.
(e)   Cash paid to G. Boyd £64 entered on the debit side of the cash book and the credit side of G. Boyd's account.
(f)   A sale of fittings £320 had been entered in the Sales account.

→

(g) Cash withdrawn from bank £200 had been entered in the cash column on the credit side of the cash book, and in the bank column on the debit side.

(h) Purchase of goods £1,182 has been entered in error in the Furnishings account.

32.4 After preparing its draft final accounts for the year ended 31 March 2009 and its draft statement of financial position as at 31 March 2009 a business discovered that the inventory lists used to compute the value of inventory as at 31 March 2009 contained the following entry:

Inventory item	Number	Cost per unit	Total cost
Y 4003	100	£1.39	£1,390

Required:
(a) What is wrong with this particular entry?
(b) What would the effect of the error have been on
  (i) the value of inventory as at 31 March 2009?
  (ii) the cost of goods sold for the year ended 31 March 2009?
  (iii) the net profit for the year ended 31 March 2009?
  (iv) the total for Current Assets as at 31 March 2009?
  (v) the Owner's Capital as at 31 March 2009?

(*Association of Accounting Technicians*)

32.5 Give the journal entries needed to record the corrections of the following. Narratives are not required.

(a) Extra capital of £5,000 paid into the bank had been credited to Sales account.
(b) Goods taken for own use £72 had been debited to Sundry Expenses.
(c) Private rent £191 had been debited to the Rent account.
(d) A purchase of goods from D. Pine £246 had been entered in the books as £426.
(e) Cash banked £410 had been credited to the bank column and debited to the cash column in the cash book.
(f) Cash drawings of £120 had been credited to the bank column of the cash book.
(g) Returns inwards £195 from G. Will had been entered in error in T. Young's account.
(h) A sale of a printer for £100 had been credited to Office Expenses.

32.6A Journal entries to correct the following are required, but the narratives can be omitted.

(a) Rent Received £430 have been credited to the Commissions Received account.
(b) Bank charges £34 have been debited to the Business Rates account.
(c) Completely omitted from the books is a payment of Motor Expenses by cheque £37.
(d) A purchase of a fax machine £242 has been entered in the Purchases account.
(e) Returns inwards £216 have been entered on the debit side of the Returns Outwards account.
(f) A loan from G. Bain £2,000 has been entered on the credit side of the Capital account.
(g) Loan interest of £400 has been debited to the Van account.
(h) Goods taken for own use £84 have been debited to the Purchases account and credited to Drawings.

32.7A Thomas Smith, a retail trader, has very limited accounting knowledge. In the absence of his accounting technician, he extracted the following trial balance as at 31 March 2011 from his business's accounting records:

	£	£
Inventory-in-trade at 1 April 2010		10,700
Inventory-in-trade at 31 March 2011	7,800	
Discounts allowed		310
Discounts received	450	
Allowance for doubtful debts	960	
Purchases	94,000	
Purchases returns	1,400	
Sales		132,100
Sales returns	1,100	
Freehold property: at cost	70,000	
Provision for depreciation	3,500	
Motor vehicles: at cost	15,000	
Provision for depreciation	4,500	
Capital – Thomas Smith		84,600
Balance at bank	7,100	
Trade accounts receivable		11,300
Trade accounts payable	7,600	
Establishment and administrative expenditure	16,600	
Drawings	9,000	
	£239,010	£239,010

Required:

(a) Prepare a corrected trial balance as at 31 March 2011.

After the preparation of the above trial balance, but before the completion of the final accounts for the year ended 31 March 2011, the following discoveries were made:

(i) The correct valuation of the inventory-in-trade at 1 April 2010 is £12,000; apparently some inventory lists had been mislaid.

(ii) A credit note for £210 has now been received from J. Hardwell Limited; this relates to goods returned in December 2010 by Thomas Smith. However, up to now J. Hardwell Limited had not accepted that the goods were not of merchantable quality and Thomas Smith's accounting records did not record the return of the goods.

(iii) Trade sample goods were sent to John Grey in February 2011. These were free samples, but were charged wrongly at £1,000 to John Grey. A credit note is now being prepared to rectify the error.

(iv) In March 2011, Thomas Smith painted the inside walls of his stockroom using materials costing £150 which were included in the purchases figure in the above trial balance. Thomas Smith estimates that he saved £800 by doing all the painting himself.

(b) Prepare the journal entries necessary to amend the accounts for the above discoveries. *Note*: narratives are required.

(*Association of Accounting Technicians*)

Suspense accounts and errors

Learning objectives

After you have studied this chapter, you should be able to:

- explain why a suspense account may be used
- create a suspense account in order to balance the trial balance
- correct errors using a suspense account
- recalculate profits after errors have been corrected
- explain why using a suspense account is generally inappropriate

Introduction

In this chapter, you'll learn how to use suspense accounts to temporarily balance an out-of-balance trial balance. You'll also learn that it is usually not a wise thing to do, even temporarily.

33.1 Errors and the trial balance

In the previous chapter, we looked at errors that do not affect the trial balance. However, many errors will mean that trial balance totals will not be equal. These include:

- incorrect additions in any account;
- making an entry on only one side of the accounts, e.g. a debit but no credit; a credit but no debit;
- entering a different amount on the debit side from the amount on the credit side.

33.2 Suspense account

We should try very hard to find errors when the trial balance totals are not equal. When such errors cannot be found, the trial balance totals can be made to agree with each other by inserting the amount of the difference between the two totals in a **suspense account**. This is shown in Exhibit 33.1 where there is a £40 difference.

Exhibit 33.1

Trial Balance as at 31 December 2011

	Dr	Cr
	£	£
Totals after all the accounts have been listed	100,000	99,960
Suspense		40
	100,000	100,000

To make the two totals the same, a figure of £40 for the suspense account has been shown on the credit side of the trial balance. A suspense account is opened and the £40 difference is also shown there on the credit side:

Suspense

	2011		£
	Dec 31	Difference per trial balance	40

Activity 33.1   Where is the debit side of this entry made?

33.3   Suspense accounts and the statement of financial position

If the errors are not found before the financial statements are prepared, the suspense account balance will be included in the statement of financial position. The balance should be included shown after the figure for net current assets, either as a negative amount (credit balance) or a positive amount (debit balance) (see Exhibit 33.5).

Activity 33.2   Does the use of a suspense account in financial statements affect the true and fair view that they are meant to portray?

33.4   Correction of errors

When errors are found they must be corrected using double entry. Each correction must first have an entry in the journal describing it, and then be posted to the accounts concerned.

One error only

We will look at two examples:

Example 1

Assume that the cause of the error of £40 in Exhibit 33.1 is found on 31 March 2012. The error was that the sales account was undercast by £40. The action taken to correct this is:

> Debit suspense account to close it: £40.
> Credit sales account to show item where it should have been: £40.

The accounts now appear as Exhibit 33.2:

Exhibit 33.2

Suspense

2012		£	2012			£
Mar 31 Sales		40	Jan 1	Balance b/d		40

Sales

			2012		£
			Mar 31	Suspense	40

This can be shown in journal form as:

The Journal

	Dr	Cr
	£	£
2012		
Mar 31 Suspense	40	
Sales		40
Correction of undercasting of sales by £40 last year		

Here's another example.

Example 2

The trial balance on 31 December 2012 had a difference of £168. It was a shortage on the debit side.

A suspense account is opened, and the difference of £168 is entered on the debit side in the account. On 31 May 2013 the error was found. We had made a payment of £168 to K. Leek to close his account. It was correctly entered in the cash book, but was not entered in K. Leek's account.

First of all, the account of K. Leek is debited with £168, as it should have been in 2009. Second, the suspense account is credited with £168 so that the account can be closed.

Exhibit 33.3

K. Leek

2013		£	2013			£
May 31 Bank		168	Jan 1	Balance b/d		168

The account of K. Leek is now correct.

Suspense

2013			£	2013		£
Jan 1	Balance b/d		168	May 31 K. Leek		168

The Journal entry is:

The Journal

	Dr	Cr
	£	£
2013		
May 31 K. Leek	168	
Suspense		168
Correction of non-entry of payment last year in K. Leek's account		

More than one error

Let's now look at Example 3 where the suspense account difference was caused by more than one error.

Example 3

The trial balance at 31 December 2010 showed a difference of £77, being a shortage on the debit side. A suspense account is opened, and the difference of £77 is entered on the debit side of the account.

On 28 February 2011 all the errors from the previous year were found.

(A) A cheque of £150 paid to L. Kent had been correctly entered in the cash book, but had not been entered in Kent's account.
(B) The purchases account had been undercast by £20.
(C) A cheque of £93 received from K. Sand had been correctly entered in the cash book, but had not been entered in Sand's account.

These three errors resulted in a net error of £77, shown by a debit of £77 on the debit side of the suspense account. These are corrected as follows:

(*a*) Make correcting entries in accounts for (A), (B) and (C).
(*b*) Record double entry for these items in the suspense account.

Exhibit 33.4

L. Kent

2011				£	
Feb	28	Suspense	(A)	150	

Purchases

2011				£	
Feb	28	Suspense	(B)	20	

K. Sand

				2011				£
				Feb	28	Suspense	(C)	93

Suspense

2011				£	2011				£
Jan	1	Balance b/d		77	Feb	28	L. Kent	(A)	150
Feb	28	K. Sand	(C)	93		28	Purchases	(B)	20
				170					170

The Journal

			Dr	Cr
2011			£	£
Feb	28	L. Kent	150	
		Suspense		150
		Cheque paid omitted from Kent's account		
	28	Purchases	20	
		Suspense		20
		Undercasting of purchases by £20 in last year's accounts		
	28	Suspense	93	
		K. Sand		93
		Cheque received omitted from Sand's account		

Note: Only errors which make the trial balance totals different from each other can be corrected using a suspense account.

33.5   The effect of errors on profits

Some of the errors will have meant that original profits calculated will be wrong. Other errors will have no effect upon profits. We will use Exhibit 33.5 to illustrate the different kinds of errors.

Exhibit 33.5 shows a set of financial statements in which errors have been made.

Exhibit 33.5

K. Davis
Income Statement for the year ending 31 December 2011

		£	£
Sales			180,000
Less	Cost of goods sold:		
	Opening inventory	15,000	
	Add Purchases	92,000	
		107,000	
	Less Closing inventory	(18,000)	
			(89,000)
Gross profit			91,000
Add Discounts received			1,400
			92,400
Less	Expenses:		
	Rent	8,400	
	Insurance	1,850	
	Lighting	1,920	
	Depreciation	28,200	
			(40,370)
Net profit			52,030

Statement of Financial Position as at 31 December 2011

	£	£
Non-current assets		
Equipment at cost		62,000
Less Depreciation to date		(41,500)
		20,500
Current assets		
Inventory	18,000	
Accounts receivable	23,000	
Bank	19,000	
	60,000	
Less Current liabilities		
Accounts payable	(14,000)	
		46,000
Suspense account		80
		66,580
Capital		
Balance as at 1.1.2011		46,250
Add Net profit		52,030
		98,280
Less Drawings		(31,700)
		66,580

The errors that have been made may be of three types.

1 Errors which do not affect profit calculations

If an error affects items only in the statement of financial position, then the original calculated profit will not need to be changed. Example 4 shows this.

Example 4

Assume that in Exhibit 33.5 the £80 debit balance on the suspense account was because of the following error:

On 1 November 2011 we paid £80 to a creditor T. Monk. It was correctly entered in the cash book. It was not entered anywhere else. The error was identified on 1 June 2012.

The journal entries to correct it will be:

The Journal

			Dr	Cr
			£	£
2012				
June	1	T. Monk	80	
		Suspense		80
		Payment to T. Monk on 1 November 2005 not		
		entered in his account. Correction now made.		

Both of these accounts appeared in the statement of financial position only with T. Monk as part of accounts payable. The net profit of £52,030 does not have to be changed.

2 Errors which do affect profit calculations

If the error is in one of the figures shown in the income statement, then the original profit will need to be amended. Example 5 shows this.

Example 5

Assume that in Exhibit 33.5 the £80 debit balance was because the rent account was added up incorrectly. It should be shown as £8,480 instead of £8,400. The error was identified on 1 June 2012. The journal entries to correct it are:

The Journal

			Dr	Cr
			£	£
2012				
Jun	1	Rent	80	
		Suspense		80
		Correction of rent undercast last year		

Rent last year should have been increased by £80. This would have reduced net profit by £80. A statement of corrected profit for the year is now shown.

K. Davis
Statement of Corrected Net Profit for the year ending 31 December 2011

	£
Net profit per the financial statements	52,030
Less Rent understated	(80)
Corrected net profit for the year	51,950

3 Where there have been several errors

Let's assume that in Exhibit 33.5 there had been four errors in the ledger accounts of K. Davis that were all identified on 31 March 2012:

(A)	Sales overcast by	£90
(B)	Insurance undercast by	£40
(C)	Cash received from a debtor, E. Silva, entered in the Cash Book only	£50
(D)	A purchase of £59 is entered in the books, debit and credit entries as	£95

Note: Error (D) is known as an 'error of transposition', as the correct numbers have been included but in the wrong order, i.e. they have been 'transposed'. It did not affect the trial balance, so it is not included in the £80 adjustment made by opening the suspense account.

The entries in the suspense account and the journal entries will be as follows:

Suspense Account

2012				£	2012					£
Jan	1	Balance b/d		80	Mar	31	Sales	(A)		90
Mar	31	E. Silva	(C)	50		31	Insurance	(B)		40
				130						130

The Journal

					Dr	Cr
2012					£	£
1	Mar	31	Sales		90	
			Suspense			90
			Sales overcast of £90 in 2005			
2	Mar	31	Insurance		40	
			Suspense			40
			Insurance expense undercast by £40 in 2005			
3	Mar	31	Suspense		50	
			E. Silva			50
			Cash received omitted from accounts receivable account in 2011			
4	Mar	31	Creditor's account		36	
			Purchases			36
			Credit purchase of £59 entered both as debit and credit as £95 in 2011			

Note: Remember that in (D), the correction of the overstatement of purchases does *not* pass through the suspense account because it did not affect the balancing of the trial balance.

Now we can calculate the corrected net profit for the year 2011. Only items (A), (B) and (D) affect figures in the income statement. These are the only adjustments to be made to profit.

K. Davis
Statement of Corrected Net Profit for the year ending 31 December 2011

			£
Net profit per the financial statements			52,030
Add Purchases overstated	(D)		36
			52,066
Less Sales overcast	(A)	90	
Insurance undercast	(B)	40	
			(130)
Corrected net profit for the year			51,936

Error (C), the cash not posted to an accounts receivable account, did not affect profit calculations.

33.6 Suspense accounts: businesses and examinations

Businesses

Every attempt should be made to find errors. A suspense account should be opened only if all other efforts have failed, and they *never* should!

Examinations

Unless it is part of a question, *do not* make your statement of financial position totals agree by using a suspense account. The same applies to trial balances. Examiners are very likely to penalise you for showing a suspense account when it should not be required.

Overall

Suspense accounts have probably been used ever since people first started keeping accounts and using them to produce financial statements. However, just because suspense accounts have been used for a very long time does not mean that they should still be used today.

Long ago, accounting records were very poorly maintained. The people maintaining them were frequently untrained. Errors were fairly common, and no one was very concerned when it proved difficult to find out what had caused a trial balance not to balance, if they even went to the extent of preparing one.

Businesses were largely owned by one person who would often also prepare the financial statements, more out of interest than in order to make much use of what they showed which, before there was some regulation concerning what they presented, was frequently little more than the excess or shortfall of revenue over expenditure.

Nowadays, accounting is far more sophisticated and the people maintaining the accounting records are much better trained. Many organisations use computerised accounting systems and very few organisations of any complexity continue to do everything manually. When they do, their records will be good enough to make tracing an error reasonably straightforward.

Errors of the types that cause trial balances not to balance are, therefore, much less common and much easier to detect. As a result, it is inconceivable that a suspense account will ever be needed in practice when an accountant is involved in preparing or auditing the financial statements.

Nevertheless, circumstances may make it impossible for a sole trader's financial statements to be ready in time, for example, to show the bank manager when asking for a loan. It is probably only in circumstances of this type that you may find suspense accounts still in use, albeit rarely. An example may be when money is received by post or credited in to the business's bank account with no explanation and no information. It needs to be put somewhere in the ledger accounts, so a suspense account is used while the reason it was sent to the business is identified.

Learning outcomes

You should now have learnt:

1 How to make the appropriate entries in setting up a suspense account.

2 How to make the correcting entries involving the suspense account when the cause of an error is identified.

3 That some errors may cause the profits originally calculated to have been incorrect.

4 That errors that do not affect profit calculations will have an effect only on items in the statement of financial position.

5 That nowadays suspense accounts very rarely need to be used, if at all.

Answers to activities

33.1 This is a major problem in the use of suspense accounts. There is no double entry and, therefore, no debit to match the credit of £40! The justification for this is that there is either a £40 hidden credit somewhere in the accounts that has been omitted when the balances were extracted for the trial balance, or that an extra £40 has been added by mistake to the debit entries in the trial balance. As a result, making this single entry is only completing the existing double entry, the other side being the mistake. Many accountants believe that it is bad practice to open a suspense account as it contravenes the basic principles of double entry. You would be wise to follow that advice and only open a suspense account if an examiner requires you to do so.

33.2 If it is material, definitely. If it is not material, it could be argued that no one will be concerned. However, the appearance of a suspense account in the statement of financial position is, by definition, material – you don't include anything in the financial statements as a separate entry that is not of interest to the users of the financial statements. There has been *at least* one error made in the accounting entries and the fact that it cannot be found may indicate a much more serious problem with the accounting system. This is of concern to anyone with a knowledge of accounting for, nowadays, when all complex accounting systems are computerised, *no* error should be that difficult to find, no matter how large or complicated the financial system or the organisation.

Multiple choice questions: Set 4

Now attempt Set 4 of multiple choice questions. (Answers to all the multiple choice questions are given in Appendix 2 at the end of this book.)

Each of these multiple choice questions has four suggested answers, (A), (B), (C) and (D). You should read each question and then decide which choice is best, either (A) or (B) or (C) or (D). *Write down your answers on a separate piece of paper.* You will then be able to redo the set of questions later without having to try to ignore your answers.

MC61 Working Capital is a term meaning

(A) The amount of capital invested by the proprietor
(B) The excess of the current assets over the current liabilities
(C) The capital less drawings
(D) The total of Non-current Assets – Current Assets

MC62 A credit balance brought down on a Rent Account means

(A) We owe that rent at that date
(B) We have paid that rent in advance at that date
(C) We have paid too much rent
(D) We have paid too little in rent

MC63 A debit balance brought down on a Packing Materials Account means

(A) We owe for packing materials
(B) We are owed for packing materials
(C) We have lost money on packing materials
(D) We have an inventory of packing materials unused

MC64 If we take goods for own use we should

(A) Debit Drawings Account: Credit Purchases Account
(B) Debit Purchases Account: Credit Drawings Account
(C) Debit Drawings Account: Credit Inventory Account
(D) Debit Sales Account: Credit Inventory Account

MC65 Capital Expenditure is

(A)   The extra capital paid in by the proprietor
(B)   The costs of running the business on a day-to-day basis
(C)   Money spent on buying non-current assets or adding value to them
(D)   Money spent on selling non-current assets

MC66 In the business of C. Sangster, who owns a clothing store, which of the following are Capital Expenditure?

(*i*)   Shop fixtures bought
(*ii*)   Wages of assistants
(*iii*) New van bought
(*iv*)   Petrol for van

(A)   (*i*) and (*iii*)
(B)   (*i*) and (*ii*)
(C)   (*ii*) and (*iii*)
(D)   (*ii*) and (*iv*)

MC67 If £500 was shown added to Purchases instead of being added to a non-current asset

(A)   Net profit only would be understated
(B)   Net profit only would be overstated
(C)   It would not affect net profit
(D)   Both gross profit and net profit would be understated

MC68 A cheque paid by you, but not yet passed through the banking system, is

(A)   A standing order
(B)   A dishonoured cheque
(C)   A credit transfer
(D)   An unpresented cheque

MC69 A Bank Reconciliation Statement is a statement

(A)   Sent by the bank when the account is overdrawn
(B)   Drawn up by us to verify our cash book balance with the bank statement balance
(C)   Drawn up by the bank to verify the cash book
(D)   Sent by the bank when we have made an error

MC70 Which of the following are not true? A Bank Reconciliation Statement is

(*i*)   Part of the double entry system
(*ii*)   Not part of the double entry system
(*iii*) Sent by the firm to the bank
(*iv*)   Posted to the ledger accounts

(A)   (*i*), (*iii*) and (*iv*)
(B)   (*i*) and (*ii*)
(C)   (*i*), (*ii*) and (*iv*)
(D)   (*ii*), (*iii*) and (*iv*)

MC71 Which of the following should be entered in the Journal?

(*i*)   Payment for cash purchases
(*ii*)   Fixtures bought on credit
(*iii*) Credit sale of goods
(*iv*)   Sale of surplus machinery

→

(A) (*i*) and (*iv*)
(B) (*ii*) and (*iii*)
(C) (*iii*) and (*iv*)
(D) (*ii*) and (*iv*)

MC72 The Journal is

(A) Part of the double entry system
(B) A supplement to the Cash Book
(C) Not part of the double entry system
(D) Used when other journals have been mislaid

MC73 Given a desired cash float of £200, if £146 is spent in the period, how much will be re-imbursed at the end of the period?

(A) £200
(B) £54
(C) £254
(D) £146

MC74 When a petty cash book is kept there will be

(A) More entries made in the general ledger
(B) Fewer entries made in the general ledger
(C) The same number of entries in the general ledger
(D) No entries made at all in the general ledger for items paid by petty cash

MC75 Which of the following do *not* affect trial balance agreement?

(*i*)   Sales £105 to A. Henry entered in P. Henry's account
(*ii*)   Cheque payment of £134 for Motor expenses entered only in Cash Book
(*iii*) Purchases £440 from C. Browne entered in both accounts as £404
(*iv*)   Wages account added up incorrectly, being totalled £10 too much

(A) (*i*) and (*iv*)
(B) (*i*) and (*iii*)
(C) (*ii*) and (*iii*)
(D) (*iii*) and (*iv*)

MC76 Which of the following are *not* errors of principle?

(*i*)   Motor expenses entered in Motor Vehicles account
(*ii*)   Purchases of machinery entered in Purchases account
(*iii*) Sale of £250 to C. Phillips completely omitted from books
(*iv*)   Sale to A. Henriques entered in A. Henry's account

(A) (*ii*) and (*iii*)
(B) (*i*) and (*ii*)
(C) (*iii*) and (*iv*)
(D) (*i*) and (*iv*)

MC77 Errors are corrected via the Journal because

(A) It saves the bookkeeper's time
(B) It saves entering them in the ledger
(C) It is much easier to do
(D) It provides a good record explaining the double entry records

MC78   Which of these errors would be disclosed by the trial balance?

(A)   Cheque £95 from C. Smith entered in Smith's account as £59
(B)   Selling expenses had been debited to Sales Account
(C)   Credit sales of £300 entered in both double entry accounts as £30
(D)   A purchase of £250 was omitted entirely from the books.

MC79   If the two totals of a trial balance do *not* agree, the difference must be entered in

(A)   The Income Statement
(B)   A Suspense Account
(C)   A Nominal Account
(D)   The Capital Account

MC80   What should happen if the balance on a Suspense Account is of a material amount?

(A)   Should be written off to the statement of financial position
(B)   Carry forward the balance to the next period
(C)   Find the error(s) before publishing the final accounts
(D)   Write it off in the Income Statement.

Review questions

33.1   A trial balance was extracted from the books of D. Wilson, and it was found that the debit side exceeded the credit side by £100. This amount was entered in the suspense account. The following errors were later discovered and corrected:

(*i*)   Purchases were over-summed by £200.
(*ii*)   An amount paid to R. Took was debited to the control account as £87 instead of £78.
(*iii*)   Sales were under-summed by £51.

Required:
Write up and rule off the suspense account as it would appear in Baker's ledger.

33.2   Your bookkeeper extracted a trial balance on 31 December 2008 which failed to agree by £400, a shortage on the credit side of the trial balance. A suspense account was opened for the difference.

In January 2009 the following errors made in 2008 were found:

(*i*)   Sales day book had been undercast by £300.
(*ii*)   Sales of £500 to T. Ball had been debited in error to T. Bell account.
(*iii*)   Rent account had been undercast by £200.
(*iv*)   Discounts allowed account had been overcast by £50.
(*v*)   The sale of a computer at net book value had been credited in error to the Sales account £400.

You are required to:
(*a*)   Show the journal entries necessary to correct the errors.
(*b*)   Draw up the suspense account after the errors described have been corrected.
(*c*)   If the net profit had previously been calculated at £30,000 for the year ending 31 December 2008, show the calculations of the corrected net profit.

33.3A   You have extracted a trial balance and drawn up accounts for the year ended 31 December 2010. There was a shortage of £78 on the credit side of the trial balance, a suspense account being opened for that amount.

During 2011 the following errors made in 2010 were found:

(*i*)   £125 received from sales of old office equipment has been entered in the sales account.
(*ii*)   Purchases day book had been overcast by £10.

(*iii*) A private purchase of £140 had been included in the business purchases.
(*iv*) Bank charges £22 entered in the cash book have not been posted to the bank charges account.
(*v*) A sale of goods to K. Lamb £230 was correctly entered in the sales book but entered in the personal account as £320.

Required:
(*a*) Show the requisite journal entries to correct the errors.
(*b*) Write up the suspense account showing the correction of the errors.
(*c*) The net profit originally calculated for 2010 was £28,400. Show your calculation of the correct figure.

33.4 Show how each of the following errors would affect trial balance agreement:

(*i*) Computer repairs £184 was debited to the computer account.
(*ii*) £819 discounts received credited to discounts allowed account.
(*iii*) Inventory at close undervalued by £1,100.
(*iv*) £145 commission received was debited to the sales account.
(*v*) Drawings £94 credited to the capital account.
(*vi*) Cheque paying £317 to T. Burnett entered in the cash book but not in the personal account.
(*vii*) Cheque £212 from J. Hare credited to J. Hair.

Use the following format for your answer:

Item	If no effect state 'No'	Debit side exceeds credit side by amount shown	Credit side exceeds debit side by amount shown
(*i*)			
(*ii*)			
(*iii*)			
(*iv*)			
(*v*)			
(*vi*)			
(*vii*)			

33.5 The following is a trial balance which has been incorrectly drawn up:

Trial Balance at 31 January 2012

	£	£
Capital 1 February 2011	7,845	
Drawings	19,500	
Inventory 1 February 2011		8,410
Trade accounts receivable		34,517
Furniture and fittings	2,400	
Cash in hand	836	
Trade accounts payable		6,890
Sales		127,510
Returns inwards		2,438
Discount received	1,419	
Business expenses	3,204	
Purchases	72,100	
	107,304	179,765

In addition to the mistakes evident above, the following errors were also discovered:

1 A payment of £315 made to a creditor had not been posted from the cash book into the purchases ledger.
2 A cheque for £188 received from a customer had been correctly entered in the cash book but posted to the customer's account as £180.
3 A purchase of fittings £407 had been included in the purchases account.

4 The total of the discounts allowed column in the cash book of £42 had not been posted into the general ledger.
5 A page of the sales day book was correctly totalled as £765 but carried forward as £675.

Show the trial balance as it would appear after all the errors had been corrected. Show all your workings.

33.6 Study the following and answer the questions below.

The trial balance of Mary Harris (Gowns) as at 31 December 2011 showed a difference which was posted to a suspense account. Draft final accounts for the year ended 31 December 2011 were prepared showing a net profit of £47,240. The following errors were subsequently discovered:

- Sales of £450 to C. Thomas had been debited to Thomasson Manufacturing Ltd.
- A payment of £275 for telephone charges had been entered on the debit side of the Telephone account as £375.
- The sales journal had been undercast by £2,000.
- Repairs to a machine, amounting to £390, had been charged to Machinery account.
- A cheque for £1,500, being rent received from Atlas Ltd, had only been entered in the cash book.
- Purchases from P. Brooks, amounting to £765, had been received on 31 December 2011 and included in the closing inventory at that date, but the invoice had not been entered in the purchases journal.

Questions:
(a) (i)   Give the journal entries, without narratives, necessary to correct the above errors.
     (ii) Show the effect of each of these adjustments on the net profit in the draft financial statements and the correct profit for the year ended 31 December 2011.
(b) (i)   State briefly the purpose of the journal, giving a suitable example of its use.
     (ii) State why it is necessary to distinguish between capital and revenue expenditure.

(*Midland Examining Group: GCSE*)

33.7A Gail Dawson is the owner of a retail business. She has employed an inexperienced book-keeper to maintain her accounting records.

(a) On 31 March 2012, the end of the business's accounting year, the bookkeeper extracted the following trial balance from the business's records:

Trial Balance at 31 March 2012

	Dr £	Cr £
Non-current assets at cost	18,300	
Provision for depreciation of non-current assets, 1 April 2011	2,800	
Inventory		
1 April 2011	3,700	
31 March 2012		2,960
Trade accounts receivable		1,825
Trade accounts payable	864	
Balance at bank (overdrawn)	382	
Capital		26,860
Drawings	7,740	
Sales	26,080	
Purchases		18,327
Running expenses	6,904	
Allowance for doubtful debts	90	
Suspense		16,888
	£66,860	£66,860

→

Required:
1 A corrected version of Gail Dawson's trial balance dated 31 March 2012 based on the above information, but with an amended figure for the suspense account.

(b) The following errors were found in the accounting system after a corrected version of the trial balance above was prepared.

(i)   The total of the sales day book for December 2011 had been overstated by £120.
(ii) In January 2009 some new office equipment had been purchased for £360; this had been debited to the purchases account.
(iii) A payment by cheque to a creditor, £216, had been entered in the books as £261.
(iv) A credit note for £37 sent to a customer had been overlooked.
(v)   The owner had withdrawn a cheque for £80 for private use in October 2008; both the bank and drawings account had been credited with this amount.

Required:
In the books of Gail Dawson
2 Journal entries to correct each of these errors.
  (**Note:** narratives are NOT required.)
3 The suspense account. (Start with the amount in the corrected trial balance given in answer to Required 1 above, and include any entries arising from the correction of the errors.)
4 An explanation of the term 'error of commission'. (Give an example of such an error to illustrate your answer.)

(*Southern Examining Group: GCSE*)

33.8 The trial balance as at 30 April 2010 of Timber Products Limited was balanced by the inclusion of the following debit balance:

Difference on trial balance suspense account £2,513.

Subsequent investigations revealed the following errors:

(i)   Discounts received of £324 in January 2010 have been posted to the debit of the discounts allowed account.
(ii) Wages of £2,963 paid in February 2010 have not been posted from the cash book.
(iii) A remittance of £940 received from K. Mitcham in November 2009 has been posted to the credit of B. Mansell Limited.
(iv) In December 2009, the company took advantage of an opportunity to purchase a large quantity of stationery at a bargain price of £2,000. No adjustments have been made in the accounts for the fact that three-quarters, in value, of this stationery was in the inventory on 30 April 2010.
(v)   A payment of £341 to J. Winters in January 2010 has been posted in the personal account as £143.
(vi) A remittance of £3,000 received from D. North, a credit customer, in April 2010 has been credited to sales.

  The draft accounts for the year ended 30 April 2010 of Timber Products Limited show a net profit of £24,760.
  Timber Products Limited has very few personal accounts and therefore does not maintain either a purchases ledger control account or a sales ledger control account.

Required:
(a)   Prepare the difference on trial balance suspense account showing, where appropriate, the entries necessary to correct the accounting errors.
(b)   Prepare a computation of the corrected net profit for the year ended 30 April 2010 following corrections for the above accounting errors.
(c)   Outline the principal uses of trial balances.

(*Association of Accounting Technicians*)

33.9A   Chi Knitwear Ltd is an old-fashioned business with a handwritten set of books. A trial balance is extracted at the end of each month, and an income statement and a statement of financial position are computed. This month, however, the trial balance will not balance, the credits exceeding debits by £1,536.

You are asked to help and after inspection of the ledgers discover the following errors.

(*i*)   A balance of £87 on a debtor's account has been omitted from the schedule of debtors, the total of which was entered as accounts receivable in the trial balance.
(*ii*)   A small piece of machinery purchased for £1,200 had been written off to repairs.
(*iii*)   The receipts side of the cash book had been undercast by £720.
(*iv*)   The total of one page of the sales day book had been carried forward as £8,154, whereas the correct amount was £8,514.
(*v*)   A credit note for £179 received from a supplier had been posted to the wrong side of his account.
(*vi*)   An electricity bill in the sum of £152, not yet accrued for, is discovered in a filing tray.
(*vii*)   Mr Smith, whose past debts to the company had been the subject of a provision, at last paid £731 to clear his account. His personal account has been credited but the cheque has not yet passed through the cash book.

Required:
(*a*)   Write up the suspense account to clear the difference, and
(*b*)   State the effect on the accounts of correcting each error.

(*Association of Chartered Certified Accountants*)

33.10A   The trial balance of Happy Bookkeeper Ltd, as produced by its bookkeeper, includes the following items:

Sales ledger control account	£110,172
Purchases ledger control account	£78,266
Suspense account (debit balance)	£2,315

You have been given the following information:

(*i*)   The sales ledger debit balances total £111,111 and the credit balances total £1,234.
(*ii*)   The purchases ledger credit balances total £77,777 and the debit balances total £1,111.
(*iii*)   The sales ledger includes a debit balance of £700 for business X, and the purchases ledger includes a credit balance of £800 relating to the same business X. Only the net amount will eventually be paid.
(*iv*)   Included in the credit balance on the sales ledger is a balance of £600 in the name of H. Smith. This arose because a sales invoice for £600 had earlier been posted in error from the sales day book to the debit of the account of M. Smith in the purchases ledger.
(*v*)   An allowance of £300 against some damaged goods had been omitted from the appropriate account in the sales ledger. This allowance had been included in the control account.
(*vi*)   An invoice for £456 had been entered in the purchases day book as £654.
(*vii*)   A cash receipt from a credit customer for £345 had been entered in the cash book as £245.
(*viii*)   The purchases day book had been overcast by £1,000.
(*ix*)   The bank balance of £1,200 had been included in the trial balance, in error, as an overdraft.
(*x*)   The bookkeeper had been instructed to write off £500 from customer Y's account as a bad debt, and to reduce the provision for doubtful debts by £700. By mistake, however, he had written off £700 from customer Y's account and *increased* the allowance for doubtful debts by £500.
(*xi*)   The debit balance on the insurance account in the nominal ledger of £3,456 had been included in the trial balance as £3,546.

Required:
Record corrections in the control and suspense accounts. Attempt to reconcile the sales ledger control account with the sales ledger balances, and the purchases ledger control account with the purchases ledger balances. What further action do you recommend?

(*Association of Chartered Certified Accountants*)

33.11   The following points were discovered in the books of a small building business before the closing entries had been made. Draft financial statements had already been prepared and showed a net profit of £23,120.

(*i*)   The purchase of a new van for £6,000 was included in the motor vehicle expenses account.
(*ii*) The drawings account included £250 for the purchase of fuel which was used to heat the business offices.
(*iii*) £300 paid by a customer, B. Burton Ltd, had been credited to B. Struton's account in error.
(*iv*) The water rates on the proprietor's home of £750 has been paid by the business and debited to the business rates account.
(*v*)   £720 included in the wages account was paid to workmen for building a greenhouse in the proprietor's garden.
(*vi*) Building materials bought on credit from K. Jarman for £500, has been delivered to the business on the date of the statement of financial position and had been included in the inventory figure at that date, but the invoice for these goods had not been entered in the purchases day book.

Required:
(*a*)   The journal entries to record the necessary adjustments arising from the above.
(*b*)   A statement showing the effect of these adjustments on the profit shown in the draft financial statements.

33.12   At the end of a financial year, the trial balance of a small company failed to agree and the difference was entered in a suspense account. Subsequently, the following errors were discovered:

(*i*)   The sales day book had been undercast by £10.
(*ii*) A customer's personal account has been correctly credited with £2 discount, but no corresponding entry was made in the discount column of the cash book.
(*iii*) Discounts allowed for July amounting to £70 were credited instead of being debited to the discount account.
(*iv*) A debit balance on the account of D. Bird, a customer, was carried forward £10 short.
(*v*)   An old credit balance of £3 on a customer's account (J. Flyn) had been entirely overlooked when extracting the balances.

Required:
(*a*)   Prepare, where necessary, the journal entries to correct the errors.
(*b*)   Draw up a statement showing the impact of these errors upon the trial balance.

33.13A   Journalise the matters arising from the following items in the books of B. Danby, including the narrative in each case. Note that for this purpose cash and bank items may be journalised.
   In the case of those items which gave rise to a difference in the trial balance you are to assume that the difference was previously recorded in a suspense account.

(*a*)   Discounts allowed during March amounting to £62 were posted to the credit of the discounts received account.
(*b*)   The sales day book was overcast by £100.
(*c*)   The motor van standing in the ledger at £1,800 was exchanged for fittings valued at £1,400 plus a cheque for £700.
(*d*)   £470 has been included in the wages account and £340 in the purchases account. These amounts represent expenditure on an extension to the business premises.
(*e*)   A cheque for £86 received from C. Blimp and discount of £4 allowed to him were correctly recorded but, when the cheque was subsequently dishonoured, no further entries were recorded.
(*f*)   A cheque for £76 paid to D. Hood was correctly recorded in the cash book but was posted in error to D. I. Hoade's account as £67.

33.14   The bookkeeper of a firm failed to agree the trial balance at 30 June, the end of the financial year. She opened a suspense account into which she entered the amount she was out of balance and carried this amount to a draft statement of financial position which she prepared.

The following errors were subsequently discovered in the books:

(*i*)   The purchase day book had been undercast by £10.

(*ii*)   Goods bought on credit from A. Supplier for £5 had been posted to his account as £50.

(*iii*)   A new machine costing £70 had been posted to the debit of the repairs to machinery account.

(*iv*)   S. Kane, a customer, returned goods valued at £10. This had been entered in the sales returns day book and posted to the debit of the customer's account.

(*v*)   The sale on credit of various items of plant and machinery at their book value of £300 had been recorded in the sales day book.

(*vi*)   £60 owed by D. Clarke, a customer, had been overlooked when drawing up a schedule of accounts receivable from the ledger.

(*vii*)   An item of cash discount allowed £2 had been correctly entered in the cash book but had not been posted to the account of B. Luckwood, the customer.

(*viii*) Business rates, treated as having been paid in advance in the previous accounting period, amounting to £45 had not been brought down as a balance on the business rates account at the start of the accounting period. Instead it was included in the prepayments account.

As a result of posting these errors to the suspense account, the balance on the suspense account was reduced to zero.

Required:

(*a*)   Prepare the suspense account, including the initial opening entry made by the bookkeeper, along with all the necessary adjusting entries identified above.

(*b*)   Explain clearly the effect of correcting the above errors:

   (*i*)   on the net profit shown in the draft income statement
   (*ii*)   on any of the items in the draft statement of financial position

Note: You will find this question easier if you prepare journal entries for each item before answering (*a*) and (*b*).

Single Entry and Incomplete Records

Single entry and incomplete records

Learning objectives

After you have studied this chapter, you should be able to:

- deduce the figure of profits where only the increase in capital and details of drawings are known
- draw up an income statement and statement of financial position from records not kept on a double entry system
- deduce the figure for cash drawings when all other cash receipts and cash payments are known
- deduce the figures of sales and purchases from incomplete records

Introduction

In this chapter, you'll learn about single entry and incomplete records. You will learn how to use the accounting equation to identify the profit for a period when only the opening and closing capital figures and drawings are known. You will also learn how to find the figure for cash drawings or the figure for cash expenses when all other cash receipts and payments are known. And you will learn how to find the figures for purchases and sales from incomplete records.

35.1 Why double entry is not used

For every small shopkeeper, market stall, Internet cafe or other small business to keep its books using a full double entry system would be ridiculous. Apart from anything else, a large number of the owners of such businesses would not know how to write up double entry records, even if they wanted to.

It is more likely that they would enter details of a transaction once only, using a single entry system. Many of them would fail to record every transaction, resulting in incomplete records.

It is, perhaps, only fair to remember that accounting is supposed to be an aid to management – accounting *is not* something to be done as an end in itself. Therefore, many small firms, especially retail shops, can have all the information they want by merely keeping a cash book and having some form of record, not necessarily in double entry form, of their debtors and creditors.

However, despite many small businesses not having any need for accounting records, most do have to prepare financial statements or, at least, calculate their sales or profits once a year. How can these be calculated if the bookkeeping records are inadequate or incomplete?

Activity 35.1

What may cause these accounting statements and figures to need to be calculated?

(*i*) profits
(*ii*) sales
(*iii*) financial statements

35.2 Profit as an increase in capital

From your knowledge of the accounting equation, you know that unless there has been an introduction of extra cash or resources into a business, the only way that capital can be increased is by making profits.

Identifying profits when opening and closing capital are known

If you know the capital at the start of a period and the capital at the end of the period, profit is the figure found by subtracting capital at the start of the period from that at the end of the period.

Let's look at a business where capital at the end of 2010 was £20,000. During 2011 there have been no drawings, and no extra capital has been brought in by the owner. At the end of 2011 the capital was £30,000.

$$\text{Net profit} = \underset{\text{capital}}{\underset{\text{This year's}}{£30,000}} - \underset{\text{capital}}{\underset{\text{Last year's}}{£20,000}} = £10,000$$

If drawings had been £7,000, the profits must have been £17,000:

$$\text{Last year's Capital} + \text{Profits} - \text{Drawings} = \text{This year's Capital}$$
$$£20,000 \quad + \quad ? \quad - \quad £7,000 \quad = \quad £30,000$$

We can see that £17,000 profits is the figure needed to complete the formula:

$$£20,000 + £17,000 - £7,000 = £30,000$$

Identifying profits when you only have a list of the opening and closing assets and liabilities

In this case, you use the accounting equation.

Activity 35.2

What is the formula for the accounting equation? Write down both (a) the normal form and (b) the alternate form.

Exhibit 35.1 shows the calculation of profit where insufficient information is available to draft an income statement. The only information available is about the assets and liabilities.

Exhibit 35.1

H. Taylor has not kept proper bookkeeping records, but she has kept notes in diary form of the transactions of her business. She is able to give you details of her assets and liabilities as at 31 December 2011 and 31 December 2012:

At 31 December 2011
   Assets: Van £6,000; Fixtures £1,800; Inventory £3,000; Accounts receivable £4,100; Bank £4,800; Cash £200.
   Liabilities: Accounts payable £1,200; Loan from J. Ogden £3,500.

At 31 December 2012
   Assets: Van (after depreciation) £5,000; Fixtures (after depreciation) £1,600; Inventory £3,800; Accounts receivable £6,200; Bank £7,500; Cash £300.
   Liabilities: Accounts payable £1,800; Loan from J. Ogden £2,000.

   Drawings during 2012 were £5,200.
   You need to put all these figures into a format that will enable you to identify the profit. Firstly, you need to draw up a **statement of affairs** as at 31 December 2011. This is really just a statement of financial position, but is the name normally used when you are dealing with incomplete records.
   From the accounting equation, you know that capital is the difference between the assets and liabilities.

H. Taylor
Statement of Affairs as at 31 December 2011

	£	£
Non-current assets		
Van		6,000
Fixtures		1,800
		7,800
Current assets		
Inventory	3,000	
Accounts receivable	4,100	
Bank	4,800	
Cash	200	
		12,100
Total assets		19,900
Current liabilities		
Accounts payable	1,200	
Non-current liability		
Loan from J. Ogden	3,500	
Total liabilities		(4,700)
Net assets		15,200
Capital^Note		15,200

Note: the accounting equation tells you that this must be the figure to use.

You now draw up a second statement of affairs, this time as at the end of 2012. The formula of *Opening Capital + Profit − Drawings = Closing Capital* is then used to deduce the figure of profit.

→

H. Taylor
Statement of Affairs as at 31 December 2012

		£	£
Non-current assets			
Van			5,000
Fixtures			1,600
			6,600
Current assets			
Inventory		3,800	
Accounts receivable		6,200	
Bank		7,500	
Cash		300	
			17,800
Total assets			24,400
Current liabilities			
Accounts payable		1,800	
Non-current liability			
Loan from J. Ogden		2,000	
Total liabilities			(3,800)
Net assets			20,600
Capital			
Balance at 1.1.2012			15,200
Add Net profit	(C)		?
	(B)		?
Less Drawings			(5,200)
	(A)		

Deduction of net profit:
Opening Capital + Net Profit − Drawings = Closing Capital. Finding the missing figures (A), (B) and (C) by deduction:

(A) is the same as the total of the top half of the statement of affairs, i.e. £20,600;
(B) is therefore £20,600 + £5,200 = £25,800;
(C) is therefore £25,800 − £15,200 = £10,600.

To check:

		£
Capital		
Balance at 1.1.2012		15,200
Add Net profit	(C)	10,600
	(B)	25,800
Less Drawings		(5,200)
	(A)	20,600

Obviously, this method of calculating profit is very unsatisfactory. It is much more informative when an income statement can be drawn up. Therefore, whenever possible, this 'comparisons of capital method' of ascertaining profit should be avoided and a full set of financial statements should be drawn up from the available records.

It is important to realise that businesses should have exactly the same income statements and statements of financial position whether they keep their books by single entry or double entry. However, as you will see, whereas the double entry system uses the trial balance in preparing the financial statements, the single entry system will have to arrive at the same answer by different means.

Drawing up the financial statements

The following example shows the various stages of drawing up financial statements from a single entry set of records.

The accountant has found the following details of transactions for J. Frank's shop for the year ended 31 December 2011.

(a) The sales are mostly on credit. No record of sales has been kept, but £61,500 has been received from persons to whom goods have been sold – £48,000 by cheque and £13,500 in cash.
(b) Amount paid by cheque to suppliers during the year = £31,600.
(c) Expenses paid during the year: by cheque: Rent £3,800; General Expenses £310; by cash: Rent £400.
(d) J. Frank took £250 cash per week (for 52 weeks) as drawings.
(e) Other information is available:

	At 31.12.2010	At 31.12.2011
	£	£
Accounts receivable	5,500	6,600
Accounts payable for goods	1,600	2,600
Rent owing	–	350
Bank balance	5,650	17,940
Cash balance	320	420
Inventory	6,360	6,800

(f) The only non-current asset consists of fixtures which were valued at 31 December 2010 at £3,300. These are to be depreciated at 10 per cent per annum.

We'll now prepare the financial statements in five stages.

Stage 1

Draw up a Statement of Affairs on the closing day of the earlier accounting period:

J. Frank
Statement of Affairs as at 31 December 2010

	£	£
Non-current assets		
Fixtures		3,300
Current assets		
Inventory	6,360	
Accounts receivable	5,500	
Bank	5,650	
Cash	320	
		17,830
Total assets		21,130
Current liabilities		
Accounts payable		(1,600)
Net assets		19,530
Financed by:		
Capital (difference)		19,530

All of these opening figures are then taken into account when drawing up the financial statements for 2011.

Stage 2

Prepare a cash and bank summary, showing the totals of each separate item, plus opening and closing balances.

	Cash	Bank		Cash	Bank
	£	£		£	£
Balances 31.12.2010	320	5,650	Suppliers		31,600
Receipts from debtors	13,500	48,000	Rent	400	3,800
			General expenses		310
			Drawings	13,000	
			Balances 31.12.2011	420	17,940
	13,820	53,650		13,820	53,650

Stage 3

Calculate the figures for purchases and sales to be shown in the trading account. Remember that the figures needed are the same as those which would have been found if double entry records had been kept.

Purchases: In double entry, 'purchases' are the goods that have been bought in the period irrespective of whether they have been paid for or not during the period. The figure of payments to suppliers must, therefore, be adjusted to find the figure for purchases.

	£
Paid during the year	31,600
Less Payments made, but which were for goods purchased in a previous year	
(accounts payable at 31.12.2010)	(1,600)
	30,000
Add Purchases made in the current year for which payment has not yet been made	
(accounts payable at 31.12.2011)	2,600
Goods bought in this year, i.e. purchases	32,600

The same answer could have been obtained if the information had been shown in the form of a total accounts payable account, the figure for purchases being the amount required to make the account totals agree.

Total Accounts Payable

	£		£
Cash paid to suppliers	31,600	Balances b/d	1,600
Balances c/d	2,600	Purchases (missing figure)	32,600
	34,200		34,200

Sales: The sales figure will only equal receipts where all the sales are for cash. Therefore, the receipts figures need adjusting to find sales. This can only be done by constructing a total accounts receivable account, the sales figure being the one needed to make the totals agree.

Total Accounts Receivable

	£		£
Balances b/d	5,500	Receipts: Cash	13,500
Sales (missing figure)	62,600	Cheque	48,000
		Balances c/d	6,600
	68,100		68,100

Stage 4

Expenses. Where there are no accruals or prepayments either at the beginning or end of the accounting period, then expenses paid will equal expenses used up during the period. These figures will be charged to the income statement.

On the other hand, where such prepayments or accruals exist, an expense account should be drawn up for that particular item. When all known items are entered, the missing figure will be the expenses to be charged for the accounting period. In this case, only the rent account needs to be drawn up.

Rent

	£		£
Bank	3,800	Profit and loss (missing figure)	4,550
Cash	400		
Accrued c/d	350		
	4,550		4,550

Stage 5

Now draw up the financial statements.

J. Frank
Income Statement for the year ending 31 December 2011

	£	£
Sales (stage 3)		62,600
Less Cost of goods sold:		
Inventory at 1.1.2011	6,360	
Add Purchases (stage 3)	32,600	
	38,960	
Less Inventory at 31.12.2011	(6,800)	
		(32,160)
Gross profit		30,440
Less Expenses:		
Rent (stage 4)	4,550	
General expenses	310	
Depreciation: Fixtures	330	
		(5,190)
Net profit		25,250

Statement of Financial Position as at 31 December 2011

	£	£
Non-current assets		
Fixtures at 1.1.2011		3,300
Less Depreciation		(330)
		2,970
Current assets		
Inventory	6,800	
Accounts receivable	6,600	
Bank	17,940	
Cash	420	
		31,760
Total assets		34,730
Current liabilities		
Accounts payable	2,600	
Rent owing	350	
Total liabilities		(2,950)
Net assets		31,780
Financed by:		
Capital		
Balance 1.1.2011 (per Opening Statement of Affairs)		19,530
Add Net profit		25,250
		44,780
Less Drawings		(13,000)
Total capital		31,780

35.4   Incomplete records and missing figures

In practice, part of the information relating to *cash* receipts or payments is often missing. If the missing information is in respect of one type of payment, then it is normal to assume that the missing figure is the amount required to make both totals agree in the *cash* column of the cash and bank summary. (This does not happen with bank items owing to the fact that another copy of the bank statement can always be obtained from the bank.)

Exhibit 35.2 shows an example where the figure for Drawings is unknown. The exhibit also shows the contra entry made in the cash book when cash receipts are banked.

Exhibit 35.2

The following information on cash and bank receipts and payments is available:

	Cash	Bank
	£	£
Cash paid into the bank during the year	35,500	
Receipts from debtors	47,250	46,800
Paid to suppliers	1,320	44,930
Drawings during the year	?	–
Expenses paid	150	3,900
Balances at 1.1.2010	235	11,200
Balances at 31.12.2010	250	44,670

Now, you need to enter this information in a cash book:

	Cash	Bank		Cash	Bank
	£	£		£	£
Balances 1.1.2010	235	11,200	Bank ¢	35,500	
Received from debtors	47,250	46,800	Suppliers	1,320	44,930
Cash ¢		35,500	Expenses	150	3,900
			Drawings	?	
			Balances 31.12.2010	250	44,670
	47,485	93,500		47,485	93,500

The amount needed to make the two sides of the cash columns agree is £10,265, i.e. £47,485 minus £(35,500 + 1,320 + 150 + 250). This is the figure for drawings.

Exhibit 35.3 shows an example where the amount of cash received from debtors is unknown.

Exhibit 35.3

Information on cash and bank transactions is available as follows:

	Cash	Bank
	£	£
Receipts from debtors	?	78,080
Cash withdrawn from the bank for business use (this is the amount which is used besides cash receipts from debtors to pay drawings and expenses)		10,920
Paid to suppliers	–	65,800
Expenses paid	640	2,230
Drawings	21,180	315
Balances at 1.1.2010	40	1,560
Balances at 31.12.2010	70	375

	Cash	Bank		Cash	Bank
	£	£		£	£
Balances 1.1.2010	40	1,560	Suppliers		65,800
Received from debtors	?	78,080	Expenses	640	2,230
Withdrawn from Bank ¢	10,920		Withdrawn from Bank ¢		10,920
			Drawings	21,180	315
			Balances 31.12.2010	70	375
	21,890	79,640		21,890	79,640

As it is the only missing item, receipts from debtors is, therefore, the amount needed to make each side of the cash column agree, £10,930, i.e. £21,890 minus £(10,920 + 40).

It must be emphasised that the use of balancing figures is acceptable *only* when all the other figures have been verified. Should, for instance, a cash expense be omitted when cash received from debtors is being calculated, this would result in an understatement not only of expenses but also, ultimately, of sales.

35.5 Where there are two missing pieces of information

Quite often, the only cash expense item for which there is some doubt is drawings. Receipts will normally have been retained for all the others.

If both cash drawings and cash receipts from debtors (or from cash sales) were not known, it would not be possible to deduce both of these figures separately. The only course available would be to estimate whichever figure was more capable of being accurately assessed, use this as if it were a 'known' figure, then deduce the other figure. However, this is a most unsatisfactory position as both of the figures are estimates, the accuracy of each one relying entirely upon the accuracy of the other.

> **Activity 35.3** Why is arriving at a figure for drawings that is as accurate as possible *very* important for the owner of a business?

35.6 Cash sales and purchases for cash

Where there are cash sales as well as sales on credit terms, then the cash sales must be added to sales on credit to give the total sales for the year. This total figure of sales will be the one shown in the trading account part of the income statement.

Similarly, purchases for cash will need to be added to credit purchases in order to produce the figure of total purchases for the trading account.

35.7 Inventory stolen, lost or destroyed

When inventory is stolen, lost or destroyed, its value will have to be calculated. This could be needed to justify an insurance claim or to settle problems concerning taxation, etc.

If the inventory had been valued immediately before the fire, burglary, etc., then the value of the inventory lost would obviously be known. Also, if a full and detailed system of inventory records were kept, then the value would also be known. However, as the occurrence of fires or burglaries cannot be foreseen, and many small businesses do not keep full and proper inventory records, the value of the inventory lost has to be calculated in some other way.

The methods described in this chapter and in Chapter 34 are used. Bear in mind that you are going to be calculating figures as at the time of the fire or theft, not at the end of the accounting period.

Let's now look at Exhibits 35.4 and 35.5. The first exhibit involves a very simple case, where figures of purchases and sales are known and all goods are sold at the same gross profit margin. The second exhibit is rather more complicated.

Exhibit 35.4

J. Collins lost the whole of his inventory in a fire on 17 March 2012. The last time that stocktaking had been done was on 31 December 2011, the last date of the statement of financial position, when the inventory was valued at cost at £19,500. Purchases from then until 17 March 2012 amounted to £68,700 and sales in that period were £96,000. All sales were made at a uniform gross profit margin of 20 per cent.

First, the trading account section of the income statement can be drawn up with the known figures included. Then the missing figures can be deduced.

J. Collins
Trading Account section of the income statement for the period
1 January 2012 to 17 March 2012

		£		£
Sales				96,000
Less Cost of goods sold:				
Opening inventory		19,500		
Add Purchases		68,700		
		88,200		
Less Closing inventory	(C)	(?)		
			(B)	(?)
Gross profit			(A)	?

Now the missing figures can be deduced:

It is known that the gross profit margin is 20 per cent, therefore gross profit (A) is 20% of £96,000 = £19,200.

Now (B) + (A) £19,200 = £96,000, so that (B) is the difference, i.e. £76,800.

Now that (B) is known, (C) can be deduced: £88,200 − (C) = £76,800, so (C) is the difference, i.e. £11,400.

The figure for inventory destroyed by fire, at cost, is therefore £11,400.

Note: you should always do this calculation in the sequence shown (i.e. A then B then C).

Exhibit 35.5

T. Scott had the whole of his inventory stolen from his warehouse on the night of 20 August 2009 along with many of his accounting records including his sales and purchases day books. The sales and purchases ledgers were found in the car park. The following facts are known:

(a) Inventory at the last date of the statement of financial position, 31 March 2009, was £12,480 at cost.
(b) Receipts from debtors during the period 1 April to 20 August 2009 amounted to £31,745. Accounts receivable were: at 31 March 2009 £14,278, at 20 August 2009 £12,333.
(c) Payments to creditors during the period 1 April to 20 August 2009 amounted to £17,270. Accounts payable were: at 31 March 2009 £7,633, at 20 August 2009 £6,289.
(d) The gross profit margin on all sales has been constant at 25 per cent.

Before we can start to construct a trading account for the period, we need to find out the figures for sales and purchases. These can be found by drawing up total accounts receivable and total accounts payable accounts, sales and purchases figures being the difference on the accounts.

Total Accounts Receivable

	£		£
Balances b/d	14,278	Cash and bank	31,745
Sales (difference)	29,800	Balances c/d	12,333
	44,078		44,078

Total Accounts Payable

	£		£
Cash and bank	17,270	Balances b/d	7,633
Balances c/d	6,289	Purchases (difference)	15,926
	23,559		23,559

Activity 35.4 You already did this for another example earlier in this chapter. Where?

The trading account section of the income statement can now show the figures so far known:

Trading Account section of the income statement for the period 1 April to 20 August 2009

		£	£
Sales			29,800
Less Cost of goods sold:			
Opening inventory		12,480	
Add Purchases		15,926	
		28,406	
Less Closing inventory	(C)	(?)	
	(B)		(?)
Gross profit	(A)		?

Gross profit can be found, as the margin on sales is known to be 25%, therefore (A) = 25% of £29,800 = £7,450.

Cost of goods sold (B) + Gross profit £7,450 = £29,800, therefore (B) is £22,350.

£28,406 – (C) = (B) £22,350, therefore (C) is £6,056.

The figure for cost of goods stolen is therefore £6,056.

The completed trading account is, therefore:

Trading Account section of the income statement for the period 1 April to 20 August 2009

		£	£
Sales			29,800
Less Cost of goods sold:			
Opening inventory		12,480	
Add Purchases		15,926	
		28,406	
Less Closing inventory	(C)	(6,056)	
	(B)		(22,350)
Gross profit	(A)		7,450

Learning outcomes
You should now have learnt:

1 The difference between a single entry system and a double entry system.

2 How to calculate net profit for a small trader when you know the change in capital over a period and the amount of drawings during the period.

3 How to prepare an income statement and statement of financial position from records not kept on a double entry system.

4 How to deduce the figures for purchases and sales from a total accounts payable account and a total accounts receivable account.

Answers to activities

35.1 There are a range of possible reasons. Of the three examples shown here, the first must be done once a year, the second must be done from time to time, and the third is done on demand:

(*i*) Profits need to be calculated for the purpose of determining the income tax payable.

(*ii*) Turnover (i.e. sales) needs to be calculated in order to know whether or not the business needs to register for VAT.

(*iii*) Financial statements may be required by the bank.

35.2 (*a*) Capital = Assets − Liabilities
(*b*) Assets = Capital + Liabilities

35.3 Normal practice would be to try to get the owner to list all the cash withdrawn as accurately as possible and then use that figure for drawings. However, care needs to be taken to make this as accurate as possible because the Revenue and Customs (the UK tax authority) has very sophisticated data on the relationship between business income and expenditure and profitability, and also on level of income and standard of living enjoyed by a taxpayer. If the drawings are underestimated, this could have very serious repercussions for the owner.

35.4 This is exactly the same as what you did in Section 35.3 Stage 3.

Review questions

35.1 A. Dodds started in business on 1 January 2011 with £40,000 in a bank account. Unfortunately, he did not keep proper books of account.

He must submit a calculation of profit for the year ending 31 December 2011 to the Inspector of Taxes. At 31 December 2011 he had inventory valued at cost £8,000, a van which had cost £9,000 during the year and which had depreciated during the year by £2,000, accounts receivable of £16,000, expenses prepaid of £400, a bank balance of £34,000, a cash balance £300, trade accounts payable £8,000, and expenses owing £800.

His drawings were: cash £500 per week for 50 weeks, cheque payments £1,000.

Draw up statements to show the profit or loss for the year.

35.2 Alice Twig is a magician. She has conjured up the following results from her non-existent accounting records.

Fees are equal to four times her direct costs. (This term is explained in Section 37.3.)
At any given time her inventory equals one week's direct costs.
She defines a month as four weeks.
Her inventory at both 31 May and 30 June was valued at £800.

Required:
Calculate her fees and profit for the month of June.

35.3A B. Barnes is a dealer who has not kept proper books of account. At 31 October 2012 his state of affairs was as follows:

	£
Cash	210
Bank balance	4,700
Fixtures	2,800
Inventory	18,200
Accounts receivable	26,600
Accounts payable	12,700
Van (at valuation)	6,800

During the year to 31 October 2013 his drawings amounted to £32,200. Winnings from the Lottery of £7,600 were put into the business. Extra fixtures were bought for £900.

At 31 October 2013 his assets and liabilities were: Cash £190; Bank overdraft £1,810; Inventory £23,900; Accounts payable for goods £9,100; Accounts payable for expenses £320; Fixtures to be depreciated £370; Van to be valued at £5,440; Accounts receivable £29,400; Prepaid expenses £460.

Draw up a statement showing the profit or loss made by Barnes for the year ending 31 October 2013.

35.4 The following is a summary of Jane's bank account for the year ended 31 December 2012:

	£		£
Balance 1.1.2012	4,100	Payments to creditors for goods	67,360
Receipts from debtors	91,190	Rent	3,950
Balance 31.12.2012	6,300	Insurance	1,470
		Sundry expenses	610
		Drawings	28,200
	101,590		101,590

All of the business takings have been paid into the bank with the exception of £17,400. Out of this, Jane has paid wages of £11,260, drawings of £1,200 and purchase of goods £4,940.

The following additional information is available:

	31.12.2011	31.12.2012
Inventory	10,800	12,200
Accounts payable for goods	12,700	14,100
Accounts receivable for goods	21,200	19,800
Insurance prepaid	420	440
Rent owing	390	–
Fixtures at valuation	1,800	1,600

You are to draw up a set of financial statements for the year ended 31 December 2012. Show all of your workings.

35.5A A. Bell has kept records of his business transactions in a single entry form, but he did not realise that he had to record cash drawings. His bank account for the year 2011 is as follows:

	£		£
Balance 1.1.2011	920	Cash withdrawn from bank	12,600
Receipts from debtors	94,200	Trade accounts payable	63,400
Loan from F. Tung	2,500	Rent	3,200
		Insurance	1,900
		Drawings	11,400
		Sundry expenses	820
		Balance 31.12.2011	4,300
	97,620		97,620

Records of cash paid were: Sundry expenses £180; Trade accounts payable £1,310. Cash sales amounted to £1,540.

The following information is also available:

	31.12.2010	31.12.2011
	£	£
Cash in hand	194	272
Trade accounts payable	7,300	8,100
Accounts receivable	9,200	11,400
Rent owing	–	360
Insurance paid in advance	340	400
Van (at valuation)	5,500	4,600
Inventory	24,200	27,100

You are to draw up an income statement for the year ending 31 December 2011, and a statement of financial position as at that date. Show all of your workings.

35.6 On 1 May 2011 Jenny Barnes, who is a retailer, had the following balances in her books: Premises £70,000; Equipment £8,200; Vehicles £5,100; Inventory £9,500; Trade accounts receivable £150. Jenny does not keep proper books of account, but bank statements covering the 12 months from 1 May 2011 to 30 April 2012 were obtained from the bank and summarised as follows:

	£
Money paid into bank:	
Extra capital	8,000
Shop takings	96,500
Received from debtors	1,400
Payments made by cheque:	
Paid for inventory purchased	70,500
Purchase of delivery van	6,200
Vehicle running expenses	1,020
Lighting and heating	940
Sales assistants' wages	5,260
Miscellaneous expenses	962

It has been discovered that, in the year ending 30 April 2012, the owner had paid into the bank all shop takings apart from cash used to pay (*i*) £408 miscellaneous expenses and (*ii*) £500 per month drawings.

At 30 April 2012:

£7,600 was owing to suppliers for inventory bought on credit.

The amount owed by trade accounts receivable is to be treated as a bad debt. Assume that there had been no sales on credit during the year.

Inventory was valued at £13,620.

Depreciation for the year was calculated at £720 (equipment) and £1,000 (vehicles).

You are asked to prepare an income statement for the year ending 30 April 2012. (Show all necessary workings separately.)

(*Edexcel Foundation, London Examinations: GCSE*)

35.7A Bill Smithson runs a second-hand furniture business from a shop which he rents. He does not keep complete accounting records, but is able to provide you with the following information about his financial position at 1 April 2011: Inventory of furniture £3,210; Trade accounts receivable £2,643; Trade accounts payable £1,598; Motor vehicle £5,100; Shop fittings £4,200; Motor vehicle expenses owing £432.

He has also provided the following summary of his bank account for the year ended 31 March 2012:

	£		£
Balance at 1 Apr 2011	2,420	Payments of trade accounts payable	22,177
Cheques received from trade debtors	44,846	Electricity	1,090
Cash sales	3,921	Telephone	360
		Rent	2,000
		Advertising	1,430
		Shop fittings	2,550
		Insurance	946
		Motor vehicle expenses	2,116
		Drawings	16,743
		Balance at 31 Mar 2012	1,775
	£51,187		£51,187

All cash and cheques received were paid into the bank account immediately.
You find that the following must also be taken into account:

- Depreciation is to be written-off the motor vehicle at 20% and off the shop fittings at 10%, calculated on the book values at 1 April 2011 plus additions during the year.
- At 31 March 2012 motor vehicle expenses owing were £291 and insurance paid in advance was £177.
- Included in the amount paid for shop fittings were:
  a table bought for £300, which Smithson resold during the year at cost,
  some wooden shelving (cost £250), which Smithson used in building an extension to his house.
  Other balances at 31 March 2012 were:

	£
Trade accounts receivable	4,012
Trade accounts payable	2,445
Inventory of furniture	4,063

Required:
(a) For the year ended 31 March 2012
   (i) calculate Smithson's sales and purchases,
   (ii) prepare his income statement.
(b) Prepare Smithson's statement of financial position as at 31 March 2012.

(*Midland Examining Group: GCSE*)

35.8 Although Janet Lambert has run a small business for many years, she has never kept adequate accounting records. However, a need to obtain a bank loan for the expansion of the business has necessitated the preparation of 'final' accounts for the year ended 31 August 2012. As a result, the following information has been obtained after much careful research:

1 Janet Lambert's business assets and liabilities are as follows:

As at	1 September 2011	31 August 2012
	£	£
Inventory	8,600	16,800
Accounts receivable for sales	3,900	4,300
Accounts payable for purchases	7,400	8,900
Rent prepaid	300	420
Electricity accrued due	210	160
Balance at bank	2,300	1,650
Cash in hand	360	330

2 All takings have been banked after deducting the following payments:

Cash drawings – Janet Lambert has not kept a record of cash drawings, but suggests these will be in the region of	£8,000
Casual labour	£1,200
Purchase of goods for resale	£1,800

Note: Takings have been the source of all amounts banked.

3 Bank payments during the year ended 31 August 2012 have been summarised as follows:

	£
Purchases	101,500
Rent	5,040
Electricity	1,390
Delivery costs (to customers)	3,000
Casual labour	6,620

4 It has been established that a gross profit of 33⅓% on cost has been obtained on all goods sold.

5 Despite her apparent lack of precise accounting records, Janet Lambert is able to confirm that she has taken out of the business during the year under review goods for her own use costing £600.

Required:
(a) Prepare a computation of total purchases for the year ending 31 August 2012.
(b) Prepare an income statement for the year ending 31 August 2012 and a statement of financial position as at that date, both in as much detail as possible.
(c) Explain why it is necessary to introduce accruals and prepayments into accounting.

(*Association of Accounting Technicians*)

35.9A Jean Smith, who retails wooden ornaments, has been so busy since she commenced business on 1 April 2011 that she has neglected to keep adequate accounting records. Jean's opening capital consisted of her life savings of £15,000 which she used to open a business bank account. The transactions in this bank account during the year ended 31 March 2012 have been summarised from the bank account as follows:

	£
Receipts:	
Loan from John Peacock, uncle	10,000
Takings	42,000
Payments:	
Purchases of goods for resale	26,400
Electricity for period to 31 December 2011	760
Rent of premises for 15 months to 30 June 2012	3,500
Rates of premises for the year ended 31 March 2012	1,200
Wages of assistants	14,700
Purchase of van, 1 October 2011	7,600
Purchase of holiday caravan for Jean Smith's private use	8,500
Van licence and insurance, payments covering a year	250

According to the bank account, the balance in hand on 31 March 2012 was £4,090 in Jean Smith's favour.

While the intention was to bank all takings intact, it now transpires that, in addition to cash drawings, the following payments were made out of takings before bankings:

	£
Van running expenses	890
Postages, stationery and other sundry expenses	355

On 31 March 2012, takings of £640 awaited banking; this was done on 1 April 2012. It has been discovered that amounts paid into the bank of £340 on 29 March 2012 were not credited to Jean's bank account until 2 April 2012 and a cheque of £120, drawn on 28 March 2012 for purchases, was not paid until 10 April 2012. The normal rate of gross profit on the goods sold by Jean Smith is 50% on sales. However, during the year a purchase of ornamental goldfish costing £600 proved to be unpopular with customers and therefore the entire inventory had to be sold at cost price.

Interest at the rate of 5% per annum is payable on each anniversary of the loan from John Peacock on 1 January 2012.

Depreciation is to be provided on the van on the straight line basis; it is estimated that the van will be disposed of after five years' use for £100.

The inventory of goods for resale at 31 March 2012 has been valued at cost at £1,900.

Accounts payable for purchases at 31 March 2012 amounted to £880 and electricity charges accrued due at that date were £180.

Trade accounts receivable at 31 March 2012 totalled £2,300.

Required:
Prepare an income statement for the year ending 31 March 2012 and a statement of financial position as at that date.

(*Association of Accounting Technicians*)

35.10   David Denton set up in business as a plumber a year ago, and he has asked you to act as his accountant. His instructions to you are in the form of the following letter.

Dear Henry,

I was pleased when you agreed to act as my accountant and look forward to your first visit to check my records. The proposed fee of £250 p.a. is acceptable. I regret that the paperwork for the work done during the year is incomplete. I started my business on 1 January last, and put £6,500 into a business bank account on that date. I brought my van into the firm at that time, and reckon that it was worth £3,600 then. I think it will last another three years after the end of the first year of business use.

I have drawn £90 per week from the business bank account during the year. In my trade it is difficult to take a holiday, but my wife managed to get away for a while. The travel agent's bill for £280 was paid out of the business account. I bought the lease of the yard and office for £6,500. The lease has ten years to run, and the rent is only £300 a year payable in advance on the anniversary of the date of purchase, which was 1 April. I borrowed £4,000 on that day from Aunt Jane to help pay for the lease. I have agreed to pay her 10 per cent interest per annum, but have been too busy to do anything about this yet.

I was lucky enough to meet Miss Prism shortly before I set up on my own, and she has worked for me as an office organiser right from the start. She is paid a salary of £3,000 p.a. All the bills for the year have been carefully preserved in a tool box, and we analysed them last week. The materials I have bought cost me £9,600, but I reckon there was £580 worth left in the yard on 31 December. I have not yet paid for them all yet, I think we owed £714 to the suppliers on 31 December. I was surprised to see that I had spent £4,800 on plumbing equipment, but it should last me five years or so. Electricity bills received up to 30 September came to £1,122; but motor expenses were £912, and general expenses £1,349 for the year. The insurance premium for the year to 31 March next was £800. All these have been paid by cheque but Miss Prism has lost the rate demand. I expect the Local Authority will send a reminder soon since I have not yet paid. I seem to remember that rates came to £180 for the year to 31 March next.

Miss Prism sent out bills to my customers for work done, but some of them are very slow to pay. Altogether the charges made were £29,863, but only £25,613 had been received by 31 December. Miss Prism thinks that 10 per cent of the remaining bills are not likely to be paid. Other customers for jobs too small to bill have paid £3,418 in cash for work done, but I only managed to bank £2,600 of this money. I used £400 of the difference to pay the family's grocery bills, and Miss Prism used the rest for general expenses, except for £123 which was left over in a drawer in the office on 31 December.

Kind regards,
Yours sincerely,
David.

You are required to draw up an income statement for the year ending 31 December 2013, and a statement of financial position as at that date.

(*Association of Chartered Certified Accountants*)

35.11 The following are summaries of the cash book and bank accounts of J. Duncan who does not keep his books using the double entry system.

Bank Summary	£	£
Balance on 1 January 2011		8,000
Receipts		
Accounts receivable	26,000	
Cash banked	4,100	30,100
		38,100
Payments		
Trade accounts payable	18,500	
Rent	1,400	
Machinery	7,500	
Wages	6,100	
Insurance	1,450	
Accounts receivable (dishonoured cheque)	250	
Loan interest	300	35,500
Balance on 31 December 2011		2,600

Cash Summary	£	£
Balance on 1 January 2011		300
Receipts		
Cash sales	14,000	
Accounts receivable	400	14,400
		14,700
Payments		
Drawings	9,500	
Repairs	300	
Electricity	750	
Cash banked	4,100	14,650
Balance on 31 December 2011		50

The following referred to 2011	£
Bad debts written-off	400
Discount received	350
Goods withdrawn by J. Duncan for own use	300
Credit note issued	1,200

The following additional information is available.	1 January 2011	31 December 2011
	£	£
Inventory	4,100	3,200
Machinery	12,600	15,900
Rent prepaid	200	
Rent owing		250
Accounts receivable	6,300	5,000
Accounts payable	2,400	2,500
Loan from bank at 8%	5,000	5,000
Loan interest owing		100

You are required to:
(*a*) Calculate the value of J. Duncan's capital on 1 January 2011.
(*b*) Prepare the Income Statement for the year ending 31 December 2011.

(*Scottish Qualifications Authority*)

35.12   Using the information in Review Question 35.11, prepare J. Duncan's statement of financial position as at 31 December 2011.

35.13A   The following are summaries of the cash book and bank accounts of P. Maclaran who does not keep her books using the double entry system.

Bank Summary	£	£
Balance on 1 January 2011		6,000
Receipts		
Accounts receivable	35,000	
Cash banked	2,200	37,200
		43,200
Payments		
Trade accounts payable	31,000	
Rent	1,100	
Machinery	3,400	
Wages	9,200	
Insurance	850	
Accounts receivable (dishonoured cheque)	80	
Loan interest	500	(46,130)
Balance on 31 December 2011		(2,930)

Cash Summary	£	£
Balance on 1 January 2011		60
Receipts		
Cash sales	9,700	
Accounts receivable	1,100	10,800
		10,860
Payments		
Drawings	6,600	
Repairs	1,400	
Electricity	570	
Cash banked	2,200	(10,770)
Balance on 31 December 2011		90

The following referred to 2011	£
Bad debts written-off	240
Discount received	600
Goods withdrawn by P. Maclaran for own use	1,200
Credit note issued	640

The following additional information is available.	1 January 2011	31 December 2011
	£	£
Inventory	2,300	5,400
Machinery	9,800	10,400
Rent prepaid		100
Rent owing	150	
Accounts receivable	8,100	9,200
Accounts payable	5,700	4,800
Loan from bank at 10%	7,000	7,000
Loan interest owing		200

You are required to:
(a)   Calculate the value of P. Maclaran's capital on 1 January 2011.
(b)   Prepare the Income Statement for the year ending 31 December 2011.

→

→ **35.14A** Using the information in Review Question 35.13, prepare P. Maclaran's Statement of Financial Position as at 31 December 2011.

35.15 A business prepares its financial statements annually to 30 April and stocktaking is carried out on the next following weekend. In 2011, 30 April was a Wednesday. Inventory was taken on 3 May and the inventory actually on the premises on that date had a value at cost of £124,620.

The following additional information is ascertained:

(*i*)   The cash and credit sales totalled £2,300 during the period 1–3 May.
(*ii*) Purchases recorded during the period 1–3 May amounted to £1,510 but, of this amount, goods to the value of £530 were not received until after 3 May.
(*iii*) Sales returns during 1–3 May amounted to £220.
(*iv*) The average ratio of gross profit to sales is 20 per cent.
(*v*)   Goods in the inventory at 30 April and included in stocktaking on 3 May at £300 were obsolete and valueless.

Required:
Ascertain the value of the inventory on 30 April 2011 for inclusion in the financial statements.

Answers to review questions for selected chapters from *Frank Wood's Business Accounting 1*

Answers to review questions

Note: All the answers are the work of the author. None has been supplied by an examining body. The examining bodies accept no responsibility whatsoever for the accuracy or method of working in the answers given.

Note: In order to save space, in most cases brackets have not been entered to indicate negative numbers. Also, £ signs have been omitted from columns of figures, except where the figures refer to £000, or where the denomination needs to be specified.

1.1

(a) 16,600	(b) 14,200	(c) 16,000	(d) 1,600
(e) 27,100	(f) 70,400		

1.3

(a) Liability	(b) Liability	(c) Asset
(d) Liability	(e) Asset	(f) Asset

1.5

Wrong Assets: Mortgage on office building;
Wrong Liabilities: Delivery van; Office supplies; Computers; Cash in hand.

1.7

Assets: Van 13,000; Market stall 1,050; Computer 450; Inventory 8,000; Bank 4,700; Cash 1,400 = total 28,600.
Liabilities: Loan 10,000; Account payable 3,000 = total 13,000
Capital: 28,600 − 13,000 = 15,600.

1.9

N. Marriott
Statement of financial position as at 31 December 2011

Non-current assets		
Equipment	7,900	
Car	8,300	
		16,200
Current assets		
Inventory	5,700	
Accounts receivable	800	
Cash at bank	1,600	
	8,100	
		24,300
Current liabilities		
Accounts payable		(3,600)
		20,700
Capital		20,700

1.11

	Assets	Liabilities	Capital
(a)	− Cash	− Accounts payable	
(b)	− Bank		
	+ Fixtures		
(c)	+ Inventory	+ Accounts payable	
(d)	+ Cash		+ Capital
(e)	+ Cash	+ Loan from J. Walker	
(f)	+ Bank		
	− Accounts receivable		
(g)	− Inventory	− Accounts payable	
(h)	+ Premises		
	− Bank		

1.13

A. Park
Statement of financial position as at 7 May 2012

Non-current assets		
Fixtures	9,600	
Car	12,300	
Computer	610	
		22,510
Current assets		
Inventory	9,700	
Accounts receivable	3,650	
Bank	1,440	
Cash	2,900	
	17,690	
		40,200
Current liabilities		
Accounts payable		(8,500)
		31,700
Capital		31,700

2.1

Debited	Credited
(a) Computer	Capital
(c) Bank	C. Ure
(e) C. Ure	J. Pike
(g) Car	Computer
	Wiley Motors

Debited	Credited
(b) P. Took	Capital
(d) Loan: J. Syme	Cash
(f) Bank	J. Pike

2.3

Bank
(1) Capital	62,000	(2) Office furn.	3,700
(23) D. Bush	450	(5) Van	9,800
		(15) VPC	1,710
		(31) Machinery	310

Capital
		(1) Bank	62,000

Office furniture
(2) Bank	3,700	(8) D. Bush	450

Machinery
(31) Bank	310		

Cash

VPC Ltd
(15) Bank	1,710	(3) Computers	1,710

Van
(5) Bank	9,800		

D Bush & Sons
(8) Off. furn.	450	(23) Bank	450

Computers
(3) VPC	1,710		

2.4

Cash
(1) Capital	17,500	(2) Bank	9,400
(25) Equipment	200		
(28) Bank	130		

Bank
(2) Cash	9,400	(8) Van	5,250
(30) F. Brown	4,000	(26) Dream	1,840
		(28) Cash	130

Capital
		(1) Cash	17,500
		(18) Office furn.	2,100

Office furniture
(5) Dream	2,100	(26) Bank	1,840

Van
(8) Bank	5,250		

Equipment
(12) Pearce & Sons	2,300	(25) Cash	200

Dream Ltd
(26) Bank	1,840	(5) Office furn.	2,100

Pearce & Sons
(25) Cash	200	(12) Equipment	2,300

F Brown (Loan)
		(30) Bank	4,000

3.1

Debited	Credited
(1) Cash	Sales
(3) Cash	Machinery
(5) H. Hardy	Returns outwards
(7) Bank	Sales
(9) Returns inwards	J. Nelson

Debited	Credited
(2) Van	H. Thomas
(4) B. Perkins	Sales
(6) Purchases	J. Reid
(8) H. Forbes	Returns outwards
(10) Purchases	D. Simpson

3.3

Cash
(1) Capital	1,600	(3) Purchases	220
(10) Sales	86	(25) F. Herd	480
(31) B. Squire	146		

Purchases
(3) Cash	220		
(7) F. Herd	600		
(18) D. Exodus	730		

Sales
		(10) Cash	86
		(24) B. Squire	146

Returns outwards
		(14) F. Herd	120
		(21) D. Exodus	52

B. Squire
(24) Sales	146	(31) Cash	146

F. Herd
(14) Returns	120	(7) Purchases	600
(25) Cash	480		

D. Exodus
(21) Returns	52	(18) Purchases	730

Capital
		(1) Cash	1,600

3.5

Bank
(1) Capital	20,000	(25) B. Brown	1,924
(6) Cash	200	(29) Aberdeen Cars	9,100

Cash
(2) D. Rupert (Loan)	5,000	(6) Bank	200
(4) Sales	1,910	(20) Purchases	770
(24) Sales	110	(31) Office furn.	365
(28) Capital	2,500		

Purchases
(3) B. Brown	1,530		
(3) I. Jess	4,162		
(11) B. Brown	560		
(20) Cash	770		

Sales
		(4) Cash	1,910
		(8) H. Rise	1,530
		(10) P. Taylor	341
		(14) G. Farm	535
		(14) R. Sim	262
		(24) Cash	110

Returns outwards
		(15) B. Brown	94
		(19) I. Jess	130

Returns inwards
(12) H. Rise	65		
(26) G. Farm	34		

Van
(17) Aberdeen Cars	9,100		

Aberdeen Cars
(29) Bank	9,100	(17) Van	9,100

Office furniture
(18) J. Winter	1,800	(27) J. Winter	180
(31) Cash	365		

J. Winter Ltd
(27) Office furn.	180	(18) Office furn.	1,800

Capital
		(1) Bank	20,000
		(28) Cash	2,500

B. Brown
(15) Returns	94	(3) Purchases	1,530
(25) Bank	1,924	(11) Purchases	560

I. Jess
(19) Returns	130	(3) Purchases	4,162

D. Rupert (Loan)
		(2) Cash	5,000

P. Taylor
		(10) Sales	341

G. Farm
(26) Returns	34	(14) Sales	535

H. Rise
(12) Returns	65	(8) Sales	1,530

R. Sim
		(14) Sales	262

4.1

Capital

	(1) Bank 18,000
	(1) Cash 2,000

Bank

(1) Capital 18,000	(3) Fixtures 2,300
(21) Rent received 240	(24) Van 8,200

Cash

(1) Capital 2,000	(2) Purchases 580
(5) Sales 280	(10) Rent 400
	(12) Stationery 90
	(30) Wages 610
(23) Sales 650	(31) Drawings 510

D. Monty

(18) Returns out 41	(2) Purchases 580

C. George

	(6) Purchases 650

G. Field

	(23) Sales 1,600

Purchases

(2) D. Monty 580	
(6) C. George 650	

Rent received

	(21) Bank 240

Sales

	(5) Cash 280
	(23) G. Field 1,600

Stationery

(12) Cash 90	

Returns out

	(18) D. Monty 41

Fixtures

(3) Bank 2,300	

Van

(24) Bank 8,200	

Rent

(10) Cash 400	

Wages

(30) Cash 610	

Drawings

(31) Cash 510	

4.2

Capital

	(1) Cash 16,000

Cash

(1) Capital 16,000	(3) Rent 870
(11) Sales 312	(4) Bank 12,500
	(20) B repairs 78
	(28) Purchases 470
	(30) Motor exps 216

Bank

(4) Cash 12,500	(7) Stationery 85
	(27) W. Young 366
	(29) Van 3,850

Purchases

(2) W. Young 420	
(28) Cash 470	

Sales

	(5) D. Unbar 192
	(11) Cash 312
	(17) J. Harper 212

Stationery

(7) Bank 85	

Returns outwards

	(14) W. Young 54

Computer

(31) B. Coal 730	

Rent

(3) Cash 870	

Building repairs

(20) Cash 78	

Motor expenses

(30) Cash 216	

Van

(29) Bank 3,850	

W. Young

(14) Returns out 54	(2) Purchases 420
(27) Bank 366	

D. Unbar

(22) Returns in 31	(5) Sales 192

J. Harper

	(17) Sales 212

Returns inwards

(22) D. Unbar 31	

B. Coal

	(31) Computer 730

4.5

(A) Bought motor vehicle £5,000, paying by bank.
(B) Paid off £4,000 creditors in cash.
(C) Lee lent us £150,000, this being paid into the bank.
(D) Bought land and buildings £125,000, paying by bank.
(E) Debtors paid cheques £80,000, being paid into bank.
(F) Land and buildings sold for £300,000, the proceeds being paid into the bank.
(G) Loan from Lee repaid out of the bank.
(H) Creditors £8,000 paid in cash.
(I) Stock costing £17,000 sold for £12,000 on credit. Loss of £5,000 shown deducted from Capital.

5.1

B. Flyn

(1) Sales 810	(10) Returns 124
(4) Sales 134	(24) Cash 440
	(31) Balance c/d 380
944	944
(1) Balance b/d 380	

F. Start

(4) Sales 480	(31) Balance c/d 720
(31) Sales 240	
720	720
(1) Balance b/d 720	

F. Lane

(1) Sales 1,100	(18) Bank 1,100

T. Fey

(1) Sales 413	(10) Returns 62
	(20) Bank 351
413	413

5.2

J. Saville

(10) Returns 65	(1) Purchases 240
(28) Cash 300	(15) Purchases 210
(30) Balance c/d 85	
450	450
	(1) Balance b/d 85

J. Fry

(10) Returns 140	(1) Purchases 1,620
(30) Balance c/d 1,480	
1,620	1,620
	(1) Balance b/d 1,480

P. Todd

(10) Returns 39	(1) Purchases 390
(30) Balance c/d 821	(3) Purchases 470
860	860
	(1) Balance b/d 821

P. Rake

(19) Cash 290	(3) Purchases 290

5.3

B. Flyn

2012		Dr	Cr	Balance	
May 1	Sales	810		810	Dr
4	Sales	134		944	Dr
10	Returns		124	820	Dr
24	Cash		440	380	Dr

F. Lane

2012		Dr	Cr	Balance	
May 1	Sales	1,100		763	Dr
18	Bank		1,100	0	

T. Fey

2012		Dr	Cr	Balance	
May 1	Sales	413		413	Dr
10	Returns		62	351	Dr
20	Bank		351	0	

F. Start

2012		Dr	Cr	Balance	
May 4	Sales	480		480	Dr
31	Sales	240		720	Dr

5.4

J. Saville

2012		Dr	Cr	Balance	
Jun 1	Purchases		240	240	Cr
10	Returns	65		175	Cr
15	Purchases		210	385	Cr
28	Cash	300		85	Cr

P. Todd

2012		Dr	Cr	Balance	
Jun 1	Purchases		390	390	Cr
3	Purchases		470	860	Cr
30	Returns	39		821	Cr

J. Fry

2012		Dr	Cr	Balance	
Jun 1	Purchases		1,620	1,620	Cr
10	Returns	140		1,480	Cr

P. Rake

2012		Dr	Cr	Balance	
Jun 3	Purchases		290	290	Cr
19	Bank	290		0	

5.5

D. Blue

Dr			Cr		
(1) Sales	780		(2) Purchases	780	

F. Rise

Dr			Cr		
(17) Returns	12		(2) Purchases	1,020	
(30) Balance c/d	1,100		(10) Purchases	92	
	1,112			1,112	
			(1) Balance b/d	1,100	

P. Lee

Dr			Cr		
(30) Balance c/d	560		(2) Purchases	560	
			(1) Balance b/d	560	

R. James

Dr			Cr		
(17) Returns	84		(10) Purchases	870	
(26) Bank	766				
(30) Balance c/d	20				
	870			870	
			(1) Balance b/d	20	

J. Bee

Dr			Cr		
(1) Sales	1,040		(24) Bank	940	
			(28) Cash	80	
			(30) Balance c/d	20	
	1,040			1,040	
(1) Balance b/d	20				

T. Day

Dr			Cr		
(1) Sales	1,260		(12) Returns	190	
(8) Sales	340		(30) Bal c/d	1,410	
	1,600			1,600	
(1) Bal b/d	1,410				

J. Soul

Dr			Cr		
(1) Sales	480		(17) Returns	25	
			(30) Balance c/d	455	
	480			480	
(1) Balance b/d	455				

L. Hope

Dr			Cr		
(8) Sales	480		(30) Bank	480	

6.1

Cash

Dr			Cr		
(1) Capital	1,800		(6) Rent	410	
			(15) Carriage in	38	
			(31) Balance c/d	1,352	
	1,800			1,800	

Bank

Dr			Cr		
(1) Capital	4,200		(12) M. Taylor	174	
(9) J. Sharpe	340		(12) J. Ward	610	
(10) F. Titmus	1,000		(31) Rent	490	
			(31) Bal c/d	4,266	
	5,540			5,540	

Capital

Dr			Cr		
			(1) Cash	1,800	
			(1) Bank	4,200	

Rent

Dr			Cr		
(6) Cash	410				
(31) Bank	490				

Purchases

Dr			Cr		
(2) J. Ward	610				
(2) P. Green	515				
(2) M. Taylor	174				
(2) S. Gemmill	345				
(2) P. Tone	542				
(18) P. Green	291				
(18) S. Gemmill	940				

Sales

Dr			Cr		
			(4) J. Sharpe	340	
			(4) G. Boycott	720	
			(4) F. Titmus	1,152	
			(21) G. Boycott	810	

G. Boycott

Dr			Cr		
(4) Sales	720				
(21) Sales	810				

F. Titmus

Dr			Cr		
(4) Sales	1,152		(10) Bank	1,000	

Carriage In

(15)	Cash	38	

J. Ward

(12)	Bank	610	(2)	Purchases	610

P. Green

		(2)	Purchases	515
		(18)	Purchases	291

M. Taylor

(12)	Bank	174	(2)	Purchases	174

S. Gemmill

		(2)	Purchases	345
		(18)	Purchases	940

P. Tone

(12)	Bank	542	(2)	Purchases	542

J. Sharpe

(4)	Sales	340	(9)	Bank	340

6.2

Bank

(1)	Capital	8,000	(17)	G. Byers	700
(24)	B. Tyler	845	(21)	Stop Ltd	740
			(31)	Van	6,250
			(31)	Bal c/d	1,155
		8,845			8,845

Cash

(5)	Sales	510	(6)	Wages	110
(30)	G. Prince (Loan)	1,000	(9)	Purchases	120
			(12)	Wages	110
			(31)	Bal c/d	1,170
		1,510			1,510

Capital

		(1)	Bank	8,000

Van

(31)	Bank	6,250

Wages

(6)	Cash	110
(12)	Cash	110

Shop fixtures

(15)	Stop Ltd	740

G. Prince (loan)

		(30)	Cash	1,000

J. Snow

(7)	Sales	295

Sales

(5)	Cash	510
(7)	J. Snow	295
(7)	K. Park	360
(7)	B. Tyler	640
(13)	K. Park	610
(13)	B. Tyler	205

Purchases

(2)	L. Frank	550
(2)	G. Byers	540
(2)	P. Lee	610
(9)	Cash	120
(10)	G. Byers	410
(10)	P. Lee	1,240

Returns outwards

(18)	P. Lee	83
(27)	L. Frank	18

Trial balance as at 31 May 2008

	Dr	Cr
Cash	1,352	
Bank	4,266	
Capital		6,000
Rent	900	
Carriage in	38	
P. Green		806
S. Gemmill		1,285
P. Tone		542
G. Boycott	1,530	
F. Titmus	152	
Purchases	3,417	
Sales		3,022
	11,655	11,655

K. Park

(7)	Sales	360
(13)	Sales	610

B. Tyler

(7)	Sales	640	(24)	Bank	845
(13)	Sales	205			

L. Frank

(27)	Returns	18	(2)	Purchases	550

G. Byers

(17)	Bank	700	(2)	Purchases	540
			(10)	Purchases	410

P. Lee

(18)	Returns	83	(2)	Purchases	610
			(10)	Purchases	1,240

Stop Ltd

(21)	Bank	740	(15)	S. fixtures	740

Trial balance as at 31 March 2008

	Dr	Cr
Bank	1,155	
Cash	1,170	
Capital		8,000
Van	6,250	
Wages	220	
Shop fixtures	740	
G. Prince (loan)		1,000
J. Snow	295	
K. Park	970	
L. Frank		532
G. Byers		250
P. Lee		1,767
Sales		2,620
Purchases	3,470	
Returns outwards		101
	14,270	14,270

6.5

Bank

Balance b/d		17,500	Central Council		2,500
Aardvarks		1,500	Klingon Corp		2,800
			Vehicle expenses		10,000
			Balance c/d		3,700
		19,000			19,000
Balance b/d		3,700			

Cash

Balance b/d	375.00	Spock		3,016.25
Sales	5,000.00	Balance c/d		2,358.75
	5,375.00			5,375.00
Balance b/d	2,358.75			

Capital

Balance c/d	49,000	Bank	49,000
	49,000		49,000
		Balance b/d	49,000

Fixtures

Balance b/d	20,000	Balance c/d	23,500
Klingon Corp	3,500		
	23,500		23,500
Balance b/d	23,500		

Inventory

Balance b/d	15,000	Cost of sales	500
Central Council	2,500	Cost of sales	250
		Balance c/d	16,750
	17,500		17,500
Balance b/d	16,750		

Cost of sales

Inventory	500	Balance c/d	750
Inventory	250		
	750		750
Balance b/d	750		

Sales

Balance c/d	6,500	Cash	5,000
		Aardvarks	1,500
	6,500		6,500
		Balance b/d	6,500

Discount received

Balance c/d	858.75	Spock	158.75
		Klingon Corp	700.00
	858.75		858.75
		Balance b/d	858.75

6.5 (cont'd)

Spock

Cash	3,016.25	Balance b/d	3,175
Discount	158.75		
	3,175.00		3,175

McCoy

Balance c/d	500	Balance b/d	500
	500		500
		Balance b/d	500

Aardvarks

Sales	1,500	Bank	1,500
	1,500		1,500

Vehicle expenses

Bank	10,000	Balance c/d	10,000
	10,000		10,000
Balance b/d	10,000		

Scott

Balance c/d	200	Balance b/d	200
	200		200
		Balance b/d	200

Central Council

Bank	2,500	Inventory	2,500
	2,500		2,500

Klingon Corp

Bank	2,800	Fixtures	3,500
Discount	700		
	3,500		3,500

USS Enterprise
Trial Balance as at 31 October 2012

	Dr £	Cr £
Bank	3,700	
Capital		49,000
Cash	2,358.75	
Fixtures	23,500	
Inventory	16,750	
Cost of sales	750	
Sales		6,500
Discount received		858.75
Scott		200
McCoy		500
Vehicle expenses	10,000	
	57,058.75	57,058.75

7.1

B. Cork
Income statement for the year ended 31 December 2012

Sales		200,500
Less Cost of goods sold:		
Purchases	120,800	
Less Closing inventory	15,600	
		105,200
Gross profit		95,300
Less Expenses:		
Salaries	58,600	
Motor expenses	2,400	
Rent	1,900	
Insurance	300	
General expenses	170	
		63,370
Net profit		31,930

7.2

G. Foot
Income statement for the year ended 30 June 2012

Sales		266,000
Less Cost of goods sold:		
Purchases	154,000	
Less Closing inventory	18,000	
		136,000
Gross profit c/d		130,000
Less Expenses:		
Salaries and wages	52,000	
Rent	3,800	
Lighting and heating	700	
Insurance	3,000	
Motor expenses	4,600	
Sundry expenses	300	
		64,400
Net profit		65,600

7.5

Bank

Bal b/d	6,000	Purchases	1,400
W. Abbot	1,200	Office cleaning	25
G. Smart	600	J. Sanders	190
Cash	312	Salaries	240
		Balance c/d	6,257
	8,112		8,112
Balance b/d	6,257		

Cash

Balance b/d	400	Wages	60
Sales	300	Sundry expenses	48
Sales	380	Wages	60
		Bank	312
		Balance c/d	600
	1,080		1,080
Balance b/d	600		

Sales

Balance c/d	1,880	W. Abbot	1,200
		Cash	300
		Cash	380
	1,880		1,880
		Balance b/d	1,880

W. Abbot

Sales	1,200	Bank	1,200
	1,200		1,200

Wages

Cash	60	Balance c/d	120
Cash	60		
	120		120
Balance b/d	120		

G. Smart

Balance b/d	640	Bank	600
		Discount allowed	40
	640		640

Discount allowed

G Smart	40	Balance c/d	40
	40		40
Balance b/d	40		

Sundry expenses

Cash	48	Balance c/d	48
	48		48
Balance b/d	48		

Purchases

Bank	1,400	Balance c/d	1,400
	1,400		1,400
Balance b/d	1,400		

J. Sanders

Bank	190	Balance b/d	210
Discount received	20		
	210		210

Office cleaning

Bank	25	Balance c/d	25
	25		25
Balance b/d	25		

Discount received

Balance c/d	20	J. Sanders	20
	20		20
		Balance b/d	20

Salaries

Bank	240	Balance c/d	240
	240		240
Balance b/d	240		

Bill Sankey

Income statement for the month ended 31 March

Sales		1,880
Less: Cost of goods sold – Purchases		1,400
Gross profit		480
Add: Discount received		20
		500
Less:		
Wages	120	
Discount allowed	40	
Sundry expenses	48	
Office cleaning	25	
Salaries	240	473
Net profit		27

8.1

B. Cork

Statement of financial position as at 31 December 2012

Non-current assets		
Premises	95,600	
Motor vehicles	17,200	112,800
Current assets		
Inventory	15,600	
Accounts receivable	26,800	
Bank	16,400	
Cash	600	59,400
		172,200
Current liabilities		
Accounts payable	17,600	
		154,600
Capital		
Balance at 1.1.2012	131,070	
Add Net profit	31,930	
	163,000	
Less Drawings	8,400	
		154,600

8.2

G. Foot

Statement of financial position as at 30 June 2012

Non-current assets		
Buildings	84,800	
Fixtures	2,000	
Vans	16,000	102,800
Current assets		
Inventory	18,000	
Accounts receivable	31,200	
Bank	15,000	64,200
		167,000
Less Current liabilities		
Accounts payable		16,000
		151,000
Capital		
Balance at 1.7.2011	114,000	
Add Net profit	65,600	
	179,600	
Less Drawings	28,600	
		151,000

8.5

A. Bell

Statement of financial position as at 30 June 2013

Non-current assets		
Premises		80,000
Current assets		
Inventory	28,000	
Accounts receivable	1,600	
Cash and bank	3,800	33,400
		113,400
Current liabilities		
Accounts payable	6,200	
Non-current liability		
Mortgage	40,000	(46,200)
		67,200
Capital		
Balance at 1.07.2012	60,000	
Capital introduced	4,000	
Net profit	15,200	79,200
Less Drawings		12,000
		67,200

9.1

J. Bell
Trading account part of the income statement for the year ending 31 December 2012

Sales	165,000	
Less Returns in	1,300	163,700
Less Cost of goods sold:		
Purchases	120,000	
Less Returns out	900	
	119,100	
Carriage inwards	1,000	
	120,100	
Less Closing inventory	11,600	
		108,500
Gross profit		55,200

9.3

G. Still
Income statement for the year ending 30 September 2013

Sales	380,400	
Less Returns in	1,540	378,860
Less Cost of goods sold:		
Opening inventory	41,600	
Add Purchases	188,430	
Less Returns out	3,410	
	185,020	
Carriage inwards	3,700	
	230,320	
Less Closing inventory	44,780	
	185,540	
Gross profit		193,320
Less Expenses:		
Salaries and wages	61,400	
Warehouse rent	3,700	
Carriage out	2,100	
Insurance	1,356	
Motor expenses	1,910	
Office expenses	412	
Lighting and heating	894	
General expenses	245	72,017
Net profit		121,303

Statement of financial position as at 30 September 2013

Non-current assets		
Premises	92,000	
Fixtures and fittings	1,900	
Motor vehicles	13,400	107,300
Current assets		
Inventory	44,780	
Accounts receivable	42,560	
Bank	5,106	92,446
		199,746
Current liabilities		
Accounts payable		(31,600)
		168,146
Capital		
Balance at 1.10.2012		68,843
Add Net profit		121,303
		190,146
Less Drawings		22,000
		168,146

9.4

F. Sorley
Income statement for the year ending 30 April 2013

Sales	210,420	
Less Returns in	4,900	205,520
Less Cost of goods sold:		
Opening inventory	9,410	
Add Purchases	108,680	
Less Returns out	3,720	
	104,960	
Carriage inwards	840	
	115,210	
Less Closing inventory	11,290	
		103,920
Gross profit		101,600
Less Expenses:		
Salaries and wages	41,800	
Motor expenses	912	
Rent	6,800	
Carriage out	1,115	
Sundry expenses	318	50,945
Net profit		50,655

Statement of financial position as at 30 April 2013

Non-current assets		
Fixtures and fittings	912	
Motor vehicles	14,400	15,312
Current assets		
Inventory	11,290	
Accounts receivable	23,200	
Bank	4,100	
Cash	240	38,830
		54,142
Less Current liabilities		
Accounts payable		14,100
		40,042
Capital		
Balance as at 1.5.2012		18,827
Add Net profit		50,655
		69,482
Less Drawings		29,440
		40,042

9.7

Capital

	01.05 Bank 1,500
	01.05 Cash 500

Bank

01.05 Capital 1,500	03.05 Fixtures 150
31.05 Cash 2,000	30.05 Wages 450
	31.05 Drawings 500

Purchases

02.05 C. Dunn 1,750
06.05 E. Farnham 115

C. Dunn

	02.05 Purchases 1,750

Fixtures and fittings

03.05 Bank 150

E. Farnham

	06.05 Purchases 115

Cash

01.05 Capital 500	10.05 Rent 300
31.05 Sales 2,500	12.05 Stationery 75
	31.05 Bank 2,000

Rent

10.05 Cash 300

Stationery

12.05 Cash 75

Sales

	14.05 G. Harlem 125
	31.05 Cash 2,500

G. Harlem

14.05 Sales 125

Van

20.05 I. Jumpstart 2,000

I. Jumpstart

	20.05 Van 2,000

Wages

30.05 Bank 450

Drawings

31.05 Bank 500

A. Baker
Trial balance as at 31 May

Capital		2,000
Bank	2,400	
Purchases	1,865	
C. Dunn		1,750
Fixtures and fittings	150	
E. Farnham		115
Cash	625	
Rent	300	
Stationery	75	
Sales		2,625
G. Harlem	125	
Van	2,000	
I. Jumpstart		2,000
Wages	450	
Drawings	500	
	7,490	7,490

Statement of financial position as at 31 May

Non-current assets		
Fixtures and fittings		150
Van		2,000
		2,150
Current assets		
Inventory	500	
Accounts receivable	125	
Bank	2,400	
Cash	625	
	3,650	
		5,800
Current liabilities – Accounts payable		(3,865)
		1,935
Capital		
Balance at 1 May		2,000
Add: Net profit*		435
		2,435
Less: Drawings		500
		1,935

*2,625 – (1,865 – 500) – (300 + 450 + 75) = 435

9.9 **Kingfire**
Income statement for the year ending 30 June 2012

Sales		35,800
Less Cost of sales		
Purchases	14,525	
Less Closing inventory	3,000	
		11,525
Gross profit		24,275
Less		
Salaries	2,325	
Motor expenses	9,300	
Rent and business rates	1,250	
Insurance – Buildings	750	
– Vehicles	1,200	
		14,825
Net profit		9,450

9.9 (cont'd)   Statement of financial position as at 30 June 2012

Non-current assets			
Motor vehicles			10,000
Fixtures			17,500
			27,500
Current assets			
Inventory		3,000	
Accounts receivable		11,725	
Cash		500	
			15,225
			42,725
Less Current liabilities			
Accounts payable	9,750		
Bank	1,250		
		11,000	
Loan		15,000	(26,000)
			16,725
Capital			
Opening balance			19,275
Net profit			9,450
			28,725
Less Drawings			12,000
			16,725

10.1
See text.

10.2
See text.

10.3
See text.

10.4
(a) See text.
(b) The historical cost convention does not make the going concern convention unnecessary. Several instances illustrate this:
(i) Non-current assets are depreciated over the assumed useful economic life of the assets. This presupposes that the business will continue to operate during the years of the assumed useful economic life of the assets.
(ii) Prepayments also assume that the benefits available in the future will be able to be claimed, because the business is expected to continue.
(iii) Inventory is also valued on the basis that it will be disposed of during the future ordinary running of the business.
(iv) The accruals concept itself assumes that the business is to continue.
All of this shows that the two complement each other.

(c) Shareholders want financial statements so that they can decide what to do with their shareholdings, whether they should sell their shares or hold on to them.
To enable them to decide upon their actions, they would really like to know what is going to happen in the future. To help them in this they would also like information which shows them what happened in the past. Ideally, therefore, they would like both types of report, those on the past and those on the future.
If they had a choice, the logical choice would be to receive a report on the future provided that it could be relied upon.

13.1   Cash book

	Cash	Bank		Cash	Bank
(1) Capital	5,000	6,000	(2) Rent	500	
(3) G. Broad (Loan)			(4) J. Fine		900
(5) Sales	400		(9) A. Moore	150	
(7) F. Love		100	(16) Bank ¢	2000	
(11) Sales		300	(19) R. Onions (Loan)		1,000
(15) P. Hood	350		(26) Motor expenses		230
(16) Cash ¢		2000	(30) Cash ¢		160
(22) Sales		600	(31) Wages	420	
(30) Bank ¢	160		(31) Balances c/d	2,840	6,710
	5,910	9,000		5,910	9,000

13.3   Cash book

	Disc	Cash	Bank		Disc	Cash	Bank
(1) Balance b/d		620	7,142	(4) Rent			430
(2) G. Slick	13		247	(8) R. White	18		702
(2) P. Fish	16		304	(8) G. Green	24		936
(2) T. Old	21		399	(8) L. Flip	40		1,560
(6) F. Black: loan			5,000	(10) Motor expenses		81	
(12) J. Pie	2		88	(15) Wages		580	
(18) A. Pony	27		513	(21) Cash			400
(18) B. Line & Son	35		665	(24) Drawings		200	
(18) T. Owen	26		494	(25) W. Peat	5	155	
(21) Bank		400		(29) Fixtures			720
(31) Commission			120	(31) Balances c/d		4	10,224
	140	1,020	14,972		87	1,020	14,972

Discounts received
(31) Total for month 87

Discounts allowed
(31) Total for month 140

13.5

Bank

		Bank			Bank
Balance b/d		10,000	Newton & Ridley		7,790
M. Baldwin		4,500	J. Duckworth		400
G. Platt		1,000			
Balance c/d		7,310			8,190
		8,190	Balance b/d		7,310

Discounts allowed
| M. Baldwin | 500 | Balance c/d | 500 |

M. Baldwin

Balance b/d	5,000	Bank	4,500
		Discount	500
	5,000		5,000

G. Platt

Balance b/d	1,000	Bank	1,000

Discount received

Balance c/d	450	Newton and Ridley	450

A. Roberts

Balance b/d	2,000	Bad debts	2,000

Newton and Ridley

Bank	7,790	Balance b/d	8,200
Discount	410		
	8,200		8,200

Bad debts

A. Roberts	2,000	Balance c/d	2,000

J. Duckworth

Bank	400	Balance b/d	400

14.1

Sales Day Book

(1) B. Hope	310
(3) T. Fine	285
(6) L. Moore	38
(10) B. Hope	74
(17) H. Tor	534
(19) J. Young	92
(27) T. Most	44
(31) R. Best	112
	1,489

Sales Ledger

B. Hope

(1) Sales	310
(10) Sales	74

T. Fine

(3) Sales	285

L. Moore

(6) Sales	38

H. Tor

(17) Sales	534

J. Young

(19) Sales	92

T. Most

(27) Sales	44

R. Best

(31) Sales	112

General Ledger

Sales Account

(31) Total for month	1,489

14.3

Workings of invoices:

(1) F. Gray			
3 rolls white tape × 10 =	30		
5 sheets blue cotton × 6 =	30		
1 dress length × 20 =	20		
		80	
Less trade discount 25%		20	
			60

(4) A. Gray			
6 rolls white tape × 10 =	60		
30 metres green felt × 4 =	120		
		180	
Less trade discount 33⅓%		60	
			120

(8) E. Hines		
1 dress length black silk × 20 =		20

(20) M. Allen			
10 rolls white tape × 10 =	100		
6 sheets blue cotton × 6 =	36		
3 dress lengths black silk × 20 =	60		
11 metres green felt × 4 =	44		
		240	
Less trade discount 25%		60	
			180

(31) B. Cooper			
12 rolls white tape × 10 =	120		
14 sheets blue cotton × 6 =	84		
9 metres green felt × 4 =	36		
		240	
Less trade discount 33⅓%		80	
			160

Sales Day Book

(1) F. Gray	60
(4) A. Gray	120
(8) E. Hines	20
(20) M. Allen	180
(31) B. Cooper	160
	540

Sales Ledger

F. Gray

(1) Sales	60

A. Gray

(4) Sales	120

E. Hines

(8) Sales	20

M. Allen

(20) Sales	180

B. Cooper

(31) Sales	160

General Ledger

Sales Account

(31) Total for month	540

15.1

Workings of purchases invoices

(1) D. Pope			
4 DVDs × 60 =	240		
3 mini hi-fi units × 240 =	720		
		960	
Less trade discount 25%		240	
			720

(3) F. Lloyd			
2 washing machines × 280 =	560		
5 vacuum cleaners × 80 =	400		
2 dishwashers × 200 =	400		
		1,360	
Less trade discount 20%		272	
			1,088

(15) B. Sankey			
1 hi-fi unit × 600 =	600		
2 washing machines × 320 =	640		
		1,240	
Less trade discount 25%		310	
			930

(20) J. Wilson			
6 CD/radios × 45		270	
Less trade discount 33⅓%		90	
			180

(30) R. Freer			
4 dishwashers × 240		960	
Less trade discount 20%		192	
			768

15.1 *(cont'd)*

Purchases Day Book

(1) D. Pope	720
(3) F. Lloyd	1,088
(15) J. Sankey	930
(20) J. Wilson	180
(30) R. Freer	768
	3,686

Purchases Ledger

D. Pope
(1) Purchases 720

F. Lloyd
(3) Purchases 1,088

J. Sankey
(15) Purchases 930

J. Wilson
(20) Purchases 180

R. Freer
(30) Purchases 768

General Ledger

Purchases Account
(31) Total for month 3,686

Purchases Ledger

C. Clarke
May 9 Purchases 240

A. Charles
May 16 Purchases 160

M. Nelson
May 31 Purchases 50

Sales
May 31 Credit sales for the month 405

15.3

Purchases Day Book

(1) Smith Stores	90
(23) C. Kelly	105
(31) J. Hamilton	180
	375

Purchases Ledger

Smith Stores
(1) Purchases 90

C. Kelly
(23) Purchases 105

J. Hamilton
(31) Purchases 180

General Ledger

Sales Account
(31) Total for month 393

Purchases Account
(31) Total for month 375

Purchases
May 31 Credit purchases for the month 450

(c)

(d) See text.

15.5 *(a)*

Sales Day Book

May	1 M. Marshall	45
	1 R. Richards	200
	23 T. Young	160
		405

Purchases Day Book

May	9 C. Clarke	240
	16 A. Charles	160
	31 M. Nelson	50
		450

Sales Ledger

M. Marshall
May 1 Sales 45

R. Richards
May 1 Sales 200

T. Young
May 23 Sales 160

(b)

16.1

Purchases Day Book

(1) F. Bean	324
(4) A. Clerk	216
(4) B. Lock	322
(4) F. Turner	64
(4) G. Rill	130
(10) B. Lock	140
(18) J. Top	230
(18) I. Gray	310
(18) F. Low	405
(18) P. Able	180
(31) F. Turner	174
(31) T. Burns	230
	2,725

Returns Outwards Day Book

(7) F. Bean	56
(7) A. Clerk	28
(25) I. Gray	140
(25) B. Lock	34
	258

Purchases Ledger

F. Bean
(7) Returns 56 | (1) Purchases 324

A. Clerk
(7) Returns 28 | (4) Purchases 216

B. Lock
(25) Returns 34 | (4) Purchases 322
(10) Purchases 140

F. Turner
(4) Purchases 64
(31) Purchases 174

G. Rill
(4) Purchases 130

J. Top
(18) Purchases 230

I. Gray
(25) Returns 140 | (18) Purchases 310

F. Low
(18) Purchases 405

P. Able
(18) Purchases 180

T. Burns
(31) Purchases 230

General Ledger

Purchases
2,725

Returns Outwards
(31) Total for month 258

16.3

Sales Day Book

(1)	T. Thompson	56
(1)	L. Rodriguez	148
(1)	K. Barton	145
(7)	K. Kelly	89
(7)	N. Mendes	78
(7)	N. Lee	257
(24)	K. Mohammed	57
(24)	K. Kelly	65
(24)	O. Green	112
(31)	N. Lee	55
		1,062

Purchases Day Book

(3)	P. Potter	144
(3)	H. Harris	25
(3)	B. Spencer	76
(9)	B. Perkins	24
(9)	H. Harris	58
(9)	N. Miles	123
(17)	H. Harris	54
(17)	B. Perkins	65
(17)	L. Nixon	75
		644

Returns Inwards Day Book

(14)	T. Thompson	12
(14)	K. Barton	22
(14)	K. Kelly	14
(28)	N. Mendes	48

Returns Outwards Day Book

(11)	P. Potter	5
(11)	B. Spencer	11
(20)	B. Spencer	14
		24
		54

Purchases Ledger

P. Potter

(11)	Returns	5	(3)	Purchases	144

H. Harris

			(3)	Purchases	25
			(9)	Purchases	58
			(17)	Purchases	54

B. Spencer

(11)	Returns	22	(3)	Purchases	76
(20)	Returns	14			

B. Perkins

			(9)	Purchases	24
			(17)	Purchases	65

H. Miles

			(9)	Purchases	123

L. Nixon

			(17)	Purchases	75

Sales Ledger

T. Thompson

(1)	Sales	56	(14)	Returns	12

L. Rodriguez

(1)	Sales	148	

K. Barton

(1)	Sales	145	(14)	Returns	22

K. Kelly

(7)	Sales	89	(14)	Returns	14
(24)	Sales	65			

N. Mendes

(7)	Sales	78	(28)	Returns	48

N. Lee

(7)	Sales	257	
(31)	Sales	55	

K. Mohammed

(24)	Sales	57	

O. Green

(24)	Sales	112	

General Ledger

Sales

	(31)	Total for month	1,062

Returns Outwards

	(31)	Total for month	48

Purchases

(31)	Total for month	644

Returns Inwards

(31)	Total for month	54

17.1

(a)	Van	Dr	6,000	:	Deedon Garage	Cr 6,000
(b)	Bad debts	Dr	100	:	P. Knight	Cr 100
(c)	Timewas Ltd	Dr	600	:	Office furniture	Cr 600
(d)	(i) Bank	Dr	200	:	R. Twig	Cr 200
	(ii) Bad debts	Dr	300	:	R. Twig	Cr 300
(e)	Drawings	Dr	20	:	Purchases	Cr 20
(f)	Drawings	Dr	80	:	Insurance	Cr 80
(g)	Machinery	Dr	2,400	:	Electrotime Ltd	Cr 2,400

17.3

The Journal

(1)

	Dr	Cr
Premises	34,000	
Van	5,125	
Fixtures	810	
Inventory	6,390	
Accounts receivable:		
P. Mullen	140	
F. Lane	310	
Bank	6,240	
Cash	560	
Accounts payable:		
S. Hood		215
J. Brown		640
Capital		52,720
	53,575	53,575

(14)

	Dr	Cr
Van	4,850	
Abel Motors		4,850

Purchases Day Book

(2)	S. Hood	145
(2)	D. Main	206
(2)	W. Tone	96
(2)	R. Foot	66
(22)	L. Mole	183
(22)	W. Wright	191
		887

Sales Day Book

(3)	J. Wilson	112
(3)	T. Cole	164
(3)	F. Syme	208
(3)	J. Allen	91
(3)	P. White	242
(3)	F. Lane	90
(9)	T. Cole	68
(9)	J. Fox	131
		1,106

Returns Inwards Day Book

(11)	J. Wilson	32
(11)	F. Syme	48
		80

Returns Outwards Day Book

(19)	R. Foot	6

17.3 (cont'd)

Cash Book

Debit side

	Disct	Cash	Bank
(1) Balances b/d		560	6,240
(16) P. Mullen	7		133
(16) F. Lane	20		380
(16) J. Wilson	4		76
(16) F. Syme	8		152
	39	**560**	**6,981**

Credit side

	Disct	Cash	Bank
(1) Storage			40
(4) Motor expenses		60	
(7) Drawings		150	
(24) S. Hood	18		342
(24) J. Brown	32		608
(24) R. Foot	6		54
(27) Salaries			740
(30) Business rates			140
(31) Abel Motors			4,850
(31) Balance c/d		350	207
	56	**560**	**6,981**

Purchases Ledger

W. Wright — Cr: (22) Purchases 191

P. Mullen — Dr: (16) Bank & disct 140 | Cr: (1) Balance 140

F. Lane — Dr: (16) Bank & disct 400 | Cr: (1) Balance 310, (3) Sales 90 — 400 / 400

J. Wilson — Dr: (16) Returns 32, (16) Bank & disct 80 | Cr: (3) Sales 112 — 112 / 112

L. Mole — Cr: (22) Purchases 183

S. Hood — Dr: (24) Bank & disc 360 | Cr: (1) Bal b/d 215, (2) Purchases 145 — 360 / 360

J. Brown — Dr: (24) Bank & disct 460 | Cr: (1) Balance b/d 460

D. Main — Cr: (2) Purchases 206

W. Tone — Cr: (2) Purchases 96

R. Foot — Dr: (19) Returns 6, (24) Bank & disct 60 | Cr: (2) Purchases 66 — 66 / 66

P. White — Dr: (3) Sales 242

J. Fox — Dr: (9) Sales 131

Sales Ledger

T. Cole — Dr: (3) Sales 164, (9) Sales 68

F. Syme — Dr: (3) Sales 208 | Cr: (11) Returns 48, (16) Bank & disct 160 — 208 / 208

J. Allen — Dr: (3) Sales 91

General Ledger

Capital — Cr: (1) Bal b/d 52,900

Storage — Dr: (1) Bank 40

Motor Expenses — Dr: (4) Cash 47

Drawings — Dr: (7) Cash 150

Salaries — Dr: (27) Bank 480

Business rates — Dr: (30) Bank 132

Sales — Cr: (31) Total for month 1,106

Purchases — Dr: (31) Total for month 887

Returns Inwards — Dr: (31) Total for month 80

Returns Outwards — Cr: (31) Total for month 6

Premises — Dr: (1) Bal b/d 34,000

Vans — Dr: (1) Bal b/d 5,125, (14) Better Motors 4,850

Fixtures — Dr: (1) Bal b/d 810

Inventory — Dr: (1) Bal b/d 6,390

Discounts Allowed — Dr: (31) Total for month 39

Discounts Received — Cr: (31) Total for month 47

Abel Motors — Dr: (31) Bank 4,850 | Cr: (14) Van 4,850

Trial Balance as at 31 May 2013

	Dr	Cr
D. Main		206
W. Tone		96
L. Mole		183
W. Wright		191
T. Cole	232	
J. Allen	91	
P. White	242	
J. Fox	131	
Capital		52,720
Storage	40	
Motor expenses	60	
Drawings	150	
Salaries	740	
Business rates	140	
Sales		1,106
Purchases	887	
Returns inwards	80	
Returns outwards		6
Premises	34,000	
Vans	9,975	
Fixtures	810	
Inventory	6,390	
Discounts allowed	39	
Discounts received		56
Bank	207	
Cash	350	
	54,564	**54,564**

18.1

(a)–(c)   Petty Cash Book

Receipts	Detail	Total	Cleaning	Motor Expenses	Postage	Stationery	Travelling
300	(1) Balance b/d						
	(2) Postage	18			18		
	(3) Travelling	12					12
	(4) Cleaning	15	15				
	(7) Petrol	22		22			
	(8) Travelling	25					25
	(9) Stationery	17				17	
	(11) Cleaning	18	18				
	(14) Postage	5			5		
	(15) Travelling	8					8
	(18) Stationery	9				9	
	(18) Cleaning	23	23				
	(20) Postage	13			13		
	(24) Motor service	43		43			
	(26) Petrol	18		18			
	(27) Cleaning	21	21				
	(29) Postage	5			5		
	(30) Petrol	14		14			
		286	77	97	41	26	45
286	(31) Cash						
	(31) Balance c/d	300					
586		586					

(d) See text.

18.2

(a) Briefly: To keep detail out of cash book.
To reduce postings to expense accounts.
To enable petty cash to be kept by someone other than main cashier.

(b)   Petty Cash Book

Receipts	Detail	Total	Postage and Stationery	Travel Expenses	Ledger Accounts
1.13	(1) Balance b/d				
23.87	(2) Cash				
	(4) Postage	8.50	8.50		
	(9) Courtney Bishop	2.35			2.35
	(11) Bus fares	1.72		1.72	
	(17) Envelopes	0.70	0.70		
0.68	(23) Telephone reimbursed				
	(26) Petrol	10.00		10.00	
		23.27	9.20	11.72	2.35
	(30) Balance c/d	2.41			
25.68		25.68			
2.41	(1) Balance b/d				
22.59	(1) Cash				

(c)

Postage and Stationery
   (30) Petty cash 9.20

Travel Expenses
   (30) Petty cash 11.72

Courtney Bishop
   (9) Petty cash 2.35

Telephone
   (23) Petty cash 0.68

18.4   Fine Teas

Receipts	Date	Details	Total	Travel	Stationery	Postage	Miscellaneous	Repairs/Replacement
24.37	May 1	Balance b/d						
115.63	1	Cash						
	2	Bus fares	0.41	0.41				
	2	Stationery	2.35		2.35			
	4	Bus fares	0.30	0.30				
	7	Postage	6.50			6.50		
	7	Trade journal	0.95				0.95	
	8	Bus fares	0.64	0.64				
	11	Tippex	1.29		1.29			
	12	Typewriter ribbons	5.42					5.42
	14	Parcel	3.45			3.45		
	15	Paper-clips	0.42		0.42			
	15	Newspaper	2.00				2.00	
	16	Photocopier repair	16.80					16.80
	19	Postage	1.50			1.50		
	20	Drawing pins	0.38		0.38			
	21	Train fare	5.40	5.40				
	22	Photo-paper	5.63		5.63			
	23	Display decorations	3.07				3.07	
	25	Tippex Wrapping paper	1.14		1.14			
	27	String	0.78				0.78	
	27	Sellotape	0.61				0.61	
	27	Pens	0.75		0.75			
	27	Pencils	0.46		0.46			
	28	Stapler repair	13.66					13.66
	30	Bus fares	2.09	2.09				
	31	Balance c/d	64.00					
140.000		140.00					
64.00	June 1	Balance b/d						
76.00	1	Cash						
			76.00	8.84	12.42	11.45	7.41	35.88

24.11

Wooden store shed

Balance b/d	850	Wooden store shed disposal 850

Office buildings

Balance b/d	179,500
Wages	109
Materials	109

Office buildings repairs

Wages	181
Materials	351

New store

Wooden store shed disposal	100
Materials	4,750
Wages	3,510
Direct expenses	85

Wooden store shed disposal

Wooden store shed	850	Bank	180
Bank	265	New store	100

24.12

(a) *Plant at Cost*

Balance 1 April 2013	372,000
Add Acquisitions during year	96,000
	468,000
Less Disposals (36,000 + 4,000 + 4,400)	44,400
Balance 31 March 2014	423,600

(b) *Provision for Depreciation of Plant*

Balance 1 April 2013	205,400
Less Depreciation on disposals (W1)	25,200
	180,200
Add Provision for year 20% × (423,600 − 180,200)	48,680
Balance 31 March 2014	228,880

Plant Sold

Cost: year to 31 March 2010		40,000
Depreciation: year to 31 March 2010	20%	8,000
		32,000
Depreciation: year to 31 March 2011	20%	6,400
		25,600
Addition		4,400
		30,000
Depreciation: year to 31 March 2012	20%	6,000
		24,000
Depreciation: year to 31 March 2013	20%	4,800
		19,200

(W1) Depreciation accumulated: 8,000 + 6,400 + 6,000 + 4,800 = 25,200.

23.1
See text.

23.2
See text.

23.3
See text.

23.4
See text.

24.1
(a) Per text.
(b) Capital: (i), (ii), machine part of (v), (vi).
Revenue: (iii), (iv), drinks part of (v).

24.3 Capital: (a), (c), (e), (g); Revenue: (b), (d), (f).

24.5 Capital: (a), (b), (e).

24.7 Capital: (a), (c), (d), (f), (j), (l); Revenue: (b), (e), (g), (h), (i), (k).

24.9
(a) Per text.
(b) PC – acquisition cost

Basic cost	4,000
Installation and testing	340
	4,340
Less 5% discount	217
	4,123
Special wiring	110
Modifications	199
Staff training	990
Total cost	5,422

(c) 1. Revenue. 2. Capital. 3. Capital. 4. Revenue. 5. Revenue.
6. Revenue. 7. Capital. 8. Revenue. 9. Capital. 10. Capital.

(c) Sale of plant

Sale of plant		13,700
Less Cost (40,000 + 4,400)	44,400	
Depreciation	25,200	
Book value at date of sale		19,200
Loss on disposal		5,500

24.14

Classifying something as a capital expense rather than a revenue expense increases non-current assets, reduces expenses and so increases net profit (and so also increases capital). This makes the business look more profitable than it would have been had the expenditure been classified instead as revenue expenditure. It also makes it look in a better financial state than it would have been (as non-current assets have increased). Misclassifying revenue expenditure as capital expenditure is misleading to users of the financial statements.

25.1

Bad Debts

2013			2013		
May 31	S. Gill & Son	600	Dec 31	Profit and loss	1,200
Sep 30	H. Black Ltd	400			
Nov 30	A. Thorn	200			
		1,200			1,200

Allowance for doubtful debts

2013		
Dec 31	Profit and loss	500

Income Statement (extracts)

Bad debts	1,200
Allowance for doubtful debts	500

Statement of Financial Position as at 31 December 2013 (extract)

Accounts receivable		15,000
Less: Allowance for doubtful debts		500
		14,500

25.2

(a)

Bad debts

2011			2011		
Dec 31	Various	700	Dec 31	Profit and loss	700

(b)

Allowance for doubtful debts

Dec 31	Balance c/d	340	Jan 1	Balance b/d	300
			Dec 31	Profit and loss	40
		340			340

Income Statement (extracts)

(c)

Bad debts	700
Allowance for doubtful debts	40

(d)   Statement of Financial Position (extract)

Accounts receivable		16,800
Less allowance for doubtful debts		672
		16,128

25.3

(i)

Bad Debts

2010			2010		
May 31	F. Lamb	200	Dec 31	Profit and loss	500
Oct 31	A. Clover	300			
		500			500
2011			2011		
Jan 31	D. Ray	100	Dec 31	Profit and loss	550
Jun 30	P. Clark	400			
Oct 31	J. Will	50			
		550			550

Allowance for Doubtful Debts

2010			2010		
Dec 31	Balance c/d	800	Dec 31	Profit and loss	800
		800			800
2011			2011		
Dec 31	Balance c/d	900	Jan 1	Balance b/d	800
			Dec 31	Profit and loss	100
		900			900

(ii)   Statement of Financial Position (extracts)

	2010		2011
Accounts receivable	55,000		59,000
Less Allowance for doubtful debts	800		900
	54,200		58,100

25.5

Allowance for Doubtful Debts

2010			2010		
Dec 31	Balance c/d	500	Jan 1	Balance b/d	400
			Dec 31	Profit and loss	100
		500			500
2011			2011		
Dec 31	Balance c/d	600	Jan 1	Balance b/d	500
			Dec 31	Profit and loss	100
		600			600
2012			2012		
Dec 31	Profit and loss	200	Jan 1	Balance b/d	600
Dec 31	Balance c/d	400			
		600			600

25.5 (cont'd)

Income Statement Extract for the year ending 31 December

2010

Gross profit	xxx
Less Expenses	
Allowance for doubtful debts	100
Bad debts	420

2011

Gross profit	xxx
Less Expenses	
Allowance for doubtful debts	100
Bad debts	310

2012

Gross profit		xxx
Add Reduction in allowance for doubtful debts		200
		xxx
Less Expenses		
Bad debts		580

(b)

Bad Debts Recovered

2010 Profit and loss	210	2010 J. Sweeny	210
2011 Profit and loss	320	2011 Various accounts receivable	320

(c)

Allowance for Doubtful Debts

2009 Balance c/d	2,600	2009 Profit and loss	2,600
2010 Balance c/d	3,680	2010 Balance b/d	2,600
		Profit and loss	1,080
	3,680		3,680
2011 Profit and loss	80	2011 Balance b/d	3,680
Balance c/d	3,600		
	3,680		3,680

(d)

Profit and Loss Account (extracts)

(2009) Bad debts	1,400		
Allowance for doubtful debts	2,600		
(2010) Bad debts	2,200	(2010) Bad debt recovered	210
Allowance for doubtful debts	1,080	(2011) Reduction in allowance for doubtful debts	80
(2011) Bad debts	3,800	Bad debt recovered	320

25.7

(a)

Allowance for Doubtful Debts

2011		2010	
May 31 Profit and loss (W1)	1,390	Jun 1 Balance b/d	2,300
31 Balance c/d	910		
	2,300		2,300
		2011	
		Jun 1 Balance b/d	910

(b)

Provision for Discounts Allowed

2011		2011	
May 31 Profit and loss (W2)	594	May 31 Profit and loss (W2)	594

Workings

(W1) Provision 1.6.2010 — 2,300

Less Provision 31.5.2011

1% × 24,000	240
2% × 10,000	200
4% × 8,000	320
5% × 3,000	150
	910
	1,390

(W2)

Accounts receivable liable for discounts	24,000
Less Allowance for doubtful debts	240
	23,760

Provision for discounts allowed $2\frac{1}{2}\% \times 23,760 = 594$

25.9

(a) (days and months omitted)

Bad Debts

2009 Debtors	1,400	2009 Profit and loss	1,400
2010 Debtors	2,200	2010 Profit and loss	2,200
2011 Debtors	3,800	2011 Profit and loss	3,800

25.10

(A) See text.
(B) See text.
(C) (1) (i)

Allowance for Doubtful Debts

2010		2010	
Dec 31 Profit and loss	33	Jan 1 Balance b/d	750*
Balance c/d	717**		
	750		750

(ii)

Bad Debts

2010		2010	
? Accounts receivable – A. Stewart	900	Dec 31 Profit and loss	3,800
? Accounts receivable –	2,300		
Dec 31 Accounts receivable – J. Smith	600		
	3,800		3,800

(2) the net profit will increase by £33.

*3% × 25,000 = 750; **3% × 23,900

26.1

Straight Line

Cost	1,200
Yr 1 Depreciation*	275
	925
Yr 2 Depreciation	275
	650
Yr 3 Depreciation	275
	375
Yr 4 Depreciation	275
	100

*1,200 − 100 = 1,100 ÷ 4 = 275

Reducing Balance

Cost	1,200
Yr 1 Depn 45% of 1,200	595
	605
Yr 2 Depn 45% of 605	272
	333
Yr 3 Depn 45% of 333	150
	183
Yr 4 Depn 45% of 183	83
	100

26.2

(a) Straight Line

Cost	8,000
Yr 1 Depreciation*	1,120
	6,880
Yr 2 Depreciation	1,120
	5,760
Yr 3 Depreciation	1,120
	4,640
Yr 4 Depreciation	1,120
	3,520
Yr 5 Depreciation	1,120
	2,400

$$\dfrac{*8,000 - 2,400}{5} = 1,120$$

(b) Reducing Balance

Cost	8,000
Yr 1 Depn 20% of 8,000	1,600
	6,400
Yr 2 Depn 20% of 6,400	1,280
	5,120
Yr 3 Depn 20% of 5,120	1,024
	4,096
Yr 4 Depn 20% of 4,096	819
	3,277
Yr 5 Depn 20% of 3,277	655
	2,622

26.3

(a) Reducing Balance

Cost	12,000
Yr 1 Depn 35% of 12,000	4,440
	7,560
Yr 2 Depn 35% of 7,560	2,797
	4,763
Yr 3 Depn 35% of 4,763	1,763
	3,000

(b) Straight Line

Cost	12,000
Yr 1 Depreciation*	3,000
	9,000
Yr 2 Depreciation	3,000
	6,000
Yr 3 Depreciation	3,000
	3,000

$$\dfrac{*12,000 - 3,000}{3} = 3,000$$

26.7

		A	B (Machines)	C
	Bought 1.1.2009 — 15% for 12 months			
2009	Cost	2,000		
	Depreciation	300		
		1,700		
	Bought 1.9.2010		4,000	
2010	Depreciation 15% × 1,700	255		
	Depreciation 15% for 4 months		200	
		1,445	3,800	
	Bought 1.5.2011			3,000
2011	Depreciation 15% × 1,445	217		
	Depreciation 15% × 3,800		570	
	Depreciation 15% for 8 months			300
		1,662	3,230	2,700

2011   Total depreciation provision 217 + 570 + 300 = 1,087

26.8

Motor Vehicle

2009		
Jan 1	Trucks Ltd	12,000

Accumulated provision for depreciation on motor vehicles

2009			2009		
Dec 31	Balance c/d	3,000	Dec 31	Depreciation	3,000
2010			2010		
Dec 31	Balance c/d	5,250	Jan 1	Balance b/d	3,000
			Dec 31	Depreciation	2,250
		5,250			5,250

26.9

Ivor Innes

Statement of Financial Position as at 31 March 2011

Non-current assets		
Fixtures (7,600 − 600)		7,000
Current assets		
Inventory	19,000	
Accounts receivable	4,440	
Bank	8,320	
Cash	700	
	32,460	
		39,460
Current liabilities		
Accounts payable		(8,800)
		30,660
Capital		
Balance at 1 April 2010*		34,900
Capital introduced		18,000
		52,900

26.9 (cont'd)

Less: Net loss	10,840	
Drawings	11,400	22,240
		30,660

*840 + 7,600 + 5,500 + 17,800 + 8,360 − 5,200 = 34,900

26.12

(a) Reducing balance. Obsolescence probably very slow and not relevant.

(b) Straight line. Obsolescence very slow and probably not relevant.

(c) Straight line. Obsolescence depends on the market and growth at the business.

(d) Reducing balance (as it is likely to be more efficient in the early years of use and susceptible to obsolescence).

(e) Machine hours. Already obsolete.

27.1

Vans

2011			2011		
Jan	1 Bank	16,000	Dec 31 Balance c/d		25,000
Aug	1 Bank	9,000			
		25,000			25,000

Provision for Depreciation: Vans

2011			2011		
Dec 31 Balance c/d		4,750	Dec 31 Profit and loss		4,750*

*16,000 × 25% = £4,000

9,000 × 25% × $^4/_{12}$ = 750

4,750

27.2

(a)

Equipment

2010			2010		
Jan	1 Bank	800	Dec 31 Balance c/d		800
2011			2011		
Jan	1 Balance b/d	800	Dec 31 Balance c/d		3,800
Jul	1 Bank	2,400			
Oct	1 Bank	600			
		3,800			3,800
2012			2012		
Jan	1 Balance b/d	3,800	Dec 31 Balance c/d		3,800
2013			2013		
Jan	1 Balance b/d	3,800	Dec 31 Balance c/d		5,200
Apr	1 Bank	1,400			
		5,200			5,200

(b)

Provision for Depreciation: Equipment

2010			2010		
Dec 31 Balance c/d		80	Dec 31 Profit and loss		80
2011			2011		
Dec 31 Balance c/d		295	Jan 1 Balance b/d		80
			Dec 31 Profit and loss		215*
		295			295
2012			2012		
Dec 31 Balance c/d		675	Jan 1 Balance b/d		295
			Dec 31 Profit and loss		380
		675			675
2013			2013		
Dec 31 Balance c/d		1,160	Jan 1 Balance b/d		675
			Dec 31 Profit and loss		485**
		1,160			1,160

*800 × 10% = 80

2,400 × 10% × $^1/_2$ = 120

600 × 10% × $^1/_4$ = 15

215

**3,800 × 10% = 380

1,400 × 10% × $^3/_4$ = 105

485

(c)

Statement of Financial Position Extracts

31 December 2010		
Equipment		800
Less Depreciation	80	720
31 December 2011		
Equipment	3,800	
Less Depreciation to date	295	3,505
31 December 2012		
Equipment	3,800	
Less Depreciation to date	675	3,125
31 December 2013		
Equipment	5,200	
Less Depreciation to date	1,160	4,040

27.4

Plant

2010			2010		
Jan	1 Bank	2,600	Dec 31 Balance c/d		4,700
Oct	1 Bank	2,100			
		4,700			4,700
2012			2012		
Jan	1 Balance b/d	4,700	Dec 31 Balance c/d		7,500
Sep	1 Bank	2,800			
		7,500			7,500
2013			2013		
Jan	1 Balance b/d	7,500	Aug 31 Disposals		2,600
			Dec 31 Balance c/d		4,900
		7,500			7,500

Provision for Depreciation: Plant

2010		**2010**	
Dec 31 Balance c/d	781	Dec 31 Profit and loss	781*
2011		**2011**	
Dec 31 Balance c/d	1,956	Jan 1 Balance b/d	781
		Dec 31 Profit and loss	1,175
	1,956		1,956
2012		**2012**	
Dec 31 Balance c/d	3,364	Jan 1 Balance b/d	1,956
		Dec 31 Profit and loss	1,408*
	3,364		3,364
2013		**2013**	
Sep 30 Plant disposals	2,383	Jan 1 Balance b/d	3,364
Dec 31 Balance c/d	2,639	Dec 31 Profit and loss	1,658*
	5,022		5,022

$2,600 \times 25\% = 650$
$2,100 \times 25\% \times 3/12 = 131.25$
$\underline{781}$

$*4,700 \times 25\% = 1,175$
$2,800 \times 25\% \times 4/12 = 233.33$
$\underline{1,408}$

$*2,600 \times 25\% \times 8/12 = 433.33$
$2,100 \times 25\% = 52.5$
$2,800 \times 25\% = 700$
$\underline{1,658}$

Plant Disposals

2013		**2013**	
Sep 30 Plant	2,600	Sep 30 Provn for depn	2,383
Dec 31 Profit and loss	593	30 Bank	810
	3,193		3,193

Statements of Financial Position

	2010	2011	2012	2013
Plant at cost	4,700	4,700	7,500	4,900
Less depn to date	781	1,956	3,364	2,639
	3,919	2,744	4,136	2,261

27.5

Machinery

2012		**2012**	
Jan 1 Balance b/d	94,500	Dec 31 Machinery disposals	1,600
Dec 31 Bank	16,000	31 Balance c/d	108,900
	110,500		110,500

Office Furniture

2012		**2012**	
Jan 1 Balance b/d	3,200	Dec 31 Balance c/d	3,660
Dec 31 Bank	460		
	3,660		3,660

Provision for Depreciation: Machinery

2012		**2012**	
Dec 31 Machinery disposals	1,280	Jan 1 Balance b/d	28,350
31 Balance c/d	48,850	Dec 31 Profit and loss	21,780
	50,130		50,130

Provision for Depreciation: Office Furniture

2012		**2012**	
Dec 31 Balance c/d	1,646	Jan 1 Balance b/d	1,280
		Dec 31 Profit and loss	366
	1,646		1,646

Machinery Disposals

2012		**2012**	
Dec 31 Machinery	1,600	Dec 31 Provision for depn	1,280
31 Profit and loss: Gain on sale	40	31 Bank	360
	1,640		1,640

Statement of Financial Position as at 31 December 2012

Machinery at cost	108,900	
Less Depreciation to date	48,850	60,050
Office furniture at cost	3,660	
Less Depreciation to date	1,646	2,014

27.6
£2,500 and £8,500.

27.8

(a) (i) Time factor (ii) Economic factors (iii) Deterioration physically (iv) Depletion.

(b) (i) Depletion (ii) Physical deterioration (iii) Time (iv) Not usually subject to depletion, but depends on circumstances (v) Economic factors, obsolescence for example (vi) Time factor.

(c)

Equipment

Balance b/d	135,620	Asset disposals	36,000
Bank	47,800	Balance c/d	147,420
	183,420		183,420
Balance b/d	147,420		

Provision for Depreciation – Equipment

Asset disposals	28,224	Balance b/d	81,374
Balance c/d	90,858	Profit and loss	37,708
	119,082		119,082
		Balance b/d	90,858

Asset Disposals

Equipment	36,000	Provision for depreciation	28,224
		Bank	5,700
		Profit and loss	2,076
	36,000		36,000

27.10

(a) (i) Straight line depreciation method

Non-current Asset

Year 1 Bank	10,000	Year 3 Asset disposals	10,000

Accumulated Provision for Depreciation

Year 2 Balance c/d	4,000	Year 1 Profit and loss	2,000
		Year 2 Profit and loss	2,000
	4,000		4,000
Year 3 Asset disposals	4,000	Year 3 Balance b/d	4,000

Asset Disposals

Year 3 Non-current asset	10,000	Year 3 Bank	5,000
		Year 3 Acc. provn for depn	4,000
		Year 3 Profit and loss	1,000
	10,000		10,000

(ii) Reducing balance method

Non-current Asset

Year 1 Bank	10,000	Year 3 Asset disposals	10,000

Accumulated Provision for Depreciation

Year 2 Balance c/d	6,400	Year 1 Profit and loss	4,000
		Year 2 Profit and loss	2,400
	6,400		6,400
Year 3 Asset disposals	6,400	Year 3 Balance b/d	6,400

Asset Disposals

Year 3 Non-current asset	10,000	Year 3 Bank	5,000
Year 3 Profit and loss	1,400	Year 3 Acc. provn for depn	6,400
	11,400		11,400

(b) (i) The purpose of depreciation provisions is to apportion the cost of non-current asset over the useful years of its life to the organisation.

The matching concept concerns the matching of costs against the revenues which those costs generate. If the benefit to be gained is equal in each year then the straight line method is to be preferred. If the benefits are greatest in Year 1 and then falling year by year, then the reducing balance method would be preferred. The impact of maintenance costs of the non-current asset, if heavier in later years, may also give credence to the reducing balance method.

(ii) The net figure at the end of Year 2 is the amount of original cost not yet expensed against revenue.

(c) The charge in Year 1 should be nil in this case. The matching concept concerns matching costs against revenues. There have been no revenues in Year 1, therefore there should be no costs.

27.12 Your letter should include the following:

● Depreciation is an expense.
● It allows the expense of an asset to be spread over its useful economic life.
● It is only a book figure and therefore 'real' money is not set aside when you depreciate an asset.
● It is not a reserve, and never can be as there are no assets of the business underpinning it.

27.14

(a) (a)

		Dr	Cr
2011	Machines	15,000	
	XY Manufacturing Co		15,000
2012	Depreciation	2,000	
	Acc. provn for depn: machine		2,000
2013	Depreciation	2,000	
	Acc. provn for depn: machine		2,000

(b)

Statement of Financial Position extract as 30 September 2013

Machine	11,000

(b) (a)

Machine

2014		2014	
Oct 1 Balance b/d	15,000	Oct 1 Machine disposal	15,000

Accumulated Provision for Depreciation: Machine

2014		2014	
Oct 1 Machine disposal	6,000	Oct 1 Balance b/d	6,000

Machine Disposal

	£			£
2014		2014		
Oct 1 Machine	15,000	Oct 1 Acc. provn for depn		6,000
		1 Cash		7,500
		2015		
		Sept 30 Profit and loss		1,500
	15,000			15,000

(b)

Machine Account and Accumulated Provision for Depreciation Account are as in (a)

Machine Disposal

	£			£
2014		2014		
Oct 1 Machine	15,000	Oct 1 Acc. provn for depn		6,000
2015		1 Cash		12,000
Sept 30 Profit and loss	3,000			
	18,000			18,000

27.16

Machinery

	£			£
2011		2011		
Jan 1 Bank	10,000	Dec 31 Balance c/d		16,000
July 1 Bank	6,000			
	16,000			16,000
2012		2012		
Jan 1 Balance b/d	16,000	Dec 31 Balance c/d		24,000
Mar 31 Bank	8,000			
	24,000			24,000
2013		2013		
Jan 1 Balance b/d	24,000	Oct 7 Machinery disposal		10,000
Nov 5 Bank	12,000	Dec 31 Balance c/d		26,000
	36,000			36,000
2014		2014		
Jan 1 Balance b/d	26,000	Feb 4 Machinery disposal		6,000
Feb 6 Bank	9,000	Oct 11 Machinery disposal		12,000
Oct 11 Machinery disposal	7,000	Dec 31 Balance c/d		24,000
	42,000			42,000

Accumulated provision for depreciation

	£			£
2011		2011		
Dec 31 Balance c/d	3,200	Dec 31 Depreciation		3,200
2012		2012		
Dec 31 Balance c/d	8,000	Jan 1 Balance b/d		3,200
		Dec 31 Depreciation		4,800
	8,000			8,000
2013		2013		
Oct 7 Machinery disposal	4,000	Jan 1 Balance b/d		8,000
Dec 31 Balance c/d	9,200	Dec 31 Depreciation		5,200
	13,200			13,200
2014		2014		
Feb 4 Machinery disposal	3,600	Jan 1 Balance b/d		9,200
Oct 11 Machinery disposal	2,400	Dec 31 Depreciation		3,800
Dec 31 Balance c/d	7,000			
	13,000			13,000

Machinery Disposal

	£			£
2013		2013		
Oct 7 Machinery	10,000	Oct 7 Acc. provn for depn		4,000
		7 Bank		5,500
		Dec 31 Profit and loss (loss on sale)		500
	10,000			10,000
2014		2014		
Feb 4 Machinery	6,000	Feb 4 Acc. provn for depn		3,600
Oct 11 Machinery	12,000	4 Bank		3,000
		Oct 11 Acc. provn for depn		2,400
		11 Machinery		7,000
		Dec 31 Profit and loss (loss on disposal)		2,000
	18,000			18,000

X Y Ltd

Statement of Financial Position extract as at 31 December

		£
2013		
Machinery at cost		26,000
Less: Accumulated depreciation		9,200
		16,800
2014		
Machinery at cost		24,000
Less: Accumulated depreciation		7,000
		17,000

27.18

Plant and machinery

	£			£
2010		2010		
Jan 1 Balance b/d	180,000	Dec 31 Balance c/d		200,000
Mar 1 Bank	20,000			
	200,000			200,000
2011		2011		
Jan 1 Balance b/d	200,000	Dec 31 Balance c/d		200,000
	200,000			200,000
2012		2012		
Jan 1 Balance b/d	200,000	Jan Plant and m/c disposal		20,000
		Dec 31 Balance c/d		180,000
	200,000			200,000

27.18 (cont'd)

Accumulated provision for depreciation

	2010	
2010 Dec 31 Balance c/d	96,000	Jan 1 Balance b/d 70,000
		Dec 31 Depreciation 26,000
	96,000	96,000
2011 Dec 31 Balance c/d	116,800	2011 Jan 1 Balance b/d 96,000
		Dec 31 Depreciation 20,800
	116,800	116,800
2012 Jan Plant and m/c disposal**	7,200	2012 Jan 1 Balance b/d 116,800
Dec 31 Balance c/d	123,067	Dec 31 Depreciation* 13,467
	130,267	130,267

*180,000 – (116,800 – 7,200) – 30,000 = 41,400 ÷ 3 = 13,467
**(20,000 × 0.2) + [(20,000 – (20,000 × 0.2)) × 0.2] = 4,000 + 3,200 = 7,200

Plant and Machinery Disposal

	2012	
2012 Jan Plant and machinery	20,000	Mar 1 Acc provn for depn 7,200
Dec 31 Profit and loss	1,200	Bank 14,000
	21,200	21,200

27.20

(a) (i) Straight line:
Cost £112,000 – trade-in £12,000 = £100,000
Per month £100,000 ÷ 48 = 2,083.33

2009	9 months	=	18,750
2010	12 months	=	25,000
2011	12 months	=	25,000
2012	12 months	=	25,000
2013	3 months	=	6,250

(ii) Diminishing (reducing) balance:

Cost	112,000
Depreciation 2009 (40%)	44,800
	67,200
Depreciation 2010	26,880
	40,320
Depreciation 2011	16,128
	24,192
Depreciation 2012	9,677
	14,515
Depreciation 2013	5,806
	8,709

(iii) Units of output (total £100,000):

2009	4,000/20,000	=	20,000
2010	5,000/20,000	=	25,000
2011	5,000/20,000	=	25,000
2012	5,000/20,000	=	25,000
2013	1,000/20,000	=	5,000
			100,000

27.18 (b)

(i) *Machine*

	2010	
2010 Jan 1 Balance b/d	112,000	Dec 31 Assets disposal 112,000

(ii) *Provision for Depreciation*

	2010	
2010 Dec 31 Assets disposal	31,250	Jan 1 Balance b/d 18,750
		Dec 31 Profit and loss 12,500
	31,250	31,250

(iii) *Assets Disposals*

	2010	
2010 Dec 31 Machine	112,000	Jun 30 Bank 80,000
		Dec 31 Depreciation 31,250
		31 Profit and loss 750
	112,000	112,000

28.1

(a) *Motor Expenses*

	2009	
2009 Dec 31 Cash and bank	800	Dec 31 Profit and loss 900
31 Owing c/d	100	
	900	900

(b) *Insurance*

	2009	
2009 Dec 31 Cash and bank	900	Dec 31 Prepaid c/d 70
		31 Profit and loss 830
	900	900

(c) *Stationery*

	2009	
2009 Dec 31 Cash and bank	400	Jan 1 Owing b/d 200
31 Owing c/d	300	Dec 31 Profit and loss 500
	700	700

(d) *Business Rates*

	2009	
2009 Jan 1 Prepaid b/d	180	Dec 31 Prepaid c/d 160
Dec 31 Cash and bank	2,000	31 Profit and loss 2,020
	2,180	2,180

(e) *Rent Received*

	2009	
2009 Jan 1 Owing b/d	190	Dec 31 Cash and bank 1,600
Dec 31 Profit and loss	1,620	31 Owing c/d 210
	1,810	1,810

28.3

Business Rates

2011		£	2011		£
Jan 1	Balance b/d	400	Dec 31	Profit and loss	3,100
Dec 31	Bank	3,600	31	Prepaid c/d	900*
		4,000			4,000

*3,600 × 3/12 = 900

Packing Materials

2011		£	2011		£
Jan 1	Balance b/d	800	Dec 31	Profit and loss	4,400
Dec 31	Bank	6,000	31	Cash: Scrap	200
31	Owing c/d	700	31	Balance c/d	1,300
		7,500			6,700

28.5

(a)

Insurance

2013		£	2013		£
Jan 1	Prepaid b/d	562	Dec 31	Profit and loss	1,236
Dec 31	Bank	1,019	31	Prepaid c/d	345
		1,581			1,581
2014					
Jan 1	Prepaid b/d	345			

Wages

2013		£	2013		£
Dec 31	Cash	15,000	Jan 1	Accrued b/d	306
31	Accrued c/d	419	Dec 31	Profit and loss	15,113
		15,419			15,419
			2014		
			Jan 1	Accrued b/d	419

Rent Receivable

2013		£	2013		£
Dec 31	Profit and loss	2,741	Jan 1	In advance b/d	36
			Dec 31	Bank	2,600
			31	Arrears c/d	105
		2,741			2,741
2014					
Jan 1	Arrears b/d	105			

(b)

Income Statement (extract)

	£
Insurance	1,236
Wages	15,113
Rent receivable	(2,741)

(c) (i) Expenses accrued increases the amount charged as expense for that period. It reduces the recorded net profit. It shows as a current liability in the statement of financial position.

(ii) Income received in advance reduces the revenue to be recorded for that period. It reduces the recorded net profit. It shows as a current liability in the statement of financial position.

(d) (i) To match up expenses charged in the income statement account with the expense cost used up in the period.

(ii) To match up revenue credited to the income statement with revenue earned for the period.

28.8

R. Giggs

Income Statement for the year ending 28 February 2010

	£	£	£
Sales			157,165
Less Cost of goods sold:			
Opening inventory		4,120	
Add Purchases		92,800	
		96,920	
Less Closing inventory		2,400	94,520
Gross profit			62,645
Add Discounts received			160
			62,805
Less Expenses:			
Wages and salaries (31,400 + 340)		31,740	
Rent (3,400 – 230)		3,170	
Discounts allowed		820	
Van running costs (615 + 72)		687	
Bad debts		730	
Doubtful debt allowance		91	
Depreciation:			
Office furniture	380		
Delivery van	1,250	1,630	
			38,868
Net profit			23,937

Statement of Financial Position as at 28 February 2010

	£	£	£
Non-current assets			
Office furniture		2,900	
Less Depreciation		380	2,520
Delivery van		3,750	
Less Depreciation		1,250	2,500
			5,020
Current assets			
Inventory		2,400	
Accounts receivable	12,316		
Less Allowance for doubtful debts	496	11,820	
Prepaid expenses		230	
Cash at bank		4,100	
Cash in hand		324	
		18,874	
			23,894
Less Current liabilities			
Accounts payable		5,245	
Expenses owing (340 + 72)		412	(5,657)
Net assets			18,237
Financed by:			
Capital			
Balance at 1.3.2009			11,400
Add Net profit			23,937
			35,337
Less Drawings			17,100
			18,237

28.9

Rent

Aug 31 Balance b/d	4,400	Aug 31 Profit and Loss	4,800
31 Accrual c/d	400		
	4,800		4,800
		Sept 1 Accrual b/d	400

Rates

Aug 31 Balance b/d	1,600	Aug 31 Prepaid c/d	300
		31 Profit and loss	1,300
	1,600		1,600
Sept 1 Prepaid b/d	300		

Income Statement for the year ending 31 August 2011

Sales		40,900
Less Cost of goods sold		
Opening inventory	8,200	
Add Purchases	26,000	
	34,200	
Less Closing inventory	9,100	
		25,100
Gross profit		15,800
Less expenses:		
Rent	4,800	
Business rates	1,300	
Sundry expenses	340	
Depreciation	1,800	
		8,240
Net profit		7,560

Statement of financial position as at 31 August 2011

Non-current assets		
Motor vehicles		9,000
Less Depreciation		3,000
		6,000
Current assets		
Accounts receivable	1,160	
Inventory	9,100	
Prepayment	300	
Bank	1,500	
	12,060	
	18,060	
Current liabilities		
Accounts payable	2,100	
Accrual	400	
		(2,500)
		15,560
Capital		
Opening balance		19,700
Add Net profit		7,560
		27,260
Less Drawings		11,700
		15,560

28.11

John Brown

Income statement for the year ending 31 December 2010

Sales		400,000
Less Returns in		5,000
		395,000
Less Cost of goods sold		
Inventory at 1.1.2010		100,000
Add Purchases	350,000	
Less Returns out	6,200	
	343,800	
	443,800	
Less Inventory at 31.12.2010	120,000	
		323,800
Gross profit		71,200
Less Wages	35,000	
Rates	5,500	
Telephone	1,220	
Bad debts	200	
Allowance for doubtful debts	180	
Depreciation: Shop fittings	4,000	
Van	6,000	
		52,100
Net profit		19,100

Statement of financial position as at 31 December 2010

Non-current assets		
Shop fittings at cost	40,000	
Less Depreciation	4,000	
		36,000
Van at cost	30,000	
Less Depreciation	6,000	
		24,000
		60,000
Current assets		
Inventory	120,000	
Accounts receivable	9,800	
Less Provision for doubtful debts	980	
	8,820	
Prepayments	500	
Bank	3,000	
	132,320	
	192,320	
Less Current liabilities		
Accounts payable	7,000	
Expenses accrued	5,220	
Net assets		(12,220)
		180,100
Financed by:		
Capital		
Balance as at 1.1.2010		179,000
Add Net profit		19,100
		198,100
Less Drawings		18,000
		180,100

28.13
Mr Chai
Income statement for the year ending 30 April 2010

Sales (259,870 – 5,624)		254,246
Less Cost of goods sold		
Inventory 1.5.2006	15,654	
Purchases (135,680 – 13,407)	122,273	
Carriage inwards	11,830	
	149,757	
Less Inventory 30.4.2010	17,750	
		132,007
Gross profit		122,239
Discounts received		1,750
		123,989
Less Expenses		
Salaries and wages	38,521	
Rent, rates and insurances (25,973 – 1,120 – 5,435)	19,418	
Heating and lighting (11,010 + 1,360)	12,370	
Carriage out	4,562	
Advertising	5,980	
Postage, stationery and telephone	2,410	
Bad debts	2,008	
Allowance for doubtful debts	223	
Discounts allowed	2,306	
Depreciation	12,074	99,872
Net profit		24,117

Statement of Financial Position as at 30 April 2010

Non-current assets			
Fixtures and fittings at cost		120,740	
Less Depreciation to date		63,020	
			57,720
Current assets			
Inventory		17,750	
Accounts receivable	24,500		
Less Allowance for doubtful debts	735	23,765	
Prepaid expenses		6,555	
Bank		4,440	
Cash		534	
		53,044	
		110,764	
Less Current liabilities			
Accounts payable	19,840		
Expenses accrued	1,360		
		(21,200)	
Net assets		89,564	
Financed by:			
Capital: Balance as at 1.5.2009		83,887	
Add Net profit		24,117	
		108,004	
Less Drawings		18,440	
		89,564	

29.1

(i) FIFO Closing Inventory 60 × £22 = £1,320

(ii)

LIFO	Received	Issued	Inventory after each transaction	
Mar	200 × £20		200 × £20	4,000
Sept	100 × £22		200 × £20	4,000
			100 × £22	2,200
				6,200
Dec		240 × £30	60 × £20	1,200

(iii)

AVCO	Received	Issued	No. of units in inventory	Average cost per unit inventory held	Total value of inventory
Mar	200 × £20		200	£20	£4,000
Sept	100 × £22		300	£20.67	£6,200
Dec		240	60	£20.67	£1,240*

* rounded to nearest £

29.2
Trading Account for the year ending 31 December

	FIFO	LIFO	AVCO
Sales	7,200	7,200	7,200
Less Cost of sales			
Purchases	6,200	6,200	6,200
Less Closing inventory	1,320	1,200	1,240
	(4,880)	(5,000)	(4,960)
Gross profit	2,320	2,200	2,240

29.5

(a) (dates and calculations omitted)

Cash

Loan: School fund	200.00	Purchases	53.50
Sales	51.36		

Purchases

Cash	53.50

Sales

Cash	51.36

(b) Inventory valuation:

34	Break × 16p =	5.44
15	Brunch × 12p =	1.80
		7.24

Stock

Trading account	7.24

(c)
Broadway School
Trading Account for the month ending 31 December 2012

Sales		53.50
Less Cost of sales		
Purchases	51.36	
Less Closing inventory	7.24	
		44.12
Gross profit		9.38

29.5 (cont'd)

(d)

Purchases (units)	Break	Brunch
	240	108
Less Sold	200	90
Inventory should have been	40	18
Actual inventory	34	15
Missing items	6	3

If there have been no arithmetical errors, one can only assume that someone has stolen 6 Breaks and 3 Brunches.

29.6

(This is a brief answer showing the main points to be covered. In the examination the answer should be in report form and elaborated.)

1 For Charles Gray

(i) The concept of prudence says that inventory should be valued at lower of cost or net realisable value. As 50% of the retail price £375 is lower than cost £560, then £375 will be taken as net realisable value and used for inventory valuation.

(ii) The sale has not taken place by 30 April 2012. The prudence concept does not anticipate profits and therefore the sale will not be assumed. The gun should therefore be included in inventory, at cost price £560.

2 For Jean Kim

It appears that it is doubtful if the business can still be treated as a going concern. If the final decision is that the business cannot continue, then the inventory valuation should be £510 each, as this is less than cost, with a further overall deduction of auction fees and expenses £300.

3 For Peter Fox

Inventory must be valued at the lower of cost or net realisable value in this case. The cost to be used is the *cost* for Peter Fox. It is quite irrelevant what the cost may be for other distributors.

It would also be against the convention of consistency to adopt a different method. The consistency applies to Peter Fox, it is not a case of consistency with other businesses. Using selling prices as a basis is not acceptable to the vast majority of businesses.

29.8

(a) In one respect the consistency convention is not applied, as at one year end the inventory may be shown at cost whereas the next year end may see inventory valued at net realisable value.

On the other hand, as it is prudent to take the lower of cost or net realisable value, it can be said to be consistently prudent to consistently take the lower figure.

(b) Being prudent can be said to be an advantage. For instance, a shareholder can know that inventory is not overvalued: if it were, it would give him a false picture of his investment.

Someone to whom money is owed, such as a creditor, will know that the inventory in the statement of financial position is realisable at least at that figure.

It is this knowledge that profits are not recorded because of excessive values placed on inventory that gives outside parties confidence to rely on reported profits.

29.9

Cobden Ltd

Computation of inventory as at 31 May 2012

	Increase	Decrease
(a) No adjustment needed	–	–
(b) Cost lower than net realisable value		130
(c) Reduction to net realisable value		126
(d) Arithmetic corrected	72	
(e) Omitted items	2,010	
(f) Transposition error		9
(g) Goods omitted	638	
(h) Hired item not to be included		347
(i) Samples to be excluded		63
(j) Sale or return items reduced to cost		184
Goods held simply on sale or return		267
	2,720	1,126
Net increase		1,594
Inventory as originally computed		87,612
		89,206

30.1

Bank Reconciliation as at 31 December 2012

Cash at bank as per cash book		3,000
Add: Credit transfers		300
		3,300
Cash at book per statement of financial position		
Less: bank lodgements		600
		2,700
Add: imprested cheques		800
Cash at bank per bank statement		3,500

Note for students

Both in theory and in practice you can start with the cash book balance working to the bank statement balance, or you can reverse this method. Many teachers have their preferences, but this is a personal matter only. Examiners sometimes ask for them using one way, sometimes the other. Students should therefore be able to tackle them both ways.

30.3

(a)

Cash Book

2012 (Totals so far)	4,129	2012 (Totals so far)		692
Dec 31 T Morris	93	Dec 31 Bank charges		47
		31 Balance c/d		3,483
	4,222			4,222

(b)

Bank Reconciliation Statement as on 31 December 2012

Balance per cash book	3,483
Add Unpresented cheque	209
	3,692
Less Bankings not yet on bank statement (319 + 246)	565
Balance per bank statement	3,127

or

Bank Reconciliation Statement as at 31 December 2012

Balance per bank statement	3,127
Add Bankings not yet on bank statement (319 + 246)	565
	3,692
Less Unpresented cheque	209
Balance per cash book	3,483

30.5

(a)

Cash Book (*bank columns*)

2011			2011		
Dec 31 Balance b/d	1,500		Dec 31 Bank charges	30	
31 Dividends	240		31 RAC	70	
31 HM Revenue & Customs	260		31 Loan repayment	200	
31 Deposit account	1,400		31 Balance c/d	3,100	
	3,400			3,400	

(b) **Bank Reconciliation Statement as on 31 December 2011**

Balance per cash book	3,100
Add Unpresented cheques (250 + 290)	540
	3,640
Less Bankings not entered on statement	690
Balance per bank statement	2,950

30.7

Cash Book

2012 (Totals so far)	853		2012 (Totals so far)	5,048
Mar 31 G. Frank	88		Mar 31 TYF	32
31 Balance c/d	4,158		31 Bank charges	19
	5,099			5,099

Bank Reconciliation Statement as at 31 March 2012

Overdraft per cash book	4,158
Add Bankings not yet in bank statement	192
	4,350
Less Unpresented cheques	504
Overdraft per bank statement	3,846

30.9

(a)

Balance per Cash Book at 31 October		
Less: Bank charges	(554)	
Sundries cheque	136	
Cheque returned – Jones	44	
Rates standing order	80	
Incorrect entry	150	
	6	(416)
		(970)
Add Dividends received not entered	62	
Error in calculation of opening balance	50	
		112
Corrected Cash Book balance		(858)

George Ltd

(b) **Bank Reconciliation Statement as at 31 October**

Balance per bank statement*	(1,353)
Add Outstanding lodgements	762
	(591)
Less Unpresented cheques	(267)
Balance per cash book	(858)

*This is the balancing figure.

31.1

Sales Ledger Control

Balances b/d	24,000		Returns inwards	1,000
Sales Day Book	14,000		Cheques and cash	18,000
			Discounts allowed	500
			Balances c/d	18,500
	38,000			38,000

31.3

2012

Sales Ledger Control

March 1 Balances b/d	12,000		March 31 Cash and bank	11,000
31 Sales	9,000		31 Discounts allowed	1,000
31 Balances c/d	50		31 Set-offs:	100
			Purchases ledger	
			31 Balances c/d	8,950
	21,050			21,050

31.5

Purchases Ledger Control

Returns outwards	1,452		Balances b/d	19,420
Bank	205,419		Purchases Day Book	210,416
Petty cash	62			
Discounts received	1,721			
Set-offs against sales ledger	640			
Balances c/d	20,210			
	*229,504			*229,836

*Difference between two sides   332

Sales Ledger Control

Balances b/d	28,227		Returns inwards	3,618
Sales Day Book	305,824		Bank and cash	287,317
			Discounts allowed	4,102
			Set-offs against	
			Purchase ledger	640
			Balances c/d	38,374
	334,051			334,051

31.6

Accounts Receivable Ledger Control

Balance b/d	46,462	Balance b/d	245
Sales	126,024	Contra	455
Cash	52	Bad debt	1,253
		Discount	746
		Cash	120,464
		Balance c/d	49,375
	172,538		172,538
Balance b/d	49,375		

Accounts Payable Ledger Control

Balance b/d	1,472	Balance b/d	25,465
Returns	2,154	Purchases	76,474
Contra	455		
Discount received	1,942		
Cash	70,476		
Balance c/d	25,440		
	101,939		101,939
		Balance b/d	25,440

31.9

Total Accounts Receivable Account

Balance b/d	26,555	Cash (600,570 − 344,890)	255,680
Credit sales	268,187	Discounts allowed	5,520
		Set-offs (Total accounts receivable)	70
		Bad debts	780
		Returns inwards	4,140
		Balances c/d	28,552
	294,742		294,742
Balances b/d	28,552		

Total Accounts Payable Account

Cash (503,970 − 14,440)	489,530	Balances b/d	43,450
Discounts received	3,510	Credit purchases	496,600
Set-offs (total accounts payable)	70		
Returns outwards	1,480		
Balances c/d	45,460		
	540,050		540,050
		Balances b/d	45,460

Note: the Allowance for doubtful debts does not affect the control accounts.

31.10

(a) To ensure an arithmetical check on the accounting records. The agreement of the total of individual accounts payable balances with that of the balance on the control account provides that check.

If the control account and the ledger are kept by separate personnel, then a check on their work and honesty is provided.

(b) (i) Increase £198 (ii) Decrease £100 (iii) No effect
(iv) Decrease £400 (v) Decrease £120.

(c) A computer will automatically enter two figures in different directions and will then confirm it in total fashion. As such there may seem at first sight to be no need for control accounts.

However, there is still the need to check on the accuracy of data input. It is important that both the skill and the honesty of the programmer are checked. Accordingly there will still be a need for control accounts.

31.11
(a) See Section 31.1.
(b) See Section 31.5.

32.1
(a) Error of omission – a credit purchase omitted from the books.
(b) Error of commission – a credit sale to J. Briggs entered in the account of H. Briggs.
(c) Error of principle – repairs debited to the asset account.
(d) Compensating errors – prepayments £15 too high and accruals £15 too high.
(e) Errors of original entry – a credit purchase for £100 recorded in the books as £10.
(f) Complete reversal of entries – payment of advertising debited to bank and credited to advertising.
(g) Transposition error – sales invoice for £263 entered as £236 in both ledger accounts.

32.2
To economise on space, all narratives for journal entries are omitted.

(a)	T. More	Dr	412	:	T. Mone Cr	412
(b)	Machinery	Dr	619	:	J. Frank Cr	619
(c)	Computer	Dr	550	:	Office expenses Cr	550
(d)	B. Wood	Dr	18	:	Sales Cr	18
(e)	Sales	Dr	164	:	Commissions rec'd Cr	164
(f)	Cash (needs double the amount)	Dr	136	:	T. Blair Cr	136
(g)	Purchases	Dr	372	:	Drawings Cr	372
(h)	Discounts allowed	Dr	48	:	Discounts received Cr	48

32.4
(a) 100 units × £1.39 = £139 not £1,390.
(b) (i) Inventory overstated by £1,251 (i.e. 1,390 − 139).
(ii) Cost of goods sold understated by £1,251.
(iii) Net profit overstated by £1,251.
(iv) Current Assets overstated by £1,251.
(v) Owner's Capital overstated by £1,251.

32.5

(a)	Sales	Dr	5,000	:	Capital Cr	5,000
(b)	Drawings	Dr	72	:	Sundry expenses Cr	72
(c)	Drawings	Dr	191	:	Rent Cr	191
(d)	D. Pine	Dr	180	:	Purchases Cr	180
(e)	Bank	Dr	820	:	Cash Cr	820
(f)	Bank	Dr	120	:	Cash Cr	120
(g)	T. Young	Dr	195	:	G. Will Cr	195
(h)	Office expenses	Dr	100	:	Printer disposals Cr	100

33.1

Suspense

			Cr
(i) Purchases			100
(ii) Accounts payable	Balance b/d	40	
(iii) Sales		9	
		51	
		100	100

33.2

(a) The Journal (narratives omitted)

	Dr	Cr
(i) Suspense	300	
Sales		300
(ii) T. Ball	500	
T. Bell		500
(iii) Rent	200	
Suspense		200
(iv) Suspense	50	
Discounts allowed		50
(v) Sales	400	
Computer disposals		400

(b) Suspense Account

Sales	300	Balance b/d	300
Discounts allowed	50	Rent	50
	350		350

(c) Net profit per financial statements

Net profit per financial statements		30,000
Add (i) Sales undercast	300	
(iv) Discounts overcast	50	350
		30,350
Less (iii) Rent undercast	200	
(v) Reduction in sales	400	600
Corrected net profit		29,750

33.4

Item	If no effect state 'No'	Debit side exceeds credit side by	Credit side exceeds debit side by
(i)	No		
(ii)	No		
(iii)	No		
(iv)		£290	
(v)			£188
(vi)			£317
(vii)	No		

33.5

Trial Balance as at 31 January 2012

	Dr	Cr
Drawings	19,500	
Inventory	8,410	
Accounts receivable (34,517 – 8)	34,509	
Furniture (2,400 + 407)	2,807	
Cash	836	
Returns inwards	2,438	
Business expenses	3,204	
Purchases (72,100 – 407)	71,693	
Discounts allowed	42	
Capital		7,845
Accounts payable (6,890 – 315)		6,575
Sales (127,510 + 90)		127,600
Discounts received		1,419
	143,439	143,439

33.6

(a) (i) C. Thomas

The Journal

Thomasson Manufacturing Ltd

	Dr	Cr
Suspense	450	
Telephone		450
Telephone	100	
Suspense		100
Suspense	2,000	
Sales account		2,000
Machine repairs	390	
Machinery		390
Suspense	1,500	
Rent received*		1,500
Purchases account	765	
P Brooks		765

* Assumed not invoiced to Atlas Ltd

(ii) Computation of Corrected Profit for year ending 31 December 2011

Profit as originally reported		47,240
Add Telephone expense overstated	100	
Sales understated	2,000	
Rent received omitted	1,500	3,600
		50,840
Less Machinery repairs understated	390	
Purchases omitted	765	1,155
Corrected profit figure		49,685

(b) (i) Per text (ii) Per text

33.8

(a)

Difference on Trial Balance Suspense

Per trial balance	2,513	J. Winters	198
Discounts received	324	Wages	2,963
Discounts allowed	324		
	3,161		3,161

(b) **Computation of Corrected Net Profit for year ending 30 April 2010**

	–	+
Net profit per draft accounts		24,760
(i) Discounts		648
(ii) Wages	2,963	
(iv) Stationery inventory		1,500
(vi) Remittance	3,000	
	5,963	2,148
Correct net profit		3,815
		20,945

(iii) and (v) did not affect profit

(c) Per text

33.11

(a)

(i)	Van	6,000	
	Motor vehicle expenses		6,000
(ii)	Fuel	250	
	Drawings		250
(iii)	B. Struton	300	
	B. Burton Ltd		300
(iv)	Drawings	750	
	Business rates		750
(v)	Drawings	720	
	Wages		720
(vi)	Purchases	500	
	K. Jarman		500

(b) Net profit per draft financial statements

			23,120
Add (i)	6,000		
(iv)	750		
(v)	720		
		7,470	
		30,590	
Less (ii)	250		
(vi)	500		
		750	
		29,840	

33.12

(a)

			Dr	Cr
(i)	Suspense		10	
	Sales			10
(ii)	Discount allowed		2	
	Suspense			2
(iii)	Discount allowed		140	
	Suspense			140
(iv)	D. Bird		10	
	Suspense			10
(v)	Suspense		3	
	J. Flyn			3

(b) The overall effect on the trial balance is that the following changes have been made:

		Dr	Cr
(i)	Sales		10
(ii) and (iii)	Discount allowed	142	
(iv) and (v)	Accounts receivable		7
(i) to (v)	Suspense		139

33.14   Workings

		Dr	Cr
(i)	Purchases	10	
	Suspense		10
(ii)	A. Supplier	45	
	Suspense		45
(iii)	Plant and Machinery Repairs	70	
	Suspense		70
(iv)	Suspense	20	
	S. Kane		20
(v)	Sales	300	
	Plant and Machinery disposals		300
(vi)	Accounts receivable	60	
	Suspense		60
(vii)	Suspense	2	
	B. Luckwood		2
(viii)	Business rates	45	
	Prepayments		45

(a)

Suspense

Balance	93	(i) Purchases	10
(iv) S. Kane	20	(ii) A. Supplier	45
(vii) B. Luckwood	2	(vi) Accounts receivable	60
	115		115

(b)

(i) The suspense account is shown in the statement of financial position, not the income statement. The following item increases net profit:

(iii) 70

The following items reduce net profit:

(i)	10
(viii)	45
	(55)
	15

Overall, net profit is increased by

Note: (v) has no effect on net profit. Sales are reduced by 300 and the loss on disposal of the plant and machinery is reduced by 300.

(ii) The following items are changed in the statement of financial position:

Suspense

	Dr	Cr
		93
(ii) Accounts payable	45	
(iii) Plant and Machinery	70	
(iv), (vi), (vii) Accounts receivable	38	
(viii) Prepayments		45
Net profit		15
	153	153

34.1

V. Fraga
Trading Account part of the Income Statement for the year ending
31 December 2013

Sales			160,000
Less Cost of goods sold:			
Inventory 1.1.2013		20,000	
Add Purchases	(D)	130,040	
	(C)	150,040	
Less Inventory 31.12.2013		27,000	
	(B)		123,040
Gross profit	(A)		36,960

Missing figures found in the order (A) to (D).
(A) Mark-up is 30%. Therefore, Margin is 23.1%. Sales are 160,000 so Margin is 23.1% × 160,000 = 36,960 Gross Profit
(B) + (A) = 160,000. Therefore, (B) + 36,960 = 155,880 and accordingly (B) is 123,040.
(C) − 27,000 = 123,040. Therefore, (C) is 150,040.
(D) + 20,000 = 150,040. Therefore, (D) is 130,040.

34.3

(a) We know that

$$\frac{\text{Cost of goods sold}}{\text{Average inventory}} = \text{Rate of inventory turnover}$$

Substituting $\dfrac{x}{14{,}000} = 10$.

x = Cost of goods sold = 140,000.

(b) If mark-up is 40%, gross profit is 40% of the cost of sales = 56,000.
(c) Turnover is (a) + (b) = 140,000 + 56,000 = 196,000.
(d) 60% × 56,000 = 33,600.
(e) Gross Profit − Expenses = Net Profit = 22,400.

34.5

(a) Sales = 230,000 + (20% × 230,000) = 276,000.
(b) 41,400 − (9% × 271,400) = 16,974.
(c) $\dfrac{230{,}000}{(34{,}000 + 41{,}000) \div 2} = \dfrac{230{,}000}{37{,}500} = 6.13$.
(d) Gross profit is 25% × 260,000 = 65,000.
Sales are 260,000 + 65,000 = 325,000.
Expenses are 9% of sales = 29,250.
Net profit = 65,000 − 29,250 = 35,750.

34.7

(a)

Capital

Balance c/d	5,000	Bank	5,000
	5,000		5,000
		Balance b/d	5,000

Bank

Capital	5,000	Cash	300
		Van	3,500
		Rent	500
		Balance c/d	700
	5,000		5,000
Balance b/d	700		

Cash

Bank	300	Sundry Expenses	50
Sales	300	Drawings	500
		Balance c/d	50
	600		600
Balance b/d	50		

34.7 (cont'd)

Van

Bank	3,500	Balance c/d	3,500
	3,500		3,500
Balance b/d	3,500		

Purchases

A. Supplier	2,500	Balance c/d	2,500
	2,500		2,500
Balance b/d	2,500		

A. Supplier

Returns	500	Purchases	2,500
Balance c/d	2,000		
	2,500		2,500
		Balance b/d	2,000

Sales

Balance c/d	1,300	Cash	300
		B. Safe	1,000
	1,300		1,300
		Balance b/d	1,300

B. Safe

Sales	1,000	Balance c/d	1,000
	1,000		1,000
Balance b/d	1,000		

Returns out

Balance c/d	500	A. Supplier	500
	500		500
		Balance b/d	500

Sundry Expenses

Cash	50	Balance c/d	50
	50		50
Balance b/d	50		

Rent

Bank	500	Balance c/d	500
	500		500
Balance b/d	500		

Drawings

Cash	500	Balance c/d	500
	500		500
Balance b/d	500		

(b)

L. Mann
Trial Balance as at 30 April

Bank	700	
Cash	50	
Van	3,500	
Purchases	2,500	
Accounts receivable	1,000	
Sundry expenses	50	
Rent	500	
Drawings	500	
Capital		5,000
Accounts payable		2,000
Sales		1,300
Returns out		500
	8,800	8,800

(c)

Income Statement for the month ending 30 April

Sales		1,300
Purchases	2,500	
– Returns out	500	
	2,000	
– Closing inventory	1,250	
Cost of sales		750
Gross profit		550
Less Expenses		
Sundry expenses	50	
Rent	500	
		550
Net profit		0

(d) *Statement of Financial Position as at 30 April*

Non-current assets		
Van		3,500
Current assets		
Inventory	1,250	
Accounts receivable	1,000	
Bank	700	
Cash	50	
		3,000
		6,500
Current liabilities		
Accounts payable		(2,000)
		4,500
Capital		5,000
Less Drawings		500
		4,500

(e) (i) $\dfrac{550}{1,300} = 42.3\%$

(ii) $\dfrac{0}{5,000} = 0\%$

(f) (i) As there has been neither a profit nor a loss, the £500 drawings are eating into capital. This is not a good sign. Drawings must not exceed net profit in the long term, or the business will fail.

(ii) Working capital is £1,000. The current ratio is 1.5, which ought to be adequate, though this would need to be confirmed by comparison with other businesses operating in the same sector.

34.9 (a)

	2010	2011	2012
Opening inventory	10,000	21,000	25,000
Purchases	70,000	86,000	77,000
	80,000	107,000	102,000
Less Closing inventory	21,000	25,000	23,000
Cost of goods sold	(59,000)	(82,000)	(79,000)
Sales	90,000	125,000	120,000
Gross profit	31,000	43,000	41,000

(b) (i) Gross profit/sales

2010
$\dfrac{31,000}{90,000} = 34\%$

2011
$\dfrac{43,000}{125,000} = 34\%$

2012
$\dfrac{41,000}{120,000} = 34\%$

(ii) Inventory turnover $= \dfrac{\text{Cost of goods sold}}{\text{Average inventory}}$

2010
$\dfrac{59,000}{(10,000 + 21,000) \div 2} = 3.8$ times

2011
$\dfrac{82,000}{(21,000 + 25,000) \div 2} = 3.6$ times

2012
$\dfrac{79,000}{(25,000 + 23,000) \div 2} = 3.3$ times

35.1

A. Dodds

Statement of Affairs as at 31 December 2011

Non-current assets			
Van at cost		9,000	
Less Depreciation		2,000	
			7,000
Current assets			
Inventory		8,000	
Accounts receivable		16,000	
Prepaid expenses		400	
Bank		34,000	
Cash		300	
			58,700
			65,700
Less Current liabilities			
Trade accounts payable	8,000		
Expenses owing	800		
			(8,800)
			56,900
Capital			40,000
Cash introduced		(C)	
Add Net profit		(B)	
Less Drawings		(A)	
			26,000

Missing figures (A), (B) and (C) deduced in that order. (A) to balance is 56,900, thus (B) has to be 82,900 and (C) becomes 42,900.

35.2

800 × 4 = 3,200 = Costs
× 4
= 12,800 = Fees

Fees	12,800
Costs	3,200
Profit	9,600

35.4

Workings:

Purchases	Bank	67,360	Sales Banked	91,190
	Cash	4,940	Cash	17,400
		72,300		108,590
− Creditors 31.12.2011		12,700	− Debtors 31.12.2011	21,200
		59,600		87,390
+ Creditors 31.12.2012		14,100	+ Debtors 31.12.2012	19,800
Purchases for 2012		73,700	Sales for 2012	107,190

Opening Capital:

Bank	4,100	
Inventory	10,800	
Accounts receivable	21,200	
Insurance prepaid	420	
Fixtures	1,800	
	38,320	
Less Accounts payable	12,700	
Rent owing	390	13,090
		25,230

Jane
Income Statement for the year ending 31 December 2012

Sales		107,190
Less Cost of goods sold:		
Opening inventory	10,800	
Add Purchases	73,700	
	84,500	
Less Closing inventory	12,200	72,300
Gross profit		34,890
Less Expenses:		
Wages	11,260	
Rent (3,950 − 390)	3,560	
Insurance (1,470 + 420 − 440)	1,450	
Sundry expenses	610	
Depreciation: Fixtures	200	17,080
Net profit		17,810

Statement of Financial Position as at 31 December 2012

Non-current assets		
Fixtures at valuation	1,800	
Less Depreciation	200	1,600
Current assets		
Inventory	12,200	
Accounts receivable	19,800	
Prepayments	440	32,440
		34,040
Current liabilities		
Trade accounts payable	14,100	
Bank overdraft	6,300	
Net current assets		(20,400)
		13,640
Capital		
Balance at 1.1.2012		25,230
Add Net profit		17,810
		43,040
Less Drawings (1,200 + 28,200)		29,400
		13,640

35.6

Jenny Barnes
Income Statement for the year ending 30 April 2012

Sales*		102,908
Less: Opening inventory	9,500	
Purchases	78,100	
	87,600	
Less: Closing inventory	13,620	73,980
Gross profit		28,928
Less: Expenses		
Sales assistants' wages	5,620	
Vehicle running expenses	1,020	
Bad debts	150	
Miscellaneous expenses**	1,370	
Light and heat	940	
Depreciation: Equipment	940	
Vehicles	1,000	10,460
Net profit		18,468

*Sales 96,500 + takings in cash later spent 6,408
(drawings 6,000 + expenses 408)
**Bank 962 + cash 408 = 1,370

35.8

(a)

Accounts Payable Control

Bank	101,500	Balances b/d	7,400
Cash	1,800	Drawings: Goods	600
Balances c/d	8,900	Purchases (difference)	104,200
	112,200		112,200

(b)

Janet Lambert

Income Statement for the year ending 31 August 2012

Sales (deduced – as margin is 25% = 4 × gross profit)		128,000
Opening inventory	8,600	
Add Purchases	104,200	
	112,800	
Less Closing inventory	16,800	
Cost of goods sold		96,000
Gross profit (33⅓% of Cost of goods sold)		32,000
Less: Casual labour (1,200 + 6,620)	7,820	
Rent (5,040 + 300 – 420)	4,920	
Delivery costs	3,000	
Electricity (1,390 + 160 – 210)	1,340	17,080
Net profit		14,920

Statement of Financial Position as at 31 August 2012

Current assets		
Inventory	16,800	
Accounts receivable	4,300	
Prepayments	420	
Bank	1,650	
Cash	330	23,500
Current liabilities		
Accounts payable	8,900	
Expenses owing	160	(9,060)
		14,440
Capital:		
Balance as at 1 September 2011 (Workings 1)		7,850
Add Net profit		14,920
		22,770
Less Drawings (Workings 2)		8,330
		14,440

Workings:

(1) Capital as on 1.9.2011. Inventory 8,600 + Accounts receivable 3,900 + Prepaid 300 + Bank 2,300 + Cash 360 = 15,460 – Accounts payable 7,400 – Accruals 210 = 7,850.

(2) Cash drawings. Step (A) find cash received from sales. Accounts receivable b/d 3,900 + Sales 128,000 – Accounts receivable c/d 4,300 = 127,600 cash received.

Step (B) find cash banked. Balance b/d 2,300 + cash received? – payments 117,550 = balance c/d 1,650. Therefore, cash banked? = 116,900. Step (C) draw up cash account:

Balance b/d	360	Labour	1,200
Sales receipts	127,600	Purchases	1,800
		Banked	116,900
		Drawings (difference)	7,730
		Balance c/d	330
	127,960		127,960

(c) Per text.

35.10

David Denton

Income Statement for the year ending 31 December 2013

Work done: Credit accounts	29,863	
For cash	3,418	33,281
Less Expenses:		
Materials (9,600 – 580)	9,020	
Secretarial salary	3,000	
Rent	225	
Rates (180 – 45)	135	
Insurance (800 – 200)	600	
Electricity (1,122 + 374 estimated)	1,496	
Motor expenses	912	
General expenses (1,349 + 295)	1,644	
Loan interest (4,000 × 10% × ¾)	300	
Allowance for doubtful debts	425	
Accounting fee	250	
Amortisation of lease (650 × ¾)	487	
Depreciation: Equipment	960	
Van	900	1,860	20,354
Net profit		12,927

Statement of Financial Position as at 31 December 2013

	Cost	Depreciation	
Non-current assets			
Lease	6,500	487	6,013
Equipment	4,800	960	3,840
Vehicle	3,600	900	2,700
	14,900	2,347	12,553
Current assets			
Inventory			580
Accounts receivable		4,250	
Less Allowance for doubtful debts		425	3,825
Prepaid expenses (75 + 200)			275
Bank (see workings)			6,084
Cash			123
			10,887
			23,440

35.10 (cont'd)

			23,440
Less Current liabilities			
Trade accounts payable	714		
Interest owing	300		
Accountancy fee owing	250		
Rates owing	135		
Electricity owing	374		
		1,773	
Net current assets			
Less Loan		4,000	
			(5,773)
			17,667

Financed by:

Capital		
Introduced (6,500 + 3,600)		10,100
Add Net profit		12,927
		23,027
Less Drawings (4,680 + 280 + 400)		5,360
		17,667

Workings:

Bank (6,500 + 25,613 + 2,600 + 4,000) = 38,713 − 4,680 − 280 − 6,500 − 300 −
3,000 − 8,886 − 4,800 − 1,122 − 912 − 1,349 − 800 = 6,084

35.11

(a)

J. Duncan
Capital Account on 1 January 2011

Bank		8,000
Cash		300
Inventory		4,100
Machinery		12,600
Rent prepaid		200
Accounts receivable		6,300
		31,500
Accounts payable	2,400	
Loan	5,000	
		(7,400)
		24,100

(b)

J. Duncan
Income Statement for the year ending 31 December 2011

Sales			40,450
Less: Sales returns			1,200
			39,250
Less: Cost of Sales			
Opening Inventory at 1 January 2011		4,100	
Add: Purchases		18,950	
		23,050	
Less: Withdrawn by the owner	300		
Less: Closing inventory at 31 December 2011	3,200		
		3,500	
			19,550
Gross profit			19,700
Add: Discount received			350
			20,050
Less: Expenses			
Rent		1,850	
Bad debts written-off		400	
Wages		6,100	
Insurance		1,450	
Loan interest		400	
Depreciation		4,200	
Repairs		300	
Electricity		750	
			15,450
Net profit			4,600

Workings:

Sales 26,000 − 250 + 14,000 + 400 − 6,300 + 5,000 + 1,200 + 400 = 40,450
Purchases 18,500 − 2,400 + 2,500 + 350 = 18,950
Depreciation = balancing figure.

35.12 J. Duncan
Statement of Financial Position as at 31 December 2011

Non-current assets			
Machinery at 1 January 2011		12,600	
Add: Additions		7,500	
		20,100	
Less: Depreciation		4,200	15,900
Current assets			
Inventory		3,200	
Accounts receivable		5,000	
Bank		2,600	
Cash		50	
			10,850
			26,750
Current liabilities			
Accounts payable		2,500	
Accrued charges			
Loan interest	100		
Rent	250	350	
		2,850	
Non-current liabilities			
Bank loan 8%		5,000	
			(7,850)
			18,900
Capital account			
Balance at 1 January 2011		24,100	
Add: Net profit		4,600	
		28,700	
Less: Drawings		9,800	
			18,900

35.15 Malcolm Phillips

Inventory value per stocktake on 3 May 2011	124,620
Less Purchases (1,510 – 530)	980
	123,640
Less Sales returns (222 @ 80%)	176
	123,464
Less Obsolete inventory	300
	123,164
Add Inventory sold (2,300 @ 80%)	1,840
Value of inventory on 30 April 2005	125,004

39.1 A. Vantuira
Statement of Cash Flows for the year ending 31 December 2012

Operating activities		
Profit from operations		26,000
Adjustments for:		
Depreciation		4,000
		30,000
Operating cash flows before movements in working capital		
Decrease in inventory	2,000	
Decrease in accounts receivable	5,000	
Decrease in accounts payable	(7,000)	
		—
Cash generated by operations		30,000
Tax paid	—	
Interest paid	—	
Net cash from operating activities		30,000
Investing activities		
Payments to acquire tangible non-current assets	(6,000)	
Net cash used in investing activities		(6,000)
Financing activities		
Loan received	25,000	
Drawings	(24,000)	
Net cash from financing activities		1,000
Net increase in cash and cash equivalents		25,000
Cash and cash equivalents at beginning of year		(17,000)
Cash and cash equivalents at end of year		8,000
Bank balances and cash		8,000

39.3
(a) Malcolm Phillips
Statement of Cash Flows for the year ending 30 April 2012

Operating activities		
Profit from operations		8,500
Adjustments for:		
Depreciation		200
		8,700
Operating cash flows before movements in working capital		
Increase in inventory	(2,800)	
Increase in accounts payable	200	
Decrease in accounts receivable	500	
		(2,100)
Cash generated by operations		6,600
Tax paid	—	
Interest paid	—	
Net cash from operating activities		6,600

39.3 (cont'd)

Investing activities
Payments to acquire tangible non-current assets	(3,000)	
Net cash used in investing activities		(3,000)

Financing activities
Capital introduced	2,000	
Drawings	(8,000)	
Net cash used in financing activities		(6,000)
Net decrease in cash and cash equivalents		(2,400)
Cash and cash equivalents at beginning of year		1,500
		(900)

Cash and cash equivalents at end of year
Bank balances and cash	(900)

(b) (i) $\dfrac{7,500}{30,000} \times \dfrac{100}{1} = 25\%$ (ii) $\dfrac{22,500}{(3,100 + 5,900) \div 2} = \dfrac{22,500}{4,500} = 5$

39.4

D. Duncan
Statement of Cash Flows for the year ending 31 December 2011

Operating activities
Profit from operations		23,240
Adjustments for		
Depreciation	1,800	
Profit on sale of tangible non-current asset	(620)	
Increase in allowance for doubtful debts	200	1,380
Operating cash flows before movements in working capital		24,620
Increase in inventory	(5,400)	
Decrease in accounts receivable (8,800 − 7,700)	1,100	
Increase in accounts payable	1,300	
Cash generated by operations		21,620
Tax paid	–	
Interest paid	(3,000)	
Net cash from operating activities		21,620
		21,620

Investing activities
Receipts from sale of tangible non-current assets	3,820	
Net cash from investing activities		3,820

Financing activities
Loan repaid to J. Fry	(2,500)	
Drawings	(22,630)	(25,130)
Net cash used in financing activities		310
Net increase in cash and cash equivalents		410
Cash and cash equivalents at beginning of year		720
		720

Cash and cash equivalents at end of year
Bank balances and cash	720

45.1

Flyer Ltd
Statements of Changes in Equity (extract)

(1) For the year ending 31 March 2012

	Retained Profits	General Reserve
Opening balance	90,200	–
Retained profit for the year		–
Transferred to general reserve	(20,000)	20,000
Preference dividend paid	(5,000)	–
Closing balance	65,200	20,000

(2) For the year ending 31 March 2013

	Retained Profits	General Reserve
Opening balance	65,200	20,000
Retained profits for the year	84,600	–
Transferred to general reserve	(15,000)	15,000
Preference dividend paid	(5,000)	–
Ordinary dividend paid	(16,000)	–
Closing balance	113,800	35,000

45.2
Trainsign Ltd
Statements of Changes in Equity

(1) *For the year ending 31 December 2011*

	Retained Profits	General Reserve	Foreign Exchange Reserve
Opening balance	–	–	–
Retained profits for the year	62,400		–
Transferred to general reserve	(10,000)	10,000	–
Preference dividend paid	(6,300)		–
Closing balance	46,100	10,000	–

(2) *For the year ending 31 December 2012*

	Retained Profits	General Reserve	Foreign Exchange Reserve
Opening balance	46,100	10,000	–
Retained profits for the year	81,900		–
Transferred to general reserve	(18,000)	18,000	–
Preference dividend paid	(6,300)		–
Ordinary dividend paid	(15,600)	–	–
Closing balance	88,100	28,000	–

(3) *For the year ending 31 December 2013*

	Retained Profits	General Reserve	Foreign Exchange Reserve
Opening balance	88,100	28,000	–
Retained profits for the year	114,190		–
Transferred foreign exchange reserve	(15,000)	–	15,000
Preference dividend paid	(6,300)	–	–
Ordinary dividend paid	(20,800)	–	–
Closing balance	160,190	28,000	15,000

45.3   Statement of Financial Position as at 30 September 2011

Non-current assets	Cost	Depn	
Buildings	330,000	40,000	290,000
Motors	74,000	41,000	33,000
Fixtures	9,200	5,100	4,100
	413,200	86,100	327,100

Current assets		
Inventory	21,400	
Accounts receivable	10,300	
Bank (difference)	6,900	
		38,600
		365,700

Current liabilities		
Accounts payable	13,700	
Loan notes		
Net current assets		
Total assets *less* current liabilities		
Non-current liabilities: repayable 30.9.2015	40,000	(53,700)
		312,000

Capital and reserves	
Called-up share capital	200,000
Non-current assets replacement reserve	30,000
General reserve	50,000
Retained profits	32,000
	312,000

45.4
OK Limited
Statements of Changes in Equity (extract) for the year ending 31 March 2012

	Retained Profits	General Reserve
Opening balance	27,000	30,000
Retained profits for the year	29,000	–
Transfer to general reserve	(10,000)	10,000
Preference dividend paid	(4,000)	
Ordinary dividend paid	(12,000)	–
Closing balance	30,000	40,000

Statement of Financial Position as at 31 March 2012

Non-current assets		167

Current assets		
Inventory	52	
Accounts receivable	24	
Bank	14	
		90
		257

Current liabilities		
Accounts payable		(37)
		220

Share Capital and Reserves		
8% preference share capital		50
Ordinary shares	100	
General reserve	40	
Retained profits	30	
Ordinary shareholder's equity		170
Total shareholder's equity		220

45.6

Select Limited
Profit and Loss Account part of the Income Statement for the year ending 31 March 2012

Gross profit		98,050
Office salaries and expenses	25,000	
Advertising	5,000	
Directors' fees	11,300	
Allowance for doubtful debts	350	
Provision for depreciation	8,000	
		49,650
Net profit		48,400

Note: the proposed dividend will be shown as a note.

Statement of Changes in Equity (extract) for the year ending 31 March 2012

	Retained Profits	General Reserve	Share Premium
Opening balance	12,000	–	20,000
Retained profits for the year	48,400	–	–
Transferred to general reserve	(25,000)	25,000	–
Closing balance	35,400	25,000	20,000

Statement of Financial Position as at 31 March 2012

	Cost	Depreciation	
Non-current assets			
Land and buildings	170,000	–	
Fixtures and fittings	80,000	40,000	
	250,000	40,000	210,000
Current assets			
Inventory	42,000		
Accounts receivable	37,600		
VAT	3,800		
Bank	12,000		
	95,400		
			305,400
Current liabilities			
Sundry accounts payable			(25,000)
			280,400
Share capital			
Authorised; 300,000 ordinary shares of £1			200,000
Allotted, called-up and fully paid			200,000
Reserves			
Share premium	20,000		
General reserve	25,000		
Retained profits	35,400		
			80,400
			280,400

45.8

Tailor Times Ltd
Income Statement for the year ending 31 December 2012

Sales		925,300
Less Cost of goods sold		
Opening inventory	81,900	
Add Purchases	563,700	
	645,600	
Less Closing inventory	94,300	
		551,300
Gross profit		374,000
Less expenses		
Wages and salaries (179,400 + 1,800)	181,200	
Business rates (6,100 – 700)	5,400	
Electricity	4,800	
Bad debts	1,400	
Allowance for doubtful debts	300	
General expenses	14,600	
Depreciation: Freehold premises	25,000	
Machinery	16,800	
		249,500
Net profit		124,500

Statement of Financial Position as at 31 December 2012

Non-current assets			
Premises		271,000	
Less Depreciation		79,000	
			192,000
Machinery		84,000	
Less Depreciation		37,800	
			46,200
			238,200
Current assets			
Inventory		94,300	
Accounts receivable	74,200		
Less Allowance for doubtful debts	1,500		
		72,700	
Prepayments		700	
Bank		16,200	
		183,900	
			422,100
Current liabilities			
Accounts payable		68,300	
Expenses owing		1,800	
			(70,100)
			352,000
Financed by:			
Authorised and issued capital			200,000
Retained profits (124,500 + 27,500)			152,000
			352,000

45.10

Partido Ltd
Income Statement for the year ending 31 December 2011

Sales		1,606,086
Less Cost of goods sold		
Opening inventory	290,114	
Add Purchases	810,613	
Add Carriage inwards	2,390	
	1,103,117	
Less Closing inventory	317,426	785,691
Gross profit		820,395
Less Expenses		
Salaries	384,500	
Business rates	16,500	
Carriage outwards	13,410	
Office expenses	9,345	
Sundry expenses	2,360	
Depreciation: Buildings	40,000	
Equipment	48,000	
Directors' remuneration	119,200	633,315
Net profit		187,080

Statement of Financial Position as at 31 December 2011

	Cost	Depn	Net
Non-current assets			
Buildings	800,000	120,000	680,000
Equipment	320,000	144,000	176,000
	1,120,000	264,000	856,000

Current assets		
Inventory	317,426	
Accounts receivable	321,219	
Bank	8,100	646,745
		1,502,745
Current liabilities		
Accounts payable	237,516	
Expenses owing	1,945	(239,461)
		1,263,284
Financed by:		
Share capital: authorised and issued		800,000
Reserves		
Foreign exchange	50,000	
General reserve	190,000	
Retained profits (187,080 + 136,204 − (70,000 + 30,000))	223,284	463,284
		1,263,284

45.12

1   Burden plc: Computation of corrected net profit

Recorded net profit		58,070
Add Profit on sale of equipment		500
		58,570
Less Bad debt written off	300	
Inventory reduced to net realisable value	700	1,000
Correct figure of net profit		57,570

2   Burden plc
Statement of Changes in Equity (extract) for the year ending 31 May 2012

	Retained Profits	General Reserve	Share Premium
Opening balance	16,200	20,000	25,000
Retained profits for the year	57,570	–	–
Transfer to general reserve	(50,000)	50,000	–
	23,770	70,000	25,000

3 (i) Current assets

Inventory	17,100	
Accounts receivable	6,540	
Prepayments	760	24,400
Less Current liabilities		
Trade accounts payable	28,500	
Accrued expenses	430	
Bank overdraft	2,400	(31,330)
Working capital (deficit)		(6,930)

Note: Figures in brackets are negative.

(ii) Capital and reserves

Ordinary share capital: called up	200,000
Share premium	25,000
General reserve	70,000
Retained profits	23,770
Shareholders' funds	318,770

4   Examples:
Issue of shares: + Bank; + Share capital.
Sales of non-current assets: + Bank; − Non-current assets.
Loan notes issued: + Bank; + Loan notes.

45.14

(a) See text.

(b) The historical cost convention does not make the going concern convention unnecessary. Several instances illustrate this:

    (i) Non-current assets are depreciated over the useful life of the assets. This presupposes that the business will continue to operate during the years of assumed useful life of the assets.

    (ii) Prepayments also assume that the benefits available in the future will be able to be claimed, because the business is expected to continue.

    (iii) Inventory is valued also on the basis that it will be disposed of during the future ordinary running of the business.

    (iv) The accruals concept itself assumes that the business is to continue.

All of this shows that the two concepts complement each other.

(c) Shareholders want financial statements so that they can decide what to do with their shareholding, whether they should sell their shares or hold on to them.

    To enable them to decide upon their actions, they would really like to know what is going to happen in the future. To help them in this they would also like information which shows them what happened in the past. Ideally, therefore, they would like both types of report, those on the past and those on the future.

    If they had a choice, the logical choice would be to receive a report on the future providing that it could be relied upon.

45.15

Extract 1

(a) The amount paid for goodwill.

(b) The excess represents share premium.

(c) Equity shares generally means ordinary shares.

(d) That although issued in 2012 a dividend will not be paid in that year. The first year that dividends *could* be paid is 2013.

Extract 2

(e) (i) A rate of 8% per annum interest will be paid on them, irrespective of whether profits are made or not.

    (ii) These are the years within which the loan stock could be redeemed, if the company so wished.

(f) (i) This is the rate per annum at which preference dividends will be paid, subject to there being sufficient distributable profits.

    (ii) That the shares could be bought back by the company.

(g) Probably because there was currently a lower interest rate prevailing at the time of redemption and the company took advantage of it.

(h) Large amounts of both fixed interest and fixed dividend funds have resulted in a raising of the gearing.

(i) Debenture interest gets charged before arriving at net profit. Dividends are an appropriation of profits in the period in which they are actually paid.

(k) Shareholders are owners and help decide appropriations. Debenture holders are external lenders and interest expense has to be paid.

45.16

(a) This is incorrect. The tax portion has to be counted as part of the total cost, which is made up of loan note interest paid plus tax. Holding back payment will merely see legal action taken by the HM Revenue & Customs to collect the tax.

(b) This cannot be done. The repainting of the exterior does not improve or enhance the original value of the premises. It cannot therefore be treated as capital expenditure.

(c) This is not feasible. Only the profit on the sale of the old machinery, found by deducting net book value from sales proceeds, can be so credited to the profit and loss account. The remainder is a capital receipt and should be treated as such.

(d) This is an incorrect view. Although some of the general reserve could, if circumstances allowed it, be transferred back to the retained profits, it could not be shown as affecting the operating profit for 2012. This is because the general reserve was built up over the years before 2012.

(e) This is not feasible. The share capital has to be maintained at nominal value as per the Companies Act. A share premium cannot be created in this fashion, and even if it could, it would still have to be credited to the *share premium account* and not the profit and loss account.

(f) Incorrect. Although the premises could be revalued the credit for the increase has to be to a capital reserve account. This cannot then be transferred to the credit of the profit and loss account.

45.17

See text. Points to be made include that there must be an expectation that sufficient profits will be made in future to make the loan note interest payments when due; also, there may be cheaper sources of finance available; also, if secured loan notes are to be issued, there must be sufficient assets available to act as security over the issue. Gearing is also an issue to be considered – see text.

47.1 $\dfrac{280,000}{40,000} = 7$ times

47.2 $\dfrac{60,000}{200,000} \times 100 = 30\%$

47.3 $\dfrac{70,000}{400,000} \times 100 = 17.5\%$

47.4 $\dfrac{45,000}{400,000} \times 100 = 11.25\%$

47.5 (a) $\dfrac{50,000}{30,000} = 1.67{:}1$

    (b) $\dfrac{22,000}{30,000} = 0.73{:}1$

47.6 (a) $\dfrac{50,000}{250,000} = 1{:}5$

(b) $\dfrac{1}{5} \times 365 = 73$ days

47.7 (a) $\dfrac{40,000}{240,000} = 1{:}6$

(b) $\dfrac{1}{6} \times 365 = 61$ days*

*60.83 should be rounded up to the next whole day.

47.8 (a) $\dfrac{(i)}{(ii)} = \dfrac{300,000}{50,000} = 60\text{p}$

(b) $\dfrac{(iii)}{(a)} = \dfrac{4.2}{0.6} = 7$

(c) $\dfrac{(iv)}{(iii)} = \dfrac{0.20}{4.20} = 4.76\%$

(d) $\dfrac{(i)+(v)}{(vi)} = \dfrac{300,000 + 10,000}{120,000} = 2.58$ times

47.9 $\dfrac{30,000}{210,000} = 14.3\%$

47.10

(a)

	X	Y
(i) Gross profit as % of sales	$\dfrac{315,000}{555,000} \times \dfrac{100}{1} = 56.8\%$	$\dfrac{420,000}{750,000} \times \dfrac{100}{1} = 56\%$
(ii) Net profit as % of sales	$\dfrac{100,000}{555,000} \times \dfrac{100}{1} = 18\%$	$\dfrac{150,000}{750,000} \times \dfrac{100}{1} = 20\%$
(iii) Expenses as % of sales	$\dfrac{215,000}{555,000} \times \dfrac{100}{1} = 38.7\%$	$\dfrac{270,000}{750,000} \times \dfrac{100}{1} = 36\%$
(iv) Inventory turnover	$\dfrac{240,000}{(100,000 + 60,000) \div 2} = 3$ times	$\dfrac{330,000}{(80,000 + 70,000) \div 2} = 4.4$ times
(v) Rate of return	$\dfrac{100,000}{(76,000 + 116,000) \div 2} \times \dfrac{100}{1} = 104.2\%$	$\dfrac{150,000}{(72,000 + 152,000) \div 2} \times \dfrac{100}{1} = 133.9\%$

(vi) Current ratio $\dfrac{210,000}{104,000} = 2.02$ $\dfrac{182,500}{100,500} = 1.82$

(vii) Acid test ratio $\dfrac{145,000}{104,000} = 1.39$ $\dfrac{112,500}{100,500} = 1.12$

(viii) Accounts receivable/sales ratio $\dfrac{125,000}{555,000} \times 12 = 2.7$ months $\dfrac{100,000}{750,000} \times 12 = 1.6$ months

(ix) Accounts payable/purchases ratio $\dfrac{104,000}{200,000} \times 12 = 6.24$ months $\dfrac{100,500}{320,000} \times 12 = 3.77$ months

(b) Business Y is the most profitable, both in terms of actual net profit, £150,000 compared to £100,000, but also in terms of capital employed; Y has managed to achieve a return of £133.90 for every £100 invested compared with £104.20 for X. Reasons – possibly only – as not until you know more about the business could you give a definite answer:

(i) Possibly managed to sell far more merchandise because of lower prices, but the margins are so similar (56.8% v. 56%) that this is unlikely.

(ii) Maybe more efficient use of mechanised means in the business. Note that Y has more equipment and, perhaps as a consequence, kept other expenses down to £35,000 as compared with X's £45,000.

(iii) Did not have as much inventory lying idle. Turned over inventory 4.4 times in the year as compared with 3 for X.

(iv) X's current ratio of 2.02 is not much higher than Y's (1.82) so it is unlikely that this has contributed significantly to the difference in profitability through money sitting around doing nothing to increase profits.

(v) Following on from (iv) the Acid Test ratio for X may be higher than necessary.

(vi) Part of the reason for (v) is that X waited (on average) 2.7 months to be paid by customers. Y managed to collect them on average in 1.6 months. Money represented by debts is money lying idle.

(vii) Another reason for (v) is that X took almost twice as long to pay its creditors (6.24 months v. 3.77). However, this may be a 'good' sign for X as long as suppliers do not object and start refusing to sell to X.

Put all these factors together, and it appears that Y may be being run more efficiently, and is more profitable as a consequence.

47.12

(a)

Durham Limited

Statement of Changes in Equity (extract) for the year ending 30.4.2012

	Retained Profits	General Reserve
Opening balance	14,500	4,000
Retained profits for the year	16,500	–
Transferred to general reserve	(5,000)	5,000
Preference dividend paid	(2,000)	–
	24,000	9,000

47.12 (cont'd)

(b)

Statement of Financial Position as at 30.4.2012

Non-current assets			
Premises at cost		86,000	
Machinery and plant at cost	60,000		
Less Depreciation	40,000	20,000	106,000
Current assets			
Inventory		60,000	
Accounts receivable	20,000		
Less Allowance for doubtful debts	4,000	16,000	
Prepayments		900	
Bank		13,100	90,000
			196,000
Current liabilities			
Accounts payable		12,900	
Expenses owing		100	(13,000)
			183,000
Equity			
8% preference shares		50,000	
Ordinary shares		100,000	
General reserve		9,000	
Retained profits		24,000	
Shareholders' funds		183,000	

(c) (i) *Return on Capital Employed (ROCE)*
This is the amount of profit earned compared with the amount of capital employed to earn it. Calculated:

$$\frac{\text{Net profit}}{\text{Average of shareholders' funds}} \times \frac{100}{1} = \frac{16,500}{(168,500 + 183,000) \div 2} \times \frac{100}{1}$$
$$= 9.39\%$$

(ii) *Current Ratio*
This calculates how well the current assets can finance current liabilities. Calculated:

$$\frac{\text{Current assets}}{\text{Current liabilities}} = \frac{90,000}{13,000} = 6.9 : 1$$

A figure of 2 : 1 is often reckoned as adequate. In this case a 6.9 : 1 figure is more than adequate.

Acid Test Ratio
This calculates whether the business has sufficient liquid resources to meet its current liabilities. Calculated:

$$\frac{\text{Current assets} - \text{Inventory}}{\text{Current liabilities}} = \frac{30,000}{13,000} = 2.3 : 1$$

(d) ROCE. The return of 9.39 per cent would appear to be adequate, but we cannot really comment further without more information.
Current Ratio. A figure of 2 : 1 is often reckoned as adequate. In this case a 6.9 : 1 figure is more than adequate.
Acid Test Ratio. All current liabilities can be met and the return is therefore adequate.

(e) 1 Previous years' figures.
2 We would need to know ratios for other similar businesses.

47.13 (a) (i) Gross profit: Sales

2011	2012
$\frac{50}{200} \times \frac{100}{1} = 25\%$	$\frac{70}{280} \times \frac{100}{1} = 25\%$

(ii) Inventory turnover

2011	2012
$\frac{150}{(50 + 20) \div 2} = 4.29$	$\frac{210}{(20 + 30) \div 2} = 8.4$

(iii) Net profit: Sales

2011	2012
$\frac{12}{200} \times \frac{100}{1} = 6\%$	$\frac{20}{280} \times \frac{100}{1} = 7.14\%$

(iv) Quick ratio

2011	2012
$\frac{25}{25} = 1$	$\frac{33}{12} = 2.75$

(v) Working capital (current ratio)

2011	2012
$\frac{45}{25} = 1.8$	$\frac{63}{12} = 5.25$

(vi) Net profit: Capital employed

2011	2012
$\frac{12}{130} \times \frac{100}{1} = 9.23\%$	$\frac{20}{191} \times \frac{100}{1} = 10.47\%$

(b) (Brief answer, but you should write more in an exam)
(i) No change.
(ii) Increase caused by lowering average inventory; also probably better sales management.
(iii) An increase in sales, without a larger increase in expenses, has led to a better return.
(iv) Issue of loan notes has improved the cash situation and therefore the quick ratio.
(v) Net current assets have increased largely due to issue of debentures, although partly offset by non-current assets bought.
(vi) Increasing sales and better inventory turnover brought about better ROCE.

47.16
(a)

Joan Street
Income Statement for the year ending 31 March 2011

Sales		(W3)	240,000
Cost of sales			
Opening inventory		21,000	
Add Purchases	(W6)	174,000	
	(W7)	195,000	
Less Closing inventory		15,000	
	(W1)		180,000
Gross profit	(W2)		60,000
Sundry expenses	(W5)		38,400
Net profit	(W4)		21,600

Statement of Financial Position as at 31 March 2011

Non-current assets		(W9)	108,000
Current assets			
Inventory		15,000	
Accounts receivable		24,000	
Bank	(W8)	9,000	
	(W14)	48,000	
			156,000
Current liabilities	(W13)		12,000
Net assets	(W12)		144,000
Financed by:			
Capital:			
Balance at 1.4.2010	(W11)		122,400
Add Net profit			21,600
	(W10)		144,000

Workings (could possibly find alternatives)

(W1) As average inventory $21,000 + 15,000 \div 2 = 18,000$ and inventory turnover is 10, this means that cost of sales = $18,000 \times 10 = 180,000$

(W2) As gross profit is 25% of sales, it must therefore be $33^1/_3$% of cost of sales

(W3) As (W1) is 180,000 and (W2) is 60,000 therefore sales = (W1) + (W2) = 240,000

(W4) Net profit = 9% of sales = 21,600

(W5) Missing figure, found by arithmetical deduction

(W6) Missing figure, found by arithmetical deduction

and (W7) Missing figures – found by arithmetical deduction

(W8) $\dfrac{\text{Accounts receivable (?)} \times 365}{\text{Sales}} = 36^1/_2$, i.e.

$\dfrac{? \times 365}{240,000} = 36^1/_2 = 36^1/_2$, by arithmetic

Accounts receivable = 24,000. Proof $\dfrac{24,000 \times 365}{240,000} = 36^1/_2$

(W9) $45\% \times 240,000 = 108,000$

(W10) Knowing that net profit 21,600 is 15% of W10, so W10 = $21,600 \times 100/15 = 144,000$

(W11) Missing figure

(W12) Put in after (W11)

(W13) If Net current assets ratio is 4, it means a factor of current assets 4, current liabilities 1 = Net current assets 3 which is (W12 − W9) assets therefore:

$4/3 \times 36,000 = 48,000$
and current liabilities
$1/3 \times 36,000 = 12,000$

(W14) Is new missing figure.

(b) Question asked for two favourable aspects and two unfavourable aspects but four of each are given here
Favourable: Inventory turnover, liquidity, net current assets, net profit on sales
Unfavourable: Gross profit to sales, accounts receivable collection, return on capital employed, turnover to net capital employed.

(c) Drawbacks include:
(i) No access to trends over recent years.
(ii) No future plans etc. given.
(iii) Each business is often somewhat different.
(iv) Size of businesses not known.

47.18
(a) (i) Current ratio: by dividing current assets by current liabilities.
(ii) Quick assets ratio: by dividing current assets less inventory by current liabilities.
(iii) Return on capital employed (ROCE): can have more than one meaning. One in common use is net profit divided by capital plus long-term liabilities (e.g. loans), and shown as a percentage.
(iv) Return on shareholders' funds (ROSF): net profit divided by capital, shown as a percentage.
(v) Accounts receivable turnover: Sales divided by average accounts receivable, expressed in days or months.
(vi) Accounts payable turnover: Purchases divided by average accounts payable, expressed in days or months.
(vii) Gross profit percentage: Gross profit divided by sales, expressed as a percentage.
(viii) Net profit percentage: Net profit divided by sales.
(ix) Inventory turnover: Cost of goods sold, divided by average inventory, expressed in days.

(b) (This part of the question tests your ability to be able to deduce some conclusions from the information given. You have to use your imagination.)
First, an assumption, is that cost of sales of these two businesses. We will assume that they are approximately of the same size.
A has a higher current ratio, 2 to 1.5, but the quick assets ratio shows a much greater disparity, 1.7 to 0.7. As inventory is not included in the quick assets ratio, it can be deduced that B has relatively greater inventory. Expected also

47.18 (cont'd)

from these ratios is that A has high amounts of accounts receivable, this being seen because accounts receivable turnover is three times as great for A as for B.

The return on shareholders' funds (ROSF) is much greater for A than for B, 30 per cent to 18 per cent, but the ROCE is not that different, 20 per cent to 17 per cent. This shows that A has far more in long-term borrowings than B. The ROCE indicates that A is somewhat more efficient than B, but not by a considerable amount.

Gross profit percentage is far greater for A than B, but net profit percentage is the same. Obviously, A has extremely high operating expenses per £100 of sales.

The last ratio shows that inventory in A lies unsold for twice as long a period as for B.

A summary of the above shows that A has lower inventory, a higher figure for accounts receivable, sells at a slower rate, and has high operating expenses. B has more inventory, and sells its goods much quicker but at lower prices as shown by the gross profit percentage.

All the evidence points to A being a firm which gives emphasis to personal service to its customers. B on the other hand emphasises cheap prices and high turnover, with not as much concentration on personal service.

47.20

(There is no set answer. In addition, as a large number of points could be mentioned, the examiner cannot expect every aspect to be covered.)

The main points which could be covered are:

(i) The financial statements are for last year whereas, in fact, the bank is more interested in what might happen to the business in the future.

(ii) The financial statements are usually prepared on a historic cost basis. These therefore do not reflect current values.

(iii) The bank manager would want a cash budget to be drawn up for the ensuing periods. This would give the manager an indication as to whether or not the business will be able to meet its commitments as they fall due.

(iv) The bank manager wants to ensure that bank charges and interest can be paid promptly, also that a bank loan or overdraft will be able to be paid off. He will want to see that these commitments can still be met if the business has to cease operations. This means that the market value of assets on cessation, rather than the cost of them, is of much more interest to the bank manager.

To say that the financial statements are 'not good enough' is misleading. What the manager is saying is that the financial statements do not provide him with what he would really like to know. One could argue that there should be other types of financial statements drawn up in addition to those drawn up on a historic basis.

47.21

(a) The basis on which financial statements are prepared is that of 'accruals'. By this it is meant that the recognition of revenue and expenditure takes place not at the point when cash is received or paid out, but instead at the point when the revenue is earned or the expenditure is incurred.

To establish the point of recognition of a sale, several criteria are necessary:

(i) The product, or the service, must have been supplied to the customer.

(ii) The buyer must have indicated willingness to pay for the product or services and have accepted liability to do so.

(iii) A monetary value of the goods or services must have been agreed to by the buyer.

(iv) Ownership of the goods must have passed to the buyer.

(b) (i) This cannot be recognised as a sale. It does not comply with any of the four criteria above.

(ii) This also cannot be recognised as a sale. Neither criterion (i) nor (iv) has been covered.

(iii) If this was a cash sale, all of the above criteria would probably be achieved on delivery, and therefore it could be appropriate to recognise the sale.

If it was a credit sale, if the invoice was sent with the goods and a delivery note stating satisfaction by the customer is signed, then it would also probably be appropriate to recognise the sale.

(iv) Usually takes place after the four criteria have been satisfied. If so, the sale should be recognised.

(v) In the case of cash sales this would be the point of recognition.

In the case of credit sales it would depend on whether or not criteria (a) (i) and (iv) had also been satisfied.

(vi) This would only influence recognition of sales if there was serious doubt about the ability of the customer to pay his/her debts.

47.22

Obviously there is no set answer to this question. However, the following may well be typical:

(a) If the business is going to carry on operating, then the going concern concept comes into operation. Consequently, non-current assets are valued at cost, less depreciation to date. Inventory is valued at lower of cost or net realisable value. The 'net realisable value' will be that based on the business realising stock through normal operations.

(b) Should the business be deemed as a case for cessation, then the going concern concept could not be used. The values on non-current assets and inventory will be their disposal values. This should be affected by whether or not the business could be sold as a whole or whether it would have to be broken up. Similarly, figures would be affected by whether or not assets had to be sold off very quickly at low prices, or sold only when reasonable prices could be achieved.

It is not only the statement of financial position that would be affected, as the income statement would reflect the changes in values.

47.23

(a) See text, Chapter 10.

(b) Various illustrations are possible, but the following are examples:

(i) Apportionment of expenses between one period and another. For instance, very rarely would very small inventories of stationery be valued at the year end. This means that the stationery gets charged against one year's profits even though it may not all have been used up in that year.

(ii) Items expensed instead of being capitalised. Small items which are, in theory, capital expenditure will often be charged up to an expense account.

(iii) The value of assets approximated, instead of being measured with absolute precision.

47.23 (cont'd)

(c) (i) An illustration could be made under (b) (iii). An inventory of oil could well be estimated; the true figure, if known, might be one or two litres out. The cost of precise measurement would probably not be worth the benefit of having such information.

(ii) What is material in one company may not be material in another.

47.24

No set answer. Question is of a general nature rather than being specific. A variety of answers is therefore acceptable.

The examiner might expect to see the following covered (this is not a model answer):

(a) Different reports needed by different outside parties, as they have to meet different requirements. Might find they therefore include:

(i) for bankers – accounts based on 'break-up' value of the assets if they have to be sold off to repay loans or overdrafts;

(ii) for investors – to include how successful business has fared against budgets set for that year to see how successful business is at meeting targets;

(iii) for employees – include details of number of employees, wages and salaries paid, effect on pension funds;

(iv) for local community – to include reports showing amounts spent on pollution control, etc.

And any similar instances.

(b) The characteristics of useful information have been stated in *The Framework for the Preparation and Presentation of Financial Statements* (see Section 10.9), and the accounting reports should be measured against this.

(c) Presentation (additional) in form of pie charts, bar charts, etc., as these are often more easily understood by readers.

47.25

(a) Accountants follow the realisation concept when deciding when to recognise revenue on any particular transaction. This states that profit is normally regarded as being earned at the time when the goods or services are passed to the customer and he/she incurs liability for them. For a service business it means when the services have been performed.

(b) The stage at which revenue is recognised could be either F or G. The normal rule is that the goods have been despatched, not delivered. For instance the goods may be shipped to Australia and take several weeks to get there.

Exactly where this fits in with F or G in the question cannot be stipulated without further information.

(c) If F is accepted as point of recognition, then £130 will be gross profit. If G is accepted as point of recognition the gross profit recognised will be £120.

(d) The argument that can be advanced is to take the prudence concept to its final conclusion, in that the debtor should pay for the goods before the profit can be recognised.

Until H is reached there is always the possibility that the goods will not be paid for, or might be returned because of faults in the goods.

(e) If the goods are almost certain to be sold, it could give a better picture of the progress of the firm up to a particular point in time if profit could be recognised in successive amounts at stages B, C and D.

47.26

(a) A 'provision' is an amount written off or retained by way of providing for depreciation, renewals or diminution in value of assets, or retained by way of providing for any known liability of which the amount cannot be determined with 'substantial' accuracy. This therefore covers such items as provisions for depreciation. A 'liability' is an amount owing which can be determined with substantial accuracy.

Sometimes, therefore, the difference between a provision and a liability hinges around what is meant by 'substantial' accuracy. Rent owing at the end of the financial year would normally be known with precision; this would obviously be a liability. Legal charges for a court case which has been heard, but for which the lawyers have not yet submitted their bill, would be a provision.

Accrued expenses are those accruing from one day to another, but not paid at the year end. Such items as rates, electricity, telephone charges will come under this heading.

Accounts payable represent persons to whom money is owed for goods and services.

Reserves consist of either undistributed profits, or else sums that have been allocated originally from such profits or have been created to comply with the law. An example of the first kind is a *general reserve*, whilst a *share premium account* is of the second type.

Provisions, accrued expenses and accounts payable would all be taken into account before calculating net profit. Reserves do not interfere with the calculation of net profit, as they are appropriations of profit or, as in the case of capital reserves, do not pass through the profit and loss account.

(b) (i) Provision made for £21,000. Charge to profit and loss and show in statement of financial position under current liabilities.

(ii) Accrued expenses, $\frac{2}{12}$ £6,000 = £1,000. Charge in profit and loss account and show as current liability in statement of financial position.

(iii) Account payable £2,500. Bring into purchases in trading account and show as current liability in statement of financial position.

(iv) Reserve £5,000. Transfer from retained profits to plant replacement reserve and show the transfer in the statement of changes in equity and in the statement of financial position under *reserves*.

47.27

(a) *The bank*

The bank will be interested in two main aspects. The first is the ability to repay the loan as and when it falls due. The second is the ability to pay interest on the due dates.

Mr Whitehall

He will be interested in the expected return on his investment. This means that recent performance of the company and its plans will be important to him. In addition the possible capital growth of his investment would be desirable.

47.27 (*cont'd*)

(*b*) *Note*: For your information; more than four ratios for bank are given below despite you having being asked for four.

Bank

Long-term ability to repay loan

(*i*) Members' equity/Total assets
(*ii*) Loan capital/Members' equity
(*iii*) Total liabilities/Members' equity
(*iv*) Operating profit/Loan interest.

Short-term liquidity

(*i*) Liquid assets/Current liabilities.
(*ii*) Current assets/Current liabilities.

Mr Whitehall

Return on investment

(*i*) Price per share/Earnings per share
(*ii*) Trends of (*i*) for past few years.
(*iii*) Net profit – Preference dividend/Ordinary dividend.
(*iv*) Trends of (*iii*) for past few years.

47.28
See text.

Answers to review questions for selected chapters from *Frank Wood's Business Accounting 2*

Answers to review questions

Note: All the answers are the work of the authors. None has been supplied by an examining body. The examining bodies accept no responsibility whatsoever for the accuracy or method of working in the answers given.

In order to save space, £ signs have been omitted from columns of figures, except where the figures refer to £000, or where the denomination needs to be specified. For the same reason, names of the organisations and dates are sometimes omitted, but only where they add little to an understanding of the answer.

10.1
(a)

Merton Manufacturing Co Ltd
Balance Sheet as at . . .

Non-current tangible assets			
Freehold land and buildings at cost			95,000
Plant and equipment at written-down value	(W1)		104,350
			199,350
Current assets			
Inventory		25,000	
Accounts receivable		50,000	
Bank	(W2)	14,150	
		89,150	
Current liabilities			
Accounts payable		63,500	
			288,500
Non-current liabilities			
8% loan notes	(W3)		150,000
			213,500
Net assets			75,000
Equity			
Called-up share capital			
150,000 50p ordinary shares	(W4)		75,000

Workings:

(W1)

	Capital Reduction	
Ordinary shares 50p (new)		Ordinary shares £1 (old) 90,000
(1 for 6 = 15,000 × 50p)	7,500	6% preference shares (old) 150,000
Ordinary shares 50p (new)		11½% loan notes (old) 100,000
(1 for 3 – preference –		Share premium written off 25,000
50,000 × 50p)	25,000	
8% loan notes		
(exchange for 11½%)	150,000	
Ordinary shares 50p		
(1 for every £4		
old loan note)	12,500	
Goodwill impaired written-off	50,000	
Retained profits written off	38,850	
Plant and equipment*	81,150	
	365,000	365,000

*Per (*vii*) of question – amount needed to balance.

(W2) Shares issued 60,000 shares × 50p = 30,000
Cash 30,000 – overdraft 15,850 = balance 14,150

(W3) See capital reduction – debit side (W1) new loan notes 150,000

(W4) See (W1) 7,500 + 25,000 + 12,500 + new shares issued for cash 30,000 =
75,000

(b) (Main points)

	Old shareholdings	*New shareholdings*
Expected profit	22,500	22,500
Less Interest 11½%	11,500	
8%		12,000
		10,500
Taxable profits	11,000	3,500
Less Corporation tax 33⅓%	3,667	7,000
Profits before dividends	7,333	–
Preference dividends – if profits sufficient	9,000	

10.1 (cont'd)

Before reconstruction

(Old) Preference shareholders

Before reconstruction it would have taken over five years at this rate before preference dividends payable, as the deficit of 38,850 of retained profits would have to be cleared off first.

(Old) Ordinary shares

Even forgetting the retained profits deficit, the preference dividends were bigger than available profits. This would leave nothing for the ordinary shareholder.

After reconstruction

The EPS is £7,000 ÷ 150,000 = 4.67p

If all profits are distributed the following benefits will be gained:

By old preference shareholders

50,000 shares × 4.67p   2,335

Plus any benefits from tax credits.

By old ordinary shareholders

15,000 shares × 4.67p   700

Plus any benefits from tax credits.

(c) Preference shareholders – points to be considered:

(i) What were prospects for income?

Based on projected earnings would have been no income for over five years, then earnings of 7,333 per annum if all profits distributed.

(ii) What are new prospects for income?

Total earnings of 7,000 per annum immediately.

(iii) Is it worth exchanging (i) for (ii)?

Obviously depends on whether forecasts are accurate or not. If the above are accurate would seem worthwhile.

(iv) What have preference shareholders given up?

The exchange consists of ordinary shares which are more risky than preference shares, both in terms of dividends and of payments on liquidation. Dividends will be lower than the 6% they were due previously, but it was not being paid.

(v) What have they gained?

Likelihood of dividends much sooner than the minimum of five years anticipated above.

10.2

(a) (*Narratives omitted*)

	Dr	Cr
Preference share capital	37,500	
Ordinary share capital	175,000	
Capital reduction		212,500
Preference shares reduced 25p each (0.25 × 150,000) and Ordinary shares reduced by 0.875 (200,000 × 0.875).		
Capital reduction	3,375	
Ordinary share capital		3,375
Ordinary shares issued re. preference dividend arrears, 27,000 × 0.125.		
Share premium	40,000	
Capital reduction		40,000
Share premium balance utilised.		
Provision for depreciation	62,500	
Capital reduction	72,500	
Plant and machinery		135,000
Plant and machinery written down to 75,000.		
Capital reduction	176,625	
Retained profits		114,375
Preliminary expenses		7,250
Goodwill		55,000
Retained profits and intangible assets written off.		
Cash	62,500	
Ordinary share applicants		62,500
Applications for shares 500,000 × 0.125.		
Ordinary share applicants	62,500	
Ordinary share capital		62,500
500,000 ordinary shares issued.		

(b)

Balance Sheet as at 31 December 2005

Non-current assets			
Leasehold property at cost	80,000		
Less Provision for depreciation	30,000		
		50,000	
Plant and machinery at valuation		75,000	
			125,000
Current assets			
Inventory	79,175		
Accounts receivable	31,200		
Bank	11,500		
		121,875	
Total assets		246,875	
Current liabilities			
Accounts payable		43,500	
Net assets		203,375	
Equity			
Share capital:			
Preference shares		112,500	
Ordinary shares			
150,000 shares £0.75			
727,000 ordinary shares £0.125		90,875	
		203,375	

Quality Yarns Ltd

Balance Sheet as at 31 March 2002

Non-current assets		
Intangible: Goodwill and trademarks		30,000
Tangible: Plant and machinery		296,000
Furniture and fittings		4,000
		330,000
Current assets		
Inventory	190,200	
Accounts receivable	74,600	
Bank	255,600	
Cash	300	
		520,700
Total assets		850,700
Current liabilities		
Accounts payable	33,200	
Non-current liabilities		
Loan notes	300,000	
		333,200
		517,500
Equity		
Called-up share capital		517,500

10.3

The Journal (narratives omitted)

	Dr	Cr
(a) Preference share capital	20,000	
Capital reduction		20,000
(b) Ordinary share capital	437,500	
Capital reduction		437,500
(c) Capital reserve	60,000	
Capital reduction		60,000
(d) Preference share capital	80,000	
Ordinary share capital	437,500	
New ordinary share capital		517,500
(e) (i) Loan note holders	300,000	
Loan notes		300,000
(ii) Bank	300,000	
Loan note holders		300,000
(f) Capital reduction	517,500	
Goodwill etc.		250,000
Plant and machinery		24,000
Furniture		4,400
Retained profits		239,100

11.1

(a) Following is a brief answer:

(i) Such closure costs should be disclosed separately.

(ii) This should be adjusted in tax charge for 2007. Because it is not material (probably) it does not need to be disclosed separately.

(iii) The excess should be credited to a reserve account, and a note attached to the balance sheet. Depreciation to be based on revalued amount and on new estimate of remaining life of the asset, to be disclosed in a note to the accounts.

(iv) Treat as bad debt and write off to profit and loss.

(v) This is a prior period adjustment. The retained profit brought forward should be amended to allow for the change in accounting policy in the current year. The reasons: (1) it is material, (2) relates to a previous year, (3) as a result of change in accounting policy. The adjustment should be disclosed in a note to the financial statements.

11.2

(i) The replacement cost is irrelevant. The inventory should be shown at the cost of £26,500. This assumes historic cost accounts.

(ii) *Paramite*: inventory to be valued at direct costs £72,600 plus fixed factory overhead £15,300 = £87,900. Under no circumstances should selling expenses be included.

Paraton: as net realisable value is lower than the costs involved, this figure of £9,520 should be used (IAS 2).

11.2 (cont'd)

(iii) In this case there is a change of accounting policy. Accordingly a prior period adjustment will be made. On a straight line basis, net book value would have been:

Cost 160,000 less 12½% × 2 years =	120,000
Value shown	90,000
Therefore prior period adjustment of	30,000

to be added to retained profit at 1 November 2004.

For 2005 and each of the following five years depreciation will be charged at the rate of £20,000 per annum (IAS 16).

(iv) The cost subject to depreciation is £250,000 less land £50,000 = £200,000. With a life of 40 years this is £5,000 per annum.

This also will result in a prior period adjustment, in this case 10 × £5,000 = £50,000. This will be debited to retained profits at 1 November 2004. For 2005 and each of the following 29 years the yearly charge of depreciation will be £5,000 (IAS 16).

(v) Write off £17,500 to profit and loss.

(vi) As this development expenditure is almost definitely going to be recovered over the next four years it can be written off over that period (IAS 38).
Charge to profit and loss.

(vii) Charge to profit and loss.

(viii) As this is over 20%, it is material and appears to be long-term. This means that Lilleshall Ltd is an associate company and should be included in the financial statements on the equity basis. The post-acquisition profits to be brought in are 30% × £40,000 = £12,000.

11.5

The fact that this is a partnership does not mean that accounting standards are not applicable; they are just as applicable to a partnership as they are to a limited company.

(a) (i) These should be included as sales of £60,000 in the accounts for the year to 31 May 2007. This is because the matching concept requires that revenue, and the costs used up in achieving it, should be matched up. Profits: increase of £60,000.

(ii) Inventory values are normally based on the lower of cost or net realisable value. In this case it depends how certain it is that the inventory can be sold for £40,000. If a firm order can definitely be anticipated, then the figure of £40,000 can be used as this then represents the lower figure of net realisable value. Profit: an increase of £15,000. However, should the sale not be expected, then the concept of prudence dictates that the scrap value of £1,000 be used. Profit: a reduction of £24,000.

(b) It is important to establish the probability of the payment of the debt of £80,000. If it is as certain as it possibly can be that payment will be made, even though it may be delayed then no provision is needed. Profit change: nil.

However, the effect on future profits can be substantial. A note to the accounts detailing the possibilities of such changes should be given.

(c) The concepts which are applicable here are (i) going concern, (ii) consistency, (iii) accruals, (iv) prudence.

Following on the revelations in (b) and the effect on sales so far of the advertising campaign, is the partnership still able to see itself as a going concern? This would obviously affect the treatment of valuations of all assets.

Given that it can be treated as a going concern, the next point to be considered is that of consistency. The treatment of the expense item should be treated consistently.

The accruals concept is concerned with matching up revenues and costs, and will affect the decision as to how much of the costs should be carried forward. Some revenue in future periods needs to be expected with a high degree of certainty before any of this expenditure should be carried forward. It does not seem highly likely that large revenues can be expected in future in this case. In any case 75% is a very large proportion of such expenditure to be carried forward. There is no easy test of the validity of the partners' estimates. Granted that under IAS 38 for development expenditure some of it, under very stringent conditions, can be carried forward. If the partners' estimates can be accepted under this, then profits would be increased by 75% × (50,000 + 60,000) = £82,500.

(d) The expected profit/loss is as follows:

	Project A	Project B	Project C
Direct costs to date	30,000	25,000	6,000
Overheads to date	4,000	2,000	500
Future expected direct costs	10,000	25,000	40,000
Future expected overheads	2,000	2,000	3,000
Total of expected costs	46,000	54,000	49,500
Sale price of project	55,000	50,000	57,500
Expected total profit/loss	9,000	(4,000)	8,000
% Complete	75%	50%	15%

When a project is sufficiently near completion then a proportion of the profits can be taken as being realised.

Project A is 75% complete and this indicates profit being taken. Whether or not 75% can be taken, i.e. £6,750, will depend on the facts of the case. If completion at the above figures can be taken for granted then it might be reasonable to do so. Prudence dictates that a lesser figure be taken.

With project B there is an expected loss. Following the prudence concept losses should always be accounted for in full as soon as they become known.

In project C it is too early in the project, 15% completed, to be certain about the outcome. No profit should therefore be brought into account.

Profit, dependent on comments about project A, will therefore be increased by £6,750 − £4,000 = £2,750.

(e) This is a case where the examiner has dipped into topics from other subjects. What is needed here is a tree diagram to show the probabilities.

Address

Date

11.6

(a)

The Chief Accountant

Uncertain Ltd

Dear Sir/Mr . . . ,

Report on Draft Income Statement for the year ending 30 September 2006

Further to your letter/our meeting of . . . I would like to offer my suggestions for the appropriate accounting treatment of items (i) to (v).

(i) Redundancy payments: £100,000

The reorganisation had a material effect on the nature and focus of the reporting entity's operations. As a result, the costs should be shown separately on the face of the income statement along with the relevant taxation effect as one figure.

(ii) Closure costs of a factory

Profits or losses on the termination of an operation should be shown separately on the face of the income statement. In calculating the profit or loss in respect of the termination, consideration should only be given to revenue and costs directly related to it. Clearly, the costs have been identified and are known and there is a loss on the termination. It should not have been deducted from reserves; it must go through the income statement.

(iii) Change of basis of depreciation: £258,000

There should only be a change in the basis of depreciation if it brings about a fairer presentation of the accounting results and financial position of the company – see IAS 16. This should be treated as a change in accounting estimate (IAS 8) and should be recognised in profit or loss for this period. It is not a change in accounting policy.

Because the item is material, a note as to the details should be appended to the accounts.

(iv) Additional expenses covered by fire: £350,000

These expenses are covered by IAS 10 as post-reporting period non-adjusting events. The fire happened after the end of the reporting period, and therefore did not affect conditions as at that date. The figures in this year's financial statements, therefore, should not be altered.

If the event was such as to call into question the continuation of the business, then there should be a note to the financial statements on the going-concern basis. In this particular instance this does not seem to be the case, but good practice, although not necessary, would be to give details of the event in notes to the financial statements.

(v) Bad debt: £125,000

The accounts have not yet been approved by the directors, and it does affect the valuation of assets at the year end. IAS 10 would treat it as a post-reporting period adjusting event. It should therefore be written off as a bad debt.

Where it is considered to be material there should also be a note attached to the financial statements.

Should you like to have further discussions concerning any of the points raised, will you please contact me. I hope that you will find my comments to be of use.

Yours faithfully,

CACA

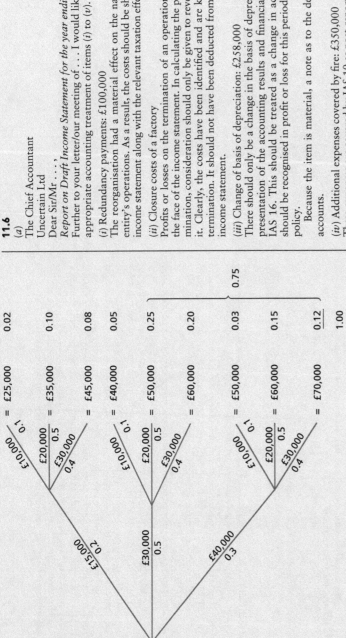

There is a probability of 0.75 of achieving £50,000 sales. As this is greater than the specified figure of 0.70 then the inventory should not be written down.

Effect on profits: nil.

(f) The opening inventory should be shown as the revised figure. If error had not been found this year's profit would have been £7,000 greater.

The adjustment should be shown as a prior period adjustment in the comparative informations in the current financial statements.

11.6 (cont'd)

(b)

Uncertain Ltd
Income Statement for the year ending 30 September 2006

Sales		5,450,490
Manufacturing cost of sales (W1)		2,834,500
		2,615,990
Administration expenses	785,420	
Selling expenses (W2)	1,013,600	
		1,799,020
Operating profit		816,970
Redundancy payments	100,000	
Discontinued operations – factory closure costs	575,000	
		675,000
Profit before tax		141,970
Corporation tax (50%) (W3)		70,985
Profit for the year		70,985

Reduction in profits for the period from draft income statement = £304,400

(W1) £3,284,500 − £100,000 (i) − £350,000 (iv) = £2,834,500
(W2) £629,800 + £258,800 (iii) + £125,000 (v) = £1,013,600
(W3) 50% of profits before tax

11.7

(a) (i) Post-reporting period events (also known as, 'post-balance sheet date events') consist of those events, whether favourable or unfavourable, which take place between the date of the balance sheet and the date on which the financial accounts and notes are approved by the directors.

(ii) Adjusting events are post-reporting period events which give extra evidence of what was happening at the balance sheet date. The events included may be included because they are either of a statutory nature or taken into account by convention.

(iii) Non-adjusting events are post-reporting period concerned with matters which did not exist at the balance sheet date.

(iv) A contingent asset/liability is concerned with something which seems to be apparent at the end of the reporting period but can only be verified by future events which are uncertain.

(b) Adjusting events: (i) debtor's inability to pay; (ii) subsequent discovery of frauds rendering accounts incorrect; (iii) when net realisable value is used for inventory valuation and later shown to be wrong when inventory sold; (iv) subsequent discovery of errors rendering accounts incorrect.
Non-adjusting events: (i) change in foreign exchange rates; (ii) strikes; (iii) nationalisation; (iv) share issues.

(c) (i) A material contingent liability should be accrued where some future event will give evidence of the loss, subject to the fact that it should be able to be determined with reasonable accuracy when the accounts are agreed by the directors.

(ii) Material contingent assets should be disclosed in the financial statements if it is very probable that they will be realised.

12.1 **Filo plc**

(i) (Internal)

Income Statement for the year ending 31 March 2005 (£000)

Sales			2,456.0
Less Returns inwards		108.0	
			2,348.0
Less Cost of sales:			
Inventory 1 April 2004		84.0	
Add Purchases	1,462.0		
Less Returns outwards	37.0		
		1,425.0	
Carriage inwards		14.7	
		1,523.7	
Less Inventory 31 March 2005		102.0	
			1,421.7
Gross profit			926.3
Distribution costs:			
Salaries and wages	34.0		
Rent and business rates	7.7		
General distribution expenses	28.0		
Motor expenses	6.4		
Depreciation: Motors	10.8		
Equipment	1.5		
		88.4	
Administrative expenses:			
Salaries and wages	102.0		
Rent and business rates	6.3		
General administrative expenses	24.0		
Motor expenses	9.6		
Auditors' remuneration	11.0		
Discounts allowed	36.0		
Bad debts	5.0		
Depreciation: Motors	18.4		
Equipment	1.2		
		213.5	
			301.9
			624.4
Other operating income: Royalties receivable			4.0
			628.4
Operating profit			
Income from associates and joint ventures		3.0	
Interest on bank deposit		6.0	
			9.0
			637.4
Interest payable: Loan-note interest			12.0
Profit before taxation			625.4
Taxation			364.0
Profit for the year			261.4
Retained profits from last year			102.0
			159.4
Transfer to general reserve		20.0	
Dividend paid		120.0	
			140.0
Retained profits carried forward to next year			19.4

(ii) (Published)   Filo plc
Income Statement for the year ending 31 March 2005 (£000)

Revenue		2,348.0
Cost of sales		1,421.7
Gross profit		926.3
Distribution costs	88.4	
Administrative expenses	213.5	301.9
		624.4
Other operating income		4.0
		628.4
Operating profit		
Income from associates and joint ventures	3.0	
Other interest receivable	6.0	9.0
		637.4
Interest payable		12.0
Profit before taxation		625.4
Taxation		364.0
Profit for the year		261.4

Administrative expenses

Salaries and wages		74.0
Rent and business rates		16.8
Motor expenses		6.0
General administrative expenses		6.0
Bad debts		2.0
Discounts allowed		11.0
Auditors' remuneration		14.0
Directors' remuneration		36.0
Depreciation: Motors		6.5
Plant and machinery		4.5
		176.8
Less Discounts received		14.0
		162.8

Operating profit		
Income from associates		5.0
Interest from government securities		3.0
		8.0
Amount written off investment in related companies		26.0
Loan-note interest		2.0
		28.0
Profit before taxation		318.5
Taxation		104.0
Profit for the year		214.5
Retained profits from last year		94.0
		308.5
Transfer to loan-note redemption reserve	25.0	
Dividend paid	60.0	85.0
Retained profits for the year		223.5

12.2

(i) (Internal)   State plc
Income Statement for the year ending 31 December 2008 (£000)

Sales			1,860.0
Less Returns inwards			9.0
			1,851.0
Less Cost of sales:			
Inventory 1 January 2008		140.0	
Add Purchases	1,140.0		
Less Returns outwards	5.0	1,135.0	
Carriage inwards		8.0	
		1,283.0	
Less Inventory 31 December 2008		160.0	
Cost of goods sold		1,123.0	
Wages		88.0	
Depreciation of plant and machinery		9.0	1,220.0
Gross profit			631.0

Distribution costs

Salaries and wages	62.0
Rent and business rates	11.2
Motor expenses	18.0
General distribution expenses	12.0
Haulage costs	4.0
Depreciation: Motors	15.0
Plant and machinery	7.5
	129.7

Distribution costs	129.7	
Administrative expenses	162.8	292.5
Operating profit		338.5

(ii) (Published)   State plc
Income Statement for the year ending 31 December 2008 (£000)

Revenue		1,851.0
Cost of sales		1,220.0
Gross profit		631.0
Distribution costs	129.7	
Administrative expenses	162.8	292.5
Operating profit		338.5
Income from associates	5.0	
Other interest receivable	3.0	8.0
		346.5
Amount written off investments	26.0	
Interest payable	2.0	28.0
Profit before taxation		318.5
Taxation		104.0
Profit for the year		214.5

12.3

(a)

Rufford plc

Income Statement for the year ended 31 March 2006

	Notes	£000	£000
Revenue	(1)		642
Cost of sales (60 + 401 – 71)			390
Gross profit			252
Distribution costs (33 + 19)		52	
Administrative expenses (97 + 8)		105	157
Operating profit	(2)		95
Loss on disposal of discontinued operations	(3)		12
			83
Income from other non-current asset investments	(4)	14	
Other interest receivable		25	39
			122
Interest payable	(5)		6
Profit before taxation			116
Taxation: Current tax	(6)	35	
Deferred tax		9	44
Profit for the year			72

Notes to the accounts:

1 Turnover is net of VAT.

2 Operating profit is shown after charging the following:

	£000	£000
Depreciation: distribution costs	19	
administrative expenses	8	27
Auditor's remuneration		20
Directors' emoluments		45
Hire of plant		12

3 Factory closure expenses.

4 Income from non-current asset investment is in respect of a listed company.

5 Interest payable is on a bank overdraft, repayable within five years.

6 Tax on profit:

	£000
Corporation tax at 50% on profits	38
Overprovision in 2005	(3)
	35

7 Dividends:

	£000
Interim 5p per share	21
Final: proposed 10p per share	42
	63

8 Earnings per share:
EPS of 17.1p per share based on earnings of £72,000 and on average 420,000 shares on issue throughout the year.

(b)

Balance Sheet extracts as at 31 March 2006

	£000	£000
Current liabilities		
Taxation (W1)		35
Non-current liabilities		
Deferred taxation (W2)		33
Workings:		£000
(W1) Corporation tax for year to 31 March 2006		35
(W2) Deferred tax as given		24
Charged to profit or loss		9
		33

13.1

Polk Ltd

Balance Sheet as at 31 March 2004 (£000)

	£000	£000	£000
Called-up share capital not paid			1
Non-current assets			
Intangible assets			
Development costs	32		
Goodwill	104	136	
Tangible assets			
Land and buildings	230		
Plant and machinery	45	275	
Investments			
Shares in associate entities		70	
			481
Current assets			
Inventory:			
Raw materials and consumables	6		
Finished goods and goods for resale	36	42	
Trade accounts receivable	24		
Amounts owed by associate entities	10		
Prepayments	2	36	
Total assets			560
Current liabilities			
Loan notes	20		
Bank overdrafts	16		
Trade accounts payable	17		
Bills of exchange payable	3	56	
Non-current liabilities			
Loan notes	30		
Bills of exchange payable	1	31	
Net assets		87	
			473

Equity

Called-up share capital		350
Share premium account		50
Other reserves:		
Capital redemption reserve	10	
General reserve	20	
		30
Retained profits		43
		473

Notes:

(i) Called-up share capital consists of:

50,000 £1 ordinary shares	250
50,000 preference shares of 50p each	100
	350

(ii) Land and buildings:

Cost		250
Depreciation to 31 March 2003	15	
Depreciation for year to 31 March 2004	5	
		20
		230

(iii) Plant and machinery:

Cost		75
Depreciation to 31 March 2003	22.5	
Depreciation for year to 31 March 2004	7.5	
		30
		45

Current liabilities

Loan notes	50	
Bank loans and overdrafts	3	
Trade accounts payable	26	
Bills of exchange payable	5	
Other accounts payable including taxation and social security	39	
		123

Non-current liabilities

Loan notes	40	
Trade accounts payable	2	
		42

Provisions:

Pensions and similar obligations	8	
Taxation, including deferred taxation	6	
		14
Net assets		179
		255

Equity

Called-up share capital	60	100
Share premium	23	
Revaluation reserve	30	
General reserve	7	
Foreign exchange reserve	35	
Retained profits		155
		255

Notes appended to the accounts on the details of tangible assets and depreciation, also exact details of items lumped under group descriptions.

13.3   **Baganza plc**

Income Statement for the year ending 30 September 2007 (£000)

Revenue		21,360
Cost of sales (W1)		14,700
Gross profit		6,660
Distribution costs	600	
Administrative expenses (W2)	1,390	
		1,990
		4,670
Other operating income (W3)		249
Profit before taxation		4,919
Taxation: Current tax (W4)	830	
Deferred tax	40	
		870
Profit for the year		4,049
Earnings per share (W6)		337.4p

13.2   **Tickers plc**

Balance Sheet as at 30 April 2007 (£000)

Non-current assets			
Intangible assets			
Concessions, patents, licences, trade marks and similar rights and assets	6		
Goodwill	42		
		48	
Tangible assets			
Land and buildings	200		
Plant and machinery	43		
		243	
			291
Current assets			
Inventory:			
Raw materials and consumables	24		
Work in progress	9		
Finished goods and goods for resale	21		
	84		
		54	
Trade accounts receivable			
Other accounts receivable	3		
Prepayments and accrued income	2		
		89	
			143
Total assets			434

13.3 (cont'd)

Workings (in £000):

(W1) Opening inventory 2,300 + Purchases 16,000 – Closing inventory 3,600 = 14,700

(W2) Per trial balance 400 + Research 75 + Depreciation: Property (5% × 2,700) 135 + Plant (15% × 5,200) 780 = 1,390

(W3) Dividends received 249

(W4) Corporation tax 850 – Overpayment last year 20 = 830

(W6) EPS = Profit 4,049,000 ÷ Shares 1,200,000 = 337.4p

Baganza plc
Balance Sheet as at 30 September 2007

	£000	£000	£000
Non-current assets			
Tangible assets			
Land and buildings	2,305		
Plant and machinery	820	3,125	
Investments		2,000	
			5,125
Current assets			
Inventory		3,600	
Accounts receivable		2,700	
Cash at bank		60	
			6,360
Total assets			11,485
Current liabilities			
Trade accounts payable	2,900		
Corporation tax	850		
	3,750		
Non-current liabilities			
Deferred tax	500		
		4,250	
		7,235	
Equity			
Called-up share capital		1,200	
Retained profits (2,022 – 36 + 4,049)		6,035	
		7,235	

Note: The proposed dividend should appear as a note to the income statement.

15.1

Operating activities; investing activities; financing activities.

15.3

Lee Ltd
Statement of Cash Flows (using the direct method)
for the year ending 31 December 2004

Cash flows from operating activities		
Cash received from customers	6,550	
Cash paid to suppliers	(2,875)	
Cash paid to employees	(2,025)	
Other cash payments	(600)	
Cash generated from operations	1,050	
Interest paid	(100)	
Net cash from operating activities		950
Cash flows from investing activities		
Payments to acquire tangible assets	(700)	
Net cash used in investing activities		(700)
Cash flows from financing activities		
Payment to repurchase loan notes	(100)	
Equity dividends paid	(50)	
Net cash used in financing activities		(150)
Net increase in cash and cash equivalents		100
Cash and cash equivalents at beginning of period		100
Cash and cash equivalents at end of period		200

15.5

See text of Chapter 15, Section 15.2.

15.6

Nimmo Limited

Statement of Cash Flows (using the indirect method) for the year ending 31 December 2009 (£000)

Cash flows from operating activities		
Profit before taxation		20,400
Adjustments for:		
Depreciation	5,050	
Loss on sale of non-current assets	700	
Increase in inventories	(7,000)	
Increase in trade accounts receivable	(18,100)	
Increase in prepayments	(100)	
Increase in trade accounts payable	4,000	
Increase in accruals	200	
		(15,250)
Cash generated from operations		5,150
Taxation paid		(3,200)
Net cash from operating activities		1,950
Cash flows from investing activities		
Purchase of tangible non-current assets	(11,800)	
Proceeds from sale of tangible non-current assets	1,000	
Net cash used in investing activities		(10,800)
Cash flows from financing activities		
Proceeds from issue of loan notes	150	
Dividends paid	(8,100)	
Net cash used in financing activities		(7,950)
Net decrease in cash and cash equivalents		(16,800)
Cash and cash equivalents at beginning of period		600
Cash and cash equivalents at end of period		(16,200)

Working:
Loss on sale of non-current asset = 1,000 − (5,500 − 3,800) = (700)

15.7

Track Limited

Statement of Cash Flows (using the indirect method) for the year ending 30 June 2011 (£000)

Cash flows from operating activities		
Profit before tax		180
Adjustments for:		
Depreciation	110	
Profit on sale of non-current assets	(5)	
Increase in inventories	(300)	
Increase in trade accounts receivable	(200)	
Increase in trade accounts payable	120	
		(275)
Cash generated from operations		(95)
Taxation paid		(230)
Net cash used in operating activities		(325)
Cash flows from investing activities		
Purchase of non-current assets	(175)	
Proceeds from sale of non-current assets	150	
Proceeds from sale of investments	20	
Net cash used in investing activities		(5)
Cash flows from financing activities		
Proceeds from issue of share capital	300	
Dividend paid	(130)	
Net cash from financing activities		170
Net decrease in cash and cash equivalents		(160)
Cash and cash equivalents at beginning of period		100
Cash and cash equivalents at end of period		(60)

Working:
Profit on sale of non-current assets = 20 − (25 − 10) = (5)

15.9

(a)

Baker Limited

Forecast net cash position for the three quarters ending 30 September 2007

	Quarter to		
	31 March 2007 £000	30 June 2007 £000	30 Sept 2007 £000
Receipts			
Trade accounts receivable (W1)	235	290	345
Tangible non-current assets	12	–	–
Investments	10	–	–
Loan notes	–	–	50
	257	290	395
Payments			
Trade accounts payable (W2)	150	230	285
Administration, selling and distribution expenses	37	40	42
Tangible non-current assets	–	240	–
Investments	–	–	5
Taxation	8	–	–
Dividend	15	–	–
	210	510	332
Forecast net cash flow	47	(220)	63
Add Opening cash	80	127	(93)
Forecast closing cash	127	(93)	(30)

Workings:

(W1) Trade accounts receivable: forecast cash receivable:

	31 March 2007 £000	30 June 2007 £000	30 Sept 2007 £000
Sales	250	300	350
Less Closing trade accounts receivable	65	75	80
	185	225	270
Add Opening trade accounts receivable	50	65	75
Forecast cash receipts from trade accounts receivable	235	290	345

(W2) Trade accounts payable: forecast cash payable:

	31 March 2007 £000	30 June 2007 £000	30 Sept 2007 £000
Opening inventory	40	30	40
Purchases (by deduction)	190	250	295
	230	280	335
Less Closing inventory	30	40	55
Cost of sales	200	240	280

	31 March 2007 £000	30 June 2007 £000	30 Sept 2007 £000
Purchases (as above)	190	250	295
Less Closing trade accounts payable	120	140	150
	70	110	145
Add Opening trade accounts payable	80	120	140
Forecast cash payments to trade accounts payable	150	230	285

(b)

Baker Limited

Forecast Statement of Cash Flows (using the direct method)
for the nine months ending 30 September 2007 (£000)

Cash flows from operating activities		
Profit before tax		34
Adjustments for:		
Depreciation	27	
Increase in inventory	(15)	
Increase in trade accounts receivable	(30)	
Increase in trade accounts payable	70	52
Cash generated from operations		86
Taxation		(23)
Net cash from operating activities		63
Cash flows from investing activities		
Purchase of non-current assets	(240)	
Proceeds from sale of non-current assets	12	
Net cash used in investing activities		(228)
Cash flows from financing activities		
Proceeds from issue of loan notes	50	
Net cash from financing activities		50
Net decrease in cash and cash equivalents		(115)
Cash and cash equivalents at beginning of period		95
Cash and cash equivalents at end of period		(20)

Workings:

Cash and cash equivalents at beginning of period = 80 + 15 = 95

Cash and cash equivalents at end of period = (30) + 10 = (20)

27.1

Solvency, profitability, efficiency, capital structure and shareholder.

27.3

Solvency	– *see* text, Section 27.3
Profitability	– *see* text, Section 27.2
Efficiency	– *see* text, Section 27.4
Capital structure	– *see* text, Section 27.6
Shareholder	– *see* text, Section 27.5

27.5

(a) inventory turnover

(i) (b) and (d).
(ii) (b) and (d).
(iii) (d).
(iv) If current liabilities greater than current assets, (b) and (d);
if current assets greater than current liabilities, (a) and (c).
(v) (b) and (d) but only after a customer takes up the offer.

27.9

(a) (i) Gross profit as % of revenue: $\dfrac{400}{1,800} \times \dfrac{100}{1} = 22.2\%$ $\dfrac{410}{2,700} \times \dfrac{100}{1} = 15.2\%$

(ii) Net profit as % of revenue: $\dfrac{60}{1,800} \times \dfrac{100}{1} = 3.3\%$ $\dfrac{90}{2,700} \times \dfrac{100}{1} = 3.3\%$

(iii) Expenses as % of revenue: $\dfrac{340}{1,800} \times \dfrac{100}{1} = 18.9\%$ $\dfrac{320}{2,700} \times \dfrac{100}{1} = 11.9\%$

(iv) Inventory turnover: $\dfrac{1,400}{(300 + 200) \div 2} = 5.6 \text{ times}$ $\dfrac{2,290}{(280 + 240) \div 2} = 8.8 \text{ times}$

(v) Rate of return (ROCE): $\dfrac{60}{(240 + 230) \div 2} \times \dfrac{100}{1} = 25.5\%$ $\dfrac{90}{(430 + 440) \div 2} \times \dfrac{100}{1} = 20.7\%$

(vi) Current ratio: $\dfrac{409}{245} = 1.67$ $\dfrac{382}{252} = 1.52$

(vii) Acid test ratio: $\dfrac{209}{245} = 0.85$ $\dfrac{142}{252} = 0.56$

(viii) Accounts receivable : revenue ratio: $\dfrac{205}{1,800} \times 12 = 1.37 \text{ months}$ $\dfrac{140}{2,700} \times 12 = 0.62 \text{ months}$

(ix) Accounts payable : purchases ratio: $\dfrac{245}{1,300} \times 12 = 2.26 \text{ months}$ $\dfrac{252}{2,250} \times 12 = 1.34 \text{ months}$

(b) Business B has made more net profit (£90,000 compared with £60,000) but, in terms of capital employed, B has only managed to achieve a return of 20.7% whereas A has managed a return of 25.5%. A is clearly more efficient in the use of its resources. Reasons are as follows – possibly – as not until you know more about the business could you give a definite answer.

(i) B managed to sell far more merchandise but at lower prices, i.e. took only 15.2% margin as compared with A's 22.2% margin.

(ii) Maybe less efficient use of mechanised means in the business by B. Note that assuming A and B both use similar depreciation rates, B has more equipment and it is considerably newer than A's.

(iii) B did not have as much inventory lying idle. B turned over inventory 8.8 times in the year as compared with 5.6. This could indicate inefficient purchasing by A and/or a likelihood of zero inventory and, so, loss of sales. B managed to sell far more merchandise but at lower prices, i.e. took only

(iv) While A waited (on average) 1.37 months to be paid by customers. B managed to collect in 0.62 months on average. Money represented by debts is money lying idle. However, A took longer (2.26 months) to pay its creditors than B (1.34 months). It appears that A was therefore less efficient in controlling its debtors whereas B was less efficient in controlling its creditors' payments. Overall, these two results probably cancel each other out so far as explaining A's higher rate of return.

It appears that the key factor may be the less efficient use of its assets by B. A has less than ⅓ of the resources tied up in fixed assets than B, yet has 67% of B's sales and 67% of B's net profit.

27.11

(a) The ratios reveal that L Ltd's relative profitability has fallen between the two years. The gross and net profit margins have both fallen, but this may be due to the new sales manager's price-cutting policy, rather than because of any change in costs.

The fall in return on capital employed is not what was hoped for from the new sales price policy. A drop from 31% to 18% is significant and suggests that the change in sales price policy and the investment in new machinery, although with the related increased borrowings, have led to short-term depressed returns. If the increased market resulting from the new sales policy can be retained, it would be worthwhile considering an increase in sales price to a point where a higher rate of return would be achieved.

The company appears solvent – there is no shortage of liquid assets. However, it has taken on considerably more long-term debt in order to fund the market expansion. This will have to be serviced and the level of profit should be monitored to ensure that margins do not fall further, raising the current level of risk to unacceptable levels. As 38.2% (£192,000) of net profits before interest (£502,000) is already being used to meet debt interest payments, compared with only 3.8% in 2002, it would not take very large changes in costs or selling price to cause this to become a major problem. The current level of gearing will also inhibit the company's ability to raise additional loan funding in future.

27.11 (*cont'd*)

Profitability

	2002	2003
Gross profit : revenue	$\frac{540}{900} \times 100 = 60\%$	$\frac{1,120}{2,800} \times 100 = 40\%$
Net profit : revenue	$\frac{302}{900} \times 100 = 34\%$	$\frac{310}{2,800} \times 100 = 11\%$
ROCE	$\frac{302 + 12}{929 + 100} = 31\%$	$\frac{310 + 192}{1,267 + 1,600} = 18\%$

Solvency

Current ratio	$\frac{125}{36} = 3.47 : 1$	$\frac{821}{186} = 4.41 : 1$
Acid test ratio	$\frac{125 - 30}{36} = 2.63 : 1$	$\frac{821 - 238}{186} = 3.13 : 1$

Capital structure

Capital gearing	$\frac{100}{100 + 929} = 10\%$	$\frac{1,600}{1,600 + 1,267} = 56\%$

(*b*) Current accounts receivable collection period = $\frac{583}{2,800} \times 365 = 76$ days.

If the collection period were 45 days, the new accounts receivable amount would be:

$$\frac{45}{76} \times 583,000 = 345,200$$

The amount released if a 45-day accounts receivable collection period could be imposed would be £237,800.

28.1

(*a*)

Income Statements for the year ended 31 December 2009

	X		Y	
Revenue		480,000		762,500*
Less Cost of goods sold		400,000		610,000
Gross profit		80,000		152,500
Less Admin. expenses	(−10,000) 40,000		(+10,000) 57,500	
Selling expenses	15,000 (−2,500)	55,000	35,000	92,500
		25,000		
Net profit				60,000

*Assumed 25% mark-up despite wrong inventory valuation.

(*b*) *Profitability:*

Gross profit %

	X	Y
	20%	25%
Net profit %	$\frac{25}{480} \times \frac{100}{1} = 5.2\%$	$\frac{60}{762.5} \times \frac{100}{1} = 7.87\%$
Inventory turnover	$\frac{400,000}{40,000} = 10$ times	$\frac{610,000}{45,000^*} = 13.6$ times

* Adjusted to take into account inaccurate valuation.

Return on capital employed (ROCE) (previous owners)

X	Y
$\frac{25,000}{200,000} \times \frac{100}{1} = 12.5\%$	$\frac{60,000}{350,000} \times \frac{100}{1} = 17.14\%$

Based on purchase price of business the ROCE for Adrian Frampton would be:

X	Y
$\frac{25,000}{190,000} \times \frac{100}{1} = 13.15\%$	$\frac{60,000}{400,000} \times \frac{100}{1} = 15\%$

All ratios are favourable for Y. If gross profit ratios remained the same in future together with other expenses then Y business is best value.

However:
(i) Can gross profit ratios of X be improved as compared with those of Y?
(ii) Can inventory turnover be improved?

If so, then X could be cheapest business to buy as it gives a better ROCE.

(*c*) (i) Need to know current assets and current liabilities in detail.
   (ii) Are these similar businesses?
       Type of business
       Areas in which situated
       Competition
       Prefer several years' financial statements to gauge trends
       Quality of staff and whether they would continue.

28.2

(*a*) 2006

	A £000		B £000		C £000	
Return on capital of 20% = Profit*		120.0		120.0		120.0
Interest *less* tax	–		24.0 — 10.8 (13.2)		66.0 — 29.7 (36.3)	
Profit for ordinary shares		120.0		109.2		90.3
Ordinary share capital		600		400		50
Profit return (%)		20		27.3		180.6

2007

Return on capital of 10% = Profit	60.0		60.0	60.0
Interest less tax	–	24.0	66.0	60.0
		13.2	36.3	
Profit for ordinary shares	60.0	10.8	29.7	
		49.2	30.3	
Ordinary share capital	600	400	50	
Profit return (%)	10	12.3	60.6	

*Profit is assumed to be after tax but before interest.

(b) High gearing accentuates the rate of return to the ordinary shareholder. In the zero-geared position of Company A the return to the shareholder simply reflects the change in profits earned on trading. In the high-geared position of Company C the return to the shareholder decreases from 180.6% to 60.6%, i.e. to a reduction of 66.5% as profits reduce by only 50%. Company B reflects an intermediate position with a relatively moderate level of gearing.

High gearing increases risk to shareholders for two reasons. First, if the profits earned are not sufficiently high to meet interest charges then the company may find itself failing since the lenders may seek a winding-up order. Second, the risk is increased simply because of exaggerated fluctuations in the returns which are accentuated in the high-geared situation.

However, it can be seen that if profits earned are higher than the interest rate, this will produce a significantly higher return to the shareholder in a high-geared company. The fact that interest is allowed as a deduction for tax purposes indicates that gearing may give an overall advantage. The market's assessment of the risk position will counter this, and will be based on the nature of the business and management.

28.4

(a) Refer to the text.

(b)

	Company A £000	%	Company B £000	%
Ordinary shares	300		800	
Revenue: Share premium	300		400	
Retained profit	400		200	
	1,000	62.5	1,400	87.5
8% preference shares	200		–	
10% loan notes			200	
12% loan notes	400		200	
	600	37.5	200	12.5
Total share capital and loan notes	1,600	100.0	1,600	100.0

Company A Debt : Equity $= \dfrac{37.5}{62.5} = 60\%$

$\dfrac{12.5}{87.5}$

B Debt : Equity $= \dfrac{12.5}{87.5} = 14.3\%$

(c) Company A is more highly geared than B since it is committed to paying a higher proportion of fixed dividend and interest payments for its profits. A higher level of gearing increases risk. (Note the answer in 28.2 (b) is appropriate.)

(d)

	A	B
Trading profit before interest	200,000	200,000
Less Interest charges	48,000	20,000
Net profit after interest charge	152,000	180,000
Preference dividend	16,000	
Ordinary dividend	45,000	
	61,000	120,000
Retained profit	91,000	60,000

28.6

(a)

	2008	2009
Equity shares	100,000	150,000
Reserves	150,000	220,000
Total equity capital	250,000	370,000
Loans	40,000	40,000
Total capital employed	290,000	410,000
Profits (net after tax)	60,000	70,000
Return on total equity	24%	18.9%

(b) To Mr C. Black

The reduction in profits from 24% to 18.9% of total equity needs to be analysed into its causal factors. During the year the net profits have increased but not as fast as the equity capital which has gone up by £120,000 over the year. If the increase reflected an investment late in 2008/9 it would reduce returns because a full year's profit could not be earned.

It is therefore essential to examine the nature of the investment and the future. Before shares are bought it is essential to examine future prospects. If these are good, the historic analysis may not be important. However, if the new funds were used – clearly prospects may not be good and shares should not be bought.

(c) Reserves are profits retained within the business. The profits may be from revenue, i.e. from profits which could be distributed as dividends to shareholders or capital – for example where fixed amounts are revalued upwards to reflect current market value.

The creation of reserves reflects an increase in capital in the organisation which would normally be to reflect an increasing scale of operation. In this sense reserves reflect an alternative to issuing new shares. In the case of capital reserves from revaluation – these are simply 'paper adjustments' to value which do not in themselves indicate more resources in the organisation.

Revenue reserves may in fact be distributed as dividends whereas capital reserves would not normally be available for this purpose and are more akin to share capital.

28.8

(a)   Income Statements for the year to 31 March 2008

	Chan plc £000	Ling plc £000	Wong plc £000
Operating profit	300	300	300
Interest payable	–	–	(10)
Profit on ordinary activities before tax	300	300	290
Taxation (30%)	(90)	(90)	(87)
Profit after tax	210	210	203

(b)   Changes in retained profits

	Chan plc	Ling plc	Wong plc
Opening balance	?	?	?
Profit for the year	210	210	203
Dividends paid: Preference	–	(20)	(30)
Ordinary	(100)	(60)	(40)
Increase over the year	110	130	133

(c) (i)   Earnings per share

	Chan plc	Ling plc	Wong plc
Net profit after tax and preference dividend	$\dfrac{210}{500}$	$\dfrac{210-20}{300}$	$\dfrac{203-30}{200}$
Number of ordinary shares in issue =			
=	42p	63.3p	86.5p

(ii)   Price/earnings ratio

	Chan plc	Ling plc	Wong plc
$\dfrac{\text{Market price of ordinary shares}}{\text{Earnings per share}}=$	$\dfrac{840}{42}$	$\dfrac{950}{63.3}$	$\dfrac{1{,}038}{86.5}$
=	20	15	12

(iii)   Gearing ratio

$$\frac{\text{Loan capital} + \text{preference shares} \times 100}{\text{Shareholders' funds}}$$

Chan plc $=$ Nil

Ling plc $= \dfrac{200}{300 + 100 + 130} \times 100 = 37.7\%$

Wong plc $= \dfrac{300 + 100}{200 + 100 + 133} \times 100 = 92.4\%$

(d) A gearing ratio expresses the relationship that exists between total borrowings (that is, preference share capital and long-term loans), and the total amount of ordinary shareholders' funds. It should be noted that other definitions of gearing are possible and are sometimes used.

Any company with a gearing ratio of, say, 70% would be considered to be high geared, while a company with a gearing ratio of, say, 20% would be low geared.

Gearing is an important matter to consider when investing in ordinary shares in a particular company. A *high*-geared company means that a high proportion of the company's earnings are committed to paying either interest on any loan notes and/or dividends on any preference share capital *before* an ordinary dividend can be declared. If a company is low geared, then a high proportion of the company's earnings can be paid out as ordinary dividends.

Chan plc has not issued any loan notes or any preference share capital. Gearing does not, therefore, apply to this company, and all of the earnings may be paid out to the ordinary shareholders.

Ling plc is a relatively low-geared company. It has no loan notes, and only a small proportion of its earnings are committed to paying its preference shareholders. The balance may then all be declared as an ordinary dividend.

Wong plc is an extremely high-geared company. A high proportion of borrowings (in this case consisting of both loan notes and preference share capital) means that a high proportion of its earnings has to be set aside for both its loan-note holders and its preference shareholders before any ordinary dividend can be declared. As a result, if the profits of the company are low, no ordinary dividend may be payable.

If profits are rising, a high-geared company may not be a particularly risky company in which to purchase some ordinary shares, but the reverse may apply if profits are falling.

For the year to 31 March 2008, Chan, Ling and Wong's operating profit is identical. Wong is committed to paying interest on its loan notes (which is allowable against tax), and both Ling and Wong have to pay a preference dividend (which is *not* allowable against tax).

In deciding whether to invest in any of the three companies, there are a great many other factors to be considered, including future prospects of all three companies. However, when profits are fluctuating an ordinary shareholder is more likely to receive a higher return by investing in Chan than by investing in either Ling or Wong. Similarly, an ordinary shareholder can expect a higher return by investing in Wong.

Based on the limited amount of information given in the question, therefore, an investor considering purchasing ordinary shares in only one of these three companies would be recommended to buy shares in Chan plc.

It should be noted that if profits were *increasing*, an investor would be recommended to buy shares first in Wong, then in Ling and finally in Chan. The earnings per share in both Ling and Wong are far higher than in Chan, so there is a much greater chance of an increase in the ordinary dividend, but this is not necessarily the case if profits are falling or fluctuating.

(i) Forecast Dividends

	2006 £000	2007 £000	2008 £000
Forecast profits	1,800	500	2,200
Less Corporation tax (30%)	540	150	660
	1,260	350	1,540
Dividends to be paid in following year	1,260	350	1,540

Balance sheet extracts

Shareholders' equity

	2006 £000	2007 £000	2008 £000
Issued ordinary shares of £1 each fully paid	6,000	6,000	6,000
Share premium account	1,000	1,000	1,000
Retained profits (1,650 + 1,260 − 630; 2,280	2,000	3,190	
2,910 − 1,260 + 350; 2,000 − 350 + 1,540)	9,280	9,000	10,190

Note

Dividends paid	630	1,260	350

(ii) Forecast Dividends

	2006 £000	2007 £000	2008 £000
Forecast profits	1,800	500	2,200
Less interest (12% × £2m)	240	240	240
	1,560	260	1,960
Less Corporation tax (30%)	468	78	588
	1,092	182	1,372
Dividends to be paid in following year	1,092	182	1,372

Balance Sheet extracts

Shareholders' equity

	2006 £000	2007 £000	2008 £000
Issued ordinary shares of £1, each fully paid	5,000	5,000	5,000
Retained profits (1,650 + 1,092; 2,742	1,832	3,022	
2,742 − 1,092 + 182; 1,832 − 182 + 1,372)	7,742	6,832	8,022

Non-current liabilities

12% loan notes	2,000	2,000	2,000

Note

Dividends paid	630	1,092	182

(b) (i) If planned expansion is financed by share issue, the forecast return on shareholders' equity for the next three years will be:

2006 1,260/9,910 × 100 = 12.7%
2007   350/9,000 × 100 =   3.9%
2008 1,540/10,190 × 100 = 15.1%

(ii) If planned expansion is financed by issuing loan, the forecast return on shareholders' equity for the next three years will be:

2006 1,092/7,742 × 100 = 14.1%
2007   182/6,832 × 100 =   2.7%
2008 1,372/8,022 × 100 = 17.1%

Note: All the above figures are, of course, net of tax and should be grossed by a factor of 100/70 if comparison with gross interest rates is to be made (on the assumption of 30% tax rate).

(c) The return on shareholders' equity for the year ended 30 September 2005 was 630/6,650 = 9.5% (although the shareholders only received 600 of the 630 profit so their actual return received was slightly less). To have the return fluctuate between 2.7% and 17.1%, as it will do if the planned expansion is financed by the loan-notes issue, will surely unnerve all but the most sturdy shareholders. Such a violent swing from year to year will confuse, confound and alarm anyone looking at the shares as an investment.

To finance the planned expansion by a share issue does not improve matters greatly, as it will be seen that the return fluctuates between 3.9% and 15.1%. But since we are told that the industry is 'subject to marked variations in consumer demand' it does seem more appropriate to use share capital (by definition risk-bearing) rather than a loan note. The poor profits forecast for 2007 suggest that it would not take much of a variation from the expected results to show no profit at all, and were this to occur, is there not a possibility that the loan note holders could not be paid their due interest? Failure to pay loan note interest on time would then be to collect not only the unpaid interest but the capital as well, as failure to pay interest would be a breach of the conditions under which the loan notes were issued.

Under both options shareholders are to miss a year's dividends as a result of the dividend for 2005 having been paid during the year and the 2006 dividend not being paid until 2007. The directors can expect a stormy annual general meeting, but that is far less dangerous than the entry of a receiver.

In practice, of course, it is unusual for a company to pay out all profits as dividends, and since shareholders will pay more attention usually to the level of dividends paid than to profits earned, it would make better financial sense if the 2006 dividend were maintained at or slightly above the 2005 level, enabling an addition to be made to retained profits. This in turn would enable a fund to be built up to supplement current profits for dividends and/or to redeem the loan notes.

The all-shares or all-loan-notes choice is also an unrealistic one. Although there is much to be said for a broad share base to support what is obviously a risky business, it could make better sense to raise part of the required £2,000,000 by shares and part by loan notes. A restrained dividend policy coupled with the use of the (probably enlarged) depreciation charge arising after the expansion had taken place could enable a loan note redemption programme to be established over the course of the next few years.

28.12

(a) (i) *Shareholders*

	2006	2007
Earnings per share (EPS)	$\frac{9,520}{39,680} = 24\text{p}$	$\frac{11,660}{39,680} = 29.4\text{p}$

Dividend cover
(= EPS ÷ dividend per share)

$$\frac{24\text{p}}{(2,240 \div 39,680)} = \frac{24\text{p}}{5.6\text{p}} = 4.3 \text{ times}$$

$$\frac{29.4\text{p}}{(2,400 \div 39,680)} = \frac{29.4\text{p}}{6\text{p}} = 4.9 \text{ times}$$

Here the most important ratio is that of ROCE (return on capital employed). A's ROCE is 27.2% as compared with B's 15.6%.

The great difference in ROCE can be explained by reference to the secondary ratios of profit and asset utilisation. Both ratios are in A's favour. The profit ratios are A 34%: B 29%. The asset utilisation ratios are A 0.9%: B 0.6%, showing that A is utilising its assets 50% better than B. It is the effects of these two ratios that give the ROCE for each company.

The very low working capital employed by A Ltd very much affects the asset utilisation ratio. How far such a low working capital is representative of that throughout the whole year is impossible to say.

Liquidity

It would not be sensible to draw a final conclusion as to the liquidity positions of the two companies based on the balance sheet figures. As a balance sheet is based at one point in time it can sometimes be misleading, as a reading of figures over a period would be more appropriate.

A Ltd does appear to have a short-term liquidity problem, as the current assets only just cover current liabilities. The 'quick' or 'acid test ratio' on the face of it appears to be very inadequate at 0.6.

By contrast, B Ltd with a current ratio of 1.4 and a 'quick ratio' of 1.0 would appear to be reasonably liquid.

However, much more light is shed on the position of the companies when the debtor collection period is examined. A collects its debts with a credit period of nine weeks. In the case of B Ltd this rises to an astonishing 36.7 weeks. Why is this so? It could be due simply to very poor credit control by B Ltd. Such a long credit period casts considerable doubt on the real worth of the accounts receivable. There is a high probability that many of the debts may prove difficult to collect. It might be that B Ltd, in order to maintain sales, has lowered its requirements as to the creditworthiness of its customers. If the credit period were reduced to a normal one for the industry it might be found that many of the customers might go elsewhere.

The problem with accounts receivable in the case of B Ltd is also carried on to inventory. In the case of A Ltd the inventory turnover is 4.3 falling to 2.8 in B Ltd. There could be a danger that B Ltd has inventory increasing simply because it is finding it difficult to sell its products.

Capital gearing

A Ltd is far more highly geared than B Ltd: 39.6% as compared with 14.1%. A comparison with this particular industry by means of interfirm comparison should be undertaken.

Limitations of ratio analysis

You should bear in mind the following limitations of the analysis undertaken:

(i) One year's financial statements are insufficient for proper analysis to be undertaken. The analysis of trends, taken from, say, five years' accounts would give a better insight.

(ii) Differences in accounting policies between A Ltd and B Ltd will affect comparisons.

(iii) The use of historical costs brings about many distortions.

(iv) The use of industry interfirm comparisons would make the ratios more capable of being interpreted.

(v) The plans of the companies for the future expressed in their budgets would be of more interest than past figures.

28.12 (cont'd)

(ii) *Trade accounts payable*

	2006	2007
Current ratio	$\frac{92,447}{36,862} = 2.5$	$\frac{99,615}{42,475} = 2.3$
Acid test	$\frac{40,210 + 12,092}{36,862} = 1.4 : 1$	$\frac{43,370 + 5,790}{42,475} = 1.2 : 1$

(iii) *Internal management*

Accounts receivable ratio/Sales*

*Assumed credit sales	$\frac{40,210}{486,300} \times 52 = 4.3$ weeks	$\frac{43,370}{583,900} \times 52 = 3.9$

Return on capital employed

(before tax)	$\frac{15,254}{40,740} = 37.4\%$	$\frac{18,686}{50,000} = 37.4\%$

(b) *Shareholders*

EPS. An increase of 5.4p per share has occurred. This was due to an increase in profit without any increase in share capital.

Dividend cover. Increased by 0.6 times because increase in profit not fully reflected in dividends.

Trade creditors

Current ratio. This has fallen but only marginally and it still appears to be quite sound.

Acid test. This has also fallen, but still seems to be quite reasonable.

Internal management

Accounts receivable ratio. There appears to have been an increase in the efficiency of our credit control.

Return on capital employed. This has stayed the same for each of the two years. The increase in capital employed has seen a proportional increase in profits.

28.14.

To the Board of G plc

From   AN Other, Accountant

Subject: *Potential acquisition of either of companies A Ltd and B Ltd as subsidiaries in the machine tool manufacturing sector. Financial performances assessed.*

As instructed by you I have investigated the financial performances of these two companies to assist in the evaluation of them as potential acquisitions.

It should be borne in mind that financial ratio analysis is only partial information. There are many other factors which will need to be borne in mind before a decision can be taken.

The calculations of the various ratios are given as an appendix.

Profitability

While the main interest to the board is what G plc could obtain in profitability from A Ltd and B Ltd, all I can comment on at present is the current profitability enjoyed by these two companies.

31.1

See text, Section 31.6.

31.2

See text, Section 31.6. Difficulties lie in trying to give these measures a value in money that would get universal acceptance. How can you place a monetary value on living conditions, for example?

31.3

See text, Section 31.7.

31.4

Basically, there are many things that could be done to improve the various parts of 'social well-being'. However, (*a*) benefits cost a lot of money in the short term, and (*b*) beneficial effects are felt only in the long term. Examples are better education and better housing.

31.5

See text, Section 31.10, social programme measurement.

31.7

The accountant's model of income measurement, with its reliance upon data that can be expressed in financial terms, can be said to be too narrow and fails to consider wider social and environmental issues. The air we breathe does not have a 'price' in financial terms. Yet, what businesses do may cause costs to be incurred by others as a result of their abuse of the air in their environment. Similarly, the true cost of a natural resource may never be accounted for – the rainforests being a very well known example: they are being removed upon payment of a financially stated price, but the price only satisfies the seller, it does little to replace the environment being destroyed. Thus the price being added into the cost of manufacturing paper from the trees in the rainforests does not include the social and environmental cost of their destruction.

Thus, in the income model, it could be argued only in a narrow sense of the term that 'capital' is being maintained. In reality, the destruction of natural resources that are not or cannot be replaced means that the 'capital' is being consumed and future consumption impaired as a result.

It is for reasons of this type that it can be argued that accountants ought to be involved in disclosing the effects of a company's business activities upon its environment, for only by doing so will a true view of a company's activities be revealed.

32.1

See text, Section 32.1.

32.2

See text, Section 32.3.

32.3

See text, Section 32.4.

32.4

See text, Section 32.6.

---

usions

... pending on the price which would have to be paid for acquisition, I would suggest that A Ltd is the company most suitable for takeover.

A N Other
Accountant

Appendix

(i) *Return on capital employed*

	A Ltd	B Ltd
$\dfrac{\text{Profits before interest and tax}}{\text{Capital employed}}$	$\dfrac{211}{775} \times 100 = 27.2\%$	$\dfrac{88}{565} \times 100 = 15.6\%$

(ii) *Assets utilisation ratios*

		A Ltd	B Ltd
Total assets revenue:	$\dfrac{\text{Revenue}}{\text{Total assets}}$	$\dfrac{985}{1,140} = 0.9$	$\dfrac{560}{990} = 0.6$
Non-current assets revenue:	$\dfrac{\text{Revenue}}{\text{Non-current assets}}$	$\dfrac{985}{765} = 1.3$	$\dfrac{560}{410} = 1.4$
Working capital revenue:	$\dfrac{\text{Revenue}}{\text{Working capital}}$	$\dfrac{985}{10} = 98.5$	$\dfrac{560}{150} = 3.7$

(iii) *Profitability ratios*

		A Ltd	B Ltd
Gross profit % Revenue	$\dfrac{\text{Gross profit}}{\text{Revenue}}$	$\dfrac{335}{985} \times 100 = 34\%$	$\dfrac{163}{560} \times 100 = 29\%$
Profit before taxation and interest as % revenue	$\dfrac{211}{985} \times 100 = 21\%$	$\dfrac{88}{560} \times 100 = 16\%$

(iv) *Liquidity ratios*

		A Ltd	B Ltd
Current ratio:	$\dfrac{\text{Current assets}}{\text{Current liabilities}}$	$\dfrac{375}{365} = 1.0$	$\dfrac{580}{425} = 1.4$
Acid test or Quick ratio:	$\dfrac{\text{Current assets} - \text{Inventory}}{\text{Current liabilities}}$	$\dfrac{220}{365} = 0.6$	$\dfrac{440}{425} = 1.0$
Accounts receivable weeks:	$\dfrac{\text{Trade accounts receivable}}{\text{Credit sales}} \times 52$	$\dfrac{170}{985} \times 52 = 9 \text{ weeks}$	$\dfrac{395}{560} \times 52 = 36.7 \text{ weeks}$

(v) *Capital structure*

		A Ltd	B Ltd
Gearing ratio:	$\dfrac{\text{Long-term borrowing}}{\text{Shareholders' funds}}$	$\dfrac{220}{555} \times 100 = 39.6\%$	$\dfrac{70}{495} \times 100 = 14.1\%$
Proprietory ratio:	$\dfrac{\text{Shareholders' funds}}{\text{Tangible assets}}$	$\dfrac{555}{1,140} = 0.5$	$\dfrac{495}{990} = 0.5$